# *Schizo*phrenia

## EMPIRICAL RESEARCH AND FINDINGS

This is a Volume in
*PERSONALITY, PSYCHOPATHOLOGY, AND PSYCHOTHERAPY*
A Series of Monographs, Texts, and Treatises
Under the Editorship of David T. Lykken and Philip C. Kendall

# *Schizo*phrenia

## EMPIRICAL RESEARCH AND FINDINGS

*by*
**ECKART R. STRAUBE**
Department of Psychiatry
University of Tubingen
Tubingen, Germany

and
**ROBERT D. OADES**
Clinic of Child and Adolescent Psychiatry
University of Essen
Essen, Germany

**Academic Press, Inc.**
Harcourt Brace Jovanovich, Publishers
**San Diego   New York   Boston   London   Sydney   Tokyo   Toronto**

Copyright © 1992 by Academic Press, Inc.

Academic Press, Inc.
1250 Sixth Avenue, San Diego, California 92101-4311

*United Kingdom Edition published by*
Academic Press Limited
24–28 Oval Road, London NW1 7DX


Library of Congress Cataloging-in-Publication Data

Straube, Eckart R., date
    Schizophrenia : Empirical Research and Findings
    Straube and Robert D. Oades.
        p.   cm. -- (Personality, psychopathology, and psychotherapy)
        Includes index.
        ISBN 0-12-673010-5
        1. Schizophrenia.   I. Oades, Robert D.   II. Title.   III. Series.
        [DNLM: 1. Schizophrenia.   WM 203 S911s]
    RC514.S8248   1991
    616.89'82--dc20
    DNLM/DLC
    for Library of Congress                                          91-18147
                                                                          CIP


PRINTED IN THE UNITED STATES OF AMERICA
92  93  94  95  96  97    MB    9  8  7  6  5  4  3  2  1

# Contents

**PART III** Psychophysiological Symptoms

# PART IV Neuropsychological Symptoms

# PART V Inheritance versus Environment

**Chapter 17**    Synopsis

# *Preface*

We have written this textbook to cover the broad field of research conducted on schizophrenia. We hope that the book will prove useful to those interested in the whole range of subject areas discussed. We have also kept in mind those who work in a specific area (e.g., evoked potential research, biochemical research, or cognitive research) and would like to read an up-to-date appraisal of work in a related field of study. Indeed, one of the reasons we put pen to paper (or, perhaps more appropriately, fingers to keyboard) was that as the component disciplines in schizophrenia research follow ever more divergent paths, it has become increasingly difficult for someone specializing in one area to know about new developments in neighboring areas of research.

The increasing divergence of specialized areas of investigation, particularly in the last 10 to 20 years, also made our task extremely difficult. This task necessitated viewing and reviewing an unholy multiplicity of published work. In order to cover the field we had to review well over 2000 publications. Nonetheless we hope that we have been just in this respect. We must, however, offer a word of warning: the extensive literature makes it impossible to represent faithfully all the details of the studies reported. Even from the selection of results we considered significant it was necessary to leave out some methodological details and important results. But we should also emphasize that it has been our intention to offer readers a useful *overview* of the current status of investigations into the phenomenon of schizophrenia.

Today all too many of us find ourselves facing major demands on our time. For those who want a brief synopsis we recommend the end of chapter summaries. On the other hand, for those intending to start out in a specific field of schizophrenia research, we emphasize the need for further reading and study of the original publications. Our text offers an introduction, and a pointer is provided in the Suggested Readings at the end of each chapter.

We have attempted to draw an objective outline of schizophrenia research in Chapters 1 through 14. The studies and their results are largely described free of theoretical interpretations. For example, we have described experimental results as "experimental symptoms." Our intention is to let the reader make a judgment and form a picture with minimal bias from extraneous sources. We have striven for objectivity; nonetheless, we have created a bias simply through our initial selection of subject areas and the emphasis on important features. Thus it is all the more important for those embarking on a schizophrenia research program to dig deeper and read the original reports.

Not until Chapter 17 do we start to discuss in more detail the pros and cons of some of the prominent hypotheses in schizophrenia research. Chapter 16 attempts to integrate these published interpretations with the results discussed in the previous chapters. From this we attempt to abstract conclusions about the current general understanding of the mechanisms underlying schizophrenia, what might be the common factors for a number of schizophrenic characteristics, and what might or might not be empirical reasons for separating these factors from those shown by other groups of psychiatrically ill patients. Readers who are particularly interested in these theoretical aspects of the subject should read these chapters first.

We have written each chapter such that it should be understandable without having read the previous chapters. But if points are expounded upon in more detail elsewhere, these are so indicated in the text (through cross-references). Only in Chapter 16 do the summaries and interpretations from the other chapters provide an important basis for the discussion.

We recognize that by splitting up specialty areas (ranging from neuropsychology, biochemistry, and experimental psychology to life-event research), certain relevant background information could remain obscure for some readers. We try to correct this by starting each chapter with an introduction to the methodology and subject area. This should assist the reader in understanding the chapters on, for example, evoked potentials or the lateral specializations of the brain, without having necessarily worked in these or related fields.

Research results from the last 10 to 15 years are central to our presentation. Important earlier results have been reviewed in the excellent books from Cutting (1985), Neale and Oltmanns (1980), and from Chapman and Chapman (1973). However, in these texts, discussions of results from neuropsychological, psychophysiological, anatomical, and biochemical fields of study are missing.

It was difficult for us to reconcile the vast experimental literature on schizophrenia in a half-way comfortable manner. The result, we hope, is a basic text useful both for those involved in their own research on schizophrenia and those interested in an overview of the results emerging from a host of research programs. No previous schizophrenia textbook covered *all* areas of research and integrated the empirical results from all the relevant subject areas. We have been fortunate that our research concentrates on different aspects of schizophrenia with complementary interests. Bob Oades specializes in neuro- and psychobiological work, and Eckart Straube concentrates on other areas of psychophysiology, experimental psychology, and therapy.

Considering the length and breadth of the work covered in this review and the number of text revisions that commuted back and forth between the authors, it would be surprising if one or two errors have not crept in—for these we must accept responsibility. But we would welcome feedback to facilitate future revision.

We could not have survived the various pressures over the months and years of preparation for this book without the love, tolerance, and support from all those close to us. In this way we want to thank our families and friends.

We are also most grateful to all those who in many diverse ways have offered help and support in the preparation of the manuscript, in particular Helga Hübner, Magaret Ruck, Elke Vuckovic, and Beate-Maria Wolf. We also thank those colleagues who read earlier versions of the text and offered their helpful criticism and advice.

Most importantly we wish to thank Joe Ingram and Eileen Favorite for their enduring patience, help, and involvement in the development and completion of our manuscript.

## References

Chapman, L. J., and Chapman, J. P. (1973). *Disordered thought in schizophrenia.* New York: Appleton-Century-Crafts.

Cutting, J. (1985). *The psychology of schizophrenia.* Edinburgh: Churchill Livingston.

Neale, J. M., and Oltmanns, T. F. (1980). *Schizophrenia.* New York: Wiley.

# PART I

# Clinical Symptoms

# Chapter 1

# Clinical Manifestation, Frequency, and Definition of Schizophrenia

## I. Prominent Features

The Glossary of Mental Disorders, International Classification of Diseases by the World Health Organization (WHO) describes schizophrenia as:

> a group of psychoses in which there is fundamental disturbance of personality, a characteristic distortion of thinking, often a sense of being controlled by alien forces, delusions, which may be bizarre, disturbed perception, abnormal affect, out of keeping with the real situation, and autism. Nevertheless, clear consciousness and intellectual capacity are usually maintained. (1978, p. 34).

*Disturbance of personality* refers to changes in the psychological functions of an individual that cause doubt or uncertainty about the individual's *identity* and are often accompanied by the feeling that the boundaries to the self disintegrate or melt away (i.e., in the former structure of the ego or conscious self is lost). Some patients state that they are another person or alternately are two different people. Many patients have the feeling that their psychological functions are being controlled by other people or that others know their thoughts.

Interfering secondary thoughts and associations, normally suppressed in purposeful thought processes, are characteristic of schizophrenic *thought disorder*. A consistent and logical train of thought is therefore no longer possible. Thoughts are interrupted or even totally blocked; the gaps are filled with odd material. The speech of thought-disordered schizophrenics, therefore, is often bizarre and unintelligible.

A similar disorder can be observed in the area of *perception*. Some elements of what is perceived, that are only secondary to the situation, can be given excessive meaning, so the schizophrenic's interpretation of the environment is not accepted by others. These changes in the interpretation of the environment and the feelings of being influenced or controlled by others are typical of schizophrenic delusions. An even more extreme form of perceptual disturbance occurs in schizophrenic *hallucinations.* These "perceptions," which have no external basis in reality, usually appear in the auditory sphere. The patients hear voices talking to and about them. Many patients explain these strange alterations in the perceived environment by *delusional ideas* (that they are persecuted and strangely influenced by others, i.e., they express paranoid ideas).

In the area of *emotions,* an inadequacy of the affective response is characteristic. The response is often inappropriate to the situation. In some patients, the capability to develop deep emotional involvement seems to be lost entirely, but seemingly trivial events can evoke great emotional agitation.

A patient with schizophrenic *autism* lacks the ability to relate to the reality of others. The patient lives encapsulated in his or her own world and private reality and is no longer able to duplicate the experiences and attitudes of others. The patient cannot change his or her mental perspective and is incapable of seeing things from the perspective of others.

## II. Incidence and Course of Illness

Women and men are affected equally, although, as Figure 1.1 shows, men tend to be hospitalized at an earlier age. The highest first-admission rate occurs between 20 and 30 years of age for men and somewhat later for women. The accumulated risk of first hospitalization at the age of 35 is 75% for men and 59% for women. In other words, a considerably higher proportion of women will have the first breakdown after the age of 35. The total frequency for both sexes, however, is equal (Gottesman and Shields, 1982).

About 1% of the population (more precisely, 0.85%) will develop schizophrenia during the course of life (lifetime morbidity risk). Apart from certain regional fluctuations, schizophrenia rates are approximately equal in all countries. Therefore in the United States, the most heavily populated country on the American continent, about 2 million of the 236 million inhabitants will be affected by schizophrenia during their lifetime; in the Federal Republic of Germany, the most heavily populated country in Europe, far more than half a million of the 78 million inhabitants will develop schizophrenia during their lifetime.

The developmental course of schizophrenia is extremely heterogeneous. The following approximate figures are often cited: somewhat less than 25% of the patients experience complete remission of symptoms. More than 75% of all

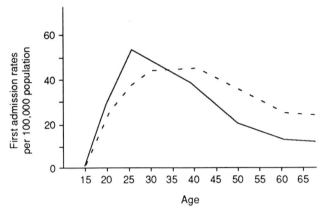

**Figure 1.1**  Age of onset distribution of British male (—) and female (– – –) first admissions with a diagnosis of schizophrenia between 1964 and 1966 (after Gottesman and Shields, 1982).

schizophrenics suffer from mental impairments throughout their life, some with symptom reduction between severe phases and relatively mild non-specific symptomatology in old age, and some with a more rapidly deteriorating course and severe schizophrenic symptomatology up to old age (for details, see Chapter 14). Chronic schizophrenics represent the largest group of long-term hospitalized psychiatric patients. During 1975, 93,000 schizophrenics, but only 10,500 patients with affective disorders, were resident in state and county hospitals in the United States (Gottesman and Shields, 1982).

The following description of schizophrenic psychopathology is subdivided into the different areas of psychological function, so the reader can compare the psychiatric symptoms with the experimentally assessed symptoms, that is, cognitive, psychophysiological, and neuropsychological symptoms as described in Chapters 2 through 9.

Modern concepts of schizophrenia are based on the work of Emil Kraepelin and Eugen Bleuler, who made their main contributions just before and after the turn of the century, respectively. Kraepelin (1899), a German psychiatrist, was the first to rearrange certain forms of insanity into one group, which he called "dementia praecox." Eugen Bleuler (1911), a Swiss psychiatrist, gave the illness the name we use today. The title of his famous book, *Dementia Praecox or the Group of Schizophrenias,* alludes to the fact that he was unsure whether schizophrenia was one disease or a group of different, but similar, illnesses.

In keeping with a well-established tradition, the description of schizophrenia in this chapter is based on the concepts of Kraepelin and Bleuler and incorporates modern diagnostic concepts.

## III. Thought Disorder

A patient with formal thought disorder often has difficulty completing a train of thought. The chain of thoughts, so to speak, falls into parts (derailment) or is blocked. The entire thought process may be replaced by mere associations to single words or parts of thoughts (through loosening of associations); the individual's speech, therefore, appears to be disorganized and incoherent. According to Bleuler, the basic pattern of this disturbance is the patient's inability to organize thoughts (or verbal utterances) according to his or her own intention. During the course of reasoning, the patient loses the conceptual goal ("Ziel-Vorstellung;" Bleuler, 1911). A modern theory in psycholinguistics conceptualizes this idea as the inability to select semantic and syntactic elements in accordance with a cognitive "plan" (see Miller *et al.*, 1960).

Drifting of reasoning through associations and loss of goal is illustrated impressively by one of Kraepelin's examples. The patient begins with a "normal" sentence and continues with mere associations and alliterations (clanging or clang associations):

> . . . up there, on the mountain range, a hunter was once discovered. On the rock wall near the alpine chalet, an alpine herdsman and an alpine dairymaid (in German: *"Senn*hütte," *"Senn*er," and *"Senn*erin") one nice day on the rock wall (and continues with meaningless words) achazant drihahol drietal up there on the wall. *V*esuv, *Vi*lz, *V*entus, *V*erlend, *V*aterland . . . (Kraepelin, 1913, p. 734)

Thought disorder, therefore, sometimes results in total disintegration, for example, a word potpourri with neologisms (nonexisting words) like those in the example just cited. Kraepelin emphasized that many patients are fully aware of these changes: "my mind sometimes goes off" or "things go around in me, thoughts, which belong in a sanatorium" (Kraepelin, 1913, p. 693, 694).

Not all patients, however, display such dramatic incoherence. The semantic coherence of the sentence is changed more frequently than the syntactic organization. As Harrow and Quinlan (1985) pointed out, often only a few minor signs of cognitive slippage are observed, or reasoning is somewhat bizarre and idiosyncratic. These authors proposed testing and rating thought disorder in a clinical setting by using standardized questions, for example, "Explain the following proverb: One swallow doesn't make a summer." One thought-disordered schizophrenic gave the following explanation: "When you swallow something, it could be all right, but the next minute you could be coughing, and dreariness and all kinds of miserable things coming out of your throat." Although the linguistic structure is not affected here, the patient was unable to refer to the total coherent contextual meaning of the words. Instead, he verbalized tangential themes associated with the dominant meaning of one word, "swallow." The patient treated the sentence as if it were composed of incoherent single parts. The absence of a connection between demand and response is characteristic of schizophrenic communication.

Although the disturbances in thought, language, and communication described are characteristic symptoms of schizophrenia (e.g., see DSM-III and Section VI), they do not appear in all patients diagnosed as "certainly schizophrenic" according to diagnostic criteria. Kendell (1987), from Edinburgh, therefore states, "More commonly there is a gradual slippage in which a sequence of minor shifts eventually produces a major change of theme (p. 10)." Rochester and Martin (1979) found massive impairment in less than one-third of the patients. The heterogeneity of the clinical manifestations of the illness will be discussed in more detail in Section XI.

## IV. **Attention Disorders**

Bleuler's statement, "The sensory response to external stimuli is quite normal" (Bleuler, 1911, p. 75), suggests that basic sensory functions are not impaired, but that the evaluation and interpretation of what has been perceived is altered. Thus, the perception of the physical features of the environment may correspond to that of a healthy person, but the patient interprets the perception in a peculiar way.

The following example, reported by Gruhle (cited in Matussek, 1952), illustrates such altered interpretation. "I noticed that the people all wore such odd coats. (How were they odd?) They wore such dark coats. (Are dark coats so strange?) Not that exactly, but I did notice something. (What did you notice then?) They wore coats that are worn to funerals." Gruhle then concluded, "With such inquiries, which you can conduct a hundred times, everything is still not perceivably 'peculiar,' but something rather usual, such as the dark color of the coat, suddenly means something. Here it alludes to a funeral . . ." (Matussek, 1952, p. 282). Cutting (1985) cites a similar example. "Most students there looked normal but one didn't. Nothing about his appearance but something about him disturbed me. The trousers he wore disturbed me—green, tweedy, loose around the bottom, which annoyed me" (p. 292)

Many researchers believe that a disturbance of attention is the basic defect in schizophrenia (e.g., Neale and Oltmanns, 1980). Such disturbances were already observed by Kraepelin and Bleuler. "The selection of normal attention from sensory impressions can be reduced to zero . . . The inhibitory as well as the facilitating qualities of attention are disturbed in an identical way" (E. Bleuler, 1911, p. 56).

Freedman (1974), as well as McGhie and Chapman (1961), has presented impressive examples of self-reports by patients. All questioned patients about their experiences and collected written comments from acute schizophrenics, such as "I am easily put off what I am doing or even what I am talking about. If something else is going on somewhere, even just a noise, it interrupts my thoughts and they get lost" (McGhie and Chapman, 1961, p. 105).

In obvious analogy to the described disturbances of speech and thought, the patient is no longer able to follow a given guideline, that is, with regard to perception, to be specifically attentive to a relevant source of stimulation. Characteristic of this inability to concentrate is a feeling of being at the mercy of the environment or of losing control.

> These patients appear to have lost the ability and freedom to direct their attention focally as required in normal concentration. Their attention is instead directed radially in a manner which is determined not by the individual's volition, but by the diffuse pattern of stimuli existing in the total environmental situation. (McGhie and Chapman, 1961, p. 105)

## V. Hallucinations

Hallucinations experienced by schizophrenics "may involve any of the five senses. However, auditory hallucinations in the form of voices are the most common, and visual, olfactory, gustatory, and tactile (somatic) hallucinations are uncommon in the absence of hallucinatory voices" (Kendell, 1985, p. 8). The latter can be observed in about two-thirds of schizophrenic patients (Sartorius et al., 1974). Schizophrenics hear voices talking to and about them in a curt, often insulting, way. The voices often comment on their behavior.

F. Krauss, a wealthy businessman of the 19th century, gave detailed descriptions of his auditory and somatic hallucinations in two autobiographical books published in 1852 and in 1867. He thought he was under the influence of other people who mesmerized him and thus produced bodily sensations. He felt that these other people were in control of his thoughts and that they spoke to him. Krauss described his experiences at the onset of his psychosis:

> I felt uneasy; I could not sleep. A hot plate entered my left ear. This plate was as wide as the palm of my hand, round, and flat like a crown piece. This mass of heat, which I could not understand, moved freely down my body; once, when it was on my hip, I put my hand on it but could not stop it. It proceeded on, but I am ashamed to say where. While she [the woman whom Krauss thought was persecuting him] moved this warm mass back, she engaged herself for quite a while in the most cynical obscenities. As if she wanted to cuddle and turn my private parts, this reprobate murmured: 'Ah vous êtes un bon mâle!'—Totally beside myself due to this infamous act, for the first time I thought that I could be electrified . . ." (Krauss, 1852, p. 37)

It should be noted that even highly intelligent patients are incapable of explaining the specific quality of their hallucinatory observations to the examiner, apparently because of the lack of a common verbal repertoire based on common experiences. F. Krauss also expresses this problem: "This nameless torture cannot be adequately described; it is far removed from our accepted notions. . ." (Krauss, 1852, pp. 64–65).

Some auditory hallucinations are described as verbalized thoughts, but they do not have the same quality as one's own thoughts; the patient therefore thinks that the thoughts cannot come from him- or herself and that they are inserted by other people.

> They [the persecutors] besiege me like stinging flies and call up in me the wretched pictures of their tasteless, obscene fantasy, they mar, distort, and make fun of my thoughts; they thwart my thoughts, fend them off; . . . they look for other thoughts to substitute for my own. . ." (F. Krauss, 1852, p. 56)

Some thoughts are described as being so intense and "loud" that the patient thinks the partner can also hear those thoughts. Sometimes the source of stimulation is transferred externally; the patient believes he hears voices talking about him, but only in short communications.

A situational variation is also observed with hallucinations. In their textbook of psychiatry, Eugen and Manfred Bleuler (1966) reported that these symptoms are promoted by situations lacking stimulation (e.g., darkness of night, isolation in a prison cell). Unstructured noisy surroundings, however, can also intensify hallucinations, whereas strongly structured activities some-times diminish them. An experiment by Hemsley and co-workers (Institute of Psychiatry, London) tends to support this assumption. They presented differ-ently structured material to schizophrenics through headphones and found that the patients' auditory hallucinations declined with the presentation of highly structured material (Margo *et al.*, 1981).

# VI. Delusional Perception—Alterations of Reality and Expectations

K. Conrad, in his monograph published in 1971, presented an impressive description of the changes that take place as the psychotic state develops. He collected reports of young German recruits at the beginning of World War II. An illustration of the increasing change in perceived reality at the onset of psychosis follows:

> For a long time, he thought that something was in the air, but he did not know exactly what. Perhaps a special mission was coming up . . . His comrades stared at him; they either refused to let him drink from the bottle or they gave it to him with peculiar glances; they were anything but friendly . . . Soon he gathered from the conversation that, during the night, he was to 'get a role,' perhaps he would be tied to a tree and somehow branded . . . They made certain hints about this. Naturally, he decided to stay awake during the night so that he could defend himself. That

night everything in the dormitory was very suspicious. By the creaking of the floor and the beds, he clearly heard how someone was trying to work his way toward him. He jumped out of bed on the side near the stove in order to recognize his adversary in its faint glow. He also saw how a glowing spot, probably the red-hot end of the poker, was being swung in the form of a hammer and sickle. At that moment he realized what was about to happen. He dashed toward the spot to catch his adversary, but the apparition disappeared. There was just enough room behind the stove for someone to hide. Outside, he frequently heard the sound of boots and a lot of rumbling in the adjacent barracks. Once someone knocked at the door. Someone wearing boots walked past the door. He also heard the clatter of buckles. All these noises told him that those outside were also informed. As soon as he jumped out of bed, the room became quiet again. The 'maneuvering,' however, started again just after he had gone back to bed. He therefore repeatedly jumped out of bed so that he could be prepared. Once he turned on a light briefly but could not see anything. Maybe the guys had crawled quickly into beds already occupied by others; the light, perhaps, was not on long enough, and there was not enough light. When the guards entered the barracks, he immediately realized that they were also 'informed': normally the guards came in often to check on the fire, but this time, it was different . . . When he returned to his barracks in the morning, everyone was informed, a hostile atmosphere surrounded him. Even his best friend 'innocently' asked him what was going on. They all disguised their feelings: they wanted, in any case, to see how he reacted. (K. Conrad, 1971, pp. 8–9)

Conrad (1971) uses this example to show that the experienced change in the meaning of the environment starts with a "delusional mood." The recruit felt that "something [was] wrong, something [was] in the air." In a next step, everyday events are given abnormal interpretations, for example, a creaking floor, a glowing spot on the stove, the noise of boots on the square. The unusual is expected to happen. Kendell (1987) points out that simply the presence of delusions is of little diagnostic value, unless the content is obviously bizarre or more elaborate.

As Feer (1970) points out, the "unconscious" or automatic consideration of probability seems changed in schizophrenia. A healthy person would be surprised by a desk on a train track, because this contradicts any expectation guided by context and experience. Schizophrenics are often surprised by "normal" events such as closed shutters in the evening or a delivery van driving around the block twice (Feer, 1970). The events of the environment become increasingly strange for the schizophrenic because, compared with the evaluation of the same events by a non-schizophrenic, they are evaluated as more improbable. The schizophrenic therefore becomes anxious and tries to find a reason for this change in the significance of the environment. Some schizophrenics attempt to put the primarily unexpected in a new context, that is, to construct a new frame of reference. They interpret the changes as made, for example, by persecutors or divine powers. These interpretations, there-fore, are delusional: the patient suspects a system of persecutions (paranoid delusion) and other strange influences.

# VII. Movement

In contrast to Bleuler (1911), the diagnostic manual of the American Psychiatric Association (DSM-III-R, 1987) classifies disturbance of motor *coordination* as a differential diagnostic sign. In fact, schizophrenics are sometimes conspicuous in a group of other patients by their lack of coordination in limb movements and facial expressions. Their movements are sometimes bizarre or curiously stereotyped. Facial motor movements may consist of grimaces without perceptible reason.

Both extremes of activity changes can be observed: slow and limited movement, especially in chronic schizophrenia, or motor agitation without visible external reason, often occurring in acute florid forms of the illness.

Another extreme form of movement change is found in the catatonic state of the illness. In states of *catatonic rigidity,* the patient maintains an uncomfortable bizarre body position for long periods of time, despite all efforts to move him or her. In *waxy flexibility,* the patient maintains an imposed posture for a longer period of time. In states of *catatonic excitement,* the patient exhibits apparently purposeless and stereotyped excited movements that are not influenced by external stimuli. During *catatonic stupor,* however, spontaneous movements and activity are extremely reduced, and reactivity to the environment is decreased.

# VIII. Memory

Major memory functions are seldom significantly changed in schizophrenia. The acute symptoms probably lead to difficulties in organizing descriptions of past events. Similarly, inability to concentrate (i.e., disturbances in attention) makes memorization and systematic learning more difficult. However, it has been observed repeatedly that patients who assume a mute seclusive role and who apparently do not participate in the environment, as in *catatonic stupor,* may later be able to recall exactly what happened during their seclusion.

# IX. Intelligence

Guertin *et al.* (1962) reviewed the results of intelligence tests in schizophrenics and reported that the IQ of *acutely* ill patients is no lower than that of healthy individuals.

Scores on the nonverbal part of the Wechsler–Bellevue IQ test are characteristically lower than on the verbal part (cf. Hunt and Cofer, 1944). Schizophrenic impairments in the areas of perception (e.g., attention, concentration) obviously interfere with performance on the nonverbal test, in which these skills are more strongly expressed. Except for these differences in the relationships of the components of intelligence, severe disturbances in intelligence *per se* are not a characteristic feature of schizophrenia (Huber, 1974). Intellectual impairments have, however, been reported in patients hospitalized for longer periods of time (see also Chapman and Chapman, 1973a,b; Fieguth and Goncalves, 1977), in subgroups of predominantly chronic schizophrenics with mild cerebral atrophy (see Johnstone *et al.*, 1978), and in severely disturbed subgroups (Robertson and Taylor, 1985; see also Goldberg *et al.*, 1988). Such impairments will be discussed more thoroughly in Chapter 8, Section I.

## X. Emotional Responses

Kraepelin and Bleuler considered the conspicuous change in emotional reactivity to be one of the basic symptoms of schizophrenia; this view is still held by most modern investigators. As for psychomotor deviations, both increases and decreases in emotion are observed. Some patients show only a blunted affect, while others, usually acute patients, are more irritable and emotionally agitated. Bleuler described this response: "At the beginning of the illness we often see a certain *hypersensitiveness* [our emphasis]; the patients deliberately isolate themselves to avoid possible occasions for emotional involvement" (Bleuler, 1911, p. 33).

In addition, a fast reversal of emotional states is sometimes observed within a short space of time (inconsistency). Bleuler assumed that these rapid emotional changes corresponded to the erratic character of thoughts. Speech content and emotional expression often are unrelated. A schizophrenic may report disturbing events such as "at night my intestines were being ripped out" in an indifferent tone of voice and, a moment later, become agitated over a seemingly banal event. Contradictory emotions for the same event may be expressed (e.g., love and hate for the same person); to the patient, however, these emotions do not appear to be contradictory (affective ambivalence).

The problems in interactions with the family and at the workplace created by such incoherent emotional responses are easy to imagine. Schizophrenics are often unable to transmit and to interpret adequately those subtly differentiated emotional signals that are important supplementary regulators of interactions of behavior and communication in a social context. Recent experimental studies by Berndl *et al.* (1986) and Cramer *et al.* (1989), in which schizophrenics were shown films of actors expressing different emotional states, demonstrated the problems schizophrenics have with the interpretation of the emotional expression of others.

As Bleuler observed during a fire in his hospital, the lack of emotional excitability in some (predominantly chronic) patients was so extreme that many schizophrenics had to be led out of the hospital; they would not have left the ward on their own. Some patients no longer respond, even to intense stimulation. For example, a schizophrenic may burn a hand with a cigarette but show no signs of emotion or pain. (As discussed in Chapter 5, the autonomic nervous system of some patients is *less* responsive, even to stressful stimulation, whereas the autonomic nervous system of certain subgroups or persons at risk seems to be *over*excitable; see also Chapter 12).

In addition to this incoherent emotional response to varying situational contexts, other more global changes in mood can be observed that are probably secondary consequences of the illness, namely anxiety, excessively strong irritation, and depressive mood. (For a discussion of depressive mood in schizophrenia, see Möller and von Zerssen, 1986.) Although these changes are relatively nonspecific (they also appear in other psychiatric diseases), they are still of interest for research and therapy.

## XI. Heterogeneity of Symptoms

The question of whether schizophrenia is one disease or a group of loosely connected diseases remains unanswered. The definition in the Glossary of Mental Disorders (WHO) quoted earlier speaks of a "group of psychoses" with good reason. The highly divergent long-term course of schizophrenia may reflect an underlying heterogeneity. The heterogeneous spectrum of symptoms may also suggest that one label includes several diseases. As Table 1.1 illustrates, not all schizophrenics exhibit even the most prominent symptoms of schizophrenia. Nearly all patients lack insight, 70–74% have hallucinations, 66% have flat affect, and only 50–52% have some type of thought disorder. Table 1.1 is based on the results of the International Pilot Study of Schizophrenia (Sartorius *et al.*, 1974). Only those patients diagnosed as schizophrenic by three different diagnostic methods are included. The study was carried out by specially trained psychiatrists in nine different countries.

This heterogeneity of symptoms, however, does not necessarily prove the existence of different underlying illnesses: the different symptoms of schizophrenia are not mutually exclusive and fluctuate considerably during the course of the illness (e.g., a patient may have symptom A at the onset of the disease and later present symptom B). In addition, heterogeneity of symptoms is observed even in diseases with an identified single cause; for example, in neurofibromatosis, some individuals who carry the gene will have only a few characteristic spots on the skin, whereas others will have severe tumors in the peripheral nerves.

Bleuler (1911) expressed his uncertainty about this question when he gave his fundamental monograph the title *Dementia Praecox or the Group of Schizophrenias*. In the text, however, he spoke only of "schizophrenia," noting, "For convenience, I use the word in the singular, although the group

**Table 1.1**  Relative Frequency of Symptoms[a]

| Symptom | Schizophrenics (%) |
|---|---|
| Lack of insight | 97 |
| Auditory hallucinations | 74 |
| Verbal hallucinations | 70 |
| Ideas of reference | 70 |
| Suspiciousness | 66 |
| Flat affect | 66 |
| Voices speaking to patient | 65 |
| Delusional mood | 64 |
| Delusions of persecution | 64 |
| Inadequate description of problem | 64 |
| Thought alienation | 52 |
| Thoughts spoken aloud | 50 |

[a]Results of International Pilot Study of Schizophrenia; only those symptoms occurring in at least 50% of schizophrenics are listed (Carpenter *et al.*, 1979).

is probably made up of several illnesses (p. 5)." The existence of *independent* subgroups within the "group of schizophrenias," however, has not been convincingly demonstrated yet, as Manfred Bleuler (1981), his son and later also head of the University Psychiatric Hospital in Zurich, stated 70 years later. Roth (1986), after reviewing the modern state of schizophrenia diagnosis, concluded, "The group of schizophrenic and schizophreniform disorders . . . are characterized by both their unity and their diversity" (Roth, 1986, p. 180). One of the objectives of this text is to discuss the empirically founded indications for diversity or unity and the possible underlying environmental, biological, and genetic factors involved.

# XII. Subgroups

In the 5th edition of Kraepelin's textbook (1896), the term "dementia praecox" included three forms of disease: *paranoid, catatonic,* and *hebephrenic.* These three types had been described already by various French and German psychiatrists as separate forms of "insanity." (For a more detailed account of the history of schizophrenia, see the short and excellent review by Cutting, 1985.) However, in the 1899 edition of his textbook, Kraepelin no longer considered these three forms of insanity distinct diseases.

Bleuler expanded the subgroups by adding the simple schizophrenia group, which was replaced by the *undifferentiated* type in the DSM-III-R, that is, these patients do not belong unequivocally to one of the other subgroups. The hebephrenic type is now called the *disorganized* type (see DSM-III-R). The essential features of this type are hallucinations or delusions that are not organized into coherent themes, as well as thought and behavioral incoherence and inappropriate or flat affect.

These classifications are based on the prominent syndromes, that is, the characteristic symptoms, and do *not* indicate a particular prognosis or crucial differences in therapeutic procedures. According to the results of the International Pilot Study on Schizophrenia, paranoid hallucinatory schizophrenia appears with the greatest frequency among the subgroups of schizophrenia. [Paranoid hallucinatory schizophrenia has to be differentiated from delusional (paranoid) disorder. The essential feature of the latter is, according to DSM-III-R, a persistent, nonbizarre delusion *without* other schizophrenic features.]

Not all these classifications are used to form subgroups for research purposes. Researchers consider "good and poor premorbid development of the illness," "acute and chronic schizophrenia," and "paranoid and nonparanoid schizophrenia" to be the most significant differentiations, without an existing valid external criterion for these differentiations. On the contrary, classification of patients according to these categories does not indicate separate forms of the illness, necessarily. Sometimes the classification may signify only that the same type of patient was examined in different phases of the developmental course of the illness. Janzarik's observations (1968) suggest that this may often be the case. This author showed that most chronic nonparanoid schizophrenics had paranoid symptoms and hallucinations at least once during the course of their illness (see similar observations by Andreasen, 1987). Similar observations of dramatic symptom shifts during the long-term course of the illness were reported by Bleuler (1972), Ciompi and Müller (1976), and Huber *et al.* (1979). (For more details, see Chapter 14.) In other words, in the absence of longitudinal data, no classification can claim to be based on discrete entities.

A concept that has become quite popular recently is the subdivision of schizophrenics according to the preponderance of *positive* or *negative symptoms* (Strauss *et al.,* 1974). Delusions, hallucinations, positive formal thought disorder, and bizarre behavior are considered to be characteristic positive (productive) symptoms. Affective flattening, motor retardation, avolition/apathy, withdrawal, anhedonia, and poverty of speech are considered typical negative (defective) symptoms. (For further details, see Andreasen, 1985.) Andreasen (1983, 1984) has developed rating scales for the assessment of positive and negative symptoms in schizophrenia. In a similar approach, Crow divides schizophrenia into *type I* (productive symptoms) and *type II* (deficit symptoms). Some of the negative symptoms assigned by Crow to type II are presumed to be indicative of mild cerebral damage, poor drug response, and poor prognosis (Crow, 1985; for more details, see Chapter 8).

Clinical experience and empirical investigation, however, show that both positive and negative symptoms are often found in the same patient (Bilder *et al.,* 1985; Guelfi *et al.,* 1989), or that patients start with positive symptoms, then, over the course of time, develop negative symptoms in the chronic stages of the illness, as already discussed. Some of these negative symptoms may even be considered secondary coping attempts to overcome the destructive effects of positive symptoms (e.g., Carpenter *et al.*, 1988). It is therefore questionable whether all, or at least which, symptoms are criteria for a separation into significant subgroups. Bilder *et al.* (1985) did not see a confirmation of a dichotomy through factor analysis, but Walker *et al.* (1988) supported the idea of two separate groups through a discriminant analysis. The situation, thus, remains equivocal.

# XIII. Diagnostic Criteria

In the last 20 years, attempts have been made to improve the reliability of psychiatric diagnoses. For research purposes, symptom inventories were developed to enhance the comparability of selected samples. The Research Diagnostic Criteria (RDC) of Spitzer *et al.* (1978) in New York and the diagnostic criteria of the Diagnostic and Statistical Manual of Mental Disorders (DSM-III-R) have become well accepted; the latter was developed by the American Psychiatric Association. These two sets of criteria are similar, because the definitions in DSM-III-R are based more or less on the RDC (Spitzer is the chairperson of the DSM task force). Both sets of criteria have now been translated into several languages and are being used increasingly, even outside the United States. Both are more detailed than the International Classification of Diseases, 9th ed. (ICD) criteria. Other sets of criteria, such as Carpenter's Flexible Checklist (Carpenter *et al.*, 1974) or the Feighner/St. Louis criteria (Feighner *et al.*, 1972) are also used; the latter, however, is not applied as frequently as in the past and has been superceded by the DSM of the American Psychiatric Association. The Carpenter criteria differ from the other sets of criteria because they are empirically selected. They consist of the 12 symptoms that best discriminate schizophrenia from non-schizophrenia, that is, they were selected statistically by discriminant analysis within the framework of the International Pilot Study on Schizophrenia.

RDC and DSM-III-R, to a certain extent, and the Feighner criteria, to a greater extent, share common elements with older criteria, namely, Schneider's first rank symptoms. It is interesting that these criteria, introduced by the German psychiatrists Schneider, became more popular in the English-speaking world than in Germany. (For more details, see the comparative evaluation of the different research criteria by Overall and Hollister, 1979.)

One stimulus to set up strict diagnostic criteria, especially in the United States, came from a direct comparison of European (British) and North American diagnostic practices. This comparison of diagnoses made by staff members of several American and British hospitals showed that the diagnoses made in the United States were considerably broader; significantly more patients with affective illnesses were diagnosed as schizophrenic (Cooper *et al.*, 1972).

The aim of the new standardized inventories, therefore, is to increase the reliability of diagnoses attained by different evaluators. Indeed, fairly good interrater reliability has been reported for most of the scales mentioned. Spitzer *et al.* (1978), for example, reported a reliability of κ = .84 for the RDC with 120 examined patients.

According to the Research Diagnostic Criteria of Spitzer *et al.* (1978), schizophrenia is *certain* when two of the following symptoms are present:

1. Thought broadcasting (spreading of thoughts to others), thought insertion, or thought withdrawal
2. Delusional idea of being controlled (or of being influenced), other bizarre delusions, or multiple delusions
3. Somatic, grandiose, religious, nihilistic, or other delusions (without persecutory or jealous content) for at least 1 week
4. Any type of delusional ideas if accompanied by any type of hallucinations for at least 1 week
5. Auditory hallucinations in which a voice keeps up a running commentary on the subject's behavior or on thoughts as they occur, or in which two or more voices converse with each other
6. Nonaffective verbal hallucinations that speak to the subject
7. Hallucinations of any type throughout the day, several days, or intermittently for at least a month
8. Definite instances of marked formal thought disorder accompanied by either blunted or inappropriate affect, delusions, or hallucinations of any type, or grossly disorganized behavior

[More detailed definitions of the symptoms are given in the manual (Spitzer *et al.*, 1978).]

Signs of the illness must persist for at least 2 weeks without symptoms of the presence of any other psychiatric illnesses.

The RDC manual by Spitzer and colleagues also presents criteria for the difficult differentiation between acute and chronic schizophrenia.

*Acute* schizophrenia is characterized by:

1. Sudden onset (onset of first appearance of illness less than 3 months from first signs of increasing psychopathology)
2. Short course (ill for less than 3 consecutive months with significant signs of schizophrenia)
3. Full recovery after a past episode

A patient is *chronically* schizophrenic when clear signs of schizophrenia are present more or less consistently for 2 years. If the course lies between these two poles, the illness is considered to be subacute or subchronic.

For the diagnosis of schizophrenia, according to the DSM-III-R, two of the following symptoms must be present:

1. Delusions
2. Prominent hallucinations (throughout the day for several days or several times a week for several weeks, each hallucinatory experience not being limited to a few brief moments)
3. Incoherence or marked loosening of associations
4. Catatonic behavior
5. Flat or grossly inappropriate affect

Despite the similarities between RDC and DSM, the DSM concept of schizophrenia is more restrictive; according to the DSM-III-R, patients are *not* diagnosed schizophrenic if continuous signs of the illness (or prodromal signs) have not persisted for at least 6 months. Some other sets of criteria (e.g., Feighner criteria) include this restriction, and some do not. The inclusion or exclusion of this restriction, however, has implications for the research and theory of schizophrenia; it therefore should always be considered before one of these sets of criteria is applied.

The DSM-III-R defines schizophrenia as a more-or-less chronic disease, excluding acute patients with intermittent course. Some of these patients may later be diagnosed as schizophrenic, if their illness shifts to chronicity. The "schizophrenic" with, for example, two short-term but severe breakdowns with the full symptom pattern of schizophrenia and recovery will never be rated schizophrenic by DSM-III-R standards. This patient, instead, is classified with a "schizophreniform disorder." "Since a 6-month duration is required for the diagnosis, there is no acute subtype" (DSM-III-R, p. 191). Good responders to neuroleptic treatment may therefore only be considered schizophreniform. Due to neuroleptic treatment or spontaneous remission, a high number of schizophrenic patients, however, recovers *before* 6 months have elapsed. As the well controlled study of Cole *et al.* (1964) shows, about 25% of schizophrenics even recover spontaneously within 6 weeks (see Chapter 13). The task force for the definition and criteria of the DSM IV discusses the dropping of the six-month duration criterion (see *Schizophrenia Bulletin, 17*(1).

Diagnostic criteria are hypothetical constructs based on different concepts of schizophrenia (e.g., Schneider's concept). The application of one or the other criterion cannot be easily justified by empirical data, until a decision is reached on what schizophrenia is.

Restrictive concepts are advantageous, because the risk of including nonschizophrenic in the investigated sample is minimized. The problem with restrictive criteria, however, is that the investigator only sees one section of the population without being able to show empirically that this section is representative. It will be shown in Chapters 10 through 12 that schizophrenia can be understood as a spectrum, including varying degrees of expression of the illness. If this hypothesis is correct, restriction to any one section of the spectrum may yield unrepresentative data.

A definition that is too broad, however, may include patients in the sample who are not truly schizophrenic. The study by Carpenter *et al.* (1974) proved that when the diagnosis is based on 5 of the 12 symptoms (broader criterion), 80% of those patients diagnosed by experienced clinicians as certainly schizophrenic are selected as schizophrenic by the criterion. When 7 signs are required (restrictive criterion), only 44% of theses patients are diagnosed as schizophrenic. With the broader 5-item criterion, however, 13% of the patients are diagnosed falsely, that is, are termed schizophrenic according to the criterion but not according to experienced clinicians. The more restrictive 7-item criterion falsely diagnoses only 1% (compared with clinical assessment). Both approaches, therefore, have advantages and disadvantages: a criterion that is too broad may overgeneralize and a criterion that is too narrow may limit research to one sector of the disease. Therefore, no fixed rule on the narrowness or broadness of sample selection can be presented. The researcher or the clinician must assess the "pros and cons" of each concept and make his or her own decision about which concept to use.

Reputable scientific journals today rarely publish articles in which the psychiatric samples have not been defined by one of these inventories. The researcher's policy should be to use any set of criteria rather than rely on clinical impressions or use no criteria at all. The best strategy is to compare the results of research on samples defined by different criteria of different broadness. Such a strategy prevents premature austerity or weakening of the diagnostic concept labeled "schizophrenia."

# XIV.  Suggested Readings

E. Bleuler (1911; Engl., 1950) and Kraepelin (1913; Engl., 1919) have written the seminal books in the field. These books still contain the most detailed descriptions of the clinical picture and they are still the basic writings on which most modern theories are founded. Kendell (1987) describes the modern view. The now very popular division of schizophrenia into a negative and a positive type is described in more detail by Andreasen (1987). The similar division into types I and II is described by Crow (1985), and includes his theory that poor prognosis and structural brain alterations are the characteristic features of the type-II schizophrenic.

The result of the important International Pilot Study of Schizophrenia, which for the first time showed that similar rates of occurrence and similar symptoms are found in different countries all over the world, is described by Sartorius *et al.*, 1974.

## Summary Statements and Interpretations

### Incidence

Slightly less than 1% of the population are at risk for schizophrenia. There is no gender difference. However, men are hospitalized at a younger age than women. The symptoms and course of the illness are extremely heterogeneous.

Schizophrenia may be several illnesses. However the similar proportion of affected persons in different cultures suggests the probability of associated forms of the same basic disease and a hereditary component. However, schizophrenia is not necessarily fully determined by hereditary factors (Chapter 10) nor is this presumption the only one that can be derived from these observations.

### Symptoms

#### Thought and Language Disorder

The thought-disordered schizophrenic easily deviates from the goal of the communication. Associative intrusions occur that are related to the words just uttered but not to the general goal of the communication. Productive and deficit forms (reduction and slowing of speech production) of the disorder occur.

The basic disturbance in the productive form of the illness is the inability to organize thoughts and speech production in accordance with paramount speech plans and demands of the situation.

Some of the deficit (negative) forms may be secondary to the illness, perhaps a coping response to the difficult experiences in the acute phase of the illness. However, this opinion is not shared by all investigators: some believe that different illnesses are represented by positive and negative symptoms.

#### Perceptual Disturbances

Intrinsic disturbances of perceptual processes are rarely evident. Nevertheless, schizophrenics interpret what they perceive differently than normal people do. They frequently consider secondary irrelevant aspects; they feel compelled to interpret events as striking and important.

The difference from normal perception is that schizophrenic perception does not consider contextual constraints. (A schizophrenic may interpret an open window on a warm summer evening as a striking event.)

## Hallucinations

Auditory hallucinations are the most common type found in two-thirds of schizophrenics. Therefore, they are integral parts of diagnostic criteria. Typical hallucinations are short comments and short dialogues.

Inner speech and thoughts are often perceived so intensely that they are interpreted as coming from outside. (Similar experiences are reported if certain areas of the temporal lobes are electrically stimulated during brain surgery.) Parallel processing of secondary information might be closer to the threshold of awareness than normal.

Clinical and experimental evidence shows that highly structured situations and tasks reduce hallucinations. Why this is so is not clear. One could speculate that "pseudo-perception" is the result of a weak cognitive organization that might be assisted by offering more clearly defined situations.

There is some evidence that schizophrenia involves the hemisphere (usually the left) dominant for speech production and for conscious experience (see Chapter 8 for further discussion of this controversy).

## Delusions

The prominent delusion is that of being under the control of other people or hidden forces.

Delusions appear to arise from hallucinations or false interpretations of events. The patient feels forced to attend to secondary phenomena and experiences his or her own thoughts as coming from outside. He or she often has the feeling of being a passive observer, that his or her own will can no longer influence events (cf. Frith and Done, 1988). He or she interprets these experiences as indicative of being under the control of others.

## Psychomotor Disturbances

Disorganization of body, limb, and facial movements can be observed. Experiments discussed in chapter 7 report a correlation with thought disorganization. (Hyperactivity and extreme retardation are rare and striking deviations.)

Whether these disturbances are more typical of different subgroups (e.g., with more or less positive or negative symptoms) or represent more widespread secondary features will be discussed in subsequent text.

A special form and possibly a special subgroup is the catatonic form of the illness, which shows extreme rigidity and sometimes extreme agitation.

### Intelligence

No *major* intellectual disturbances are found. Possible exceptions are those patients who are hospitalized for longer periods of time and those with mild cerebral atrophy.

Experimental evidence shows that schizophrenics show deviant performance under certain task conditions (cf. Chapter 3). However, this performance may not be specific and is probably a minor deviation, which does not lead to striking difficulties in daily life, unlike the handicaps experienced by patients with cerebral damage.

### Emotions

As with motor behavior, vacillation between intense and reduced emotional expression occurs. Often intense emotional excitement predominates in the acute phase of the illness, but an extreme poverty of emotional expression may also be found. In chronic long-term phases, the reduction of emotional excitability predominates (e.g., affective blunting, flatness of affect).

The question arises of whether there is one illness, two, or only a change during the course of the illness.

A common feature is a discrepancy between the actual situation and the appropriate emotional expression.

This feature may parallel the inadequate verbal responses that do not fit contextual requirements.

## Heterogeneity and Problems of Definition and Diagnosis

The heterogeneity of manifestations and differences in diagnostic habits requires strict diagnostic criteria, especially if patients are selected for research programs.

Available diagnostic criteria result in different concepts. The researcher, therefore, can never be absolutely sure that the selected sample is truly representative.

## References

Andreasen, N. C. (1983). *The scale for assessment of negative symptoms (SANS)*. Iowa City, Iowa: The University of Iowa.

Andreasen, N. C. (1984). *The scale for assessment of positive symptoms (SAPS)*. Iowa City, Iowa: The University of Iowa.

Andreasen, N. C. (1985). Positive vs. negative schizophrenia: A critical evaluation. *Schizophrenia Bulletin, 11*, 380–389.

Andreasen, N. C. (1987). The diagnosis of schizophrenia. *Schizophrenia Bulletin*, *13*, 9–22.

Berndl, K., von Cranach, M., and Grüsser, O.-J. (1986). Impairment of perception and recognition of faces, mimic expression and gestures in schizophrenic patients. *European Archives of Psychiatry and Neurological Science*, *235*, 282–291.

Bilder, R. M., Mukherjee, S., Rieder, R. O., and Pandurangi, A. K. (1985). Symptomatic and neuropsychological components of defect states. *Schizophrenia Bulletin*, *11*, 409–419.

Bleuler, E. (1911). *Dementia praecox oder die Gruppe der Schizophrenien.* (Translation: J. Zinkin, *Dementia praecox or the group of schizophrenias.* International Universities Press, 1950). Leipzig: Deuticke Verlag.

Bleuler, E., and Bleuler, M. (1966). *Lehrbuch der Psychiatrie*, 10 Ed. Berlin: Springer.

Bleuler, M. (1972). *Die schizophrenen Geistesstörungen im Lichte langjähriger Kranken- und Familiengeschichten.* Stuttgart: Thieme.

Bleuler, M. (1981). Einzelkrankheiten in der Schizophreniegruppe? In G. Huber (Ed.), *Schizophrenie. Stand und Entwicklungstendenzen der Forschung.* Stuttgart: Schattauer.

Carpenter, W. T., Heinrichs, D. W., and Wagman, A. M. I. (1988). Deficit and nondeficit forms of schizophrenia: The concept. *American Journal of Psychiatry*, *145*, 578–583.

Carpenter, W. T., Strauss, J. S., and Bartko, J. J. (1974). Use of signs and symptoms for the identification of schizophrenic patients. *Schizophrenia Bulletin*, *11*, 37–49.

Chapman, L. J., and Chapman, J. P. (1973a). *Disordered thought in schizophrenia.* New York: Appleton-Century-Crofts.

Chapman, L. J., and Chapman, J. P. (1973b). Selection of subjects in studies of schizophrenic cognition. *Journal of Abnormal Psychology*, *86*, 10–15.

Ciompi, L., and Müller, C. (1976). *Lebensweg und Alter der Schizophrenen. Eine katamnestische Langzeitstudie bis ins Senium.* Berlin: Springer.

Cole, J. O., Klerman, G. L., and Goldberg, S. C. (1964). Phenothiazine treatment in acute schizophrenia. *Archives of General Psychiatry*, *10*, 246–261.

Conrad, K. (1971). *Die beginnende Schizophrenie.* Stuttgart: Thieme.

Cooper, J. E., Kendell, R. E., Gurland, B. J., Sharpe, L., Copeland, J. R. M., and Simon, R. (1972). *Psychiatric diagnosis in New York and London: A comparative study of mental hospital admissions.* New York: Oxford University Press.

Cramer, P., Weegmann, M., and O'Neil, M. (1989). Schizophrenia and the Perception of Emotions. How accurately do schizophrenics Judge the Emotional States of others? *British Journal of Psychiatry*, *155*, 225–228.

Crow, T. J. (1985). The two-syndrome concept: Origins and current status. *Schizophrenia Bulletin*, *11*, 471–486.

Cutting, J. (1985). *The psychology of schizophrenia.* Edinburgh: Churchill Livingstone.

Feer, H. (1970). *Kybernetik in der Psychiatrie. Schizophrenie und Depression.* Basel: Karger.

Feighner, J. P., Robins, P., Guze, S. B., Woodruff, R. A., Winokur, G., and Muñoz, R. (1972). Diagnostic criteria for use in psychiatric research. *Archives of General Psychiatry*, *26*, 57–63.

Fieguth, G., and Goncalves, N. (1977). Testleistung chronisch Schizophrener im HAWIE. *Archiv für Psychiatrie und Nervenkrankheiten*, *222*, 139–149.

Freedman, B. J. (1974). The subjective experience of perceptual and cognitive disturbances in schizophrenia. *Archives of General Psychiatry*, *30*, 333–340.

Frith, C. D., and Done, D. J. (1988). Towards a neuropsychology of schizophrenia. *British Journal of Psychiatry*, *153*, 437–443.

Goldberg, T. E., Karson, C. N., Lelesni, J. P., and Weinberger, D. R. (1988). Intellectual impairment in adolescent psychosis: A controlled psychometric study. *Schizophrenia Research*, *1*, 261–266.

Gottesman, I. I., and Shields, J. (1982). *Schizophrenia: The Epigenetic Puzzle.* Cambridge: Cambridge University Press.

Guelfi, G. P., Faustman, W. O., and Csernansky, J. G. (1989). Independence of positive and negative symptoms in a population of schizophrenic patients. *Journal of Nervous and Mental Disease, 177*, 285–290.

Guertin, W. H., Raabin, A. I., Frank, G. H., and Ladd, C. E. (1962). Research with the Wechsler intelligence scales for adults. *Psychological Bulletin, 59*, 1–26.

Harrow, M., and Quinlan, D. Q. (1985). *Disordered thinking and schizophrenic psychopathology.* New York: Gardner Press.

Huber, G. (1974). *Psychiatrie.* Stuttgart: Schattauer.

Huber, G., Gross, G., and Schüttler, R. (1979). *Schizophrenie. Eine verlaufs- und sozialpsychiatrische Langzeitstudie.* Berlin: Springer.

Hunt, J. McV., and Cofer, C. N. (1944). Psychological deficit. In J. McV. Hunt (Ed.), *Personality and behavior disorders.* New York: Ronald Press.

Janzarik, W. (1968). *Schizophrene Verläufe.* Berlin: Springer.

Johnstone, E. C., Crow, T. J., Frith, C. D., Stevens, M., Kreel, L., and Husband, J. (1978). The dementia of dementia praecox. *Acta Psychiatrica Scandinavica, 57*, 305–324.

Kendell, R. E. (1985). Schizophrenia: Clinical features. In R. Michels and J. O. Cavenar (Eds.) *Psychiatry*, Vol. 1. London: Basic Books.

Kendell, R. E. (1987). Schizophrenia: Clinical Features. In: R. Michels, J. O. Cavenar, Jr., A. M. Cooper, S. B. Guze, L. L. Judd, G. L. Klerman and A. J. Solnit (Eds.) *Psychiatry, Volume 1.* New York: Basis Books.

Kraepelin, E. (1896). *Psychiatrie*, 5th Ed. (Translation: J. C. Cutting and M. Sheperd (Eds.), *Schizophrenia: The origin and development of its study in Europe.* Cambridge University Press, 1986). Leipzig: Barth.

Kraepelin, E. (1899). *Psychiatrie: Ein Lehrbuch für Studierende und Ärzte.* Leipzig: Barth.

Kraepelin, E. (1913). *Psychiatrie*, Vol. 3, 8th Ed. (Translation: *Dementia praecox and paraphrenia*, Edinburgh: Livingston, 1919). Leipzig: Barth.

Krauss, F. (1852). *Nothschrei eines Magnetisch-Vergifteten.* Stuttgart: Selbstverlag des Herausgebers.

Krauss, F. (1867). *Nothgedrungene Fortsetzung meines Nothschrei gegen meine Vergiftung mit concentriertem Lebensäther.* Stuttgart: Selbstverlag des Herausgebers.

Leff, J. P., Kuipers, L., Berkowitz, R., Eberlein-Fries, R., and Sturgeon, D. (1982). A controlled trial of social intervention in the families of schizophrenic patients. *British Journal of Psychiatry, 141*, 121–134.

Lehmann, H. E. (1975). Schizophrenia: Clinical features. In A. M. Freedman, H. I. Kaplan, and B. J. Sadock (Eds.), *Comprehensive Textbook of Psychiatry, II*, Vol. 1, pp. 890–923. Baltimore: Williams & Wilkins.

Margo, A., Hemsley, D. R., and Slade, P. D. (1981). The effect of varying auditory input on schizophrenic hallucinations. *British Journal of Psychiatry, 139*, 122–127.

Matussek, P. (1952). Untersuchungen über die Wahrnehmung. 1. Mitteilung. *Archiv für Psychiatrie und Zeitschrift für Neurologie, 189*, 279–319.

McGhie, A., and Chapman, J. (1961). Disorders of attention and perception in early schizophrenia. *British Journal of Medical Psychology, 34*, 103–116.

Miller, G. A., Galanter, E., and Pribram, K. H. (1960). *Plans and the structure of behavior.* New York: Holt, Rinehart, & Winston.

Möller, H. J., and von Zerssen, D. (1986). Depression in schizophrenia. In G. D. Burrows, T. R. Norman, and G. Rubinstein (Eds.), *Handbook of studies on schizophrenia.* Part I Amsterdam: Elsevier.

Neale, J. M., and Oltmanns, T. F. (1980). *Schizophrenia.* New York: Wiley.

Overall, J. E., and Hollister, L. E. (1979). Comparative evaluation of research diagnostic criteria for schizophrenia. *Archives of General Psychiatry, 36*, 1198–1205.

Robertson, G., and Taylor, P. J. (1985). Some cognitive correlates of schizophrenic illnesses. *Psychological Medicine, 15*, 81–98.

Rochester, S. R., and Martin, J. R. (1979). *Crazy Talk. A Study of the Discourse of Schizophrenic Speakers.* New York: Plenum Press.

Roth, M. (1986). Diagnosis and prognosis of schizophrenia. In G. D. Burrows, T. R. Norman, and G. Rubinstein (Eds.), *Handbook of studies on schizophrenia*, Part I. Amsterdam: Elsevier.

Sartorius, N., Shapiro, R., and Jablonsky, A. (1974). The international pilot study of schizophrenia. *Schizophrenia Bulletin, 1*, 21–35.

Schneider, K. (1957). Primary and secondary symptoms in schizophrenia. (Translation in S. R. Hirsch and M. Sheperd (Eds.), *Themes and variations in European psychiatry*, 1974). Bristol: Wright.

Spitzer, R. L., Endicott, J., and Robins, E. (1978). Research diagnostic criteria. *Archives of General Psychiatry, 35*, 773–782.

Strauss, J. S., Carpenter, W. T., Jr., and Bartko, J. J. (1974). The diagnosis and understanding of schizophrenia: Part III. Speculations on the processes that underlie schizophrenic symptoms and signs. *Schizophrenia Bulletin, 1*, 61–69.

Walker, E. F., Harvey, P. D., and Perlman, D. (1988). The positive/negative symptom distinction in psychoses. A replication and extension of previous findings. *Journal of Nervous and Mental Disease, 176*, 359–363.

World Health Organization. (1978). *Manual of the International Classification of Diseases, Injuries, and Causes of Death.* 9th Revision. Geneva, Switzerland: The Organisation.

# PART II

# Cognitive Symptoms

## General Introduction: Methodological Issues in Cognitive Research with Clinical Groups

The terms *cognitive* and *cognition* are used to refer to activities of the central nervous system involved in information processing. These activities can be regarded as analogous, but far from identical, to those performed by computers, insofar as they involve the uptake and processing of information. Consequently, we refer to processes that start with the receipt of sensory data (input), pass through various comparisons with internally stored data, modulations, and transformations, after which responses are executed (output). The actual result of this processing (unlike a computer) is under the influence of momentary internal contextual conditions (e.g., vigilance, motivation, emotional state, abilities), as well as the external contextual conditions constraining a given situation. Further constraints include prior experience and the general background of the individual (e.g., knowledge, personality). In clinical research, one tries to eliminate these influences on cognitive processing when comparing the peculiarities of information processing apparent in various groups of patients. Here, however, lies the basic methodological problem of clinical research. Clinical populations, especially schizophrenics, often deviate from healthy subjects with respect to such internal states. To decide whether a given deviation of task performance is due to a genuine failure in information processing or due to some temporary and unspecific effect of severe illness is difficult. In other words, very disturbed schizophrenics can be expected to do all sorts of tasks badly.

Chapman and Chapman (1973) suggested some rules for experimental design with clinical groups that are still valid. They discussed the importance of considering factors such as IQ, education, medication, and severity and length of the illness when matching subjects for experimental study.

The Chapmans were also concerned with the difficulty of proving a differential deficit. They argued that, through a generally reduced capability, the poor performance of a psychotic on a particular task is probably an expression of task difficulty rather than of differential cognitive deficit. The experimenter can show a differential deficit only with a *matched task* design.

Experimental and control tasks should be matched according to degree of difficulty found in the control subjects. Only if controls perform equivalently on both tasks (i.e., performances are highly correlated) can one assume that impaired task performance by schizophrenics is not due to a *generalized deficit* (Chapman and Chapman, 1973).

For example, let us examine two types of a digit-span task in which the subject has to repeat a series of digits immediately after hearing them, once in the presence and once in the absence of distracting stimuli. The controls perform similarly on both presentations. If, in contrast, the performance of schizophrenics is impaired only under distraction conditions, then the experimenter can assume that he or she has demonstrated merely a generalized deficit in this group. This experiment may be compared with the experiments by Oltmanns and his colleagues (1978; see subsequent text), in which these two tasks were equated for difficulty by presenting a long series of digits *without* and a short series *with* distracting stimuli.

A careful design with matched groups and matched tasks is indispensable in schizophrenia research. "The most appropriate design for measuring cognitive deficit is almost always that of matched tasks . . . It is unfortunate that these very useful designs have seldom been used" (Chapman and Chapman, 1973, p. 101). This statement is, to an extent, still valid today. However, an increasing number of researchers has become aware of this fundamental methodological problem in clinical research.

Another reason for the inconclusive nature of many studies, as pointed out previously, is the absence of adequate psychiatric comparison groups controlling, for example, for severity and length of illness. One aspect of this problem deserves special mention. Close matching of IQ scores can lead to the comparison of low-IQ normals and schizophrenics, who are only temporarily performing at this level because of their illness. Under these circumstances, it may be preferable to match according to the degree of education achieved. (For further discussion, see Chapman and Chapman, 1973.)

In this part we will first consider thought processes of schizophrenics and the extent to which their speech mirrors thought disturbance (Chapter 2). We shall then consider the contribution of memory performance (Chapter 3) and perceptual performance (Chapter 4) to the dysfunction of cognitive processes.

# Chapter 2

# Thought and Speech

## I. Thought Processes

In 1973, our understanding of schizophrenic thought processes was admirably reviewed by Chapman and Chapman, at the University of Wisconsin, in their book, *Disordered Thought in Schizophrenia*. Consequently, this chapter will concentrate on results obtained since then. Older literature is only cited to help illuminate newer findings.

Thought disorder, formally assessed by the nature and content of speech, is one of the diagnostic criteria of schizophrenia (e.g., RDC, Spitzer *et al.*, 1978; DSM-III-R, 1987). Bleuler (1911) viewed a particular form of thought disturbance, the loosening of associations, as one of the basic symptoms of schizophrenia (cf. Chapter 1). Formal thought disorder is still regarded as one of the core features of schizophrenia (Harrow and Quinlan, 1985). Therefore, we will begin this chapter on cognitive function with a discussion of this feature.

## A. Clinical Measurement of Thought Disturbance

Thought processes may deviate in many ways and still be considered "thought disorder" (Chapter 1). However, a basic distinction is drawn between formal thought disorder and thought content. *Formal* thought disorder denotes deviations in the way thought is expressed. These deviations may include disorganized speech flow and deviations from the original line of thought or from the goal of the conversation. Disturbances of thought *content* are usually determined by the bizarre nature of the subject's delusions.

Although certain impairments of speech or the thought process can be clear indicators of schizophrenia, we are still faced with the problem that not all subjects diagnosed with schizophrenia show these "deviations from the norm." Within the sample examined by Andreasen and Grove (1979), only 41% of the schizophrenics showed thought disorder according to speech peculiarities. Rochester and Martin (1979) reported an even lower proportion.

At the University of Iowa, Andreasen and Grove (1986) divided thought disturbances into those with positive or negative features. Generally, positive thought disturbance consists of incoherence, disorganization, and a loss of the goal in a train of thought. The main negative features are a reduction in the amount and content of speech (poverty of speech) and the blocking of thought processes. At Harvard, Holzman and colleagues (1986) ran a factor analysis of 32 items listed in their thought disorder index (TDI). They describe five major factors: (1) irrelevant intrusions, (2) combinatory thinking, (3) fluid thinking, (4) confusion, and (5) idiosyncratic verbalization.

The list shows that thought disturbance consists of changes of verbal behavior as well as of thought processes, which, of course, one cannot measure directly. Both in diagnosis and in empirical research, these two features are seldom treated separately.

Schizophrenics are not the only psychiatric subjects to show thought disorder. Andreasen and Grove (1986) used their Thought, Language, and Communication scale (TLC) to tackle the differentiation of manic and schizophrenic thought disorders. Their rather sparse results revealed that schizophrenics tended to show more marked negative features. A comparison with depressives' poverty of speech (a prominent negative symptom) did not differentiate the schizophrenics (Ragin *et al.*, 1989). Using the TDI, Holzman and colleagues (Holzman *et al.*, 1986; Solovay *et al.*, 1987) at the McLean Hospital and Harvard University, Massachusetts, found no apparent differences between schizophrenic and manic patients concerning the severity of the disturbance. However, they were able to describe features that qualitatively distinguished between manic and schizophrenic subjects: manic subjects showed significantly more "combinatory thinking." In contrast, "disorganization" (e.g., difficulty finding the right word, vagueness, confusion, and incoherence) and "idiosyncratic verbalization" characterized the schizophrenic group. "Associative looseness" did not differentiate the groups (cf. Figure 2.1). In short, certain positive "cognitive" symptoms and not negative symptoms seem to be more specific to schizophrenics.

The TDI is a relatively lengthy procedure to administer since it includes the assessment of utterances during the performance of the Rorschach Test and the verbal tests of the Wechsler Adult Intelligence Scale (WAIS). However, it probably considers more subtle features of thought deviation than the TLC (cf. Solovay *et al.*, 1987).

Perhaps one of the most detailed assessments of thought disorder was developed by Harrow at the Michael Reese Hospital, Chicago (for numerous examples, see Harrow and Quinlan, 1985). The basic assessment derives from presenting an object-sorting test, a test of proverb interpretation, and the social-comprehension subscale of the WAIS for the patient to comment on and to explain. (For a description of the short form of this test, its reliability, and validity, see Marengo *et al.*, 1986).

In agreement with others mentioned, Harrow and Marengo (1986) found that manic patients could not be distinguished by the severity of positive

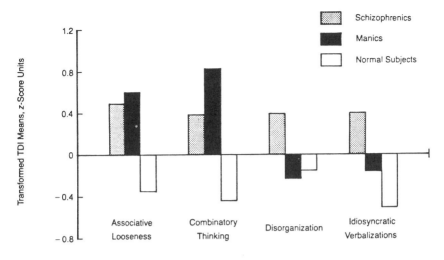

**Figure 2.1** Frequencies with which subject groups produce thought-disordered responses under four *a priori* conditions based on categories from the Thought Disorder Index. Values are *z*-scores of transformed data (from Solovay *et al.,* 1987, © American Medical Association).

thought disturbance shown at the first assessment. However, at the follow-up after 1.5–2 yr, the disturbance in manic subjects had nearly disappeared. In contrast, schizophrenics showed clear disturbances at both assessments, even if the disturbances were somewhat less at follow-up. The relative stability of the schizophrenic (positive) thought disturbance over time has been confirmed by Harvey *et al.* (1984), Harrow and Marengo (1986), Earle-Boyer *et al.* (1986), and Ragin *et al.* (1989), and of the negative form of the disturbance by Andreasen and Grove (1986). Thus, the disturbance seems to resemble more of a trait in cases of schizophrenia. However, an investigation of positive thought disorder by Ragin and Oltmanns (1987) could not confirm this.

If one accepts that thought disturbance is central to schizophrenic diagnosis, then it is natural to ask if such disturbances have been seen in biological relatives of schizophrenics. Using the TLC scale, Berenbaum *et al.* (1985) found little concordance in mono- and dizygotic twins of schizophrenic patients. Their cases came from the same population studied by Gottesman and Shields (1982) in London (see Chapter 10). These results may be evidence for the absence of thought disturbance in non-schizophrenic relatives of schizophrenics. However, the TLC was designed for clinical use; it is not very sensitive to minor disturbances (e.g., "cognitive slippage"). Studies of the children of schizophrenics have shown the presence of a slight cognitive disturbance (Chapter 12). Callahan and Saccuzzo (1986) have shown that biological relatives of schizophrenics make many more intrusive errors on associative learning tasks than control populations (for reviews, see Romney, 1988; Rund, 1988).

## B. Experimental Studies: Ability to Abstract

### 1. Introduction

The ability to abstract refers to the ability to "look beyond" concrete matters. The ability to abstract is a feature of the highest level of phylogenetic development and is part of the final phase of human ontogenetic development. Only with cognitive maturity is the ability to consider an object consciously from an abstract or theoretical point of view fully developed. Thus, a child may view objects strewn across the floor as toys; an adult can more easily adopt a different point of view and see a subgroup of them as useful, perhaps as kitchen tools.

The ability to abstract information from objects or situations has been divided into (at least) three major types of activity: (1) to order and to classify items, that is, categorical thinking; (2) to form concepts from features imputed to these items; and (3) to transfer a literal meaning into a figurative (more abstract) meaning, that is, metaphorical thinking. These features, along with the nature of strategies used to solve problems, and the ability to proceed with consequential *logical* trains of thought, have been the subject of study.

### 2. Categorical and Conceptual Thinking

An early major impetus for the study of conceptual thought processes came from the work of the Russian psychologist Vigotsky (1934). He postulated that schizophrenic thought regressed to a child-like pre-abstractive stage (the regression hypothesis). This hypothesis inspired the experimental investigations by Cameron (1939), a professor of psychiatry and psychology in Wisconsin. He compared schizophrenic reasoning to that of six-year-old children. After consultation with the well-known Swiss developmental psychologist, Piaget, he divided the thought processes of children into different classes; the result was that schizophrenic reasoning could be clearly differentiated from that of children.

A more recent report from Sackeim and Shapiro (1981) illustrates the difficulty of validating the regression hypothesis. They compared word-association performance in paranoid and nonparanoid schizophrenic and healthy adults with norms for 3rd-, 4th-, and 5th-grade school children. The crucial difference lay between a free-choice and a forced-choice test in which four alternatives were presented. Free-choice associations of the words produced no clear results, but limited(forced)-choice associations selected by the nonparanoid group were similar to those selected by young children. It is questionable whether this partial similarity really represents a regression of schizophrenic thinking to earlier stages of development. This question has not been researched thoroughly, apparently because the regression hypothesis has lost its appeal.

The theory of Goldstein (1959), a neuropsychologist who was trained in Germany, provided an early impetus to the experimental investigation of categorical thinking. He examined the ability to abstract in patients with brain damage by using an "Object-Sorting Test," which he and others used subsequently to test schizophrenics. In his first analysis, Goldstein (1959) saw parallel trends between the schizophrenic thought process and the weakness in abstract thinking shown by brain-damaged patients. Strangely, Goldstein only made qualitative analyses of his patients sorting the objects according to substance, color, or function. Later, however, he did draw a distinction between the performance of brain-damaged and psychiatric subjects. The former subjects were characterized by a more-or-less complete loss of the ability to make abstract connections when ordering the items. The latter subjects were able to abstract features, but the process was unstable. They showed a transitory disturbance with interference from different loosely connected or idiosyncratic associations. For example, a schizophrenic patient may group the match boxes and the pipe together (Figure 2.2) and say that these belong together, because "Miller's barn was set on fire last week, and Miller has a pipe."

Indeed, this feature of the schizophrenic disturbance, namely distractive interference, rather than the absence of abstract thinking, was also demonstrated by Chapman in 1956. Schizophrenics cannot only be distracted by actual physical stimuli, but also by abstract associations (categories). Reich and Cutting (1982) showed that schizophrenics used abstract expressions to describe pictures just as often as depressed subjects and that these expressions were a good deal more abstract than those used by subjects with organic brain damage. Using Lovibond's (1954) object-sorting task (which grades the nature of the category selected by the subject), Dykes and McGhie (1976) found that an acutely ill schizophrenic group sorted according to a greater variety of unusual categories and were reminiscent of a highly creative group of subjects studied for comparison. Chapman and Chapman (1973) were convinced that the idiosyncratic nature of categorization—the "private" meaning common to a series of items—gave the impression of impaired abstract thinking or *concrete thinking* in the terms used by Cameron (1938, 1939; see example in the next paragraph).

More recent use of Goldstein's object-sorting test convinced Harrow and Quinlan (1985) that an impairment of categorizing abilities is not specific to acute schizophrenia, and can be found in other acutely ill psychiatric subjects as well. However, except for chronic schizophrenics who remain hospitalized

**Figure 2.2**   Items used in an Object Sorting Test (from Payne and Hewlett, 1960).

for long periods, the impairment disappears in all groups in remission. Those who remain in the hospital or relatively isolated from verbal and social stimulation for long periods of time, whatever the original cause may be, seem to be at risk for concrete thinking. (An example of one such answer is "you need all these things for baking" instead of "household objects".) Similarly, Tutko and Spence (1962) claimed to provide evidence for the thesis that chronic rather than acute schizophrenic categorical thinking resembled that of brain-damaged subjects. However, when medication and duration of hospitalization were controlled, Daut and Chapman (1974) were unable to replicate these results.

Nevertheless, difficulties with categorical thinking by schizophrenics have been reported recently using the Wisconsin card-sorting test, in which the subjects are asked to sort card images varying according to color, form, and number. Schizophrenics "discover" fewer categories than most other groups of psychiatric or even brain-damaged patients (except for those with frontal damage; see Kolb and Whishaw, 1983; Chapter 8).

Unfortunately, it remains difficult to say whether "concrete thinking" is a feature of a particular group of schizophrenics, a consequence of long-term hospitalization (social isolation), or perhaps an indicator of organic deterioration. (This issue will be pursued further in Chapters 7 and 8, in which initial comparisons with subjects sustaining localized brain damage suggest that a subgroup of schizophrenics may sustain similar organic impairments.)

A further peculiar feature of schizophrenic thought processes that occupied the attention of research workers for some time is the notion of *overinclusive thinking* (Cameron, 1939). In terms of the often-used object-sorting test, this means that schizophrenics tend to order objects into the same category, even if in the expected sense, they do not belong to it. For example, a schizophrenic subject was asked to select the objects related to a ball from those in front of him. To this the subject responded "Kindergarten," and searched for relevant items. In addition to toys, these included knives and forks ("which the children used for eating") and matches ("with which they also played;" Harrow and Quinlan, 1985). From a wide range of tests, similar results have been reported by innumerable authors (including Straube and Klemm, 1975). In contrast, chronic schizophrenics, according to the many studies of Payne and colleagues, tend to be underinclusive, that is, they include fewer objects in a category than is expected (Payne and Hewlett, 1960; Hawks and Payne, 1971).

However, we do not wish to overemphasize findings about overinclusive thinking. It does not seem to have specific significance for schizophrenia (Andreasen and Powers, 1974), and seems to be correlated with the tendency for acute patients to be increasingly talkative (Hawks and Payne, 1971). Even in 1965, Gathercole suggested that such characteristics were a feature of the inability of schizophrenics to suppress inappropriate solutions for the question at hand (see Payne, 1971; Chapman and Chapman, 1973; Cutting, 1985; for further critical discussion).

One of the methodological weaknesses of the notion of overinclusiveness was that it was couched in terms too general for specific testing. Consequently, specific and useful conclusions were not forthcoming.

### 3. Proverb and Metaphor Comprehension

A useful method for illustrating schizophrenic impairment in abstract thinking is asking the subject to describe the meaning of a proverb. This "traditional" method of investigation has been thoroughly studied, especially by Gorham (1956). In all cases it was difficult for schizophrenics to transfer from the literal meaning of a sentence to a second metaphorical level of meaning (paralogia).

Two examples illustrate the problem. For the proverb "Shallow brooks are noisy," one schizophrenic explained, "The water hits the rocks and makes noises;" another replied, "There's a lot of rocks in shallow brooks. Sin and grief." When asked to elaborate on this answer, the reply was "The rocks kind of symbolize sin and grief" (Harrow and Quinlan, 1985).

Do these examples really show an absence of the capability for abstract thought? An impairment, perhaps, but not an inability. Interestingly, Chapman and Chapman (1973) found that if three proverbs with the same metaphorical meaning were presented, the schizophrenics were able to arrive at the meaning, as if the constraints set by the three clues enable the schizophrenic to follow the appropriate abstract line of thought.

Hamlin and Folsom (1977) compared the performance of five groups matched according to age and education (paranoid schizophrenic, chronic undifferentiated nonparanoid schizophrenic, neurotic, brain-damaged, and healthy). As the Chapmans did, Hamlin and Folsom found a trend, albeit not significant, for improved explanations in all the schizophrenic subgroups when several similar proverbs were presented. However, the subjects did improve with practice, especially on the multiple proverb task! In contrast, the organically impaired group performed worse generally and showed *no* sign of improvement. Curiously, the neurotic group performed worse on the multiple proverb test than when each proverb was presented separately.

Neuroleptic treatment can reduce the deficit in abstract thought, as recorded by a test of speech, or bring about an associated clinical improvement (e.g., thought disorder). Wahba *et al.* (1981) compared the effects on abstract thinking of standard doses of three types of neuroleptic with the performance of a healthy control group. The performance of acutely ill subjects was recorded at the beginning and end of a 10-day treatment period. All three treated groups improved on measures of abstract thought and on the digit-span test (cf. Chapter 3), with or without the distraction of emotional stimuli. The controls showed no change in performance on retest.

Even before the era of neuroleptic treatment, Cameron (1938) observed that bizarre idiosyncratic answers, typical of acute schizophrenics, declined in clinical remission. The following list shows examples of responses when patients had to complete the sentences presented:

| *At the height of psychosis* | *After partial remission* |
|---|---|
| | *H. is blond because . . .* |
| "Something, its on my head, | "Because I have inherited |
| it comes from my mother." | it from my parents." |
| | *A man fell down on the street because . . .* |
| . . its a world war." | ". . he slipped over." |
| | *The sun rises in the morning because . . .* |
| ". . . she's run out of gas." | ". . the earth rotates around |
| | the sun." |
| | *The wind blows because . . .* |
| ". . its indeed cosmic dust." | ". . the currents of air in |
| | the atmosphere change." |

Idiosyncratic and personal associations make up the bizarre and inappropriate answers. These answers dominate temporarily and disrupt the train of thought, whereas abstract thinking itself is not impaired—at least not in all subgroups (Harrow and Quinlan, 1985). Some investigators have suggested that schizophrenics use more abstract thought than healthy subjects. Shimkunas (1972) cites an example of a WAIS question, "What do an ax and a saw have in common?", to which the answer was "Building blocks of modern society" (quoted by Cutting, 1985, p. 336).

In conclusion, it seems that in some schizophrenics the ability to abstract is disturbed because they are more easily distracted by associations, whereas in other schizophrenics (perhaps a subgroup with mild brain damage) the ability may have been lost. (See Chapter 8 for a more detailed discussion of this topic.)

## C. Logical and Rational Deductive Abilities

The examples presented in the previous section lead to the area of schizophrenic logic. Do false thought processes contribute to the construction of delusions? Consider the examples of a supposedly schizophrenic syllogism favored by the German Von Domarus (1944, 1964) and the American psychiatrist Arieti (1955). "The devil influences some people. I feel influenced, therefore I am being influenced by the devil" (Harrow and Quinlan, 1985, p. 12). Delusional beliefs of schizophrenics do not seem to follow the rules of logical reasoning. Von Domarus claimed that for schizophrenics, shared attributes imply identity. Arieti was of the opinion that this breaking of a "logical rule" was most often seen when emotionally loaded themes were discussed with the patient (see also Bleuler, 1911; Chapter 1).

However, has a schizophrenic form of reasoning been established experimentally? Numerous negative results of such experiments have been reported. Chapman and Chapman (1973) could find no empirical demonstration that forms of nonrational thinking are more frequent among schizophrenics. Watson and Wold (1981) compared the performance of 100 schizophrenics with that of 50 subjects with psychiatric problems and 50 with organic problems on 158 syllogisms (e.g., All men are mortal. Socrates is a man, therefore Socrates is . . . ? The correct answer is "a mortal"). All groups were medicated. At first the comparison groups showed more errors than the schizophrenics. After the investigators had matched the subjects according to IQ and education, and attempted to match them according to the difficulties between the four conditions, all differences in performance disappeared.

Harrow's opinion is that a temporary "breaking of the rules of logic" originates from productive or positive symptoms, especially as seen in young untreated patients (Harrow and Prosen, 1978). The themes that come to mind when they try to answer a question preoccupy schizophrenics. The alternative responses cannot be efficiently suppressed. Harrow's explanation resembles Frith's (1979) description of the problem. When facing any stimulus or task, several parallel internal processes are initiated. Some of these, perhaps more in schizophrenics, are carried out consciously, rather than unconsciously as in healthy subjects.

## D. Problem-Solving Abilities

An analysis of the *strategies* used by schizophrenics to solve certain types of tasks would seem to be a particularly appropriate way to try to understand the nature of schizophrenic thought and reasoning.

Maier and Rey (1974), in Mannheim, Germany, asked 20 acute schizophrenics, including some with clinical thought disturbance, to determine which of four possible letters was represented in an incomplete dot matrix (the letter was made up of dots but was not complete). The optimal strategy minimizes the number of guesses about the position of dots missing from the complete letter. Their main finding was that schizophrenics asked more questions than members of a healthy control group and that thought-disturbed patients performed worst of all. These results led the investigators to conclude that schizophrenics were not able to select the optimal strategy. Interestingly, reduced questioning in the controls correlated with increased IQ. The schizophrenics displayed no significant correlation, despite matching according to IQ, age, and education. This result seems to imply that schizophrenic subjects were less able to apply their basic intellectual abilities to the practical solution of this type of task. However, without a psychiatric control group we do not know if the problem is specific for schizophrenics (however, see subsequent text).

A different type of test of task-solving strategies yielded similar conclusions. Malenka and colleagues (1986), at Stanford, asked small groups of chronic schizophrenic, depressed, and healthy subjects to follow a target on a video screen with a cursor. Schizophrenics had no problems in starting the exercise; however, when the cursor moved inadvertently, they made many more errors, especially when parts of the screen were blanked off. The authors concluded that the schizophrenics were impaired in their abilities to monitor internal cues in the absence of external cues. The result is consistent with the notion that schizophrenics are more dependent on externally cued structure, as indicated by the multiple-proverbs test. That their schizophrenic subjects were not regarded as thought disordered is interesting. However, those subjects with positive symptoms performed worse than those with negative ones.

Frith and Done (1989) in England extended this task. They presented two duck-shooters on a monitor, with guns pointing in opposite directions. Ducks could appear on either side, and in one version the trajectory of the bullet was hidden by a wall. The subjects—unmedicated schizophrenics with and without delusions of alien control, schizoaffective subjects, and healthy controls—all made many mistakes in the choice of and control of the duck-shooters. Most subjects could correct the errors, even in the absence of (complete) visual feedback. Only those patients suffering from delusions failed to attempt to make corrections. Here emerges a potential explanation for the behavior of a subgroup of schizophrenics, namely, a failure to monitor responses internally in order to guide further behavior.

The question of distraction in contrast to perseverance (switching or no switching between sensory channels) was investigated in a study comparing hallucinating (a positive symptom) and nonhallucinating patients, as well as poor and good premorbid patients (Heilbrun *et al.*, 1986). Subjects were asked either to concentrate on a visual pattern task and ignore words they heard or to switch their attention and repeat the words they heard. Nonhallucinators were able to perform with both strategies. Some hallucinatory patients were able to switch; others were not. Poor premorbid subjects could control distraction when required, but were impaired in repeating the word when required. Perseverance was marked; voluntary or involuntary switching was suppressed. Good premorbid patients (often acutely ill) showed the opposite effect.

Perseverance in the chronically ill was shown by a Danish group (Lyon and Gerlach, 1988). Their subjects included chronic schizophrenics (34 paranoid and undifferentiated), as well as 14 with affective, 9 with neurotic, and 9 with schizoid syndromes, and 34 healthy controls. The subjects were asked to press buttons on the left (L) and right (R) in order to make a cross appear on a screen. The authors analyzed the response sequences (e.g., LR, LRR, LLRR, L × 6). The schizophrenic *and* the emotionally disturbed showed more perseverance (i.e., choosing one side or simple alternation). The other groups switched to more complex strategies and did not differ from each other. The stereotypical nature of schizophrenic responses was not related to the length of stay in the hospital. Only the neurotic group showed an inverse relationship between the length of the hospital stay and the number of responses.

The strategies used by schizophrenic, neurotic, and healthy adolescents has also been studied (R. D. Oades, unpublished observations). Once the subjects have learned to discriminate two colored patterns appearing on a monitor, an unsignalled shift or reversal occurs on one or both of the stimulus dimensions. As in the Danish study just discussed, the schizophrenics develop a more marked perseverance of response to one or the other cue. Further, like the findings of Heilbrunn, Frith, and Malenka, they are less responsive to feedback. When the stimuli are repeated in the same position, they are less likely to show an adaptive strategy (i.e., win–stay, lose–shift).

## II. Speech

### A. Methodological Comments

Despite the variety of investigations discussed in the previous sections, it remains difficult to conclude if a type of thought disorder is specific to schizophrenia, what cognitive mechanisms are disturbed, and if the various subtypes of thought disorder differ between subgroups of patients. One of the principal problems is the term thought disorder itself. It is a term formulated from clinical experience, but difficult to apply effectively in experimental settings.

In the following sections we will consider the verbal performance of schizophrenics. One may hope that the deviance in this feature is more clearly definable and better translatable to empirical analysis and experimental tests.

### B. Spontaneous Speech

#### 1. Prosody and Pauses in Speech Flow

At the level of clinical observation, schizophrenics do not show phonetic disturbances in the strict sense, but the flow of speech often differs from the norm. Sometimes it is rapid, sometimes it is extremely slow; it may even be completely blocked.

Changes of vocal intonation were described by Ostwald (1978). Changes of emphasis may appear independent of content and sentence structure or the patient may use a monotonous sing-song. Note that some patients cannot appropriately adjust how loud they speak; they may shout at someone standing right by them or whisper inaudibly. Meaningless noises may intrude or the patient may start to laugh or giggle inappropriately. (However, we should emphasize that not all these characteristics appear in one patient.) On the basis of impaired speech modulation, schizophrenics can be distinguished reliably from healthy subjects by evaluators who are blind to the diagnosis (Todt and Howell, 1980). This identification is particularly easy in patients with blunted affect (Leff and Abberton, 1981).

A Canadian group from Toronto taped examples of speech from 40 young medicated schizophrenic patients, half of whom were thought disordered (Rochester et al., 1977). Half-hour interviews were assessed by two psychiatrists unfamiliar with the cases. Pauses occurred much more often in the speech of thought-disordered subjects than in the speech of either healthy or non-thought-disordered subjects. In particular, the length of the pause at the beginning of a sentence correlated with the lack of coherence of speech content (see Section II, B, 4). However, the authors emphasized that these were—even in thought-disordered patients—transient phenomena and a mean of less than 20% of utterances was evaluated as highly disrupted.

Nonetheless, the Americans Resnick and Oltmanns (1984) could not entirely confirm these results. Their schizophrenics certainly showed more pauses between clauses in comparison with a group of students. However, the difference did not prove to be significant when compared with healthy subjects matched according to IQ and education. They found no correlation with incoherence, but did find correlation with the degree of poverty of speech. However, since the groups only consisted of 10 subjects each, one may argue that the results were not representative.

## 2. Creativity and the Choice of Words

Schizophrenic speech often sounds "original." The appearance of new words may make a witty impression. Bleuler (1911) gave several examples. One patient says "handklar" ("hand-clear"), by which he was referring to the German expression, "Es liegt auf der Hand" ("it lies on the hand", meaning it is immediately obvious). Another patient spat on the floor of his cell and called this "Käfig-Wetter-Brühe" ("cage-weather-soup"). Such formulations have led some authors to consider schizophrenics, especially in the acute phase of their illness, highly creative.

Some schizophrenics are renowned for their "artistic productions." Although there is abundant literature of interest about this concept, it should also be noted that most artists who developed unequivocal schizophrenia either stopped producing or were unable to maintain their standards [e.g., the Swiss author Robert Walser (1878–1956) did not write during the last 27 years of his life, during which he was ill.]

Karlson (1968) claimed to observe an increased incidence of intellectually highly capable citizens with leadership qualities among the close relatives of schizophrenics in Iceland. Schuldberg *et al.* (1988) found higher creativity test scores in (nonpsychiatric) subjects with signs of schizotypal personality traits. (The authors used the Perceptual Aberration—Magical Thinking scales developed by the Chapmans; cf. Chapter 12). On the other hand, Solana (1988) interpreted the peculiarities he found in the speech of parents of schizophrenics studied in Spain as impairments, close to psychiatric thought disorder, and not as signs of a creative use of language. Further, since such impairments were more frequent among parents of schizophrenics than among parents of mentally handicapped subjects, he concluded that this characteristic was less likely to be a result of the onus of supporting a disturbed member of the family than an indicator of the specific risk status of some of the parents.

In the United States, Rothenberg (1983) compared word-association performances of a group of Nobel laureates (12), creative students (63), and schizophrenics (18). The first two groups responded significantly more often with antonyms, and the Nobel laureates responded most quickly. (For example, the Nobel laureates and the creative students responded to the stimulus word "bright" more often with the antonym "dark" than with "shining"). Of course, how one judges this result depends on societal assumptions about creativity. These assumptions refer as much to the selection of students by a "creativity test" as to the differentiation of "lateral thinking" in schizophrenics. Rothenberg postulated that productive creativity requires mental clarity and therefore cannot be compared with the schizophrenic state. We have already mentioned Dykes and McGhie's (1976) study of schizophrenic and creative subjects selected by Cropley's (1968) revision of the Wallach and Kogan test. Although both groups sorted objects into more unusual categories than normal, creative subjects made far fewer naming errors under distraction conditions, except when the words were very closely related to the test stimulus. Regardless of evaluation technique, both studies point out a qualitative difference between the cognitive styles of creative and schizophrenic subjects.

Some research workers have examined the speech of schizophrenics for other putative signs of originality. They looked at the richness of the vocabulary rather than the unusual conjunction of words. Their criterion for originality was the total number of different types of words used in samples of writing and spontaneous speech of schizophrenics. These numbers were related to the total number of words used (i.e., the type–token ratio). According to Maher's review (1972), schizophrenic speech is notable for a *reduction* of the type–token ratio. Even the choice of words of thought-disordered patients is no different from the normal range (Maher *et al.,* 1966; Manschreck, 1984). Indeed, they used fewer types of words.

One of the more detailed investigations of the spontaneous speech of schizophrenics came from the Austrian psychologist Mittenecker (1951, 1953). He found that schizophrenics repeated words, parts of words, or syllables far more frequently than healthy subjects. Repetitions occurred at much shorter intervals in the sentences of nonparanoid than paranoid patients.

Siegel *et al.* (1976), in the United States, investigated whether the length of hospital stay could influence poverty of speech. Inpatients showed significantly more repetition and perseverance. However, such features were less typical in a chronically ill outpatient population. It is difficult to know if the difference arose through hospital-induced isolation or an increased severity of illness in the inpatient population. However, Siegel and colleagues found no correlation between length of hospital stay and the poverty of speech.

Another reason for the difference between in- and outpatient populations could lie in the (more recent) division of symptoms into those with positive and those with negative features. For example, Allen (1984), from Crow's group in Harrow, England found that schizophrenics with negative symptoms used fewer words to describe pictures than those with positive symptoms or healthy subjects. The latter two groups did not differ from each other.

In conclusion, it seems that, because the acutely ill (with positive symptoms) do not show any clear increase of originality (in terms of different types of words), earlier claims in the literature probably referred to anecdotal descriptions of short-lived outbursts of expression. Systematic empirical analysis of these outbursts is not reflected in the larger part of communications with the acutely ill (cf. Rochester *et al.*, 1977). Once again we see the discrepancy between the traditional case-study approach and the results of empirical investigations.

## 3. Unusual Content

The best-known systematic method for analysis of speech content is the Gottschalk and Gleser method (1969). With this procedure, probands are asked to recount an interesting, perhaps dramatic, event they have experienced. An increased incidence of certain themes has been recorded for schizophrenics by both Gottschalk *et al.* (1969) in the United States and Angermeyer and Timpe (1980) in Germany. However, the principal finding was that the speech of schizophrenics provided relatively little new information beyond what one might expect from the symptoms. Similar results can be extracted from conventional psychiatric scales that are less laborious to administer. Nevertheless, it is worth mentioning two points recorded by both research groups. First, if the interview is *structured*, the utterances were significantly less deviant, in contrast to the patients' spontaneous accounts. Second, it seems remarkable that both groups found a 5-minute unstructured interview long enough to form a valid first impression. Both points confirm general clinical experience.

The result also sheds some light on the difficulty of producing an objective psychiatric diagnosis. On the one hand, a structured interview must be conducted in order to obtain reliability in the assessment of different subjects; on the other hand, unstructured procedures are more likely to trigger the symptoms that can be florid in an acute psychosis. An important area for further research would be the systematic comparison of the effect of different degrees of interview structure on revealing psychotic symptoms in schizophrenic patients.

## 4. Coherence and Predictability

The less coherent a text is, the more the ability to predict missing words is reduced. A simple and widely practiced method for making this kind of measurement is the Cloze technique. With this method, every 4th, 5th, or 10th word (for example) is blocked out. Excerpts of schizophrenic speech and of that of healthy controls are given to a group of raters who are blind to the origin of the transcripts. The raters are asked to suggest from the context what the missing word might be. As one would expect, the success of the raters is usually worse on excerpts of schizophrenic speech (Salzinger *et al.*, 1964a,b, 1966; Ragin and Oltmanns, 1987). However, this is not always the case (Cheek and Amarel, 1967; Rutter *et al.*, 1978), which is probably caused by including subjects with and without thought disorder in the study group. Thus, Manschreck *et al.* (1979) found no deviation when predicting the speech of non-thought-disordered schizophrenics.

It is interesting to compare these results with those from normal subjects under the influence of the psychostimulant psilocybin (Honigfeld, 1963). At first, surprisingly, the missing words became more predictable, but during the remainder of the drug's effect (about 1 hr) the sentences became extremely difficult to follow.

To help the listener follow a communication, there are not only contextual constraints but also referential ties between clauses such as the conjunctions "and", "but", and "therefore". Rochester and colleagues (1977) suggested that the unusual or surprising aspects of schizophrenic speech may also arise from the patients' neglect to carry themes over from one sentence to another and to relate what is being said to what has just been said. In this study, schizophrenics in general ($n = 40$), especially those with thought disorder ($n = 20$), used fewer referential ties between the different parts of a sentence. Unfortunately, methodological shortcomings of this study compromised the findings. The schizophrenics had had less education and showed an IQ that was an average of 10 points lower than that of control subjects. Further, whereas about half the non-thought-disordered subjects, like the controls, reported a steady employment history, this was true only for 7% of the thought-disordered group. Nonetheless, we have quoted these findings because they were the starting point of this aspect of schizophrenia research, and the results have been confirmed to a great extent by the better controlled studies that followed (Tress *et al.*, 1984; in Germany; Allen and Allen, 1985; Rutter, 1985; in England; Harvey *et al.*, 1986; Ragin and Oltmanns, 1986; in the USA; Schonauer and Buchkremer, 1986; in Germany). An example of what a schizophrenic might say illustrates the problem. "The two boys went up the hill. Then she turned around and left" (without explaining to whom he was referring) (Harvey *et al.*, 1986, p. 275). The schizophrenic, communicating in this way, seems incapable of considering the perspective of the listener.

Ragin and Oltmanns (1986) point out that such referential impairments may also be found in thought-disordered manic patients. The crucial difference between manic and schizophrenic speech, according to the authors, is that the latter shows less lexical coherence (fewer referential clues) *within a clause,* while the former displays fewer referential clues *between larger blocks of speech.* Thus, the manic subject, unlike the schizophrenic, is more likely to utter coherent sentences. This study also reported that, whereas the problem tended to remain with the schizophrenic in remission, it disappeared in the remitted manic. The results are largely supported by Andreasen's group in Iowa (Hoffman *et al.*, 1986). Thus, the reduced use of referential cues, as an aid to the listener, appears to be a candidate trait marker in schizophrenia. However, we should note that Allen and Allen (1985) claimed that low referential speech was restricted to schizophrenics with positive symptoms.

## C. Experimental Assessment of Verbal Responses in the Laboratory

### 1. Associations

*a. Loosening of Associations*   According to Bleuler (1911), one of the basic symptoms of schizophrenia is that a train of thought is not followed through to the end. Associations with any of the items in the train are likely to intrude. For example, to the question "With whom did you go for a walk today?", the answer was "with father, son," and continued after a brief pause with "and holy ghost." The fact that Bleuler attributed a fundamental importance to the *loosening of associations* was a stimulus to many early empirical tests of his ideas.

What gives rise to such loose associations? In part, naturally, their occurrence depends on the nature of the word eliciting them. Goldstein *et al.* (1972), for example, found that emotional words provoked more unusual responses. Others found that the more the meaning of the eliciting or stimulus word was ambiguous, the more the associations of schizophrenics differed from those of neurotic or healthy subjects (Penk and Kidd, 1977; Penk, 1978), but these studies have still not clarified the possible origin of the loosening process in schizophrenics.

One proposal is that the latent connections or associations between words, the semantic network (Anderson, 1985), are more easily accessible to schizophrenics, or that the normal contextual constraints on these latent connections in goal-directed discourse are impaired in schizophrenics.

The patient seems to be distracted by the possible connections and loses track of the goal of the conversation. This hypothesis has been investigated with Chapman's card-sorting task (L. Chapman, 1958; Roberts and Schuham, 1974; Hirsch and De Wolfe, 1977). In this task, cards are presented showing words that have to be ascribed to a particular category. For example, if the word "gold" is the target word, the correct response would be to choose the card with the word "metal," because "gold" belongs to the category of metals. In this case a typical schizophrenic result was to choose the card "fish." The patients were distracted by the latent associative connection between "gold" and "fish" formed by the frequently used term "goldfish." Such results are not usually found in other psychiatric subjects or alcoholics (Roberts and Schuham, 1974); they seem to be typical of newly admitted schizophrenics with a poor premorbid course, as assessed by the Phillips scale (Hirsch and De Wolfe, 1977).

The hypothesis that associative links within the semantic network are

**Table 2.1** Reaction Time to Primed Associated and Nonassociated Words[a]

| Groups | Primed associated | | Primed nonassociated | |
|---|---|---|---|---|
| | Mean | (SD) | Mean | (SD) |
| Normal | 605 | (92) | 642 | (85) |
| Unipolar | 556 | (116) | 612 | (146) |
| Non-thought disordered | 594 | (82) | 630 | (66) |
| Thought disordered | 478 | (167) | 561 | (178) |

[a]Means and standard deviations for all groups reported in milliseconds (from Manschreck *et al.*, 1988).

facilitated in schizophrenia was further supported by a research group in Boston and at Harvard University (Manschreck *et al.*, 1988). The subjects were shown a string of letters and asked to decide whether the string was a word or not. Reaction time was the main dependent variable. The target string could also be preceded by a prime (a word or a string of letters not forming a word). Here, the critical condition of interest was when the prime and target words were semantically associated. From previous studies in normal cognitive psychology it would be expected that, when prime and target words are semantically associated, the response latency is shorter. According to cognitive theory, associated semantic units can be activated even if only one element is activated through speech, hearing, or reading. The spread of activation within the semantic (neuronal) network decays rapidly or is inhibited by new elements.

Manschreck *et al.* (1988) found that thought-disordered schizophrenics had the shortest reaction time when the target word was primed by a semantically associated word, about 500 msec, which was faster than the non-thought-disordered, psychiatric, and healthy control groups (cf. Table 2.1). The groups were selected by research diagnostic criteria (now common in modern research). The authors suggest that their results may speak for an enhanced facilitation of responses in thought-disordered schizophrenics when target and prime word are associated. They also pointed out that one cannot conclude from the results whether a higher activation within the semantic network, a slower decay of the activation of associations, or a greater inhibition of concurrent associations is responsible for the differences.

***b. Unusual Associations*** Bleuler (1911) was influenced by an American study which reported that insane patients (mostly with dementia praecox) produced *unusual associations* when asked about the meanings of proverbs (Kent and Rosanoff, 1910). Here the term "unusual associations" means that the replies deviated from those given by a normal group; this response is also called "lowered communality" (i.e., they were not the sort used by society at large). Kent and Rosanoff went on to report that, when the tests were repeated, the earlier associations did not reappear. This finding of unstable associations between words has been confirmed with proverb and picture tests by Sommer *et al.* (1960), Rey and Cohen (1973) in Germany, and for paranoid schizophrenics by Neufeld (1975) in Canada. (Such evidence speaks against a widely held view of psychoanalysts that schizophrenics use a "private language." Ask a chronically ill schizophrenic to *deliberately* produce unusual associations and, unlike control subjects, he or she cannot do it.)

Some authors have been interested to see if associations that deviate from the norm occur any more frequently in particular subgroups of schizophrenics. Thus, Dokecki *et al.* (1965) found an increased frequency in those patients with a poor premorbid course (e.g., including isolation, conflict, unemployment, and social withdrawal). This did not arise in Fuller and Kates' (1969) study of nonparanoid schizophrenics, but light was shed on this discrepancy by a study done by Ries and Johnson (1967). In their subjects, unusual associations were frequent in those with both a poor premorbid course *and* a longer hospital stay. (Note that all three studies used the Kent–Rosanoff test and assessed the premorbid course with the Phillips scale.) From this last result one may suppose that the loss of the chance to communicate (i.e., through social isolation, whether through self-imposed withdrawal or withdrawal imposed by hospitalization) can give rise to both a poverty of speech and a lack of the sense of what constitutes socially usual forms of language. In support of this interpretation, O'Brian and Weingartner (1970) found no difference in the incidence of socially usual associations in the expressions of schizophrenics and institutionalized patients with tuberculosis. The previously mentioned study led by Siegel found no signs of loose associations in the expressions of either group in chronically ill hospitalized schizophrenics and chronic patients living in the community (Siegel *et al.*, 1976).

Of course, a further contributory factor is undoubtedly long-term neuroleptic treatment. Such treatment can lead to a marked reduction in the amount of abnormal associations, or thought disturbance in general, after 2–5 weeks of treatment, depending on the type of group tested (Goldstein *et al.*, 1972; Storms, 1977; Penk, 1978; Lienert and Straube, 1980).

## 2. Word Interpretations—Common and Uncommon Meanings

The vocabulary of even the most highly developed languages is not such that each item, thing, or concept has its specific descriptors. Many words have several meanings; the use of one meaning or another is usually discernible from the context. Words in routine use often have meanings that are more common or preferred than others. Chapman and Chapman (1973) claimed that schizophrenics prefer to use the more common meanings, independent of the context; the result can be ambiguous if not paradoxical. The Chapmans called this tendency "excessive yielding to normal biases." Thus, for example, chronic schizophrenics interpret the word "rare" in the statement "Robert likes rare meat" according to the more common meaning, "infrequent," and ignore the context-appropriate meaning, "partially cooked."

These results were confirmed for chronic schizophrenics in two studies (Williams *et al.*, 1976; Sackeim and Shapiro, 1981), but were refuted by L. Chapman himself when testing a heterogeneous group of subjects (Chapman *et al.*, 1976) and by others (Deckner *et al.*, 1971; Neuringer *et al.*, 1972; Naficy and Willerman, 1980).

## 3. Linguistic Competence and Performance

A disturbance of the spoken language, if not of motor origin, can relate to a defect of semantic or syntactic abilities. According to Chomsky (1965), who introduced the concepts of competence and performance to the discipline of linguistics, *competence* refers to the knowledge of the speaker or listener and *performance* is the actual *use* of language in a given situation. A working hypothesis is that *competence* is available to the schizophrenic, but *performance* is disturbed (i.e., an appropriate translation for the situation and an application of knowledge is unsuccessful). If *semantic* competence were disturbed then the basic set of semantic knowledge (semantic repertoire) would differ from that of a healthy person. A communication might not be possible if the schizophrenic were unable to call upon the same repertoire as a healthy subject (cf. schematic representation of case B, Figure 2.3). If performance were disturbed, then a schizophrenic listener would understand a non-schizophrenic since he could call upon a repertoire that was largely the same as that of the speaker (case A, Figure 2.3). However, despite the fact that the repertoire is intact, the communications from the patient would not be understood. Thus, the disturbance could result from a faulty editing process (i.e., the process of selecting appropriate words).

By analogy, the breaking of syntactic rules may derive from a disturbance of the repertoire of syntactic rules (*disturbed competence*) or from the faulty selection of a syntactic element (*disturbed performance*).

*a. Semantic Competence* Bertram Cohen and colleagues from the Rutgers Medical School have been using a simple and elegant model to examine the origin of the disturbance of communication in schizophrenia. The experiment takes the form of a game between two persons: one person plays the role of a speaker and the other person plays the role of a listener in a conversation between the two (like case A or B in Figure 2.3). The speaker is asked to describe an object or event in such a way that the listener can guess as rapidly as possible what it is. Both the speaker and the listener are shown two or more objects or object names. The speaker is not allowed to name the object.

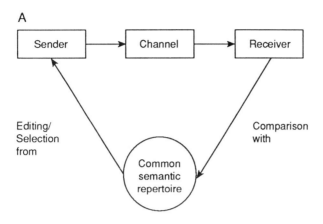

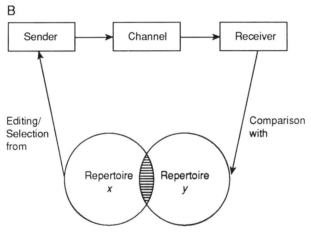

**Figure 2.3** Two different models of communication. (A) Sender and receiver have a common repertoire. (B) Sender and receiver have partially overlapping repertoires (after Hörmann, 1971).

If, for example, both see the words "lady" and "woman," then the response "distinguished" may tell the listener which word was selected by the speaker. A satisfactory performance by the speaker requires selection of appropriate descriptors from the semantic repertoire. The task of the listener is to look for the meanings of this word in an internal "lexicon," the semantic repertoire. If this repertoire is intact, then there will be no difficulty playing the role of a listener; later the speaker and listener exchange roles. This is an experiment testing communication abilities that asks which individual in which role has the greatest difficulties.

**Table 2.2**  Test of Transfer of Messages[a]

| Subject in the role of the speaker | Subject in the role of the listener | |
| --- | --- | --- |
| | Schizophrenic | Healthy |
| Schizophrenic | 0.66 | 0.67 |
| Healthy | 0.72 | 0.74 |

[a]Mean proportion of correct word selections in each group, four speaker–listener combinations (from Cohen and Camhi, 1967).

The main result of Cohen's extensive series of experiments follows: The schizophrenic often fails as a speaker or producer of appropriate descriptors. However, as a listener and decoder of information the schizophrenic is as capable as any healthy subject (Table 2.2). In detail, the absolute performance difference of schizophrenics is relatively small, but it is always significant, and occurs in the same direction (Cohen, 1978).

The conclusion of Cohen's studies is that, when communication is unsuccessful because of an inadequate choice of descriptors (or "editing," in Cohen's terms), the schizophrenic, who as listener can decode the intended meaning, must have a repertoire similar to that of the healthy conversation partner (case A, Figure 2.3). Thus, it appears that the schizophrenic has problems selecting the appropriate word, even though semantic competence, the semantic rule repertoire, remains untouched by psychosis.

In an interesting sequel to this experiment, Cohen played back the tape recording of the session 1 week later. The schizophrenic was unable to identify the object he was describing himself. (Of course, he remained capable of identifying what the healthy subject described.) This result adds to the evidence against the notion that schizophrenics have their own private language, or, as Cohen puts it, against the "tower of Babel" hypothesis. (According to the Bible, the building of the tower of Babel led to the splitting of languages.)

Is it possible that the schizophrenic's performance is unsuccessful simply because of a lack of motivation? Certainly it seems that schizophrenics are not impulsive speakers in this situation; they do not simply sit there and spout (Cohen et al., 1974). Schizophrenics often faltered longer than their healthy partners at the start of a description, especially when the stimuli presented were very similar (cf. similar results in previous sections). On the one hand, this could mean that the search for just the right expression was more difficult for the schizophrenic; only inappropriate alternatives occurred to him. On the other hand, once he began his answer, he expressed himself more profusely.

These behaviors do not describe a subject who is not motivated to solve the problem. However, Cohen (1978) also observed that, when the objects to distinguish were difficult, the schizophrenic typically wandered further and further from the goal of the description. Such deviant descriptive sequences are reminiscent of Bleuler's description of thought disturbance (Chapter 1).

In this sequence of reports, a number of subgroups—acute, chronic, paranoid, nonparanoid, thought- and non-thought-disturbed, and medicated and nonmedicated patients—have been studied with different types of stimulus material. In all cases, semantic competence was established, but performance was impaired under the described conditions. Neither treatment nor the length of hospital stay influenced the results (B. Cohen and Camhi, 1967; B. Cohen et al., 1974; B. Cohen, 1976; 1978). From these results we may deduce a basic underlying cognitive weakness in schizophrenia. Independent of the subgroup concerned, there is an impaired ability to select from the semantic repertoire. Unfortunately, whether or not the deficit is specific to schizophrenia remains unresolved. Other psychiatric groups were not studied.

More recently the ability of chronic schizophrenics to describe objects was compared with that of chronic alcoholics by a group in Constance, Germany (Heim and R. Cohen, 1981). They found no basic difference between the groups, but impaired precision of description (role of a speaker) was correlated with the severity of paranoia, symptoms of anergia, and psychiatric problems of patients in either group. This result does not affect the previous conclusion that the semantic repertoire (competence) of schizophrenics is intact, since this aspect was not tested by the group in Constance, but it does question whether the impairment of communication described by B. Cohen is, in fact, specific to schizophrenia.

***b. Syntactic Competence*** It was formerly assumed that language was generated and decoded by means of the associations between words. Now psycholinguists state that "it must be emphasized that the experimental procedures such as word association tests cannot yield the answers to these questions as normal speech is not produced by associating one word with another" (Chaika, 1982; p. 190).

Of course, this superficially surprising statement does not mean that associative connections play no role. If speech is not produced by associating one word with another, then this may partly explain why schizophrenic speech deviates from the norm, since schizophrenics follow associative links between words.

Following the change of paradigm initiated by Chomsky (1957), the idea of high-order "speech plans" has become part of the dogma of psycholinguistics. Speech plans are set up according to systems of syntactic and semantic rules and are decisive for the perception and generation of speech. Since an introductory review of this subject is beyond the scope of this book (see

Hörmann, 1978; Anderson, 1985), it will suffice to illustrate the "psychological reality" of the influence of syntactic structures with the following example.

There are two grammatical ways to illustrate the fact that a dog and a man are present and that barking is occurring:

1. Karl was barked at by the dog;
2. The dog barked at Karl.

"Karl" is the center of the first statement; the dog is the center of the second. Grammar allows two different perspectives to be expressed; in other words, the two statements are under the control of different "plans" (Miller *et al.*, 1960). The "plans" determine the position of the words (syntactic connections) and the intended meaning in the sentence. This represents a structuring of linguistic elements that may have some cognitive aspects in common with the structuring of perceptual elements, such as the organization of stimuli into figure and ground or changing the focus in a selective attention task (cf. Engelkamp, 1974).

This short diversion into linguistics illustrates the importance of syntactic competence for the generation of language. Whether the inadequate formulations (performance) of schizophrenics are a result of their impaired *syntactic* competence must still be evaluated. For example, clinical and empirical evidence suggests that schizophrenics construct sentences with a less complex syntax. Morice (1986) has reviewed this literature and his own work carried out in Australia. Thomas *et al.* (1987) from Scotland found that reduced syntactic complexity is more frequent in subjects with predominantly negative symptoms.

Laboratory tests of syntactic competence usually examine whether schizophrenics are able to recognize various linguistic structures of sentences. Thus, sequences of words with different degrees of syntactical organization are presented. The subject is asked how many words he recalls. It would be expected that the more the sequences are organized and approach normal speech, the larger the number of words remembered would be. For example, the sentence "Colorful thoughts dream behind green towels" is more likely to be remembered than "Thoughts towels dream colorful green behind." Of course, recall also depends on the meaning of the words and their relationships within a sequence, yet changes of the syntactic organization alone can improve recall (e.g., Miller and Selfridge, 1950; Miller and Isard, 1963).

A series of studies in the 1960s first showed that schizophrenics were not able to make use of linguistic structure to the degree shown by healthy subjects (i.e., reduced recall; Lawson *et al.*, 1964; Nidorf, 1964; Truscott, 1970). Raeburn and Tong (1968) found that only some patients were in a position to make use of sentence structure at all. On the other hand, Gerver (1967) could find no difference between schizophrenics and healthy controls.

Some of these studies contain serious methodological weaknesses. Lawson *et al.* and Truscott presented sentences that successively increased syntactic structure. Their patients could have tired by the time the structured sentences were presented and offered poor responses. In some cases, long sequences of words were used, severely testing the capacity of short-term memory. (The effect of sentence order and length is illustrated by the poor recall of complex sequences by depressive subjects in Levy and Maxwell's 1968 study.) Further, because only chronic schizophrenics were studied, factors such as hospitalization and isolation were not considered for their possible contribution to the differences from healthy controls. Apart from Levy and Maxwell (1968), comparisons with other psychiatric groups were not made; therefore, the specificity of the findings has not been established (cf. Rochester and Martin, 1979).

Straube *et al.* (1979) tried to avoid some of these sources of error by presenting short sentences in an order balanced according to structure (e.g., (1) random word sequences, (2) grammatical sequences of words whose meanings were unrelated, (3) grammatically correct and meaningful sentences). To examine the susceptibility to disturbance of schizophrenic perceptual and linguistic performance, different levels of noise were introduced to the test. With respect to the specificity of the results, the performance of acute and chronic schizophrenics was compared with psychiatric controls.

The recall of words improved with increasing linguistic structure for *all* groups (Figure 2.4). There was a remarkably sharp improvement between meaningless word sequences (W) and the grammatically correct but meaningless examples (G). Distracting noise did not lead to a reduction of performance specific to the schizophrenic group. The performance of all groups was impaired by loud noise. (Healthy and psychiatric controls differed somewhat in their level of performance, but not in their degree of improvement.)

Patients with and without thought disorder were studied by Maher *et al.* (1980) in the United States. Thought-disordered patients improved their recall ability less as sentence structure increased. However, it is important to note that their performance *did* improve, even if the degree of improvement was less than that of the others. When Straube *et al.* made a similar division between their subjects, a difference was not evident.

Another variable that could affect word recognition is whether the word has a prominent syntactical position (e.g., at the beginning of a clause), but Oltmanns (1982) found no differences between schizophrenic, psychiatric, and nonpsychiatric groups in the perception of syntactic structures.

An elegant technique to examine syntax competence was provided by Fodor and Bever (1965). They found that points of transition between grammatical units misled *normal* subjects about the timing of a click that was slightly displaced with respect to the transition point. Let us clarify the finding with

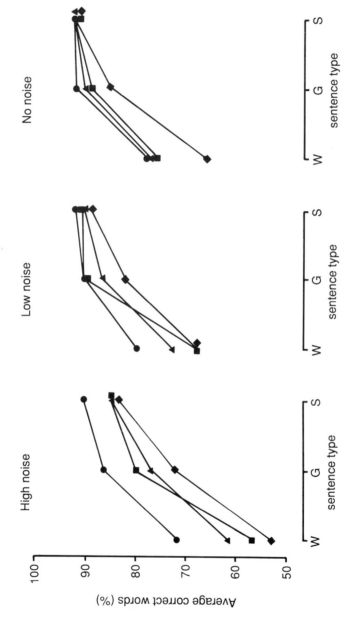

**Figure 2.4** Average percentage of correct words for each sentence type and noise condition. Performance of acute (▲) and chronic (◆) schizophrenics, and of a psychiatric (■) and a healthy (●) control group. Meaningful sentences; M; grammatical but meaningless sentences, G; meaningless word chains, W (after Straube *et al.*, 1979).

an example. The following sentence was presented 5 times over headphones; the click occurred in a different position each time.

"That he was happy was evident from the way he smiled."
$$x \quad x \quad x \quad \quad x \quad \quad x$$
$$a \quad b \quad c \quad \quad d \quad \quad e$$

The click is usually correctly localized by healthy subjects in position $c$, where it marks a transition between parts of the sentence. In other positions a click is incorrectly localized; for example $e$ is usually thought to occur between the words "evident" and "from" rather than at the end of the word "evident." The investigators claim that this means that syntax affects the perception of the click in normal subjects. This effect was also seen in schizophrenics (Rochester *et al.*, 1973).

In a similar study, with longer passages of text, Carpenter (1976) found that schizophrenics oriented to the clicks occurring after syntactic units and could more easily remember words when they were represented in the same syntactic structure. Indeed, it would seem that schizophrenics depend very strongly on syntactic structures. If the clicks were removed more from the grammatical transitions, the schizophrenics were even more biased than the normal subjects, that is, they located the click more often and incorrectly at the grammatically prominent position. This type of performance does not depend on the nature of the premorbid course nor on the level of medication (Rochester *et al.*, 1973; Grove and Andreasen, 1985). Grove and Andreasen also reported no differences between paranoid, hebephrenic, and schizoaffective groups.

Particular problems with the understanding of syntactically *complex* structures were shown by the newly admitted schizophrenic and manic patients of Morice and McNicol (1985). However, because the tasks were not matched according to difficulty we can assume that the deficit reflected problems that severely disturbed patients can have with difficult tasks (see also previous text; Chapman and Chapman, 1973). Results from experiments that do not raise these objections indicate that schizophrenic syntactic competence is usually intact.

## 4. Contextual Constraints: Predictability of Semantic Sequences

Modern languages have vocabularies that range from approximately 60,000 to over 200,000 words. Thus, it seems surprising that on most occasions we have no problem finding adequate terms or expressions without recourse to a dictionary. It is said that only 2000 words in any language are adequate for normal daily usage. Even with this small number of words, the range of combinations is enormous. Clearly, there must be a mechanism that channels the selection of expressions. It must restrict selection to a limited range of terms potentially appropriate to the situation or the goal of a communication. Semantic context is one of the guiding influences (the contextual constraint). The word or range of words resulting from application of the constraint can activate other terms within the semantic network (see previous text). The more numerous the semantic and syntactic items in a meaningful sequence of words are, the more restricted the possibilities for selection of missing words are. In other words, the *probability* for a certain word rises with the amount of contextual information given.

Let us illustrate the role of context. We are sitting in a restaurant waiting for a meal to arrive. One of us says, "The waiter is just coming with a warm bowl of s . . ." The word is lost in a sudden uproar on the other side of the room, but the context has so restricted the range of possibilities that we expect that the intended word was "soup." As listeners, we probably subconsciously weighed other alternatives (e.g., soup seemed more likely than semolina, which in turn was more likely than samovar, saffron, or socks).

The question is, do schizophrenics make use of differential probabilities in tasks in which the amount of contextual information is manipulated by the experimenter? The answer is that they have obvious difficulties with this type of task. If they try to guess what words are missing from a piece of prose with blank spaces, they are far less successful at finding the right word than healthy subjects are (Honigfeld, 1963; Blaney, 1974; Rutter *et al.*, 1975; Straube and Klemm, 1975). Schizophrenics seem less capable of recognizing the limits on probability imposed by the context.

This aspect of schizophrenia was specifically tested by De Silva and Hemsley (1977). They deleted each 5th, 7th, or 10th word from a piece of prose (Cloze procedure). Remember that the degree of restriction placed on the probable identity of the word increases with the length of text between the blank. (The task becomes easier, at least for non-schizophrenics!) This fact was reflected by an increased number of correct choices made by normal subjects (Figure 2.5). However, as the figure shows, chronic schizophrenics showed no improvement with the increase of contextual information available. Surprisingly, the acute patients showed a nonsignificant trend toward making even fewer correct choices in the presence of increased contextual information. Increasing difficulty provides no explanation here, because longer passages make the task easier for healthy subjects. The increased information in the longer passages may have distracted the schizophrenics from the appropriate word selection, compounding their inability to apply contextual constraints.

If we accept the earlier conclusions that the semantic and syntactic competence of schizophrenics is intact, then it seems surprising that they are unable to benefit from the increasing contextual constraints. However, we shall see from results reported in subsequent paragraphs and from psychophysiological data (Chapter 3) that schizophrenics are not completely unaware

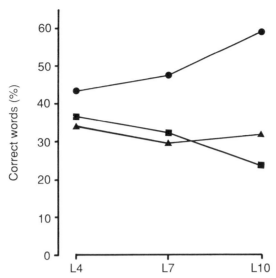

**Figure 2.5** Average percentage of correct words under each "word-omission" condition in acute (■) and chronic (▲) schizophrenics and in a healthy (●) control group. L4, 4 words between omissions; L7, 7 words between omissions; L10, 10 words between omissions (after De Silva and Hemsley, 1977).

of the probability structure associated with linguistic or other types of sequences, but their behavior seems to be less determined by these constraints. Thus highly probable or highly structured sequences do influence the performance.

This interpretation arises also out of Blaney's study (1974). He pointed out that syntactic relations in a verbal sequence have a more determined probability structure than the semantic relations in verbal sequences. For example, in the sentence "Bob went to the . . . ", the grammatical (syntactic) element is highly determined (i.e., a noun), in contrast to the missing semantic element—"house," "school," or "supermarket." Indeed, schizophrenics may have fewer problems using syntactic rules (see Section II, C, 3 and evidence from clinical observations). This conclusion also follows from other findings mentioned earlier (i.e., highly structured interview versus less structured interview).

The use of probability structures in predicting the missing semantic element was a subject that particularly interested the Russian psychologist Poljakov (1969, 1973). In his wide ranging series of experiments, he examined the effects of varying probability in word sequences (sentences). In these sentences, understanding the last word was hampered by a noise. The discrimination was made more difficult by using similar sounding words (with different meanings) at the end of each sentence. For example, in Russian the words for

**Table 2.3**   Frequency of Giving the Correct End to Sentences
Presented with the End Masked by Noise[a]

|  | Schizophrenic subjects | | Healthy controls | |
|---|---|---|---|---|
|  | I | II | I | II |
| The hunter said that this is a genuine horn/destiny (rog/rok) | 37 | 13 | 44 | 6 |
| Under the tree lay a fruit/raft (plod/plot) | 25 | 25 | 45 | 5 |
| The children found a long stick/pond (prut/prud) | 33 | 17 | 46 | 4 |
| Across his shoulders the old man carried a few scythes/ goats (kos/koz) | 12 | 18 | 27 | 3 |
| He shot a bird in flight/in ice (vlet/vled) | 20 | 10 | 29 | 1 |
| Total | 127 | 83 | 191 | 19 |

[a]Russian words are given in brackets. Sentences were presented with two levels of probability for the correct ending: I, highly likely sentence ending; II, less likely sentence ending. For further explanations see text. Data after Poljakov, 1973.

fruit (*plod*) and raft (*plot*) sound similar, so the subject might hear "Under the tree lies a fruit" or "Under the tree lies a raft." In such trials, the subject had to listen very carefully and not be misled by the semantic context.

The results were surprising: often schizophrenics were able to recognize the barely audible word, if it was one that was contextually unlikely, when normal subjects had difficulties (e.g., with "raft"). It seems from the results, shown partially in Table 2.3, that schizophrenics are less inhibited by the semantic contextual restrictions. Healthy subjects made more errors because the search procedure seems to be dominated by the probability structure of the verbal sequence, which is, of course, usually advantageous outside some artificial laboratory test situations.

Poljakov also looked into the perceptual abilities of his patients on auditory and visual discriminations, but could find no differences that could help to explain the "better" performance of schizophrenics. He did find signs of other changes. In contrast to healthy subjects, schizophrenics showed similar reaction times to tones occurring with different frequencies (i.e., different probabilities).

Further, Poljakov recorded EEGs from his subjects during the presentation of the complete sentences (in the absence of interfering noise). Normally, the novelty or surprise of an unexpected end to a sentence elicits a block of the alpha rhythm dominant up to that point. (The alpha block is one of the physiological components of the orienting response; see Chapters 5 and 6.) Poljakov's schizophrenics did not show an alpha block. When considered together, these deviations seem to indicate that cognitive, behavioral, and psychophysiological parameters are, under certain circumstances, less determined by the probability structure of sequential events. We will discuss a similarly reduced physiological responsiveness of schizophrenics to events of low probability in Chapter 6.

The advantage of the study of Poljakov (1973) is that he used the same patient sample in all of his experiments. Further, the better performance of schizophrenics in the more difficult (less predictable) condition is one of the methodological advantages of the study. The criticism of generalized deficit is therefore not applicable. There are, however, methodological problems that cloud the issue. Unfortunately, Poljakov made no precise statement about the sort of patients he investigated. From the symptoms he described, we can guess that they were young hebephrenic subjects (disorganized type, DSM-III-R) who were free of florid productive symptoms at the time of the study and were not receiving medication. His report is also frustratingly short of details on the statistical assessment of the results.

A point in Poljakov's results is worth noting. The greatest difference between schizophrenic and healthy subjects occurred when the probability associated with sentence endings lay in the middle and not at either extreme of the usual–unusual continuum. Thus, although the schizophrenics were apparently less influenced by the context, they did not perform entirely independently of it.

This evidence could help explain the discrepancy with the results obtained by Done and Frith (1984) from the Northwick Park Harrow group in England. They investigated acute and chronic schizophrenics with and without hallucinations. They were unable to find any difference between the performance of schizophrenic and healthy subjects when briefly presented with probable and highly improbable sentence endings in the visual or auditory modality. As in the Russian study, they used auditory and visual masks for the crucial last words. In contrast to Poljakov, who used a continuum of verbal sequences with respect to degrees of predictability, Done and Frith tested only endings that were semantically highly compatible (predictable) or incompatible (unpredictable). However, as mentioned earlier, Poljakov (1973) found a difference between schizophrenic and normal subjects in the *middle range* of predictability. The other difference was that Done and Frith did not use any words that sounded or looked similar to a more probable (but incorrect) word. Thus, an improved schizophrenic response resulting from a relatively context-independent performance would not necessarily follow.

On the other hand, the Done and Frith (1984) results show again that linguistic competence is not destroyed. In certain task conditions, schizophrenics showed a deviant performance, the origin of which has still to be determined.

## 5. Aphasic Speech

*a. Schizophasia as a Type of Aphasia*   Many authors have commented on a qualitative similarity between aphasia and schizophrenic thought and speech

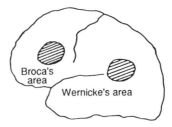

**Figure 2.6**  The two main language centers of the cortex (adapted from Morice, 1986).

disturbances. Faber *et al.* (1983) asked five specialists to try to distinguish samples of aphasic speech from speech of schizophrenics with thought disorder, among others; only one could reliably discriminate the passages presented.

It should be remembered that there are two basic sorts of aphasia, Wernicke and Broca aphasia. The area named after Broca, a French surgeon, lies anteriorly in the left cerebral hemisphere close to the motor cortex (Figure 2.6). The area named after the German neurologist Wernicke also lies on the left side, but more posteriorly on the temporoparietal border close to the auditory cortex. In Broca's aphasia, the expressive and executive (output) functions of language are disturbed. In Wernicke's aphasia, the comprehension of speech (input) is disturbed.

In the milder forms of motor or Broca aphasia, patients can speak but the grammatical structure is poor. The articulation and melody of language (prosody) is disordered. Speech is laborious and somewhat telegraphic. Sometimes the words just do not come. We might assume that dysfunction of this area has little in common with the schizophrenic disturbance. Schizophrenics, in general, produce sentences with an intact grammatical structure. On the other hand, according to Morice (1986), the absence of helpful conjunctions between the ideas expressed is reminiscent of Rochester's results (see previous section). Furthermore, as Morice observed, grammar used by schizophrenics is much simpler than that used by healthy subjects.

Despite the difficulty that patients with a sensory or Wernicke aphasia have understanding what has been said, they often talk fluently, but their speech is often remarkably devoid of meaning. Such patients have difficulty in appreciating and adapting to the requirements of the situation, particularly the needs of the listener to understand what is being talked about. The appearance of neologisms, a lack of coherence, and a lack of referential structures, both within and between sentences, seems to be reminiscent of the problems of some speech- and thought-disturbed schizophrenics.

   ***b. Comparison with Speech Changes in Aphasia***   Aphasic speech differs from schizophrenic communications both in its persistence over time and the relative frequency of some particular items. Correctness or deviance of

**Table 2.4**  Comparison of Those Aspects of Comprehension and Expression of Language Impaired in Severely Thought-Disturbed Patients with Schizophrenia, Mania, and Wernicke's Aphasia[a,b]

| Disturbance | Schizophrenia | Mania | Wernicke's aphasia |
|---|---|---|---|
| Comprehension (spoken language) | − | − | + |
| Reading | − | − | + |
| Naming | + | − | + + |
| Repeating | − | − | + + |
| Flow | − | − | − |
| Phonemic paraphasia | − | − | + |
| Semantic paraphasia | + | + | + + |
| Insight (own disturbance) | + | + | + |
| Syntax | − | − | − |
| Semantics | + + | + | + + |
| Pragmatics | + + | + | + + |

[a]After Andreasen and Grove, 1979.
[b]Level of impairment: +, present; + +, severe; −, absent.

schizophrenic speech is much more dependent on situational and experimental conditions (i.e., structure of the interview, emotional stimuli). In contrast to the condition in aphasic patients, in schizophrenics speech disturbance occurs irregularly because, in 80–90% of schizophrenics, speech rules are only broken in certain situations. About 16% of the cases show a considerable and continuous impairment (including incoherence, neologisms, imprecise expressions, and echolalia). These proportions were derived from interviews with 45 patients (Andreasen and Grove, 1979). The distribution is closer to 50:50 for manic subjects ($n = 32$; see Table 2.4). The experience of Faber and colleagues (1983) shows that the relative incidence of specific features also separates schizophrenics from aphasics (e.g., use of private meanings, derailment, relative anomia, and features of poverty).

Over the last 15 years, a number of linguists have viewed schizophrenic speech increasingly as an aspect of aphasia (e.g., Chaika, 1974; contrast criticism from Fromkin, 1975; Lecours and Vanier-Clement, 1976). It is not surprising that Chaika's claimed similarity between schizophrenic speech and fluent aphasia ("jargon aphasia") has been criticized; the analysis was based on only one patient. Nonetheless, experimentalists such as Cohen's group in Constance (List *et al.*, 1977) found—despite obvious differences—that schizophrenics have a series of features in common with aphasics.

In the study from the Constance group, the subjects listened to a sentence, after which one word of the sentence was repeated. The task was to name another word, associated with this word, that was in the sentence. The subjects were aphasics with diffuse brain damage (with and without fluent speech production), schizophrenics, brain-damaged patients without aphasia, and a healthy control group. Schizophrenics and aphasics with fluent speech often suggested a term associated with the word, but not part of the sentence. Further, they oriented much less toward the syntactic aspects of the sentence than the other groups (List *et al.*, 1977). This type of similarity with aphasics seems to occur most often in tasks which place fairly high demands on the performance of attentional mechanisms (R. Cohen *et al.*, 1977, 1981). Even on relatively simple associative tasks, tests of so-called restrictive associations (e.g., list things that are typically yellow), chronic schizophrenic performance is similar to that of aphasics. Both groups have a tendency to produce frequent repetitions or "false" associations (R. Cohen *et al.*, 1976).

Similarities are only partial; other features distinguish schizophrenics from aphasics, that is, the schizophrenic performance often lies between that of aphasics and that of healthy controls (R. Cohen *et al.*, 1976; List *et al.*, 1977; Strohner *et al.*, 1978; Andreasen and Grove, 1979; cf. Table 2.4). For example, if subjects were asked to make up sentences from a list of words provided, then, according to Rausch *et al.* (1980), schizophrenic performance was generally no different from that of healthy subjects, but aphasics had great difficulties on this task.

Further discussion of the similarities and differences between aphasic and schizophrenic characteristics will be found in the sections on lateralization (Chapter 9).

## III. Suggested Readings

Harrow and Quinlan (1985) gave a comprehensive description of the clinical characteristics and the results from their own extensive empirical investigations of thought disorder. Still, the basic book worth reading is the textbook by Chapman and Chapman (1973). The entire field of empirical schizophrenia research is reviewed in more detail (than we were able to provide) in Neale and Oltmanns (1980). The emphasis of the textbook by Cutting (1985) is on a most comprehensive review of cognitive disturbances in schizophrenia.

## IV. Summary Statements and Interpretations

## A. Thought Processes

### 1. The Question of Specificity of Thought Disorder

Thought disorder also exists in manic patients, but more evidence supports it representing a trait of the illness schizophrenia.

More detailed analysis shows that "combinatory thinking" is more common in manic subjects, and that disorganization and idiosyncratic speech are more typical for schizophrenics.

Only certain features of schizophrenic thought disorder are typical. The trait characteristic supports the idea that thought disorder is a central and important feature of schizophrenia.

## 2. Conceptual and Categorical Thinking

The ability to use conceptual and categorical thinking is, unlike in some brain-damaged patients, not completely lost. However, conceptual tasks often are not solved adequately, due to frequent interfering and inadequate associations. Nevertheless, some studies report contradictory results, for example, concrete instead of conceptual thinking and a complete failure to categorize objects.

It is evident from brain imaging studies that a subgroup of patients has mild cerebral atrophy. Frontal and temporal lobe alterations of structure or function are reported. Poor performance on a categorizing task and a concomitant reduced frontal blood flow has been observed in some schizophrenics (cf. Chapter 8). Thus, one cannot exclude the existence of subgroups with similarities to "organic" patients. Even patients who can categorize quite well may have difficulties and may use categories that are idiosyncratic or too broad.

## 3. Abstract and Metaphorical Thinking

This ability is, as with conceptual thinking, not completely lost in the majority of patients (unlike brain-damaged patients). Frequent disturbances occur, especially during the acute phase of the illness. The failure to find the metaphorical (abstract) interpretations or proverbs can be reduced by giving more cues (e.g., several proverbs with the same meaning).

No systematic evaluation of subgroup performance exists.

It seems easy to disturb the train of thought, but providing more external cues can stabilize the thought process. The failure is often transient. It is usually reduced during remission of clinical symptoms.

## 4. Logical Deductive Ability (Syllogistic Reasoning)

No unequivocal evidence for a loss of this ability exists. The thought processes appear illogical because of the schizophrenic preoccupation with task-irrelevant subject matter.

It seems that the schizophrenic is unable to suppress parallel internal processes activated by the verbal material of the task. In syllogistic tasks, the degrees of freedom are quite high and no external cues to channel the thought process are given. The thought processes seem to stray easily in situations in which no constraints for the selection of the alternatives are given. One could therefore predict an amelioration of performance correlated with the number of constraints given (see also Section I, B, 3).

### 5. Problem Solving and Use of Strategies

The schizophrenic fails if external cues or feedback from his own performance are experimentally reduced (e.g., feedback from movements carried out on a monitor screen).

Data from this field seem to support the hypothesis that schizophrenics have special problems with tasks requiring the establishment of an internal model and the constant integration of the varying external feedback into the model. Thus, Frith and Done (1988) propose that the difficulty of schizophrenics arises from a failure of "internal monitoring of self-initiated acts." They assume that this is the case with positive symptom (delusional) patients. There is a hint in one of the studies reported that such a failure may characterize this subgroup. (We have to wait for more information from other fields before coming to a conclusion about the probable mechanisms underlying the failures in thought disorder.)

### 6. Switching and Perseverance in Problem-Solving Performance

Good premorbid patients switch more easily between different aspects of task content than poor-premorbid negative-symptom patients who show more perseverative tendencies.

There is possibly a link to the problem some schizophrenics have suppressing parallel task-irrelevant thoughts, as described earlier. There may also be a link to the higher distractability by task-irrelevant stimuli shown by many, but not all, schizophrenics.

## B. Speech

### 1. Spontaneous Speech

*a. Voice Modulation*    Pauses, emphases, and volume are inadequate with respect to the content and the situation.

This finding seems to reflect a lack of coordination between basic speech programs and the requirements for communication in a given situation.

*b. Choice of Words; Creativity*    Despite indications from individual cases, the choice of words is neither creative nor original with respect to current societal norms. In those patients with negative symptoms, there are marked decreases in both the frequency and range of words used.

Schizophrenics, especially with positive symptoms, sometimes appear to use language in a creative way. However, this creativity seems to be a rather transitory phenomenon, since statistical analyses do not confirm it. There are also claims that relatives of schizophrenics are creative. Some findings seem to support this, since first degree relatives sometimes reach outstanding vocational positions. Other findings appear contradictory, especially from investigators who found indications for slight cognitive deviation in first degree relatives (cf. Chapter 4). Both features may be true to some extent. "Borderline" personalities may indeed oscillate between cognitive "deviancy," which can be characterized as creative, and more "pathological" cognitive deficits (e.g., vagueness, cognitive slippage, loss of goal in thought processes). However, after a severe psychotic breakdown creativity comes to a standstill (e.g., several writers and poets; see text).

*c. Content and Structure of the Interview* An increased bizarre content of responses in noticeable if the questions are less structured (i.e., if the degree of freedom with regard to the possible answers is high).

This characteristic is reminiscent of deviant behavior described elsewhere (e.g., proverb interpretation), when schizophrenics do worse in less constrained situations (e.g., only one proverb to interpret). A rigid external structure seems to stabilize the performance of schizophrenics. We will see in the material discussed subsequently that this pattern can often be found.

*d. Speech Coherence/Referential Cues* Thought-disordered schizophrenics and manic subjects do not impart the context and connections of their communication to the listener. For the former group this is evident within a sentence and for the second group between longer blocks of speech. The lack of referential cues is more transient in manic subjects and has more of a trait character in schizophrenics. One study reports that this type of speech is more common for positive-symptom schizophrenics.

Linguistic theory claims that the imaginary listener is an essential factor in speech production. Schizophrenics do not seem to take the perspective of the listener into account. Thus, important cognitive components do not work together; they lose their coherence.

## 2. Experimental Tests

*a. Loosening of Associations* Experimental evidence shows that semantically related words (neighboring positions in the semantic network) are more easily facilitated; schizophrenics prefer semantically associated responses ("gold-fish") to responses referring to the category (i.e., gold is metal). A "loosening" of associations can also be provoked by ambiguous or emotional words. Not much is known about subgroup differences. One study reported that newly admitted poor premorbid patients showed this type of performance. Another study reported a lack of associative loosening with chronic patients.

However, it seems that "loosening" of associations can be provoked more easily in more thought-disturbed schizophrenics.

It seems that the basic mechanism of lateral inhibition and facilitation within the semantic network is destabilized in schizophrenia. Word selection is obviously guided less by paramount speech plans, as is the case in normal speech production. The schizophrenic with thought disorder switches instead to associated words, that is, to words that have a neighboring position in the semantic network. This reduced dominance of contextual or hierarchical speech plans on speech production may lead to the paradoxical advantage of schizophrenics in certain experimental speech situations. One experiment showed that schizophrenics respond more quickly than normal controls in a primed-response situation.

*b. Communality* Lack of communality does not characterize the whole group of schizophrenics. It seems to be a by-product of long-term hospitalization.

These findings are compatible with those mentioned earlier that priming facilitates the (normal) associative links, even in schizophrenics.

*c. Semantic and Syntactic Repertoire* The repertoire of semantic rules remains untouched in the schizophrenic psychosis. Deviance is therefore due to performance differences from normal subjects as described earlier.

Syntactic competence also seems to be intact. Some contradictory findings are flawed with methodological problems. No subgroup differences are evident at this time. (Exception: A simpler grammar structure is found in negative-symptom patients.)

There is some evidence that language disorder may be caused by an impaired process of editing from an intact repertoire. However, the specificity of this characteristic is not beyond doubt.

The latter disturbance is reminiscent of selective perceptual disturbances in the presence of salient alternative but irrelevant stimuli (see Chapter 3).

*d. Contextual Constraints* The language performance of schizophrenics is less influenced by contextual constraints (see previous text). The differential probabilities of semantic elements do not guide the selection process as much as they do in control groups. It can therefore be shown that schizophrenics perform better when contextual cues are misleading the healthy subjects. This does not mean that the schizophrenic is completely unaware of the semantic (and probability) relations, since the performance of the schizophrenic does not differ from that of controls in semantic contexts with high constraints.

We will see in Chapter 6 that the schizophrenic P 300 response is less differentiated with regard to varying probabilities of stimulus events, but patients are capable of perceiving the stochastic (probable) structure of the stimulus series. It seems that the correlated physiological processes are less marked and may break down if not guided by a strong external (structuring) input.

*e. Comparison with Speech Production in Aphasics* Similarities exist, especially with the so-called Wernicke aphasics (i.e., those with fluent speech production).

Clinical features are neologisms, lack of coherence, and lack of use of referential cues.

Experimental features are difficulty producing restricted associations, that is, associations guided by the semantic constraints of the verbal task. However, schizophrenics show higher semantic competence in some tasks than do aphasics.

Clinical observations also do not support a frequent appearance of "aphasic" signs in schizophrenia. The overlap between the performance of aphasics and schizophrenics is only partial and may depend on the subgroup tested.

It seems that the same centers may be affected in both groups. However, since schizophrenic disturbances are more widespread, one cannot restrict the cause, anatomically or functionally, to the temporal lobe, parietal lobe (language), or left hemisphere alone. For example, schizophrenics have difficulties recognizing emotional facial expressions, which is not a left temporal function (cf. Chapter 1).

# References

Allen, H. A. (1984). Positive and negative symptoms and the thematic organisation of schizophrenic speech. *British Journal of Psychiatry*, *144*, 611–617.

Allen, H. A., and Allen, D. S. (1985). Positive symptoms and the organization within and between ideas in schizophrenic speech. *Psychological Medicine*, *15*, 71–80.

American Psychiatric Association (1987). *Diagnostic and statistical manual of mental disorders (DSM-III-R)*. Washington, D.C.: American Psychiatric Association.

Anderson, J. R. (1985). *Cognitive psychology and its Implications*. New York: Freeman.

Andreasen, N. C., and Grove, W. (1979). The relationship between schizophrenic language, manic language, and aphasia. *In* J. Gruzelier and P. Flor-Henry (Eds.), *Hemisphere asymmetries of function in psychopathology*. Amsterdam: Elsevier.

Andreasen, N. C., and Grove, W. M. (1986). Thought, language, and communication in schizophrenia: Diagnosis and prognosis. *Schizophrenia Bulletin*, *12*, 348–359.

Andreasen, N. C., and Powers, P. S. (1974). Overinclusive thinking in mania and schizophrenia. *British Journal of Psychiatry*, *125*, 452–456.

Angermeyer, M. C., and Timpe, F. H. (1980). Psychopathology and language behavior in schizophrenics. *Archiv für Psychiatrie und Nervenkrankheiten*, *228*, 151–160.

Arieti, S. (1955). *Interpretation of schizophrenia*. New York: Brunner.

Barnett Ragin, A., and Oltmanns, T. F. (1987). Communicability and thought disorder in schizophrenics and other diagnostic groups. *British Journal of Psychiatry*, *150*, 494–500.

Barnett Ragin, A., Pogue-Geile, M., and Oltmanns, T. F. (1989). Poverty of speech in schizophrenia and depression during in-patient and post-hospital periods. *British Journal of Psychiatry*, *154*, 52–57.

Berenbaum, H., Oltmanns, T. F., and Gottesman, I. I. (1985). Formal thought disorder in schizophrenics and their twins. *Journal of Abnormal Psychology*, *94*, 3–16.

Blaney, P. H. (1974). Two studies on the language behavior of schizophrenics. *Journal of Abnormal Psychology*, *83*, 23–31.

Bleuler, E. (1911). *Dementia praecox oder die Gruppe der Schizophrenien.* Leipzig: Deuticke.

Bobon, J. (1967). Schizophrasie et schizoparaphrasie. *Acta Neurologica et Psychiatrica Belgica*, *67*, 924–938.

Callahan, L. A., and Saccuzzo, D. P. (1986). Associative intrusions in the verbal behavior of the first-degree relatives of adult schizophrenics: A preliminary study. *Journal of Nervous and Mental Disease*, *174*, 240–242.

Cameron, N. (1938). Reasoning, regression, and communication in schizophrenics. *Psychological Monographs*, *50*, 221.

Cameron, N. (1939). Schizophrenic thinking in a problem-solving situation. *Journal of Mental Science*, *85*, 1012–1035.

Carpenter, M. D. (1976). Sensitivity to syntactic structure: Good versus poor premorbid schizophrenics. *Journal to Abnormal Psychology*, *85*, 41–50.

Chaika, E. (1974). A linguist looks at "Schizophrenic" language. *Brain and Language*, *1*, 257–276.

Chaika, E. (1982). Thought disorder or speech disorder in schizophrenia? *Schizophrenia Bulletin*, *8*, 587–591.

Chapman, L. J. (1956). Distractability in the conceptual performance of schizophrenics. *Journal of Abnormal and Social Psychology*, *53*, 286–291.

Chapman, L. J. (1958). Intrusion of associative responses into schizophrenic conceptual performance. *Journal of Abnormal and Social Psychology*, *56*, 374–379.

Chapman, L. J., and Chapman, J. P. (1973). *Disordered thought in schizophrenia.* Englewood Cliffs, New Jersey: Prentice Hall.

Chapman, L. J., Chapman, J. P., and Daut, R. L. (1976). Schizophrenic inability to disattend from strong aspects of meaning. *Journal of Abnormal Psychology*, *85*, 35–40.

Cheek, F. E., and Amarel, M. (1967). Some techniques for the measurement of changes in verbal communication. *In* K. Salzinger and S. Salzinger, (Eds.), *Research in verbal behavior and some neurophysiological implications.* New York: Academic Press.

Chomsky, N. (1957). *Syntactic structures.* 's Gravenhage: Mouton.

Chomsky, N. (1965). *Aspects of the theory of syntax.* Cambridge, Massachusetts: MIT Press.

Cohen, B. D. (1976). Referent communication in schizophrenia: The perseverative-chaining model. *Annals of the New York Academy of Science*, *270*, 124–141.

Cohen, B. D. (1978). Referent communication disturbances in schizophrenia. In S. Schwartz (Ed.), *Language and cognition in schizophrenia.* Hillsdale, New Jersey: Lawrence Erlbaum.

Cohen, B. D., and Camhi, J. (1967). Schizophrenic performance in a word communication task. *Journal of Abnormal Psychology*, *72*, 240–246.

Cohen, B. D., Nachmani, G., and Rosenberg, S. (1974). Referent communication disturbances in acute schizophrenia. *Journal of Abnormal Psychology*, *83*, 1–13.

Cohen, R., Kelter, S., and Schäfer, B. (1977). Zum Einfluß des Sprachverständnisses auf die Leistungen im Token Test. *Zeitschrift für klinische Psychologie*, *6*, 1–14.

Cohen, R., Woll, G., and Ehrenstein, W. H. (1981). Recognition deficits resulting from focussed attention in aphasia. *Psychology Research*, *43*, 391–405.

Cohen, R., Engel, D., Kelter, S., List, G., and Strohner, H. (1976). Restricted associations in aphasics and schizophrenics. *Archiv für Psychiatrie und Nervenkrankheiten*, *222*, 325–338.

Cropley, A. J. (1968). A note on the Wallach-Kogan test of creativity. *British Journal of Educational Psychology*, *38*, 197–201.

Cutting, J. (1985). *The psychology of schizophrenia.* Edinburgh: Churchill Livingstone.

Cutting, J., and Murphy, D. (1988). Schizophrenic thought disorder. A psychological and organic interpretation. *British Journal of Psychiatry*, *152*, 310–319.

Daut, R. L., and Chapman, L. J. (1974). Object sorting and the heterogeneity of schizophrenia. *Journal of Abnormal Psychology*, *83*, 581–584.

De Silva, W. P., and Hemsley, D. R. (1977). The influence of context on language perception in schizophrenia. *British Journal of Social and Clinical Psychology*, *16*, 337–345.

Deckner, W. C., Greenberg, H. C., and Cash, T. F. (1971). The relationship of cue strength and temporal interval to schizophrenic associative disorders. *The Journal of Psychology*, *79*, 123–130.

Dokecki, P. R., Polidoro, L. G., and Cromwell, R. L. (1965). Commonality and stability of word association responses in good and poor premorbid schizophrenics. *Journal of Abnormal Psychology*, *70*, 312–316.

Done, D. J., and Frith, C. D. (1984). The effect of context during word perception in schizophrenic patients. *Brain and Language*, *23*, 318–336.

Done, D. J., and Frith, C. D. (1989). Automatic and stategic volitional saccadic eye movements in psychotic patients. *European Archives of Psychiatry and Neurological Science*, *239*, 27–32.

Dykes, M., and McGhie, A. (1976). A comparative study of attentional strategies of schizophrenic and highly creative normal subjects. *British Journal of Psychiatry*, *128*, 50–56.

Earle-Boyer, E. A., Levinson, J. C., Grant, R., and Harvey, P. D. (1986). The consistency of thought disorder in mania and schizophrenia. II. An assessment at consecutive admissions. *Journal of Nervous and Mental Disease*, *174*, 443–447.

Engelkamp, J. (1974). *Psycholinguistik*. München: Wilhelm Fink.

Faber, R., Abrams, R., Taylor, M. A., Kasprison, A., Morris, C., and Weisz, R. (1983). Comparison of schizophrenic patients with formal thought disorder and neurologically impaired patients with aphasia. *American Journal of Psychiatry*, *140*, 1348–1351.

Fodor, J. A., and Bever, T. G. (1965). The psychological reality of linguistic segments. *Journal of Verbal Learning and Verbal Behavior*, *4*, 414–420.

Frith, C. D. (1979). Consciousness, information processing, and schizophrenia. *British Journal of Psychiatry*, *134*, 225–235.

Frith, C. D., and Done, D. J. (1988). Towards a neuropsychology of schizophrenia. *British Journal of Psychiatry*, *153*, 437–443.

Frith, C. D., and Done, D. J. (1989). Experiences of alien control in schizophrenia reflect a disorder in the central monitoring of action. *Psychological Medicine*, *19*, 359–363.

Fromkin, V. A. (1975). A linguist looks at "A linguist looks at 'schizophrenic language' ". *Brain and Language*, *2*, 498–503.

Fuller, G. D., and Kates, S. L. (1969). Word association repertoires of schizophrenic and normals. *Journal of Consulting and Clinical Psychology*, *33*, 497–500.

Gathercole, C. E. (1965). A note on some tests of overinclusive thinking. *British Journal of Medical Psychology*, *38*, 59–62.

Gerver, D. (1967). Linguistic rules and the perception and recall of speech by schizophrenic patients. *British Journal of Social and Clinical Psychology*, *6*, 204–211.

Goldstein, K. (1959). Concerning the concreteness in schizophrenia. *Journal of Abnormal and Social Psychology*, *59*, 146–148.

Goldstein, M. J., Rodnick, E. H., Jackson, N. P., Evans, J. R., Bates, J. E., and Judd, L. L. (1972). The stability and sensitivity of measures of thought, perception, and emotional arousal. *Psychopharmacologia (Berlin)*, *24*, 107–120.

Gorham, D. R. (1956). Use of the proverbs test for differentiating schizophrenics from normals. *Journal of Consulting Psychology*, *20*, 435–440.

Gottesman, I. I., and Shields, J. (1982). *Schizophrenia: The epigenetic puzzle*. Cambridge: Cambridge University Press.

Gottschalk, L. A., and Gleser, G. C. (1969). *The measurement of psychological states through the content analysis of verbal behavior*. Berkeley: University of California Press.

Grove, W. A., and Andreasen, N. C. (1985). Language and thinking in psychosis. *Archives of General Psychiatry*, *42*, 26–32.

Hamlin, R. M., and Folsom, A. T. (1977). Impairment in abstract responses of schizophrenic neurotics, and brain-damaged patients. *Journal of Abnormal Psychology*, *86*, 483–491.

Harrow, M., and Marengo, J. T. (1986). Schizophrenic thought disorder at followup: Its persistence and prognostic significance. *Schizophrenia Bulletin, 12,* 373–393.

Harrow, M., and Prosen, M. (1978). Intermingling and disordered logic as influences on schizophrenic "Thought disorders." *Archives of General Psychiatry, 35,* 1213–1218.

Harrow, M., and Quinlan, D. M. (1985). *Disordered thinking and schizophrenic psychopathology.* New York: Gardner Press.

Harrow, M., Silverstein, M., and Marengo, J. (1983). Disordered thinking: Does it identify nuclear schizophrenia? *Archives of General Psychiatry, 40,* 765–771.

Harvey, P. D., Earle-Boyer, E. A., and Wielgus, M. S. (1984). The consistency of thought disorder in mania and schizophrenia. An assessment of acute psychotics. *Journal of Nervous and Mental Disease, 172,* 458–463.

Harvey, P. D., Earle-Boyer, E. A., and Levinson, J. C. (1986). Distractability and discourse failure. Their association in mania and schizophrenia. *Journal of Nervous and Mental Disease, 174,* 274–279.

Hawks, D. V., and Payne, R. W. (1971). Overinclusive thought disorder and symptomatology. *British Journal of Psychiatry, 118,* 663–670.

Heilbrun, A. B., Diller, R., Flemming, R., and Slade, L. (1986). Strategies of disattention and auditory hallucinations in schizophrenics. *Journal of Nervous and Mental Disease, 174,* 265–273.

Heim, G., and Cohen, R. (1981). Referent communication of chronic schizophrenics and chronic alcoholics under simultaneous and successive task presentation. *Archiv für Psychiatrie und Nervenkrankheiten, 230,* 325–337.

Hirsch, C. L., and DeWolfe, A. S. (1977). Associative interference and premorbid adjustment in schizophrenia. *Journal of Abnormal Psychology, 85,* 589–596.

Hörmann, H. (1971). *Psycholinguistics.* Heidelberg: Springer.

Hörmann, H. (1978). *Psycholinguistics.* Heidelberg: Springer.

Hoffman, R. E., Stopek, S., and Andreasen, N. C. (1986). A comparative study of manic vs. schizophrenic speech disorganization. *Archives of General Psychiatry, 43,* 831–838.

Holzman, P. S., Shenton, M. E., and Solovay, M. R. (1986). Quality of thought disorder in differential diagnosis. *Schizophrenia Bulletin, 12,* 360–371.

Honigfeld, D. (1963). The ability of schizophrenics to understand normal, psychotic, and pseudopsychotic speech. *Diseases of the Nervous System, 24,* 692–694.

Karlsson, J. L. (1968). Genealogical studies of schizophrenia. In D. Rosenthal and S. S. Kety (Eds.), *The transmission of schizophrenia.* New York: Pergamon Press.

Kent, G. H., and Rosanoff, A. J. (1910). A study of associations in insanity. *American Journal of Insanity, 67,* 37–96.

Kolb, B., and Whishaw, I. Q. (1983). Performance of schizophrenic patients on tests sensitive to left or right frontal, temporal, or parietal function in neurological patients. *Journal of Nervous and Mental Disease, 171,* 435–443.

Lawson, J. S., McGhie, A., and Chapman, J. (1964). Perception of speech in schizophrenia. *British Journal of Psychiatry, 110,* 375–380.

Lecours, A. R., and Vanier-Clement, M. (1976). Schizophasia and jargonaphasia: A comparative look at "schizophrenic" language. *Brain and Language, 3,* 516–565.

Leff, J. P., and Abberton, E. (1981). Voice pitch measurements in schizophrenia and depression. *Psychological Medicine, 11,* 849–852.

Levy, R., and Maxwell, A. E. (1968). The effect of verbal context on the recall of schizophrenics and other psychiatric patients. *British Journal of Psychiatry, 114,* 311–316.

Lienert, G. A., and Straube, E. (1980). Die Konfigurationsfrequenzanalyse. XI. Strategien des Symptom-Konfigurations-Vergleichs. *Zeitschrift für Klinische Psychologie und Psychotherapie, 28,* 110–124.

List, G., Cohen, R., Engel, D., and Kelter, S. (1977). Zum Einfluß von syntaktischer Struktur und Proximität auf Assoziationen zu Satzteilen bei aphatischen und schizophrenen Patienten. *Zeitschrift für klinische Psychologie*, *6*, 100–115.

Lovibond, S. H. (1954). The object sorting test and conceptual thinking in schizophrenia. *Australian Journal of Psychology*, *6*, 52–70.

Luria, A. R. (1977). *Neuropsychological studies in aphasia*. Amsterdam: Swets & Zeitlinger.

Lyon, N., and Gerlach, J. (1988). Perseverative structuring of responses by schizophrenic and affective disorder patients. *Journal of Psychiatric Research*, *22*, 261–277.

Maher, B. (1972). The language of schizophrenia: A review and interpretation. *British Journal of Psychiatry*, *120*, 3–17.

Maher, B. A., Manschreck, T. C., and Rucklos, M. E. (1980). Contextual constraint and the recall of verbal material in schizophrenia: The effect of thought disorder. *British Journal of Psychiatry*, *137*, 69–73.

Maher, B. A., McKean, K. O., and McLaughlin, B. (1966). Studies in psychotic language. In P. J. Stone, D. C. Dunphy, M. S. Smith, and D. M. Olgivie (Eds.), *The general inquirer: A computer approach to content analysis*. Cambridge, Massachusetts: M.I.T. Press.

Maier, S., and Rey, E.-R. (1974). Eine experimentelle Untersuchung über Strategienlernen denkgestörter Schizophrener. *Psychologische Forschung*, *36*, 359–374.

Malenka, R. C., Angel, R. W., Thiemann, S., Weitz, C. J., and Berger, P. A. (1986). Central error-correcting behavior in schizophrenia and depression. *Biological Psychiatry*, *21*, 263–273.

Manschreck, T. C., Maher, B. A., Rucklos, M. E., and White, M. T. (1979). The predictability of thought-disordered speech in schizophrenic patients. *British Journal of Psychiatry*, *134*, 595–601.

Manschreck, T. C., Maher, B. A., Hoover, T. M., and Ames, D. (1984). The type-token ratio in schizophrenic disorders: Clinical and research value. *Psychological Medicine*, *14*, 151–157.

Manschreck, T. C., Maher, B. A., Milavetz, J. J., Ames, D., Weisstein, C. C., and Schneyer, M. L. (1988). Semantic priming in thought disordered schizophrenic patients. *Schizophrenia Research*, *1*, 61–66.

Marengo, J., and Harrow, M. (1985). Thought disorder. A function of schizophrenia, mania, or psychosis? *Journal of Nervous and Mental Disease*, *173*, 35–41.

Marengo, J. T., Harrow, M., Lanin-Kettering, I., and Wilson, A. (1986). Evaluating bizarre-idiosyncratic thinking: A comprehensive index of positive thought disorder. *Schizophrenia Bulletin*, *12*, 497–509.

Miller, G. A., Galanter, E., and Pribram, K. H. (1960). *Plans and the structure of behavior*. New York: Holt, Rinehart & Winston.

Miller, G. A., and Isard, S. (1963). Some perceptual consequences of linguistic rules. *Journal of Verbal Learning and Verbal Behavior*, *2*, 217–228.

Miller, G. A., and Selfridge, J. A. (1950). Verbal context and the recall of meaningful material. *American Journal of Psychology*, *63*, 176–185.

Mittenecker, E. (1951). Eine neue quantitative Methode in der Sprachanalyse und ihre Anwendung bei Schizophrenen. *Monatsschrift für Psychiatrie und Neurologie*, *121*, 364–375.

Mittenecker, E. (1953). Perseveration und Persönlichkeit. *Zeitschrift für Experimentelle und Angewandte Psychologie*, *1*, 5–31.

Morice, R. (1986). The structure, organization, and use of language in schizophrenia. In G. D. Burrows, T. R. Norman, and G. Rubinstein (Eds.), *Handbook of studies on schizophrenia. Part 1: Epidemiology, etiology and clinical features*. Amsterdam: Elsevier.

Morice, R., and McNicol, D. (1985). The comparison and production of complex syntax in schizophrenia. *Cortex*, *21*, 567–580.

Naficy, A., and Willerman, L. (1980). Excessive yielding to normal biases is not a distinctive sign of schizophrenia. *Journal of Abnormal Psychology*, *89*, 697–703.

Neale, J. M., and Oltmanns, T. F. (1980). *Schizophrenia*. New York: Wiley.

Neufeld, R. W. J. (1975). A multidimensional scaling analysis of schizophrenics and normals perception of verbal similarity. *Journal of Abnormal Psychology*, *84*, 498–507.

Neuringer, C., Fiske, J. P., Schmidt, M. W., and Goldstein, G. (1972). Adherence to strong verbal meaning definitions in schizophrenics. *The Journal of Genetic Psychology*, *121*, 315–323.

Nidorf, L. J. (1964). The role of meaningfulness in the serial learning of schizophrenics. *Journal of Clinical Psychology*, *20*, 92.

O'Brian, J. P., and Weingartner, H. (1970). Associative structure in chronic schizophrenia. *Archives of General Psychiatry*, *22*, 136–142.

Oltmanns, T. F. (1982). The effect of distraction on sensitivity to syntactic structure in schizophrenic and affective disorders. *British Journal of Clinical Psychology*, *21*, 191–198.

Oltmanns, T. F., Ohayon, J., and Neale, J. M. (1978). The effect of antipsychotic medication and diagnostic criteria on distractability in schizophrenia. *Journal of Psychiatric Research*, *14*, 81–91.

Ostwald, P. F. (1978). Language and communication problems with schizophrenic patients—A review, commentary, and synthesis. In W. E. Fann, I. Karacan, A. D. Pokorny, and R. L. Williams (Eds.), *Phenomenology and treatment of schizophrenia*. New York: Spectrum.

Payne, R. W. (1971). Cognitive defects in schizophrenia: Overinclusive thinking. In J. Hellmuth (Ed.), *Cognitive studies*, Vol. 2, pp. 53–89. New York: Brunner & Mazel.

Payne, R. W., and Hewlett, J. H. G. (1960). Thought disorder in psychiatric patients. In H. J. Eysenck (Ed.), *Experiments in personality*, Vol. II. New York: The Humanities Press.

Penk, W. E. (1978). Effects of ambiguous and unambiguous stimulus word differences on popular responses of schizophrenics. *Journal of Clinical Psychology*, *34*, 838–843.

Penk, W. E., and Kidd, R. V. (1977). Differences in word association commonality of schizophrenics: The self-editing-deficit model vs. the partial-collapse-of-response-hierarchy hypothesis. *Journal of Clinical Psychology*, *33*, 32–39.

Pishkin, V., and Bourne, L. E., Jr. (1981). Abstraction and the use of available information by schizophrenic and normal individuals. *Journal of Abnormal Psychology*, *90*, 197–203.

Poljakov, J. (1973). *Schizophrenie und Erkenntnistätigkeit*. Stuttgart: Hippokrates.

Polyakov, V. F. (1969). The experimental investigation of cognitive functions in schizophrenia. In M. Cole and J. Maltzman (Eds.), *Handbook of contemporary Soviet psychiatry*. New York: Basic Books.

Raeburn, J. M., and Tong, J. E. (1968). Experiments on contextual constraint in schizophrenia. *British Journal of Psychiatry*, *114*, 43–52.

Ragin, A. B., and Oltmanns, T. F. (1986). Lexical cohesion and formal thought disorder during and after psychotic episodes. *Journal of Abnormal Psychology*, *95*, 181–183.

Ragin, A. B., and Oltmanns, T. F. (1987). Communicability and thought disorder in schizophrenics and other diagnostic groups. A follow-up study. *British Journal of Psychiatry*, *150*, 494–500.

Ragin, A. B., Pogue-Geile, M., and Oltmanns, T. F. (1989). Poverty of speech in schizophrenia and depression during in-patient and post-hospital periods. *British Journal of Psychiatry*, *154*, 52–57.

Rausch, M. A., Prescott, T. E., and DeWolfe, A. S. (1980). Schizophrenic and aphasic language: Discriminable or not? *Journal of Consulting and Clinical Psychology*, *48*, 63–70.

Reich, S. S., and Cutting, J. (1982). Picture perception and abstract thought in schizophrenia. *Psychological Medicine*, *12*, 91–96.

Resnick, H. S., and Oltmanns, T. F. (1984). Hesitation patterns in the speech of thought-disordered schizophrenics and manic patients. *Journal of Abnormal Psychology*, *93*, 80–86.

Rey, E.-R., and Cohen, R. (1973). Zur Erfassung von Assoziationsstörungen Schizophrener. *Zeitschrift für Klinische Psychologie*, *2*, 164–182.

Ries, H. A., and Johnson, M. H. (1967). Commonality of word associations and good and poor premorbid schizophrenia. *Journal of Abnormal Psychology, 72*, 487–488.

Roberts, M. A., and Schuham, A. I. (1974). Word associations of schizophrenics and alcoholics as a function of strength of associative distracter. *Journal of Abnormal Psychology, 83*, 426–431.

Rochester, S. R., Harris, J., and Seeman, M. V. (1973). Sentence processing in schizophrenic listeners. *Journal of Abnormal Psychology, 82*, 350–356.

Rochester, S. R., and Martin, J. R. (1979). *Crazy talk*. New York: Plenum Press.

Rochester, S. R., Martin, J. R., and Thurston, S. (1977). Thought process disorder in schizophrenia. The listener's task. *Brain and Language, 4*, 95–114.

Romney, D. M. (1988). Thought disorder among the relatives of schizophrenics. A reaction to Callahan and Saccuzzo. *Journal of Nervous and Mental Disease, 176*, 364–367.

Rothenberg, A. (1983). Psychopathology and creative cognition. A comparison of hospitalized patients, nobel laureates, and controls. *Archives of General Psychiatry, 40*, 937–942.

Rund, B. R. (1988). Cognitive disturbances in schizophrenics: What are they and what is their origin? *Acta Psychiatrica Scandinavica, 77*, 113–123.

Rutter, D. R. (1985). Language in schizophrenia. The structure of monologues and conversations. *British Journal of Psychiatry, 146*, 399–404.

Rutter, D. R., Wishner, J., and Callaghan, B. A. (1975). The prediction and predictability of speech in schizophrenic patients. *British Journal of Psychiatry, 126*, 571–576.

Rutter, D. R., Wishner, J., Kopytynska, L, and Button, M. (1978). The predictability of speech in schizophrenic patients. *British Journal of Psychiatry, 132*, 228–232.

Sackeim, H. A., and Shapiro, H. E. (1981). Schizophrenic cognition. Regression or yielding to normal biases. *Journal of Nervous and Mental Disease, 169*, 591–598.

Salzinger, K., Portnoy, S., and Feldman, R. S. (1964a). Verbal behavior of schizophrenic and normal subjects. *Annals of the New York Academy of Science, 105*, 845–860.

Salzinger, K., Portnoy, S., and Feldman, R. S. (1964b). Experimental manipulation of continuous speech in schizophrenic patients. *Journal of Abnormal and Social Psychology, 68*, 508–516.

Salzinger, K., Portnoy, S., and Feldman, R. S. (1966). Verbal behavior in schizophrenics and some comments toward a theory of schizophrenia. *Proceedings of Annual Meetings of the American Psychopathology Association, 54*, 98–128.

Schonauer, K., and Buchkremer, G. (1986). Zur sprachlichen Manifestation schizophrenen Denkens außerhalb akuter Krankheitsepisoden. *European Archives of Psychiatry and Neurological Science, 236*, 179–186.

Schuldberg, D., French, C., Stone, L., and Heberle, J. (1988). Creativity and schizotypal traits. *Journal of Nervous and Mental Disease, 176*, 648–657.

Shimkunas, A. (1972). Conceptual deficit in schizophrenia: A reappraisal. *British Journal of Medical Psychology, 45*, 149–157.

Siegel, A., Harrow, M., Reilly, F. E., and Tucker, G. J. (1976). Loose associations and disordered speech patterns in chronic schizophrenia. *Journal of Nervous and Mental Disease, 162*, 105–112.

Solana, R. M. (1988). Communication disturbances in parents of schizophrenics. *Acta Psychiatrica Scandinavica, 77*, 427–434.

Solovay, M. R., Shenton, M. E., and Holzman, P. S. (1987). Comparative studies of thought disorders. I. Mania and schizophrenia. *Archives of General Psychiatry, 44*, 13–35.

Sommer, R., Dewar, R., and Osmond, H. (1960). Is there a schizophrenic language? *Archives of General Psychiatry, 3*, 665–673.

Spitzer, R. L., Endicott, J., and Robins, E. (1978). Research diagnostic criteria: Rationale and reliability. *Archives of General Psychiatry, 35*, 773–782.

Storms, L. H. (1977). Changes in schizophrenics' word association commonalities during hospitalization. *Journal of Nervous and Mental Disease*, *164*, 284–286.

Straube, E., Barth, U., and König, B. (1979). Do schizophrenics use linguistic rules in speech recall? *British Journal of Social and Clinical Psychology*, *18*, 407–415.

Straube, E., and Klemm, W. (1975). Sprachverhalten Schizophrener. *Archiv für Psychiatrie und Nervenkrankheiten*, *221*, 67–85.

Strohner, H., Cohen, R., Kelter, S., and Wolf, G. (1978). "Semantic" and "acoustic" errors of aphasic and schizophrenic patients in a sound–picture matching task. *Cortex*, *14*, 391–403.

Thomas, P., King, K., and Fraser, W. I. (1987). Positive and negative symptoms of schizophrenia and linguistic performance. *Acta Psychiatrica Scandinavica*, *76*, 144–151.

Todt, E. H., and Howell, R. J. (1980). Vocal cues as indices of schizophrenia. *Journal of Speech and Hearing Research*, *23*, 517–526.

Tress, W., Pfaffenberger, U., and Frommer, J. (1984). Zur Patholinguistik schizophrener Texte. *Der Nervenarzt*, *55*, 488–495.

Truscott, I. P. (1970). Contextual constraint and schizophrenic language. *Journal of Consulting and Clinical Psychology*, *35*, 189–194.

Tutko, T. A., and Spence, J. T. (1962). The performance of process and reactive schizophrenics and brain injured subjects on a conceptual task. *Journal of Abnormal and Social Psychology*, *65*, 387–394.

Vigotsky, L. S. (1934). Thought in schizophrenia. *Archives of Neurology and Psychiatry*, *31*, 1063–1077.

Von Domarus, E. (1944). The specific laws of logic in schizophrenia. In J. S. Kasanin (Ed.), *Language and thought in schizophrenia*. Berkeley: University of California Press.

Wahba, M., Donlon, P. T., and Meadow, A. (1981). Cognitive changes in acute schizophrenia with brief neuroleptic treatment. *American Journal of Psychiatry*, *138*, 1307–1310.

Watson, C. G., and Wold, J. (1981). Logical reasoning deficits in schizophrenia and brain damage. *Journal of Clinical Psychology*, *37*, 466–471.

Williams, R. M., Hemsley, D. R., and Denning-Duke, C. (1976). Language behaviour in acute and chronic schizophrenia. *British Journal of Social and Clinical Psychology*, *15*, 73–83.

# Chapter 3

# Memory

Psychiatric textbooks generally state that there is no disturbance of memory in schizophrenia. However, the results of some experiments discussed in this chapter suggest that this judgment should be qualified.

Since structural changes to the brain—such as can occur after injury, atrophy, or infection—are often accompanied by a disturbance of memory, it is of interest to take a close look to see if schizophrenics, or a subgroup thereof, suffer from similar problems of memory. Clinical interviews show that schizophrenics, in general, have no difficulty in recalling past events, but occasionally may give a somewhat distorted interpretation, possibly as a result of paranoid delusion or perhaps a wish to suppress recent experiences associated with their illness. It is thus clear that schizophrenics do not show gross amnesia as do some patients with focal brain damage (Adams and Victor, 1986).

In our discussion of cognitive function (Chapter 2) we noted that, with respect to language, schizophrenics have an intact repertoire (competence). It is therefore reasonable to deduce from this specific example that an intact memory exists for knowledge or for procedural information, that is, a so-called *semantic memory* seems to be intact. Schizophrenics have no major problems recalling events established before the onset of the illness, that is, they seem to have an intact so-called *episodic memory*. Thus, it seems unlikely that the majority of schizophrenics have long-term memory problems. (Exceptions in subgroups are possible; for example, see Tsuang, 1982, and subsequent text.) What about short-term memory failures? Experiments discussed in this chapter indicate that certain short-term memory functions are impaired in some schizophrenics.

Let us first have a brief look at models of information storage derived from results with normal subjects. The literature is vast; divergent views are too numerous to discuss here. Indeed, not all these views are relevant, because not all the aspects of memory to which they refer have been investigated with schizophrenic subjects.

"Conventional" short-term memory usually refers to a brief and limited storage which occurs about 1 sec after the sensory information has arrived centrally and lasts perhaps half a minute to several minutes. Ultra-short-term stores are usually considered to contain unprocessed sensory information for up to 1 sec. This is a large-capacity store of unprocessed data. It is also called a *sensory* or *buffer* store (an *icon* in the visual modality or *echoic memory* in the auditory modality). We will consider this type of store in our discussion of perceptual processes (Chapter 4).

The "conventional" short-term store is involved with two functions—to make data of internal or external origin available for several seconds and to allow the data to be evaluated, selected, and transformed (Cowan, 1988). The latter function is an aspect of *working memory* (a store of events specific to the individual and not directly relating to semantic knowledge). Long-term stores replace the short-term and can last a lifetime (Figure 3.1).

The short-term store contains data that are being processed; it is not a passive store. One of the functions of short-term memory processing concerns the selection of task-relevant external data (from the sensory buffer, b1, in Figure 3.1) and the selection of task-relevant data from the long-term memory (b2 in Figure 3.1). The selection from semantic memory may fail in some schizophrenics, although the semantic long-term repertoire is intact (Chapter 2). The problems of schizophrenics in selecting relevant external cues for processing is discussed in Chapter 4.

The main topic of this chapter is the effectiveness of the storing functions of short-term memory (and to a lesser degree of long-term memory). However, some researchers define the short-term or working memory as part of the long-term memory. These researchers suggest that the short-term memory is the momentarily active part of the long-term memory (cf. review by Anderson, 1985). How effectively are data stored in the short-term memory for later recall or recognition in schizophrenics? It is easy to see how this can be tested. Normally, certain processing strategies assist short-term memory storage. Thus, a monotonous series of items is hard to recall, but if the data differ in certain attributes, processing can use these differences to facilitate organization. Likewise, recognition or recall of organized material from the short- or long-term store is better than recall of unorganized material. Further, the effectiveness of the storage process can be tested by its resistance to distraction or to interference in processing by irrelevant features (Baddeley, 1988). The reader is referred to recent texts in normal psychology (e.g., Matlin, 1983; Anderson, 1985) and research reviews (e.g., Tulving, 1984; Cowan 1988) for a more complete treatment of the subject. (For neuropsychological and neuropathological interactions, see Markowitsch and Pritzel, 1985; Squire, 1986; Thompson, 1986.)

## I. Memory Performance

### A. Cognitive Organization

A large amount of research on the question of memory performance in schizophrenia has come from Koh and colleagues at the Michael Reese

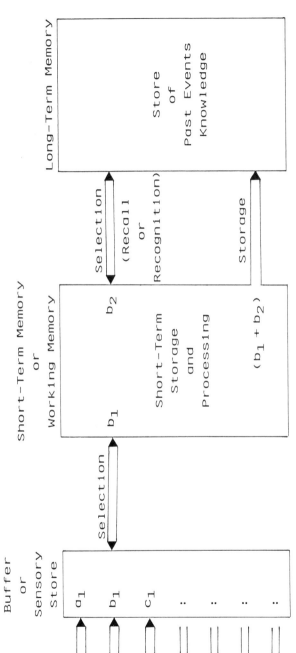

**Figure 3.1** Model of the function of different memory systems in human information processing.

Hospital in Chicago. Koh reviewed the literature and his series of studies in
1978. He reported several studies on the same group of patients, thereby
increasing the comparability of the results from different tests. Basically, 59
schizophrenics were contrasted with 31 psychiatric controls (mainly with
depression). The former were either chronic schizophrenics or were suffering
an acute episode in a chronic course. Subjects had been hospitalized, on
average, for 2–3 mos. Phenothiazine medication was administered to 63% of
the schizophrenics and 29% of the psychiatric control group, (cf. Section VI).
Patients were carefully diagnosed and matched in many ways, often with a
normal control group.

All in all the results of several experiments showed that schizophrenics
were notably poorer in recalling lists of words, but only if the words were not
organized into categories. If the words were grouped according to themes
(e.g., agricultural associations, office equipment, or plants), recall problems
disappeared. Other researchers confirm that schizophrenics find it easier to
recall semantically organized material than, for example, strings of digits
(Oltmanns and Neale, 1975; Grove and Andreasen, 1985).

How can one explain this simple method to help improve performance?
Koh (1978) said that the schizophrenics were not able to *spontaneously*
structure the material according to the semantic content of the words to be
learned. However, Larsen and Fromholt (1976), working in Denmark, noted
that if one suggested to the subjects that they choose their own categories, the
learning performance of schizophrenics improved. The schizophrenics required more time to do the test, presumably to organize the material, but they
could then recall the lists as well as healthy controls. (However, it is fair to
note that not all the patients were capable of categorizing the material.)

In San Diego, Traupmann (1980) confirmed that schizophrenics could form
conceptual categories for words based on semantic content, but that they used
less elaborate codes. A poorer cognitive organizational ability has been
attributed to schizophrenics in general, not just those with thought disorder
(Harvey *et al.,* 1986; see also Chapter 2).

In agreement with this observation, Koh and colleagues were repeatedly
able to show that schizophrenics could recall material as well as controls if
they were involved in semantic organization of the material (e.g., allowed to
form sentences from the words presented or were required via instruction to
group words according to given categories; Koh, 1978; Koh *et al.,* 1980). It is
also important to note that in this series of experiments the subjects were not
warned that, after the sentence-forming exercise, they would be asked to
recall the words used. (Thus, Koh made use of the *incidental learning*
procedure, which has the advantage that motivational factors play a far less
important role than in conventional learning tasks.) These and other studies
confirm that if schizophrenics were helped to organize word material, later

recall was improved; interestingly, they do not organize word material spontaneously. (Knight and Sims-Knight, 1979; McClain, 1983; Sengel and Lovallo, 1983).

Sengel and Lovallo (1983) noted that offering a clue for the recall of a relevant category was helpful for healthy subjects and nonparanoid schizophrenics, but less so for paranoid and depressed patients. However, increasing the delay before recall was required proved particularly detrimental to the performance of both groups of schizophrenics. [Increasing the intervals may result in more opportunity for distractions and intrusions to interfere with rehearsal of the initial information. Other investigators have also noted that schizophrenic rehearsal processes may be impaired. (Carr, 1980; Broga and Neufeld, 1981).]

These results show again that semantic competence or knowledge is intact in schizophrenics (Chapter 2), but this knowledge is not applied to the encoding of new material to the same extent as in healthy controls.

What can one conclude? Compared with healthy or depressed subjects, schizophrenics are impaired in the active organization and treatment of material for storing in memory, but are not impaired if the material to be remembered is already structured.

However, the neatness of this interpretation is challenged by the results of Russel and Beekhuis (1976), working in New Zealand. They found that schizophrenics and depressives were able to organize word material in the same way as healthy subjects, yet *both* patient groups showed poorer recall. The authors suspected that they were not able to make full use of the structure perceived in the word material. Hemsley (1982), in the United Kingdom, also noted that, whereas giving instructions on how to perform a task can enhance performance in normal subjects, such instruction did not always help schizophrenic and depressive patients. Thus, the findings raise the question of specificity and are at variance with those reported by Koh (1978) with a depressive psychiatric control group. However, Weingartner (1984), a specialist on memory performance in depressives, working at the National Institutes of Mental Health (NIMH) in Bethesda, claims that a failure to organize memory material spontaneously also characterizes the performance of depressives. He suggests that this may be explained by a failure in effortful, capacity demanding processes (which some researchers also think to be the basis of the cognitive disturbances of schizophrenics, see Chapters 4 and 16 for a more detailed assessment of the problem).

Currently, on the basis of but a few direct comparisons between these patient groups, it is difficult to determine whether conflicting results arise from specific differences in the tasks used or if an impairment in the active organization of material held in short-term memory is a nonspecific characteristic of schizophrenic and depressive patients.

## B. Effects of Emotion

A peculiar property of our memory seems to be that we are more able to
retain words or events with a positive emotional connotation than those with
neutral or negative associations. This is the so-called Polyanna principle,
named after the optimistic heroine of a novel by E. Porter (1913; see Matlin,
1983). However, schizophrenic apparently differ from healthy people and
other psychiatric subjects in this respect. According to Koh (1978), schizophrenics remember fewer words with a positive emotional loading from a list
of emotional and neutral words than do psychiatric or healthy controls. It is
not easy to find a convincing explanation for this lack of bias among
schizophrenics. Inappropriate or blunted affect is a common symptom of
schizophrenics, but Koh did not report any relationship between the lack of
the (positive) emotional bias and symptoms.

   A possible interpretation can be drawn from the cognitive theory of
emotions by Leventhal and Tomarken (1986). Here the emotions are included
as a significant attribute within the semantic network. Thus, one could simply
postulate that, in encoding and retrieval processes, schizophrenics do not
organize words according to their emotional associations nor do they organize
them the way healthy subjects do, according to other attributes (see Section I,
A, and other experiments on emotional attributes of words in Koh, 1978).

## II. Encoding with and without Distraction: The Digit-Span Test

In the test of the span of attention or capacity of short-term memory,
originally devised by Jacobs (1887), words or digits are displayed on a screen
or spoken from a tape recorder. In experiments done by Oltmanns (1978), the
subject heard a list of five digits or words and immediately afterwards was
asked to report what he or she had heard. The task has become a ubiquitous
part of intelligence testing (e.g., Wechsler, 1944). Innumerable reports in the
psychology literature show that it is easier to recall the items at the beginning
or end of a list or at the edges of visual displays. The last number or word is
particularly easy to remember (*recency effect*), presumably because it is still
held in the sensory buffer (ultra-short-term memory). The first items in a
series have a more prominent position than those in the middle and are also
more easy to remember than those in the middle (*primacy effect*). Healthy
subjects use these effects both in encoding and retrieval (Figure 3.2).

   It seems that these positional attributes may again represent cognitive
organizational procedures facilitating storage and recall, this time on a more
automatic level of processing. This would help explain that these positional
effects (in normals) are also evident in the presence of distracting items (e.g.,
relevant item spoken by a male and irrelevant items by a female voice).

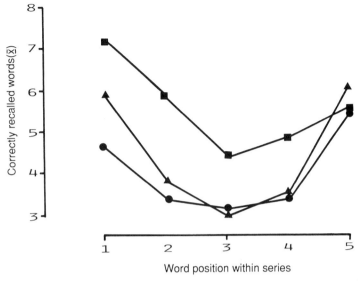

**Figure 3.2**  Average quantity of words correctly recalled by manics (▲), schizophrenics (●), and healthy controls (■), with respect to the position of the word in the series (after Oltmanns, 1978).

Under conditions of distraction, schizophrenics often seem to lose hold of the position of the stimulus and show a significantly weaker primacy effect. The performance of manic subjects lies midway between that of schizophrenic and healthy controls (and significantly differs from neither; Oltmanns and Neale, 1975; Oltmanns, 1978).

With respect to the *recency effect,* these tests show that schizophrenic performance is *not* different from that of the other groups. Retrieval of the last item requires no special cognitive organization, because it is still available in the sensory buffer, which contains largely unorganized material (see previous text). Interestingly, patients with frontal lobe damage are impaired in discriminations of primacy *and* recency (Milner *et al.,* 1985; see subsequent text).

Oltmanns and colleagues continued to show that this relative impairment of mental organization in schizophrenics remained evident even after a marked improvement of their symptoms. In this respect, they differed from the control subjects with affective disorder (Frame and Oltmanns, 1982).

Naturally one might object that impairments of learning and recall under distraction could easily just reflect the generalized nonspecific problems of severely disturbed psychiatric patients. In fact these authors had already approached this problem (Oltmanns and Neale, 1975). They presented series of digits with and without distraction, balanced for the degree of difficulty of the task in controls, and found that a differential impairment was still present.

The importance of this result is shown not only by the persistence of a deficit in remission but also by its significantly higher incidence among the (still symptom-free) offspring of schizophrenic parents (Harvey *et al.*, 1981). As a potential indicator of risk and in view of the persistence of a performance deficit, it may be argued that the impairment is potentially a schizophrenic trait and a vulnerability marker.

## III. Recall versus Recognition

Nuechterlein and Zaucha (1990) argue in their review that "because recognition memory tasks do not appear to require use of specific mnemonic strategies during encoding (Kintsch, 1970), they usually do not show performance deficits in schizophrenia" (p. 88; cf. Calev, 1984a,b; Koh *et al.*, 1981). It is appropriate here to cite a salutary warning for those contemplating research in this area from the work of Calev (1984b). At first these investigators appeared to find a memory deficit in a group of chronic schizophrenics and not in one of acute schizophrenics, but later analysis showed that the deficit was restricted to those receiving anticholinergic medication as a precaution against the development of Parkinsonian problems. It is well known that a functioning cholinergic system is important for performance on tests of memory.

A special problem seems to be the well-documented poor recognition of faces, which was already mentioned in Chapter 1 (Berndl *et al.*, 1986a,b; Cramer *et al.*, 1989). The influence of anticholinergic medication was not controlled in these studies. However, problems with facial recognition (déjà-vu phenomenon) were already observed before psychopharmaceutical therapy was administered in schizophrenia. It should be noted that in the experiments mentioned, the patients failed not only in face recognition but also in the correct interpretation of the emotional expression.

## IV. Poor Memory Performance and Schizophrenic Subgroups

We have seen that one can experimentally enhance the semantic organization abilities of schizophrenics (i.e., the use of the semantic memory). However, some of these patients still showed an impaired memory (e.g., Russel and Beekhuis, 1976, from New Zealand; Knight and Sims-Knight, 1979, from the United States; Calev *et al.*, 1983, from the United Kingdom). The latter studies found that this impaired memory was particularly apparent in chronic schizophrenics with a poor premorbid course. It seemed that in some patients there was a general decrease in the level of performance of all cognitive operations involved in encoding and retrieval that could not be alleviated by giving clues for the organization of material.

In this connection, Tsuang (1982) noted that some schizophrenics (mostly hebephrenic and nonparanoid) have problems with memory from the time they first appear in the clinic (22 from a sample of 178). These subjects had deficient recall for both recent and distant events (i.e., *episodic memory*), somewhat reminiscent of the milder forms of amnesia. The degree of disorientation shown by these patients is suggestive of a state of confusion. If we look at Tsuang's 30-yr retrospective study, we can see that these subjects had a poor outcome (cf., Chapter 14). Indeed, judging from the report of Cutting and Ryan (1982) in the United Kingdom, it was apparent that the chronic rather than the acute schizophrenic group was unable to benefit from the expressiveness provoked by the images of the words used in a verbal recognition task. (In general, words that readily generate images are more easily recalled than those that do not.) Calev and Monk (1982) also reported a general decrease in the ability of chronic process schizophrenics to recall verbal material, emphasizing the poor premorbid course of these patients. In a later study in Israel, Calev *et al.* (1987) reported that chronic patients, hospitalized for a long time, had a poor memory for recent material but performed better with respect to remote events. (No patient in this study was receiving anti-Parkinson's medication.)

The results cannot be attributed easily to the effects of age. The schizophrenics had the same average age as the normal controls, and the patients in Tsuang's (1982) longitudinal project were all quite young when first examined. Some of these memory failures are reminiscent of deficits shown by patients with structural alterations in the brain, for example, Alzheimer's disease (poor recall for recent events, relatively intact memory for remote events).

Reports are contradictory for patients with signs of tardive dyskinesia. One American group even claimed that chronic schizophrenics with tardive dyskinesia performed better on cued recall than those without. There were no differences on tests with no cues (Collerton *et al.*, 1985). The latter result contrasts with the slightly worse performance reported by Sorokin *et al.* (1988) for patients with dyskinesia. The prescription of antipsychotic medication was not controlled. (It is difficult to interpret such results when the information about changes of structure and neurotransmitter activity in the brain that are associated with tardive dyskinesia remain contentious; cf. Chapter 8).

# V. Patients with Brain Damage: A Similarity of Performance?

In our discussion we have occasionally referred to the possibility that there might be some similarity of memory performance between patients with brain damage and some schizophrenic subgroups (e.g., poor premorbid, poor prognosis patients). Unfortunately, direct comparisons of subgroups and "brain patients" concerning their performance on different types of tasks do not exist.

The most obvious group of schizophrenic patients to be examined first are those suspected to have organic damage, as seen in computer tomographic scans. From performance on the Luria–Nebraska test battery, Golden *et al.* (1980) could find *no* correlation between memory and any atrophic changes assessed by computer tomography in 42 chronic schizophrenics. However, other investigators have found correlations. When intellectual deterioration was assessed by the Withers–Hinton battery, a decline in memory performance was evident in patients with increased ventricular brain ratios (Johnstone *et al.*, 1976).

Shoqueirat and Mayes (1988) examined 16 acute schizophrenics with positive symptoms in more detail. The subjects were matched with healthy controls according to age, gender, and education. Schizophrenic performance was not impaired for recognition of faces or words, for recall of lists over a period of 2 min to 24 hr, or for spatial memory. The authors assume that the latter results, possibly indicative of the temporal lobe function, imply intact function in the acutely ill patients examined.

The ability to acquire associations and use these as attributes for the organization of stimulus material in short-term memory can differentiate between patients with frontal and temporal damage. For example, if asked to associate six cards on a table either with a particular light on the table or a hand posture in space, patients with frontal damage have difficulties learning the associations and identifying the sequence. If the neurologic patients have temporal lobe damage that extends to the hippocampus, there can be material-specific deficits in these patients (Petrides, 1985).

Gruzelier *et al.* (1988) in the United Kingdom used these types of tests with schizophrenics and depressives. Both groups of psychiatric patients were impaired in comparison with healthy controls (Gruzelier *et al.*, 1988). However, the depressive patients performed far worse on the spatial than on the nonspatial form of the test. The opposite result was more usual for the schizophrenics in this sample.

We will now consider three extensions of the digit-span test as a test of short-term memory: the Sternberg test, Hebb's recurring digits, and the Corsi block test.

The basic Sternberg test consists of presenting a number of items (e.g., 1–4 digits) and asking the subject if an item in a subsequent set was already presented in the first set. Checkosky (cf. Sternberg, 1975) examined acute and chronic schizophrenics along with alcoholic controls. Although there were effects implicating perhaps differences in the speed of processing, there was no evidence of a specific deficit. Thus, no useful comparison was obtained for an interpretation in terms of effects that might be attributable to brain damage. These results and conclusions are supported by Wishner *et al.* (1978) and Marusarz and Koh (1980).

In the Hebbian version of this task, a series of short spans of digits is presented. Every third or fourth span consists of the same digits. Normally, memory improves rapidly to a peak with the recurrent spans but more slowly and gradually with the nonrecurring spans. Deficits in this task are reliably shown by patients with temporohippocampal brain damage (Milner, 1971). They can also occur in chronic institutionalized (Crow and Stevens, 1978) and chronic remitted (Gruzelier *et al.*, 1988) schizophrenics.

In the Corsi block test, the experimenter taps six blocks on a table in a given sequence. The subject is asked to repeat the sequence. Patients with brain damage, particularly to the parietal cortex, are impaired in this task (Milner, 1971). Kolb and Whishaw (1983) found the "block span" of 30 chronic schizophrenics to be no different from that of healthy controls. Gruzelier and colleagues in London (1988) found that the performance of 36 schizophrenics, with both active and withdrawn symptoms, did not differ from that of other groups of healthy, manic, depressed, or emotionally disturbed psychotic subjects.

In the same subjects who did not produce differences in tests of memory span, Kolb and Whishaw found impairments in numerous tests sensitive to temporal lobe function (e.g., recall of paired associates, stories with and without delays).

Let us now briefly consider one study that attempted to directly compare the potential frontal contribution to schizophrenic memory performance. A group of 16 leucotomized schizophrenics (with remission varying from none to nearly complete) were compared with 5 nonoperated schizophrenics and 5 healthy subjects matched according to age, education, and socioeconomic status (Stuss *et al.*, 1982). Brain damage, checked tomographically, was located in the inferior medial prefrontal cortex. Despite careful preparation for this difficult study, problems arose in the interpretation of the results of this small number of subjects and in the separation of putative schizophrenic from putative postoperative effects. However, the results offer some support and some qualification for our foregoing discussion.

Briefly, the results were as follows. General performance on the Wechsler memory scale and particularly the ability to recall discursive stories was better in healthy and recovered patients. This suggests that contributions to the impairment in other subjects came from schizophrenic symptoms *and* brain damage. Notable is that a mild retrograde amnesia was apparent when schizophrenic symptoms and brain damage were combined. The intact schizophrenics performed worse than all others on the test of paired associates with or without delays and on recall of a complex figure 20 min after presentation. A primacy effect in the recall of word lists was absent in this group but, unexpectedly, more-or-less observable in all the others. Symptomatic schizophrenic groups, with or without brain damage, were impaired in revisualizing objects they had seen and performed poorly on Wechsler's memory test.

In conclusion, it is very disappointing to note the lack of controlled studies directly comparing brain-damaged and schizophrenic patients on the same tests of short-term memory function. In most cases, comparisons can only be made between studies using different tests, albeit designed on similar principles. Such an exercise is bound to yield equivocal results, because important details in the task presentation will differ. Another problem is the combination of schizophrenic symptoms among subjects tested. The chance of a short-term memory problem occurring seems to be higher in schizophrenics with a poor premorbid course, negative symptoms, and tomographic signs of cerebral atrophy (Johnstone *et al.*, 1976; Crow and Stevens, 1978; Tsuang, 1982; Keilp *et al.*, 1988). A few aspects of their performance on tests of memory show a partial similarity with brain-damaged subjects, some with frontal and some with temporal lesions. These similarities of function may not mean a similar organic disturbance in both groups, but this is a good place to start investigation.

## VI. Memory and Medication

Limited intake of drugs that stimulate the metabolism of dopamine and noradrenaline tend to improve the learning performance of healthy subjects. (For a review, see Weingartner, 1984.)[1] From this evidence we might conclude that antidopaminergic neuroleptic agents could lead to a depression of performance. That this is not necessarily so indicates the difficulty of extrapolating the effects of pharmacological agents on normal adults to adults with suspected pathological change.

Calev (1984b) found no particular deficit of schizophrenic memory performance caused by neuroleptic medication. Koh and Kayton (1974) found that neuroleptics made their subjects even more alert. However, perhaps the more usual finding is that neuroleptic medication does not assist performance. The amount administered seems unrelated to the impairments recorded (Neurfeld and Broga, 1981).

The administration of anticholinergic medication that is prescribed to counteract extrapyramidal effects of neuroleptics seems to be particularly problematical. This extra medication has been shown to impair performance on tests of memory (e.g., recall of unstructured word lists and the primacy effect) in schizophrenic and healthy subjects (Calev, 1984a; Frith, 1984; Weingartner, 1984; Spohn and Strauss, 1989; Strauss *et al.*, 1990). Indeed, recently a vast amount of literature has been written on this subject as a result of interest in the degeneration of cholinergic neurons in Alzheimer's disease.

---

[1]Psychostimulants, which tend to facilitatae the release of catecholamines but suppress overall turnover, probably have little effect on learning in normal adults, but by attenuating fatigue they may enhance vigilance. (For a review, see Solanto, 1984.)

Memory deficits occur both in these patients and in animal models of the disease (Hardy *et al.*, 1985; Becker *et al.*, 1988).

We should therefore ask whether the memory impairments of schizophrenics could, at least in part, be attributable to anticholinergic medication. This problem cannot be resolved at this time, because only Calev's study has compared groups of patients with and without this medication. Certainly not all patients that have been studied were receiving anticholinergic medication. In Koh's study, 27% were untreated. However, more systematic comparisons are necessary. The finding of a reduced influence of primacy in recall under conditions of distraction in untreated and nonsymptomatic offspring of schizophrenics (Harvey *et al.*, 1981) suggests, however, that not all of the results reported in this chapter are due to anticholinergic effects.

## VII. Suggested Readings

There exists, to our knowledge, no recent comprehensive review of the field, with the exception of a small chapter in Cutting's book. Still, the best review comes from Koh (1978), who made a major contribution to the field.

## VIII. Summary Statements and Interpretations

There is no gross memory deficit in schizophrenics. Specific aspects of performance in specific subgroups may, however, be selectively impaired.

## A. Performance

Less spontaneous cognitive organization of unstructured word lists in encoding processes has been recorded. However, it must be clarified whether this impairment differs from the performance of depressive patients. (Some schizophrenics show differences; some do not.) It is established that memory processes requiring effort are impaired in depressives.

On the other hand, more automatic organizational processes in encoding and rehearsal (primacy effect) seem to be specifically impaired, but only under conditions of distraction. (This seems to be a vulnerability marker, since children of schizophrenics can also be affected; cf. Chapter 12.)

Knowledge, that is, procedural or semantic memory, seems to be largely unaffected. The majority of the patients tested were able to organize the material (associative structure, etc.), albeit this was not done spontaneously.

Nevertheless, the extent to which these deficits are due to anticholinergic medication has to be clarified.

One must await new studies controlled for anticholinergic medication before coming to a final conclusion. However, at least the reduction of the primacy effect does not seem to be a pure side effect of anticholinergic medication, since it can be observed in remitted patients and in symptom-free unmedicated children of schizophrenics. It must, however, be kept in mind that an effect specific to schizophrenics only occurs when additional distracting irrelevant material is presented.

## B. Subgroup Differences: Comparison with Brain-Damaged Patients

Some poor premorbid schizophrenics showed severe memory deficits, that, unlike those of other subgroups, were not ameliorated by giving clues for the mnemonic organization of the material. Systematic comparisons with brain-damaged patients are rare. The role of the mild atrophy found in some schizophrenics remains equivocal. The few studies available report contradictory results.

The origin of more severe and generalized memory failures in a subgroup of schizophrenics remains unclear without direct measurement of structural changes. (See Chapter 8 for a more detailed discussion of this topic.)

## References

Adams, R., and Victor, M. (1986). *Principles of neurology*. New York: Mc Graw-Hill.

Anderson, J. R. (1985). *Cognitive psychology and its implications*. New York: Freeman.

Baddeley, A. (1988). Cognitive psychology and human memory. *Trends in Neuroscience, 11*, 176–181.

Becker, J. I., Huff, F. J., Nebes, R. D., Holland, A., and Boller, F. (1988). Neuropsychological function in Alzheimer's disease. Pattern of impairment and rates of progression. *Archives of Neurology, 45*, 263–268.

Berndl, K., Gruesser, O. J., Martin, M., and Remschmidt, H. (1986a). Comparative studies on recognition of faces, mimic, and gestures in adolescent and middle-aged schizophrenic patients. *European Archives of Psychiatry and Neurological Science, 236*, 123–130.

Berndl, K., von Cranach, M., and Gruesser, O. J. (1986b). Impairment of perception and recognition of faces, mimic expression, and gestures in schizophrenic patients. *European Archives of Psychiatry and Neurological Science, 235*, 282–291.

Calev, A. (1984a). Recall and recognition in chronic nondemented schizophrenics. Use of matched tasks. *Journal of Abnormal Psychology, 93*, 172–177.

Calev, A. (1984b). Recall and recognition in mildly disturbed schizophrenics: The use of matched tasks. *Psychological Medicine, 14*, 425–429.

Calev, A., and Monk, A. F. (1982). Verbal memory tasks showing no deficit in schizophrenia— Fact or artefact? *British Journal of Psychiatry, 141*, 528–530.

Calev, A., Berlin, H., and Lerer, B. (1987). Remote and recent memory in long-hospitalized chronic schizophrenics. *Biological Psychiatry, 22*, 79–85.

Calev, A., Venables, P. H., and Monk, A. F. (1983). Evidence for distinct verbal memory pathologies in severely and mildly disturbed schizophrenics. *Schizophrenia Bulletin, 9*, 247–264.

Carr, S. A. (1980). Interhemispheric transfer of stereognostic information in chronic schizophrenics. *British Journal of Psychiatry*, *136*, 53–58.

Collerton, D., Fairbairn, A., and Britton, P. (1985). Cognitive performance of medicated schizophrenics with tardive dyskinesia. *Psychological Medicine*, *15*, 311–315.

Cowan, N. (1988). Evolving conceptions of memory storage, selective attention, and their mutual constraints within the human information-processing system. *Psychological Bulletin*, *104*, 163–191.

Cramer, P., Weegmann, M., and O'Neil, M. (1989). Schizophrenia and the Perception of Emotions. How Accurately do Schizophrenics Judge the Emotional States of Others? *British Journal of Psychiatry*, *155*, 225–228.

Crow, T. J., and Stevens, M. (1978). Age disorientation in chronic schizophrenia: The nature of cognitive deficit. *British Journal of Psychiatry*, *133*, 137–142.

Cutting, J., and Ryan, K. (1982). The appreciation of imagery by schizophrenics: An interpretation of Goldstein's impairment of the abstract attitude. *Psychological Medicine*, *12*, 585–590.

Frame, C. L., and Oltmanns, T. F. (1982). Serial recall by schizophrenic and affective patients during and after psychotic episodes. *Journal of Abnormal Psychology*, *91*, 311–318.

Frith, C. D., (1984). Schizophrenia, memory, and anticholinergic drugs. *Journal of Abnormal Psychology*, *93*, 339–341.

Golden, C. J., Moses, J. A., Zelazowski, R., Graber, B., Zatz, L. M., Horvath, T. B., and Berger, P. A. (1980). Cerebral ventricular size and neuropsychological impairment in young chronic schizophrenics: measurement by the standardized Luria–Nebraska neuropsychological battery. *Archives of General Psychiatry*, *37*, 619–623.

Grove, W. M., and Andreasen, N. C. (1985). Language and thinking in psychosis. Is there an input abnormality? *Archives of General Psychiatry*, *42*, 26–32.

Gruzelier, J., Seymour, K., Wilson, L., Jolley, A., and Hirsch, S. (1988). Impairments on neuropsychological tests of temporohippocampal and frontohippocampal functions and word fluency in remitting schizophrenia and affective disorders. *Archives of General Psychiatry*, *45*, 623–629.

Hardy, J., Adolfsson, R., Alafuzoff, I., Bucht, G., Marusson, J., Nyberg, P., Perdahl, E., Wester, P., and Winblad, B. (1985). Transmitter deficits in Alzheimer's disease. *Neurochemistry international*, *7*, 545–563.

Harvey, P., Winters, K., Weintraub, S., and Neale, J. M. (1981). Distractability in children vulnerable to psychopathology. *Journal of Abnormal Psychology*, *90*, 298–304.

Harvey, P. D., Earle-Boyer, E. A., Wielgus, M. S., and Levinson, J. C. (1986). Encoding memory and thought disorder in schizophrenia and mania. *Schizophrenia Bulletin*, *12*, 252–261.

Hemsley, D. R. (1982). Cognitive impairment in schizophrenia. In A. Burton (Ed.), *The pathology and psychology of cognition*, pp. 169–202. London: Methuen.

Jacobs, J. (1887). Experiments of "prehension." *Mind*, *12*, 75–79.

Johnstone, E. C., Crow, T. J., Frith, C. D., Husband, J., and Kreel, L. (1976). Cerebral ventricular size and cognitive impairment in chronic schizophrenia. *Lancet*, *2*, 924–926.

Keilp, J. G., Sweeney, J. A., Jacobsen, P., Solomon, C., Louis, L., Deck, M., Frances, A., and Mann, J. J. (1988). Cognitive impairment in schizophrenia: Specific relations to ventricular size and negative symptomatology. *Biological Psychiatry*, *24*, 47–55.

Kintsch, W. (1970). Models for free recall and recognition. In D. A. Norman (Ed.), *Models of human memory*. New York: Academic Press.

Knight, R. A., and Sims-Knight, J. E. (1979). Integration of linguistic ideas in schizophrenics. *Journal of Abnormal Psychology*, *88*, 191–202.

Koh, S. D. (1978). Remembering of verbal materials by schizophrenic young adults. In S. Schwartz (Ed.), *Language and cognition in schizophrenia*. Hillsdale, New York: Erlbaum.

Koh, S. D., Grinker, R. R., Marusarz, T. Z., and Forman, P. L. (1981). Affective memory and schizophrenic anhedonia. *Schizophrenia Bulletin*, *7*, 292–307.

Koh, S. D., and Kayton, L. (1974). Memorization of "unrelated" word strings by young nonpsychotic schizophrenics. *Journal of Abnormal Psychology*, *83*, 14–22.

Koh, S. D., Marusarz, T. Z, and Rosen, A. J. (1980). Remembering of sentences by schizophrenic young adults. *Journal of Abnormal Psychology*, *89*, 291–294.

Kolb, B., and Whishaw, I. Q. (1983). Performance of schizophrenic patients on tests sensitive to left or right frontal, or parietal function in neurological patients. *Journal of Nervous and Mental Disease*, *171*, 435–443.

Larsen, S. F., and Fromholt, P. (1976). Mnemonic organization and free recall in schizophrenia. *Journal of Abnormal Psychology*, *86*, 61–65.

Leventhal, H., and Tomarken, A. J. (1986). Emotion: Today's problems. *Annual Review of Psychology*, *37*, 565–610.

Markowitsch, H. J., and Pritzel, M. (1985). The neuropathology of amnesia. *Progress in Neurobiology*, *25*, 189–287.

Marusarz, T. Z., and Koh, S. D. (1980). Contextual effects on the short-term memory retrieval of young schizophrenic adults. *Journal of Abnormal Psychology*, *89*, 683–696.

Matlin, M. (1983). *Cognition*. New York: Holt, Rinehart & Winston.

McClain, L. (1983). Encoding and retrieval in schizophrenic free recall. *Journal of Nervous and Mental Disease*, *171*, 417–479.

Milner, B. (1971). Inter-hemispheric differences in the localization of psychological processes in man. *British Medical Bulletin*, *27*, 272–277.

Milner, B., Petrides, M., and Smith, M. L. (1985). Frontal lobes and the temporal organization of memory. *Human Neurobiology*, *4*, 137–142.

Neufeld, R. W. J., and Broga, M. I. (1981). Evaluation of informational sequential aspects of schizophrenic performance. 1. Framework and current findings. *Journal of Nervous and Mental Disease*, *169*, 558–568.

Nuechterlein, K. H., and Zaucha, K. M. (1990). Similarities between information-processing abnormalities of actively symptomatic schizophrenic patients and high-risk children. In E. R. Straube and K. Hahlweg (Eds.), *Schizophrenia. Concepts, vulnerability, and intervention*, pp. 77–96. Berlin: Springer, 1990.

Oltmanns, T. F. (1978). Selective attention in schizophrenia and manic psychoses: The effect of distraction on information processing. *Journal of Abnormal Psychology*, *87*, 212–225.

Oltmanns, T. F., and Neale, J. M. (1975). Schizophrenic performance when distractors are present: Attentional deficit or differential task difficulty? *Journal of Abnormal Psychology*, *84*, 205–209.

Petrides, M. (1985). Deficits on conditional associative-learning tasks after frontal- and temporal-lobe lesions in man. *Neuropsychologia*, *23*, 601–614.

Russell, P. N., and Beekhuis, M. E. (1976). Organization in memory: A comparison of psychotics and normals. *Journal of Abnormal Psychology*, *85*, 527–534.

Sengel, R. A., and Lovallo, W. R. (1983). Effects of cueing on immediate and recent memory in schizophrenics. *Journal of Nervous and Mental Disease*, *171*, 426–430.

Shogeirat, M., and Mayes, A. R. (1988). Spatiotemporal memory and rate of forgetting in acute schizophrenics. *Psychological Medicine*, *18*, 843–853.

Solanto, M. V. (1984). Neuropharmacological basis of stimulant drug action in attention deficit disorder with hyperactivity: a review and synthesis. *Psychological Bulletin*, *95*, 387–409.

Sorokin, J. E., Giordani, B., Mohs, R. C., Losonczy, M. F., Davidson, M., Siever, L. J., Ryan, T. A., and Davis, K. L. (1988). Memory impairment in schizophrenic patients with tardive dyskinesia. *Society of Biological Psychiatry*, *23*, 129–135.

Spohn, H. E., and Strauss, M. E. (1989). Relation of neuroleptic and anticholinergic medication to cognitive functions in schizophrenia. *Journal of Abnormal Psychology*, *98*, 367–380.

Squire, L. R. (1986). Mechanisms of memory. *Science*, *232*, 1612–1619.

Sternberg, S. (1975). Memory scanning: New findings and current controversies. *Quarterly Journal of Experimental Psychology*, *27*, 1–32.

Strauss, M. E., Reynolds, K. S., Jayaram, G., and Tune, L. E. (1990). Effects of anticholinergic medication on memory in schizophrenia. *Schizophrenia Research*, *3*, 127–129.

Stuss, D. T., Kaplan, E. F., Benson, D. F., Weir, W. S., Chiulli, S., and Sarazin, F. F. (1982). Evidence for the involvement of orbitofrontal cortex in memory functions: an interference effect. *The Journal of comparative Psychology*, *96*, 913–925.

Thompson, R. F. (1986). The neurobiology of learning and memory. *Science*, *233*, 941–947.

Traupmann, K. L. (1980). Encoding processes and memory for categorically related words by schizophrenic patients. *Journal of Abnormal Psychology*, *89*, 704–716.

Tsuang, M. T. (1982). Memory deficit and long-term outcome in schizophrenia: A preliminary study. *Psychiatry Research*, *6*, 355–360.

Tulving, E. (1972). Episodic and semantic memory. In E. Tulving and W. Donaldson (Eds.), *Organization and memory*. London: Academic Press.

Tulving, E. (1984). Precis of elements of episodic memory. *The Behavioral and Brain Sciences*, *7*, 223–268.

Wechsler, D. (1944). *The measurement of adult intelligence*. Baltimore: Williams and Wilkins.

Weingartner, H. (1984). Psychobiological determinants of memory failures. In L. R. Squire and N. Butters (Eds.), *Neuropsychology of memory*. New York: The Guilford Press.

Weingartner, H., Grafman, J., Bouteille, W., Kaye, W., and Martin, P. R. (1983). Forms of memory failure. *Science*, *221*, 380–382.

Wishner, J., Stein, M. K., and Peastrel, A. L. (1978). Stages of information processing in schizophrenia: Sternberg's paradigm. In L. C. Wynne, R. L. Cromwell, and S. Mattysse (Eds.), *The nature of schizophrenia: New approaches to research and treatment*. New York: Wiley.

# Chapter 4

# Perception and Response

We are only capable of perceiving a small bit of all the things around us. We see only a part of the spectrum of light waves and hear only a restricted range of sound waves. We do not see ultraviolet light, the wavelength of which is less than 380 nm, and we do not hear sound waves with a frequency higher than 20 kHz. Even within the range of what we are capable of hearing and seeing, we notice some, but not other, things. Thus, one of the basic features of perception seems to be the selective aspect. We are unaware of most of these processes.

One feature of the selective aspect of perception, called selective attention, seems to be altered in schizophrenia, as already noted at the turn of the century by Kraepelin (1909) and Bleuler (1911). If we accept that schizophrenics tend to select "other" aspects of the environment as relevant, then we can understand why "healthy" observers believe that schizophrenics live in and experience another sort of reality. After all, we can only agree or identify successfully with another individual if we refer to the same environment.

Currently, most researchers still believe that a disturbance of selective attention is the core deficit of schizophrenia. In this chapter, however, we will see that this statement requires some qualification. Schizophrenics do not have problems with *all* aspects of the selective processing of information and, subgroups appear to differ.

One approach is to look at putative difficulties schizophrenics have at the different stages of information processing. This approach guides our treatment of the subject in the following sections and is illustrated in Figure 4.1. This scheme is based on dividing information processing into *automatic* and *controlled* processes as formulated by the Americans Posner, Shiffrin, and Schneider (Posner, 1975; Schneider, 1976; Massaro, 1977; Shiffrin and Schneider, 1977a,b).

## I. Automatic and Controlled Processes

Not all aspects of the environment are necessarily analyzed during all stages of information processing; much can be achieved automatically during an early

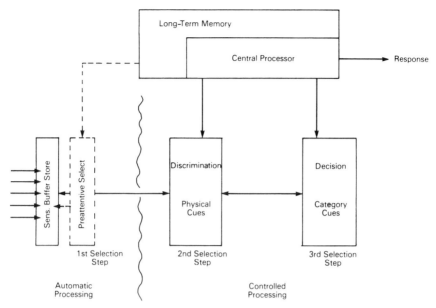

**Figure 4.1**   Model of human information processing.

stage. *Automatic* stimulus processing does not require a conscious participation in the active organization of the input material. The presence of the moon in the sky may be noted without consciously involving active attention processes.

In contrast, *controlled* processes require an active engagement which may involve a search procedure to ascertain the relevant feature. Typically, in task solution, several items may have to be analyzed for their potential relevance. Such selective attention procedures also require awareness and effort.

However, we should not overlook that automatic *discriminatory* processes also exist. These are often referred to as *preattentive* processes.

One characteristic function of preattentive mechanisms is the categorization of stimulus configurations into figure and ground, as described in Gestalt psychology. Stimulus configurations can be split into patterns that are coherent and salient; certain elements may be automatically grouped together or they may have signal value (figure) and contrast with the remainder of what is perceived (ground) (see Figures 4.2 and 4.8). If this structuring of the perceived environment is immediately evident to the subject who is perceiving, without further selective procedures, then the process is automatic or preattentive. This part of selective processing usually occurs without active or conscious intervention by the observer (see discussion in Robertson, 1986). However, if an *active* search procedure is necessary to separate the stimuli (e.g., a "T" is the relevant signal in Figure 4.2) then controlled processes are used rather than a more holistic separation into figure and ground.

**Figure 4.2**  Demonstration of "automatic" structuring of perception (gestalt perception) (after Julesz, 1984).

The tendency to perceive objects as the same despite their apparent changes (*perceptual constancy*) is also usually regarded as an automatic process. For example, one can estimate the size of a *distant* circle appropriately even though the actual dimensions on the retina are smaller than if the same circle were closer (*size constancy*).

For convenience, and because no active transformation procedures are usually required, we will also consider studies of the *perceptual threshold* and the sensory buffer under the rubric of "automatic processes."

Another important feature of automatic stages of perception is the processing of different items of information in parallel. In contrast, controlled processes involve processing of perceived material in sequential steps, that is, serial processing (according to the Schiffrin–Schneider model; see Cowan 1988 for recent qualifications of this model). For example, it is not too difficult for an experienced driver to hold a conversation while successfully negotiating the roads to work. If practiced in the art, attending to the potential hazards of driving can be an automatic process. On the other hand, even with practice, it is difficult to solve mental arithmetic problems efficiently and conduct a conversation at the same time. Nevertheless, the distinction is a relative one (cf. Section III, 4).

Another distinction between automatic and controlled processes lies in the limited capacity of the latter. For processing that involves a sequence of steps, only a certain amount of information can be treated at a given moment. To some extent, the limits are set by the number of channels available for conducting information; in another theoretical perspective, the limit is set by the amount of effort attached to a task. In the theory of Kahneman (1973), effort is necessary to "allocate processing resources" to a certain stimulus or task. The amount of processing capacity is limited by the number of processing resources available.

Controlled processes can be divided into two types. In the first type, stimuli are discriminated according to physical features (e.g., stimulus modality or light versus sound). In the second type, stimuli are separated into categories according to their meanings or associations (e.g., concepts or groups of items with common features or semantic interpretations). An example of a type-1 process is trying to concentrate on a red signal and ignore those signals appearing in other colors. An example of a type-2 process is if, while stock-taking, a salesman makes separate lists for food and nonfood items, thereby ignoring the size and color of the packages[1] (see Figure 4.1). Another way to separate these two different modes of perceptual, that is, cognitive, procedures often given in textbooks is that of stimulus-driven and concept-driven processes. The latter is identical with most of the theories dealt with in Chapter 2 and will only be treated briefly here.

The following sections are organized according to this scheme. We will discuss empirical investigations of the performance of schizophrenics on

---

[1]The distinction made here is related to Broadbent's distinction between stimulus set and response set (pigeon holing), originally made over 30 yr ago (1958). It is important that the reader not take dichotomous formulations of the serial or parallel processing of response and stimulus set, automatic and controlled, as mutually exclusive. In practice, the two can overlap and interact. For example, the preparation of a response based on automatic processing can be inhibited by the controlled evaluation of the stimulus. For reviews of the last 100 and last 30 yr of research, the reader may wish to consult Eysenck (1982) and Johnston and Dark (1986), respectively. For an extensive formulation of the role of effort, the book by Kahneman (1973) remains seminal.

functional tests and the characteristics of the series of processes to which the reader has been briefly introduced. The processes described cannot be directly observed. However, through controlled manipulation of the input, the investigator constrains the possibilities for processing and hence for the measurable output. A particular measure of output, reaction time, has occupied a special position historically and will be considered separately at the end of this chapter (Section III, B).

## II. Perception: Basic and Automatic Functions

### A. Perceptual Thresholds

#### 1. Critical Stimulus Intensity

Several studies appear to show that untreated patients as well as acutely ill or long-term hospitalized schizophrenics do *not* show abnormal thresholds for auditory stimulus detection (Bartlett, 1935; Ludwig *et al.*, 1962, 1963; Bruder *et al.*, 1975). This contrasts with depressive patients, in whom increased thresholds seem to be more commonly encountered (Bruder *et al.*, 1975).

In the visual modality, Litwack *et al.* (1979) noted that the subliminal presentation of messages with emotional content selectively aggravated the symptoms of their chronic schizophrenic subjects. This appears to show, in a rather indirect way, that the sensory perceptual mechanisms were intact in their patients.

On occasion, increased auditory thresholds have been reported (e.g., Levine and Whitney, 1970), but in this particular report the interest derives from the extension the authors made to the threshold measures. In their second experiment, they allowed the subjects to alter the loudness of the stimuli themselves. The subjects were asked to adjust the loudness of the stimuli to a level that could just about be called pleasant. Their chronic schizophrenics chose to adjust the loud speakers to a lower intensity than normal controls to make the stimuli more pleasant. From this result, one might conclude that the higher thresholds determined for these subjects may be functionally related to their lower tolerance to louder tones. (A similar observation has been made for pitch. Higher tones were judged to be unpleasant more readily by schizophrenics than by healthy subjects. R. D. Oades, unpublished observations.) One is tempted to speculate that a down regulation of the sensitivity of sensory perceptual mechanisms as a result of central influences may have occurred here (centrifugal mechanisms). Indeed, it is known from normal psychology that an increase of the perceptual threshold can occur for unpleasant stimuli (cf. Rosen, 1970). Bruder *et al.* (1975) reported that their chronic schizophrenics seemed to be more easily disturbed by the sounds with which they were presented. Thus, we may have a reason for an increase of auditory perceptual threshold in some schizophrenics.

An alternative explanation for the raised thresholds could be that the presence of hallucinations could interfere with the perception of exogenous stimuli. (Even the susceptibility to hallucinations might have an effect, so the reduced tolerance to loud stimuli may be a result of increased sensitivity to perceptual experiences such as hallucinations.) This interpretation receives support from studies of the visual modality. Kietzman *et al.* (1980), at the New York Psychiatric Institute, recorded increased visual thresholds for a range of psychiatric patients who had visual hallucinations. Bazhin *et al.* (1973) reported similar findings for the auditory modality, but only for the right ear in hallucinating schizophrenics. (We should remember that there are "stronger" auditory neuronal projections to the contralateral hemisphere, in this case the left hemisphere.) However, a study conducted at the Institute for Psychiatry in London on schizophrenic patients with auditory hallucinations, occurring at least once a week at the time of testing, found no significant threshold changes with respect to healthy controls (Collicut and Hemsley, 1981).[2]

## 2. Critical Stimulus Duration

The *temporal threshold* refers to the minimal duration of a stimulus necessary for recognition and is also known as the *critical stimulus duration*. In the experiments described here, the subjects were asked to identify a stimulus. In other words, in the detection (intensity) threshold experiments, the subjects were asked, "Was something there?" In the identification experiments they were asked, "What was there?" For example, in the studies of Saccuzzo and Braff in San Diego, the subjects were asked if they had seen a "T" or an "F." (Note: in the previous section, the independent variable was intensity; now it is the time necessary to identify a stimulus.) There has been no indication that the duration necessary for noticing the presence of a stimulus is different, but the duration required for identification, according to American studies, is longer (Saccuzzo *et al.*, 1974; Saccuzzo and Braff, 1981; Schwartz *et al.*, 1983). These results refer to chronic schizophrenics and particularly to subgroups with a poor premorbid course.

Saccuzzo and Braff showed that manics required an average of 9.3 msec to

---

[2]These authors hypothesized that auditory hallucinations could have their origin in the impaired suppression of endogenously generated noise. This would change the signal-to-noise ratio. Thus, random events in central nervous background activity run the risk of being misinterpreted as external signals. In turn, these signals would interfere with genuinely exogenous signals, resulting in raised perceptual thresholds. However, for most patients hallucinations are an irregular phenomenon, making it difficult if not impossible to arrange for threshold determinations during a hallucinatory episode.

identify the letter "T." Healthy and good premorbid schizophrenia needed 1–3 msec longer, respectively, but poor premorbid patients required twice as much time (18.3 msec). Absolute measures will, of course, vary with the nature of the stimulus to be identified. However, even with more complex stimuli a 2:1 relationship is maintained (Kostandov, 1980). Particularly interesting about this report is that a group of schizophrenics in remission was compared with a group of healthy controls. The implication is that the alterations found in some schizophrenics may not be strongly dependent on symptom severity or on the amount of medication.

Some of these experiments described here are part of the backward-masking experiments which will be discussed in detail in subsequent sections. The critical stimulus duration tests were "pretests" to examine the subjects' basic perceptual abilities (cf. Saccuzzo and Braff, 1981).

## B. Spatial Frequency

The term "spatial frequency" refers to the perception of the frequency of certain visual elements of a pattern in a specific field of view or in the retinal field onto which the stimulus projects. There is evidence from experiments, many of them performed on cats, of special neuronal detectors that respond selectively to altering spatial frequencies (Lindsay and Norman, 1977). These seem to correspond with the cortical mechanisms for the detection of spatial position, contours, and lines as described by the Nobel prize winners Hubel and Wiesel (1965). [Note, however,, that other peripheral mechanisms are also involved in spatial frequency perception (details in Schwartz and Winstead, 1988).]

Studies of function involve presentation at millisecond intervals of gratings with high or low spatial frequency. Broadly speaking, high spatial frequency means many lines are presented and low spatial frequency means only a few lines are presented to a given retinal field. Gratings with a high spatial frequency elicit a high level of neuronal activity in the detectors. If a grating is re-presented during the period of activity elicited by its first presentation, then the subject reports seeing only one presentation (see curves from healthy controls in Figure 4.3). As can be seen from Figure 4.3, the critical duration of the interstimulus interval for determining the presence of two stimuli in healthy subjects is linearly related to spatial frequency.

Schwartz and Winstead (1988) in New Orleans basically asked if there were characteristics of the neuronal activity shown by the spatial frequency detectors of schizophrenics that were different from those seen in normal subjects. They found that paranoids could separate two gratings at *shorter* presentation intervals than healthy controls, but only under the condition of high spatial frequency (see Figure 4.3). All the paranoid patients were receiving neuroleptic medication and had been diagnosed using DSM-III-R

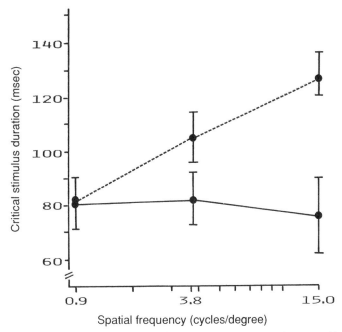

**Figure 4.3**   Critical stimulus duration for three frequency patterns presented to two subject groups. Note the typical linear increase in slope as a function of spatial frequency for normal individuals (- -), contrasted with the flat slope for paranoid schizophrenics (—) (from Schwartz and Winstead, 1988, reprinted by permission of Elsevier Publishing Company, Inc., Copyright 1988 by the Society of Biological Psychiatry.)

criteria. The authors could find no correlation between performance and the amount of medication.

A possible implication of these results is, according to the authors, that the shorter intervals required by the paranoid schizophrenics "may reflect a premature termination of information necessary for synthesis into accurate percepts" (Schwartz and Winstead, 1988, p. 3). Unfortunately, these results come from only a single laboratory in which only 15 paranoid patients have been studied at this time. No psychiatric control group has been examined.

A recent report from this group used a slightly different method. They varied the duration of the stimulus presentation rather than its spatial frequency. They claimed to find an increased *visual* persistence in chronic schizophrenics compared with healthy controls. They did not discuss what appears to be a contradiction to the earlier result (Schwartz *et al.*, 1988). Thus, it would be premature to draw conclusions. Nevertheless, the method is interesting and might be able to uncover further differences in basic perceptual mechanisms within or among psychiatric groups.

## C. Foveal and Extrafoveal Perception

There are variations in the number and type of retinal receptors in the foveal and extrafoveal areas and there are also differences in the neuronal connectivities of the two fields. A group from Yale looked for differences in the function of these two fields by presenting dots (2–5) on a monitor at different angles from the midline fixation point to a range of acute and chronic, paranoid and nonparanoid schizophrenics (Cegalis and Tegtmeyer, 1980; Cegalis and Deptula, 1981). Acutely ill subjects were far better at detecting peripheral stimuli, whereas the chronic patients' abilities were restricted to the midline range. The performance of a neurotic comparison group lay somewhat between that of the other two groups. The investigators performed a signal-detection analysis and showed that the perceptual sensitivity ($d'$) was lower for chronic nonparanoids in the periphery, where the detection abilities of the acute paranoids were best. (Sensitivity measure for healthy control subjects lay between these extremes.) The New Haven team also found that the group differences could not be explained by differences in response criteria (which is expressed by the beta-value in the signal-detection theory), that is, the paranoid patients did not guess more wildly than the other groups. They had rather low beta values.

## D. Sensory Buffer/Sensory Memory

### 1. Introduction

Between the appearance of a stimulus and its further processing by central mechanisms, there is a buffer store. A similar situation exists between the periphery and the central processor of a computer. As we have already discussed, the sensory buffer holds a largely unprocessed picture of external stimulus events for a short period of time after the stimuli have disappeared. To be sure, certain physical stimulus features may be changed under certain conditions (e.g., a reduction of intensity), but the stimulus has not been processed by the receiver for content, value, or meaning. The existence of such a store clearly has an adaptive advantage for an organism. If shortly after the disappearance of a picture one can still retrieve its image, then one can still respond to it, even though it is no longer physically there.

The sensory buffer is sometimes called an *icon,* in the visual modality, and sometimes called *echoic memory,* when referring to auditory perception (Neisser, 1967). The information in this store can be retrieved under certain circumstances, even after momentary neglect, for up to 1 sec. This phenomenon can be illustrated by an example with which most readers will be familiar. If distracted by something else, one often responds to a statement with "Sorry, what (did you say)?", and before the statement is repeated one is aware of what was said. However, after an interval of more than 1 sec, the statement

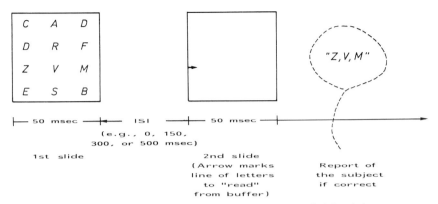

**Figure 4.4** Procedure for the Sperling technique. For a more detailed description, see text.

will have to be repeated in order to be understood. (Background information on experimental psychological and neurophysiological investigations of the sensory buffer can be found in Sperling, 1960; Neisser, 1967; Sakitt, 1976; Long, 1980; Haber, 1983; Balogh and Merritt, 1987.)

## 2. Tests of the Span of Apprehension

In order to illustrate the standard experimental situation, we will describe an example from the original demonstration of this phenomenon by Sperling (1960). A large number of letters was presented in a tachistoscope for a very short time (50 msec). Subjects were unable to identify all the letters: their span of apprehension was not sufficient to decode completely the semantic content of the stimuli (i.e., to read the letters). Some individuals, however, said they could call up an image *after* the presentation and report some of the letters.

Sperling followed this result with an elegant modification (cf. Figure 4.4). Immediately after the very short presentation of several rows of letters, an arrow appeared on the screen so it pointed to one of the rows that had just been presented. The subject was asked to read the line of letters that was apparently indicated by the arrow (so-called partial report technique). (Note that the arrow appeared *after* the letters had disappeared from the screen.) Most of Sperling's subjects were able to report the target letters. The partial report performance is normally better than the full report performance. (This result has been confirmed many times; see Neisser, 1967.)

Knight *et al.* (1977) at Brandeis University compared the performance of a range of schizophrenic subgroups with a psychiatric comparison group in the Sperling test and found that one subgroup of schizophrenics was unable to make such a selection from the sensory store. They also presented their subjects with Payne's object-classification test (Chapter 2). They found that patients who used a reduced number of categories to classify the objects (i.e., underinclusive) were only able to retrieve a few letters on the Sperling test. In contrast, the overinclusive schizophrenics who used more numerous categories (sometimes inappropriate ones) could recall as many letters on the Sperling test as the psychiatric controls. The same problem was shown by subjects with a poor premorbid history (as assessed by the widely used Phillips scale). Thus, it seems that some schizophrenic subgroups can experience difficulty retrieving sufficient information from the short-term buffer. Is the buffer deficient in these patients?

This question was examined with the *picture-integration test*. The principle of this test is to superimpose a second image on the icon. Knight *et al.* (1978) provided an elegant demonstration of the intact function of the buffer or icon in schizophrenics. In this test, a part of a picture was presented. It consisted of an apparently nonsensical arrangement of dots and dashes. The second half of the picture came some milliseconds later. Only at this stage could the subject identify the letter or digit represented. The assumption underlying the test was that a meaningful picture could only be identified if the stimulus trace of the first half of the picture was still in the buffer store when the second half was presented on the screen. If the two halves made up a meaningful picture, it would be recognized as such (Figure 4.5). The performance of schizophrenics with a good and a poor premorbid course was investigated. The investigators also subdivided over- or underinclusive groups according to Payne's object-sorting task. The performance of these groups differed neither between groups nor from that of healthy subjects. With a similar method, Spaulding *et al.* (1980; see Figure 4.3) also concluded that there was no evidence that the information in the schizophrenic sensory store

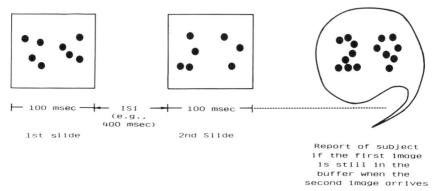

**Figure 4.5**  Procedure for the Picture Integration Test. For a more detailed description, see text.

was physically insufficient or that it decayed any more rapidly than normal. (However, it does seem that, independent of diagnosis, age can play a role. Younger subjects perform better.)

Are these two sets of results compatible? It seems that schizophrenics (even those using broad and vague concepts in a test of thought disorder) show *intact* storing in the sensory buffer, but may have difficulty retrieving the information effectively (Sperling test). Is the problem on the Sperling test caused by a weakness in the appropriate selection of relevant letters in the presence of irrelevant letters?

Results of studies in the United States (e.g., Neale, 1971; Cash *et al.,* 1972; Asarnow *et al.,* 1981) seem to show that interference from irrelevant stimuli can be a problem. These studies examined schizophrenics with the so-called *Estes technique,* a variant of the span-of-apprehension test.

In essence, arrays of letters were presented, as in the Sperling test, for very short time periods. Two measures were derived. In the *full report* condition, subjects were asked what letters they had seen. In the *partial report* condition, they were asked whether a certain letter was present (stimulus selection condition).

The results of these studies showed that schizophrenics did not differ in the full report condition, but failed in the partial report condition. Presenting only one letter (i.e., without irrelevant letters) does not lead to recognition problems for schizophrenics. However, it does seem that the selection of relevant from irrelevant letters is difficult.

It is obviously of interest whether the phenomenon with irrelevant letters (interference) could be found in schizophrenics in remission. Could this impairment take on the features of a schizophrenic trait? Asarnow *et al.* (1981) found that subjects in remission were similarly impaired, but only if their scores on the Global Assessment Scale (GAS) were above a certain threshold (which means that schizophrenic symptoms must be present in order to show the impairment). Dobson and Neufeld (1987) from London, Ontario, were able to confirm Asarnow's results with actively symptomatic subjects, they found *no* impairment with schizophrenics in remission. Recently, Asarnow and Granholm (1991) found deviant span of apprehension performance only in a subgroup on schizophrenics (40% of the sample tested; no further characteristics given) which may explain the discrepant findings. Nevertheless, Wagener *et al.* (1986) demonstrated span problems in high-risk children and their mothers.

The study by Strauss *et al.* (1984) in Baltimore questioned the specificity of the span-of-apprehension test findings. Here manic patients were also found to experience difficulties in the interference condition. According to Harris *et al.* (1985) at Arizona State University, schizophrenics had more problems finding the target letter than subjects who were affect disordered, excluding manic patients, and healthy subjects. Further study is required to resolve the similarity or difference between the problems shown by manic and schizophrenic patients.

For the sake of completeness, it should be noted that no differences were found by Harris *et al.* (1985) with an auditory version of the Estes test. However, the two methods are not equivalent and we will not go into further details here.

### 3. Visual Masking

Visual masking is a way to test how well stimuli can be stored in the sensory buffer and how rapidly they can be removed for further processing. In a form frequently used by Braff, Saccuzzo, and colleagues in San Diego, four letters are briefly presented, as in the Sperling test. The duration of presentation (circa 10–50 msec) is just long enough for a subject to say if a target letter (e.g., "T") was among those presented. However, if, shortly thereafter (circa 100 msec), four more letters are flashed onto the screen in exactly the same position, then a normal subject is unable to retrieve anything from the icon formed by the original row of letters. The second stimulus pattern is the *masking* stimulus. In our example, the masking stimulus consists of four "X"s (Figure 4.6). In this case, the subject has not had time to decode information in the sensory buffer about the first stimulus; he or she is only able to report seeing "X"s. Therefore, the interval between the first and second presentation is critical. This time period is called the critical interstimulus interval (ISI). A very short ISI prevents full retrieval from the buffer, and the subject reports only the letters of the last presentation.

The basic result of this well-replicated procedure is that schizophrenics require a *longer* ISI than healthy subjects to be able to report the target letter

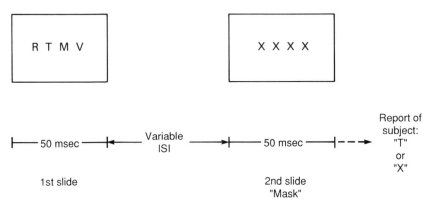

**Figure 4.6**  Procedure for the Backward Masking Test. For a more detailed description, see text.

in the original presentation (Saccuzzo *et al.*, 1974; Saccuzzo and Miller, 1977; Saccuzzo and Braff, 1981). As has been confirmed elsewhere (e.g., Schwartz *et al.*, 1983), compared with healthy subjects, the maximum number of errors in recall is made with ISIs in the range of 100–200 msec. A difference between the two groups can be recorded with ISIs up to at least 500 msec (Braff and Saccuzzo, 1985).

Many of the factors that could contribute to these basic findings have been investigated by this group in San Diego over nearly two decades. The first factor to consider is medication. First and most important, neuroleptic treatment did not impair, but in fact significantly improved, performance, particularly at shorter ISIs (circa 100 msec; Braff and Saccuzzo, 1982). As we might expect from this result, treatment of nonschizophrenic subjects with the catecholamine agonist methylphenidate impaired performance. Scores were then comparable with those shown by schizophrenics (Braff and Huey, 1988). (The subjects had minor depression or personality disorders, but apparently these features did not contribute to performance changes.) Impairment was more marked than the mild general depression of performance seen when subjects took benzodiazepines or marijuana (Braff *et al.*, 1981a,b; Braff and Huey, 1988). Thus, if neuroleptics (dopamine antagonists) can improve, and psychostimulants (dopamine agonists) can impair, it seems reasonable to suspect that dopamine activity modulates the mechanisms underlying the basic perceptual or the more advanced cognitive (rapid letter decoding) requirements of the task.

The second category of factors to consider is the specificity of the impairment to schizophrenia. Saccuzzo and Braff (1981) showed that small groups ($n = 8$) of manics and depressives performed at the same level as healthy controls, but depressives performed worse than healthy subjects and better than schizophrenics in other experiments (Braff and Saccuzzo, 1982, 1985). (The variability of the performance of various groups of depressive subjects suggests that the nature and severity of their illness is significant; e.g. Saccuzzo and Braff, 1981.) Thus, it appears that the impairment is not *qualitatively* different from that seen in some other psychiatric disturbances, but is *quantitatively* distinctive.

This point is emphasized by studies of schizotypal and schizophrenic subjects in remission. In a study of teenagers (average age, 15.5 yr) with borderline, schizotypal, or full schizophrenic diagnoses (10 per group; RDC), Saccuzzo and Schubert (1981) found impaired masking in the schizotypal group. However, the effect was even worse in the schizophrenics. Reviewing five visual masking studies of students with high schizotypal personality disturbance scores (Minnesota Multiphasic Personality Inventory, MMPI), Balogh and Merritt (1987) confirmed the presence of an impairment. However, we should beware of making a global generalization. In their study, an impairment was seen in those subjects with schizophrenic, depressive, and psychasthenic traits assessed by the MMPI (21 of 1000 subjects) and not in those showing other anomalous features (according to the MMPI), including a combination of schizophrenic and hypomanic characteristics (Merritt *et al.*, 1986). It should be emphasized that an MMPI schizotypal personality is not the same as the schizotypal group defined by the DSM-III-R. Thus, the relevance and interpretation of the findings in these groups with various combinations of personality features (including some with only a remote similarity to schizophrenic symptoms) is not clear.

Broadly speaking, results similar to those of Saccuzzo and Schubert were found in a study of patients in remission in the same laboratory (Miller *et al.*, 1979). In Tübingen, we were unable to replicate these results (Zaunbrecher *et al.*, 1990). Patients in remission showed no impairment. However, this difference may be explained by the fact that the California group studied older patients showing remission after a longer course of illness than the patients in Tübingen, many of whom remitted soon after an acute onset.

This result makes us consider whether the nature of the subgroup or the symptom displayed is important for visual masking performance. In Tübingen (Zaunbrecher *et al.*, 1990) and in San Diego (Brody *et al.*, 1980; Saccuzzo and Braff, 1981), acutely ill patients and those with a good premorbid course were impaired. However, like healthy subjects (Loeb and Holding, 1975), good premorbid patients were able to improve their performance with practice (e.g., four sessions), as shown by the San Diego group, but poor premorbid subjects did not show an improvement over eight sessions (Figure 4.7). Results from another group at Cornell University tend to support the idea that chronic patients (i.e., those with negative symptoms) show the more severe and the more lasting impairment in this type of performance (Green and Walker, 1984, 1986b). However, a closer look at the results reveals that only alogia, one of the negative symptoms, actually correlated with masking performance. (These authors noted *no* correlation between negative symptoms and digit-span performance.)

Could intellectual or sensory detection abilities affect visual masking scores? On the one hand, it is not surprising that the severely mentally retarded (IQ < 50) also show impaired processing on this test (Saccuzzo *et al.*, 1979). On the other hand, a comparison of the performances of a schizophrenic group and a group with minor depressive disorders (mean IQ = 102–109) with those of a group with spectrum diagnosis (cf. Chapter 10) of schizophrenia (mean IQ = 67) showed an impairment in the two schizophrenia-like groups, whose performance was markedly worse than that of the depressed group. All in all the results indicate that, in the extreme case, poor intellectual performance can interfere, but this interference does not explain the other findings reported here.

An objection concerning the specificity of the results could be raised on the grounds that the critical duration necessary for the stimulus to be successfully

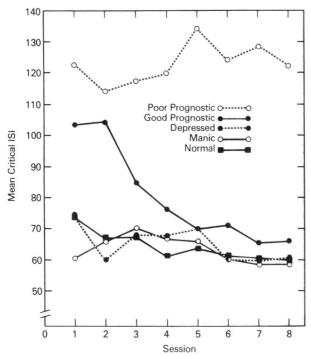

**Figure 4.7** The development across sessions of the mean critical interstimulus interval required to identify a target letter in a sample presentation before the onset of the mask in the visual backward-masking task. The subject groups tested were schizophrenics with a poor prognosis (poor premorbid) or a good prognosis (good premorbid), manic and depressive patients, and normal controls (from Saccuzzo and Braff, 1981, © American Medical Association).

identified also varies with the psychiatric group tested. As we have mentioned already, poor premorbid chronic schizophrenics need longer to identify a letter without a mask (critical stimulus duration) than depressed or healthy subjects (e.g., 6.3 versus 18.8 msec, Braff and Saccuzzo, 1985; 20 versus 50 msec, Kostandov, 1980). The problem here is that the subjects start the main masking experiment with large differences in basic perceptual abilities. A 2–3-fold increase (12–30 msec) of critical stimulus duration (threshold) may not be independent of the greater than 4-fold increase of the (masking) ISI (100–500 msec) over which schizophrenics make more mistakes. However, it is important to note that the presentation of stimuli for visual masking was balanced according to the amount of processing. This means that the target appeared approximately at the critical stimulus duration appropriate for the individual patient, whatever the actual value of the patient's threshold was. It may still be argued that, whatever the factor responsible for increasing the duration threshold, it may also be at work in the process of retrieval, as measured by visual masking. It is difficult to exclude this possibility, because the worse the masking performance, the longer the basic stimulus duration threshold. Registration in the stimulus store could take place at the same neurophysiological "locus" as or at a different "locus" as the further processing of the stimulus.

Braff and Saccuzzo (1985) presented some evidence of two separate "loci" for the stimulus duration and ISI effects. The removal of 4 of 19 subjects who had very high duration thresholds did not affect visual masking differences for the schizophrenic group as a whole. Indeed, high duration thresholds are more typical of the aged and the brain-damaged patient. Furthermore, concerning the possibility of a common innervation of the two reputed loci, a distinct but very small increase in the critical duration threshold with methylphenidate was found, as well as a decrease with neuroleptic treatment (in both cases, a mean difference of 1.5 msec; Braff and Saccuzzo, 1982; Braff and Huey, 1988).

Thus, one may conclude that each case shows a quantitative but not a qualitative difference. Antidopaminergic drugs affect (ameliorate) masking more than critical (first) stimulus duration thresholds; masking may be partially independent of the critical stimulus duration necessary for perceptual identification of stimuli presented alone; masking impairments are more exaggerated in schizophrenic than in other psychiatric or mentally retarded subjects; masking impairments are worse in actively symptomatic patients than in those supposedly at risk or in remission and are worse in schizophrenics with poor rather than good premorbid histories.

What (impaired) cognitive process is measured by visual masking? The physical quality of the stimulus trace in the sensory store may be poorer and more labile or may decay more rapidly. However, this seems rather unlikely. Schizophrenic performance can attain a normal level if the ISI is long enough. Thus, it seems more likely that the weakness is in "further processing," retrieval, or decoding. However, if poor premorbid patients with negative symptoms can still attain normal levels, given a long enough ISI (~700 msec), then even the vague explanation of *slowed* information processing may be somewhat plausible, at least for the poor premorbids.

An alternative argument follows. Normal performance of schizophrenics is achieved at ISIs long enough to permit further processing of the icon before the mask appears. The impairment at shorter ISIs reflects an interaction between the mask and the original stimulus, during which the irrelevance of the mask stimulus cannot be suppressed (as a result of poor perceptual organization). The interaction of the two stimuli degrades the original image. It is no longer salient enough for retrieval. (For a discussion, see Nuechterlein and Dawson, 1984.)

This possibility was studied by Knight et al. (1985). The authors used meaningful and meaningless images as masks (ranging from random dot assemblies to pictures of routine scenes). Schizophrenics with poor premorbid course were less distracted when the picture had meaningful content than those with a good premorbid course or other psychiatric and healthy subjects. Thus, the meaningful mask had less of a disrupting influence on the letter-decoding performance of the poor premorbid subject. Therefore the hypothesis of a stronger interference between stimulus and mask as an explanation of the generally poorer performance of the poor premorbid subjects (in the studies mentioned earlier) does not seem to explain the findings.

If poor storage in the buffer is not the cause, and if an interaction between stimulus and mask does not explain the findings, then only a slower transfer or decoding may provide an explanation for the especially poor performance (even after task replication) of patients with a poor premorbid course.

## E. Preattentive Gestalt Organization

Preattentive Gestalt organization refers to the structuring of material in automatic perceptual processes. In Figure 4.2, and 4.8 we immediately see some patterns. There is no need for further controlled data processing. The figures are perceived to be different from the hatched background. However, if asked whether a "T" is present in Figure 4.2 and 4.8, a controlled and demanding attentional process is required. Broadly speaking, one must generate an imaginary "T" and search through the items in the figure, comparing each one with the internally generated pattern.

The first type of structuring or organization can take place in automatic

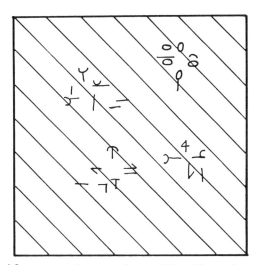

**Figure 4.8**  Procedure for testing "automatic" gestalt grouping processes.

perceptual processes. The rules of Gestalt psychology—the forerunner of modern cognitive psychology—are followed. Another law of Gestalt psychology states that perceptual elements that are closer to one another than to other elements in a given perceptual field are seen as one Gestalt or group separate from the other elements. In Figure 4.8 for example, one can identify four groups and separate elements on the basis of the closeness of the lines to each other. This is the Gestalt principle of *proximity*.

Cox and Leventhal (1978) at Bowling Green State University, Ohio, looked into the ability of different groups of schizophrenics to apply the principles of Gestalt perception. They presented pictures similar to those in Figure 4.8, consisting of a mixture of symbols, digits, and letters. The pictures were arranged so that the less frequent elements would be perceived as *figures* contrasting with the rest in the *background*. Whereas paranoid schizophrenics with good premorbid histories, as well as psychiatric controls, saw the appropriate figures (the latter often after a mere 10 msec presentation), nonparanoid schizophrenics with a poor premorbid course were unable to perceive figures.

In a second experiment, Cox and Leventhal increased the salience of the figures by introducing color, increasing the breadth of the elements, and reducing the number of items in the presentation. This change was enough to allow the nonparanoids, on at least two of three presentations, to improve their performance to the level of the paranoid, the acutely ill, and the control groups. Such results indicate that these mechanisms of automatic processing may function poorly in subgroups of schizophrenics under certain conditions, but are not entirely absent.

A further basic principle in Gestalt theory is that the whole (Gestalt) is seen before the pieces that make up the whole. This perception process seems to be reversed in some schizophrenics. Bemporad (1967; cited in Cutting, 1985) examined this principle with a simple experiment. A digit made of dots was presented against a diffuse out-of-focus background. Whereas healthy subjects first saw the digit (the whole) and then perceived that it was composed of dots (the parts), schizophrenics first reported the dots and then the whole digit. In contrast to the previously described results, no differences were recorded among the performances of acute or chronic schizophrenics in remission. This evidence agrees with our own results obtained with a closure test presented in the context of a perception test battery (Straube, 1975). Both acute and chronic schizophrenics first saw only the parts that made up the figure; only after the experimenter intervened could they make out the whole figure.

A similar characteristic of schizophrenic perception, what might be called a bit-by-bit analytical procedure, was observed in a British study by Reich and Cutting (1982). In this task, healthy subjects used a more "global" approach. Rather than first describing the general theme represented by a picture (e.g., preparation for a journey), as the controls did, schizophrenics started by listing the details of what they saw (e.g., suitcase, ball). Of course this task is not one concerned specifically with the study of automatic preattentive mechanisms, but the theme is pertinent.

A frequently cited investigation study of whether schizophrenics can apply Gestalt rules of perception as efficiently as healthy subjects was reported by Schwartz-Place and Gilmore (1980) and replicated by Wells and Leventhal (1984). These investigators presented patterns of dashes tachistoscopically (15 msec) that could be perceived as grouped figures, similar to those in Figure 4.8 but less complicated. In some presentations the patterns were more heterogeneous and contained a feature that was not immediately apparent and that probably could not be perceived automatically. The subjects were required to count the lines.

Both studies agreed that the healthy subjects reported the grouped items better, that is, they preferred to use the concept of Gestalt grouping to facilitate counting. Interestingly, both studies found that schizophrenics were relatively better than controls in making out the heterogeneous patterns (Wells and Leventhal used both healthy and psychiatric controls; see Table 4.1). It would seem, perhaps, that the bit-by-bit procedure used by schizophrenics is advantageous in this situation (whereas the nonschizophrenic controls may still rely on a Gestalt-grouping approach). Further, this procedure seems to be common to both paranoid and nonparanoid schizophrenics (Wells and Leventhal, 1984; Table 4.1).

This result is particularly interesting because one cannot object that anomalous schizophrenic performance could be attributable to the difficulty of the task (i.e., a generalized deficit), which in turn might imply a nonspecific impairment in the more severely ill (cf. Introduction to Chapter 2). However, the possibility should be investigated whether other nonspecific factors could underlie the improved reporting of non-Gestalt-grouped patterns. For example, Tyler and Tucker (1982) found that strategies employing a sequential analysis

**Table 4.1**  Mean Proportion of Correct Scores under Condition under Which Gestalt Principles Are More Difficult to Apply[a]

| Groups | Display size (number of lines) | | | |
|---|---|---|---|---|
| | 3 | 4 | 5 | 6 |
| Nonparanoid schizophrenic | 0.64 | 0.59 | 0.43 | 0.46 |
| Paranoid schizophrenic | 0.75 | 0.63 | 0.53 | 0.48 |
| Psychiatric controls | 0.60 | 0.44 | 0.35 | 0.24 |
| Healthy controls | 0.60 | 0.39 | 0.29 | 0.34 |

[a]Adapted from Wells and Leventhal, 1984.

rather than a global approach were typical of markedly anxious (non-psychiatric) subjects. It would be intriguing to compare the performance of anxious and schizophrenic subjects in the same test.

Finally, it is of interest to mention a study of Gestalt perception performed by brain-damaged patients with lesions either in the right or the left temporal lobe (Robertson *et al.*, 1988). The results suggested an analysis of global forms in the right and analysis of details in the left temporal lobe (cf. Chapter 8).

## F. Perceptual Constancy

Mechanisms to preserve perceptual constancy ensure that objects are identified for what they are, independent of the angle from which they are perceived and the actual dimensions projected onto the retina. A distant object may project a small image on the retina. By automatic evaluation of referential cues, the size is corrected and one responds to the actual size. If referential cues are removed (e.g., in a laboratory test), then the size of an object is estimated to be different from (i.e., smaller than) what it actually is. Reduced perceptual constancy is shown if one estimates the size of the object to be smaller than it is. Another type of perceptual constancy relates to color. Differences in illumination are automatically corrected (e.g., the same wall in bright sunlight or in twilight). Such adjustments provide further evidence that automatic analysis mechanisms are switched on before controlled and cognitive mechanisms take over to process information. Similar to other preattentive mechanisms, their correct function is a precondition to an appropriate and optimal interpretation of environmental signals.

To our knowledge, no recent investigations of constancy have been published (Raush, 1952; Hamilton, 1972). The most recent report appears to be that of Meyer-Ostercamp and R. Cohen (1973) in Germany. The inconsistency of older findings might be due to the difficulty in assessing the exact diagnosis of the subjects. Diagnosis was neither explicit nor exact by current standards. In contrast, Meyer-Osterkamp and R. Cohen presented psychopathological profiles of their chronic nonparanoid and paranoid patients, controlled the presentation conditions, and systematically varied the referential cues. Their most important result was that only the nonparanoids showed reduced size constancy. However, differences from healthy controls were only apparent when the number of referential cues was diminished; then the paranoids performed in the same way as the controls. Thus, the nonparanoids did not use referential cues as much as the controls, and underestimated object size. The object was judged to be smaller and, hence, closer to the actual retinal size.

A second interesting observation was made. Changes of the stimulus conditions had less effect on the formation of new judgments by the paranoid group than on the similar activity by the other groups. Here Meyer-Osterkamp and R. Cohen saw a parallel with the earlier results of Rausch (1952). In his report, paranoid schizophrenics were found to show an unusually stable size constancy under changing stimulus conditions.

# III. Controlled Processing

## A. Selection by Physical Cues

Two operational features of controlled processing figure prominently in the following discussion on schizophrenia. One relates to the processing of stimuli according to their physical characteristics (e.g., color or shape) and is also called stimulus-driven processing. The other concerns guidance of the selection of stimuli according to concepts and is also called concept-driven processing (cf., Figure 4.1).

Another process is important here: *selective focused attention*. With respect to our discussion of the selection of central stimulus representations, focused attention is related to the serial processing feature of working memory. Although several stimulus elements may be available for a short time for further processing, only one element is within the focus of attention at a given moment. In recalling, for example, the name and location of the house of a friend, the peculiar pink color of the house might come into the momentary focus of attention although all the other elements are available. The serial feature can be compared to the beam of a flashlight. The focus of attention moves like the beam from one element of the working memory to the next. Thus, focal attention can be considered to result from an activated subset within working or short-term memory, which in turn, in some circumstances, can be an activated subset of long-term memory (see also Introduction to Chapter 2).

### 1. Early Systematic and Clinical Observations

A good example of a way in which careful clinical observations can provide substance for experimental investigation is shown in the report of Freeman, Cameron, and McGhie (1958) in the United Kingdom. At first, they defined schizophrenic symptoms in terms of pathological defense strategies of a weak "ego," according to the psychoanalytic theory of Paul Federn (1953). However, on the basis of numerous accounts presented by schizophrenics in systematically conducted interviews, McGhie and J. Chapman (1961) discarded this concept and came to the conclusion that many schizophrenic symptoms in fact derive from a disturbance of selective attention. (The article can be recommended for the quotes from many of the observations made by the participating schizophrenics about themselves.) We will cite part of their abstract as a motto for the subject of this section.

These patients appear to have lost the ability and freedom to direct their attention focally as required in normal concentration. Their attention is instead directed radially in a manner which is determined, not by the individual's volition but by the diffuse pattern of stimuli existing in the total environmental situation. In effect, what seems to be happening is that the individual finds himself less free to direct his attention at will. Instead, his control of attention is now being increasingly determined for him by concrete changes in the environment. To this extent, the patient feels "open", vulnerable, and in danger of having his personal identity swamped by the incoming tide of impressions which he cannot control. (McGhie and Chapman, 1961, p. 105)

Hence, a major symptom of schizophrenia is an inability to exert a conscious control and the inability to control his or her particular focus of attention.

Today we can no longer be satisfied with the mere conclusion that "schizophrenia is a result of a disturbance of attention." A more precise definition of the aspect of the disturbed information processing is required. However, this should not detract from the fact that this simple statement was a minor revolution at the start of the 1960s.

The simplicity of the statement has also been at the root of some of the problems of the "attentional hypothesis." It is too global and too vague. Posner (1975) stated, "Attention is not a single concept but the name of a complex field of study (p. 475)." Thus, on the one hand, it led to the interpretation of nearly all schizophrenic cognitive deficits in terms of attention and, on the other, to claims of repeated proofs and disproofs of the hypothesis (depending on what one understood by the "hypothesis"). It is our opinion that, by differentiating between the various aspects of performance affected in schizophrenia (often all subsumed under the attention-disorder headline) and the subgroups of schizophrenics showing these effects, one can arrive at a clearer picture of what is happening in the various forms of the illness.

As we have said, the review of the American authors Chapman and Chapman (1973) provided a turning point between the older and newer work. In the following sections we will concentrate on the more recent work. Here we should briefly reiterate the major points that emerge from this review. First, and of historical interest, are the results of Chapman and McGhie's (1962) experimental test of the theory they developed based on clinical interviews. Second are a series of reports on the performance of schizophrenics in the presence or absence of distracting stimuli by these and other investigators (e.g., Ludwig et al., 1962, 1963; Stilson and Kopell, 1964; Stilson et al., 1966). However, one aspect was left unresolved by most authors. If schizophrenics (or a group thereof) show impairments under distraction, is this a result of increased task difficulty or does it really show a disturbance of selective attention? (See the methodological discussion in

Chapter 2, Section I, concerning generalized deficit and matched task design.) In short, the critique points out that it is always harder to solve a task with than without distracting conditions. Schizophrenia is one of the more debilitating illnesses. One may expect that when a task gets more difficult schizophrenics may be disproportionally impaired, no matter what cognitive ability is required. Thus, some older findings could be considered rather trivial since the more severely ill subjects performed worse on harder tasks. Hence, the Chapmans recommend not only matching psychiatric controls according to severity but also matching the tasks presented according to their difficulty.

## 2. Discrimination of Auditory and Visual Signals

According to Rappaport *et al.* (1972), from the United States, only a group of paranoid schizophrenics had considerably more trouble detecting an auditory signal embedded in white noise than did healthy subjects; in contrast, the nonparanoid group had much less difficulty. Neither group was being treated with neuroleptics. Despite the small numbers in each test group (5 paranoid and 9 nonparanoid subjects), the tests were unusually thoroughly documented and the results carefully analyzed (Figures 4.9 and 4.10).

The seminal finding for later studies was that the paranoid schizophrenics frequently made a particular type of error. They would report having detected a signal when there was none. This is known in signal-detection theory as a "false alarm." Such false alarms were recorded from these patients at two levels of difficulty (at 17- and 22-dB differences between noise and signal, Figures 4.9 and 4.10). Were the patients hearing internally generated signals that had no basis in external events (cf. Chapter 1)? The authors did not consider this possibility but preferred to interpret their acutely ill patients' responses in terms of increased sensitivity. They rejected the possibility that paranoid patients were more ready to respond to stimuli, because the groups made errors of omission (failure to respond to actual stimuli) with approximately equal probability. This latter form of readiness to "take a risk" and respond (known as beta, the criterion for response) can be differentiated from the detection sensitivity ($d'$) in signal-detection theory, as discussed earlier. Paranoid schizophrenics did not differ from other groups according to response criterion (beta).

Again, the generalized deficit cannot be entirely refuted, but it is more unlikely than in the other studies, since the paranoid patients were not more severely ill than the nonparanoids. Further, the nonparanoids gave more false alarms under the easier detection conditions. Thus, the task was not more difficult for one of the groups.

Intriguing were the observations of Rappaport and colleagues on the differential responses to neuroleptic treatment (administered in a counterbalanced order with placebo). Most of the medicated nonparanoid subjects

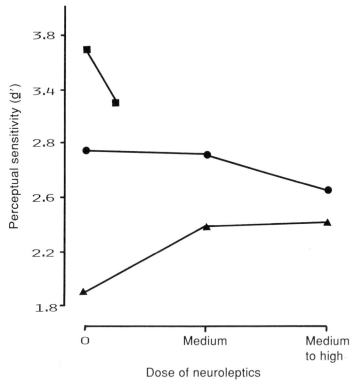

**Figure 4.9**   Average $d'$, perceptual sensitivity, in a signal detection task under relatively easy
detection conditions (background noise 17 dB louder than signal). Paranoid (▲) and nonparanoid
(●) schizophrenics were tested without medication and under medium and high doses of
medication. Healthy controls (■) performed without and with medication, that is, a single dose
of neuroleptics (after Rappaport *et al.*, 1972).

showed impaired performance at each level of task difficulty. However, the
paranoids showed an improving trend that just missed reaching conventional
levels of significance. Healthy controls also received a dose of 50 mg
chlorpromazine, which impaired their signal detection performance.

However, before accepting that neuroleptics impaired the sensitivity of the
nonparanoids, two points should be considered. First, at the time of the
experiment current research diagnoses were not being used (cf. Chapter 1). It
is conceivable that some members of this group were depressive. Second,
chlorpromazine has a strong sedative effect. It would be interesting to
examine the effect of an agent with less of a sedative effect, for example, a
butyrophenone (e.g., haloperidol). The issue deserves closer examination in
future experiments and will be raised again later in the chapter.

Hemsley, a psychologist at the Institute of Psychiatry in London, has

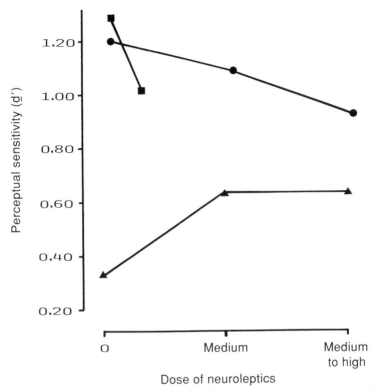

**Figure 4.10** Average *d'*, perceptual sensitivity, in a signal detection task under relatively difficult detection conditions (background noise 22 dB louder than signal). Other conditions as in Figure 4.9 (after Rappaport *et al.*, 1972).

carried out numerous stimulus-selection experiments. For example, Hemsley and Zawada (1976) asked if schizophrenics had difficulty discriminating between messages with similar content spoken by voices with different physical characteristics. A list of numbers was spoken by a female or male voice. Healthy controls had no trouble attending to the one and ignoring the other. Schizophrenics (diagnostic profile missing) were less precise and slower, but generally did not make significantly more errors than depressive subjects.

Using DSM-III-R criteria and Andreasen's scales for positive and negative symptoms (cf. Chapter 1), Green and Walker (1986a) from the United States selected two groups of schizophrenics for a dichotic listening study. The subjects listened to three numbers presented to each ear and were asked to repeat what they heard in either the left or the right ear. At this level, when the subject merely had to distinguish the ear (channel) receiving the message

**Table 4.2**  Correct Identification of a Figure on a
Monitor Which Is Partially Covered by Visual Noise[a]

| | Mean amount of information perceived under different signal to noise ratios (bits) | | |
| --- | --- | --- | --- |
| | 2.8 | 4.0 | 6.6 |
| Healthy controls | 2.9 | 3.0 | 3.0 |
| Schizophrenics | 2.8 | 2.9 | 3.0 |
| Occipital lesion patients | 0.3 | 0.5 | 0.8 |
| Temporal lesion patients | 2.4 | 2.7 | 3.0 |
| Frontal lesion patients | 2.7 | 2.8 | 3.0 |

[a] Adapted from Bazhin *et al.*, 1973.

and to recall the three digits, there were no differences between the schizophrenic and healthy subjects. The patients were able to temporarily store information from both ears and to select one of the stored items as required by the experimenter. This seems surprising, because, as described earlier (Chapter 3), schizophrenics with more positive than negative symptoms made more mistakes recalling visual stimuli in a digit-span test presented under conditions of distraction. Of course, there were more items to recall in the digit-span test, and the main effect was that of a reduced role for primacy in the organization of data in the short-term store.

A basic question that keeps recurring is whether the type of impairment found in some studies (e.g., Rappaport *et al.*, 1972) results from early disruption at the level of input or at later stages of processing.

Widespread damage to the occipital cortex disrupts input processing in such a way that patients can no longer discriminate signals from the background noise, as clearly shown by Bazhin *et al.* (1973) at the Bechterev Institute in Leningrad. Exceptionally, these authors compared the performance of patients with damage in different areas of the brain with that of schizophrenics. Whereas patients with occipital damage were incapable of discriminating figure from background, even under conditions of marked contrast, those with temporal or frontal damage were not much impaired (Table 4.2). Schizophrenics were quite capable and performed in a manner similar to healthy subjects, even under difficult conditions. The authors tested schizophrenics with paranoid symptoms and hallucinations as the prominent features. It should be recalled that Rappaport *et al.* (1972) found a deficit in this group which improved somewhat under simpler conditions of discrimination. In contrast, the test figures of Bazhin *et al.* (1973) are easier to discriminate (cf. signal–noise differences; Table 4.2; Figures 4.9 and 4.10).

Other early studies from the United States (Yates and Korboot, 1970) and the United Kingdom (Hemsley, 1976; Hemsley and Zawada, 1976) showed that schizophrenics were slower to discriminate auditory or visual signals from the background. They did not make more mistakes; thus, their error performance was indistinguishable from that of other psychiatric subjects. Royer and Friedman (1973) came to the same conclusion using a form-discrimination test. Thus, an interpretation of these results in terms of a genuine selective-attention disorder in schizophrenia depends on the criterion required for confirmation; the presence of a main effect alone or of an interaction seems to depend on the precise test conditions.

Marshall (1973) found that the schizophrenic slowness of response correlated with the degree of complexity of the presentation. Hirt *et al.* (1977) reported that this was particularly true for the nonparanoid schizophrenics. However, both of these studies may be criticized for not adequately distinguishing the possibility of a generalized deficit (Chapman and Chapman, 1973; Chapter 2, Section I).

A study that did attempt to match according to the discriminating power of the task-forms was done by R. G. Knight *et al.* (1985) in New Zealand. (In other words they compared the difficulty of different subtests in a group of healthy subjects in a pilot study.) Subjects were asked to discriminate rows of letters on the basis of whether "o"s or "x"s were more frequent. Increasing selective attention demand was provided by adding more irrelevant letters. It should be of no surprise that in this study the chronic schizophrenics (DSM-II-R) performed no differently from healthy controls. Acutely ill patients were not tested.

Broen and Nakamura (1972) reversed the question. They ingeniously assumed that acute patients who may be more distractable on difficult tasks may, through this facility, be able to handle multiple tasks, as long as the tasks are kept simple. Their assumption was confirmed. The patients were asked to perform a sensorimotor coordination test simultaneously with a simple auditory discrimination. The chronically ill were not able to perform both tasks, though neither was very difficult. The acute schizophrenic group, despite or because of what the authors called a "pathological" ability to distribute their attention, were quite capable of performing both tasks perfectly. These authors and Venables (1977) indicate that the chronically ill showed too limited a span of attention to concentrate simultaneously on both tasks. Thus, we can see from these and the other studies described that schizophrenics cannot, as a group, be regarded as showing a general "pathological" increase of their attention span. The performance of subgroups must be differentiated.

## 3. Visual Vigilance Tests: The Continuous Performance Test

In the last section we discussed selective aspects of perception and the performance of schizophrenics on tests of their ability to selectively attend to aspects of a stimulus complex and to ignore irrelevant messages presented simultaneously. Here we will concentrate on another form of attention—the ability to sustain attention and maintain vigilance. The conventional test here is the continuous performance test (CPT) developed by Rosvold *et al.* (1956) and first applied to a study of schizophrenics in the United States by Orzack and Kornetsky (1966). Since then it has become one of the most frequently used tests in schizophrenia research. The test concerns discriminating relevant "target" from irrelevant "nontarget" stimuli when the stimuli are presented sequentially rather than simultaneously. The discrimination is often simple itself, but is presented over an extended period to measure sustained attentional performance, vigilance, and ability to maintain concentration.

Typically a series of letters is presented briefly in a rapid sequence. The subject is asked to press a button when a particular letter appears (e.g., "x"). The task may be presented at different levels of difficulty (e.g., press only if an "a" is followed by an "x", or press if a letter is repeated). Perhaps the most difficult version is the presentation of degraded letters that are difficult to recognize (cf. studies of those at risk for schizophrenia, Chapter 12). Originally letters were presented on a rotating drum; later tachistoscopes and, more recently, computer monitors have been used.

Orzack and Kornetsky (1966) used the simple form of the task ("x" as target) with letters presented for 100 msec. They were able to show that about half of the chronic schizophrenics showed a lower "hit" rate than either chronic alcoholic or healthy subjects. (In contrast, chronic alcoholics were more impaired on the digit–symbol-substitution test of the Wechsler–Bellevue scale.)

From the studies that followed, some using more difficult versions of the CPT, the deficit seemed to be relatively specific. Thus, schizophrenic deficits could be demonstrated with respect to comparison groups, including subjects with schizoaffective or affective disturbances (diagnosed with research criteria; e.g., Walker, 1981; Walker and Shaye, 1982).

If the deficit seems relatively specific then it is natural to ask if it seems to be more of a "state" or a "trait" variable. Here the results of Wohlberg and Kornetsky (1973) are notable, because they retested a group of acute schizophrenics after spontaneous remission, who, with one exception, were free of medication. (Symptom severity had attained a level equivalent to that reported 6 mo before their current phase.) In this instance, the stimuli consisted of a series of digits projected for only 50 msec onto a screen. Tests were also carried out under distracting conditions, that is, either flashes of light appeared on the periphery of the screen or a metronome was heard over headphones. Under conditions of distraction, the schizophrenics in remission made more mistakes. This was confirmed by Asarnow and MacCrimmon (1978) in a similar situation, in which the distractor consisted of irrelevant numbers being presented over a loudspeaker. It was striking in Wohlberg and

Kornetsky's experiment that the schizophrenics made more errors of commission, that is, they responded as if a target were present when in fact none had been presented. This is reminiscent of the results from Rappaport *et al.* (1972), which we discussed earlier. Both laboratories were studying patients who were showing or had shown paranoid symptoms in the acute phase of the illness. Cornblatt *et al.* (1989) assumed that the distraction effect was not specific since depressed patients were distracted to a similar degree in a version of the CPT in which distracting stimuli were presented simultaneously. Also of interest is that the authors reported no *specific* vigilance deficit, that is, attention did not decline from the initial level over time.

The CPT deficit seems to be unrelated to other measures of cognitive function, diagnostic subgroup, duration of illness, hospitalization, age of onset, or education (Kornetsky and Orzack, 1978). Some authors report improvements following the calming effect of neuroleptic treatment (e.g., Kornetsky and Orzack, 1978), others an improving trend (Walker, 1981), and yet others, after thioridazine treatment, for example, no improvement at all (Erickson *et al.*, 1984).

Is there enough evidence that a CPT impairment could in fact be a specific trait or marker for schizophrenia? The persistence of a CPT deficit in remission implies the possibility that CPT performance could serve as a trait marker. Further, the findings by Walker and Shaye (1982) indicating that CPT impairments are more frequently found in schizophrenics with a family history of schizophrenia supports the hypothesis. However, we will see in Chapter 12 that biological relatives of schizophrenic do not typically show a deficit in these types of CPT tests (in contrast to the use of *degraded stimuli*). Results from a number of laboratories support these findings (Wegener *et al.*, 1986).

In the "a–x" version of the CPT, mothers of schizophrenics did not show any performance deficit (Wagener *et al.*, 1986). However, it is remarkable that in the same study, in contrast to the CPT test, on the span-of-apprehension test the performance of the mothers correlated with that of their impaired schizophrenic progeny (60% of the variance was explained, 48% after correcting for extreme values). (In this test, target digits were briefly presented with a number of irrelevant nontargets, more a test of selective perception than of vigilance.) One possible implication of the different results produced on these two tests is that the schizophrenic CPT impairment reflects vigilance problems and therefore only part of the underlying cognitive problem, that is, shares only a certain degree of common variance with the theoretical basic cognitive disturbance.

## 4. Competing Verbal Messages: Selection by Physical Cues

Human information processing has the ability to select the relevant signals from a cacophony, independent of intensity or other salient features. Representative is

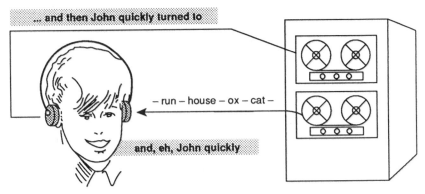

**Figure 4.11** Experimental procedure for the dichotic shadowing task. The subject has to attend to and repeat ". . . and then John quickly tuned to . . ." and has to ignore the message "run, house, ox, cat" simultaneously presented to the other ear (after Lindsay and Norman, 1977).

the classic example of the cocktail party, described in most texts on perception. In such a situation, many people are herded together in a small room and stand in small groups engrossed in animated conversation. Here, despite the general noise level, one is usually able to hear what one's partner is saying and tune out other conversations. The features we use at this moment include physical ones such as the direction of the source of conversation (e.g., partner is on the right/left) and its pitch (e.g., partner is male/female). These are the selection criteria to be discussed here; in the next section we will discuss the use of conversation content as a guide (data selection by content) or concept-driven selection.

Selection through physical cues can be easily simulated and controlled in the laboratory. The subject, using headphones, is asked to listen to a message played from a tape recorder to the right ear and to ignore another played to his left ear (or vice versa). In this *dichotic* presentation, the subject is usually asked to repeat or "shadow" the attended message (Figure 4.11). The selection takes place through the difference in location of the two earphones.

A large number of studies have been carried out on normal healthy subjects using the dichotic listening paradigm. The results have contributed considerably to the development of various theories of attention (e.g., Broadbent, 1958; Deutsch and Deutsch, 1963; Treisman, 1967; Kahneman and Treisman, 1984). Despite different theoretical interpretations, all who have done such experiments agree that the normal subject is amazingly proficient at following a message in one ear and ignoring another played at equivalent intensity in the other ear. Such a subject is often unaware of what was said to the unattended ear; he or she is unable to answer questions about the unattended message, as if the irrelevant message had been discarded; there is no "conscious" trace of it. If the message was not checked for its semantic content then it presumably did not pass through a stage of controlled processing.

However, after a while, exceptions to Broadbent's (1958) postulate of a total filtering out of irrelevant material, the bottleneck theory, became so frequent that these conceptions were undermined. These important exceptions included irrelevant material with strong emotional content or marked semantic similarity to the attended message. Such material "disturbed" healthy subjects enough to induce short delays in shadowing the attended message. This effect was recorded even when the subjects were not aware of what was being said to the unattended ear at the critical moments when the shadowing of the relevant message was delayed. Therefore, it is now believed that the unattended material is not completely filtered out. Instead more or less processing capacity is attached to the "unattended" material, even if this does not always reach a level of awareness or controlled stages of processing (Moray, 1959; Lewis, 1970; Treisman *et al.*, 1974; Kahneman and Treisman, 1984).

The first studies with schizophrenics on the dichotic task were reported by Payne, Hochberg, and Hawks (1970) in the United Kingdom. They deliberately chose to study overinclusive thinkers, (i.e., those who had difficulty in suppressing irrelevant thoughts). Subjects were asked to shadow single words or texts heard in one ear and to ignore words repeatedly presented to the other. The schizophrenics made many mistakes. However, these mistakes usually did not consist of mixing up the relevant and irrelevant words. This was an important indication to the authors that the patients always knew which trace was relevant, despite being more easily disturbed.

However, the results were somewhat less clear when the patients had to shadow a text as opposed to a short series of independent words. All the patients, with and without overinclusive thinking, made more mistakes under both conditions (i.e., with and without distracting messages).

Hawks, a member of this group, along with Robinson (1971) investigated this point and asked a group of 18 chronic nonparanoid schizophrenics to note digits heard on one side and ignore those heard on the other. The stimuli were not repeated aloud. Patients were asked after the presentation how many of the digits they could recall. Schizophrenic performance was poorer than that of the healthy subjects. It should be noticed, however, that under this condition not just the ability to select, but also the ability to store and recall, was being tested. Further, without the need to respond to each digit immediately, the demands for concentrated focus of attention may be less on what is being heard in one ear. The subject, consciously or unconsciously, switches more often between the channels of information in one ear and the other, which itself might pose a source of interference.

Extended experience with dichotic tasks has shown that the precise nature of the instructions and the task conditions are very important for the interpretation of the results. Instructions can influence whether attention will be focused on only one side and the extent to which the subject can switch attention between the content of relevant and irrelevant channels. The latter can be decisive for the performance of schizophrenics.

    With the use of an appropriate task design, it has indeed been demonstrated
that schizophrenics are able to tune out irrelevant information (Korboot and
Damiani, 1976). Their patients included acute and chronic, paranoid and
nonparanoid schizophrenics and psychiatric and healthy controls. The subjects
were asked to shadow digits heard in one ear and to ignore those heard in the
other. All the schizophrenic groups could do this as well as the psychiatric
controls. The chronic nonparanoids were just a bit slower. The same patients
were also given a signal-detection task, similar to that used by Rappaport *et
al.* (1972) and Bazhin *et al.* (1973). Once again none of the groups, not even
the slow responders, could be differentiated. These results, along with those
presented in the last section, cast doubt on whether the slowness of information processing in schizophrenics with negative symptoms can be regarded as
fundamental to the illness or whether it relates to selective attention mechanisms as measured by the dichotic listening task.
    Maloney *et al.* (1976) performed dichotic tests with a group of schizo-
phrenics in which those with a poor premorbid course had already shown
themselves to be slower on a series of sensorimotor tests than those with an
unremarkable premorbid course (as assessed by the Phillips and Ullman–
Giovannoni scales). The authors were exemplary in using precise diagnostic
criteria and provided a detailed assessment of symptoms. The range and
severity of the symptoms shown by the two groups was similar. Unfortunately, no other comparison group was studied. However, the investigators were
able to test patients before and after neuroleptic treatment in monaural as well
as dichotic conditions (Figure 4.12).
    Word pairs were presented separately and simultaneously to each ear. The
subjects were instructed to listen only to one ear. The interesting finding here
was not the performance under distraction, but the performance of the poor
premorbid group in the easy monaural condition without distraction. This
group made more mistakes than the good premorbid group. This result could,
perhaps, be attributed to a general slowness, already demonstrated on the
sensorimotor tests, because the presentation rate was relatively fast (50 wpm).
After all, it can be seen in Figure 4.12 that their performance was already as
low as that of the good premorbid patients with external distraction. The
impairment improved after neuroleptic treatment. There was no differential
impairment when there were two competing messages.
    A somewhat similar experimental design was used by Straube and Germer
(1979). In the dichotic condition they presented word pairs to one ear (to be
attended) and, simultaneously, words to the other ear (to be ignored). The
distracting message was varied to include words for which the content was
neutral, emotional, or synonymous with that presented to the attended ear.
The ability to shadow was also examined in a condition without competing
messages. In contrast to Maloney *et al.* (1976), the presentation rate was a
little slower (40 wpm) and neurotic and healthy subjects were also tested.
    Acute schizophrenic patients, tested immediately after admission, did not

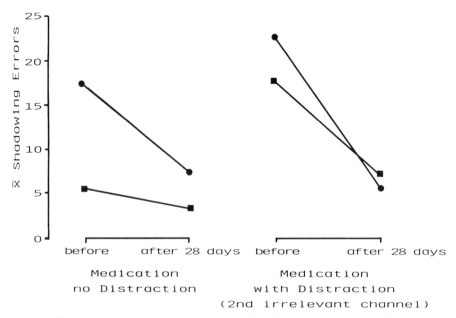

**Figure 4.12** Average shadowing errors in a dichotic listening task with and without distraction in good (■————■) and poor (●————●) premorbid schizophrenics, before and 28 days after neuroleptic medication (after Maloney *et al.*, 1976).

perform differently from the psychiatric and healthy controls. All groups made more errors in the dichotic presentation in which emotional words were used in the competing irrelevant channel. Unfortunately, unlike the study of Maloney *et al.*, not all patients could be tested before they were treated with neuroleptics, but a *post hoc* analysis showed that there was no performance difference between patients free of medication and those who had received neuroleptic treatment prior to admission (i.e., the absence of a specific disturbance was not due to the short-term treatment patients had received in the clinic). Performance was unrelated to the number of prior hospitalizations. Furthermore, neither the presence nor absence of paranoid symptoms, nor their severity, had an effect on the disturbance shown.

After this study, Straube *et al.* (1984) looked into the effect of varying the rate of presentation of the same material with another, but comparable, group of schizophrenics. The results showed that, even at slower rates, the schizophrenics did not show any more intrusions from the competing messages than the controls. There was no increase in the incidence of switching attention between channels. This is important, because studies with normal subjects with slow presentation rates have shown a slight reduction of the efficacy of focusing attention.

It seems that schizophrenics have relatively fewer problems focusing attention when stimulus selection is guided by physically defined cues and switching to the other channel is restricted by instruction or task condition. This was confirmed by Pogue-Geile and Oltmanns (1980). They found that acute schizophrenics had no more difficulty shadowing than did other psychiatric or healthy subjects. However, these schizophrenic subjects showed poorer recall of the stimuli that had been presented under distracting conditions (i.e., in the second irrelevant channel) than for those items they had previously shadowed without distraction. This evidence suggests that, although selective abilities function adequately under clearly defined conditions, the presence of other traces (of irrelevant stimuli) can lead to decrements of the encoding or recall processes.

On the other hand, dichotic studies of divided attention have produced different results. When the subject is asked to shadow words heard in one ear, but also to notice (for later recall) what is heard in the other ear, a disturbance provided by a second trace becomes clear (Wishner and Wahl, 1974; Wahl, 1976). Wahl's instructions were "Try to listen to both ears, while repeating only from the right." Unfortunately, one feature that must be criticized here is that the degree to which the subject directs his attention to the other ear is uncontrolled. This decision is left to the subject, but perhaps the difference between precise and ambivalent instructions in fact helps to uncover a specific deficit in schizophrenic cognitive abilities. It seems that selection according to physical cues does not always lead to a net breakdown of the selection process *per se*. However, when the instructions allow temporary changes of attentional focus, the content of the irrelevant message can intrude into the relevant trace.

A first look at the results of an experiment by Schneider (1976) seems to constitute a contradiction. Although Schneider's instructions made it clear that only the words from the relevant channel were to be shadowed, the schizophrenics performed poorly when themes from their own delusions were interpolated in the irrelevant channel. However, the specificity of these findings must remain doubtful, because the healthy control groups did not have to perform under similar (meaningful and aversive) conditions. However, it should be remembered that the performance of normal subjects is also disturbed if personal and emotionally significant material is presented to one ear. Bearing this in mind, when emotional material was interpolated in the irrelevant channel, Straube and Germer (1979) found that the number of shadowing mistakes increased in roughly equivalent proportions for both patient groups and for the healthy control group. Although Heilbrun and Norbert (1971) have claimed that a particular subgroup of schizophrenics is especially disturbed by irrelevant stimuli with emotional content (see Section III, B), there is generally no convincing demonstration of a special disturbance of performance on this test of selective attention in schizophrenia.

Superficially, another shadowing experiment appears to contradict again the claim that selection by physical cues is relatively unimpaired in schizophrenia. In the widely cited experiment by Spring (1980) in the United States, the subjects had to repeat words in the relevant channel and to ignore irrelevant words played at the same time into the other channel (headphone). This procedure was very similar to those mentioned earlier. In order to be sure the authors did not report a breakdown in the total selective performance of their subjects, a closer analysis of the recorded responses revealed a significant increase of minor intrusions (letters, syllables) from the irrelevant channel (Spring *et al.*, 1989).

The methodological difference with respect to other studies was that the pairs of words (the relevant and the irrelevant word) were deliberately less clearly synchronized between the two ears (for example, in the experiment of Straube and Germer, 1979). Thus, the subjects were able to hear part of the irrelevant word before the start or after the termination of the relevant word. This could attract the attention of the subjects and lead to switches between channels (Spring, personal communication). The effect parallels results in other studies in which the likelihood of the material in the irrelevant channel to be processed and evaluated is increased through instructions or experimental conditions.

The study was regarded as important, not as much for this methodological variant as for the inclusion in the investigation of the performance of biological relatives of the schizophrenics tested. Even this symptom-free group produced significantly more intrusions than the healthy control group (cf., Figure 4.13).

It seems quite reasonable to postulate that schizophrenics (and possibly also some of their first degree relatives) are less capable of suppressing meaningful stimuli once these have reached a certain stage of elaboration in information processing. Results in the next section also pertain to this hypothesis.

## B. Selection by Category or Concept: The Mental Set

Selection by conceptual cues instead of by a physical (spatial or pitch) separation of the two messages in a shadowing paradigm requires full processing of the irrelevant material in order to decide which is and which is not relevant. In the study of Hemsley and Richardson (1980) from the United Kingdom, two different passages of continuous prose were presented over headphones simultaneously to both ears. Both passages were spoken here by the same person to prevent the possibility of separation according to the pitch of the voice. Separation was only possible on the basis of content. The subjects had to form a concept of the passages just heard in order to select the relevant items from the incoming material.

Hemsley and Richardson (1980) asked their subjects to shadow the novel they could hear being read to one ear and to ignore the account from a

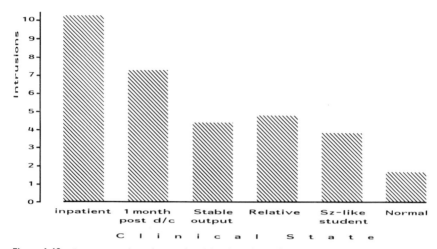

**Figure 4.13**  Average number of errors involving intrusions of distractors in the shadowing responses of clinical and healthy subject groups performing a dichotic listening task. All groups made significantly more shadowing errors than the normal controls. The groups included schizophrenics varying in clinical state (inpatients, patients a month after discharge, and clinically stable outpatients), first degree relatives of schizophrenics, and schizotypal college students (after Spring *et al.*, 1989).

physiology textbook presented to the other. (The relevant passage started some seconds ahead of the irrelevant one.) Whereas healthy or depressive subjects had relatively little difficulty differentiating the texts on the basis of their semantic content, the shadowing of schizophrenics was markedly disorganized. The texts were presented at two rates. The performance of both comparison groups tended to be slightly better with the higher speed of presentation, but this variation of conditions had no influence on the performance of the schizophrenics. Unfortunately, the obvious conclusion of a failure of conceptually guided selection is compromised without a control condition, requiring selection of a text by physical cues in a task matched according to difficulty. We therefore do not know whether the conceptual condition is really critical for schizophrenics.

The Stroop test is a classical test for showing a conflict between a discrimination based on the physical features and one based on the semantic meaning of stimuli. In its most usual form, the test consists of presenting a series of words that are names of colors. Confusion and difficulty arise because some of the color names are printed in another color (e.g., the word "blue" is printed in red). The subject may be asked to name either the meaning of the word or the color in which it appears. Psychologists often use this test as a measure of the ability to form and maintain a "mental set" (i.e., the ability to process information according to a criterion of meaning ignoring

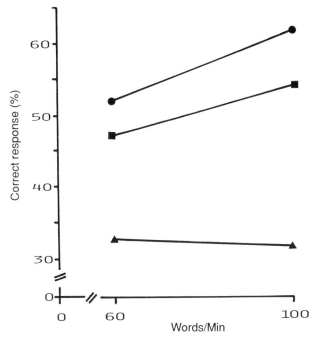

**Figure 4.14**  Average percentage of correct responses of schizophrenics (▲), depressives (■), and healthy controls (●) when shadowing for content in a dichotic listening task under two different word presentation rates (after Hemsley and Richardson, 1980).

physical features). The difficult version requires the subject to follow the semantic concept but the word is written in a different color. In other words, it is a test of the stability of the mental set. The increase in reaction time and error is interpreted as a measure of interference between sets.

Bush (1977), however, was unable to find a specific schizophrenic performance deficit. Response latencies correlated with the severity of psychiatric illness, independent of the patient group tested. Another report attributed a relatively poor Stroop performance by schizophrenics to the lower IQ shown by this particular group (Stuss *et al.*, 1981). Andreasen and colleagues (1986) found no relationship between Stroop performance in schizophrenics and the degree of frontal atrophy shown on tomographic scans. Much earlier, Heilbrun and Norbert (1971) had reported a slight tendency for paranoids to perform better than nonparanoid schizophrenics. Interesting in this report was the addition of an unusual test condition. While performing the Stroop test, the subjects listened to a tape of a mother scolding her son. The performance of paranoids worsened considerably whereas that of the nonparanoid and healthy subjects tended, if anything, to improve slightly.

It is possible that acute paranoid schizophrenics do have problems with the selective processing of information under certain conditions. Straube (1975) found that hallucinating paranoid patients had little difficulty in performing a discrimination according to the criterion of the physical shape of the stimuli. However, the same patients had great difficulty in a card-sorting test in which they had to discover the criterion (concept) for the selection themselves. The cards showed either rings or snake-like lines on a Rorschach-like background. Healthy subjects and neurotic patients immediately perceived that there was a pattern present and divided the cards accordingly. The task required that subjects checked every pattern for its potential relevance. They were not instructed about which pattern they should pay attention to. This led the schizophrenics to treat the background as relevant and to include it in their attempts to categorize the cards. The task required subjects to attend to and process the irrelevant background. One can imagine that this led to a categorization of cards according to quite bizarre associations (e.g., those with green spots were categorized as maps of woodland, while others supposedly showed skulls and were placed in the cemetery category!).

It seems reasonable to suppose that a protracted involvement with irrelevant stimulus material leads to increased distraction on tasks concerning concept formation and correlates with the paranoid hallucinatory state of schizo-phrenics. Chronically ill nonparanoid schizophrenics were not distracted by the background in Straube's experiments. These chronic nonparanoids were exclusively drawn from a pool of patients who had been initially admitted with a paranoid hallucinatory syndrome. Thus, the conceptual difficulty tested in this experiment seems to be more of a state than a trait marker. (See further discussion on concept formation and card sorting, Chapter 2.

## IV. Studies of Reaction Time

Investigations of reaction time have a long history in experimental psycholo-gy. It is therefore no wonder that they obtain a certain classical status in schizophrenia research. The vast literature available by 1978 has been thoroughly reviewed by Nuechterlein (1977), Shakow (1979), and Mannuzza (1980). Thus, we will only attempt a brief overview here.

### A. Simple Reaction Time

The reaction time of schizophrenics began to be studied in the renowned laboratories of Huston and Shakow at the Worcester State Hospital in the 1930s and 1940s (Huston *et al.*, 1937). The simple, clear, and frequently replicated results showed that chronic schizophrenics were slower to push a button when they perceived a target stimulus. The interesting aspect of the older studies remains that the schizophrenics were studied prior to the era of neuroleptic medication. Thus, the results appearing in chronic patients cannot be discarded simply as an artifact of such treatment.

As real as the results may be, it remains questionable whether it is a specific characteristic of schizophrenic performance. Slowed responses have been recorded from patients suffering from other psychoses (King, 1954). (However, nearly 40 years later the diagnostic criteria used may be questioned.) Twenty years ago Goldberg *et al.* (1968) reported that there was a strong correlation between slowed response times and withdrawal, which would be called a negative symptom today. Other psychiatric groups (e.g., depressives) showed slow latencies also (Giedke *et al.*, 1981), and a direct comparison between schizophrenic and depressive patients has shown no significant differences (Bruder *et al.*, 1980). However, the effect is possibly not limited to psychotic subjects in the affect-disordered group (Schwartz *et al.*, 1989); elderly subjects (Botwinik *et al.*, 1959) and subjects with brain damage also show slowed responses (Olbrich, 1972).

For some schizophrenics, a slowed reaction time can result from direct interference by hallucinations (Goldberg *et al.*, 1968). Indeed, Inouye and Shimizu (1972) reported that visual reaction times were slowed at times of auditory hallucination compared with periods without hallucinations. (The amplitude of evoked potentials was similarly reduced during hallucination. Putative auditory hallucinations were identified with EMGs from the muscles involved in speech.)

In contrast to a common preconception, a number of studies have reported that neuroleptic treatment has either no effect on *simple* reaction times (Heilizer, 1959; Wynne and Kornetsky, 1960; Pearl, 1962; Pugh, 1968; Held *et al.*, 1970) or can improve reaction time (Brooks and Weaver, 1961; Spohn *et al.*, 1977; Cesarec and Nyman, 1985). Higher doses (Venzky-Stalling *et al.*, 1985) or, more pertinently, higher serum levels of neuroleptic (Strauss *et al.*, 1985) have been claimed to correlate with shorter latencies in chronic schizophrenics.

## B. Preparatory Intervals and the Crossover Effect

In this type of task the subject is presented with a warning signal shortly before the imperative stimulus to which he or she is required to respond. The general type of experimental design is as follows. When a light appears one must press a button and release it only when one hears or sees the expected imperative stimulus. The crucial variable her is the duration of the forewarning period or the "preparatory interval" between the warning and the imperative stimuli. This interval may be the same or may vary on each trial (regular or irregular sequences).

If regular and irregular sequences are employed in reaction-time experi-

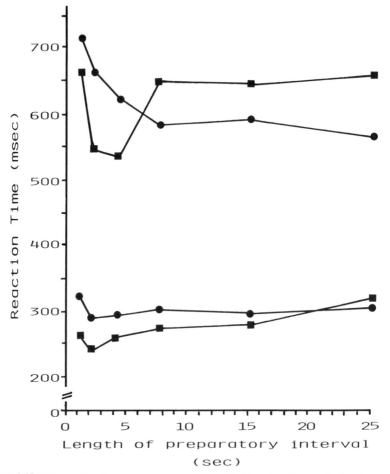

**Figure 4.15**   The reaction time crossover or crossover effect in schizophrenics (top) and responses of healthy controls (bottom), who do not show the effect. Reaction times after a regular preparatory interval (■) are compared with reaction times after irregular preparatory intervals (●) (modified from Rodnik and Shakow, 1940).

ments, then the frequently replicated *crossover effect* occurs (Rodnik and Shakow, 1940, Figure 4.15). Healthy subjects respond faster on regular than on irregular sequences. With interstimulus intervals greater than 6 sec, schizophrenics show the opposite effect; that is, at short intervals schizophrenics respond like healthy subjects (faster on regular, slower on irregular intervals). At longer intervals, the effect "crosses over." The result is remarkably stable over a range of variations of the basic experimental design. Even if the subject is informed about the duration of the coming preparatory interval, the crossover effect can still be recorded. (For a review, see Nuechterlein, 1977.) The crossover effect is also not unduly influenced if one makes the estimation of interval length easier with additional marker stimuli to structure the preparatory interval (Borst, 1986).

Perhaps the simplest interpretation is that chronic schizophrenics (the group in which the deficit is most frequently demonstrated) show less of a vigilance decrement with irregular preparatory intervals. This would lead to a relatively shorter reaction time. (The condition in which the interstimulus interval varies is the less monotonous of the two investigated.) As can be seen in Figure 4.15, a slight increase of response latency in the regular sequence can also be recorded from healthy subjects, yet it remains questionable whether the dramatic increase of latency shown by schizophrenics at intervals longer than 5 sec is adequately explained by vigilance levels.

Bellissimo and Steffy (1972) introduced a variation of the basic experiment, the embedded procedure. Sequences of up to four stimulus pairs with regular intervals were embedded in a longer series of stimuli with irregular preparatory intervals. Here, too, they found that the longer the regular interval was, the longer was the reaction time; the longer the interval in the irregular sequence, the shorter was the reaction time (cf. Figure 4.16). These authors attributed the crossover effect to a "redundancy deficit." By this they meant that the

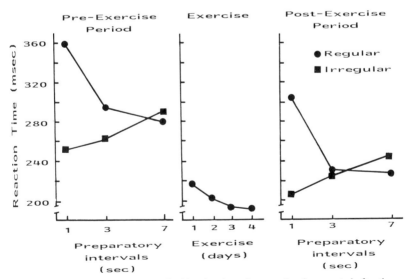

**Figure 4.16** Average reaction times of schizophrenic patients to signals presented after three different mean lengths of regular (●) and irregular (■) preparatory intervals during the pre-exercise (before test practice), exercise, and post-exercise (after practice) period using the embedded procedure (after Steffy and Galbraith, 1980).

schizophrenics were unable to make use of the information offered by regular preparatory intervals to predict when the imperative stimulus would appear. On the other hand, Shakow (1979) believed that schizophrenics operate with a less stable mental set. ("Mental set" here refers to the state of cognitive preparedness after the warning signal.) An unstable mental set would have the consequence that schizophrenics were less able to use the information available from the regular intervals for prediction as the intervals increase in length (i.e., relatively longer reaction times after longer intervals compared with those shown at shorter intervals).

In this situation, as elsewhere, the argument is often raised whether psychiatric patients in general, and schizophrenics in particular, perform poorly due to a lack of motivation. Steffy and Galbraith (1980) attempted to answer this criticism in a particularly worthy way. They took a group of chronic schizophrenics with a poor premorbid course and subjected them to several days of training. They developed a good personal relationship with the subjects, offered encouragement and praise, and a small financial reward for good performance. Yes, with practice the reaction-time performance improved and they responded faster but, intriguingly, the crossover effect remained (Figure 4.16).

Reviewing the subject in 1984, Nuechterlein and Dawson at the University of California at Los Angeles came to the conclusion that the crossover effect was most reproducible among poor premorbid schizophrenics (e.g., in two to three of every four patients tested). To an extent this observation was supported by the results of Spaulding *et al.* (1984). They found that a co-variance existed between the crossover effect and chronicity of the illness. However, the results also raised questions concerning the specificity of the crossover effect. A similar correlation was found for the length of illness shown by other psychiatric control groups. At least we may note that, with Steffy's embedded variation of the test, there was no correlation with the patients' age (DeAmicis *et al.*, 1986). However, even in the most severely depressed bipolar patients, the crossover effect is not found in more than one in four patients (Bohannon and Strauss, 1983).

Unexpected, at first glance, is the report from Greiffenstein *et al.* (1981) that epileptic patients, in whom the focus was located on either side of the temporal lobe but not elsewhere, also showed a marked crossover effect. This becomes less unexpected if we recall that such patients, particularly if the focus is on the left side, frequently show a number of clinical symptoms common to schizophrenics. However, at this stage we must leave the question open whether the crossover effect is specific to schizophrenia and reflects underlying temporal lobe pathology (cf. Chapter 8 on neurophysiological and lateralization characteristics in schizophrenia).

The plausibility of one hypothesis or another on the specificity of the crossover effect is influenced to some extent by whether the effect takes on the appearance of a schizophrenic trait. Does it occur in patients in remission or in persons at risk for the illness? The prevalence of the crossover effect among schizophrenics in remission (maintained on neuroleptic therapy) is approximately the same as for the chronically ill inpatients described earlier. (For a review, see Nuechterlein and Dawson, 1984.)

However, at first glance, the picture is less clear when one looks at the performance of persons who may be regarded to be at risk for schizophrenia. Rosenbaum and colleagues (1988) selected a schizotypal group from a population of students according to the MMPI (combination of scales 2-7-8). This group was reported to show a crossover effect, but it is curious that, from their figures, even "unremarkable" students tended to show a crossover at longer preparatory intervals. This becomes even clearer in the group defined by the MMPI as "remarkable" (but not schizotypal). Interpretation is made more difficult by the performance of the chronic schizophrenic group also tested. They showed a rather flat curve with no dramatic increase of reaction time at regular intervals longer than 5 sec. Nonetheless, despite our qualifying these results, it should be noted that Simons *et al.* (1982) had already reported the crossover effect from (nonpsychiatric) subjects who showed "perceptual aberrations" according to the Chapman questionnaire (see Chapter 12).

From these results alone, one might suspect that the crossover effect was not any more or any less a symptom or state marker correlating with some of the features rated by the scales used. The alternative, that it may be a vulnerability marker indicative of an underlying disturbance, received only marginal support from studies of the biological relatives of schizophrenics. Van Dyke *et al.* (1975) obtained negative results in their Danish adoption study. However, in the United States, DeAmicis and Cromwell (1979) used the embedded procedure and found a 17% incidence of crossover in first degree relatives of poor premorbid schizophrenics (who themselves showed a 47% incidence). Interesting here is that the more marked the crossover effect was in the patients, the more numerous were the relatives who had sought psychiatric assistance (independent of the nature of the problem).

In a reanalysis of their work (DeAmicis *et al.*, 1986; see previous text), the authors uncovered an unexpected paradox (unexpected in the sense that most of us tend to make extrapolations from results to other areas of function and interest). There were healthy first degree relatives of poor premorbid schizo-phrenics in their study who showed a marked crossover effect. This group reached a significantly higher socioeconomic level than the relatives with a relatively small crossover effect. Was this due to increased compensatory effort, as is sometimes seen with other handicaps, or due to other special cognitive abilities (e.g., creativity) that were inherited as a consequence of being related to a schizophrenic? (See Chapter 2 for a more detailed treatment of the issue).

Perhaps the crossover test situation places demands on specific and non-specific cognitive functions of the subject, of which one is the more important in schizophrenia. In support of this idea it should be noted that the crossover effect in chronic schizophrenics correlates with their simple reaction-time performance. This does not hold true for the relatives (DeAmicis *et al.*, 1986). The sometimes nonspecific findings with respect to the crossover effect may further support the idea of a generalized impairment. If there is any truth in this thesis, it will be necessary for future investigations to alter the conditions of testing so that one can separate the putative schizophrenia-specific and schizophrenia-nonspecific component of the reaction-time performance.

## C. The Modality Shift Effect

The pattern of reaction times shown when one changes stimulus modality is an experimental paradigm closely associated with the renowned schizophrenia investigator Zubin and his former group at the New York Psychiatric Institute. The basic result of changing the modality of the stimulus from, perhaps, a tone to a light (or vice versa) is that the response times become slower (Sutton and Zubin, 1965; Figure 4.17). In fact, even a change of stimulus quality or intensity can bring about a certain slowness of response (Rist and Thurm, 1984), although this did not turn out to be significant in the work by Sutton and Zubin (1965) shown here.

Slowed reaction times are recorded from acutely ill schizophrenics with a good premorbid course as well as from those with a more chronic course. The latter usually show longer latencies than the acutely ill, independent of the stimulus conditions (Brooks and Weaver, 1961; Mannuzza *et al.*, 1984; Williams *et al.*, 1984). Mannuzza and colleagues showed that, even if one controls the degree of difficulty of the modality shift task, the effect remains. Longer latencies have also been reported for schizophrenics in remission by Rey and Oldigs (1982) in Mannheim.

As with the crossover effect discussed in the previous section, the increase of reaction time is still recorded if patients are told in advance of the change of modality, as was shown by the group in New York (Waldbaum *et al.*, 1975). In fact, it is in this condition that the slowing is more clearly seen, in comparison with the control groups who better utilize the information. On the other hand, if there is uncertainty concerning the modality of the coming stimulus then a difference is not always clearly seen. However, a more marked slowing of the reaction time with respect to healthy subjects becomes clear if the patient is asked to guess the modality and the guess turns out to be correct. It appears again that healthy subjects use information from their own estimates to improve sensorimotor performance. These results were obtained by Waldbaum, working in Sutton's group, for acute untreated

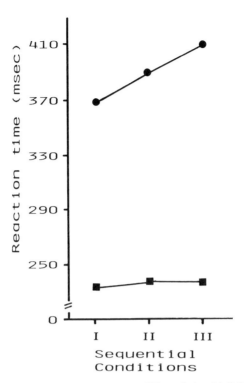

**Figure 4.17** Average reaction time to signals in two different ipsimodal (I: blue, blue or II: blue, yellow) and in one contramodal (III: light, tone) condition (so-called cross-modal reaction time) in schizophrenics (●) and healthy controls (■) (after Sutton and Zubin, 1965).

patients. But Verleger and Cohen (1978), working in Constance, were unable to reproduce the effect with a group of chronic schizophrenics who had received long-term treatment as inpatients.

The two studies do vary on certain points of methodology, but it is perhaps more likely that the difference can be attributed to the nature of the groups studied. After reviewing the literature, Mannuzza (1980) concluded that the decisive factor may, in fact, be not so much medication status, but the presence or absence of acute paranoid symptoms. However, the difference is perhaps relatively minor, because Cohen's group was able to record the specific effect of modality change on reaction time in further experiments. Indeed, they found that almost any change led to an increase of the schizophrenics' reaction time (e.g., even the task-irrelevant change of presenting stimuli to the other ear; R. Cohen et al., 1984).

According to Spring (1980), a former colleague of the New York group, the effect cannot be found among first degree relatives. However, since only 12 family members at risk for schizophrenia were studied, one should not overinterpret these results. The chance of uncovering an inherited feature in such a small sample is very small. A more significant finding of this report was the lack of differences between the reaction times of schizophrenic and depressive patients, despite the former recording significantly slower responses than healthy subjects under at least one condition.

Neuroleptic treatment does not appear to significantly alter the effect of changing modality (e.g., without medication, Sutton and Zubin, 1965; Kristofferson, 1967; with medication, Spring, 1980).

## D. Choice Reaction-Time Experiments

In a choice reaction-time experiment, the subject is asked to respond only when a specific stimulus appears. Zahn (1970) reports that schizophrenics have no difficulty performing simple choices. Also, if complexity is increased somewhat, so that the subject must press the left button after a red light and the right one after a green light, then, with a little practice, schizophrenics are still able to perform similarly to healthy controls. It is probably helpful for a schizophrenic in this situation that the task has a very clearly defined structure. (Such aids are used as a part of cognitive therapies with schizophrenics; see Chapter 13.)

Nuechterlein's review (1977) confirms the generalization of Zahn's finding, and the more recent study of Williams and Hemsley (1986) in London confirm and extend it by including a depressive group. With increasing complexity, *all* subjects tend to make more mistakes, as one would expect from Chapman and Chapman's remarks (1973) about the need for experimental design to take account of generalized deficits (see Section I).

The early work of Payne and Caird (1967) in the United Kingdom, on the performance of paranoid and nonparanoid schizophrenic and healthy subjects is of particular interest. They tested subgroups of schizophrenics, varying both the number of stimuli (i.e., more irrelevant stimuli) and the number of response possibilities. Distracting stimuli included tones, laughter, and conversation played back from a tape recorder. External distraction was minimized by covering the eyes or ears, condition "0" shown in Figure 4.18. They compared the choice response performance with simple reaction times.

It can be seen that the paranoid schizophrenics were more easily distracted than the others when the number of response possibilities (i.e., number of response keys) was increased in addition to distraction (Figure 4.18). The nonparanoid group responded in a heterogeneous fashion. Some were as distracted as the paranoids; others performed the same as the healthy controls. Thus, the overall group performance was not significantly different from that of the healthy controls, although the average was close to that of the paranoids, as can be seen from Figure 4.18. (One would suppose that the

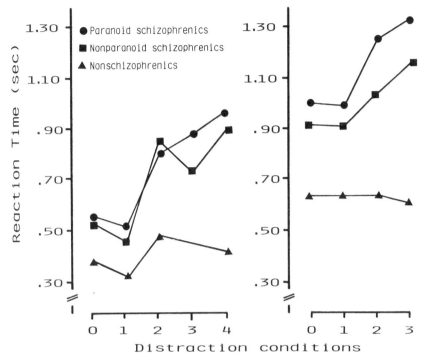

**Figure 4.18**  Average reaction time in a simple (*left*) and a choice (*right*) reaction time task under conditions of increasing distraction (after Payne and Caird, 1967).

nonparanoid group was a poorly defined heterogenous group. It could have included acute hebephrenic "disorganized" schizophrenics in addition to long-term inpatients with few positive symptoms.)

Neufeld (1977), from Canada, also found in his study that the paranoid schizophrenics were slower on choice reaction time tasks, and that the nonparanoid group performed the same as healthy controls. At least here the cumulative stay in the hospital did not exceed 2.5 yrs.

However, paranoid schizophrenics had no difficulty mastering a task that involved reacting to 5 lights, each with its respective response key [cf. the work of Scherer and Storms (1981) from San Francisco, Figure 4.19]. In this case, there is a clear structured stimulus–response relationship. However, the authors did note that the nonparanoid patients (who had been hospitalized for a long time) were limited in their ability to pay attention to all the stimuli. Imperative stimuli that appeared in the periphery of the display elicited notably longer reaction times. This effect did not correlate with the age or education of the subjects nor with the amount of neuroleptic medication they were receiving. The possibility that such a change in perceptual style (reduced

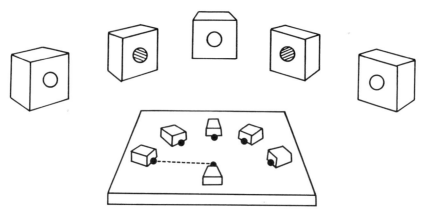

**Figure 4.19**   Experimental set-up for measuring choice reaction times (Scherer and Storms, 1981, ©
Williams and Wilkins). Response keys are shown with the relevant light signals behind them.

range of attention) is characteristic of a subgroup of patients was found with
other types of tasks as well (see Chapter 2 and previous text of this chapter)
and is reminiscent of a hypothesis of Venables (1977).

Frith and Done (1983), Lyon *et al.* (1986), and Lyon and Gerlach (1988)
found schizophrenics, especially chronic schizophrenics, to show "pre-
severative switching" in their pattern of responses in a free-choice task. (We
discussed this study already in Chapter 2.) The task was, in essence, to make
a cross appear on a monitor screen. This was possible with different
combinations of two computer keys (right key and left key). The schizophrenics were less variable in the combinations used. Lyon and Gerlach
(1988), however, showed that, in addition to the chronic patients, the patients
with affective disorders were also more rigid in their response performance.
They were not different from schizophrenics. Schizoid probands showed the
same variable response pattern as the healthy controls.

## V. Suggested Readings

As in Chapter 2, the textbook of Chapman and Chapman (1973) is still the
basic book with an excellent and comprehensive survey of cognitive research
prior to 1973, to which they made and are still making important contributions. The literature after 1973 is covered in detail by Neale and Oltmanns
(1980) and Cutting (1985). Nuechterlein and Dawson (1984) wrote an
influential review of experiments and hypotheses (including their own hypothesis).

# VI. Summary Statements and Interpretations

## A. Basic and Automatized Functions

### 1. Perceptual Thresholds

*a. Variation of Stimulus Intensity (Detection Threshold)*   There is no general change of absolute stimulus detection threshold. However, there may be exceptions for subgroups. Thresholds may be higher in some chronic and some hallucinating patients.

Two explanations emerge from additional tests of patients with exceptionally high thresholds. (1) Such patients rated the stimuli as more unpleasant and disturbing. Thus, a psychological rather than a purely sensory explanation may be relevant. (2) Hallucinations or their underlying cause may interfere with the perception of the stimulus. The presence of changed thresholds correlated with the presence of hallucinations. In one report, the auditory threshold was only higher in the right ear. This was suggested to result from interference from the left hemispheric production of auditory hallucinations.

*b. Variation of Stimulus Duration (Identification Threshold)*   There is no evident change across groups, but again subgroup differences emerge. It takes longer for some schizophrenics to identify the semantic content of stimuli. This seems particularly true for poor premorbid patients (they need longer to identify a tachistoscopically presented letter).

Stimulus identification is a more complex process than stimulus detection (it requires "higher" processing). One explanation often used in the interpretation of schizophrenia research is that data processing is slower in the poor premorbid schizophrenic. An alternative is that stimulus recognition is slower because other ongoing processes interfere if "higher" processes are involved (i.e., lower signal-to-noise ratio).

### 2. Spatial Frequency

The few experiments carried out indicate the possibility that paranoid schizophrenics are able to discriminate two spatial stimuli at shorter intervals than healthy subjects.

It is premature to found a theory on these results, but there are other isolated but similar findings. In his review, Sutton (1973) mentioned an interesting result from his institute that showed that schizophrenics discriminated two light flashes when the normal control group could see only one. These results are related to the findings of Freedman's group in Colorado (e.g., Nagamoto *et al.,* 1989; Chapter 6), who basically found less interference between two short-interval click-evoked potentials in schizophrenics than in normals. Although the latter findings were not confirmed elsewhere, it might be possible that at least a subgroup of patients (paranoid perhaps) have different perceptual processes. If confirmed, this might then be a physiological candidate for the basis of the misinterpretation of the external world by (paranoid) schizophrenics.

### 3. Extrafoveal Perception

Here again a better performance by acute paranoid patients was reported, in contrast to that of nonparanoid chronic patients. (The performance of the psychiatric controls was average.)

The higher sensitivity of the paranoid group may again be an indication that basic perceptual processes are altered in this group. It is unfortunate that not much research has been done in this field.

### 4. Sensory Buffer Store

Several tests using the technique of sequential picture integration show that the "hardware" is not altered in schizophrenics. Information is stored without alteration for the same time span as in the controls.

However, if selection of information is involved, then several aspects appear to be altered.

*a. Span of Apprehension Test* If schizophrenics are asked to report which target letters they saw in a tachistoscopically presented array of irrelevant letters, they usually fail. The same is true for high risk children and acute patients. However, reports exist questioning the specificity of these findings. Manic patients also failed. Furthermore, the trait character of the disturbance is doubtful because schizophrenics in remission do not always show the deficit.

Data selection in the presence of similar irrelevant stimuli may simply be more difficult and, thus, (1) disappear in full remission and (2) be seen in other psychiatric disturbances (cf. Chapman and Chapman, 1973). Furthermore, subgroup difference and differences in the method used may also explain the discrepant results.

*b. Full Report and Partial Report (Sperling Test)* Schizophrenics are less impaired when unselected information is at issue (i.e., a full report is required). They are as good or as bad as controls, but it is easier for healthy subjects and overinclusive schizophrenic patients to report only a part of the material presented. Underinclusive patients do not show this advantage. (This group shows underinclusive sorting in an object-sorting test.)

The selective impairment of the underinclusive group is striking. Why is partial report not advantageous for them? How does the reduction in the range of categories influence this? The data do not provide any answer to this question. The interest in this result lies in the fact that deviations of perceptual and cognitive ability are present in subgroups of schizophrenics, that is, on quite different levels of performance.

   *c. Visual Masking*   Good and poor premorbid schizophrenics have difficulty selecting a target from a row of three letters before a second stimulus appears and masks the first. However, good premorbid patients learn to do so when the test is repeated several times. The performance remains impaired in poor premorbid patients.

   A putatively poorer quality of the iconic storage does not seem to explain the findings, since it was shown with the picture-integration task that schizophrenics could perform correctly. A stronger interference of the target letters with the mask is also unlikely, since the poor premorbids were less influenced by the meaningfulness of the mask in an additional task. (Only the good premorbid and healthy subjects were disturbed only by a meaningful mask.) The only alternative explanation is that the *selective* transfer of the target from the sensory store to central cognitive units is less effective in the poor premorbids (slower; more easily disturbed?). The latter is possibly reminiscent of the lack of advantage of the underinclusive group (which may be also poor premorbid) with the partial report of stimulus material from the sensory store (as discussed earlier).

## 5. Gestalt Perception

Schizophrenics, although they are not unaware of the principles of Gestalt perception, are less inclined to take them into account. There are reports that nonparanoid poor premorbid patients are especially affected, but other studies show that the impairment is not restricted to this group. Of special interest are those studies in which schizophrenics perform *better* than controls in that part of a number task in which Gestalt principles are less apparent.

   Healthy controls try to apply global grouping strategies to an array of stimuli and fail when stimulus counting is required. Here, the bit-by-bit analysis typical of the schizophrenic is advantageous. However, there are reports from other tests that anxious subjects also use a bit-by-bit strategy. Thus, direct comparisons of anxious subjects and schizophrenics are required.

   Evidence from patients with brain lesions suggests that global Gestalt perception is a function of the nondominant (right) hemisphere (temporal lobe). However, again direct comparisons are lacking.

## 6. Perceptual Constancy

Little research has been done in this field recently. Evidence from older studies shows that nonparanoids use too few environmental referents. In contrast, paranoids tend to be "super-stable" and insensitive to changes in experimental conditions.

The reduction of the use of cues in nonparanoids is reminiscent of the reduced span of attention in chronic schizophrenics in a choice reaction-time task (Section IV).

# B. Controlled Processes

## 1. Selection through Physical Cues (Stimulus-Driven Processing)

*a. Signal–Noise Discrimination*   Paranoid schizophrenics have difficulty discriminating signals from noise. They more often report the signal when only noise was present (i.e., more "false alarms"). Nonparanoids do not differ from normals. The poor performance of the paranoid group improves under neuroleptic treatment.

These "misperceptions" provide an interesting contrast to the higher sensitivity of paranoid schizophrenics (e.g., spatial-frequency test). It seems as though they interpret irrelevant signals under difficult signal–noise conditions more often as significant as a result of their higher perceptual sensitivity. However, whether this type of perceptual "style" really characterizes this subgroup cannot be answered from this rather isolated result. The role of task difficulty also requires definition.

A comparison between schizophrenics and brain-damaged subjects in an easier version of the signal–noise discrimination task shows that the latter group has more fundamental problems with this type of task, especially those with occipital lesions, but not those with frontal lesions.

*b. Stimulus Recognition in the Presence of Irrelevant Material*   The error rate is low in schizophrenics if the task is to recognize physically defined stimuli (color, pitch of voice, location, etc.) in the presence of other but irrelevant stimuli. Some studies, however, find that schizophrenics react more slowly; others show that the slowness was correlated with task difficulty. In a task matched for task difficulty, no selective-attention disorder was apparent.

There is indication that distractors disturb chronic patients less than acute patients. This result probably parallels the better performance of acute patients in a (simple) dual task. Here chronic patients have problems attending to and performing both tasks simultaneously.

The popular hypothesis that schizophrenics have a fundamental disturbance in selective attention abilities is less clearly supported than expected, at least concerning experiments in which stimulus-guided processing is required. The subgroup of paranoid acute patients may be an exception since they attend more to the second task in a dual task experiment, and since they give more false alarms in a signal detection task.

Disturbances of selective attention differs in its nature between subgroups and may not be apparent under all conditions (e.g., see subsequent text).

*c. Sustained Attention (Vigilance Tasks)*   All groups, including patients in remission, have difficulty maintaining vigilance on the continuous performance task (CPT). Interestingly, under distracting conditions the rate of "false alarms" is again higher in paranoid schizophrenics.

The latter finding task is reminiscent of a similar finding in the signal–noise discrimination task reported earlier.

The CPT is of special interest, because children of schizophrenics perform poorly, particularly under difficult discrimination conditions (e.g., with blurred or degraded stimuli; cf. Chapter 12). Performance on the (nondegraded) CPT is also worse in patients with a family history of schizophrenia. These findings suggest that CPT performance may show a fundamental deficit underlying the schizophrenic disorder, especially under the more difficult discrimination condition.

Nuechterlein and Dawson (1984) interpret these results in terms of limited processing capacity, since high risk subjects fail under the more demanding perceptual conditions. We have already seen that not all results can be so interpreted. Further, these tests have seldom been controlled for task difficulty; see discussion by Chapman and Chapman, 1973; methodological criteria in the previous text).

**d. Dichotic Shadowing**   If the duration and depth of processing of irrelevant material is limited by the instruction and procedure, then schizophrenics have no selective attention problems. This is generally the case if the information to be processed is defined by physical features (location, channel, pitch of the voice, etc.).

It seems that physically defined material can be rejected at an early level of information processing. In this case it is not disturbing. However, when authors require subjects to monitor the irrelevant material or when switches between ears are possible, then intrusions occur (i.e., when the irrelevant material has a greater chance to be processed more deeply).

An old hypothesis of Cromwell and Dokecki (1968) may be applicable— schizophrenics have difficulty "disattending." It may be difficult for them to disregard material which has reached a certain level of controlled processing.

## 2. Selection through Content (Concept-Driven Processing)

**a. Dichotic Shadowing**   Selection through content instead of physical cues leads to a net breakdown of the shadowing ability of schizophrenics. This is the case when the content of a story has to be monitored, but the narrative of another story has to be analyzed in some detail in order to reject it by contextual criteria.

Here, in order to know what is relevant, a feed-forward mechanism has to operate. Each incoming item has to be checked for relevance. The selection is guided by a concept of the subject and not primarily by stimulus features (i.e., conceptually driven data selection). Instead, past stimulus events create a model that sets up the probability of the next events (i.e., a concept to which incoming events are compared; the probability of fit is estimated and finally selected or rejected). The material presented in two stories is compared with this model. A similar hypothesis from Frith and Done (1988) will be discussed later. Unfortunately there is, so far, only one study with dichotic shadowing. However, conceptually guided data processing was already shown to be deviant in Chapter 2 and will be discussed again along with the P 300 results in Chapter 6.

## C. Reaction Time

### 1. Simple Reaction Time

Schizophrenics, especially those with negative symptoms, have slower reaction times (RTs), but a slow RT is not specific to schizophrenia. (There are reports that hallucinations interfere with performance.)

Results show that slow RTs are not sufficient to characterize schizophrenics specifically. This questions the assumption that slow information processing is specific to schizophrenia.

### 2. Crossover Paradigm (Shakow Method)

Warning periods at longer regular intervals lead to slower RTs than warnings at longer irregular intervals. This crossover of performance with respect to the effect of warnings at short intervals correlates with the length of illness in schizophrenics and other psychiatric patients. It is also seen in patients with temporal lobe epilepsy. High risk children do not show this feature.

Shakow's (1979) interpretation is that schizophrenics have a less stable mental set and, therefore, cannot use the information in the regular contingencies. However, why should this pertain to other long-term patients?

The discovery that temporal lobe patients show the same peculiarity is of interest, but is difficult to integrate. Does it imply that the temporal lobes (including the hippocampus) are involved in this type of performance? Is there a link to other similar symptoms shown by temporal lobe patients?

### 3. Embedded Procedure (Steffy Method)

This variation of the crossover paradigm does not present blocks of regular and irregular warning intervals in a random order, but presents the regular intervals as a block within irregular periods. With this procedure, it is more evident that schizophrenics do not use the regularity information to speed up their RT. There is some evidence that, with the Steffy method, the effect may be more specific and not dependent on the length of the illness. Perhaps it is even more important that there are several reports that show that, with the Steffy method, deviant performance can also be seen in first degree relatives and in persons with schizotypal traits.

It seems that the Steffy method is more successful as a specific marker for vulnerability. Steffy interprets the performance shown by the schizophrenics and their relatives as a redundancy deficit. They seem to be unable to use the redundancy of the regular intervals, that is, they do not use the higher predictability of the regular intervals between warning and go signals. It may be that the more massive serial redundancy of the Steffy procedure (with a blockwise presentation) leads to a more pronounced differentiation of schizophrenics from other groups. However, this has to be tested by a direct comparison between the two methods.

## 4. Modality Shift Effect

A change of the modality of the signal leads to a slowing of the RT of acute and chronic schizophrenics. Results from persons at risk are less clear-cut than with the Steffy procedure. One report raises doubt about the specificity of the findings.

In normal and experimental psychology, impairments on such tests of extradimensional shifts are interpreted in terms of disturbances of response-set selection in information processing. This interpretation is compatible with the impairment proposed in concept-driven selection processes. However, we should emphasize that the specificity of the effect is not beyond doubt.

## 5. Choice RT

Schizophrenics show *no* deficit if the stimulus–response contingencies are clearly structured and if no distractions are present. If distractions are present, then paranoid patients, unlike nonparanoids, make more errors.

One interesting report concerns the position of the stimulus: Long-term nonparanoid chronic patients respond more slowly to peripherally located signals.

Both results show some similarity with previously discussed findings. Patients with paranoid symptoms seem to be more easily distracted by irrelevant stimuli. Chronic patients, perhaps with negative symptoms are only able to respond to a reduced range of stimuli effectively (i.e., they respond more slowly to stimuli on the periphery of the visual display of the signals). They are less distracted, are less influenced by external but related stimuli, and are poor performers in dual tasks. That chronic patients (with negative symptoms) show reduced scanning of the environment is plausible from clinical observations and is a hypothesis derived from experiments quite early in the history of schizophrenia research (cf. Venables, 1964; Broen, 1968).

# References

Anderson, J. R. (1985). *Cognitive psychology and its implications*. New York: Freeman.

Andreasen, N. C., Nasrallah, H. A., Dunn, V., Olson, S. A., Grove, W. M., Erhardt, J. C., Coffman, J. A., and Crosset, H. W. (1986). Structural abnormalities in the frontal system in schizophrenia: A magnetic resonance imaging study. *Archives of General Psychiatry*, 43, 136–144.

Asarnow, R. F. and Granholm, E. (1991). The Contributions of Cognitive Psychology to Vulnerability Models. In H. Häfner and W. F. Gattaz (Eds). *Search for the Causes of Schizophrenia*. Berlin: Springer.

Asarnow, R. F., and MacCrimmon, D. J. (1978). Residual performance deficit in clinically remitted schizophrenics: A marker of schizophrenia? *Journal of Abnormal Psychology*, 87, 597–608.

Balogh, D. W., and Merritt, R. D. (1987). Visual masking and the schizophrenia spectrum: Interfacing clinical and experimental methods. *Schizophrenia Bulletin*, 13, 679–698.

Bartlett, M. R. (1935). The sensory acuity of psychopathic individuals. *Psychiatric Quarterly*, 9, 422–425.

Baruch, I., Hemsley, D. R., and Gray, J. A. (1988). Differential performance of acute and chronic schizophrenics in a latent inhibition task. *Journal of Nervous and Mental Disease*, 176, 598–606.

Bazhin, E. F., Meerson, Y. A., and Tonkonogii, I. M. (1973). On distinguishing a visual signal from noise by patients with visual agnosia and visual hallucinations. *Neuropsychologia*, 11, 319–324.

Bellisimo, A., and Steffy, R. A. (1972). Redundancy-associated deficit in schizophrenic reaction time performance. *Journal of Abnormal Psychology*, 80, 299–307.

Bemporad, J. R. (1967). Perceptual disorders in schizophrenia. *American Journal of Psychiatry*, 123, 971–976.

Bleuler, E. (1911). *Dementia praecox oder die Gruppe der Schizophrenien*. Leipzig: Deuticke

Bohannon, W. E., and Strauss, M. E. (1983). Reaction time crossover in psychiatric outpatients. *Psychiatry Research*, 9, 17–22.

Borst, U. (1986). *Der Einfluß zeitlicher Information auf den "Crossover"-Effekt bei chronisch Schizophrenen*. Konstanz: Hartung-Gorre.

Botwinik, J., Brinley, J. F., and Robbin, J. S. (1959). Maintaining set in relation to motivation and age. *American Journal of Psychology*, 72, 585–588.

Braff, D. L., and Huey, L. (1988). Methylphenidate-induced information processing dysfunction in nonschizophrenic patients. *Archives of General Psychiatry*, 45, 827–832.

Braff, D. L., and Saccuzzo, D. P. (1982). Effect of antipsychotic medication on speed of information processing in schizophrenic patients. *American Journal of Psychiatry*, 139, 1127–1130.

Braff, D. L., and Saccuzzo, D. P. (1985). The time course of information processing deficits in schizophrenia. *American Journal of Psychiatry*, 142, 170–174.

Braff, D. L., Silverton, L., Saccuzzo, D. P., and Janowsky, D. S. (1981a). Impaired speed of visual information processing in Marijuana intoxication. *American Journal of Psychiatry*, 138, 613–617.

Braff, D. L., Silverton, L., Saccuzzo, D. P., and Janowsky, D. S. (1981b). Information processing deficit in acute marijuana intoxication. *American Journal of Psychiatry*, 138, 608–612.

Broadbent, D. E. (1958). *Perception and communication*. New York: Pergamon.

Brody, D., Saccuzzo, D. P., and Braff, D. L. (1980). Information processing for masked and unmasked stimuli in schizophrenia and old age. *Journal of Abnormal Psychology*, 89, 617–622.

Broen, W. E. (1968). *Schizophrenia. Research and theory. Personality and psychopathology.* New York: Academic Press.

Broen, W. E., Jr., and Nakamura, C. Y. (1972). Reduced range of sensory sensitivity in chronic nonparanoid schizophrenia. *Journal of Abnormal Psychology*, 79, 106–111.

Brooks, G., and Weaver, L. (1961). Some relations between psychiatric and psychomotor behavior changes associated with tranquilizing medications. *Comprehensive Psychiatry*, 2, 203–210.

Bruder, G., Yozawitz, A., Berenhaus, I., and Sutton, S. (1980). Reaction time facilitation in affective psychotic patients. *Psychological Medicine*, 10, 549–554.

Bruder, G. E., Sutton, S., Babkoff, H., Gurland, B. J., Yozawitz, A., and Fleiss, J. L. (1975). Auditory signal detectability and facilitation of simple reaction time in psychiatric patients and non-patients. *Psychological Medicine*, 5, 260.

Bush, M. (1977). The relationship between impaired selective attention and severity of psycho-pathology in acute psychiatric patients. *British Journal of Medical Psychology*, 50, 251–265.

Cash, T. F., Neale, J. M., and Cromwell, R. L. (1972). Span of apprehension in acute schizophrenics: Full-report technique. *Journal of Abnormal Psychology*, 79, 322–326.

Cegalis, J. A., and Deptula, D. (1981). Attention in schizophrenia. Signal detection in the visual periphery. *Journal of Nervous and Mental Disease*, 169, 751–760.

Cegalis, J. A., and Tegtmeyer, P. F. (1980). Visual selectivity in schizophrenia. *Journal of Nervous and Mental Disease*, 168, 229–235.

Cesarec, Z., and Nyman, A. K. (1985). Differential response to amphetamine in schizophrenia. *Acta Psychiatrica Scandinavica*, 71, 523–538.

Chapman, J., and McGhie, A. (1962). A comparative study of disordered attention in schizo-phrenia. *Journal of Mental Science*, 108, 487–500.

Chapman, L. J., and Chapman, J. P. (1973). *Disordered thought in schizophrenia.* Englewood Cliffs, New Jersey: Prentice Hall.

Cohen, R., Hermanutz, M., and Rist, F. (1984). Zur Spezifizität sequentieller Effekte in den Reaktionszeiten und ereignisbezogenen Potentialen chronisch Schizophrener. In A. Hopf and H. Beckmann (Eds.), *Forschungen zur biologischen Psychiatrie.* Berlin: Springer.

Collicut, J. R., and Hemsley, D. R. (1981). A psychological investigation of auditory functioning in schizophrenia. *British Journal of Clinical Psychology*, 20, 199–204.

Cornblatt, B. A., Lenzenweger, M. F., and Erlenmeyer-Kimling, L. (1989). The continuous performance test, identical pairs version. II. Contrasting attentional profiles in schizophrenic and depressed patients. *Psychiatry Research*, 29, 65–85.

Cowan, N. (1988). Evolving conceptions of memory storage, selective attention, and their mutual constraints within the human information-processing system. *Psychological Bulletin*, 104, 163–191.

Cox, M. D., and Levanthal, D. B. (1978). A multivariate analysis and modification of a preattentive, perceptual dysfunction in schizophrenia. *Journal of Nervous and Mental Disease*, 166, 709–718.

Cromwell, R. L., and Dokecki, P. (1968). Schizophrenic language: A disattention interpretation. In S. Rosenberg and J. H. Koplin (Eds.), *Developments in applied psycholinguistics research.* New York: McMillan.

Cutting, J. (1985). *The psychology of schizophrenia.* Edinburgh: Churchill Livingstone.

DeAmicis, L. A., and Cromwell, R. L. (1979). Reaction time crossover in process schizophrenic patients, their relatives, and control subjects. *Journal of Nervous and Mental Disease*, 167, 593–600.

DeAmicis, L. A., Wagstaff, D. A., and Cromwell, R. L. (1986). Reaction time crossover as a marker of schizophrenia and of higher functioning. *Journal of Nervous and Mental Disease*, 174, 177–179.

Deutsch, J. A., and Deutsch, D. (1963). Attention: Some theoretical considerations. *Psychological Review*, 70, 80–90.

Dobson, D. J. G., and Neufeld, W. J. (1987). Span of apprehension among remitted schizophrenics using small visual angles. *Journal of Nervous and Mental Disease*, 175, 362–366.

Erickson, W. D., Yellin, A. M., Hopwood, J. H., Realmuto, G. M., and Greenberg, L. M. (1984). The effect of neuroleptics on attention in adolescent schizophrenics. *Biological Psychiatry*, 19, 745–753.

Eysenck, M. W. (1982). *Attention and arousal: Cognition and performance*. Heidelberg: Springer.

Federn, P. (1953). *Ego psychology and the psychoses*. London: Imago.

Freeman, T., Cameron, J. L., and McGhie, A. (1958). *Chronic schizophrenia*. New York: International Universities Press.

Frith, C. D., and Done, D. J. (1983). Stereotyped responding by schizophrenic patients on a two-choice guessing task. *Psychological Medicine*, 13, 779–786.

Frith, C. D., and Done, D. J. (1988). Towards a neuropsychology of schizophrenia. *British Journal of Psychiatry*, 153, 437–443.

Giedke, H., Thier, P., and Bolz, J. (1981). The relationship between P3-latency and reaction time in depression. *Biological Psychology*, 13, 31–49.

Goldberg, S. C., Schooler, N. R., and Mattsson, N. (1968). Paranoid and withdrawal symptoms in schizophrenia: Relationship to reaction time. *British Journal of Psychiatry*, 114, 1161–1165.

Green, M., and Walker, E. (1984). Susceptibility to backward masking in schizophrenic patients with positive or negative symptoms. *American Journal of Psychiatry*, 141, 1273–1275.

Green, M., and Walker, E. (1986a). Attentional performance in positive- and negative-symptom schizophrenia. *Journal of Nervous and Mental Disease*, 174, 208–213.

Green, M., and Walker, E. (1986b). Symptom correlates of vulnerability to backward masking in schizophrenia. *American Journal of Psychiatry*, 143, 181–186.

Greiffenstein, M., Lewis, R., Milberg, W., and Rosenbaum, G. (1981). Temporal lobe epilepsy and schizophrenia: Comparison of reaction time deficits. *Journal of Abnormal Psychology*, 90, 105–112.

Haber, R. N. (1983). The impending demise of the icon! A critique of the concept of iconic storage in visual information processing. *The Behavioral and Brain Sciences*, 6, 1–54.

Hamilton, V. (1972). The size constancy problem in schizophrenia: A cognitive skill analysis. *The British Journal of Psychology*, 63, 73–84.

Harris, A., Ayers, T., and Leek, M. R. (1985). Auditory span of apprehension deficits in schizophrenia. *Journal of Nervous and Mental Disease*, 173, 650–657.

Hawks, D. V., and Robinson, K. N. (1971). Information processing in schizophrenia: The effect of varying the rate of presentation and introducing interference. *British Journal of Social and Clinical Psychology*, 10, 30–41.

Heilbrun, A. B., and Norbert, N. (1971). Sensitivity to maternal censure in paranoid and nonparanoid schizophrenics. *Journal of Nervous and Mental Disease*, 152, 45–49.

Heilizer, J. (1959). The effects of chlorpromazine upon psychomotor and psychiatric behavior of chronic schizophrenic patients. *Journal of Nervous and Mental Disease*, 128, 358–364.

Held, J. M., Cromwell, R. L., Frank, E. J., Jr., and Fann, W. E. (1970). Effect of phenothiazines on reaction time in schizophrenics. *Journal of Psychiatric Research*, 7, 209–213.

Hemsley, D. R. (1976). Stimulus uncertainty, response uncertainty, and stimulus-response compatibility as determinants of schizophrenic reaction time performance. *Bulletin of the Psychonomic Society*, 8, 425–427.

Hemsley, D. R., and Richardson, P. H. (1980). Shadowing by context in schizophrenia. *Journal of Nervous and Mental Disease*, 168, 141–145.

Hemsley, D. R., and Zawada, S. L. (1976). "Filtering" and the cognition deficit in schizophrenia. *British Journal of Psychiatry*, 128, 456–461.

Hirt, M., Cuttler, M., and Genshaft, J. (1977). Information processing by schizophrenics when task complexity increases. *Journal of Abnormal Psychology*, 86, 256–260.

Hubel, D. H., and Wiesel, T. N. (1965). Receptive fields and functional architecture in two nonstriate visual areas (18 and 19) of the cat. *Journal of Neurophysiology*, 28, 229–289.

Huston, P. E., Shakow, D., and Riggs, L. A. (1937). Studies of motor function in schizophrenia. II. Reaction time. *The Journal of General Psychology*, 16, 39.

Inouye, F., and Shimizu, A. (1972). Visual evoked response and reaction time during visual hallucination. *Journal of Nervous and Mental Disease*, 155, 419–426.

Johnston, W. A., and Dark, V. J. (1986). Selective attention. *Annual Review of Psychology*, 37, 43–75.

Julesz, B. (1984). A brief outline of the texton theory of human vision. *Trends in Neuroscience*, 2, 41–45.

Kahneman, D. (1973). *Attention and effort*. Englewood Cliffs, New Jersey: Prentice-Hall.

Kahneman, D., and Treisman, A. (1984). Changing views of attention and automaticity. In R. Parasuraman and D. R. Davies (Eds.), *Varieties of attention*. New York: Academic Press.

Kietzman, M. L., Spring, B., and Zubin, J. (1980). Science of human behavior: Contributions of the psychological sciences. In H. I. Kaplan, A. M. Freedman, and B. W. Sadock (Eds.), *Comprehensive textbook of psychiatry*, III. Baltimore: Williams & Wilkins.

King, H. A. (1954). *Psychomotor aspects of mental illness*. Cambridge, Massachusetts: Harvard University Press.

Knight, R. A., Elliot, D. S., and Freedman, E. G. (1985). Short-term visual memory in schizophrenics. *Journal of Abnormal Psychology*, 94, 427–442.

Knight, R. A., Sherer, M., Putchat, C., and Carter, G. (1978). A picture integration task for measuring iconic memory in schizophrenics. *Journal of Abnormal Psychology*, 87, 314–321.

Knight, R. A., Sherer, M., and Shapiro, J. (1977). Iconic imagery in overinclusive and nonoverinclusive schizophrenics. *Journal of Abnormal Psychology*, 86, 242–255.

Knight, R. G., Youard, P. J., and Wooles, I. M. (1985). Visual information-processing deficits in chronic schizophrenic subjects using tasks matched for discriminating power. *Journal of Abnormal Psychology*, 94, 454–459.

Korboot, P. J., and Damiani, N. (1976). Auditory processing speed and signal detection in schizophrenia. *Journal of Abnormal Psychology*, 85, 287–295.

Kornetsky, C., and Orzack, M. H. (1978). Physiological and behavioral correlates of attention dysfunction in schizophrenic patients. *Journal of Psychiatric Research*, 14, 69.

Kostandov, E. A. (1980). Asymmetry of visual perception and interhemispheric interaction. *Neuroscience*, Behavior and Physiology, 10, 36–47.

Kraepelin, E. (1909). *Psychiatrie: Ein Lehrbuch für Studierende und Ärzte*, Vol. 1. Leipzig: Barth.

Kristofferson, M. W. (1967). Shifting attention between modalities: A comparison of schizophrenics and normals. *Journal of Abnormal Psychology*, 72, 388–394.

Levine, F. M., and Whitney, N. (1970). Absolute auditory threshold and threshold of unpleasantness of chronic schizophrenic patients and normal controls. *Journal of Abnormal Psychology*, 75, 74–77.

Lewis, J. L. (1970). Semantic processing of unattended messages using dichotic listening. *Journal of Experimental Psychology*, 85, 225–228.

Lindsay, P. H., and Norman, D. A. (1977). *Human information processing*, 2d ed. New York: Academic Press.

Litwack, T. R., Wiedemann, C. F., and Yager, J. (1979). The fear of object loss, responsiveness to subliminal stimuli, and schizophrenic psychopathology. *Journal of Nervous and Mental Disease*, 167, 79–90.

Loeb, M., and Holding, D. H. (1975). Backward interference by tones or noise in pitch perception as a function of practice. *Perception and Psychophysics*, 18, 205–208.

Long, G. M. (1980). Iconic memory: A review and critique of the study of short-term visual storage. *Psychological Bulletin*, 88, 785–820.

Ludwig, A. M., Stilson, D. W., Wood, B. S., and Downs, M. P. (1963). Further studies in audition in schizophrenia. *American Journal of Psychiatry*, 120, 70–71.

Ludwig, A. M., Wood, B. S., and Downs, M. P. (1962). Auditory studies in schizophrenia. *American Journal of Psychiatry*, 119, 122–127.

Lyon, N., and Gerlach, J. (1988). Perseverative structuring of responses by schizophrenic and affective disorder patients. *Journal of Psychiatric Research*, 22, 261–277.

Lyon, N., Nejsholm, B., and Lyon, M. (1986). Stereotyped responding by schizophrenic outpatients: Crosscultural confirmation of perseverative switching on a two-choice task. *Journal of Psychiatric Research*, 20, 137–150.

Mackintosh, N. J. (1975). A theory of attention: Variations in the associability of stimuli with reinforcement. *Psychological Review*, 82, 276–298.

Maloney, M. P., Sloane, R. B., Whipple, K., Razani, J., and Eaton, E. M. (1976). Auditory attention in process and reactive schizophrenia. *Biological Psychiatry*, 11, 325–333.

Mannuzza, S. (1980). Cross-modal reaction time and schizophrenic attentional deficit: A critical review. *Schizoprenia Bulletin*, 6, 654–675.

Mannuzza, S., Kietzman, M. L., Berenhaus, I. J., Ramsey, P. H., Zubin, J., and Sutton, S. (1984). The modality shift effect in schizophrenia: Fact or artifact? *Biological Psychiatry*, 19, 1317–1331.

Marshall, W. L. (1973). Cognitive functioning in schizophrenia. I. Stimulus analyzing and response selection processes. *British Journal of Psychiatry*, 123, 413–423.

Massaro, D. W. (1977). Capacity limitations in auditory information processing. In S. Dornic (Ed.), *Attention and performance*, IV. Hillsdale, New Jersey: Erlbaum.

McGhie, A., and Chapman, J. (1961). Disorders of attention and perception in early schizophrenia. *British Journal of Medical Psychology*, 34, 103–116.

Merrit, R. D., Balogh, D. W., and Leventhal, D. B. (1986). Use of a metacontrast and a paracontrast procedure to assess the visual information processing of hypothetically schizotypic college students. *Journal of Abnormal Psychology*, 95, 74–80.

Meyer-Osterkamp, S., and Cohen, R. (1973). *Zur Größenkonstanz bei Schizophrenen*. Berlin: Springer.

Miller S., Saccuzzo, D. P., and Braff, D. L. (1979). Information processing deficit in remitted schizophrenics. *Journal of Abnormal Psychology*, 88, 446–449.

Moray, N. (1959). Attention in dichotic listening: Affective cues and the influence of instructions. *Quarterly Journal of Experimental Psychology%,RR 11*, 56–60.

Nagamoto, H. T., Adler, L. E., Waldo, N. C., and Freedman, R. (1989). Sensory gating in schizophrenics and normal controls: Effects of changing stimulation interval. *Biological Psychiatry*, 25, 549–561.

Neale, J. M. (1971). Perceptual span in schizophrenia. *Journal of Abnormal Psychology*, 77, 196–204.

Neale, J. M., and Oltmanns, T. F. (1980). *Schizophrenia*. New York: Wiley.

Neisser, U. (1967). *Cognitive psychology*. New York: Appleton-Century-Crofts.

Neufeld, R. W. J. (1977). Response-selection processes in paranoid and nonparanoid schizophrenia. *Perceptual and Motor Skills*, 44, 499–505.

Nuechterlein, K. H. (1977). Reaction time and attention in schizophrenia: A critical evaluation of the data and theories. *Schizophrenia Bulletin*, 3, 373–428.

Nuechterlein, K. H., and Dawson, M. E. (1984). Information processing and attentional functioning in the developmental course of schizophrenic disorders. *Schizophrenia Bulletin*, 10, 160–203.

Olbrich, R. (1972). Reaction time in brain-damaged and normal subjects to variable preparatory intervals. *Journal of Nervous and Mental Disease*, 155, 356–362.

Orzack, M. H., and Kornetzky, C. (1966). Attention dysfunction in chronic schizophrenia. *Archives of General Psychiatry*, 14, 323–326.

Payne, R. W., and Caird, W. K. (1967). Reaction time, distractability, and overinclusive thinking in psychotics. *Journal of Abnormal Psychology*, 72, 112–121.

Payne, R. W., Hochberg, A. C., and Hawks, D. V. (1970). Dichotic stimulation as a method of assessing disorder of attention in over-inclusive schizophrenic patients. *Journal of Abnormal Psychology*, 76, 185–193.

Pearl, D. (1962). Phenothiazine effects in chronic schizophrenia. *Journal of Clinical Psychology*, 18, 86–89.

Pogue-Geile, M. F., and Oltmanns, T. F. (1980). Sentence perception and distractability in schizophrenic, manic, and depressed patients. *Journal of Abnormal Psychology*, 89, 115–124.

Posner, M. (1975). Psychobiology of attention. In M. S. Gazzaniga and C. Blakemore (Eds.), *Handbook of psychobiology*, pp. 441–498. New York: Academic Press.

Pugh, L. A. (1968). Response time and electrodermal measures in chronic schizophrenia: The effects of chlorpromazine. *Journal of Nervous and Mental Disease*, 146, 62–70.

Rappaport, M., Hopkins, H. K., Silverman, J., and Hall, K. (1972). Auditory signal detection in schizophrenia. *Psychopharmacologia (Berlin)*, 24, 6–28.

Raush, H. L. (1952). Perceptual constancy in schizophrenia: I. Size constancy. *Journal of Personality*, 21, 176–187.

Reich, S. S., and Cutting, J. (1982). Picture perception and abstract thought in schizophrenia. *Psychological Medicine*, 12, 91–96.

Rey, E.-R., and Oldigs, J. (1982). Ergebnisse einer experimentellen zweijährigen Verlaufsunter-suchung zu Störungen der Informationsverarbeitung Schizophrener. In G. Huber (Ed.), *Endogene Psychosen: Diagnostik, Basissymptome, und biologische Parameter*. Stuttgart: Schattauer.

Rist, F., and Thurm, I. (1984). Effects of intramodal and crossmodal stimulus diversity on the reaction time of chronic schizophrenics. *Journal of Abnormal Psychology*, 93, 331–338.

Robertson, L. C. (1986). From gestalt to neo-gestalt. In T. J. Knapp and L. C. Robertson (Eds.), *Approaches to cognition: Contrast and controversies*, pp. 159–188. Hillsdale, New Jersey: Erlbaum.

Robertson, L. C., Lamb, M. R., and Knight, R. T. (1988). Effects of lesions of temporal-parietal junction on perceptual and attention processing in humans. *Journal of Neuroscience Research*, 8, 3757–3769.

Rodnick, E., and Shakow, D. (1940). Set in the schizophrenic as measured by a composite reaction time index. *American Journal of Psychiatry*, 97, 214–225.

Rosen, A. C. (1970). Change in perceptual threshold as a protective function of the organism. In M. D. Vernon (Ed.), *Experiments in visual perception*, 2d ed. Harmondsworth: Penguin Books.

Rosenbaum, G., Chapin, K., and Shore, D. L. (1988). Attention deficit in schizophrenia and schizoptypy: Marker versus symptom variables. *Journal of Abnormal Psychology*, 97, 41–47.

Rosvold, H. E., Mirsky, A. F., Sarason, I., Bransome, E. D., and Beck, L. H. (1956). A continuous performance test of brain damage. *Journal of Consulting Psychology*, 20, 343–350.

Royer, F. L., and Friedman, S. (1973). Scanning time of schizophrenics and normals for visual design. *Journal of Abnormal Psychology*, 82, 212–219.

Saccuzzo, D. P., and Braff, D. L. (1981). Early information processing deficit in schizophrenia: New findings using schizophrenic sub-groups and manic controls. *Archives of General Psychiatry*, 38, 175–179.

Saccuzzo, D. P., Hirt, M., and Spencer, T. J. (1974). Backward masking as a measure of attention in schizophrenia. *Journal of Abnormal Psychology*, 83, 512–522.

Saccuzzo, D. P., Kerr, M., Marcus, A., and Brown, R. (1979). Input capability and speed of processing in mental retardation. *Journal of Abnormal Psychology*, 88, 341–345.

Saccuzzo, D. P., and Miller, S. (1977). Critical interstimulus interval in delusional schizophrenics and normals. *Journal of Abnormal Psychology*, 86, 261–266.

Saccuzzo, D. P., and Schubert, D. L. (1981). Backward masking as a measure of slow processing in schizophrenia spectrum disorders. *Journal of Abnormal Psychology*, 90, 305–312.

Sakitt, B. (1976). Iconic memory. *Psychological Review*, 83, 257–276.

Scherer, M., and Storms, L. (1981). Attention and visual reaction time in schizophrenia. *Journal of Nervous and Mental Disease*, 169, 348–356.

Schneider, S. J. (1976). Selective attention in schizophrenia. *Journal of Abnormal Psychology*, 85, 167–173.

Schwartz, B. D., Mallott, D. B., and Winstead, D. K. (1988). Preattentive deficit in temporal processing by chronic schizophrenics. *Biological Psychiatry*, 23, 664–669.

Schwartz, B. D., and Winstead, D. K. (1988). Visible persistence in paranoid schizophrenics. *Biological Psychiatry*, 23, 3–12.

Schwartz, B. D., Winstead, D. K., and Adinoff, B. (1983). Temporal integration deficit in visual information processing by chronic schizophrenics. *Biological Psychiatry*, 18, 1311–1320.

Schwartz, F., Carr, A. C., Munich, R. L., Glauber, S., Lesser, B., and Murray, J. (1989). Reaction time impairment in schizophrenia and affective illness: The role of attention. *Biological Psychiatry*, 25, 540–548.

Schwartz-Place, E. J., and Gilmore, G. C. (1980). Perceptual organization in schizophrenia. *Journal of Abnormal Psychology*, 89, 409–418.

Shakow, D. (1979). *Adaptation in schizophrenia. The theory of segmental set*. New York: Wiley.

Shiffrin, R. M., and Schneider, W. (1977). Controlled and automatic human information processing. II. Perceptual learning, automatic attending, and a general theory. *Psychological Review*, 84, 127–190.

Simons, R. F., MacMillan, F. W., and Ireland, F. B. (1982). Reaction-time cross-over in preselected schizotypic subjects. *Journal of Abnormal Psychology*, 91, 414–419.

Spaulding, W., Huntzinger, R. S., Le Compte, P., and Cromwell, R. L. (1984). Clinical and etiological implications of a specific attention deficit in schizophrenia. *Journal of Nervous and Mental Disease*, 172, 279–286.

Spaulding, W., Rosenzweig, L., Huntzinger, R., Cromwell, R. L., Briggs, D., and Hayes, T. (1980). Visual pattern integration in psychiatric patients. *Journal of Abnormal Psychology*, 89, 643–653.

Sperling, G. (1960). The information available in brief visual presentations. Psychological Monographs, 74(12), Whole No. 498.

Spohn, H. E., Lacoursiere, R. B., Thompson, K., and Coyne, L. (1977). Phenothiazine effects on psychological and psychophysiological dysfunction in chronic schizophrenics. *Archives of General Psychiatry*, 34, 633–644.

Spring, B. J. (1980). Shift of attention in schizophrenics, siblings of schizophrenics, and depressed patients. *Journal of Nervous and Mental Disease*, 168, 133–140.

Spring, B., Lemon, M., Weinstein, L., and Haskell, A. (1989). Distractibility in schizophrenia: state and trait aspects. *The British Journal of Psychiatry*, Suppl. July 5, 63–68.

Steffy, R. A., and Galbraith, K. J. (1980). Relation between latency and redundancy-associated deficit in schizophrenic reaction time performance. *Journal of Abnormal Psychology*, 89, 419–427.

Stilson, D. W., and Kopell, B. S. (1964). The recognition of visual signals in the presence of visual noise by psychiatric patients. *Journal of Nervous and Mental Disease*, 139, 209–221.

Stilson, D. W., Kopell, B. S., Vandenbergh, R., and Downs, M. P. (1966). Perceptual recognition in the presence of noise by psychiatric patients. *Journal of Nervous and Mental Disease*, 142, 235–247.

Straube, E. (1975). Experimente zur Wahrnehmung Schizophrener. *Archiv für Psychiatrie und Nervenkrankheiten*, 220, 139–158.

Straube, E., Maier, H.-A., Lemcke, C., and Germer, Ch. (1984). Attention abilities and verbal reaction time of schizophrenics in a dichotic shadowing task. Unpublished manuscript.

Straube, E. R., and Germer, Ch. K. (1979). Dichotic shadowing and selective attention to word meaning in schizophrenia. *Journal of Abnormal Psychology*, 88, 346–353.

Strauss, M. E., Bohannon, W. E., Stephens, J. H., and Pauker, N. E. (1984). Perceptual span in schizophrenia and affective disorders. *Journal of Nervous and Mental Disease*, 172, 431–435.

Strauss, M. E., Lew, M. F., Coyle, J. T., and Tune, M. D. (1985). Psychopharmacologic and clinical correlates of attention in chronic schizophrenia. *American Journal of Psychiatry*, 142, 497–499.

Stuss, D. T., Benson, D. F., Kaplan, E. F., Weir, W. S., and Della Malva, C. (1981). Leucotomized and non-leucotomized schizophrenics: Comparison on tests of attention. *Biological Psychiatry*, 16, 1085–1100.

Sutton, S. (1973). Fact and artifact in the psychology of schizophrenia. In M. Hammer, K. Salzinger, and S. Sutton (Eds.), *Psychopathology*. New York: Wiley.

Sutton, S., and Zubin, J. (1965). Effect of sequence on reaction time in schizophrenia. In A. T. Welford and J. E. Birren (Eds.), *Behavior. Aging and the nervous system*. Springfield, Illinois: Charles C. Thomas.

Treisman, A., Squire, R., and Green, J. (1974). Semantic processing in dichotic listening? A replication. *Memory & Cognition*, 2, 641–646.

Treisman, A. M. (1967). Selective attention: Perception or response? *Quarterly Journal of Experimental Psychology*, 19, 1–17.

Tyler, S. K., and Tucker, D. M. (1982). Anxiety and perceptual structure: Individual differences in neuropsychological function. *Journal of Abnormal Psychology*, 91, 210–220.

Van Dyke, J. L., Rosenthal, D., and Rasmussen, P. V. (1975). Schizophrenia: Effects of inheritance and rearing on reaction time. *Canadian Journal of Behavioral Science*, 7, 223–236.

Venables, P. H. (1964). Input dysfunction in schizophrenia. In B. A Maher (Ed.), *Progress in experimental personality research*, Vol. 1. New York: Academic Press.

Venables, P. H. (1977). Input dysfunction in schizophrenia. In B. Maher (Ed.), *Contributions to the psychopathology of schizophrenia*, pp. 1–56. New York: Academic Press.

Venzky-Stalling, I., Mussgay, L., and Cohen, R. (1985). Kognitive Beeinträchtigung bei chronisch Schizophrenen im Buchstabenvergleich nach Posner. *Zeitschrift für Klinische Psychologie*, 14, 228–237.

Verleger, R., and Cohen, R. (1978). Effects of certainty, modality shift, and guess outcome on evoked potentials and reaction times in chronic schizophrenics. *Psychological Medicine*, 8, 81–93.

Wagener, D. K., Hogarty, G. E., Goldstein, M. J., Asarnow, R. F., and Browne, A. (1986). Information processing and communication deviance in schizophrenic patients and their mothers. *Psychiatry Research*, 18, 365–377.

Wahl, O. (1976). Schizophrenic patterns of dichotic shadowing performance. *Journal of Nervous and Mental Disease*, 163, 401–407.

Waldbaum, J. K., Sutton, S., and Kerr, J. (1975). Shift of sensory modality and reaction time in schizophrenia. In M. L. Kietzman, S. Sutton, and J. Zubin (Eds.), *Experimental approaches to psychopathology*. New York: Academic Press.

Walker, E. (1981). Attentional and neuromotor functions of schizophrenics, schizoaffectives, and patients with other affective disorders. *Archives of General Psychiatry*, 38, 1355–1358.

Walker, E., and Shaye, J. (1982). Familial schizophrenia: A predictor of neuromotor and attentional abnormalities in schizophrenia. *Archives of General Psychiatry*, 39, 1153–1156.

Wells, D. S., and Leventhal, D. (1984). Perceptual grouping in schizophrenia. *Journal of Abnormal Psychology*, 93, 231–234.

Williams, R. M., Alagaratnam, W., and Hemsley, D. R. (1984). Relationship between subjective self-report of cognitive dysfunction and objective information-processing performance in a group of hospitalized schizophrenic patients. *European Archives of Psychiatry and Neurological Science*, 234, 48–53.

Williams, R. M., and Hemsley, D. R. (1986). Choice reaction time performance in hospitalized schizophrenic patients and depressed patients. *European Archives of Psychiatry and Neurological Science*, 236, 169–173.

Wishner, J., and Wahl, O. (1974). Dichotic listening in schizophrenia. *Journal of Consulting and Clinical Psychology*, 42, 538–546.

Wohlberg, G. W., and Kornetsky, C. (1973). Sustained attention in remitted schizophrenics. *Archives of General Psychiatry*, 28, 533–537.

Wynne, R. D., and Kornetzky, C. (1960). The effects of chlorpromazine and secobarbital on the reaction times of chronic schizophrenics. *Psychopharmacologia*, 1, 294–302.

Yates, A. J., and Korboot, P. (1970). Speed of perceptual functioning in chronic nonparanoid schizophrenics. *Journal of Abnormal Psychology*, 76, 453–461.

Zahn, T. P. (1970). Effects of reduction in uncertainty on reaction time in schizophrenic and normal subjects. *Journal of Experimental Research in Personality*, 4, 135–143.

Zaunbrecher, D., Himer, W., and Straube, E. (1990). Sind frühe Stufen der visuellen Informationsverarbeitung bei Schizophrenen gestört? *Der Nervenarzt*, 61, 418–425.

# PART III

# Psychophysiological Symptoms

# Chapter 5

# Responses of the Autonomic Nervous System to External Stimuli

## I. Introduction

Not only does the central nervous system (CNS) change activity in response to external stimuli, but the autonomic nervous system (ANS) does so as well. Changes in some measures of functions modulated by the ANS are considered to be indicators of this response. Examples of frequently used measures include changes of heart rate, dilation of the pupils, glandular secretion in the palm of the hand, and associated electrodermal or skin conductance changes.

The word "autonomic" refers to physiological actions that are not usually influenced by conscious or willed intent. The ANS plays a large role in mediating information about hunger and thirst, and sexual and emotional reactions. However, ANS changes can also be observed as concomitant to controlled data processing in the CNS, especially if the task is demanding, that is, requires effort.

Simple autonomic reactions are easily observable in ourselves. Consider how we flush in an embarrassing situation, our heart beats faster with excitement and expectation, or our hands sweat when we are fearful. Combinations of these and more complex reactions are experienced in emotional or stressful situations. Some of these responses are easily measured (e.g., pulse rate) and are the subject of numerous laboratory investigations. These functions are adaptive, since their purpose is basically to activate the organism in situations of potential threat or excessive demand. They are phylogenetically very old functions.

Another basic adaptive and also automatically elicited function of the ANS is the so-called orienting response (OR), which is a brief phasic change of ANS activity due to a sudden change in the environment.

From behavioral observation alone it might be expected that the adaptive reactions of the ANS are, to some extent, impaired in many schizophrenics. At the turn of the century, Bleuler (1911) already reported changes in the "psychogalvanic" reaction of schizophrenics. These were results obtained by his assistants at the time: Veraguth and a certain C. G. Jung, who later became a student of Freud. Summarizing the results, Bleuler wrote

> indifference and stupor are currently expressed as a totally straight line on the recorder during the resting period, but unstable graphs are also found, namely in hallucinatory patients. All reactions to psychological and physical stimuli are reduced to zero in severe cases (1911, p. 41).

It is amazing that these two early findings, namely, spontaneous fluctuations during hallucinations (e.g., Cooklin *et al.*, 1983) and nonresponding in emotionally withdrawn patients (see subsequent text, have been widely confirmed by more recent work.

## II. The Orienting Response—Neutral Stimuli

The OR is a phasic change of ANS activity following the sudden occurrence of stimuli of mild intensity. If the stimulus is repeated several times and if no harmful or demanding consequences follow, then the ANS response habituates. However, no habituation occurs if the stimulus signals a threat or that a task has to be performed. The OR is thought to be adaptive because it prepares the organism for a quick response to a change in the environment (in animals, this is "fight or flight"). The following method is usually used for studying the OR. A series of 10–15 unexpected stimuli is presented. The stimuli may be visual but are more commonly auditory tones of moderate intensity (75–80 dB) without any consequence (i.e., they are nonthreatening and neutral). The ANS response includes the following components: increased skeletal muscle tone, peripheral vasoconstriction (as measured, for example, by finger pulse volume), increased glandular activity in the palm of the hand and the sole of the foot (as measured by the electrodermal response),[1] reduction in the frequency and depth of breathing, transient brief cardiac acceleration followed by a deceleration (and eventually by a further acceleration), and pupillary dilation.[2]

The most frequently investigated component of the orienting reaction is the change in skin conductance or electrodermal response (EDOR). Increased sweating on the palm or the finger pads brings about a change in electrical conductance. Some laboratories use the reciprocal measure, the change in

[1]The biological reason for this response would seem to be that it increases the grip on the substratum (e.g., by primates in trees).

[2]Electrophysiological recordings show increased activity of retinal neurons with the increased incident light that follows pupillary dilation (cf. Sokolov, 1963).

electrical resistance. It is believed that the change in electrodermal conductivity (or resistance) is due to a change in the number of active glands under the electrode surface (cf. Thomas and Korr, 1957; Venables and Christie, 1980). The brain centers which may be involved in triggering the EDOR are the limbic structures, especially the amygdala and the hippocampus, but other centers— such as the hypothalamus, reticular formation, and some cortical areas—may also be involved.

The electrodermal response is very simple to measure. It only requires the application of two surface electrodes to the skin and a means of recording the potential differences. Ease and reliability of measurement are considerable advantages in the investigation of the responsiveness of severely disturbed patients.

## A. The Electrodermal Orienting Response

Early studies in the 1960s showed that there were many schizophrenics who did not show an EDOR to neutral stimuli. It appeared from these studies that the more the schizophrenics were cognitively disturbed, the more likely they were to be nonresponders (Bernstein, 1964).

Later on, Gruzelier and Venables in London (1972) reported a bimodal distribution of electrodermal responses in schizophrenics. One peak represented EDOR nonresponders and the other peak represented those who showed delayed habituation (hyperresponders). However, despite studying a heterogeneous sample of schizophrenic patients, the investigators could find no relationship between response type and the conventional subgroups of schizophrenia.

The English study was heuristically useful and stimulated much new research, but subsequent work has only clearly confirmed the existence of a group of nonresponding schizophrenics and that nonresponse is much more frequent in schizophrenics than in the healthy population at large (Patterson, 1976; Zahn, 1976; Straube, 1979; Alm et al., 1984). Nonresponse can even be found in schizophrenic outpatients who are in remission (Iacono, 1982). Hyperresponders (i.e., those who do not habituate after 10–15 stimuli) can be found among schizophrenics if more intense stimuli are used, but they are not more numerous than in the general population (Bernstein, 1987).

Some researchers, however, found that nonresponders were underrepresented in their sample (e.g., Frith et al., 1979; Toone et al., 1981; Bartfai et al., 1983). In order to clarify whether differences in methodology or in evaluation of the data were responsible for these discrepancies, six research groups from three countries (the United States, the United Kingdom, and the Federal Republic of Germany) followed the proposal of Bernstein to reanalyze their already published or still unpublished data. The result of this analysis was that, with only limited exceptions, nearly all schizophrenics deviated in comparison with the healthy control groups in the nonresponder category (Bernstein *et al.*, 1982). This is corroborated by the results of a review of the literature by Öhman (1981) in Sweden, who found that, in 29 studies by 22 authors, nonresponding was the dominant finding in schizophrenia. The median for all studies reviewed by Öhman (1981) was 40% schizophrenic nonresponders. (see also Figure 5.1).

The proportion of nonresponse, habituation, or nonhabituation is independent of medication status (Straube, 1979, 1980; Gruzelier *et al.*, 1981; Straube and Öhman, 1990; Spohn and Strauss, 1989; see Section III, G for further discussion), as can be seen in Figure 5.1.

In the studies that showed a reduced proportion of nonresponders, patients with largely positive symptoms had been tested (Frith *et al.*, 1979, 1982; Toone *et al.*, 1981; Zahn *et al.*, 1981a,b; Bartfai *et al.*, 1983). Indeed, both Frith's and Bartfai's group explicitly excluded subjects with negative symptoms from their study. Furthermore, Bartfai and colleagues (1983, p. 186) commented that the absence of nonresponders in their study "might be explained as partly an effect of studying unmedicated highly aroused patients with positive symptoms." Indirectly confirming their supposition, a recent study from their laboratory showed that 33% of a mixed group of schizophrenics were electrodermal nonresponders (Bartfai *et al.*, 1987). This result is more in accord with the consensus elsewhere. As we will see later, it seems that nonresponse is frequently associated with the presence of negative symptoms. Medication status does not explain the difference between the studies, as already discussed.

Another critical factor is the instruction given to the subjects: nonresponders change to responders when the instruction attaches a signal value to the stimuli (Gruzelier and Venables, 1973; Bernstein *et al.*, 1988). It is therefore possible that, in addition to differences in the composition of the group, slight differences in the instruction may have caused changes in the percentage of nonresponders. This point will be discussed further in a later section.

In conclusion, since there has been an unbiased selection of subjects and an instruction assuring a nonsignal value to the stimulus, there is a greater-than-expected incidence of electrodermal nonresponse among schizophrenic subjects than among healthy or neurotic control subjects. A differential incidence for EDOR hyperresponding has not been demonstrated. An increased likelihood of nonresponse to neutral stimuli may not, however, be specific to schizophrenia. A similar proportion of nonresponders has been reported among depressive patients (Giedke *et al.*, 1982; Bernstein *et al.*, 1988) and chronic alcoholics (Sommer, 1985).

## 1. Tonic Arousal Level

The tonic level of arousal (i.e., the basal conductance level) of nonresponders is significantly lower than that of responders in most studies (Gruzelier and

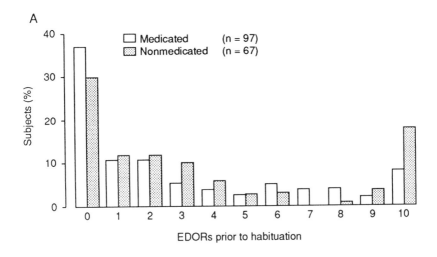

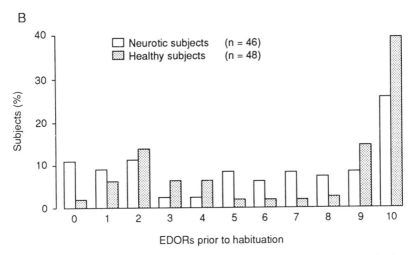

**Figure 5.1** The number of EDORs elicited by neutral auditory stimuli prior to habituation in groups of (A) medicated and nonmedicated schizophrenics and (B) neurotic and healthy subjects (after Straube, 1979).

Venables, 1972, 1974; Patterson and Venables, 1978; Rubens and Lapidus, 1978; Rippon, 1979). Thus, this heterogeneity in the skin conductance level values of schizophrenics may explain why no clear differences have been found between healthy subjects and the total group of schizophrenics (i.e., when grouping nonresponders and responders together; for review, see Öhman, 1981).

## 2. EDOR Recovery

Another aspect of the EDOR that has received some attention in the past is the recovery time of the phasic response (i.e., the time for the EDOR to return to the prestimulation level). Early studies claimed that there was a relationship between increased recovery latency and schizophrenic illness (Ax and Bamford, 1970; Gruzelier and Venables, 1972). However, more recent work has failed to confirm such a relationship. We will not pursue this controversy here, but the interested reader may refer to Öhman's review (1981).

## 3. Other Autonomic Components of the Orienting Response

The electrodermal component is not the only component of the OR that has an abnormal response pattern in schizophrenia. The finger pulse volume is a measure of peripheral vasoconstriction. The reduction of the pulse amplitude during the OR has an incidence similar to that of EDOR nonresponse in schizophrenics (Figure 5.2). About 68–85% of chronic (Bernstein et al., 1981) and 64% of acute (Straube, 1983) schizophrenics are both electrodermal *and* cardiovascular nonresponders. Straube (1983) found a total frequency of cardiovascular nonresponse of 34% in acute schizophrenia; there was a correlation with EDOR nonresponse of $r_s = 0.43$ for schizophrenics and $r_s = 0.34$ for healthy subjects). In agreement with these results, Gruzelier and Venables (1975) found a weaker heart rate OR in electrodermal nonresponders than in responders. Electrodermal nonresponders also showed relatively low activity in related measures, such as tonic heart rate level, systolic blood pressure, and skin temperature (Gruzelier and Venables, 1975).

Two studies reported that electrodermal nonresponders showed reduced pupillary constriction in response to light stimuli (Patterson, 1976; Straube, 1982). However, Straube (1983) could not confirm this relationship in a second study.

What other parameters might warrant further study? One such parameter might be serum cortisol. Gruzelier and Hammond (1978) claimed that electrodermal responders showed a higher serum level of cortisol than nonresponders. Another potentially important correlate of OR is the alpha block in the electroencephalogram (EEG). Curiously, this correlation has only been investigated by Bernstein and colleagues (1981). Their findings were surprising because they found no difference between electrodermal responders and nonresponders.

One of the useful features of these other measures of the OR is that they help discriminate other psychiatric populations. For example, Bernstein et al. (1988) found that very few depressive patients were cardiovascular nonresponders, although a high percentage of depressives showed EDOR

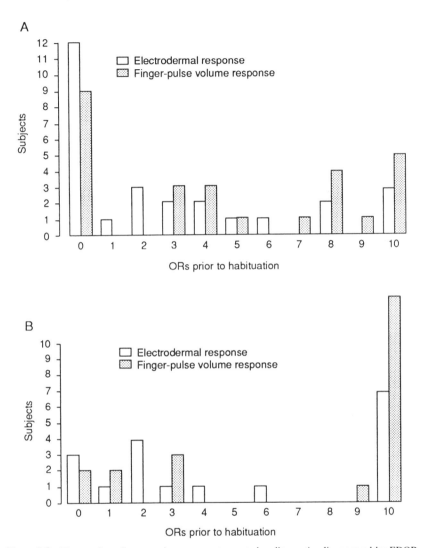

**Figure 5.2** The number of autonomic responses to neutral auditory stimuli measured by EDOR and finger-pulse volume prior to habituation in (A) schizophrenics (n = 27) and (B) healthy controls (n = 18) (Straube, 1983).

nonresponse. However, schizophrenics were nonresponders in both components of the orienting response. This confirms the results obtained with measures of the finger pulse volume by Bruno *et al.* (1983). Öhman *et al.* (1989) confirmed the higher consistency of ANS arousal patterns in schizophrenics ("low and high responsive") compared with healthy controls. Several phasic and tonic electrodermal and cardiac measures were recorded under different stimulus conditions.

In summary, the different autonomic measures of the OR give a relatively clear picture of a decreased level of excitability, both in the phasic response to neutral stimuli and in the background level of arousal. Unfortunately, the relationship is not, as is so often the case in psychobiology, so robust that the one measure can be replaced by the other. (For further discussion of the general problems of low correlations between psychophysiological measures, see Fahrenberg, 1987.)

## B. Characteristics of a Subgroup of Schizophrenics

Some studies showed that significant differences exist between EDOR responders and nonresponders with respect to their pattern of psycho-pathological symptoms. Schizophrenic EDOR nonresponders more frequently have negative symptoms than EDOR responders. (Responders were defined as those producing at least three responses.) This result has been reported by several research groups: Gruzelier (1976) in the United Kingdom, Straube (1979) in Germany, and Bernstein et al. (1981) in the United States. The last two studies used the same rating scale—the Brief Psychiatric Rating Scale (BPRS) of Overall and Gorham (1962). The common result of these last two studies was that nonresponding schizophrenics more often showed emotional withdrawal, drive reduction, slowed motor reactions, and anergia as assessed by the BPRS than did responders. However, Bartfai et al. (1983) in Sweden, Sommer (1982) in Constance, Germany and Green et al. (1989) in California reported no relationship between the electrodermal response type and symptomatology. These differences might have arisen from the selection of a certain subgroup, as already discussed in the case of Bartfai et al. (1983), but this does not explain the negative findings of Sommer (1982) and Green et al. (1989).

Alm and colleagues in Uppsala, Sweden (1984), reported an association between a family history of schizophrenia and nonresponse. Bartfai et al. (1987) could not confirm this relationship in their study, but did find an increased incidence of mild cerebral atrophy (increased ventricle width) among the responders. Since this was not confirmed by Öhman's group (Alm et al., 1984), the relationship of these two features to the nature of the EDOR remains decidedly unclear.

Finally, it is interesting that nonresponders also occur in the population belonging to the subclinical spectrum of schizophrenia. Two studies with adolescents found a greater incidence of nonresponse in those showing schizoid personality characteristics (Simons et al., 1983; Raine and Venables, 1984). About 7% of healthy subjects are nonresponders (Venables, 1966).

Here it is important to note that Simons and colleagues found spectrum features only in those adolescents who were nonresponders on *repeated* tests.

## C. The EDOR as a Component of Information-Processing Systems

According to several theories, the functional role of the OR is that of initiating information processing for stimuli that appear unexpectedly and to which the subject has not attended previously (Venables, 1973). Öhman speaks about the OR as "a call for central processing capacity." Similarly, Bernstein (1987, p. 623), in reviewing new Western studies, says that the OR can be identified "with the allocation of a limited capacity central processor (or with a call for such a processor)." The result of this processing determines the occurrence of habituation or nonhabituation of the OR (Sokolov, 1963).

Since a disturbance of information processing can be observed in schizophrenics (cf. Chapter 2), it can be expected that OR changes are linked to changes in information processing. Astonishingly, few studies have looked for a direct link between the nature of the OR and cognitive processing.

There is only a small amount of evidence for such a link in the work of German and English laboratories and no evidence in a Swedish laboratory. Patterson and Venables (1980) in the United Kingdom also found impaired performance of nonresponders on a signal-detection task, but this English group also found that the responders made more mistakes. Only the schizophrenics whose EDOR habituated rapidly after the first or second tone showed no impairment and performed as well as the healthy controls did. Straube (1979) found that the performance of nonresponders was poor compared to responders when asked to repeat words, even without irrelevant stimuli. Thus, distractability does not appear to play a role here. Alm *et al.* (1984) in Sweden found no differences between responders and nonresponders on a stimulus-selection task.

Without further studies, an interpretation of these results would point more toward a general increase in the threshold for response to external stimuli in nonresponders and less toward a disturbance of stimulus selection mechanisms. This idea is supported by a result of Gruzelier and Venables (1974) concerning the flicker-fusion thresholds of their subjects. They found that at an interstimulus interval at which responders could still perceive two flashing lights separately, nonresponders perceived only one. Also relevant here is the description of stimulus registration in nonresponders by Rubens and Lapidus (1978). On the Bellak scale, they were said to show a higher "stimulus barrier function," referring to their reduced awareness of potentially disturbing external stimuli and, indeed, their reduced irritability in general.

Of course, on the basis of such a small number of studies we cannot tell if these findings truly reflect a sensory or even an information processing correlate to the absence of responding in the electrodermal system. We can only reiterate the remark of Dawson and Nuechterlein that "the relationship between SCR-ORs [EDORs] and information processing in schizophrenia is in need of further investigation and appears to be a particularly promising area for future research" (1984, p. 213).

## III. ANS Responses to Demanding Stimuli

## A. Response to Orienting Stimuli Compared with Signal Stimuli

So far we have used the term OR to refer to a reaction of the organism to neutral nonsignal stimuli. In order to avoid confusion in the interpretation of results, particularly from psychiatric populations, it is important to emphasize the difference between autonomic reactions to nonsignal stimuli and those to signal stimuli that have consequences.

One can easily imagine the importance of this distinction by referring to electrodermal nonresponders. If the neutral stimulus, to which a proportion of schizophrenics have shown no EDOR, becomes a signal stimulus (for example, in a reaction-time task), then the majority of the EDOR nonresponders show an electrodermal response (Gruzelier and Venables, 1973; Bernstein et al., 1988). The normalizing of the EDOR of nonresponders was apparently as true for the schizophrenics as for the depressives as was demonstrated in the study of Gruzelier and Venables (Figure 5.3). Indeed, any kind of increase in the significance of the stimuli seems to reduce the proportion of EDOR nonresponders dramatically (e.g., if the test requires counting the stimuli, or if the subject unexpectedly hears his or her name; Straube, 1983). Even an increase in stimulus intensity leads to a reduction in the number of nonresponders (Bernstein, 1970; Bernstein et al., 1981), that is, with an increase in stimulus intensity from 60 to 90 dB, the proportion of nonresponders falls from 50 to 25% of the chronic schizophrenics tested. At the same time, the habituation of the EDOR is increasingly delayed in the responders (Bernstein et al., 1980). However, it should also be noted that a similar shift of responsiveness occurs in the healthy population (Siddle et al., 1979; Turpin and Siddle, 1979). Stimulus intensities of 90 dB and higher give rise to what the researchers in this field call the defensive or startle response. In contrast to the OR, the startle response does not habituate or habituates much more slowly.

From these results we can conclude that the threshold of electrodermal response is raised in a subgroup of schizophrenics, but that this raised threshold can be overcome with more salient, significant, or intense stimuli. This fact, in turn, seems to indicate that a defect in the mechanism involves a relative functional shift in the excitability of the ANS.

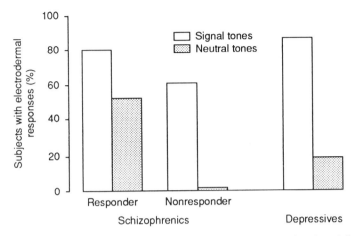

**Figure 5.3** Percentage of subjects showing an EDOR to signal tones as a function of diagnosis (schizophrenia, depression) and EDOR response to neutral stimuli (schizophrenic subjects) (after Gruzelier and Venables, 1973).

## B. Response to Increased Demands and Emotion

Of the many controversial fields of schizophrenia research, this particular area of endeavor has provided one of the most heterogeneous series of results. The heterogeneity reflects not only the range of schizophrenic groups studied, but also the methods used by the different investigators for presenting stimuli and recording responses. We attempt here the difficult task of reviewing the literature, selecting themes from it, and constructing hypotheses that may be useful for future investigations.

## C. Early Studies and Remarks on Methodology

At first, the older literature, well-reviewed by Lang and Buss (1965), presents a simple story. According to a range of measures of ANS function, schizophrenics, or at least some schizophrenics, hardly react to external stimuli, even if the stimuli are painful or have an emotional connotation.

Similar, but even earlier, reports support this conclusion but were of an anecdotal nature and were not based on systematic investigations. For example, Bumke and Kehrer (1910, p. 945) found that "changes of the pulse rate and breathing frequency following sensory stimulation (especially cold and painful stimuli) are absent on the catatonic state." Interesting case studies were reported by Peterson (Columbia University) and Bleuler's assistant Jung from their work at the psychiatric clinic in Zurich (Peterson and Jung, 1907).

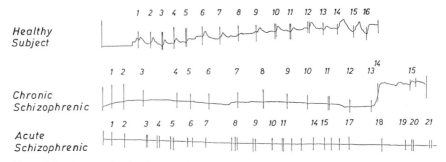

**Figure 5.4** An example of early "psychogalvanic" (electrodermal) measures with an acute schizophrenic, a chronic schizophrenic, and a healthy subject. Reduced responsiveness is shown in both schizophrenic subjects (after Peterson and Jung, 1907).

These early investigators believed schizophrenia to reflect a deep emotional disturbance, only the form of the disturbance appeared to vary considerably [e.g., "emotional atrophy" (Kraepelin, 1913); "lack of emotional coordination," "ataxia between emotion and meaning" (Stransky, 1904)]. Elements of emotional excitation might be present, but in all forms the responses were inappropriate to the situation. These views, the heterogeneity of the nature of schizophrenic reactions and, above all, the discrepancy between the response requirements and the actual reactions to a stimulus, are reflected in the "psychogalvanic" curves of Peterson and Jung (1907) (e.g., one of these is reproduced in Figure 5.4). The chronic patient scarcely responded to a series of innocuous stimuli (words), but when told that the next stimulus would be a pin prick (No. 13 and 14, Figure 5.4), the patient responded strongly to the stimulus. Even this response was absent in the acute catatonic patient whose electrodermal recordings are shown in the lower curve. However, paranoid hallucinatory patients were observed to show increased reactions to emotional words (e.g., love) in a word-association test (not in Figure 5.4).

These earliest observations demonstrate well the breadth of individually inappropriate and interindividually heterogeneous types of schizophrenic responses. Response deficiency predominates, as has been confirmed statistically in later group studies (Hoskins, 1946; Lang and Buss, 1965). Indeed, early Russian work reported diminished autonomic reactivity, even to painful stimuli (for review, see Lynn, 1963). Only when the authors differentiated subgroups did they find that, far from reduced responsiveness, some schizophrenics show exaggerated reactions on some measures.

Clearly, these early studies show that hyporesponsiveness in demanding situations was characteristic of some schizophrenics before the era of psychopharmacotherapy, but they also show that no single type of response is to be expected from schizophrenics in stressful situations.

## D. Recent Studies on Increased Mental Stress and Stimulus Intensity

A team at the University Psychiatric Clinic in Munich made a thorough study of biochemical and ANS variables in 12 untreated acute schizophrenics (Albus *et al.*, 1982). Their protocol included two rest phases, a cold pressure test (foot in iced water), noise, "active relaxation," and an arithmetic test (repeated subtraction of 7 from 500). They recorded the EEG, EMG, EDOR, finger pulse volume and temperature, heart and pulse rates, respiratory volume, and an electrogastrogram. Blood samples were taken six times during the study from an implanted catheter for determination of plasma levels of cortisol and noradrenaline.

Perhaps it is not surprising that these subjects were already stressed before the experiment started. First, the cortisol level, an indicator of stress (Frankenhaeuser, 1975), was increased even during the initial rest phase. Second, increased arousal was registered in the initial rest phase according to tonic measures of electrodermal conductance, finger temperature, EMG frequency, and noradrenaline levels. In the actual stress phase, three of the already increased variables showed only a minor phasic response in comparison with the responses seen in healthy controls. There were no significant differences in the other measures taken. Clearly, if the experimental setting was apparently so stressful, it is questionable whether the relatively small phasic response can be attributed to a lower reactivity in this acute schizophrenic group. Indeed, the initial values indicate that the schizophrenics were, in one sense, more reactive than the healthy controls.

In a study by Straube (1982), electrodermal, cardiovascular, and pupillary responses were measured after presentation of neutral and emotional stimuli and during a cognitive test. He found there to be no overall lowered responsiveness in the acute unmedicated schizophrenic subjects. The only significant finding, in contrast to Albus *et al.* (1982), was of an increased pupillary response in schizophrenics (for a given performance level in both groups) on a digit-span test compared with the healthy controls.

At the National Institutes of Mental Health (NIMH) in Bethesda, Zahn and colleagues investigated changes of heart rate and electrodermal responses to neutral and stressful stimuli (1981a,b; further details in Chapter 13). Their schizophrenic subjects were investigated on admission and also prior to medication. The patients showed a heterogeneous range of responses. But a *post hoc* subdivision of the subjects according to whether they improved after their period of inpatient treatment produced a clearer and more consistent picture. Those with a poor prognosis initially showed a reduced level of autonomic responsiveness in a demanding situation (reaction-time task). In contrast, those who improved later, as well as the healthy controls, showed increased responsiveness that paralleled the increased demands. In contrast to these findings, the two groups could not be separated on the basis of psychopathology.

One could come to the conclusion from the results of Zahn and colleagues that schizophrenic patients whose illness will ultimately follow an unfavorable course show a deficient adaptation to demand. Further studies make this proposal plausible (see Chapter 13 for more details). Chronic, often untreated, schizophrenics show a fairly uniform picture of low basal arousal and reduced responses to simple stimuli, even to unpleasant noises and loud tones (Gray, 1975; Waddington *et al.*, 1978).

Waddington *et al.* (1978) monitored the heart rate telemetrically during an avoidance task. In this task, the subjects had to learn to switch off an unpleasantly loud noise that followed a signal stimulus. The cardiac response to the signal stimulus was significantly lower in the schizophrenic patients than in the healthy controls. Unfortunately, although the set-up for this experiment was not as complicated as in some of the tests described previously, one still cannot exclude a confounding bias in the selection of subjects as a result of their experimental procedure. Only 14 of 38 chronic patients were able to complete the experiment. Was a subgroup of highly reactive chronic patients excluded as a result of the stressful procedure?

A particularly interesting experimental design was used in the doctoral dissertation of A. L. Gray, supervised by cardiophysiologist Paul Obrist at the University of Waterloo, Canada. In addition to a healthy control group, he used a group of prisoners to control for the institutional experience of the chronically ill experimental subjects. In the end, there appeared to be no difference between the prisoners and the healthy control group so these results were combined. The neuroleptic treatment of the schizophrenic group was replaced with a placebo 3 weeks before the test. Gray recorded heart rate and electrodermal responses during a reaction-time test in which tones of low intensity (70 dB) and very high intensity (110 dB) were presented in a counterbalanced sequence. The subjects were additionally instructed to either simply listen to the tones in one condition or make a motor response to them in the other condition (for four conditions in all).

Paradoxically, Gray found that the schizophrenics showed a relative reduction of ANS activity arousal level in the part of the experiment in which the high intensity tones were played independent of instructions [i.e., whether a response was demanded or not (Figure 5.5)]. (Since the ANS activity levels at the start of the experiment were the same in both groups, this was not due to different basal levels of arousal.)

As can be seen in Figure 5.5, the heart rate in response to the loud tones was similar in both groups, but much higher rates in response to the low intensity tones were shown in the schizophrenics than in the controls (Figure 5.5).

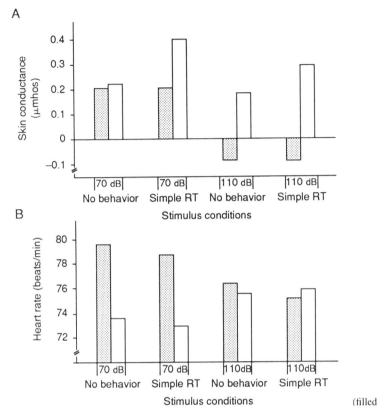

**Figure 5.5** (A) Average skin conductance and (B) heart rate response of schizophrenic (filled bars) and healthy (open bars) subjects to two tone intensities in two behavioral conditions (no behavior or simple button-press response required). Response differences to baseline (after Gray, 1975).

A similar paradox was found in the electrodermal recordings of the anticipatory tonic level of conductance (Figure 5.5). This term refers to the difference between pre- and postsignal conductance levels. Interestingly, there was a co-variance between the reduction of the tonic level of conductance in the intense stimulus condition and improved performance in the reaction-time task.

Finally, Gray also measured the patients' heart rate at rest during their stay on the ward. Since the heart rate levels were lower in the laboratory compared with those measured on the ward, the "clinical" result seems to support the assumption derived from the experimental results that stressful stimulation leads to a paradoxical reduction in ANS arousal level in the chronic schizophrenics tested.

## E. Information Processing: Signal and Non-signal Stimuli

Autonomic responses to signal, nonsignal, and irrelevant distracting stimuli have been studied in chronic schizophrenics (under neuroleptic treatment) by Öhman *et al.* (1986) in Sweden. Their main finding is that, in their patients, independent of the level of task performance, heart rate and electrodermal measures did not "differentiate" between signal, nonsignal, and distracting stimuli. This confirms a report from Frith *et al.* (1981) in the United Kingdom, who only reported on electrodermal responses. Although the schizophrenics certainly showed a greater response to the task-relevant stimuli, the difference between relevant and irrelevant stimuli was significantly less than that shown by the controls. (Here the control group included healthy and neurotic patients.) Zahn *et al.* (1987) in the United States also found reduced heart rate and electrodermal responses in schizophrenics, compared with healthy controls, when performing a reaction-time task. This pattern of response was shared by a group of autistic patients.

These results appear to complement those already discussed (Chapter 4) and point to a parallel between autonomic responses accompanying relevant and irrelevant stimuli and the difficulty that schizophrenics have in stimulus discrimination tasks. However, we should note that schizophrenics show lower differential autonomic responses even when they make a correct discriminatory response (cf. Zahn, 1988). Similar results have been obtained in evoked potential studies of the P 300 (see Chapter 6).

## F. Emotional Stimuli

When observing schizophrenics, it cannot escape notice that many scarcely respond to emotional stimuli and rarely express their feelings. On the other hand there are others, often acute patients, who are extremely sensitive and often become emotional at the slightest cause. It is noticeable that schizophrenics, more than other groups, have difficulty interpreting facial expressions and "body language" (Berndl *et al.,* 1986a,b; Mandal and Raj, 1987). Schizophrenics show marked impairments on tasks that use emotional stimuli, whether they be relevant or irrelevant distracting stimuli (Chapters 2 and 3).

This range of schizophrenic response from overreaction to lack of reaction is also reflected in autonomic measures. In the United States, Payne and Shean (1975) recorded smaller electrodermal and cardiovascular responses in schizophrenics being shown murder scenes on film than in healthy controls. Rist and R. Cohen (1979) from Constance found that although schizophrenics responded in the same way as controls, with a heart-rate change, to words with a positive connotation, they showed a selectively reduced response to words with a negative social connotation. This finding of a differential response seems to be relatively specific, because the German group found that their psychiatric control group responded in the same way as the healthy subjects. Strength is added to these results by their finding that a co-variance exists between the absence of a response to negative stimuli and the symptom of "flat affect." The chronic schizophrenics in both studies were receiving treatment with neuroleptics. Whereas it might be supposed that treatment might reduce reactivity in general, it seems unlikely that neuroleptics would cause a differential response to negative and positive stimuli.

Tarrier *et al.* (1979) and Sturgeon *et al.* (1981) report diametrically opposed results. They describe increased spontaneous electrodermal fluctuations in young schizophrenics in the presence of an emotionally involved or critical relative (cf. Chapter 11). Valone *et al.* (1984) also found increased electrodermal conductance in behaviorally disturbed youngsters who were being monitored for the putative development of schizophrenia in the UCLA project we shall describe in Chapters 11 and 12. Some of these youngsters eventually developed schizophrenia or a schizotypal personality. However, because the group was small it should not be concluded that there is necessarily a connection between increased electrodermal arousal and the later diagnosis.

The heterogeneity of emotional reactions found in schizophrenics is also illustrated by the studies of White *et al.* (1987) in the United States and Schlenker (1988) in Germany. White *et al.* studied chronic schizophrenics who were EDOR nonresponders in an interaction session with the experimenter. In this situation, the schizophrenics became responders in the same way as the healthy controls. Schlenker studied acutely ill EDOR responders and nonresponders in the presence of a relative. She found no change in either group, whether or not the relative was highly emotional or critical.

Do the negative results (for example, of Schlenker) reflect a heterogeneity of schizophrenic response reflecting diverse symptomatology or a heterogeneity of experimental methodology? It is difficult to assess, in most of these studies, precisely what constituted the emotional stress and how it was manipulated. For example, neither Sturgeon *et al.* nor Tarrier *et al.* described what interactions actually took place. In order to be more confident in generalizing about the effects of emotional stress from the results of experimental studies, it will be necessary to conduct further studies using (and reporting) a more standard protocol with clearly defined subgroups (e.g., acute versus chronic; negative versus positive symptoms; with and without neuroleptic treatment).

## G. Effects of Neuroleptic Treatment

Some of the studies discussed in the previous sections were performed on untreated patients or patients who had not received neuroleptic treatment for 3–4 weeks. Thus, one simple conclusion is possible: the absence of, or the paradoxical drop in, responsiveness, as recorded with autonomic measures, cannot always be attributed to medication (cf. older studies, Chapter 6).

As already indicated, neuroleptic treatment does not appear to systematically affect autonomic responses to neutral (orienting) stimuli (Bernstein, 1967, 1970; Pugh, 1968; Tecce and Cole, 1972; Spohn et al., 1977; Gruzelier and Hammond, 1978; Spohn and Strauss, 1989; Straube and Öhman, 1990). It is possible, however, that neuroleptics cause small changes of heart rate as reported for the rest period by Spohn et al. (1977), but not confirmed by Straube and Heimann (1985). One exception for this was found by Green and Nuechterlein (1988) and Green et al. (1989); they obtained a correlation between the anticholinergic properties of some neuroleptics and reduced electrodermal responding. This result has important implications, since the synapse of the sweat gland is cholinergic. Treatment with anticholinergic agents should be taken into account in future studies.

It is more likely that neuroleptics have an effect on autonomic responsiveness in demanding situations. A neuroleptic-induced drop in ANS activity—as indicated by the responses to signal, stressful, and emotional stimuli—has been observed (Goldstein et al., 1966; Pugh, 1968; Spohn et al., 1977; Gruzelier and Hammond, 1978). This presumably "protective" type of treatment effect is to be expected, considering the usefulness of neuroleptics in reducing the risk of relapse in patients released into the care of highly emotional relatives (Chapter 11). However, such potential neuroleptic effects on autonomic responsiveness do not seem to have been accorded in specific, thorough, and systematic study.

## IV. Suggested Readings

Bernstein (1987) and Bernstein et al. (1982) give comprehensive surveys of the orienting response research with schizophrenics. The latter also contains a direct comparison of orienting response research from different laboratories in different countries. Dawson and Nuechterlein (1984) and Zahn (1986, 1988) reviewed the entire field.

## V. Summary Statements and Interpretations

### A. Responses to Nondemanding Stimuli (Orienting)

Electrodermal nonresponse to nondemanding stimuli is characteristic of a subgroup of schizophrenic patients. They show a considerable number of negative symptoms and thought disorder. The prevalence of nonresponse is higher in chronic than in acute populations. The electrodermal nonresponse is also an indicator of the reduction of other ANS parameters in schizophrenia.

Electrodermal nonresponse also occurs in patients with affective and other disorders. One report claims that nonresponse in affective patients, in contrast to schizophrenics, is limited to the electrodermal response component (i.e., schizophrenics also showed cardiovascular nonresponse).

Electrodermal nonresponse is rare in healthy persons.

Electrodermal nonresponse is clearly not specific, but a combination of reduced ANS response with other parameters may indicate a somewhat more specific pattern. The latter result requires confirmation.

One interpretation of the meaning of nonresponse is that it reflects a raised threshold for responding to external stimuli. This interpretation is supported by the fact that the response reappears if the stimuli gain salience or significance. There are also some, albeit inconsistent, findings that attention to external stimuli in cognitive tasks is reduced in nonresponders. (This could indicate that nonresponse may have a protective function, at least in some schizophrenics.)

No unequivocal relationship is seen between nonresponse and cerebral atrophy (CT studies; cf. Chapter 8). Differences in family history do not seem to explain electrodermal nonresponse. No systematic effect of neuroleptics is seen on the OR.

An interpretation in terms of a nonspecific protective response, more common in chronic patients with negative symptoms, seems to be supported by the absence of nonresponse in high risk children (cf. Chapter 12). It can, however, be observed in (older) schizotypal probands, in whom it may also be regarded as a coping response.

## B. ANS Response to Demanding or Stressful Stimuli

Autonomic responses to demanding or stressful stimuli are exaggerated in some schizophrenic patients but are reduced in most of the schizophrenic patients studied. Some of these patients even show a paradoxical reduction of electrodermal or cardiovascular response to aversive stimuli, but a relatively elevated response to mild nonstressful stimuli. This type of response may be more specific to schizophrenia, but this variable was not controlled in all studies.

Neuroleptic treatment leads to a reduction of the reactivity to demanding stimuli (contrast orienting; see previous section). However, reduced responsiveness can also be observed in untreated patients.

Differences between reports may reflect the testing of different subgroups, but information on symptom correlations is less frequent than for the OR. One prospective study reported that reduced response to demanding stimuli in untreated patients indicates poor prognosis, but several reports claim that high responses to nondemanding stimuli also indicate poor short-term prognosis. A maladapted physiological response (indicative of poor prognosis) seems to consist of a relatively high reaction to nondemanding and a relatively low one to demanding stimuli. However, the relationship does not hold for long-term prognosis (cf. Chapter 13). ANS parameters and stimulus conditions differ widely among studies. We suspect that some of the reductions reported may again reflect attempts to cope (e.g., reduced responses to aversive film scenes). An alternative interpretation may be that a maladapted ANS responsiveness (too low in demanding situations and too high in nondemanding situations) may be another aspect of disturbed information processing (like the reduction of the P 300 evoked potential amplitude in response to meaningful stimuli). Firm conclusions require more information, particularly from tasks that involve ANS and information processing measures in the same experiment.

Neuroleptic-induced reductions of ANS reactivity to demanding or stressful stimuli, but not to neutral stimuli, may be indicative of their protective effects (i.e., lower relapse rates in medicated remitted patients living with a "high-expressed-emotion" relative; Chapter 11).

# References

Albus, M., Ackenheil, M., Engel, R. R., and Müller, F. (1982). Situational reactivity of autonomic functions in schizophrenic patients. *Psychiatry Research*, 6, 361–370.

Alm, T., Lindström, L. H., Öst, L. G., and Öhman, A. (1984). Electrodermal nonresponding in schizophrenia: Relationships to attentional, clinical, biochemical, computed tomographical and genetic factors. *International Journal of Psychophysiology*, 1, 195–208.

Ax, A. F., and Bamford, J. L. (1970). The GSR recovery limb in chronic schizophrenia. *Psychophysiology*, 7, 145–147.

Barry, R. J. (1977). Failure to find evidence of the unitary OR concept with indifferent low-intensity auditory stimuli. *Physiological Psychology*, 5, 89–96.

Bartfai, A., Levander, S., Edman, G., Schalling, D., and Sedvall, G. (1983). Skin conductance responses in unmedicated recently admitted schizophrenic patients. *Psychophysiology*, 20, 180–187.

Bartfai, A., Levander, S. E., Nybäck, H., and Schalling, D. (1987). Skin conductance nonresponding and nonhabituation in schizophrenic patients. *Acta Psychiatrica Scandinavica*, 75, 321–329.

Berndl, K., Grusser, O. J., Martin, M., and Remschmidt, H. (1986a). Comparative studies on recognition of faces, mimic and gestures in adolescent and middle-aged schizophrenic patients. *European Archives of Psychiatry and Neurological Sciences*, 236, 123–130.

Berndl, K., von Cranach, N., and Grusser, O. J. (1986b). Impairment of perception and recognition of faces, mimic expression and gestures in schizophrenic patients. *European Archives of Psychiatry and Neurological Sciences*, 235, 282–291.

Bernstein, A. S. (1964). The galvanic skin response orienting reflex among chronic schizophrenics. *Psychonomic Science*, 1, 391–392.

Bernstein, A. S. (1967). The orienting reflex as a research tool in the study of psychotic populations. In I. Ruttkay-Nedecky, V. Ciganek, V. Zikmund, and E. Kellerova (Eds.), *Mechanisms of the orienting reflex in man*. Bratislava: Slovak Academy of Science.

Bernstein, A. S. (1970). Phasic electrodermal orienting response in chronic schizophrenics. II. Response to auditory signals of varying intensity. *Journal of Abnormal Psychology*, 75, 146–156.

Bernstein, A. S. (1987). Orienting response research in schizophrenia: Where we have come and where we might go? *Schizophrenia Bulletin*, 13, 623–640.

Bernstein, A. S., Frith, C. D., Gruzelier, J. H., Patterson, T., Straube, E. R., Venables, P. H., and Zahn, T. P. (1982). An analysis of the skin conductance orienting response in samples of American, British, and German schizophrenics. *Biological Psychology*, 14, 155–211.

Bernstein, A. S., Riedel, J. A., Graae, F., Seidman, D., Steele, H., Connolly, J., and Lubowsky, J. (1988). Schizophrenia is associated with altered orienting activity; Depression with electrodermal (cholinergic?) deficit and normal orienting response. *Journal of Abnormal Psychology*, 97, 3–12.

Bernstein, A. S., Schneider, S. J., Juni, S., Pope, A. T., and Starkey, P. W. (1980). The effect of stimulus significance on the electrodermal response in chronic schizophrenia. *Journal of Abnormal Psychology*, 89, 93–97.

Bernstein, A. S., Taylor, K. W., Starkey, P., Juni, S., Lubowsky, J., and Paley, H. (1981). Bilateral skin conductance, finger pulse volume and EEG orienting response to tones of differing intensities in chronic schizophrenics and controls. *Journal of Nervous and Mental Disease*, 169, 513–528.

Bleuler, E. (1911). *Dementia praecox oder die Gruppe der Schizophrenien*. Leipzig: Deuticke.

Bleuler, E., and Bleuler, M. (1966). *Lehrbuch der Psychiatrie*. Berlin: Springer.

Bruno, R., Mayers, S., and Glassman, A. (1983). A correlational study of cardiovascular autonomic functioning and unipolar depression. *Biological Psychiatry*, 18, 227–235.

Bumke, O., and Kehrer, F. (1910). Plethysmographische Untersuchungen an Geisteskranken. *Archiv für Psychiatrie*, 47, 945–946.

Cooklin, R., Sturgeon, D., and Leff, J. (1983). The relationship between auditory hallucinations and spontaneous fluctuations of skin conductance in schizophrenia. *British Journal of Psychiatry*, 142, 47–52.

Dawson, M. E., and Nuechterlein, K. H. (1984). Psychophysiological dysfunction in the developmental course of schizophrenic disorders. *Schizophrenia Bulletin*, 10, 204–232.

Fahrenberg, J. (1987). Theory in psychophysiology: The multi-component analysis of psychophysiological reactivity. *Journal of Psychophysiology*, 1, 9–11.

Frankenhaeuser, M. (1975). Experimental approaches to the study of catecholamines and emotion. In L. Levi (Ed.), *Emotions—Their parameters and measurement*. New York: Raven Press.

Frith, C. D., Stevens, M., Johnstone, E. C., and Crow, T. J. (1988). Acute schizophrenic patients fail to modulate their level of attention. *Journal of Psychophysiology*, 2, 195–200.

Frith, C. D., Stevens, M., Johnstone, E. C., and Crow, T. J. (1979). Skin conductance responsivity during acute episodes of schizophrenia as a predictor of symptomatic improvement. *Psychological Medicine*, 9, 101–106.

Frith, C. D., Stevens, M., Johnstone, E. C., and Crow, T. J. (1982). Skin conductance habituation during acute episodes of schizophrenia: Qualitative differences from anxious and depressed patients. *Psychological Medicine*, 12, 575–583.

Giedke, H., Heimann, H., and Straube, E. (1982). Vergleichende Ergebnisse psychophysiologischer Untersuchungen bei Schizophrenien und Depressionen. In G. Huber (Ed.), *Endogene Psychosen: Diagnostik, Basissymptome, und biologische Parameter*. Stuttgart: Schattauer.

Goldstein, M., Acker, C., Crockett, J., and Riddle, J. (1966). Psychophysiological reactions to films by chronic schizophrenics. *Journal of Abnormal Psychology*, 71, 335–344.

Gray, A. L. (1975). Autonomic correlates of chronic schizophrenia: A reaction time paradigm. *Journal of Abnormal Psychology*, 84, 189–196.

Green, M., and Nuechterlein, K. H. (1988). Neuroleptic effects on electrodermal responsivity to soft tones and loud noise in schizophrenia. *Psychiatry Research*, 24, 79–86.

Green, M., Nuechterlein, K. H., and Satz, P. (1989). The relationship of symptomatology and medication to electrodermal activity in schizophrenia. *Psychophysiology*, 26, 148–157.

Gruzelier, J. H. (1976). Clinical attributes of schizophrenic skin conductance responders and non-responders. *Psychological Medicine*, 6, 245–248.

Gruzelier, J. H., Eves, F., Connolly, J., and Hirsch, S. (1981). Orienting, habituation, sensitization, and dishabituation in the electrodermal system of consecutive, drug free admissions for schizophrenia. *Biological Psychology*, 12, 187–209.

Gruzelier, J. H., and Hammond, N. (1978). The effect of chlorpromazine upon psychophysiological, endocrine, and information processing measures in schizophrenia. *Journal of Psychiatric Research*, 14, 167–182.

Gruzelier, J. H., and Venables, P. H. (1972). Skin conductance orienting activity in a heterogeneous sample of schizophrenics. *Journal of Nervous and Mental Disease*, 155, 277–287.

Gruzelier, J. H., and Venables, P. H. (1973). Skin conductance responses to tones with and without attentional significance in schizophrenic and nonschizophrenic psychiatric patients. *Neuropsychologia*, 11, 221–230.

Gruzelier, J. H., and Venables, P. H. (1974). Two-flash threshold, sensitivity, and beta in normal subjects and schizophrenics. *Quarterly Journal of Experimental Psychology*, 26, 594–604.

Gruzelier, J. H., and Venables, P. H. (1975). Evidence of high and low arousal in schizophrenia. *Psychophysiology*, 12, 66–73.

Hoskins, R. G. (1946). *The biology of schizophrenia*. New York: Norton.

Iacono, W. G. (1982). Bilateral electrodermal habituation–dishabituation and resting EEG in remitted schizophrenics. *Journal of Nervous and Mental Disease*, 170, 91–101.

Kraepelin, E. (1913). *Psychiatry*, Vol. 3, 8th ed. Translated as *Dementia praecox and paraphrenia*, 1919. Edinburgh: Livingstone.

Lang, P. J., and Buss, A. H. (1965). Psychological deficit in schizophrenia. II. Interference and activation. *Journal of Abnormal Psychology*, 70, 77–106.

Lynn, R. (1963). Russian theory and research on schizophrenia. *Psychological Bulletin*, 60, 486–498.

Mandal, P. A., and Raj, A. (1987). Responses to facial emotion and psychopathology. *Psychiatry Research*, 20, 317–323.

Öhman, A. (1981). Electrodermal activity and vulnerability to schizophrenia: A review. *Biological Psychology*, 12, 87–145.

Öhman, A., Nordby, H., and D'Elia, G. (1986). Orienting and schizophrenia: Stimulus significance, attention, and distraction in a signaled reaction time task. *Journal of Abnormal Psychology*, 95, 326–334.

Öhman, A., Nordby, H., and D'Elia, G. (1989). Orienting in schizophrenia: Habituation to auditory stimuli of constant and varying intensity in patients high and low in skin conductance responsivity. *Psychophysiology*, 26, 48–61.

Overall, J., and Gorham, D. (1962). The Brief Psychiatric Rating Scale. *Psychological Reports*, 10, 799–812.

Patterson, T. (1976). Skin conductance responding/nonresponding and pupillometrics in chronic schizophrenia. *Journal of Nervous and Mental Disease*, 163, 200–209.

Patterson, T., and Venables, P. H. (1978). Bilateral skin conductance and skin potential in schizophrenics and normal subjects: The identification of the fast habituator group of schizophrenics. *Psychophysiology*, 15, 556–560.

Patterson, T., and Venables, P. H. (1980). Auditory vigilance: Normals compared to chronic schizophrenic subgroups defined by skin conductance variables. *Psychiatry Research*, 2, 107–112.

Payne, P., and Shean, G. (1975). Autonomic responses of paranoid, nonparanoid, schizophrenic, and normal subjects to affective visual stimulation. *Journal of Nervous and Mental Disease*, 161, 123–129.

Peterson, F., and Jung, C. G. (1907). Psycho-physical investigations with the galvanometer and pneumograph in normal and insane individuals. *Brain*, 30, 11–218.

Pugh, L. (1968). Response time and electrodermal measures in chronic schizophrenia: The effect of chlorpromazine. *Journal of Nervous and Mental Disease*, 146, 62–70.

Raine, A., and Venables, P. H. (1984). Electrodermal nonresponding, antisocial behavior, and schizoid tendencies in adolescents. *Psychophysiology*, 21, 424–433.

Rippon, G. (1979). Bilateral differences in skin conductance level in schizophrenic patients. In J. Gruzelier and P. Flor-Henry (Eds.), *Hemisphere asymmetries of function in psychopathology*. New York: Elsevier/N. Holland Biomedical Press.

Rist, F., and Cohen, R. (1979). Paradoxical response reduction and flattening of affect in schizophrenia. *SPR Abstracts*, 201.

Rubens, R. L., and Lapidus, L. B. (1978). Schizophrenic patterns of arousal and stimulus barrier functioning. *Journal of Abnormal Psychology*, 87, 199–211.

Schlenker, R. (1988). Unpublished manuscript. Tübingen.

Siddle, D. A. T., and Spinks, J. A. (1979). Orienting response and information-processing: Some theoretical and empirical problems. In H. D. Kimmel, E. H. van Olst, and J. F. Orlebeke (Eds.), *The orienting reflex in humans*. Hillsdale, New Jersey: Erlbaum.

Simons, R. F., Losito, B. D., Rose, S. C., and MacMillan, F. W. (1983). Electrodermal nonresponding among college undergraduates: Temporal stability, situational specificity, and relationship to heart rate change. *Psychophysiology*, 20, 498–506.

Sokolov, E. N. (1963). Higher nervous functions: The orienting reflex. *Annual Review of Physiology*, 25, 545–580.

Sommer, W. (1982). *Event-related potentials in electrodermal responders and nonresponders*. University of Konstanz: Ph.D. Thesis.

Sommer, W. (1985). Selective attention differentially affects brainstem auditory evoked potentials of electrodermal responders and nonresponders. *Psychiatry Research*, 16, 227–232.

Spohn, H. E., Lacoursiere, R. B., Thompson, K., and Coyne, L. (1977). Phenothiazine effects on psychological and psychophysiological dysfunction in chronic schizophrenia. *Archives of General Psychiatry*, 34, 633–644.

Spohn, H. E., and Strauss, M. E. (1989). Relation of neuroleptic and anticholinergic medication to cognitive functions in schizophrenia. *Journal of Abnormal Psychology*, 98, 367–380.

Stransky, E. (1904). How to understand certain symptoms of dementia praecox. Translated in J. C. Cutting and M. Shepherd (Eds.), *Schizophrenia: The origin and development of its study in Europe*, 1986. Cambridge: Cambridge University Press.

Straube, E. (1979). On the meaning of electrodermal nonresponding in schizophrenia. *Journal of Nervous and Mental Disease*, 167, 601–611.

Straube, E. R. (1980). Reduced reactivity and psychopathology—Examples from research on schizophrenia. In M. Koukkou, D. Lehmann, and J. Angst (Eds.), *Functional states of the brain: Their determinants*. Amsterdam: Elsevier.

Straube, E. R. (1982). Pupillometric, cardiac, and electrodermal reactivity of schizophrenic patients under different stimulus conditions. Meeting of the Society for Psychophysiological Research Abstracts. *Psychophysiology*, 19, 589.

Straube, E. R. (1983). *Psychophysiologische Untersuchung Schizophrener. Reaktivität des autonomen Nervensystems unter besonderer Berücksichtigung der elektrodermalen Orientierungsreaktion*. Tübingen: Habilitationsschrift.

Straube, E. R., and Heimann, H. (1985). Kompensatorische Mechanismen—Spezifisch oder unspezifisch? In G. Huber (Ed.), *Basisstadien endogener Psychosen und das Borderline-Problem*. Stuttgart: Schattauer.

Straube, E. R., and Öhman, A. (1990). Functional role of the different autonomic nervous system activity patterns found in schizophrenia. In E. R. Straube and K. Hahlweg (Eds.), *Schizophrenia: Concepts, vulnerability, and intervention*, pp. 135–157. Berlin: Springer.

Straube, E. R., Wagner, W., Förster, K., and Heimann, H. (1989). Findings significant with respect to short- and medium-term outcome in schizophrenia—A preliminary report. *Progress in Neuropsychopharmacology and Biological Psychiatry*, 12, 185–197.

Sturgeon, D., Kuipers, L., Berkowitz, R., Turpin, G., and Leff, J. (1981). Psychophysiological responses of schizophrenic patients to high and low expressed emotion relatives. *British Journal of Psychiatry*, 138, 40–45.

Tarrier, N., Vaughn, C., Lader, M. H., and Leff, J. P. (1979). Bodily reactions to people and events in schizophrenics. *Archives of General Psychiatry*, 36, 311–315.

Tecce, J. J., and Cole, J. C. (1972). Psychophysiologic responses of schizophrenia to drugs. *Psychopharmacologia*, 24, 159–200.

Thomas, P. E., and Korr, I. M. (1957). Relationship between sweat gland activity and electrical resistance of the skin. *Journal of Applied Physiology*, 10, 505–510.

Toone, B. K., Cooke, E., and Lader, M. H. (1981). Electrodermal activity in the affective disorders and schizophrenia. *Psychological Medicine*, 11, 495–508.

Turpin, G., and Siddle, D. A. T. Effects of stimulus intensity on electrodermal activity. *Psychophysiology*, 16, 582–591.

Valone, K., Goldstein, M. J., and Norton, J. P. (1984). Parental expressed emotion and psychophysiological reactivity in an adolescent sample at risk for schizophrenia spectrum disorders. *Journal of Abnormal Psychology*, 93, 448–457.

Venables, P. H. (1966). Psychophysiological aspects of schizophrenia. *British Journal of Medical Psychology*, 39, 289–295.

Venables, P. H. (1973). Input regulation and psychopathology. In U. Hammer, K. Salzinger, and S. Sutton (Eds.), *Psychopathology*. New York: Wiley.

Venables, P. H., and Christie, M. J. (1980). Electrodermal activity. In I. Martin and P. H. Venables (Eds.), *Techniques in Psychophysiology*. New York: Wiley.

Waddington, J. L., Macculloch, M. J., Schalken, M. L., and Sambrooks, J. E. (1978). Absence of cardiac deceleration in a signalled escape paradigm: A psychophysiological deficit in chronic schizophrenia. *Psychological Medicine*, 8, 157–162.

White, C., Farley, J., and Charles, P. (1987). Chronic schizophrenic disorder. I. Psychophysiological responses, laterality and social stress. *British Journal of Psychiatry*, 150, 365–373.

Zahn, T. P. (1976). On the bimodality of the disturbance of electrodermal orienting response in schizophrenic patients. *Journal of Nervous and Mental Disease*, 162, 195–199.

Zahn, T. P. (1986). Psychophysiological approaches to psychopathology. In M. G. H. Coles, E. Donchin, and S. W. Porges (Eds.), *Psychophysiology*, pp. 508–610. New York: Guilford Press.

Zahn, T. P. (1988). Studies of autonomic psychophysiology and attention in schizophrenia. *Schizophrenia Bulletin*, 14, 205–208.

Zahn, T. P., Carpenter, W. T., and McGlashan, T. H. (1981a). Autonomic nervous system activity in acute schizophrenia. I. Method and comparison with normal controls. *Archives of General Psychiatry*, 38, 251–258.

Zahn, T. P., Carpenter, W. T., and McGlashan, T. H. (1981b). Autonomic nervous system activity in acute schizophrenia. II. Relationships to short term prognosis and clinical state. *Archives of General Psychiatry*, 38, 260–266.

Zahn, T. P., Rumsey, J. M., and Van Kammen, D. P. (1987). Autonomic nervous system activity in autistic, schizophrenic, and normal men: Effects of stimulus significance. *Journal of Abnormal Psychology*, 96, 135–144.

# Chapter 6

# Electroencephalogram and Evoked Potentials

## I. Electroencephalogram

### A. General Introduction

In the 1930s, Berger in Jena, Germany, discovered that the changing electrical activity of the brain could be measured through electrodes positioned on the scalp. He called the resulting tracing made by the recording device an electroencephalogram (EEG). Today, the EEG is the most widely used routine electrophysiological diagnostic technique. It is a polygraphical measure of the frequencies and amplitudes of electrical potential shifts recorded between two electrodes on the scalp. The EEG presumably results from a complex summation of excitatory and inhibitory postsynaptic potentials in the brain. Regions generating this electrical activity are presumed to lie in the neocortex, close to the recording electrodes. However, subcortical volume-conducted influences are likely (e.g., from the hippocampus). Pacemaker activity for the various frequency bands of EEG activity may derive from pathways ascending from limbic (e.g., septum), thalamic (e.g., intralaminar), and reticular (e.g., Nucleus gigantocellularis) nuclei.

Different states of brain activity are expressed on the EEG as higher or lower frequencies of potential shifts within a given period of time; higher frequencies are regarded as signs of cerebral activation (cf. Figure 6.1). The exact nature of the neurophysiological mechanism on which the EEG is based, however, has not been fully clarified yet. (For a more detailed discussion, see Creutzfeld, 1971; Lindsley and Wicke, 1974; Rockstroh et al., 1982.) The different frequency bands and respective amplitudes are shown in Figure 6.1. It should be noted that the division of the EEG into four frequency bands is merely a matter of convention; other divisions are possible but seldom used.

| Type | Frequency band | Amplitude (mV) | Idealized examples of EEG traces |
|------|----------------|----------------|----------------------------------|
| delta | 0.5 – 4 | 20 – 200 | 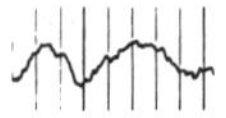 |
| theta | 5 – 7 | 5 – 100 | 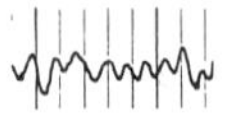 |
| alpha | 8 –13 | 5 – 100 | 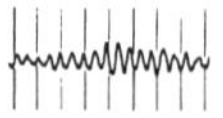 |
| beta | 14 – 30 | 2 – 20 | 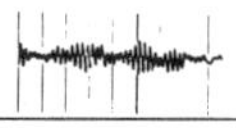 |

**Figure 6.1**  Examples and typical amplitudes for the four main categories of EEG frequencies.

## B. Spontaneous EEG Activity in Schizophrenia

### 1. Early Research

As early as 1937, Berger used this new tool to investigate mentally ill patients. He reported a prevalence of beta waves in schizophrenia. Other researchers, however, reported divergent findings. Several investigators observed the same shifts toward faster frequencies (beta activity) reported by Berger, while others found a predominance of the lower frequency bands (slow alpha or theta activity). Since both faster and slower activity was reported, one possible common denominator could be decreased activity in the middle (alpha) frequency range for all schizophrenics examined in these studies. A further review of the literature suggests different activity shifts in subgroups: a predominant shift toward lower activity in chronic schizophrenics and a predominant shift toward higher activity in acute schizophrenics.

The database for these earlier studies, however, is questionable. In most cases no control groups were set up; basic requirements of experimental design, such as standardization of the examination and sampling procedures, were also lacking. Most of these studies were made during the course of routine medical examinations in the EEG laboratory of the hospital.

A comprehensive review of early EEG research was compiled by Shagass (1976), an American EEG researcher who, with his research team in

Philadelphia, has carried out many EEG and evoked-potential investigations over the last 35 years.

## 2. Recent Research

The team associated with Hirsch in London (Fenton *et al.*, 1980) found spontaneous activity to be faster in acute schizophrenics than in the control groups, a finding that corroborates the earlier findings. (This frequency shift was more pronounced at the temporal sites.) However, faster alpha as well as beta activity is decreased in chronic schizophrenic outpatients and inpatients, that is, the proportion of very slow frequencies, especially delta waves, is higher. The control groups tested included healthy and neurotic subjects. This finding confirms some of the results reported by Lifshitz and Gradijan (1972) and Laurian *et al.* (1984). Karson *et al.* (1988) from the National Institutes of Mental Health (NIMH) in Bethesda, Maryland, found less alpha activity to be associated with an enlargement of the lateral ventricles (CT scans) in medication-free chronic inpatients.

An increase in slow-activity delta waves was found to be especially pronounced in frontal leads from the EEG in most medication-free chronic schizophrenics (e.g., Karson *et al.*, 1987; Morisha *et al.*, 1983; both from NIMH: Mukundan, 1986, from India) but was not different from that of healthy controls in acute schizophrenics (Williamson and Mamelak, 1987, from Canada). This finding is also of interest in light of the reduced blood flow findings discussed in Chapter 8.

Some of the chronic schizophrenics in the study performed by Fenton *et al.* (1980) were tested without neuroleptics; no difference was found between the EEG results of patients on medication and those not, but based on two investigations by his research team, Itil (1977) reported an increase in slow activity caused by neuroleptics. Lifshitz *et al.* (1987) from the United States observed an increase in alpha activity after neuroleptic medication in chronic schizophrenics. Tarrier *et al.* (1978) working in the United Kingdom found no differences between chronic schizophrenics with and without medication. However, it could be argued that the long-acting effects of neuroleptics may cause a shift toward decreased activity even after their withdrawal in so-called drug-free chronic patients. This argument is refuted since some of the investigations already mentioned showed a tendency for slow activity in chronic schizophrenics before the neuroleptic era. The effect of neuroleptics has been investigated less systematically in acute schizophrenics. Why, however, should neuroleptics lead to faster activity in this group, when they usually reduce it?

In the already mentioned study, Tarrier *et al.* (1978) examined the resting EEGs of schizophrenic outpatients from the London Psychiatric Institute, who were in remission and living with their families, and compared them with those of long-term inpatients at the same institution and with those of a healthy control group. Drugs were discontinued for 4 weeks. In partial confirmation of the previously reported results, relatively slower (theta) activity was seen in the resting EEGs of long-term inpatients than in those of the normal control group. Moreover, the amount of fast (beta) activity was also higher in the inpatient group. No difference in EEG activity, however, was found between the outpatients and the healthy control group. These results indicate that global changes of the resting EEG in the inpatient group do not represent a biological marker for schizophrenia, since outpatients in remission show no EEG changes. These EEG findings are obviously not specific for schizophrenia, since they also appear in chronic alcoholics (Coger *et al.*, 1979) and manics (Shagass *et al.*, 1984). Giannitrapani (1988) from the United States stated that the fast beta activity (29 Hz) that was found by some researchers in the past, especially in young schizophrenics, is also not pathognomonic for this group.

The team at the Institute of Psychiatry in London was unable to establish any effect of emotional stress on the EEG tracing; Tarrier *et al.* (1978) examined whether daily contact with a relative with a high expressed emotion (high EE) could lead to long-term change in the resting EEG of the outpatients. No difference was established between outpatients living with a high EE person and those living with a low EE person. By contrast, in the electrodermal recording a significantly higher arousal with respect to spontaneous fluctuations was found in outpatients exposed to an emotionally overreactive relative (see Chapter 5). This discrepancy may be due to procedural differences; the patient had no direct contact with the high EE person during the EEG examination, whereas in the electrodermal study the "key person" was announced to the patient and eventually entered the room while electrodermal activity was being recorded (see Chapter 5).

Since patients from high EE homes are at considerably higher risk for early relapse, the question of the underlying biological mechanisms is important. (For further discussion of this issue, see Chapters 11 and 13).

Topographic EEG findings, particularly lateralized EEG findings, will be discussed in greater detail in Chapter 8.

## C. Stimulus-Related Changes in EEG Frequency Band

Only spontaneous activity of the EEG has been discussed until now. Although systematic shifts in the frequency band can be induced under experimental conditions in healthy subjects, it is questionable whether the same response is demonstrable in all schizophrenics, since, as mentioned in Chapter 5, a considerable proportion of schizophrenics shows extremely reduced ANS activity (e.g., to orienting stimuli).

The EEG equivalent of the ANS orienting response is an alpha rhythm block. As already reported, however, Bernstein *et al.* (1981) observed no covariation between the ANS and EEG components of the orienting response in schizophrenics (i.e., no nonresponse was discernible on the EEG). Koukkou (1980), who was on the staff of the Psychiatric Hospital in Zürich, found less EEG change in acute schizophrenics than in healthy controls after presentation of verbal stimulus material. Furthermore, Colombo *et al.* (1989) in Milan (Italy) found less alpha (block) reduction due to a simple visual task. This group tested 84 undifferentiated and disorganized schizophrenics, some without medication. Since neither research team measured ANS parameters, and their methods of stimulation differed considerably (meaningless sentences instead of pure tones), the results are not comparable with the results from the usual ANS orienting-response research. Koukkou (1980) also observed a normalization of the EEG when the patient reached remission, confirming the report of Tarrier *et al.* (1978).

In schizophrenics, EEG changes apparently do not persist longer than the clinical symptoms. This result contrasts with some evoked-potential measures derived from averaging EEG responses to repeated events (see subsequent text). Should this be corroborated by further experiment, EEG changes must be considered to reflect a state rather than a trait of schizophrenia.

Less order (i.e., more entropy) in the EEG of schizophrenics was reported by a research group associated with Kornhuber in Ulm (Germany) (Diekmann *et al.*, 1985). This finding may be significant with respect to schizophrenic information processing and the higher variability of the evoked potentials in schizophrenics (see subsequent text). Further investigations should determine whether these findings are related.

The possible impact of EEG findings on schizophrenia research can be summarized by stating that the use of EEG in experimental designs is limited by the method used by each research group. Such limitations include the length and number of epochs of EEG activity studied, the poorly defined situation in which spontaneous or resting EEGs are recorded and the lack of precise stimulus–response relationships. A better solution to some of these problems may be achieved by measuring stimulus-evoked potentials (see next section).

# II. Evoked Potentials

## A. General Introduction

In the 1960s, it was noticed that a stimulus "evokes" short-term voltage shifts in the EEG. As a rule, however, these voltage shifts are not much higher than concurrent spontaneous oscillations in the EEG. Early investigators first saw evoked potentials when they superimposed identical EEG sections on the screen of an oscilloscope. This superposition of 15 to 20 stimulus-related EEG sections resulted in a characteristic waveform (see Figure 6.2). This wave occurs because potential shifts evoked by the repeated stimulation have a consistent temporal

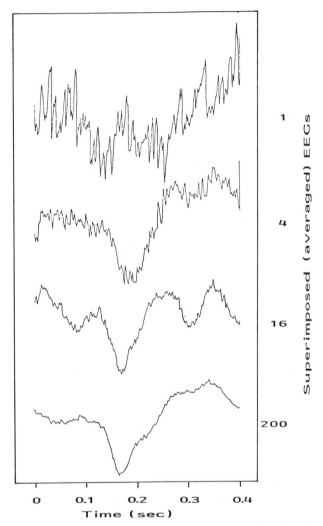

**Figure 6.2** Demonstration of how the superposition (i.e., averaging) of an increasing number of EEG samples recorded 0.4 sec after an event leads to smooth event-related-potential waveform. Examples of averaging 1, 4, 16, and 200 repetitions are shown (0 = stimulus onset). Further details are presented in the text.

relation to the stimulus (i.e., they are "time locked" to the event). The peaks and troughs of the evoked potential, therefore, almost always appear at the same position, whereas concurrent spontaneous oscillation is unrelated to the event (i.e., the spontaneous voltage shifts of the EEG do not add up to a certain waveform). This "superpositioning" is currently done with modern laboratory computers that calculate the average poststimulus waveform on the basis of the sum of repeated identical EEG sections. The baseline is usually obtained by averaging the negative and positive potentials over a given prestimulus period.

The evoked potential is composed of several waves that represent positive and negative voltage shifts (N, negative; P, positive potentials). These waves appear with latencies ranging from 1 to 1000 msec after the stimulus. Not all peaks in Figure 6.3 can be measured in one experiment. The peak that appears depends on the type of stimulation, for example, the positive peak around 300 msec after stimulation ($P_{300}$) is only found with certain cognitive tasks. The small waves that appear up to 10 msec after stimulation are brainstem potentials (roman numerals in Figure 6.3). They reflect the passage of the "stimulus" through different nuclei of the brainstem. Peaks between 10 and approximately 80 msec reflect the transmission of the "stimulus" from brainstem to sensory projection areas of the cortex. Evoked potentials in the association areas (after 80–100 msec or more) vary increasingly in amplitude with the amount of selective attention allocated to the stimulus by the observer (e.g., $N_1$ *amplitude* in Figure 6.3). Peaks after 200 msec, that is, $P_3$ and later components (see Figure 6.3), reflect more complex decision making processes. The different components of the evoked potential, therefore, indicate the temporal course of neuronal events in subcortical and cortical areas of the brain that are evoked by a stimulus (i.e., different steps of data evaluation in human information processing). For this reason, Hillyard and Kutas (1983) referred to the measurement of evoked potentials as "mental chronometry." An explanation of the functional significance of the respective evoked-potential segments is presented at the beginning of each of the sections below. (For further information, consult Hillyard and Kutas, 1983; Hansen and Hillyard, 1988; or Naatanen, 1990.)

By measuring potentials evoked by stimulus events, the researcher attempts to determine which step and which type of data processing is disturbed in schizophrenia.

## B. Prerequisites for Intact Cognitive Processing of Stimulus Information

### 1. Intact Neuronal Transmission in the Brainstem

*a. Short-Latency Brainstem Evoked Potentials* During the first 10 msec after onset of stimulation, short potential shifts of low amplitude appear, due to transmission of the stimulus in neuronal centers of the brainstem. These brainstem evoked potentials (BSEPs) are demonstrated by using fast sequences of simple clicks. The evoked electrophysiological phenomena are detectable by electrodes placed at a central position on the head (electrode positions: Cz).

*b. Schizophrenia* According to investigations by the research team

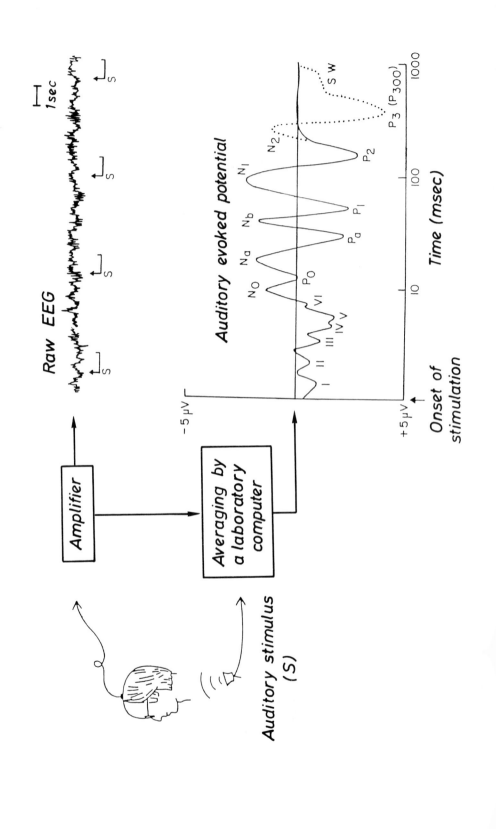

Raw EEG

1sec

Amplifier

Averaging by a laboratory computer

Auditory stimulus (S)

Auditory evoked potential

−5 μV

+5 μV

Onset of stimulation

Time (msec)

10    100    1000

N₀    Nₐ    N_b    N₁    N₂    S w

P₀

I II III IV V VI    Pₐ    P₁    P₂    P₃ (P₃₀₀)

associated with Roth at Palo Alto, California, BSEPs of schizophrenics do not differ from those of healthy controls (Pfefferbaum et al., 1980). This finding was confirmed by Brecher and Begleiter (1985) in New York and by Bolz and Giedke (1982) in Tübingen. In all studies, the controls were healthy subjects; Bolz and Giedke (1982) also examined patients with an affective disorder.

BSEPs are also of interest to the neurologist, since they examine intactness of sensory pathways (i.e., "hardware of the brain"). As suggested by the results reported by Lukas (1980) and Hackley et al. (1987), some of these subcortical processes in healthy subjects may already be influenced by cognitive factors. Lukas observed that, in healthy subjects, allocation of attention to a stimulus influences BSEPs, beginning with wave V (see Figure 6.3). (This wave represents the passage of the stimulus through the inferior colliculus of the brainstem.) Lukas assumed that this effect could be attributed to efferent neuronal pathways from the cortex to the brainstem. In contrast, Picton et al. (1974) and Connolly et al. (1989) observed no alterations in BSEPs during experimental manipulation of the allocation of attention. Therefore, the contexts in which central effects on (at least) wave V may and may not occur remain to be defined.

The following results obtained in schizophrenics, however, could possibly be regarded as indirect confirmation of those findings reported by Lukas (1980). The research team associated with R. Cohen in Constance (Cohen et al., 1981; Sommer, 1985) reported that the latency of wave V in electrodermal nonresponders is longer when they are asked to ignore stimuli that are task irrelevant than when the stimuli are task relevant. This nonresponder group consisted of chronic schizophrenics and alcoholics. However, in schizophrenics and alcoholics who are electrodermal responders, as well as in normal subjects, the latency of wave V is not altered by experimental manipulation of selective attention. In other words, in patients lacking an electrodermal orienting response, relevant and irrelevant information is treated differentially in subcortical and cortical centers, since the concomitant neurophysiological effects of the irrelevant information are slowed down (see subsequent text).

This finding, however, also indicates that the slowing phenomenon is not specific to schizophrenia; nonresponsive alcoholics are also affected. Skoff et

---

**Figure 6.3**   Idealized form of the averaged event-related evoked potential to a sequence of auditory stimuli (S). Brainstem potentials, waves I to VI; early potentials, 10–80 msec; middle potentials, 80–200 msec; late potentials, N2, P3/P300, and SW after about 200 msec (dotted line). P300 appears only under certain conditions reflecting endogenous influences on stimulus processing (see text). SW, slow wave (a late positive, sometimes negative, potential shift up to 1000 msec after stimulus onset; N, negative potential shift; P, positive potential shift. Component numbers represent approximate latency × 100 msec, e.g., N1, negative potential 100 msec after stimulation. Note log units on time axis (after Hillyard and Kutas, 1983). Reproduced with permission from the *Annual Review of Psychology*, **34**, © 1983 by Annual Reviews Inc.

*al.* (1980) also observed longer latencies in autistic children, although this finding has not been confirmed in nonretarded autistic individuals (Courchesne *et al.*, 1985). Longer brainstem latencies were also observed in diabetics (Donald *et al.*, 1980).

Regarding schizophrenics, it should be emphasized that apparently only one subgroup was concerned in the studies just discussed. Similarly, Hayashida *et al.* (1986) in Kagawa, Japan, established deviant BSEPs only in "deteriorated" schizophrenics. Schizophrenics were considered deteriorated when they displayed thought disorder (volitional and catatonic) and delusional disturbances, and scored low on the Kraepelin Performance Test (i.e., BSEP amplitudes were lower and the latencies were longer). The differences between nondeteriorated schizophrenics and normal controls were minimal; however, since the effect of selective attention was not examined by Hayashida and co-workers, these results are not directly comparable with those of Cohen and co-workers, although the subgroups tested were different. In addition, it is questionable whether these slight latency shifts indicate an alternation of the brainstem hardware. However, Lindström *et al.* (1987) from Uppsala, Sweden, observed more pathological changes in the brainstem waves (severe reductions in amplitudes of waves I to V), mostly in schizophrenics who reported auditory hallucinations within the week preceding the recording. Most of these patients were not on medication. The nonhallucinating schizophrenics had normal BSEPs. The authors have speculated on an organic background for these alterations but found no evidence for such a cause with computerized tomography (CT) (i.e., no signs of cerebral atrophy or ventricular enlargement; see Chapter 8).

### 2. Intact Stimulus Transmission to the Forebrain

*a. Mid-Latency Potentials*   After 10 msec or more, the neural impulses gradually "fan out" in the CNS, and neuronal intercommunication and feedback loops become more frequent. Consequently, more and more brain centers influence the "fate" of the stimulus. Nevertheless, the primary neurophysiological origin of evoked potentials between 10 and 80 msec can be identified. They are triggered by the passage of the "stimulus" from the thalamus (at about 15 msec) to the primary sensory projection areas of the cortex (arriving between 45 and 80 msec). The length of the transmission time depends on the type of stimulation.

For example, when the *left* arm of a subject is repeatedly stimulated, a negative potential can be recorded over the contralateral (*right*) somatosensory area about 45 msec after stimulus onset. After about 65 msec, an additional potential can be identified over the related somatosensory area of the *left* hemisphere (e.g., Desmedt, 1977).

Thus, early evoked potentials reflect the transmission of the "stimulus" from the periphery (i.e., subcortex) to the first modules of the central units (i.e., primary sensory projection field). Even at this point, the level of proper cortical data processing has not been reached yet. Such processes are possible only when the next step, the stimulation of the secondary projection field, is attained. For example, patients with intact primary visual projection fields and lesions of the secondary fields do not understand what they see (i.e., they have visual agnosia).

Therefore, these early evoked potentials express primarily physical properties (e.g., intensity of stimulation) and not data evaluation. As has been seen with the BSEPs, however, these early evoked potentials may also be influenced by global descending regulation from (higher) units in the cortex (e.g., Baner and Bayles, 1990).

***b. Schizophrenia*** Even though only a few experiments have been conducted with schizophrenics to date, the findings obtained in these studies are extremely interesting, although sometimes controversial.

The research team associated with Shagass in Philadelphia (Shagass *et al.,* 1974; Shagass, 1977) as well as Ikuta in Japan (1974) report that the amplitude of early components (e.g., $N_{60}$, $N_b$, in Figure 6.3) of somatosensory evoked potentials is *greater* in schizophrenics than in healthy controls. This finding is surprising, since all potentials after about 80 msec are consistently reported to be reduced in schizophrenics (see subsequent text). The increased amplitude of such potentials, however, is not specific for schizophrenia, since patients with an affective disorder also show increases. Within the group of schizophrenics, this increased amplitude appears to be limited to chronic schizophrenics (acute schizophrenics do not differ from healthy controls in this respect). The increase found in chronic schizophrenics cannot be explained by possible effects of medication because the same pattern is found in drug-free schizophrenics (Shagass, 1979).

A different type of stimulation was conducted in several experiments by research groups from Denver, Colorado (e.g., Adler *et al.,* 1982; Nagamoto *et al.,* 1989). This group administered the conditioning-testing paradigm, which examines the (neuronal) inhibitory effect of a first (conditioning) stimulus on a second (test) stimulus presented within a short interval (0.5–2 msec). The resulting amplitude of the evoked potential to the second click is a function of the strength and duration of the inhibitory effect elicited by the first stimulus in the neuronal pathways. In other words, the lower the second amplitude, the stronger (or longer), the inhibitory aftereffects of the first neuronal event. The normal control group showed a pronounced reduction (relative to the first evoked potential), while the schizophrenics did not. This was interpreted by the authors as a weak inhibitory effect or as reduced sensory gating (Adler *et al.,* 1982; Siegel *et al.,* 1984). The difference between schizophrenics and normal subjects was most pronounced by the positive peak at about 50 msec (P 50, i.e., $P_a$ in Figure 6.3) and with a click interval of 0.5 sec. Adler *et al.*

(1982, 1985), from the Colorado group, reported only a 15% decrement of the second amplitude in acutely psychotic unmedicated schizophrenics, whereas a decrement of more than 80% was observed in normal subjects (amplitude of the first click was 100%).

According to Waldo *et al.* (1986), from the same group, chronic schizophrenics and psychotic manic patients have the same low decrement rates; euthymic manic patients, however, do not differ from normal subjects. More recently, Baker *et al.* (1987) examined every second admission to two psychiatric hospitals in Colorado. The schizophrenics as a group were different from other types of patients, but a correlation with the severity of psychopathology was found even in nonschizophrenic patients (DSM-III diagnosis).

The most interesting aspect of the research from Colorado, however, is the examination of first degree relatives of schizophrenics and patients with an affective disorder. Siegel *et al.* (1984) reported a reduced inhibitory effect in approximately 50% of the first degree relatives of schizophrenics, but "normal" inhibitory functions in first degree relatives of patients with an affective disorder. Therefore, weakness of neuronal inhibitory effects as seen in the P 50 to the double click is interpreted as a genetic marker for schizophrenia. This finding could have strong implications for schizophrenia theory. According to the interpretation of the authors, it may serve as an explanation for the cognitive disturbances caused by the weakness of inhibitory effects of an early filter mechanism.

However, some notes of caution are necessary. All the reports are from only one lab; the measurement of these early evoked potentials is very difficult due to multiple sources of artifacts; an exact prestimulus baseline is difficult to obtain; and later evoked potentials (i.e., $N_1$) superimpose in some cases. (This is a special problem, since the Colorado group used prestimulus and poststimulus epochs to determine a baseline; see, for example, Baker *et al.*, 1987. As stated earlier, the EEG of schizophrenics can be considered disordered. The resulting amplitude deviation could therefore be a function of this general disorder and of the problem of exact baseline determination.) A further problem is that the Colorado group based their statements on relative amplitudes only (i.e., % decrement). However, a full evaluation of the differential effects can be made only when the absolute amplitude values are given.

The research group of Engel in Munich was not able to replicate these findings with acute schizophrenics (although they did find a trend in the expected direction), possibly because of these multiple methodological problems and slight differences in the stimulation method (Kathmann and Engel, 1990). The authors also questioned the stability of the phenomenon because of their negative retest results. The use of medication does not seem to explain these discrepancies, since Freedmann *et al.* (1983) found no influence.

## C. Cortical Evoked Potentials

### 1. Poststimulus Latency of 100 to 200 msec—Stimulus-Driven Assessment of Environment

*a. Introduction* The amplitude of negative peaks with latencies of approximately 100 msec varies depending on the amount of selective attention allocated to the events in the environment that elicit them. Using computer processing as an analogy, the actual data evaluation by the CNS is reflected in these evoked components. When, for example, an individual is only interested in certain sounds and ignores concurrently presented visual stimuli, the trace of the evoked potentials shows a strong negative shift at about 100 msec ($N_1$) that is evoked by sounds, but shows little or no amplitude deflection ($N_1$) in response to the lights. It is therefore assumed that evoked potentials between 100 and 200 msec reflect a certain type of data processing (i.e., stimulus discrimination or selection). The negative shift of $N_1$ is sensitive to physical properties of the stimulus, that is, it is influenced by factors of an exogenous nature (Hillyard *et al.*, 1973). $N_1$, therefore, largely reflects stimulus-driven information processing (see also Chapter 4). However, a small effect of endogenous control is evident if, for example, one directs attention to one ear. Sounds to the other ear elicit a slightly smaller $N_1$ wave. In contrast, later components (e.g., $P_3$) are considered to be largely endogenous; they are less dependent on the physical properties of the stimuli, but more dependent on conceptual aspects of processing.

A particular physical property of a related set of stimuli can be regarded as a sensory channel for the observer, or, as Pritchard (1986) states, "'Channel' is defined as a set of stimuli that can easily be discriminated from other stimulus sets based on some shared physical characteristic" (p. 51) (Chapter 4; see also Hansen and Hillyard, 1988).

*b. Potentials Evoked by Neutral Stimuli in Schizophrenia* In experiments in which a series of stimuli without task demands is presented (i.e., passive evoked-potential paradigms), amplitudes between 100 and 200 msec were found to be smaller in schizophrenics than in healthy controls. The $N_1/P_2$ differences (i.e., the voltage) between the negative peak at about 100 msec ($N_1$) and the positive peak at about 200 msec ($P_2$) was measured in most of the studies reported here. Several authors confirmed that a reduction of the $N_1/P_2$ amplitude for auditory stimuli characterized the schizophrenic group (Jones and Callaway, 1970; Saletu *et al.*, 1971; R. Cohen, 1973). Similar results were reported in the somatosensory area (Shagass, 1977; see also Schooler *et al.*, 1976). Regarding visual evoked potentials, however, reduction seemed to occur only under certain experimental conditions (i.e., in a certain intensity range; Shagass, 1977). As mentioned earlier, Shagass observed increased amplitudes of early evoked potentials in the same group of chronic schizophrenics!

When differences in latencies (i.e., latency of the amplitude peak) between schizophrenics and normal subjects were considered, the picture was less clear. Some studies reported longer latencies, while others found they were shorter. (For a review, see Shagass, 1979.) The latency issue will be discussed in more detail in subsequent sections.

What causes amplitude reduction, and is it a specific finding? An obvious conjecture is that neuroleptics are responsible. According to a review by Buchsbaum (1977), neuroleptics appear to reduce the amplitude of $N_1$ (and later evoked-potential components) in schizophrenic patients. Domino *et al.* (1979) from the United States and Schlör *et al.* (1985) from Germany reported indirect evidence. They found no amplitude difference between untreated schizophrenics (chronic and acute) and normal subjects. A separate analysis, however, revealed that the $N_1$ amplitude was reduced in very disturbed (untreated) chronic schizophrenics. Rappaport *et al.* (1975) from the United States reported findings that contradict any generalizations from Buchsbaum's conclusion (1977) and, to a certain extent, those of findings of Domino *et al.* (1979) and Schlör *et al.* (1985). Rappaport *et al.* (1975) found that visual evoked potentials ($N_1$) did not differ between treated and untreated chronic schizophrenics, but they did find that amplitudes were lower in both schizophrenic groups than in the healthy controls.

Apart from medication status and the stimulus modality studied, another reason for the discrepancy could be the sample of patients examined. Before the application of research diagnostic criteria became a general practice, some patients in the United States with an affective disorder were misdiagnosed as schizophrenic (see Chapter 1), so it is possible that a mixed group was tested. According to the results of Shagass and co-workers, which were substantiated in several experiments, a reduction of $P_2$ component amplitudes is found in patients with an affective disorder (Shagass, 1979; see also Giedke *et al.*, 1980).

Apart from the question of specificity and diagnostic criteria, methodological flaws in some earlier investigations complicate the interpretation of the results. Although artifact control is crucial in evoked-potential research, it was often lacking. Common sources of artifacts are the interspersion of muscle potentials (especially eye movements) on the EEG and the effects of the background EEG on evoked potentials.

A recent investigation by Shagass' Philadelphia group again draws attention to another possible source of discrepancy: the variability of evoked-potential form and latency in the schizophrenic sample was considerably higher than that in the healthy group (Josiassen *et al.*, 1988). Variability was also higher in individual schizophrenics, as will be discussed in a later section.

*c. Evoked Potentials to Attended and Ignored Stimuli in Schizophrenia*   In a carefully controlled study including artifact control and a psychiatric control group, R. Cohen and his colleagues from the University of Constance (Germany) examined the effect of selective attention on evoked potentials in chronic schizophrenic patients. The slow late potentials measured in the study will be discussed in a later section, and the BSEP results have been described already (Cohen *et al.*, 1981; Sommer, 1985). (Early, middle, and late components of the evoked potential were measured within one experimental setting.)

In both the healthy and the psychiatric controls (alcoholics), the $N_1$ amplitude was significantly larger for attended stimuli than it was for task-irrelevant stimuli. This, however, was not the case in the chronic schizophrenics (Cohen *et al.*, 1981). Paradoxically, $N_1$ amplitudes to task-irrelevant stimuli were relatively higher than those in the control groups. Does this, therefore, suggest general attention problems of schizophrenics? As we will see in the following paragraph, there is no simple answer to this question.

A well-established test of selective attention is the dichotic shadowing task (see Chapter 4). Interestingly, the study carried out by Baribeau-Braun *et al.* (1983) in Ottawa, Canada, using this test showed no reduction of $N_1$ amplitude in schizophrenics when stimuli were played at a fast presentation rate in the relevant channel of the headphones. Saitoh *et al.* (1984) from Tokyo replicated this finding with the same presentation rate. With a slower presentation rate, however, the $N_1$ amplitude was lower than that in the normal control group (Baribeau-Braun *et al.*, 1983; See also discussion in Chapter 4: possibility of a switching of attention to the irrelevant channel with slow presentation rate in dichotic shadowing tasks.). The patients were thought-disordered subacute and chronic schizophrenics, selected by research diagnostic criteria. Unfortunately, no psychiatric control group was examined.

In a second investigation, carried out in a French laboratory, Baribeau-Braun and Laurent (1986) confirmed their earlier findings and also demonstrated that the amplitude of middle-latency potentials in non-thought-disordered schizophrenics was lower at both speeds of presentation. The authors therefore concluded that this stage of information processing is more severely affected in this group than in thought-disordered schizophrenics. As will be shown in later sections, the more deviant late evoked-potential component is displayed by patients with formal thought disorder. These findings suggest that different sites are disturbed during information processing in thought-disordered and non-thought-disordered patients.

The evoked-potential experiments by Baribeau and co-workers represent a rare example of research that attempts to differentiate within the group of schizophrenias and which possibly demonstrates that not all schizophrenics display the same type of information processing deficit. These observations, which corroborate those reported in Chapter 4, point out again the need for a more differential theory of information processing deficit in schizophrenia (see Chapters 15 and 16).

   *d. Variability of Evoked Potentials*    Several investigators have established that the variability of middle and late components of evoked potentials (e.g., variability of shape and peak latency) is higher in schizophrenics than in healthy subjects (Jones *et al.*, 1965; Lifshitz, 1969; Jones and Callaway, 1970; Saletu *et al.*, 1971, 1973; Borge, 1973; R. Cohen, 1973; Rappaport *et al.*, 1975; Baribeau *et al.*, 1988; Josiassen *et al.*, 1988). Unfortunately, since these authors used different measures of variability and different stimulus presentations, the apparent agreement is less impressive when the material is more closely scrutinized. A detailed description of these methodological problems, however, goes beyond the scope of this textbook. Those readers who are particularly interested in such questions are referred to Callaway (1975), Coppola *et al.* (1978), and Buchsbaum and Coppola (1979).

   It is interesting to note that Shagass (1979) established a higher stability of evoked potentials in the very early potential sections and lower stability of components after 100 msec in schizophrenics than in psychiatric or healthy controls.

   The results of R. Cohen's studies (1973) indicate that the greater variability of middle and late potentials may be of pathophysiological significance. The variability of the evoked potential is more strongly influenced by task-irrelevant changes in the stimulus material in chronic schizophrenics than in the control groups. Saletu *et al.* (1971) found this instability of evoked potentials to be related to thought disorders.

   The effect of neuroleptics on the variability of evoked potentials has not yet been satisfactorily clarified. Rappaport *et al.* (1975) demonstrated an increase in stability due to neuroleptics, but Shagass (1976) was unable to establish any neuroleptic-induced effect. Unfortunately, the two research groups again used different criteria for evoked-potential variability.

   *e. Variation of Stimulus Intensity (Augmenting/Reducing)*    The ANS response to intense stimulation is paradoxically reduced in some schizophrenics (Chapter 5). Is there a similar response pattern with evoked potentials?

   The research group formerly associated with Buchsbaum at the NIMH reported a paradoxical reduction of $P_1/N_1$ amplitude in a subgroup of schizophrenics when stimulus intensity was increased. These patients were referred to as "reducers." Other schizophrenics displayed the expected response, since the increase in intensity was paralleled by an increase of $P_1/N_2$ amplitude (i.e., "augmenters"). Most healthy subjects also respond similarly (see, for example, Buchsbaum and Silverman, 1968; Landau *et al.*,

1975; Asarnow *et al.,* 1978; Buchsbaum *et al.,* 1986). The hypothesis of these researchers was that paradoxical reduction of $P_1/N_1$ in a subgroup of schizophrenics is due to a protective mechanism.

The allocation of subjects to the augmenter or the reducer group is usually based on the $P_1/N_1$ voltage difference. It is sometimes also based on $N_1/P_2$ or on the area under the waveform. Most studies focus on the visual modality (i.e., light flashes of varying intensity).

Iacono *et al.* (1982) in Canada, however, pointed out a methodological problem by suggesting that the reduction in these studies is due to artifacts. They demonstrated that, in normal subjects, eye blink artifacts (i.e., electrical potentials on the EEG caused by eye blinks) have a reducing effect in normal subjects. However, this was not confirmed by Soskins and Shagass (1974). Since Asarnow *et al.* (1978) measured augmenting and reducing on subjects with closed eyes (i.e., light flashes at a short distance in front of the closed eyes), an artifact-related reduction, at least in this study, is less probable. Nevertheless, the possibility that the reducing pattern in other investigations was a secondary phenomenon cannot be ruled out, since schizophrenics often have higher blink rates (see Chapter 7). This and other methodological problems, which Iacono *et al.* (1982) and Connolly and Gruzelier (1986) discuss in more detail, complicate the evaluation of the theoretical implications of this type of investigation (see also Pritchard, 1986).

More and better controlled studies are needed, in view of the considerable heuristic value of the augmenting/reducing concept. One may postulate a relationship between negative symptoms and reducing similar to that between negative symptoms and electrodermal nonresponse (see Chapter 5). Reducing is found in both acute and chronic patients, but the literature indicates that it is rarely seen in paranoid schizophrenics (Schooler *et al.,* 1976).

On the basis of the results of manipulating attention to auditory stimuli, Baribeau *et al.* (1988; France/Canada) interpreted reduction as secondary to inattention in schizophrenics and in some normal subjects. However, the authors found no differential effect in the schizophrenics. The very mild intensity stimuli used and the small group tested (schizophrenics, $n = 10$) make comparisons with the results of other studies difficult.

The augmenting/reducing concept is again one of the rare attempts in experimental research to uncover psychobiological processes underlying the well-known clinical heterogeneity of the group of schizophrenias (see Chapter 1). In this context, the finding of Landau *et al.* (1975) is particularly interesting. Schizophrenic subjects with the greatest $P_1/N_1$ reduction during hospitalization showed the greatest improvement several weeks after discharge.

An experiment carried out by a former NIMH research group (Davis *et al.,* 1979) may reveal one of the (protective?) biological mechanisms underlying the reducing phenomenon. Evoked potentials produced by mildly painful stimuli were significantly smaller in chronic schizophrenics than in healthy controls. Correspondingly, the patients rated the different stimulus intensities as less painful than did the control group. Since endorphins are transmitters that respond to painful stimulation, the authors hypothesized that the raised threshold for pain perception in schizophrenics is due to a higher activity of the endorphin system. Davis *et al.* (1979), therefore, "treated" the patients with naloxone, an endorphin antagonist. The "treatment" resulted in normalization of the pain-evoked potentials. The authors' hypothesis is also indirectly supported by results reported by Von Knorring *et al.* (1979) in Sweden, who observed that (nonschizophrenic) pain patients with an elevated endorphin level in the cerebrospinal fluid had significantly lower middle evoked-potential amplitudes to stimuli of varying light intensities. Since endorphins are transmitters belonging to the endogenous opiate system, it is tempting to speculate on a possible relationship between high endorphin levels and hallucinations in schizophrenia (see Chapter 13).

The results reported by Davis *et al.* (1979) seem to contradict the heterogeneity assumption of reducing and augmenting mentioned previously. However, these authors only examined a small group: indeed, a high percentage of schizophrenics refused to participate in their experiment. The response of the tested sample, therefore, is probably not representative of the presumably heterogeneous psychobiological response patterns in schizophrenia (i.e., some schizophrenics may not show reduced potentials to painful stimulation).

### 2. Poststimulus Latency Longer than 200 msec—Concept-Driven Assessment of Environment

*a. Introduction: $P_3$ and Late Slow Waves*   Information processing before approximately 200 msec is primarily stimulus-driven. By contrast, the $P_3$ component of the evoked potential is primarily determined by concept-driven processes (see Chapters 2 and 3). Concept-driven information processing is based on stored knowledge of past events and the expectations that are formed through this knowledge.

The discovery of the $P_3$ potential is a result of experimental schizophrenia research. In the mid-1960s, Sutton and colleagues at the Psychiatric Institute in New York were curious to know if there were cerebral electrophysiological correlates of the crossmodal increase in reaction time seen in schizophrenics (Chapter 4). They applied the newly developed event-related potential (ERP) averaging technique and found that a change of stimulus modality induced a large positive deflection around 300–350 msec poststimulus. This proved to be independent of the nature of the modality and thus seemed to reflect the information delivered by an unexpected event (Sutton *et al.*, 1965).

Duncan-Johnson and Donchin (1977) suggested that $P_3$ reflects the updating of the subject's neuronal model of the current environmental context, since new events are compared with an inner categorical model of the environment. As mentioned earlier, $P_3$ and later components are referred to as endogenous waveforms. This terminology indicates that the major contribution to the waveform characteristics comes from cognitive processing (or "category state;" Broadbent, 1971).

In a typical $P_3$ experiment, for example, two events occur with different frequencies. One event may be the syllable "vat" and the other event the syllable "bat." The syllable "vat" may occur very frequently and the syllable "bat" very infrequently. After several repetitions, the subject presumes that the two syllables belong to two different categories that are defined by the different probabilities of appearance. Due to this newly formed model of the environment, the subject expects the event "vat" but not the event "bat." This is reflected in different amplitudes of the $P_3$s corresponding to the events belonging to different categories.

The heights of the amplitude of both middle and late components are also a function of the significance of the event or stimulus. A high $N_1$ amplitude is elicited by stimuli, the significance of which is defined by physical features. A higher $P_3$ amplitude is elicited by stimuli belonging to a significant category. Since greater significance is usually attached to rare events, the $P_3$ reaction to the infrequent event (for example, tones) is higher as demonstrated in Figure 6.4. Figure 6.4 shows that relevance plays a role too. (For further discussion of this special topic, see Donchin, 1980; Donchin and Coles, 1988.)

The latency of $P_3$ reflects the duration of the evaluation process, which may be up to 500 msec or longer, depending on the complexity of the task. However, the term $P_3$, or $P_{300}$ has been adopted as a generalized symbol for positive peaks with latencies longer than 200 msec and up to 500 msec. It is usually largest over the vertex or parietal sites (i.e., Cz and Pz, respectively).

A positive component occurring even later is the so-called slow wave (SW), which peaks after 500–800 msec (for schematic outline, see Figure 6.3). The SW appears to indicate ongoing cognitive processing. A late negative shift is sometimes observed at Fz (frontal sites) with a more positive deflection at Pz. Both components are subsumed under the term late positive components (LPC). The reader interested in a broader overview of the research on $P_3$ is referred to Hillyard and Kutas (1983).

*b. Assessment of Stimulus Probabilities by Schizophrenics*  As Roth and Cannon (1972) demonstrated, schizophrenics display lower $P_3$ amplitudes to rare events than did normal controls. These authors, from Stanford University and the Veterans Administration, Palo Alto, California, used the "oddball paradigm." Here a random sequence of two distinctive stimuli is presented to the subject, with one class of stimuli in the category of rare events (i.e., the "oddballs"). Roth and Cannon (1972) used a passive version of this paradigm to examine schizophrenic patients on medication. In this version, the patient

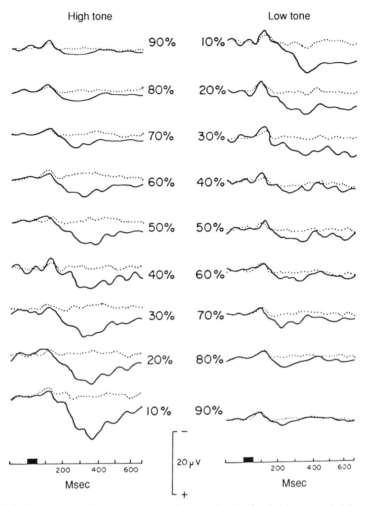

**Figure 6.4** Evoked potentials elicited by stimuli at nine levels of probability, recorded from the midline parietal scalp area and averaged over ten subjects. High- and low-frequency tones were presented in random order at complementary probabilities. Data are superimposed for two task conditions in which subjects either counted the high tone or ignored the tones and performed a word puzzle (dotted lines). Stimulus occurrence is indicated by a black rectangle on the time scale (after Duncan, 1990).

was not required to make a discriminatory response. Further studies with medication-free schizophrenic patients showed that the reduction in $P_3$ is not due to medication (e.g., Shagass *et al.*, 1975; Brecher *et al.*, 1987a; see also a review by Pritchard, 1986). The habituation of $P_3$ to simple stimuli (without task demand), however, is not different from that seen in normal subjects, as was demonstrated by Laurian *et al.* (1988) from Lausanne, Switzerland. As in the passive version, $P_3$ is also reduced in the target version of the oddball paradigm (button press to infrequent stimuli; Brecher *et al.*, 1987b). This finding corroborates the results of a large number of earlier studies reviewed by Mirsky and Duncan (1986) and Duncan (1988).

One obvious interpretation of these results is that schizophrenics are apparently unable to register the different probabilities and significances of the events. This interpretation, however, is refuted by the results of Duncan-Johnson *et al.* (1984) from the Stanford research group. These authors found that, even in schizophrenics, a co-variance exists between the amplitude of $P_3$ and the different stimulus probabilities, although the absolute $P_3$ response is smaller than that seen in healthy controls. This is also true when the experimenter announces what the patient should expect next (i.e., whether a frequent or rare event will follow) (Levit *et al.*, 1973). An experiment by Scrimali *et al.* (1988) from Catania, Italy, further supports these findings. The authors discriminated between two modes of late processing steps represented by $P_{3a}$ and $P_{3b}$.

$P_{3a}$, with a latency varying from 220 to 280 msec in this experiment, usually has a more frontal distribution and correlates, in normal subjects, with the registration of infrequent or unexpected stimuli. $P_{3b}$ has a higher amplitude and its latency varies from 310 to 380 msec. Its peak signifies more elaborate processing steps such as, for example, target discrimination from background noise in an oddball experiment.

The most interesting result of the study by Scrimali *et al.* was that schizophrenics did not differ from the controls in the $P_{3a}$ amplitude to the infrequent stimuli (passive listening to the stimuli), but had significantly lower $P_{3b}$ amplitudes on the target version of the oddball experiment. This may be interpreted as indicating that they register the infrequent stimuli, but that they are less efficient in target discrimination and further evaluation processes that are necessary to make the correct response. This is corroborated by the fact that the schizophrenics were significantly slower in responding to the targets and that they made more errors. The eight patients examined belonged to the disorganized subgroup according to DSM-III criteria and were all on neuroleptics. (In the light of results already mentioned, it is improbable that the findings can be interpreted as pure medication effects.)

The just-mentioned study by Levit *et al.* (1973) from the Institute of Psychiatry in New York also examined a psychiatric control group composed of patients with an affective disorder. These affective-disordered patients also showed reduced responses, but the reduction was less than that found in schizophrenics. Levit *et al.* (1973) also employed a modality shift paradigm. (For further discussion of modality shift experiments, see Chapter 4.) When the modality of the stimuli changes, the reaction time of schizophrenics is prolonged and the $P_3$ amplitudes are lower than in controls. In a replication study, Verleger and R. Cohen (1978) from the University of Constance (Germany), however, found only an insignificant trend toward less $P_3$ "responsiveness" in schizophrenics in this paradigm. Since Duncan (1980, 1988), now at the NIMH, and Pfefferbaum et al. (1989) in Palo Alto, California, showed that schizophrenics have a significantly reduced $P_3$ to infrequent auditory stimuli but not to infrequent visual stimuli, it is necessary to further examine whether the discrepancies and divergent findings in other studies are due to this differential effect. Duncan (1988, 1990) further showed that the reduction in $P_3$ to auditory infrequent stimuli was more stable over time (on and off medication, change in psychopathology) than $P_3$ to visual infrequent stimuli. These findings may suggest a marker function of auditory $P_3$, possibly based on a more dysfunctional auditory system than visual system. But Duncan (1990), based on new results, is more cautious: "The data on $P_{300}$ as a vulnerability marker are incomplete, for want of repeated measure designs and systematic family studies" (p. 131).

*c. Assessment of Relevance by Schizophrenics*   The difficulties schizophrenics have in correctly evaluating relevant cues in the environment is expressed by decreased $P_3$ amplitudes to signal stimuli, as already suggested by the previously mentioned lower $P_3$ amplitude to target stimuli in the oddball experiment. Pass et al. (1980) in the United States examined schizophrenics with the continuous-performance test (see Chapter 4). The $P_3$ amplitude of schizophrenics to target stimuli was as great as that of healthy controls to nontargets. A similar finding was obtained by the Constance research group (R. Cohen et al., 1981), but this was not confirmed by the research team of Engel (Wagner et al., 1989) in Munich. In the former experiment (some of the results of which have already been discussed in the section on BSEPs), evoked potentials and the electrodermal orienting response were examined in schizophrenics, alcoholics, and healthy controls. Cohen and co-workers (1981) reported a significant reduction in $N_2$ amplitude to signal stimuli and a decreased slow wave in electrodermal nonresponders, but found no difference for $P_3$ between electrodermal responders and nonresponders. Schizophrenics and alcoholics were found in both the responder and the nonresponder groups; the normal controls were almost all in the responder group (see also previous text). Similarly, Brecher et al. (1987b) found no $P_3$ difference between alcoholics and schizophrenics on a perceptual discrimination task (i.e., the findings were not specific for schizophrenia). The Palo Alto group found $P_3$ to be reduced in schizophrenic demented patients and patients with an affective disorder when compared with normal controls. However, amplitudes of the $P_3$s of the patients with an affective disorder were higher than those of the schizophrenics and demented patients, in whom $P_3$ was reduced to a similar extent (Pfefferbaum et al., 1984).

*d. The Mental Chronometric Aspect*   At what level does a disturbance in the sequence of information processing steps occur? Studies by Baribeau-

Braun *et al.* (1983) revealed that, in fast stimulus presentation conditions, $N_1$ does not differ from that of normal subjects, but $P_3$ is smaller in both presentation conditions (dichotic shadowing). Kemali *et al.* (1988) from Naples, Italy, reported that earlier components (such as $N_1$) were no different in DSM-III schizophrenics, than in normal subjects, but the late components of the response to the target (consonants) were significantly smaller. The patients were not on medication and did not differ in their task performance from the normal subjects. This again suggests a more severe disturbance of the later stages of information processing or, as Mirsky and Duncan (1986) stated, "the modulation of $N_{100}$ amplitude by attention indicates integrity of early stimulus selection."

This interpretation is also supported by the results of Saitoh *et al.* (1984) from Tokyo, Japan, who reported that siblings of schizophrenics displayed a normal $N_1$ effect, but a reduced $P_3$ on the dichotic shadowing task. (A Canadian research group reported a $P_3$ reduction in patients with borderline personality disorder, some of them with a schizotypal personality disorder as well; Kutcher *et al.*, 1987; Blackwood *et al.*, 1986.)

However, as has already been shown, other investigators also found altered responses at earlier levels of information processing. This discrepancy may be due to subgroup differences among schizophrenics. As discussed earlier, Baribeau-Braun and Laurent (1986) demonstrated that, in all conditions of the selective attention task, the middle ($N_1$) (stimulus-driven) components are more severely affected in non-thought-disordered schizophrenic patients than in thought-disordered schizophrenics. These data, therefore, suggest that information processing in one subgroup of schizophrenics may already be deviant at the stimulus-selection level (early negativity) and that other subgroups show stronger disturbances at the conceptual level of information processing. However, the exact (subgroup) specificity of these findings requires evaluation.

*e. Latency of the $P_3$*   One final remark should be made about differences in cognitive evaluation time expressed by $P_3$ latency. The findings are contradictory: Roth and Cannon (1972) found no time difference, whereas Pfefferbaum *et al.* (1984), from the same laboratory, reported longer latencies for 20–30% of the schizophrenics and 50% of the demented patients when compared with the normal subjects. Barrett *et al.* (1986) saw no latency shift in schizophrenics with predominantly positive symptoms. Obiols *et al.* (1986) from Barcelona, Spain, found no difference in chronic (DSM-III) schizophrenics. Further studies, therefore, should clarify whether these discrepancies can be explained by subgroup differences, since Schwarzkopf *et al.* (1988) found longer latencies in schizophrenics with no family history of schizophrenia and Hegerl *et al.* (1988) in Germany reported that schizophrenics with higher doses of neuroleptic medication and without symptoms of anxiety or depression would be likely to show longer $P_3$ latencies.

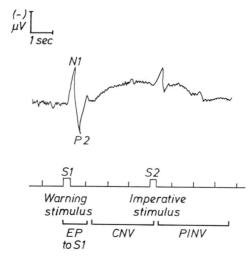

**Figure 6.5**   Schematic diagram of CNV and PINV with interstimulus interval of 4 sec. For further explanation, see text.

## 3. Slow Potential Shifts—Preparation for and Appraisal of Response

*a. Contingent Negative Variation*   The typical contingent negative variation (CNV) paradigm is a fixed-foreperiod reaction-time task in which a warning stimulus ($S_1$) is followed by an imperative stimulus ($S_2$) (see Figure 6.5). The function of $S_1$ is to inform the subject whether or not it is necessary to answer $S_2$ with a response (e.g., button press). When an EEG with a long time constant is measured during this experiment, a slowly building negative voltage shift develops between $S_1$ and $S_2$, since the CNV preparation represents anticipation of $S_2$.

The CNV is larger over the hemisphere contralateral to the performing hand. This indicates a relatively close relationship to motor areas of the cortex, that is, to the preparation of the motor response. (Further and more detailed information on functional significance can be found in Rockstroh *et al.*, 1982, and Rohrbaugh and Gaillard, 1983.)

*b. Schizophrenia*   As already discussed (see Chapter 4), the reaction time of schizophrenics is generally slower than that of healthy controls. It is therefore reasonable to assume that schizophrenics have altered CNVs. Indeed, as the results of McCallum and Abraham (1973), Abraham *et al.* (1976) in the United States, Timsit-Berthier *et al.* (1973a,b) in Belgium, and Rizzo *et al.* (1983) in Italy show, this is the case. Since general slowness in reaction-time tasks is a nonspecific finding, it may well be that the same is true for concomitant CNVs. Timsit-Berthier and co-workers reported low amplitudes (defined as less than 5 $\mu$V) in 8% of the healthy controls, 10% of the neurotics, 23% of the depressed patients, and 24% of the schizophrenics they studied (Timsit-Berthier *et al.*, 1973a,b). CNV was also found to be reduced in patients with brain injury (Rizzo *et al.*, 1978). A subsequent investigation by the Belgian research group, however, showed that the reduction is significantly more pronounced in schizophrenics than in patients with an affective disorder (Timsit-Berthier *et al.*, 1984).

According to Timsit-Berthier *et al.* (1973a,b) and Abraham *et al.* (1976), reduced CNVs were still found after remission, although some patients did show an increase in amplitude (McCallum and Abraham, 1973). CNVs partly normalized with neuroleptic treatment, at least in patients responsive to such medication (Knott *et al.*, 1976; Rizzo *et al.*, 1983). This indicates that medication effects are not likely to be responsible for CNV reduction in schizophrenics.

Higher CNV amplitudes were observed in patients with obsessive–compulsive or psychosomatic disorders (Timsit-Berthier *et al.*, 1973a,b; Dongier *et al.*, 1977).

A thorough and critical review was published by Roth (1977) from Palo Alto, California. Roth points out substantial deficiencies in the earlier studies. The control of possible artifacts caused by eye movement and sweating is often not described; effects of putative differences in the task performance on the CNV are not discussed. The interpretation of the results, therefore, is somewhat difficult. A subsequent study by Roth *et al.* (1979) showed that the CNV of schizophrenics is not necessarily always reduced. In this study, Roth and co-workers examined young schizophrenics, some of whom were untreated. A great effort was made to control possible sources of artifacts (e.g., analysis of eye movements, needle electrodes to reduce sweating artifacts). It is interesting to note that differences appeared only within the group of schizophrenics. The CNV amplitudes of schizophrenics who had had hallucinations in the preceding month were lower than those of schizophrenics who had had no hallucinations during the same interval. This was confirmed by similar results from McCallum and Abraham (1973) and Abraham and McCallum (1977). Roth *et al.* (1979) also analyzed reaction time, which was found to correlate with the magnitude of CNV in the schizophrenics but not in the normal controls.It is also noteworthy that intraindividual and interindividual variability is substantially higher in schizophrenics than in healthy subjects (see previous section on EP variability).

With regard to the long-term development of schizophrenia and its concomitant bodily responses, Rizzo and co-workers' (1984) observation of paranoid and disorganized schizophrenics is of interest: a progressive reduction of the CNV amplitude occurs with the change from the acute to the chronic state of the illness. This reduction was more pronounced in the disorganized than in the paranoid schizophrenics. Taking this finding and those of Roth and co-workers into consideration, the CNV may be more closely related to secondary long-term effects of the illness than to a primary and specific deficit.

*c. Postimperative Negative Variation*    The postimperative negative variation (PINV) sometimes appears after the patient's motor response, that is after $S_2$ (See Figure 6.5). It has been proposed that this slow negative shift reflects ongoing assessments of the last response by the patient. (For a general discussion of the method, see Rockstroh *et al.*, 1982.)

Here again, there is some evidence in the literature that PINV does not differ among schizophrenic, depressive, anxious, and obsessive–compulsive patients (Timsit-Berthier *et al.*, 1973a,b; Bolz and Giedke, 1981; Bachneff and Engelsmann, 1983). In contrast to the CNV, the PINV amplitude is significantly higher in these patient groups than in healthy controls. A rise of PINV amplitude in healthy subjects, however, can be seen in experimentally induced helplessness and other forms of loss of control over aversive stimulation (Rockstroh *et al.*, 1979).

Other studies suggest that PINV more likely reflects state rather than trait characteristics, since the PINV deviation in schizophrenics disappears after the remission of acute symptoms or is found in only a small percentage (11%) of chronic patients in remission (Rizzo *et al.*, 1983, 1984).

## III. Suggested Readings

Pritchard (1986) and Zahn (1986) reviewed the entire field of evoked-potential research in schizophrenics. In addition, Zahn (1986) surveyed the entire field of psychophysiology under consideration of all mental disorders. Mirsky and Duncan (1986) also covered the field with respect to schizophrenia. Naatanen (1990) and Duncan (1990) have also presented reviews, the former primarily concerned with $N_1$, $N_2$, and the interpretation of difference waves in normal subjects, the latter dealing primarily with $P_3$ research relating to schizophrenia.

## IV. Summary Statements and Interpretations

## A. EEG

A shift towards faster EEG activity can be observed in acute schizophrenics. The chronic schizophrenic EEG is characterized by a shift toward slower activity and a less marked alpha block. Several authors report a shift to slower frontal activity in studies of chronic patients.

Neuroleptics may reduce EEG activity, but reports are inconsistent. Reduction of schizophrenic EEG activity was observed before the era of neuroleptics.

The results may indicate differences in cortical arousal and reflect prevailing symptom patterns in acute and chronic illness. Thus some patients with more positive symptoms tend to show less alpha power and more beta power to salient stimuli. As the deviations disappear in remission, EEG changes should be considered as state-dependent symptom markers.

Reduced activity in frontal leads (i.e., more slow delta activity) is reminiscent of the relatively reduced frontal blood flow most often found in withdrawn chronic patients (see Chapter 9).

One finding of special interest may be the report of a higher entropy in the EEG of schizophrenics than in those of the control group.

A more "disorganized" EEG may be connected with less stable information processing (see similar interpretation of variable evoked-potential amplitude).

## B. Evoked Potentials

### 1. Brainstem Potentials

Most authors report that evoked potentials indicative of brainstem transmission do not show significant changes in schizophrenia (i.e., for unaltered early stimulus transmission).

Exceptions are seen in subgroups (e.g., skin conductance nonresponders). This is the case for chronic schizophrenics and chronic alcoholics. In such patients, brainstem transmission (for nonsignal stimuli) is retarded, that is, a higher wave V latency.

An increased wave V latency is nonspecific and limited to a subgroup, but may be heuristically valuable. It may reflect a stronger dampening of nonsignal input in a group of patients who are electrodermal nonresponders to nondemanding stimuli. Speculation could be made about an inhibitory or protective influence of higher or lower center function. This suggestion is controversial in the neurophysiological literature.

Another exception is a reduction of brainstem evoked-potential amplitudes in patients with thought disorder or hallucinations.

It is difficult to interpret a report of an association between reduced brainstem evoked-potential amplitude and these symptoms. However, the possibility that the basis for these symptoms interferes with brainstem stimulus transmission cannot be entirely ruled out, since they seem to interfere at other levels of data processing (e.g., stimulus threshold; cf. Chapter 3). No correlation with CT evidence of mild atrophy was found.

### 2. Early Potentials (Poststimulus Latency Less Than 100 msec Reflecting Transmission between Brainstem and Sensory Projection Fields

Increased $N_{60}$ amplitudes are recorded in some chronic schizophrenic and depressed patients, but not in acute schizophrenic patients. The findings are therefore not specific.

Interestingly, but controversially, a few reports show less P$_{50}$ suppression in a conditioning–testing paradigm (interpreted as reduced sensory gating by the Colorado research group). The Colorado research group found this phenomenon in acute schizophrenics, chronic schizophrenics, and, interestingly, in about 50% of the first degree relatives of these patients. Unfortunately, replication has not been successful elsewhere.

The problem is that small amplitudes are very difficult to distinguish from noise in the brain wave recordings. Nevertheless the findings are attractive in light of possibly related findings on perception (e.g., better discrimination of two stimulus events in the millisecond domain in schizophrenics as shown with spatial frequency tests; see Chapter 3). Further studies are needed to determine whether methodological or subgroup differences explain the discrepancies.

### 3. Evoked Potentials (100–200 msec Poststimulus Latency)

*a. Selective Attention Tasks (Selection by Physical Cues)* Reduced amplitudes to the relevant stimulus have been found in schizophrenics by most authors. One exception is that amplitudes do not differ from controls in a dichotic listening study when the possibility of attentional switches is reduced by a fast presentation rate.

Deviance in the physiological component of stimulus data selection by physical cues seems to be more pronounced than in the results reported in Chapter 4. However, according to one unconfirmed report, as with the behavioral measures, effects are reduced if selectivity is enhanced by experimental manipulation. Nevertheless the evoked-potential data suggest that a disturbed attentional effect may be present at the physiological level, but may only appear at the behavioral level under more difficult selection conditions. (There may be differences between thought-disordered and non-thought-disordered schizophrenics.)

However, there are fewer evoked-potential studies than behavioral studies of selective attention, which means that interpretations in the domain of evoked potentials are not based on the same wealth of data.

*b. Variability of Evoked Potentials* There are many reports of significantly higher amplitude and latency variability in schizophrenics.

This is possibly an indication that information processes are unstable in schizophrenics, which is supported by the correlation between variability and thought disorder, and that variability increases by task-irrelevant changes only in schizophrenics.

*c. Stimulus Intensity and EPS with a Latency of 100–200 msec* Findings of reduced amplitude with increased stimulus intensity are predominant. The variability of the results could be due to the multiple artifacts discussed and possibly to uncontrolled subgroup differences.

If the effect were replicated in new artifact-free studies, then two interpretations are possible. (1) A protective mechanism is at work. This interpretation is supported by a study that relates endorphin levels and reduced evoked potentials to painful stimuli in schizophrenics. Furthermore, a better short-term prognosis for "reducers" also supports this suggestion (cf. better short-term prognosis for schizophrenics with reduced electrodermal responding: Chapters 5 and 13). (2) Attention is generally reduced. This could be argued to be due to the absence of augmentation of waves with a latency of 100–200 msec. However, there are no clear results concerning subgroups of schizophrenics.

## 4. Late Positive Evoked Potentials ($P_{300}$)

*a. Assessment of Stimulus Probability (Oddball Paradigm)* Schizophrenics show reduced $P_{300}$ amplitudes to rare events. This remains significant in patients in remission, but they are able to register stimulus probabilities (corroboration of results in Chapter 2). Depressed and demented patients can also show $P_{300}$ reduction. The deviation seems to be more marked in the auditory modality in schizophrenics.

$P_{300}$ may represent the degree of mismatch (i.e., meaningfulness) of an event with a model of the external world constructed on the basis of past events. This model must adapt to changing external events and expectations (cf. Donchin and Coles, 1988).

Reduced $P_{300}$ amplitudes may further support the idea that concept-driven data evaluation is altered in schizophrenia. There may be a less stable model or template for the matching process.

However, schizophrenics are able to recognize the large differences in event probability usually used in the $P_3$ paradigm, although the amplitude differences between signal and nonsignal amplitudes are smaller than in the healthy controls. (Note that in Chapter 2 schizophrenics' estimates were deviant in the middle probability range but not at the extremes where the relationships are very obvious.)

Reduced $P_{300}$ amplitudes are also recorded in nonschizophrenic psychiatric groups. (However, these may not show the superiority in middle probability tasks; Chapter 2.)

The deviation is more pronounced in the auditory modality. It could be speculated that there are links to the preponderance of auditory hallucinations and possibly also to a disturbance in the serial processing of auditory stimuli. This leaves unexplained, for example, evidence for disturbances of visual holistic (Gestalt) processes.

*b. Assessment of Relevance* Some interesting reports show intact $N_{100}$ in certain selective attention tasks. However, a reduction of $P_{300}$ is seen in the same schizophrenic group. ($N_{100}$ is often reduced, possibly as a result of medication.) Some researchers observed that the $P_{300}$ amplitude to task-relevant stimuli in schizophrenics was as high as that of normal subjects to task-irrelevant stimuli. However, not all studies demonstrate a specific deviance in schizophrenics.

The latter finding is reminiscent of the lack of an adaptive ANS that responds to low- and high-demanding stimuli as reported in Chapter 5.

One study reports a $P_{300}$ reduction in siblings of schizophrenics; these siblings had a normal $N_{100}$. Another study reports $P_{300}$ deviation in schizotypal probands.

Again, the results support the idea that concept-driven information processing is more seriously affected in schizophrenia than stimulus-driven data selection. The difference between schizophrenics and other psychiatric groups may become clearer if the whole pattern of evoked potentials (early to late components) is evaluated. Reduced $P_{300}$ in schizotypal probands may suggest that it is a vulnerability indicator. However, studies of high risk children (children of a schizophrenic parent) did not always report $P_{300}$ changes (cf. Chapter 12).

There are also reports of $P_{200}$ and $P_{300}$ anomalies, especially over temporal regions; however, such anomalies have proved difficult to confirm (cf. Chapter 8).

## 5. CNV

Measures of CNV parallel the predominant findings of slow RTs. Both deviations are nonspecific (e.g., both can be observed in depressed patients). The role of artifacts was not investigated in all studies. If this were done, then subgroup differences would have become evident (e.g., lower CNVs in hallucinating subjects). One study reported that the reduction paralleled the change from acute to chronic states of the illness.

CNV reduction seems to be state dependent and nonspecific. The correlation between hallucinations and CNV reduction may be indicative of interference (e.g., at the level of input sensitivity or response organization), as with other similar correlations reported previously.

## 6. PINV

Findings here are the inverse of those from CNV studies. A higher PINV was observed in the schizophrenics.

This is also observed in other psychiatric patients, and is therefore not a specific phenomenon. A net reduction of the effect is observed after symptom remission.

# References

Abraham, P., and McCallum, W. C. (1977). A permanent change in the EEG (CNV) of schizophrenics. *Electroencephalography and Clinical Neurophysiology*, 43, 533.

Abraham, P., McCallum, W. C., and Gourlay, J. (1976). The CNV and its relation to specific psychiatric syndromes. In W. C. McCallum and J. R. Knott (Eds.), *The responsive brain.* Bristol: Wright.

Adler, L. E., Pachtmann, E., Franks, R. D., Pecevich, M., Waldo, M. C., and Freedman, R. (1982). Neurophysiological evidence for a defect in neuronal mechanisms involved in sensory gating in schizophrenia. *Biological Psychiatry*, 17, 639–654.

Adler, L. E., Waldo, M. C., and Freedman, R. (1985). Neurophysiologic studies of sensory gating in schizophrenia: Comparison of auditory and visual responses. *Biological Psychiatry*, 20, 1284–1296.

Asarnow, R. F., Cromwell, R. L., and Rennick, P. M. (1978). Cognitive and evoked response measures of information processing in schizophrenics with and without a family history of schizophrenia. *Journal of Nervous and Mental Disease*, 166, 719–730.

Bachneff, S. A., and Engelsmann, F. (1983). Correlates of cerebral event-related slow potentials and psychopathology. *Psychological Medicine*, 13, 763–770.

Baker, N., Adler, L. E., Franks, R. D., Waldo, M., Berry, S., Nagamoto, H., Muckle, A., and Freedman, R. (1987). Neurophysiological assessment of sensory gating in psychiatric inpatients: Comparison between schizophrenia and other diagnosis. *Biological Psychiatry*, 22, 603–617.

Baribeau, J., and Laurent, J. P. (1986). Neurophysiological indices of two distinct attentional dysfunctions in schizophrenics with and without formal thought disorder. In C. Shagass, R. C. Josiassen, and R. A. Roemer (Eds.), *Brain electrical potentials and psychopathology.* Amsterdam: Elsevier.

Baribeau, J C., Laurent, J. P., and Braun, C. (1988). Individual differences, the augmenting/reducing effect and selective attention in schizophrenia. *Research Communications in Psychology and Psychiatry Behavior*, 13, 17–33.

Baribeau-Braun, J., Picton, T. W., and Gosselin, J. (1983). Schizophrenia: A neurophysiological evaluation of abnormal information processing. *Science*, 219, 874–876.

Barrett, K., McCallum, W. C., and Pocock, P. V. (1986). Brain indicators of altered attention and information processing in schizophrenic patients. *British Journal of Psychiatry*, 148, 414–420.

Bauer, L. O., and Bayles, R. L. (1990). Precortical filtering and selective attention: An evoked potential analysis. *Biological Psychology*, 30, 21–33.

Bernstein, A. S., Taylor, K., Starkey, P., Juni, S., Lubowsky, J., and Paley, H. (1981). Bilateral skin conductance, finger pulse volume, and EEG orienting response to tones of differing intensities in chronic schizophrenics and controls. *Journal of Nervous and Mental Disease*, 169, 513–528.

Blackwood, D. H. R., St. Clair, D. M., and Kutcher, S. P. (1986). P300 event-related potential abnormalities in borderline personality disorder. *Biological Psychiatry*, 21, 557–560.

Bolz, J., and Giedke, H. (1981). Controllability of an aversive stimulus in depressed patients and healthy controls: A study using slow brain potentials. *Biological Psychiatry*, 16, 441–452.

Bolz, J., and Giedke, H. (1982). Brain stem auditory evoked responses in psychiatric patients and healthy controls. *Journal of Neural Transmission*, 54, 285–291.

Borge, G. F. (1973). Perceptual modulation and variability in psychiatric patients. *Archives of General Psychiatry*, 29, 760–763.

Brecher, M., and Begleiter, H. (1985). Brain stem auditory evoked potentials in unmedicated schizophrenic patients. *Biological Psychiatry*, 20, 199–202.

Brecher, M., Porjesz, B., and Begleiter, H. (1987a). Late positive component amplitude in schizophrenics and alcoholics in two different paradigms. *Biological Psychiatry*, 22, 848–856.

Brecher, M., Porjesz, B., and Begleiter, H. (1987b). The N2 component of the event-related potential in schizophrenic patients. *Electroencephalography and Clinical Neurophysiology*, 66, 369–375.

Broadbent, D. E. (1971). *Decision and Stress*. New York: Academic Press.

Buchsbaum, M. S. (1977). The middle evoked response components and schizophrenia. *Schizophrenia Bulletin*, 3, 93–104.

Buchsbaum, M. S., Awsare, S. V., Holcomb, H. H., DeLisi, L. E., Hazlett, E., Carpenter, W. T., Pickar, D., and Morihisa, J. M. (1986). Topographic differences between normals and schizophrenics: The N120 evoked potential component. *Neuropsychobiology*, 15, 1–6.

Buchsbaum, M. S., and Coppola, R. (1979). Signal-to-noise ratio and response variability in affective disorders and schizophrenia. In H. Begleiter (Ed.), *Evoked brain potentials and behavior*. New York: Plenum.

Buchsbaum, M. S., and Silverman, J. (1968). Stimulus intensity control and the cortical evoked response. *Psychosomatic Medicine*, 25, 12–22.

Callaway, E. (1975). *Brain electrical potentials and individual psychological differences*. New York: Grune & Stratton.

Coger, R. W., Dymond, A. M., and Serafetinides, E. A. (1979). Electroencephalographic similarities between chronic alcoholics and chronic, nonparanoid schizophrenics. *Archives of General Psychiatry*, 36, 91–94.

Cohen, R. (1973). The influence of task-irrelevant stimulus variations on the reliability of auditory evoked responses in schizophrenia. In A. Fessard and G. LeLord (Eds.), *Human neurophysiology, psychology, psychiatry: Average evoked responses and their conditioning in normal subjects and psychiatric patients*. Paris: Inserm.

Cohen, R., Sommer, W., and Hermanutz, M. (1981). Auditory event-related potentials in chronic schizophrenics. *Advances in Biological Psychiatry*, 6, 180–185.

Colombo, C., Gambini, O., Macciardi, F., Bellodi, L., Sacceti, E., Vita, A., Cattaneo, R., and Scarone, S. (1989). Alpha reactivity in schizophrenia and in schizophrenic spectrum disorders: Demographic, clinical and hemispheric assessment. *International Journal of Psychophysiology*, 7, 47–54.

Connolly, J. F., Aubry, K., McGillivary, N., and Scott, D. W. (1989). Human brainstem auditory evoked potentials fail to provide evidence of efferent modulation of auditory input during attentional tasks. *Psychophysiology*, 26, 292–303.

Connolly, J. F., and Gruzelier, J. H. (1986). Persistent methodological problems with evoked potential augmenting-reducing. *International Journal of Psychophysiology*, 3, 299–306.

Coppola, R., Tabor, R., and Buchsbaum, M. S. (1978). Signal to noise ratio and response variability measurements in single trial evoked potentials. *Electroencephalography and Clinical Neurophysiology*, 44, 214–222.

Courchesne, E., Courchesne, R. Y., Hicks, G., and Lincoln, A. J. (1985). Functioning of the brain-stem auditory pathway in nonretarded autistic individuals. *Electroencephalography and Clinical Neurophysiology*, 61, 491–501.

Creutzfeld, O. (1971). Neurophysiologische Grundlagen des Elektroencephalogramms. In M. Haider (Ed.), *Neuropsychologie*. Bern: Hans Huber.

Davis, G. C., Buchsbaum, M. S., van Kammen, D. P., and Bunney, W. E. (1979). Analgesia to pain stimuli in schizophrenics and its reversal by naltrexone. *Psychiatry Research*, 1, 61–69.

Desmedt, J. (1977). Some observations on the methodology of cerebral evoked potentials in man. In J. Desmedt (Ed.), *Attention, voluntary contraction, and event-related cerebral potentials*. Basel: Karger.

Dieckmann, V., Reinke, W., Grözinger, B., Westphal, K. P., and Kornhuber, H. H. (1985). Diminished order in the EEG of schizophrenic patients. *Naturwissenschaften*, 72, 541–542.

Domino, E. F., Demetriou, S., Tuttle, T., and Klinge, V. (1979). Comparison of the visually evoked response in drugfree chronic schizophrenic patients and normal controls. *Electroencephalography and Clinical Neurophysiology*, 46, 123–127.

Donald, M. W., Bird, C. E., El-Sawy, R., Hart, P., Lawson, S., Letemendia, F. J., Surridge, D. H., and Wilson, D. L. (1980). Cortical evoked potentials and auditory decision times of diabetics. *Progress in Brain Research*, 54, 516–521.

Donchin, E. (1980). Surprise! . . . Surprise? *Psychophysiology*, 18, 493–513.

Donchin, E., and Coles, M. G. H. (1988). Is the P300 component a manifestation of context updating? *The Behavioral and Brain Sciences*, 11, 357–374.

Dongier, M., Dubrovsky, B., and Engelsmann, F. (1977). ERSP in psychiatry: Problems of methodology and symptom evaluation. In D. Otto (Ed.), *Multidisciplinary perspectives in event-related brain potential research*. Washington, D.C.: U.S. Government Printing Office.

Duncan, C. C. (1988). Event-related brain potentials: A window on information processing in schizophrenia. *Schizophrenia Bulletin*, 14, 199–203.

Duncan, C. C. (1990). Current issues in the application of P300 to research in schizophrenia. In E. Straube and K. Hahlweg (Eds.), *Schizophrenia: Concepts, vulnerability, and intervention*. Berlin: Springer.

Duncan, J. (1980). The locus of interference in the perception of simultaneous stimuli. *Psychological Review*, 87, 272–300.

Duncan-Johnson, C. C., and Donchin, E. (1977). On quantifying surprise: The variation of event-related potentials with subjective probability. *Psychophysiology*, 14, 456–467.

Duncan-Johnson, C. C., Roth, W. T., and Kopell, B. S. (1984). Effects of stimulus sequence on P300 and reaction time in schizophrenics: A preliminary report. In R. Karrer, J. Cohen, and P. Tueting, (Eds.), *Brain and information: Event-related potentials*, pp. 570–577. New York: The New York Academy of Sciences.

Fenton, G. W., Fenwick, P. B. C., Dollimore, J., Dunn, T. L., and Hirsch, S. R. (1980). EEG spectral analysis in schizophrenia. *British Journal of Psychiatry*, 136, 445–455.

Freedman, R., Adler, L. E., Waldo, M. C., Pachtman, E., and Franks, R. D. (1983). Neurophysiological evidence for a defect in inhibitory pathways in schizophrenia: Comparison of medicated and drug-free patients. *Biological Psychiatry*, 18, 537–551.

Giannitrapani, D. (1988). Do specific EEG frequencies have a role in schizophrenia? *Research Communications in Psychology and Psychiatry Behavior*, 13, 83–96.

Giedke, H., Bolz, J., and Heimann, H. (1980). Evoked potentials, expectancy wave, and skin resistance in depressed patients and healthy controls. *Pharmakopsychiatrie*, 13, 91–101.

Hackley, S. A., Wolldorf, M., and Hillyard, S. A. (1987). Combined use of microreflexes and event-related potentials as measures of auditory selective attention. *Psychophysiology*, 24, 632–647.

Hansen, J. C., and Hillyard, S. A. (1988). Temporal dynamics of human auditory selective attention. *Psychophysiology*, 25, 316–329.

Hayashida, Y., Mitani, Y., Hosomi, H., Amemiya, M., Mifune, K., and Tomita, S. (1986). Auditory brain stem responses in relation to the clinical symptoms of schizophrenia. *Biological Psychiatry*, 21, 177–188.

Hegerl, U., Gaebel, W., and Ulrich, G. (1988). Relationship between residual symptomatology and auditory evoked potentials in schizophrenic outpatients. *Pharmacopsychiatry*, 21, 329–330.

Hillyard, S. A., and Kutas, M. (1983). Electrophysiology of cognitive processing. *Annual Review of Psychology*, 34, 33–61.

Hillyard, S. A., Hink, R. F., Schwendt, V. L., and Picton, T. W. (1973). Electrical signs of selective attention in the human brain. *Science*, 182, 177–180.

Iacono, W. G., Gabbay, F. H., and Lykken, D. T. (1982). Measuring the average evoked response to light flashes: The contribution of eye-blink artifact to augmenting-reducing. *Biological Psychiatry*, 17, 897–911.

Ikuta, T. (1974). Somatosensory evoked potentials (SEP) in normal subjects, schizophrenics, and epileptics. *Fukuoka Acta Medica*, 65, 1010–1019.

Itil, T. M. (1977). Qualitative and quantitative EEG findings in schizophrenia. *Schizophrenia Bulletin*, 3, 61–79.

Jones, E. T., Blacker, K. H., Callaway, E., and Layne, R. S. (1965). The auditory evoked responses as a diagnostic and prognostic measure in schizophrenia. *American Journal of Psychiatry*, 122, 33–41.

Jones, R. T., and Callaway, E. (1970). Auditory evoked responses in schizophrenia—A reassessment. *Biological Psychiatry*, 2, 291–298.

Josiassen, R. C., Shagass, C., and Roemer, R. A. (1988). Somatosensory evoked potential correlates of schizophrenic subtypes identified by the Millon clinical Multiaxial Inventory. *Psychiatry Research*, 23, 209–219.

Karson, C. N., Coppola, R., and Daniel, D. G. (1988). Alpha frequency in schizophrenia: An association with enlarged cerebral ventricles. *American Journal of Psychiatry*, 145, 861–864.

Karson, C. N., Coppola, R., Morihisa, J. M., and Weinberger, D. R. (1987). Computed electroencephalographic activity mapping in schizophrenia. *Archives of General Psychiatry*, 44, 514–517.

Kathmann, N., and Engel, R. R. (1990). Sensory gating in normals and schizophrenics: a failure to find strong *P50* suppression in normals. *Biological Psychiatry*, 27, 1216–1226.

Kemali, D., Galderisi, S., Maj, M., Mucci, A., Cesarelli, M., and D'Ambra, L. (1988). Event-related potentials in schizophrenic patients: Clinical and neurophysiological correlates. *Research Communications in Psychology and Psychiatry Behavior*, 13, 3–16.

Knott, J. R., Peters, J. F., Robinson, M. D., Smith, A., and Andreasen, N. C. (1976). The contingent negative variation in schizophrenic and depressed patients. *Electroencephalography and Clinical Neurophysiology*, 40, 329–330.

Koukkou, M. (1980). EEG reactivity in acute schizophrenics reflects deviant (ecotropic) state changes during information processing. In M. Koukkou, D. Lehmann, and J. Angst (Eds.), *Functional states of the brain: Their determinants*. New York: Elsevier–North Holland Biomedical Press.

Kutcher, S. P., Blackwood, D. H. R., St. Clair, D., Gaskell, D. F., and Muir, W. J. (1987). Auditory P300 in borderline personality disorder and schizophrenia. *Archives of General Psychiatry*, 44, 645–650.

Landau, S. G., Buchsbaum, M. S., Carpenter, W., Strauss, J., and Sacks, M. (1975). Schizophrenia and stimulus intensity control. *Archives of General Psychiatry*, 32, 1235–1245.

Laurian, S., Bryois, C., Gaillard, J.-M., Le, P. K., and Schöpf, J. (1984). Some aspects of brain electrical activity in schizophrenia. In B. Saletu, C. Perris, and D. Kemali (Eds.), *Neurophysiological correlates of mental disorders. Advances in biological psychiatry*, Vol. 15. Basel: Karger.

Laurian, S., Gaillard, J.-M., Grasset, F., Oros, L., and Schöpf, J. (1988). Short-term habituation of auditory evoked responses in schizophrenics. *Research Communications in Psychology and Psychiatry Behavior*, 13, 35–42.

Levit, R. A., Sutton, S., and Zubin, J. (1973). Evoked potential correlates of information processing in psychiatric patients. *Psychological Medicine*, 3, 487–494.

Lifshitz, K. (1969). Intra- and inter-individual variability in the averaged evoked potential in normal and chronic schizophrenic subjects. *Electroencephalography and Clinical Neurophysiology*, 27, 688–689.

Lifshitz, K., and Gradijan, J. (1972). Relationship between measures of the coefficient of variation of the mean absolute EEG voltage and spectral intensities in schizophrenic and control subjects. *Biological Psychiatry*, 5, 149–163.

Lifshitz, K., Lee, K. L., and Susswein, S. (1987). Long-term replicability of EEG spectra and auditory evoked potentials in schizophrenic and normal subjects. *Neuropsychobiology*, 18, 205–211.

Lindsley, D. B., and Wicke, J. D. (1974). The electroencephalogramm: Autonomous electrical activity in man and animals. In R. F. Thompson and M. M. Patterson (Eds.), *Bioelectric recording techniques. Part B. Electroencephalography and human brain potentials.* New York: Academic Press.

Lindström, L., Klockhoff, I., Svedberg, A., and Bergstrom, K. (1987). Abnormal auditory brainstem responses in hallucinating schizophrenic patients. *British Journal of Psychiatry*, 151, 9–14.

Lukas, J. H. (1980). Human auditory attention: The olivocochlear bundle may function as a peripheral filter. *Psychophysiology*, 17, 444–452.

McCallum, W. C., and Abraham, P. (1973). The contingent negative variation in psychosis. *Electroencephalography and Clinical Neurophysiology*, 33, 329–395.

Mirsky, A. F., and Duncan, C. C. (1986). Etiology and expression of schizophrenia: Neurobiological and psychosocial factors. *Annual Review of Psychology*, 37, 291–319.

Morihisa, J. M., Duffy, F. H., and Wyatt, R. J. (1983). Brain electrical activity mapping (BEAM) in schizophrenic patients. *Archives of General Psychiatry*, 40, 719–728.

Mukundan, C. R. (1986). Computed EEG in schizophrenics. *Biological Psychiatry*, 21, 1221–1225.

Naatanen, R. (1990). The role of attention in auditory information processing as revealed by event-related potentials and other brain measures of cognitive function. *The Behavioral and Brain Sciences*, 13, 201–288.

Nagamoto, H. T., Adler, L. E., Waldo, M. C., and Freedman, R. (1989). Sensory gating in schizophrenics and normal controls: Effects of changing stimulation interval. *Biological Psychiatry*, 25, 549–561.

Obiols, J. E., Bachs, J. S., and Masana, J. (1986). Event-related potentials in young chronic schizophrenics. *Biological Psychiatry*, 21, 856–859.

Pass, H. L., Klorman, R., Salzman, L. F., Klein, R. H., and Kaskey, G. B. (1980). The late positive component of the evoked response in acute schizophrenics during a test of sustained attention. *Biological Psychiatry*, 15, 9–20.

Pfefferbaum, A., Ford, J. M., White, P. M., and Roth, W. T. (1989). P3 in schizophrenia is affected by stimulus modality, response requirements, medication status, and negative symptoms. *Archives of General Psychiatry*, 46/11, 1035–1044.

Pfefferbaum, A., Horvath, T. B., Roth, W. T., Tinklenberg, J. R., and Kopell, B. S. (1980). Auditory brain stem and cortical evoked potentials in schizophrenia. *Biological Psychiatry*, 15, 209–223.

Pfefferbaum, A., Wenegrat, B. G., Ford, J. M., Roth, W. T., and Kopell, B. S. (1984). Clinical application of the P3 component of event-related potentials. II. Dementia, depression and schizophrenia. *Electroencephalography and Clinical Neurophysiology*, 59, 104–124.

Picton, T. W., Hillyard, S. A., Kransz, H. I., and Galambos, R. (1974). Human auditory evoked potentials. I. Evaluation of components. *Electroencephalography and Clinical Neurophysiology*, 36, 179–190.

Pritchard, W. S. (1986). Cognitive event-related potential correlates of schizophrenia. *Psychological Bulletin*, 100, 43–66.

Rappaport, M., Hopkins, H. K., Hall, K., and Belleza, T. (1975). Phenothiazine effects on cerebral-evoked potentials and eye movements in acute schizophrenics. *International Pharmacopsychiatry*, 10, 111–124.

Rizzo, P. A., Albani, G. F., Spadaro, M., and Morocutti, C. (1983). Brain slow potentials (CNV), prolactin, and schizophrenia. *Biological Psychiatry*, 18, 175–183.

Rizzo, P. A., Amabile, G., Caporall, M., Spadaro, M., Zanasi, M., and Morocutti, C. (1978).

A CNV study in a group of patients with traumatic head injuries. *Electroencephalography and Clinical Neurophysiology*, 45, 281–285.

Rizzo, P. A., Spadaro, M., Albani, G. F., and Morocutti, C. (1984). Contingent negative variation and schizophrenia: A long-term follow-up study. *Biological Psychiatry*, 19, 1719–1724.

Rockstroh, B., Elbert, T., Birbaumer, N., and Lutzenberger, W. (1982). *Slow brain potentials and behavior*. Baltimore: Urban & Schwarzenberg.

Rockstroh, B., Elbert, T., Lutzenberger, W., and Birbaumer, N. (1979). Slow cortical potentials under conditions of uncontrollability. *Psychophysiology*, 16, 374–380.

Rohrbaugh, J. W., and Gaillard, A. W. K. (1983). Sensory and motor aspects of the contingent negative variation. In A. W. K. Gaillard and W. Ritter (Eds.), *Tutorials in event related potentials research: Endogenous component. Advances in psychology*, Vol. 10. Amsterdam: North-Holland.

Roth, W. T. (1977). Late event-related potentials and psychopathology. *Schizophrenia Bulletin*, 3, 105–120.

Roth, W. T., and Cannon, E. H. (1972). Some features of the auditory evoked response in schizophrenics. *Archives of General Psychiatry*, 27, 466–471.

Roth, W. T., Horvath, T. B., Pfefferbaum, A., Tinklenberg, J. R., Mezzich, J., and Kopell, B. S. (1979). Late event-related potentials and schizophrenia. In H. Begleiter (Ed.), *Evoked brain potentials and behavior*. New York: Plenum Press.

Saitoh, O., Niwa, S. I., Hiramatsu, K. L., Kameyama, T., Rymar, K., and Itoh, K. (1984). Abnormalities in late positive components or event-related potentials may reflect a genetic predisposition to schizophrenia. *Biological Psychiatry*, 19, 293–303.

Saletu, B., Itil, T. H., and Saletu, M. (1971). Auditory evoked response, EEG, and thought process in schizophrenics. *American Journal of Psychiatry*, 128, 336–344.

Saletu, B., Saletu, M., and Itil, T. M. (1973). The relationship between psychopathology and evoked responses before, during, and after psychotropic drug treatment. *Biological Psychiatry*, 6, 46–74.

Schlör, K.-H., Moises, H. W., Haas, S., and Rieger, H. (1985). Schizophrenia, psychoticism, neuroleptics, and auditory evoked potentials. *Pharmacopsychiatry*, 118, 293–296.

Schooler, C., Buchsbaum, M. S., and Carpenter, W. T. (1976). Evoked response and kinesthetic measures of augmenting/reducing in schizophrenia: Replications and extensions. *Journal of Nervous and Mental Disease*, 163, 221–232.

Schwarzkopf, S. B., Chapman, R. M., Jimenez, M., Treglia, L., Kane, C. F., Lamberti, J. S., and Nasrallah, H. A. (1988). Familial and sporadic schizophrenia: Visual evoked potential differences. *Biological Psychiatry*, 24, 828–833.

Scrimali, T., Grimaldi, L., and Rapisarda, V. (1988). The passive eliciting of P300 versus the "odd-ball + time reaction" paradigm in healthy subjects and schizophrenic patients. *Research Communications in Psychology and Psychiatry Behavior*, 13, 97–102.

Shagass, C. (1976). An electrophysiological view of schizophrenia. *Biological Psychiatry*, 11, 3–30.

Shagass, C. (1977). Early evoked potentials. *Schizophrenia Bulletin*, 3, 80–92.

Shagass, C. (1979). Sensory evoked potentials in psychosis. In H. Begleiter (Ed.), *Evoked brain potentials and behavior*. New York: Plenum Press.

Shagass, C., Overton, D. A., and Straumanis, J. J. (1974). Evoked potential studies in schizophrenia. In H. Mitsuda and T. Fukuda (Eds.), *Biological mechanisms of schizophrenia and schizophrenia-like psychoses*. Tokyo: Igaku-Shoin.

Shagass, C., Roemer, R. A., Straumanis, J. J., and Josiassen, R. C. (1984). Psychiatric diagnostic discriminations with combinations of quantitative EEG variables. *British Journal of Psychiatry*, 144, 581–592.

Shagass, C., Straumanis, J. J., and Overton, D. A. (1975). Psychiatric diagnosis and EEG-evoked response relationships. *Neuropsychobiology*, 1, 1–15.

Siegel, C., Waldo, M., Mizner, G., Adler, L. E., and Freedman, R. (1984). Deficits in sensory gating in schizophrenic patients and their relatives. *Archives of General Psychiatry*, 41, 607–612.

Skoff, B. F., Mirsky, A. F., and Turner, D. (1980). Prolonged brainstem transmission time in autism. *Psychiatry Research*, 2, 157–166.

Sommer, W. (1985). Selective attention differentially affects brainstem auditory evoked potentials of electrodermal responders and nonresponders. *Psychiatry Research*, 16, 227–232.

Soskins, D. A., and Shagass, C. (1974). Evoked potentials tests of augmenting-reducing. *Psychophysiology*, 11, 175–180.

Sutton, S., Braren, M., and Zubin, J. (1965). Evoked-potential correlates of stimulus uncertainty. *Science*, 150, 1187–1188.

Tarrier, N., Cooke, E. C., and Lader, M. H. (1978). The EEGs of chronic schizophrenic patients in hospital and in the community. *Electroencephalography and Clinical Neurophysiology*, 44, 669–673.

Timsit-Berthier, M., Gerono, A., Rousseau, J. C., Mantanus, H., Abraham, P., Verhey, F. H., Lamers, T., and Emonds, P. (1984). An international pilot study of CNV in mental illness. Second report. *Annals of the New York Academy of Science*, 425, 629–673.

Timsit-Berthier, M., Delaunoy, J., Koninckx, N., and Rousseau, J. C. (1973a). Slow potential changes in psychiatry. I. Contingent negative variation. *Electroencephalography and Clinical Neurophysiology*, 35, 355–361.

Timsit-Berthier, M., Delaunoy, J., and Rousseau, J. C. (1973b). Slow potential changes in psychiatry. II. Motor potential. *Electroencephalography and Clinical Neurophysiology*, 35, 363–367.

Verleger, R., and Cohen, R. (1978). Effects of certainty, modality shift, and guess outcome on evoked potentials and reaction times in chronic schizophrenics. *Psychological Medicine*, 8, 81–93.

Von Knorring, L., Aimay, B. G. L., Johansson, F., and Terenius, L. (1979). Endorphins in CSF of chronic pain patients, in relation to augmenting-reducing response in visual averaged evoked response. *Neuropsychobiology*, 5, 322–326.

Wagner, M., Kurtz, G., and Engel, R. R. (1989). Normal P300 in acute schizophrenics during a continuous performance test. *Biological Psychiatry*, 25, 788–792.

Waldo, M., Adler, L., Franks, R., Baker, N., Siegel, C., and Freedman, R. (1986). Sensor gating and schizophrenia. *Biological Psychology*, 23, 108.

Williamson, P., and Mamelak, M. (1987). Frontal spectral EEG findings in acutely ill schizophrenics. *Biological Psychiatry*, 22, 1021–1024.

Zahn, T. P. (1986). Psychophysiological approaches to psychopathology. In M. G. H. Coles, E. Donchlin, and S. W. Porges (Eds.), *Psychophysiology*. New York: The Guilford Press.

# PART IV

# Neuropsychological Symptoms

Neuropsychological investigations that will be described in Chapter 7 use a variety of methods with which to approach the question of whether schizophrenics suffer a breakdown of certain prescribed neurological functions. Many of these concern motor activity and reflexes, and their elaboration and modulation in the service of "higher" central nervous function. Chapter 8 discusses structural changes of the brain, as might underlie atrophic changes seen with computer tomography (CT), as well as the functions that these affected regions of the brain may mediate. Chapter 9 deals with lateralized functions of the brain.

If it could be unequivocally shown that specific brain regions were structurally damaged or were not functioning well in schizophrenics or in particular schizophrenic subgroups, then it might be possible to attribute the psychophysiological changes described in the previous chapters and the neuropsychological changes described in Chapters 7 through 9 to a localized dysfunction in the schizophrenic central nervous system (CNS).

However, it should be kept in mind that checking only the output variable, the neuropsychological function, does not necessarily mean that the underlying defect will localize a structural alteration, even if the same functional disturbance is seen in patients with a clearly demonstrable brain lesion. Neurological functions depend to varying degrees on the psychological state at the time of measurement (e.g., anxiety, arousal, vigilance). Since psychotic states are accompanied by extreme psychological alterations, the influence of the subject's state during testing is particularly important for schizophrenic patients. This should always be kept in mind when evaluating the validity and significance of the results of neuropsychological examinations in psychiatric patients.

# Chapter 7

# Neurological Tests: Examination and Experiment

## I. Neurological Soft Signs, Locomotor Coordination, and Motor and Neuromuscular Function

### A. Neurological Soft Signs

Originally the term "neurological soft signs" was applied to mild developmental disturbances noted in children (e.g., impaired coordination). It was supposed that these signs were indicative of "minimal brain dysfunction." Since they usually could not be attributed to specific structural changes, they were termed "soft." In contrast, "hard" signs represent severe disabilities such as pathological reflexes or loss of neuronal control of muscular activity.

Today the term usually refers to small qualitatively assessed deviations from the norm found in routine neurological examinations, such as slight alterations of the basic reflexes, sensory motor coordination (see finger–nose test) of gait and limb movements, stereognosis (capacity to appreciate three-dimensional structure), or graphesthesia (recognition of symbols "written" on the hand). As the reader can see, this is a heterogeneous collection of functions. Reports on soft signs often refer to different subsets of tests and usually do not include quantitative measures. It is therefore difficult to interpret the range of deviations found by different groups.

As early as the turn of the century, slight neurological dysfunctions in schizophrenics were reported by Kraepelin (1909) and Bumke (1911), both in Germany. These reports were reviewed by Hoskins (1946) from the United States, who included his own findings in a monograph that is still well worth reading.

Reports of the presence of neurological soft signs in schizophrenic patients are numerous (e.g., Cox and Ludwig, 1979; Torrey, 1980; Johnstone and Owens, 1981; Walker, 1981; Kolakowska *et al.*, 1985; Kinney *et al.*, 1986; Woods *et al.*, 1986, 1987; Bartkó *et al.*, 1988; Silverstein and Arzt, 1985).

There are also reports of the absence of such signs (e.g., Nasrallah *et al.*, 1983).

Ruling out one potential reason for the different findings, Kolakowska *et al.* (1985) found no relationship between the presence of soft signs and neuroleptic dose. Furthermore, the slowing of responses found by Silverstein and Arzt (1988) in the Luria–Nebraska test battery cannot easily be attributed to medication since schizophrenics with and without the impairment were receiving neuroleptics at the time of testing.

After a routine investigation, Johnstone and Owens (1981) claimed that 355 of 456 schizophrenics in one psychiatric hospital had some mild neurological signs. The majority of the abnormalities were related to extrapyramidal disturbances that are well known as side effects of long-term neuroleptic treatment. Nonetheless, 27 of 52 medication-free patients showed some neurological signs. These signs mostly consisted of abnormalities of motor coordination and in the tone of the face and limb musculature. However, the result should be treated with caution since the patients were relatively old and no control groups were tested.

Using the Halstead–Reitan test battery, Lewis *et al.* (1979) compared a group with a range of brain injuries to a group of schizophrenics. Their paranoid patients showed fewer abnormalities than the brain-damaged group, and no differences when compared with other psychiatrically ill patients. However, this study may be criticized for using heterogeneous comparison groups of different ages.

Other sources for discrepant findings are putative subgroup differences. Torrey (1980), using the graphesthesia and face–hand test (identify with eyes closed the spot on the body touched by the examiner), reported impairments in only 8% of an acutely ill group, but in nearly 50% of the chronically ill patients. He reported that the longer the patient had been psychotic and the earlier the apparent onset, the more likely the impairment was to be shown. The questions of whether (and how) the length of illness or even of a long period of neuroleptic treatment can contribute to these deficits remain unanswered.

Balogh *et al.* (1979) reported that nonparanoid poor premorbid schizophrenics, compared with healthy and psychiatric controls, had difficulty in spatially locating the source of a noise. (It is questionable whether this really represents an examination of neurological signs.) Liddle (1987) found that some but not all negative symptoms correlate with the incidence of soft signs. Green and Walker (1985) found that the only abnormality relating to the presence of negative symptoms was in visuomotor and visuospatial ability. In contrast, patients with positive symptoms showed short-term memory deficits. However, Kolakowska *et al.* (1985), Bartkó *et al.* (1988), and Faustman *et al.* (1988) could find no relationship between soft signs and negative symptoms.

If studies comparing subgroups of schizophrenics have produced equivocal results, how specific to schizophrenia are these characteristics with respect to other patient groups? Cox and Ludwig (1979) examined healthy subjects as well as groups showing schizophrenic, mixed-character neurotic, alcoholic, and unipolar and bipolar disorders ($n = 11-21$/group). In the opinion of the authors, probable signs of cortical lobe functioning separated all but the schizophrenic and depressed groups. The latter groups were separated by the increased incidence of functional disturbances in the schizophrenic group that were regarded as frontal signs by the authors. These so-called frontal signs included various perseverative functions and grasp and palmomental reflexes (i.e., a movement that follows stroking the palm with an object). In a study restricted to schizophrenics, Bartko *et al.* (1988) also commented on a relatively high incidence of the palmomental reflex ($n = 22$ of 58).

Since some neurological signs might be present in schizophrenics, it is interesting to ask if some of these signs would relate to inherited schizophrenic traits. Kinney's group reported mild neurological signs among schizophrenics and their close relatives. These signs included unilateral reflexes, hyperactivity, Babinski reflex, hypotonia, and choreiform and awkward movements, potentially reflecting changes in corticospinal, cerebellar, and extrapyramidal systems (Kinney *et al.*, 1986; Woods *et al.*, 1986, 1987). However, a close look at the data reveals that many relatives showed only one of the 18 neurological signs sought. It is doubtful if the appearance of one sign, such as, for example, an awkward gait, can really be regarded as a neurological disturbance, let alone an indicator of the presence of focal cerebral changes. However, in fairness to Woods *et al.* (1987), it should be noted that the test protocols of the subjects were examined again in a blind analysis, the relatives of the more severely ill schizophrenics were found to have more signs.

Is an increase of neurological signs an indicator of genetically linked schizophrenia? While Walker and Shaye (1982) did report finding more neurological signs in schizophrenics with a family history of the illness, Torrey (1980) and Kolakowska *et al.* (1985) did not find that schizophrenics with a relatively high incidence of soft signs were more likely to have a family history of schizophrenia.

In their short review of the subject, Heinrichs and Buchanan (1988) noted that neurological signs are more frequent among schizophrenics than among nonpsychiatric controls. They even noted that it is a tenable hypothesis that schizophrenics show more such signs than do subjects with nonpsychotic and affective disorders, but that the evidence is inconsistent on this point. They recommend that the functions to be studied should be more closely defined in the future, and, whenever possible, methods should be applied to follow up on the neurological changes implicated.

The following sections are concerned with tests of more closely described functional abilities in an effort to derive some less equivocal conclusions.

## B. Motor and Neuromuscular Function and Locomotor Coordination

Extreme forms of motor disturbance (e.g., bizarre postures, stupor, or hyperactivity) can be seen in the subgroup of catatonic schizophrenics. Slight oddities, such as clumsiness, jerkiness, stereotypes, mannerisms, or loss of smooth muscular coordination, had been observed in other subgroups even before the era of neuroleptics (see Manschreck, 1986, for a detailed clinical description).

Experimental studies of fine motor movements of schizophrenics in reaction-time tasks by Vrtunski *et al.* (1986, 1989) in the United States revealed (1) less smooth, more discontinuous movement; (2) less motor steadiness prior to response; (3) impaired agonist–antagonist muscle synchrony; and
(4) motor responses made with excessive force (compared with psychiatric and healthy control groups). There were no differences between those who did or did not receive medication. Furthermore, Günther *et al.* (1986) from Germany were able to distinguish between untreated schizophrenics and a group with depressive psychosis on the basis of a factor analysis of the motor disturbances.

In fact, abnormal movements such as those involved in facial expression had been studied long before these two reports. Using film records of interviews, Heimann and Spoerri (1957) from Switzerland showed that facial movements of untreated schizophrenics were much more broken up than those of other psychiatric groups. Even earlier studies in the United States, prior to the era of neuroleptic treatment, reported that, under stressful conditions, the electromyogram (EMG) showed an increased level of neuromuscular tension (Malmo *et al.*, 1948; Malmo and Shagass, 1949). Thirty years later, this was confirmed in EMG records of schizophrenics with a poor premorbid course (average age, 35 years) performing a reaction-time task. Compared with healthy controls, the schizophrenics showed more tension and a longer recovery time (Schneider and Grossi, 1979). The authors argued that the widely reported slowed reaction times of schizophrenics reflected not only a cognitive change but also inefficient motor function.

Tardive dyskinesia is a relatively frequent motor disturbance, with stereotyped movements that often involve facial muscles (e.g., rolling and smacking of the tongue; see Chapter 13). In general, it is considered to be a long-term effect of neuroleptic treatment. However, the incidence of tardive dyskinesia is variable. It has been suggested that early minor neurological damage may have occurred in those who later develop tardive dyskinesia. Chronic neuroleptic treatment then exacerbates the effect of this damage. A variation of this hypothesis suggests that such patients do not suffer as much from an earlier neurological insult as from a sensitization of dopamine receptors. In either case, it is important to note that there were case studies of disorders similar to tardive dyskinesia before the era of neuroleptic treatment (cf. Kraepelin, 1909; for a review, see Lohr *et al.*, 1986).

According to Kane's group at the Long Island Jewish Hillside Medical Center, tardive dyskinesia occurred in about one-fourth of all cases of schizophrenia. This group also found more neurological signs among schizophrenics with tardive dyskinesia. The patient most at risk was one who had a poor premorbid course (Wegner *et al.*, 1985; confirmed by Youssef and Waddington, 1988), yet Iagar *et al.* (1986) found no association with the occurrence of symptoms of defect as such.

According to a group of Tübingen (Germany), the genetic background seemed to be different in patients with and patients without tardive dyskinesia; the schizophrenic with the impairment was less likely to have a family history of schizophrenia (Bartels *et al.*, 1985). Kane and colleagues reported a similar trend (Wegner *et al.*, 1985).

Meltzer's group at the Illinois State Psychiatric Institute (Chicago) looked more closely at neuromuscular function in schizophrenics and, in particular, studied the speed of conductance in the tibial nerve (H reflex). At first, their results suggested that conductance in this reputedly monosynaptic reflex was abnormal. They later qualified this result and suggested that their finding was not specific (Goode *et al.*, 1977, 1979; Metz *et al.*, 1980).

Manschreck's group at Harvard concentrated on the question of the coordination of movement. Schizophrenics (average age, 27 years) were asked to follow a given rhythm by tapping. Compared with the performance of healthy and psychiatric controls, the tapping of schizophrenics was often desynchronized. However, the psychiatric controls (depressive and schizoaffective patients) were unable to keep up if the rhythm increased much in pace (Figure 7.1; Manschreck, 1983). The specific difference was restricted to the slower frequencies. It may be that at higher frequencies the patients, particularly the depressives, were simply less able to follow. Manschreck *et al.* (1981) claim that medication status did not affect the result, although tapping is a standard test for bradykinesia in Parkinson's patients, an illness with known alterations in the dopamine system (Matthews and Haaland, 1979).

One of the interesting outcomes of this investigation was that the impairment of tapping accuracy correlated with measures from clinical rating scales of the motor disturbance and thought disorder. This finding gives the impression that the motor abnormality is but a facet of a more global impairment of integrative functions in schizophrenia. The observation of Holzman (1972) that, during phases of increased thought disturbance, there was an increased inability to coordinate movement supports this thesis. Indeed, Manschreck and Ames (1984) found that a number of neurological abnormalities that showed up on a test battery correlated with formal thought

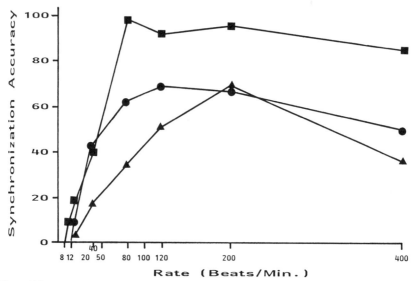

**Figure 7.1**   Accuracy of the synchronization of subjects' tapping with that of the experimenter versus increasing rates of tapping. Subject groups consisted of normal controls (■), schizophrenics (▲), and patients with affective disorder (●) (after Manschreck *et al.,* 1981).

disturbance. The motor tests included standing (with eyes open and closed), walking, finger–nose (with eyes open and closed), and a number of prescribed limb movements. The highest correlation with thought disorder ($r = 0.67$) was achieved by the total motor score. The authors found no relationship between neuroleptic treatment and the appearance of extrapyramidal side effects nor between neuroleptic dose and motor coordination scores.

Berger's group at Stanford (Malenka *et al.,* 1982, 1986) asked their subjects to follow targets on a video monitor with a cursor under conditions when they could or could not see the movement errors they made. They could correct their movements by reference to external cues or to their internal "model" of the task situation if no feedback was available (see Chapter 2 on problem solving). The schizophrenics were less able than other groups (including depressives) to coordinate movements with their internal "model" and correct their errors. (This ability may reflect frontal lobe function, as suggested by Welsh and Pennington, 1988, and Frith and Done, 1988.) On comparison with the study of Manschreck and Ames (1984), it is surprising to find that the schizophrenics did not show formal thought disorder and that their inability to monitor movements did not correlate with the severity of positive symptoms. Nevertheless, those with negative symptoms did perform somewhat better.

## II. Eye Movements: Neuro-opthalmological Studies

### A. Nystagmus

Nystagmus is a rhythmical eye movement that can occur spontaneously or is elicited by a moving stimulus. The former may reflect dysfunction in the vestibular system, cerebellum, or brainstem. Voluntary nystagmus can be elicited in normal persons by looking at the passing landscapes from a train window, or in the laboratory by moving vertical black and white stripes around the person (or vice versa). The eyes follow the stimulus for a short time (slow component), then flick back to the opposite side of the visual field to pick up the reappearing pattern (fast component). This is called a jerk nystagmus. Other methods of eliciting such movements (for clinical assessment) include irrigating the ear with warm and cold water, which causes the caloric nystagmus (see Adams and Victor, 1986, for more details).

Among neurological signs used in studies of schizophrenia, measures of nystagmus (along with pupillary reflexes) have perhaps the longest history of application. As early as 1921, Pekelsky from Germany reported on the reduction of induced nystagmus in two stuporous catatonic schizophrenics. This was confirmed in 23 reports in the older literature. It became accepted as a feature of schizophrenics and was viewed as reflecting disturbed vestibular function. (For a review, see Levy *et al.*, 1983.) However, it should be noted that there are no reports of a truly pathological (i.e., disturbed) spontaneous nystagmus.

More recent reports in no way confirm this early confidence. Holzman and his colleagues at Boston and Cambridge could find only slight "irregularities" and increased intraindividual variability of the jerk nystagmus (Levy *et al.*, 1978). Huddleston (1978) compared poor and good premorbid schizophrenics (as determined by the Phillips scale); only the former group showed some irregularities (i.e., shorter jumps for the fast component). Hirsch *et al.* (1980) reported a number of abnormal features, but they did not study healthy subjects. This is a critical weakness, since normal nystagmus varies considerably with the conditions for its elicitation and measurement.

None of the studies used a control group for the influence of treatment. All the patients had received or were receiving neuroleptic medication. A Russian group examined the question of a possible effect of treatment (Szymczewska, 1971; Levy *et al.*, 1983). Only the untreated catatonic patients showed deviations (slow or no nystagmus at all). Haloperidol treatment largely restored function, although, in comparison to noncatatonic patients and healthy controls, the difference was still apparent.

As noted in the introduction to this chapter, the psychological state can influence the measures of neurological function obtained during an examination. Levy *et al.* (1978) cited an earlier report that suggested that experimentally induced emotional excitement could lead to a reduction of the abnormality in nystagmus (Bourguignon, 1931). Levy and colleagues made an effort to control and maintain vigilance in their subjects and yet, as previously mentioned, they could find very little difference between schizophrenics (treated) and healthy subjects. It would not be too difficult in future work to systematically study whether the abnormalities reported for chronic, process, and catatonic schizophrenics could be attributed to changes in the level of activation or arousal.

Whatever the outcome, the results to date are not strong enough to implicate damage to the cerebellar–vestibular–brainstem system responsible for nystagmus.

The results from other methods examined in Holzman's laboratory were mixed. They found no differences with caloric nystagmus (Levy *et al.*, 1978). Another method comparing "whole-field" with "partial-field" nystagmus was more interesting (Latham *et al.*, 1981).

"Partial-field" stimulation means that the subject tries to hold part of the environment in a foveal position on the retina. "Whole-field" stimulation means there is no foveal fixation; the subject, who attempts to hold the whole visual field on the retina, is simply rotated to elicit nystagmus. Animal studies show that different cerebral areas are involved in these two types of effect.

The examination of the "whole-field" nystagmus obtained negative results. Latham *et al.* (1981) tested the "partial-field" by rotating colored stripes across a 125-cm screen. Fixation and attention were assured by asking subjects to name the colors. Perhaps it is not surprising that their schizophrenic patients showed abnormal pursuit movements, since the test situation approximates the more specific tests performed by this group in the study of smooth pursuit eye movements (SPEM), which will be discussed at length subsequently. Suffice it to say that the authors interpret the result in terms of a cortical, perhaps parietal, dysfunction, since "partial-field" responses are unaffected by damage to the labyrinth or brainstem.

## B. Saccadic Eye Movements (Stationary Target)

A saccade is a rapid ballistic eye movement usually intended to bring an extrafoveal stimulus onto the fovea for detailed inspection. Normally, the saccade often undershoots the target and is followed, after feedback about the target's position, by a corrective saccade approximately 100 msec later ("double saccades").

Various other categories of saccades have been described, depending on the situation in which they occur. For example, there are those that occur during the tracking and pursuit of a stimulus moving through the visual field (see Section II, C).

By contrast, this section deals with saccades (eye movements) toward a stationary target. These saccades may occur spontaneously (e.g., reflex), in response to the sudden appearance of an external stimulus in the periphery, or be more under the command of voluntary control (e.g., if the instruction asks for eye movements in the opposite direction to a new stimulus).

Important neuronal centers involved in saccades are the frontal eye fields, the superior colliculus, and the reticular formation as well as the caudate nucleus and the substantia nigra. It may be important to note that the frontal eye fields are especially involved in voluntary purposeful saccadic eye movements (Marx, 1989).

We will see in the following sections that schizophrenics have more problems with voluntary than with involuntary saccades.

In earlier experimental studies of saccadic function, there was much agreement that some basic features such as velocity and accuracy of the saccades toward a stationary object were not impaired in schizophrenics (Couch and Fox, 1934; Cegalis *et al.*, 1981; Iacono *et al.*, 1981; Levin *et al.*, 1981, 1982; Mather and Putchat, 1982).

Schmidt-Burgk *et al.* (1983) from Germany reported that undershooting was more marked in schizophrenics and schizoaffectives than in other patients or in healthy groups. However, since undershooting is basically a normal feature, it is difficult to say that their report refers to a pathological function.

Two groups in the United States have shown that intriguing abnormalities occur after experimental manipulations that make the task more difficult for the subject (Levin, 1981; Mather and Putchat, 1982). Mather and Putchat found that if there were fewer referents in the area of the target for guiding the movement, then overshooting was more likely, and that there were twice as many corrective saccades. Further study by Mather (1986) showed that this effect can also occur in normal controls, but under more extreme conditions. Additionally, Levin *et al.* (1984) found that latencies tended to increase if the movement covered a relatively wide angle ($>10°$, particularly to the right). Reminiscent of Mather and Putchat's finding, Levin's group found that schizophrenics had difficulty maintaining the target on the fovea (i.e., more corrective movements were needed).

Thus it seems that schizophrenics experience difficulties if there are relatively few cues to use in planning or voluntarily controlling saccades. Here, fine modulation over the sensory feedback loop seem to be less efficient in schizophrenics.

Demand on voluntary control is also high if the subject is instructed to switch gaze from a central point of fixation to a peripheral stimulus. A higher latency of shift again was particularly evident for the production of strategic (voluntary) saccades, but not for automatic (reflexive) saccades in the study by Done and Frith (1984) at the Clinical Research Center in England. These authors compared medicated and unmedicated schizophrenics with depressive patients and healthy controls.

**Table 7.1**  Correlations between Saccadic Reaction
Time and Psychopathology as Assessed with Brief
Psychiatric Rating Scale (BPRS)[a]

| | Saccadic reaction time correlation | |
| Psychopathology | r | p |
| --- | --- | --- |
| BPRS Items | | |
| Suspiciousness | .28 | .10 |
| Motor retardation | .41 | .01 |
| Unusual thought content | .29 | .05 |
| Blunted affect | .34 | .05 |
| BPRS Factor | | |
| Withdrawal/retardation | .41 | .01 |
| BPRS Total | .28 | .05 |

[a] Adapted from Mackert and Fletchner, 1989.

The research group of Gaebel in Berlin found no difference in simple
"normal" saccadic movement tasks, but a significantly higher rate of incorrect
eye movement was seen when the subject inspected drawings (i.e., scan with
an arrow and name the number the arrow is pointing to; Reischies et al.,
1988).

Frith and Done (1988) speculate that in those tasks in which the demands
on planning and voluntary control of eye movements are high, the underlying
deficit may reflect inefficient function of the frontal eye fields.

There is only one more direct indication of an involvement of the frontal
lobes in deviant voluntary saccadic movement in schizophrenia (see also
Section I). Fukushima et al. (1988) from Japan reported a longer latency for
so-called antisaccades in schizophrenic patients with mild atrophy of the
frontal fields. (They asked their subjects to look *away* from the target as
quickly as possible.) They interpreted their findings as a difficulty in the
voluntary control of saccadic movement.

Mackert and Flechtner (1989) at the Psychiatric Clinic in Berlin found that
the increase of latency to fixate a peripheral light flash could be 20 msec
longer in schizophrenics than in healthy controls. The degree of slowing
correlated with a poor course and negative symptoms, such as withdrawal and
psychomotor impairment (Table 7.1).

Thaker et al. (1989) found that schizophrenics with or without tardive
dyskinesia showed more inappropriate saccades and an increased latency;
those with tardive dyskinesia performed worse.

## C. Smooth Pursuit Eye Movements

Relatively early in the history of modern psychiatry, it was observed that certain psychiatric patients had difficulty fixating and following objects moving across the visual field (Diefendorf and Dodge, 1908).

In contrast to the (ballistic) saccadic jerk of the eyes toward a stationary object described in the previous section, the basic task here requires the eyes to follow the movements of an object, such as a pendulum swinging from side to side. The patient is asked to keep the bottom of the pendulum in the center of vision (i.e., on the fovea). Here, saccades are considered tracking errors since they represent interruptions of the smooth tracking performance and other off-target movements. Today, the experiment would be run with a stimulus oscillating on a video monitor and an electrooculogram (EOG) recording.

This situation elicits SPEMs. The neural circuitry controlling SPEM still has not been described fully and satisfactorily, but is known to involve the occipital and temporal cortex and the cerebellum (Adams and Victor, 1986).

Movement is detected by the retinal ganglion cells. Input passes up to the lateral geniculate nucleus, the visual cortex, and then over the occipitoparietal pathway. Processing under certain conditions can be modulated by influences from the temporal lobe and frontal eye fields. Output may occur over an occipitomesencephalic pathway (via the superior colliculus and thalamic pulvinar nucleus to the pontine reticular formation) or, alternatively, over a frontal mesencephalic pathway (Levin, 1984; Marx, 1989).

In contrast to nystagmus, SPEM cannot be viewed as an automatic process. This is apparent when subjects are encouraged to cooperate in the requirements of experimental investigations. Inattentiveness often leads to the pursuit movement lagging behind the stimulus. The subject can make up for this with a quick corrective saccade. Inattentiveness can also lead to overshooting of the target (see previous section). In Figure 7.2, an unadulterated pursuit movement is shown emerging from the EOG as a smooth sine wave. Saccades and other intrusions lead to irregular curves that, in the extreme case, almost obscure the underlying sine form.

The early studies of Diefendorf and Dodge (1908) and Couch and Fox (1934) reported no unusual saccadic movements among schizophrenics. However, the former study reported that such saccades intruded on the SPEM, presenting a steplike pattern. This occurred in other psychiatric patients, but not as often. Couch and Fox found a similar pattern among their psychiatric patients.

Only in the 1970s was this paradigm again taken up. The work of Holzman's group, initially in Chicago and subsequently at Harvard and Boston, is responsible for the resurgence of interest. The first of many reports from this group received wide attention. The investigators established that there were more frequent interruptions of the SPEM in both paranoid and

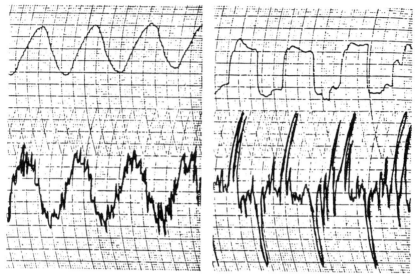

**Figure 7.2** Examples of two different SPEM recordings. The top of each sample shows the direct eye signal, the bottom shows the derivative of that signal displaying eye velocity. *Left,* Good tracking performance with few velocity arrests per cycle. *Right,* Poor tracking performance with many more arrests per cycle (from Holzman *et al.,* 1976, © 1976 American Medical Association).

nonparanoid groups than in manic depressive and nonpsychotic patients (Holzman *et al.,* 1973). (All patients were receiving neuroleptic treatment.) The curves shown for all patient groups in this study were significantly more irregular than those shown for healthy controls. (The question of specificity is immediately raised.) The authors found that encouraging the subjects to concentrate on the task could lead to a reduction of intrusions—particularly of saccades overshooting the target—but the differences between the groups remained.

The data do seem to indicate that, even when trying to focus their attention on the task, the schizophrenics show more interruptions than other psychiatric patients. In retrospect, it seems somewhat surprising that the EOGs in this and several subsequent studies were evaluated by visual inspection. A five category scale was used to rate the number of positive saccadic intrusions on the SPEM curve.

The study by Holzman's group was replicated by Shagass' group in Philadelphia a year later, also using a qualitative scale with which to rate the interruptions. This group confirmed the result for several medicated schizophrenic subgroups but could not differentiate the performance of manic depressives (Shagass *et al.,* 1974). However, other patients without either of these types of psychoses showed unremarkable SPEMs that were no different from those of the healthy controls.

From the latter result, one may conclude that the increase of saccadic intrusions was not specific to schizophrenia but specific to the endogenous psychoses. Another more extreme interpretation would be that the data show that poor SPEM is linked to the more severe psychiatric disturbances, and thus represents a nonspecific "generalized deficit" (cf. Chapter 2). This issue will be discussed again later.

## 1. The Role of Attention and Distraction

In 1976, both Holzman's and Shagass' groups published reports in which they took a closer look at the role played by attentional mechanisms in the production of irregular SPEMs. Attention was assured by asking the subjects to read numbers written on the base of the swinging pendulum or on the oscillating object on the video screen. The performance of patients, in particular those who had previously shown a poor performance in the absence of the numbers, improved dramatically. Nonetheless, the difference between the schizophrenics and healthy subjects remained significant (Figure 7.3; Holzman *et al.*, 1976; Shagass *et al.*, 1976).

Of special interest is that Holzman included a group of first degree relatives

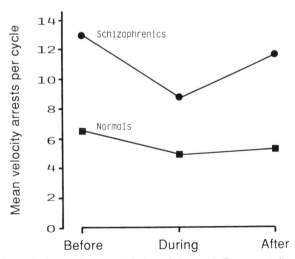

**Figure 7.3** Mean velocity arrests per cycle before, during, and after presentation of numbers for silent reading on the base of the swinging pendulum. (Attention condition, number to be read during tracking performance). Differences between schizophrenics (●) and normal individuals (■) remain significant under all three conditions (after Holzman *et al.*, 1976).

of the schizophrenics in this and later studies. Even under the condition that resulted in an improvement of attention and performance, 45% of the healthy subjects "at risk" showed abnormal SPEMs. This result should be compared with an incidence of 70% in the schizophrenic group. The questions of specificity and heredity will be discussed again subsequently.

Cegalis and Sweeney (1979) at Syracuse University, were also able to report on an improvement in their group of acute schizophrenics under similar conditions that required focused attention. (The information on the moving object varied over time.) However, as soon as they introduced distracting stimuli, SPEM quality deteriorated. This result has been confirmed by Pass *et al.* (1978) from Rochester, New York; Lipton *et al.* (1980) from Holzman's group; Tomer *et al.* (1981) in Israel; Galley *et al.* (1982) from Cologne, Germany; and Pivik *et al.* (1987) from Ottawa, Canada.

From these studies it can also be seen that distraction reduces the ability of the healthy subject to focus on the moving object. Brezinova and Kendell (1977), working in Edinburgh, showed that in the extreme case it was no longer possible to distinguish between the curves produced by the healthy and by the schizophrenic subjects. They found that, under conditions of mild distraction, schizophrenics responded in much the same way as healthy subjects in the presence of more salient irrelevant stimulation. Apparently, the schizophrenics were more sensitive to externally generated "noise" or had additional sources of internally generated interference. This point of view was suggested in a collaborative study between Dutch and American researchers (Wertheim *et al.*, 1985). These authors found that the threshold for the detection of rapid movement was significantly increased in the schizophrenics they studied. They supposed that this could arise as a result of increased noise or interference in the relevant CNS pathways.

## 2. Relationship to Activation, Metabolism, and Mild Cerebral Atrophy

The question of whether there are any correlations between the occurrence of abnormal SPEM and general indicators of pathological change, such as sympathetic arousal, monoamine metabolism, or signs of cerebral atrophy, is posed here. Unfortunately, few investigators have risen to the challenge of instigating such interdisciplinary studies.

In the Karolinska Hospital, Stockholm, Bartfai *et al.* (1983) recorded both the SPEM and the electrodermal orienting response (EDOR) in acute, unmedicated schizophrenics. The authors found a correlation between the incidence of abnormal SPEM and the number of EDORs during habituation to auditory orienting stimuli. Interestingly, there was no such correlation in the healthy controls. Since the finding did not also relate to basal skin conductance level, it is not entirely clear if there really was a relation between autonomic arousal and poor tracking. Owen (cited in Venables, 1978) reported findings that indirectly support Bartfai's results. Disturbed SPEM occurred among schizophrenics who displayed electrodermal response to orienting stimuli, but not among the electrodermal nonresponders.

The problem of ascertaining which variable is related to which response is illustrated by results from an interdisciplinary study conducted at the Menninger Foundation, Topeka, Kansas, by Spohn and colleagues (1985). They found that the patients most likely to show tardive dyskinesia usually had received high doses of neuroleptics; they also showed worse SPEM, slowed reaction times, decreased basal levels of skin conductance, and an increase of nonspecific electrodermal responses.

Siever *et al.* (1987), working at the National Institutes of Mental Health (NIMH) in Bethesda, Maryland, treated nonschizophrenic psychotic patients with amphetamine; the nature of the SPEM worsened in some patients but improved in others. This result could suggest a change of the level of activation (rate-dependent effect, which depended on the initial levels of activation), but the investigators could find no correlation with peripheral measures of monoamine metabolism. The just-mentioned study by Bartfai also included cerebrospinal fluid (CSF) measures of the metabolites of dopamine, noradrenaline, and serotonin in schizophrenics. These tests also failed to correlate with SPEM. Thus the implication of these variables for SPEM quality is not strong.

Other groups have asked whether cerebral atrophy in schizophrenia might be related to poor SPEM (cf. Chapter 8). The limited evidence available does not speak strongly for the hypothesis. Siever *et al.* (1986) found no relationship between SPEM and cerebroventricular size. However, since the number of subjects was very small, a relationship could easily have been missed (type 2 statistical error). With a much larger group of schizophrenics ($n = 67$; 101 healthy controls), Smeraldi *et al.* (1987) in Milan, Italy, even found an inverse relationship. The patients whose ventricle size was within the control range were the ones most likely to have abnormal SPEM. It must be kept in mind, though, that only more specific degenerative changes (e.g., frontal sulci) might be expected to influence areas that modulate eye movement (e.g., frontal eye field).

## 3. SPEM and Methodological Questions: Assessment Methods, Subgroup Characters, and Medication

In the work just discussed, a range of different criteria and methods for the evaluation of data have been used. The analysis methods range from the qualitative to the quantitative, from inspection of EOG sine waves or counting of saccadic jumps, to a full Fourier analysis. However, the degree of agreement between studies is surprisingly high (e.g., Holzman *et al.*, 1974; Lindsey *et al.*, 1978; Levin *et al.*, 1981). There is even agreement with such different procedures as EOG and infrared measurement, despite the possibility, for example, that large EEG variations can produce artifacts in the EOG record (e.g., Lindsey *et al.*, 1978; Iacono and Lykken, 1979; Ross *et al.*, 1988). Recently, the Holzman group corroborated their findings with the "search-coil technique." Here, the subject wears a scleral contact lens containing a small coil of wire. The signal is basically generated by the movement of the coil through a magnetic field (Levin *et al.*, 1988). The advantage of this method is that the incidence of artifacts is further reduced; the disadvantage is that not all schizophrenic patients tolerate the contact lens.

Repeated testing showed a high degree of reproducibility between measures taken over a 2-yr period ($r = 0.64$–$0.75$, depending on the nature of the procedure; Iacono and Lykken, 1981).

Even when taking different diagnostic habits into account, it can be said that abnormal eye movements are not restricted to any conventional subgroup of schizophrenics. Cegalis and Sweeney (1979) and Mather and Putchat (1982) found no difference in the incidence of abnormal SPEM between acute and chronic schizophrenics. However, more recent studies explicitly taking saccades into account indicate a slightly higher probability of occurrence of abnormalities in patients with a poor premorbid history and poor course or tardive dyskinesia (Spohn *et al.*, 1988; Thaker *et al.*, 1989).

In studies of motor function, there is always a suspicion that neuroleptic treatment, by way of its effect on dopaminergic systems, could be responsible for the deviations found. However, in the case of SPEM the consistency of the negative results in reports comparing effects of treatment, no treatment, dose effects, and the withdrawal of medication argue against the need for this suspicion (Spohn *et al.*, 1978; Karson, 1979; David, 1980; Mialet and Pichot, 1981; Levy *et al.*, 1983; Holzman *et al.*, 1984; Siever *et al.*, 1986). The absence of an effect on SPEM at the time of withdrawal from treatment did not distinguish between four families of neuroleptic used in the treatment of a group of 64 schizophrenics (Spohn *et al.*, 1988).

The uniformity of results suggesting that neuroleptics in the normal therapeutic dose range do not adversely affect SPEM in schizophrenics contrasts with preliminary data from studies of Rhesus monkeys (Ando *et al.*, 1986). They report that cumulative doses of methamphetamine ($<1.0$ mg/kg), apomorphine ($<0.5$ mg/kg), and haloperidol ($<0.03$ mg/kg) disrupted SPEMs in EOG records.

However, other types of agents with effects on CNS function do affect smooth pursuit eye movements (e.g., barbiturates and tranquilizers; for a review, see Lipton *et al.*, 1983). Even lithium, frequently used in the therapy of patients with affective disturbances, can exacerbate SPEM abnormalities (Iacono *et al.*, 1982; Levy *et al.*, 1985). The difference, in comparison to the absence of a provocative effect of neuroleptics, has important repercussions for the question of differentiating these two groups of psychiatrically disturbed patients (see the next section). The question of the specificity of variant SPEM to one or the other group, and the specificity of lithium's effect to one, is important enough to demand further study.

### 4. Are Deviant SPEMs Specific for Schizophrenia?

The results of the studies discussed thus far have not shown that irregular eye movements are a problem restricted to schizophrenia. Other studies confirm the suspicion that they may be a nonspecific feature (Lipton et al., 1980). Although Kobatke et al. (1983) from Japan did not study a psychotic group, they found irregular eye movements in 82% of their alcoholic group, which is reason enough to question claims of specificity. In Canada, Pivik (1979a,b) found much larger abnormalities among a group of psychiatric inpatients than among a group that had been released, without differentiating between diagnostic groups. This would seem to suggest a contribution of the severity of illness to the abnormalities recorded. The results of another Canadian group (Iacono et al., 1981) could be interpreted in the same way. They found no difference in the abnormalities of groups of schizophrenic and bipolar patients. The differences between the bipolar and unipolar patients could be explained by the reported increase of episodes of illness in the bipolar group. Furthermore, neither Kornhuber's group in Germany (Schmidt-Burgk et al., 1982) nor the Dutch group of Van den Bosch et al. (1987) found any specific eye movement problems of schizophrenics in comparison with other psychiatric groups.

Schizophrenics in remission were the subject of further study by the Canadian group of Iacono and Koenig (1983), whose comparison groups consisted of unipolar (25) or bipolar (24) depressives and nonpsychiatric controls (46). They reported that the specific type of disturbance in the schizophrenic group was that their eye movements lagged behind the swing of the pendulum. This "phase lag" consisted of many instances in which pursuit stopped. The number of stops correlated ($r = 0.61$) more with the previous severity of the illness rather than with the actual psychiatric status (e.g., psychosocial adjustment problems). These findings in schizophrenic patients with a relatively remitted symptom picture contrast with conclusions drawn to this point about the role of the severity of the illness.

### 5. Are Deviant SPEMs a Genetic Marker for Schizophrenia?

Having noted that the question of the specificity of SPEM deviance for schizophrenia has not been unequivocally established, it may seem surprising to learn that the SPEM abnormality is one of the prime candidates for a genetic marker for schizophrenia. This opinion is largely attributable to Holzman's group and their intensive studies of the twins (Holzman et al.,

**Table 7.2**   Quality of SPEM Performance$^{a,b}$

|  |  | Parents | |
|---|---|---|---|
|  |  | Good | Poor |
| Schizophrenics | Good ($n = 13$) | 16 | 7 |
|  | Poor ($n = 9$) | 9 | 6 |
| Manics | Good ($n = 4$) | 12 | 1 |
|  | Poor ($n = 8$) | 7 | 1 |

$^a$ Adapted from Holzman *et al.*, 1984.
$^b$ Performance of parents of schizophrenics ($n = 38$) in relation to the performance of their schizophrenic sons or daughters ($n=22$) and performance of parents of manics ($n = 21$) in relation to the performance of their manic sons or daughters ($n = 12$).

1978, 1980) and first degree relatives of schizophrenics (Holzman *et al.*, 1984).

Considering the potential consequences of confirming that a particular variable is a genetic marker, it is appropriate to be very strict about the definitions and methods used for obtaining the results and for their interpretations.

If deviant SPEM is a genetic marker for schizophrenia, then such abnormalities must occur with a higher than random incidence among the relatives of schizophrenics. Of special interest here is the question of whether the nonschizophrenic partners of monozygotic twins discordant for the illness also show abnormal SPEM.

Holzman's group studied parents of patients with schizophrenia and with bipolar affective disorders. In 1984 they reported that the incidence of poor SPEM was higher in the parents of schizophrenics than in the parents of manic–depressives (Table 7.2). The schizophrenic patients themselves showed a higher incidence of SPEM abnormalities, but this was not statistically different from the bipolar patients (59% vs. 41%). Holzman *et al.* (1988) interpreted the nonspecific findings in the patients and the putative specificity in the relatives as a genuine defect underlying schizophrenia.

The higher incidence of poor SPEM in the affective patients was explained by Holzman and co-workers (1984) with reference to the exacerbating influence of lithium on eye movements (Iacono *et al.*, 1982). At the time of the test, most of the manic–depressive patients were receiving this medication and the schizophrenics were receiving neuroleptic treatment, but whether lithium was, in fact, causing poor SPEM in one case while neuroleptic treatment was causing no change in the other is a debatable point. A direct comparison between untreated groups of schizophrenics and untreated manic–

depressives has not been made yet. A further problem with this study was the small database. There were only 12 sets of parents, from which not every parent was available for the investigation.

Other researchers sought support for the postulated heritability of SPEM by examining persons with schizotypal personality disorder. There is indeed some evidence that this group is genetically linked to schizophrenia (cf. Chapter 10). Both Smeraldi *et al.* (1987) from Italy and Siever *et al.* (1984) from the United States found that individuals with DSM-III schizotypal personality characteristics (in part, blind rating) showed more deviant SPEM than did controls.

Holzman's group also investigated the marker status of SPEM in twins. Holzman's subjects originated in Kringlen's twin study in Norway and a blind evaluation was made in the United States. The study covered three experiments on both monozygotic (MZ) and dizygotic (DZ) twins. Independent evaluators divided the EOG curves into categories of "good" and "poor."

The results of successive studies of schizophrenic and bipolar twins largely agree with one another (Holzman and Levy, 1977; Holzman *et al.*, 1978, 1980). The main result was that the concordance rate for SPEM impairment was higher than that for the schizophrenic illness in MZ twins, that is, there were several cases in which one MZ twin was schizophrenic but both showed poor SPEM, although their genetic material was identical (i.e., concordant for poor SPEM, discordant for schizophrenia). Thus, the hypothesis of a marker status for poor SPEM seems to be supported.

However, this hypothesis does require some qualification: SPEM performance is, to a high degree, concordant in healthy MZ twins (Iacono and Lykken, 1979). Therefore, it can be supposed that poor SPEM is also genetically transmitted, irrespective of the diagnostic status of the MZ twins. Thus, concordance for SPEM in schizophrenic MZ twins does not necessarily mean that poor SPEM performance is genetically associated with schizophrenia.

Another finding also questions the position of poor SPEM as a genetic marker. As with the study of parents of schizophrenics (Holzman *et al.*, 1984), some schizophrenics did not show disorganized eye tracking but the unaffected MZ twin did (e.g., Holzman *et al.*, 1980). (That some schizophrenics with good tracking have relatives with poor tracking was also confirmed in the previously mentioned studies with first degree relatives.)

The presence of a considerable proportion of MZ twins discordant for SPEM and schizophrenia leads to the conclusion that the link between deviant SPEM and a hereditary basis for schizophrenia is not as close as assumed by Holzman's group. Therefore, it is surprising to read that Matthysse, Holzman, and Lange (1986) strongly simplify the matter by invoking pleiotropy, that is, they conclude that there is a latent genetic agent expressing itself as a schizophrenic phenotype, a poor SPEM phenotype (i.e., a genotype that results in two different phenotypes), or both. The genotype is called a "latent trait" by the authors. Holzman *et al.* (1988, p. 641) suggest that poor SPEM and schizophrenics "may be transmitted as independent manifestations of an autosomal dominant trait." Thus, Matthysse, Holzman, and co-workers opt for the single major locus model, which is not supported by most of the genetic transmission analysis described in Chapter 10.

Since this supposition, if true, would have considerable consequences for the understanding of schizophrenia, it is necessary to very carefully inspect the database for this assumption. The data in the report by Holzman *et al.* (1980) show that only 4 of the 10 MZ pairs of twins included a partner who was ill with an unequivocal diagnosis of schizophrenia. Thus, at least in their second twin study, the database for the concordance analysis is decidedly limited. The other pairs seem more likely to show a manic–depressive illness. (We refer to the data presented in their review; Lipton *et al.,* 1983). Another problem is that poor SPEM is not limited to schizophrenia, as discussed earlier.

However, the recent hypothesis of Holzman and colleagues were derived from another examination of the Norwegian twin project but this time based on a larger sample, where besides Holzman, Kringlen and Matthysse were the principal investigators. Eye tracking was examined in the offspring (children and grandchildren) of MZ and DZ twins, at least one of which had schizophrenia (details of the diagnosis were not given) a major affective disorder, or a reactive psychosis (Holzman *et al.,* 1988). The latter group was the control group. The authors were able to demonstrate that poor SPEM was much more common in the offspring of the MZ and DZ twins with schizophrenic probands than in the offspring of the twin groups with affective or reactive probands. For example, from the schizophrenic MZ group with 57 offspring, 3 had a diagnosis of schizophrenia and 18 showed poor SPEM (rated without knowledge of the subject status). From the control group of MZ twins with affective disorder or reactive psychosis, in 41 offspring no schizophrenia was reported and only 4 subjects showed poor SPEM. Judging from previous studies, the authors expected poor SPEM in 8% of normal probands. They found 10% probands with poor SPEM in the control group and 32% in the index offspring group. In the index offspring group, 5% of the probands had schizophrenia.

Precisely what can be deduced from these data? The incidence of poor SPEM is clearly higher in the index group. Therefore, the possibility that the determination of some characteristic forms of eye movement may have a genetic component and that this component is somehow linked with schizo-phrenia cannot be completely refuted. Some reservations are nevertheless necessary concerning the question of specificity, the role of medication, the diagnosis of some of the probands, the still puzzling low concordance between schizophrenia and poor SPEM performance in the studies including relatives, and that in some families "more subjects than expected" had neither the SPEM abnormalities nor schizophrenia. Holzman *et al.* (1988) therefore suggest that one can study the "symptom-free family members for other indications of the same latent structure" (p. 646). These investigators assume that it is likely that not all the phenotypic features of the hypothetical latent trait have been revealed by now.

## III. Eye Blinking

### A. Rate of Blinking

It has long been observed that the rate of blinking increases in some schizophrenics (Kraepelin, 1913) and decreases in Parkinson's patients (Ponder and Kennedy, 1928). However, a surge of interest in the increases shown by schizophrenics only occurred at the end of the 1970s (e.g., Stevens, 1978; Cegalis and Sweeney, 1979; Karson, 1979). Such an increased blink rate could have an exogenous psychological or an endogenous biological origin. Excitement, fear, or increased dopaminergic activity can lead to an increased rate of blinking. Their sources can be relevant for schizophrenics.

Dopamine agonists (e.g., apomorphine, methamphetamine, L-DOPA) can lead to an increase of blinking in monkeys whereas antagonists (neuroleptics) can lead to a decrease (Karson *et al.*, 1981a; Ando *et al.*, 1986). In patients with Parkinson's disease, who suffer from an insufficiency of dopaminergic activity as do patients treated with neuroleptics, there is usually a reduced rate of eye blinking (Karson *et al.*, 1982; Kleinman *et al.*, 1984b). L-DOPA can raise low blink rates and dopamine metabolism in patients with Parkinson's disease (Karson *et al.*, 1984). Neuroleptics can suppress high blink rates in patients with Tourette syndrome and schizophrenia (Cohen *et al.*, 1980; Karson *et al.*, 1982).

Not all authors found a neuroleptic-induced decrease in schizophrenics to be significant (Mackert *et al.*, 1988). However, the latter authors did find that blink rate correlated with scores for the Brief Psychiatric Rating Scale (BPRS) factor of hostility. It is interesting to note that Kleinman *et al.* (1984) found that the decreased blink rate in schizophrenics correlated with the haloperidol-induced reduction of thought disturbance, but only in the patients with normal cerebral ventricles (cf. Chapter 8).

Both Stevens (1978) and Karson (1983) noted that, after withdrawal of neuroleptic treatment, their subjects showed an increased blink rate. Karson argued against the possibility that the recorded increase merely reflected a rebound effect of neuroleptic withdrawal by emphasizing that he could find no relationship between blink rate and the incidence of tardive dyskinesia. Indeed, blink rates decreased again to normal levels with the reinstatement of neuroleptic treatment.

Rates of blinking may vary enormously between individuals in a group of schizophrenics (e.g., 22 ± 13/min), but high rates correlate with low levels of monoamine oxidase, the catabolic enzyme for dopamine (a feature that could enhance synaptic activity of dopamine; Freed et al., 1980; Karson et al., 1983).

Considering that normal adult blink rates are sometimes 4–5 times higher than those basically required for lubrication of the eyes (Doane, 1980), it becomes clear that many factors can affect the rate of blinking. These include affect states (e.g., fear and anxiety; McEwen and Goodner, 1969), gender (McLean et al., 1985), level of somatic activity shown (Obrist et al., 1970), and the season when the subjects are studied (Karson et al., 1984a).

There is also no doubt that changes of blink rate occur in a number of psychiatric conditions other than schizophrenia. These include the depressed and the demented as well as those with schizoaffective psychoses (Freed et al., 1980; Mackintosh et al., 1983; Boutros et al., 1988). Thus the interest in blinking has nothing to do with an abnormality specific to schizophrenia. The interest lies in the extent to which it may point to those patients, established by other criteria to be schizophrenic, who have raised levels of dopamine activity, and through this identification to see what other features are common to the subtype (e.g., perhaps type 1 schizophrenia of Crow and Kleinman et al., 1984). The results mentioned earlier point to the possibility that a subgroup of schizophrenics with raised dopamine activity may exist, but much work remains to be done to sort out the relationships between the factors that can contribute to changes of eye blink rates (i.e., intervening variables such as emotional arousal) and on the symptoms associated with high (and low) rates of blinking in psychiatric patients.

## B. Blink Reflex

The blink reflex, in contrast to spontaneous blinking, is induced by a quick movement of an object toward the eye, by an airpuff, or by a sudden high intensity noise. The blink or startle reflex was examined in a very mixed group of schizophrenics by Braff et al. (1978). They used high intensity tones and recorded both a longer latency and a greater amplitude for the blink reflex in schizophrenics. However, the result is difficult to assess because all but one of the patients were treated with neuroleptics and no psychiatric control group was included in the study. Later, Geyer and Braff (1982) compared the habituation of the blink reflex between patients and healthy controls and found a slower rate of habituation in medicated schizophrenic patients. Geyer and Braff concluded that startle habituation was impaired in schizophrenics. In addition, they inferred from animal studies that neuroleptics do not influence habituation rate. Stevens (1978) noted, however, that after withdrawal of neuroleptic treatment their patients showed a decrease of the blink reflex; in some cases it vanished altogether. Although Stevens did not test habituation directly, the two results seem to be contradictory and any conclusion is equivocal.

## IV. Pupillary Responses

Two different responses have been measured in schizophrenics: the pupillary reflex and the pupillary response to events or stimuli with emotional or motivational content. The pupillary reflex is the response of the pupil to an increase in light intensity (the diameter decreases in response to light flashes). The response of the pupil to a stimulus with cognitive, emotional, or motivational relevance is to increase in diameter. This "psychological" reaction is most easily demonstrated in task situations requiring cognitive effort.

As early as 1911, Bumke reported unusual features of the pupillary response in the mentally ill patient. Approximately 60% of patients with dementia praecox showed some abnormality. "That symptom, that is really typical of dementia praecox, is the absence of psychoreflexes, the presence of pupillary restlessness, and the absence of reflex of increasing in size in response to sensitive (sic) stimuli" (Bumke, 1911, p. 255; translated by the authors). In fact, Westphal (1907) had already noted that catatonics showed no pupillary response to bright light and maintained unusually dilated pupils. This observation was confirmed by Koester (1927) and Levine and Schilder (1942).

However, these were episodic reports; systematic study only slowly got under way in the 1930s as the techniques for measurement improved, first with the use of the cine camera and later with videorecording combined with computer analysis.

## A. Pupillary Reflex

The main reason for expressing an interest in the reflex response to light is that a positive result could imply impaired neural function in schizophrenia. The nature of such an impairment might yield in investigation since the normal circuitry is relatively well understood (Adams and Victor, 1986). Furthermore, since dopamine is a neurotransmitter in the retina (Kramer, 1971; Kramer et al., 1971) and the dopamine hypothesis plays a significant role in schizophrenia research (Chapter 13), positive results could have considerable heuristic value. An indication of this potential is provided by the repeatedly observed decrease of pupil width (miosis) after treatment with dopamine-blocking neuroleptics (Lauber, 1973; Smolen et al., 1975; review by Buchsbaum, 1977).

Lowenstein, stimulated by Westphal's earlier finding, joined him in the first cinematic investigation of pupillary responses in Germany at the end of the

1920s. Together they found a number of different types of response to light. Most frequently seen were delayed and reduced reactions to light. However, some subjects showed considerable variation of responses, some of which were much stronger than usual. Notable here is that they recorded a decreased amplitude of the pupillary reflex in schizophrenics in the period before the introduction of neuroleptic therapy (Lowenstein and Westphal, 1933).

About 25 years later, a team from the New York Psychiatric Institute repeated and extended such studies using an infrared television camera to record pupil changes, analyzing the data online (Hakerem *et al.,* 1964). They reported two basic results: (1) Acute schizophrenics showed a smaller pupil diameter under baseline conditions at the start of the experiment, even when unmedicated. (2) Both acute and chronic schizophrenics showed a smaller maximal contraction in response to intense light.

The result for acute subjects could be explained by Wilder's law of initial values (1958). If the diameter was smaller at the start of the experiment, it could not decrease in diameter as much as pupils of normal subjects that were wider to begin with. The team from New York checked this point and found that maximal contraction was still reduced in acute patients when only those patients with initial pupil widths that matched the normal control group were tested (Hakerem and Lidsky, 1975).

Patterson (1976) achieved the same result for chronic medicated schizophrenics; in fact, he differentiated between patients within this group. Schizophrenics who did not show EDORs showed smaller responses to light than electrodermal responders (cf. Chapter 5). However, generalizations cannot be made from these results. In Tübingen, Straube and colleagues studied a group of untreated acute schizophrenics diagnosed according to Bleuler's criteria (Straube, 1982; Straube *et al.,* 1987). They could confirm neither the reduced response to light nor the relationship of response amplitude to EDOR reactivity. Based on the initial pupil width and the amplitude of their response to light of different intensities, the patients were no different from healthy controls. In contrast to this negative result, the Tübingen group was able to show that after 14 days of treatment with the neuroleptic Perazine, the latency for the light response was delayed (Straube *et al.,* unpublished). This delay correlated with the dose and plasma level of neuroleptic but not with any change of psychopathology as assessed by the BPRS. The pupil diameter of the healthy subjects remained stable for given conditions during all repeat sessions.

As mentioned earlier, if the results cannot be generalized, perhaps the impairments may be specific to particular subgroups. A series of studies from Rubin in the 1960s and 1970s at the Eastern Psychiatric Institute in Philadelphia lent support to this idea (Rubin, 1974, 1976). Rubin studied the light and dark reflexes in patients with functional psychoses (i.e., not only schizophrenics) and found both reduced and excessive responses. However, this does not mean that only extreme responses were recorded; some patients showed unremarkable reflexes. Unfortunately, the nature of the subgroups showing one type of response or the other was not described. Instead, the author preferred to attempt an interpretation in terms of an imbalance of the sympathetic–parasympathetic nervous system (adrenergic–cholinergic balance). (We will not elaborate on this concept here since such studies alone provide insufficient evidence for the argument.) Rubin's results were partly a replication of those of Stilson *et al.* (1966) but, in general, his findings have not been followed up.

It is thus concluded that there is no general and uniform pattern of the light reflex in schizophrenics. As far as reduced responsiveness is concerned, it appears that a subgroup of perhaps chronic schizophrenics with negative symptoms, may be so characterized. However, the exact features characterizing this subgroup have not been described yet.

## B. "Psychological" Modulation of the Pupillary Response

Very little systematic research has been carried out on pupil dilation in schizophrenic patients faced with stressful, emotional, or cognitive stimuli. Hakerem (1973) investigated both event-related potentials and pupillary reactions to the rare tones in an oddball discrimination (cf. Chapter 5). The rare stimulus was meaningful since it required a response. The amplitudes of both the $P_{300}$ potential and the pupillary response to the stimulus were attenuated. This combined deficit was confirmed for the schizophrenics studied by Steinhauer and Zubin (1982) and Friedman *et al.* (1973).

In Tübingen, Straube (1982) combined measures of pupillary response with electrodermal and heart rate recordings in the study of responses to cognitive and emotional stimuli (see Chapter 5). The acutely ill untreated schizophrenics reacted more strongly, with larger pupillary diameters, than did the healthy controls during the presentation of a cognitive task (the digit-span task), despite comparable recall performance.

This result is in contrast to the findings mentioned previously. Differences in the stimulation conditions or the subgroups tested (acute patients here and more chronic patients in the previous studies) may explain the conflicting result, but the contrast is more likely due to differences in the drug status. In the Tübingen study, all patients were unmedicated. Unfortunately, since no psychiatric control group was tested, no conclusion on the specificity of the finding could be made. In addition, no differences in electrodermal and heart rate responses were recorded among the groups studied. Responses to emotional words did not differ among groups for all three psychophysiological measures. Thus, it is possible to draw the tentative conclusion that the psychophysiological responses of schizophrenics performing cognitive tasks do not always show a uniform pattern of attenuation. This conclusion qualifies but does not contradict the often reported finding of a decreased responsiveness, as mentioned in Chapters 5 and 6.

# V. Suggested Readings

The monograph of Hoskins (1946) is still well worth reading; he presents discussions of early neurological and psychological investigations and the book contains good clinical descriptions of patients (high and low active group) before the era of neuroleptics, done at the famous Worcester Research Laboratories. (Shakow was one of the other well-known researchers at these laboratories; see RT research, Chapter 4.) The handbook edited by Nasrallah and Weinberger (1986) contains important contributions to the field of neurological impairments in schizophrenia, for example, Manschreck (1986) gives a comprehensive survey of motor problems in schizophrenia and Lohr *et al.* (1986) review the possible co-variations between tardive dyskinesias and neurological signs. Holzman *et al.* (1988) is suggested, because the authors develop their hypothesis about the putative relationship between SPEM deviance and the mode of genetic transmission in schizophrenia.

# VI. Summary Statements and Interpretations

## A. Neurological Soft Signs

Many, but not the majority of, schizophrenics may show a neurological soft sign. The absence of clear-cut results reflects the number and heterogeneous nature of the tests applied. The likelihood of neurological signs is highest in chronic or poor premorbid schizophrenics. There are reports for and against an increased incidence of such signs in patients with negative symptoms and subjects with a family history of mental illness.

Some of the neurological soft signs reported are probably effects of long-term neuroleptic treatment, but a subgroup with such signs may also show an increased incidence of cerebral atrophy (see Chapter 8) and negative symptoms.

## B. Motor Coordination

Case reports and experimental studies of patients with and without medication suggest that motor disorganization can be prominent in schizophrenia.

Sensorimotor coordination problems correlate with the incidence of formal thought disorder. If visual feedback is reduced, schizophrenics are less able to use feedback from their own movements.

Tardive dyskinesia is often considered a consequence of long-term neuroleptic treatment, although it was originally reported before the era of neuroleptics. Interesting are findings of a poor premorbid course in those who later developed tardive dyskinesia. There are also reports that tardive dyskinesia is more common in patients with no family history of schizophrenia.

The latter results point to a subgroup with a low genetic load but more prominent neurological signs. Mild cerebral atrophy, which itself may occur more in schizophrenics without a family history for the illness, may be associated with tardive dyskinesia. However, not all motor deviations are signs for a subgroup of schizophrenics with a low genetic load.

More central to schizophrenia are signs of impaired sensorimotor coordination. Could the correlation between poor sensorimotor performance and thought disorder imply a common central disturbance? Also of interest is the difficulty schizophrenics have in using motor feedback when the visual cues for task performance are removed (see also similar findings with saccadic and smooth eye movements).

Both findings suggest the involvement of higher centers responsible for the integration of feedback from ongoing behavior into the internal motor plans [Abbs and Cole, 1982; see similar mechanisms in speech production and perhaps in integrating feedback from various sources, for example, contextual cues in thought processes (Rosenbaum, 1982, 1987) and goal-setting]. In a similar vein, Frith and Done (1988) argue that schizophrenics with positive symptoms have difficulty monitoring actions. These authors speculate that delusional symptoms may be based on a split between one's own action and the central monitoring of these actions. (See Chapters 15 and 16 for more details.)

## C. Nystagmus

Older reports of reduced (experimentally induced) nystagmus have not been confirmed, but there are reports of minor irregularities in poor premorbid and catatonic patients.

Anomalous vestibular function is therefore unlikely to underlie schizophrenic symptoms.

## D. Saccadic Eye Movements (Fixed Target)

Under usual stimulus conditions (fixation saccades toward a suddenly appearing object), no deviations are found. Saccadic movements are deviant if the demand on voluntary control or planning is higher than under conditions under which more spontaneous (reflexive) saccades occur. The first conditions are conditions under which a voluntary movement away from the target is required or where referential cues are reduced.

These findings seem to suggest that the deviance is stronger if the control of higher cortical centers is required. A neuroanatomical candidate for this may be the frontal eye fields. There is one direct hint for this possibility: schizophrenics with mild atrophy in the frontal lobe perform more poorly in a task in which the demands on voluntary control of the saccadic movements are high. In addition, neurophysiological evidence exists that the frontal eye fields play an important role in voluntary saccades (see text; for review, see Marx, 1989).

It is interesting, indeed striking, that the saccadic failures under reduction of referential cues seem to parallel the behavioral (see Chapter 2) and SPEM (see Section VI) failures of schizophrenics under reduction of referential cues. It seems possible that a common neurophysiological basis is the cause (weakness of performance control if execution of control has to rely on an internal model of the environment; Frith and Done, 1988).

## E. Smooth Pursuit Eye Movements (SPEM)

### 1. SPEM in Actively Symptomatic Patients

Irregular SPEM is obvious in schizophrenics and patients with an affective disorder. Deviations can be reduced by enhancing the conditions for focused attention. However, deviations remain apparent, particularly in schizophrenics.

The schizophrenic SPEM is similar to that produced by normal subjects when distracted; it is present in treated and untreated patients. (Some authors claim that lithium causes SPEM deviation in the affectively disordered patient.)

Poor SPEM performance correlates with delayed habituation of the EDOR and is more common in schizophrenics without signs of cerebral atrophy. No correlations with other physiological indicators (e.g., metabolites) have been reported.

The question of whether lithium treatment can induce poor SPEM in the affectively disordered patient requires resolution. This would also answer the question of the specificity of SPEM anomalies. (Is the difference from depressives merely a quantitative one?) Distraction seems to play a significant role in the performance of schizophrenics. Some authors are therefore of the opinion the poor SPEMs in schizophrenics are the result of a "higher internal neuronal noise." Viewed critically, the data seem to show that the most disturbed patients are the poorest SPEM performers. However some symptom-free relatives of schizophrenics may also show poor SPEM (see Section VI, E, Z).

### 2. SPEM in Asymptomatic Probands

There are three reasons for suggesting that poor SPEM is related to a basic deficit in schizophrenia. (1) Some reports claim that remitted schizophrenic patients show a poorer SPEM than patients in remission from an affective disturbance. (2) Other reports show a higher incidence of poor SPEM in the first degree relatives of schizophrenics than in those of patients with an affective disorder. (3) Poor SPEM is reported from schizotypal probands. However, a report from the Holzman group creates some conceptual problems: schizophrenics frequently may show no deviations when the relative does.

The Holzman group claims that a genetic mechanism is involved in poor SPEM as a latent trait that can appear in the schizophrenic, the "healthy" carrier, or both. Even if the findings are genuine, the interpretations are puzzling. Discrepant cases are assumed to show the "independent manifestations of an autosomal dominant trait" (Holzman *et al.*, 1988). This is a courageous theory.

An alternative but more conservative interpretation follows: SPEM deviations are unspecific features and not necessarily linked with schizophrenia or the genetic risk. (There are indications, as mentioned in the text, that schizophrenics who show a reduction of the EDOR or mild cerebral atrophy show fewer signs of SPEM deviance. Somewhat contradictory are the reported associations of tardive dyskinesias with SPEM disorder.)

## F. Blink Rate

The observation of an increased blink rate in untreated schizophrenics can be a sign of raised dopaminergic activity. However, higher blink rates are not limited to schizophrenia and may reflect psychological factors (e.g., anxiety, arousal).

Examination of blink rates may serve as an additional tool to identify a putative subgroup with raised dopamine activity.

## G. Blink Reflex

There are contradictory findings on the blink (startle) reflex. Both decreases and a lack of inhibition have been recorded.

## H. Pupillary Reflex

There may be subgroup differences. Chronic schizophrenics, perhaps with negative symptoms, show reduced pupillary reactivity to light stimuli. These patients more often may be EDOR nonresponders, but this was not confirmed in a study of acute patients. Reports of higher reflex activity receive less support.

There are similar findings of the reduction of physiological responses in chronic negative-symptom schizophrenics in other fields. However, the existence of a subgroup is less clearly supported.

## 1. Psychological Response of the Pupil

The simultaneous measurement of $P_{300}$ and pupillary response reveals a concomitant lower response to infrequent events.

This shows that the failure of schizophrenics to respond adequately to events of different probability (concept-driven information processing) is not limited to brain potentials (see Chapters 2, 4, and 6).

Stronger pupil responses are observed in an acute untreated group with positive symptoms in a digit-span task. Both patients and healthy controls showed the same recall performance.

The study requires replication. Depending on the type of task and the subgroup tested, schizophrenics seem to exert more effort to attain the performance level of healthy controls.

# References

Abbs, J. H., and Cole, K. J. (1982). Memorial mechanism of motor equivalence and goal achievement. In S. P. Wise (Ed.), *Higher brain functions. Recent explorations of the brain's emergent properties.* New York: Wiley.

Abel, L. A., Ziegler, A. S. (1988). Smooth pursuit eye movements in schizophrenics—What constitutes quantitative assessment? *Biological Psychiatry, 24*, 747–761.

Adams, R., and Victor, M. (1986). *Principles of neurology*, 3d. ed. New York: McGraw-Hill.

Ando, K., Johanson, C. E., and Schuster, C. R. (1986). Effects of dopaminergic agents on eye tracking before and after repeated methamphetamine. *Pharmacological and Biochemical Behavior, 24*, 693–699.

Balogh, D. W., Schuck, J. R., and Leventhal, D. B. (1979). A study of schizophrenics' ability to localize the source of a sound. *Journal of Nervous and Mental Disease, 167*, 484–487.

Bartels, M., Mann, K., and Friedrich, W. (1985). Tardive dyskinesia: Marked predominance of nongenetic schizophrenia. *Biological Psychiatry, 20*, 94–119.

Bartfai, A., Levander, S. E., and Sedvall, G. (1983). Smooth pursuit eye movements, clinical symptoms, CSF metabolites and skin conductance habituation in schizophrenic patients. *Biological Psychiatry,18*, 971–987.

Bartko, G., Zador, G., Horvath, S., and Herczeg, I. (1988). Neurological soft signs in chronic schizophrenic patients: Clinical correlates. *Biological Psychiatry, 24*, 458–460.

Bourguignon, G. (1931). Relations de la chronaxie vestibulaire avec l'emotivité, à l'etat normal et dans le pseudomongolisme et la demence precoce. *Comptes Rendus des Seances de l'Academie des Science, 193*, 250–253.

Boutros, N. N., and Hatch, J. P. (1988). Blink rate on routine EEGs: Possible psychiatric significance. *Biological Psychiatry, 24*, 717–720.

Braff, D., Stone, C., Callaway, E., Gever, M., Glick, I., and Bali, L. (1978). Prestimulus effects on human startle reflex in normals and schizophrenics. *Psychophysiology, 15*, 339–343.

Brezinová, V., and Kendell, R. E. (1977). Smooth pursuit eye movements of schizophrenics and normal people under stress. *British Journal of Psychiatry, 130*, 59–63.

Buchsbaum, M. S. (1977). Psychophysiology and schizophrenia. *Schizophrenia Bulletin, 3*, 7–14.

Bumke, O. (1911). *Die Pupillenstörungen bei Geistes- und Nervenkrankheiten.* Jena: Fischer.

Cegalis, J. A., and Deptula, D. (1981). Attention in schizophrenia: Signal detection in the visual periphery. *Journal of Nervous and Mental Disease, 169*, 751–760.

Cegalis, J. A., and Sweeney, J. A. (1979). Eye movements in schizophrenia: A quantitative analysis. *Biological Psychiatry, 14*, 13–26.

Cohen, D. J., Detlor, J., Young, J. G., and Shaywitz, B. A. (1980). Clonidine ameliorates Gilles de la Tourette's syndrome. *Archives of General Psychiatry, 37*, 1350–1357.

Couch, F. H., and Fox, J. C. (1934). Photographic study of ocular movements in mental disease. *Archives of Neurology and Psychiatry, 34*, 556–578.

Cox, S. M., and Ludwig, A. M. (1979). Neurological soft signs and psychopathology. I. Findings in schizophrenia. *Journal of Nervous and Mental Disease, 167*, 161–165.

David, I. (1980). Disorders of smooth pursuit eye movements in schizophrenics and the effect of neuroleptics in therapeutic doses. *Activitas Nervosa Superior*, (Praha) *22*, 156–157.

Diefendorf, A. R., and Dodge, R. (1908). An experimental study on the ocular reactions of the insane from photographic records. *Brain, 31*, 451.

Doane, M. G. (1980). Interaction of eyelids and tears in corneal wetting and the dynamics of the normal human eye blink. *American Journal of Opthalmology, 89*, 507–516.

Done, D. J., and Frith, C. D. (1984). Automatic and strategic control of eye movements in schizophrenia. In A. G. Gale and F. Johnson (Eds.), *Theoretical and applied aspects of eye movement research.* Amsterdam: Elsevier.

Done, D. J., and Frith, C. D. (1984). The effect of context dunnig word perception in schizophrenic patients. *Brain and Language, 23*, 318–336.

Done, D. J., and Frith, C. D. (1989). Automatic and strategic volitional saccadic eye movements in psychotic patients. *European Archives of Psychiatry and Neurological Science, 239*, 27–32.

Faustman, W. O., Moses, J. A., Jr., and Csernansky, J. G. (1988). Luria–Nebraska performance and symptomatology in unmedicated schizophrenic patients. *Psychiatry Research, 26*, 29–34.

Freed, W. J., Kleinman, J. E., Karson, C. N., Potkin, S. G., Murphy, D. L., and Wyatt, R. J. (1980). Eye-blink and rates and platelet monoamine oxidase activity in chronic schizophrenic patients. *Biological Psychiatry, 15*, 329–332.

Friedman, D., Hakerem, G., Sutton, S., and Fleiss, J. (1973). Effect of stimulus uncertainty on the pupillary dilation response and the vertex evoked potential. *Electroencephalography and Clinical Neurophysiology, 34*, 475–484.

Frith, C. D., and Done, D. J. (1988). Towards a neuropsychology of schizophrenia. *British Journal of Psychiatry, 153*, 437–443.

Fukushima, J., Fukushima, K., Chiba, T., Tanaka, S., Yamashita, I., and Kato, M. (1988). Disturbances of voluntary control of saccadic eye movements in schizophrenic patients. *Biological Psychiatry, 23*, 670–677.

Galley, N., Widera-Bernsen, M., and Ishak, H. B. (1982). Eye movements in schizophrenics— Revisited. In R. Gruner, C. Merz, D. F. Fisher, and R. A. Monty (Eds.), *Eye movements—An international perspective.*, Hillsdale, New Jersey: Erlbaum.

Geyer, M. A., and Braff, D. L. (1982). Habituation of the blink reflex in normals and schizophrenic patients. *Psychophysiology, 19*, 1–6.

Goode, D. J., Meltzer, H. Y., Crayton, J. W., and Mazura, T. A. (1977). Physiologic abnormalities of the neuromuscular system in schizophrenia. *Schizophrenia Bulletin, 3*, 121–138.

Goode, D. J., Meltzer, H. Y., and Mazura, T. A. (1979). Hoffman reflex abnormalities in psychotic patients. *Biological Psychiatry, 14*, 95–110.

Green, M., and Walker, E. (1985). Neuropsychological performance and positive and negative symptoms in schizophrenia. *Journal of Abnormal Psychology, 94*, 460–469.

Groner, R., and Groner, M. T. (1989). Attention and eye movement control: An overview. *European Archives of Psychiatry and Neurological Science, 239*, 9–16.

Günther, W., Günther, R., Eich, F. X., and Eben, E. (1986). Psychomotor disturbances in psychiatric patients as a possible basis for new attempts at differential diagnosis and therapy. II. Cross validation study on schizophrenic patients. *European Archives of Psychiatry and Neurological Science, 235*, 301–308.

Hakerem, G. (1973). The effect of cognitive manipulation on pupillary diameter and evoked vertex potentials. In E. Dodt and K. E. Schrader (Ed.), *Die normale und die gestörte Pupillenbewegung*. München: Bergmann.

Hakerem, G., and Lidsky, A. (1975). Characteristics of pupillary reactivity in psychiatric patients and normal controls. In M. L. Kietzman, S. Sutton, and J. Zubin (Eds.), *Experimental approaches to psychopathology*. New York: Academic Press.

Hakerem, G., Sutton, S., and Zubin, J. (1964). Pupillary reactions to light in schizophrenic patients and normals. *Annals of the New York Academy of Science, 105*, 820–831.

Heimann, H., and Spoerri, T. (1957). Das Ausdruckssyndrom der mimischen Desintegrierung bei chronischen Schizophrenen. *Schweizerische Medizinische Wochenschrift, 87*, 1126.

Heinrichs, D. W., and Buchanan, R. W. (1988). Significance and meaning of neurological signs in schizophrenia. *American Journal of Psychiatry, 145*, 11–18.

Hirsch, B., Lesinski, S. G., Hirschowitz, J., and Garver, D. L. (1980). "Vestibular responses in schizophrenia." Presented at the Annual Meeting of the American Psychiatric Association, San Francisco.

Holzman, P. (1972). Assessment of perceptual functioning in schizophrenia. *Psychopharmacology, 25*, 29–41.

Holzman, P. S., and Levy, D. L. (1977). Smooth pursuit eye movements and functional psychoses: A review. *Schizophrenia Bulletin, 3*, 15–27.

Holzman, P. S., Kringlen, E., Levy, D. L., and Haberman, S. (1980). Deviant eye tracking in twins discordant for psychosis: A replication. *Archives of General Psychiatry, 32*, 627–631.

Holzman, P. S., Kringlen, E., Levy, D. L., Proctor, L. R., and Haberman, S. (1978). Smooth pursuit eye movements in twins discordant for schizophrenia. *Journal of Psychiatric Research, 14*, 111–122.

Holzman, P. S., Kringlen, E., Matthysse, S., Flanagan, S. D., Lipton, R. B., Cramer, G., Levin, S., Lange, K., and Levy, D. L. (1988). A single dominant gene can account for eye tracking dysfunctions and schizophrenia in offspring of discordant twins. *Archives of General Psychiatry, 45*, 641–647.

Holzman, P. S., Levy, D. L., and Proctor, L. R. (1976). Smooth-pursuit eye movements, attention, and schizophrenia. *Archives of General Psychiatry, 33*, 1415–1420.

Holzman, P. S., Proctor, L. R., and Hughes, D. W. (1975). Eye-tracking patterns in schizophrenia. *Science, 181*, 179–181.

Holzman, P. S., Proctor, L. R., Levy, D. L., Yasillo, N. J., Meltzer, H. Y., and Hurt, S. W. (1974). Eye-tracking dysfunction in schizophrenic patients and their relatives. *Archives of General Psychiatry, 31*, 143–151.

Holzman, P. S., Solomon, C. M., Levin, S., and Waternaux, C. S. (1984). Pursuit eye movement dysfunctions in schizophrenia. Family evidence for specificity. *Archives of General Psychiatry, 41*, 136–139.

Hoskins, R. G. (1946). *The biology of schizophrenia*. New York: Norton.

Huddleston, C. J. (1978). Differentiation between process and reactive schizophrenia based on vestibular reactivity, grasp strength, and posture. *American Journal of Occupational Therapy, 32*, 438–444.

Iacono, W. G. (1983). Young psychophysiologist award address, 1982. Psychophysiology and genetics. A key to psychopathology research. *Psychophysiology, 20*, 371–381.

Iacono, W. G., and Koenig, W. G. R. (1983). Features that distinguish the smooth-pursuit eye-tracking performance of schizophrenic, affective-disorder, and normal individuals. *Journal of Abnormal Psychology, 92*, 29–41.

Iacono, W. G., and Lykken, D. T. (1979). Electro-oculographic recording and scoring eye tracking: A parametric study using monozygotic twins. *Psychophysiology, 16*, 94–107.

Iacono, W. G., and Lykken, D. T. (1981). Two-year retest stability of eye tracking performance and a comparison of electro-oculographic and infrared recording techniques evidence of EEG in the electro-oculogram. *Psychophysiology, 18*, 49–55.

Iacono, W. G., Peloquin, L. J., Lumry, A. E., Valentine, R. H., and Tuason, V. B. (1982). Eye tracking in patients with unipolar and bipolar affective disorders in remission. *Journal of Abnormal Psychology, 91,* 34–44.

Iacono, W. G., Tuason, V. B., and Johnson, R. A. (1981). Dissociation of smooth-pursuit and saccadic eye tracking in remitted schizophrenics. *Archives of General Psychiatry, 38,* 991–996.

Iager, A.-C., Kirch, D. G., Jeste, D. V., and Wyatt, R. J. (1986). Defect symptoms and abnormal involuntary movement in schizophrenia. *Biological Psychiatry, 21,* 751–755.

Johnstone, E. C., and Owens, D. G. C. (1981). Neurological changes in a population of patients with chronic schizophrenia and their relationship to physical treatment. *Acta Psychiatrica Scandinavica, 63*/Suppl. *291,* 103–110.

Karson, C. N. (1979). Oculomotor signs in a psychiatric population: A preliminary report. *American Journal of Psychiatry, 136,* 1057.

Karson, C. N. (1983). Spontaneous eye-blink rates and dopaminergic systems. *Brain, 106,* 643–653.

Karson, C. N., Berman, K. F., Donnelly, E. F., Mendelson, W. B., Kleinman, J. E., and Wyatt, R. J. (1981a). Speaking, thinking, and blinking. *Psychiatry Research, 5,* 243–246.

Karson, C. N., Berman, K. F., Kleinman, J. E., and Karoum, F. (1984a). Seasonal variation in central dopamine activity. *Psychiatry Research, 11,* 111.

Karson, C. N., Bigelow, L. B., Kleinman, J. E., Weinberger, D. R., and Wyatt, R. J. (1982). Haloperidol-induced changes in blink rates correlate with changes in BPRS score. *British Journal of Psychiatry, 140,* 503–507.

Karson, C. N., Burns, S., LeWitt, P. A., Foster, N. L., and Newman, R. P. (1984b). Blink rates and disorders of movement. *Neurology, 34,* 677–678.

Karson, C. N., Freed, W. J., Kleinman, J. E., Bigelow, L. B., and Wyatt, R. J. (1981b). Neuroleptics decrease blinking in schizophrenic subjects. *Biological Psychiatry, 16,* 679–682.

Karson, C. N., Kleinman, J. E., Berman, K. F., Phelps, B. H., Wise, C. D., Delisi, L. E., and Jeste, D. V. (1983). An inverse correlation between spontaneous eye-blink rate and platelet monoamine oxidase activity. *The British Journal of Psychiatry, 142,* 43–46.

Kinney, D. K., Woods, B. T., and Yurgelun-Todd, D. (1986). Neurologic abnormalities in schizophrenic patients and their families. II. Neurologic and psychiatric findings in relatives. *Archives of General Psychiatry, 43,* 665–668.

Kleinman, J. E., Karson, C. N., Weinberger, D. R., Freed, W. J., Berman, K. F., and Wyatt, R. J. (1984). Eye blinking and cerebral ventricular size in chronic schizophrenic patients. *American Journal of Psychiatry, 141,* 1430–1432.

Kobatke, K., Yoshii, F., Shinohara, Y., Nomura, K., and Takagi, S. (1983). Impairment of smooth pursuit eye movement in chronic alcoholics. *European Neurology, 22,* 392–396.

Koester, A. (1927). Frequency of loss pupillary reaction. *Archiv für Psychiatrie, 81,* 601–605.

Kolakowska, T., Williams, A. O., Jambor, K., and Ardern, M. (1985). Schizophrenia with good and poor outcome. III. Neurological 'soft' signs, cognitive impairment and their clinical significance. *British Journal of Psychiatry, 146,* 348–357.

Kraepelin, E. (1909). *Psychiatrie.* Leipzig: Barth.

Kraepelin, E. (1913). *Psychiatrie, Vol. 3, 8th ed. Translated as Dementia praecox and paraphrenia, 1919.* Edinburgh: Livingstone.

Kramer, S. G. (1971). Dopamine: A retinal neurotransmitter. I. Retinal uptake, storage and lightstimulated release of H3–dopamine *in vivo. Investigative Ophthalmology, 10,* 438–452.

Kramer, S. G., Potts, A. M., and Mangnall, Y. Dopamine: A retinal neurotransmitter. II. Autoradiographic localization of H3–dopamine in the retina. *Investigative Ophthalmology, 10,* 617–624.

Latham, C., Holzman, P. S., Manschreck, T. C., and Tole, J. (1981). Optokinetic nystagmus and pursuit eye movements in schizophrenia. *Archives of General Psychiatry, 38,* 997–1003.

Lauber, H. (1973). Die Wirkung von Psychopharmaka auf die menschliche Pupille. In E. Dodt and K. E. Schrader (Ed.), *Die normale und die gestörte Pupillenbewegung.*, München: Bergmann.

Levin, S. (1984). Frontal lobe dysfunctions in schizophrenia. 1. Eye movement impairments. *Journal of Psychiatric Research, 18,* 27–55.

Levin, S., Holzman, P. S., Rothenberg, S. J., and Lipton, R. B. (1981). Saccadic eye movements in psychotic patients. *Psychiatry Research, 5,* 47–58.

Levin, S., Jones, A., Stark, L., Merrin, E. L., and Holzman, P. S. (1982). Identification of abnormal patterns in eye movements of schizophrenic patients. *Archives of General Psychiatry, 39,* 1125–1130.

Levin, S., Luebke, A., Zee, D. S., Hain, T. C., Robinson, D. A., and Holzman, P. S. (1988). Smooth pursuit eye movements in schizophrenics: Quantitative measurements with the search-coil technique. *Journal of Psychiatric Research, 22,* 195–206.

Levine, A., and Schilder, P. (1942). The catatonic pupil. *Journal of Nervous and Mental Disease, 96,* 1.

Levy, D. L., Holzman, P. S., and Proctor, L. R. (1978). Vestibular responses in schizophrenia. *Archives of General Psychiatry, 35,* 972–981.

Levy, D. L., Lipton, R. B., Holzman, P. S., and Davis, J. M. (1983). Eye tracking dysfunction unrelated to clinical state and treatment with haloperidol. *Biological Psychiatry, 18,* 813–819.

Levy, D. L., Dorus, E., Shaughnessy, R., Yasillo, N. J., Pandey, G. N., Janicak, P. G., Gibbons, R. D., Gaviria, M., and Davis, J. M. (1985). Pharmacologic evidence for specificity of pursuit dysfunction to schizophrenia. *Archives of General Psychiatry, 42,* 335–341.

Lewis, R. F., Nelson, R. W., and Eggertsen, C. (1979). Neuropsychological test performances of paranoid schizophrenic and brain-damaged patients. *Journal of Clinical Psychology, 35,* 54–59.

Liddle, P. F. (1987). Schizophrenic syndromes, cognitive performance and neurological dysfunction. *Psychological Medicine, 17,* 49–57.

Lindsey, D. T., Holzman, P. S., Haberman, S., and Yasillo, N. J. (1978). Smooth-pursuit eye movements: A comparison of two measurement techniques for studying schizophrenia. *Journal of Abnormal Psychology, 87,* 491–496.

Lipton, R. B., Levin, S., and Holzman, P. S. (1980). Horizontal and vertical pursuit eye movements, the oculocephalic reflex, and the functional psychoses. *Psychiatry Research, 3,* 193–203.

Lipton, R. B., Levy, D. L., Holzman, P. S., and Levin, S. Eye movement dysfunctions in psychiatric patients: A review. *Schizophrenia Bulletin, 9,* 13–32.

Löwenstein, C., and Westphal, A. (1933). *Experimentelle und klinische Studien zur Physiologie und Pathologie der Pupillenbewegungen mit besonderer Berücksichtigung der Schizophrenie.* Berlin: Karger.

Lohr, J. B., Wisniewski, A., and Jeste, D. V. (1986). Neurological aspects of tardive dyskinesia. In H. A. Nasrallah and D. R. Weinberger (Eds.), *Handbook of schizophrenia, Vol. 1, pp. 97–119.* Amsterdam: Elsevier.

Mackert, A., and Flechtner, M. (1989). Saccadic reaction times in acute and remitted schizophrenics. *European Archives of Psychiatry and Neurological Science, 239,* 33–38.

Mackert, A., Woyth, C., Flechtner, M., and Frick, K. (1988). Increased blink rate in acute and remitted schizophrenics. *Pharmacopsychiatry, 21,* 334–335.

Mackintosh, J. H., Kumar, R., and Kitamura, T. (1983). Blink rate in psychiatric illness. *British Journal of Psychiatry, 143,* 55–57.

Malenka, R. C., Angel, R. W., Hampton, B., and Berger, P. A. (1982). Impaired central error-correcting behavior in schizophrenia. *Archives of General Psychiatry, 39,* 101–107.

Malenka, R. C., Angel, R. W., Thiemann, S., Weitz, C. J., and Berger, P. A. (1986). Central error-correcting behavior in schizophrenia and depression. *Biological Psychiatry, 21,* 263–273.

Malmo, R., and Shagass, C. (1949). Physiologic studies of reaction to stress in anxiety and early schizophrenia. *Psychosomatic Medicine,, 11,* 9–24.

Malmo, R., Shagass, C., and Davis, J. (1948). A method for the investigation of somatic response mechanisms in psychoneurosis. *Science, 112*, 325–328.

Manschreck, T. C. (1986). Motor abnormalities in schizophrenia. In H. A. Nasrallah and D. R. Weinberger (Eds.), *Handbook of schizophrenia, Vol. 1, pp. 65–96. Amsterdam: Elsevier.*

*Manschreck, T. C. (1983). Psychopathology of motor behavior in schizophrenia. In B. A. Maher and W. B. Maher (Eds.), Progress in experimental personality research,* Vol. 12. New York: Academic Press.

Manschreck, T. C., and Ames, D. (1984). Neurologic features and psychopathology in schizophrenic disorders. *Biological Psychiatry, 19*, 703–719.

Manschreck, T. C., Maher, B. A., Rucklos, M. E., Vereen, D. R., and Ader, D. N. (1981). Deficient motor synchrony in schizophrenia. *The Journal of Abnormal Psychology, 90*, 321–328.

Marx, P. (1989). Supratentorial structures controlling oculomotor functions and their involvement in cases of stroke. *European Archives of Psychiatry and Neurological Science, 239*, 3–8.

Mather, J. A. (1986). Saccadic eye movements to seen and unseen targets: Oculomotor errors in normal subjects resembling those of schizophrenics. *Journal of Psychiatric Research, 20*, 1–8.

Mather, J. A., and Putchat, C. (1982). Motor controls of schizophrenics. I. Oculomotor control of schizophrenics: A deficit in sensory processing, not strictly in motor control. *Journal of Psychiatric Research, 17*, 343–360.

Matthews, C. G., and Haaland, K. Y. (1979). The effect of symptom duration on cognitive and motor performance in Parkinsonism. *Neurology, 29*, 951–956.

Matthysse, S., Holzman, P. S., and Lange, K. (1986). The genetic transmission of schizophrenia: Application of mendelian latent structure analysis to eye-tracking dysfunctions in schizophrenia and affective disorder. *Journal of Psychiatric Research, 20*, 57–76.

McEwen, W. K., and Goodner, K. (1969). Secretion of tears and blinking. In H. Davidson (Ed.), *The eye*, Vol. 3, pp. 341–378. New York: Academic Press.

McLean, W. E., Lewis, M., Bryson-Brockmann, W. A., Ellis, D. N., Arendt, R. E., and Baumeister, A. A. (1985). Blink rate and stereotyped behavior: Evidence for dopamine involvement? *Biological Psychiatry, 20*, 1321–1325.

Metz, J., Goode, D. J., and Meltzer, H. Y. (1980). Descriptive studies of H-reflex recovery curves in psychiatric patients. *Psychological Medicine, 10*, 541–548.

Mialet, J. P., and Pichot, P. (1981). Eyetracking patterns in schizophrenia. An analysis based on incidence of saccades. *Archives of General Psychiatry, 38*, 183–186.

Nasrallah, H. A., Tippin, F., and McCalley-Whitters, M. (1983). Neurological soft signs in manic patients: A comparison with schizophrenic and control groups. *Journal of Affective Disorders, 5*, 45–50.

Nasrallah, H. A., and Weinberger, D. R. (1986). The neurologie of schizophrenia. Vol. 1. In: H. A. Nasrallah (Ed.). *Handbook of schizophrenia*. Amsterdam: Elsevier.

Obrist, P. A., Webb, R. A., Sutterer, J. R., and Howard, J. L. (1970). Cardiac deceleration and reaction time: An evaluation of two hypotheses. *Psychophysiology, 6*, 695–706.

Pass, H. L., Salzman, L. F., Klorman, R., Kaskey, G. B., and Klein, R. H. (1978). The effect of distraction on acute schizophrenics' visual tracking. *Biological Psychiatry, 13*, 587–593.

Patterson, T. (1976). Skin conductance responding/nonresponding and pupillometrics in chronic schizophrenia. *Journal of Nervous and Mental Disease, 163*, 200–209.

Pekelsky, A. (1921). Transitorischer Nystagmus bei Katatonie. Ist der Nystagmus willkürlich unterdrückbar? *Revue Neuropsychopathologie, 18*, 97–102.

Pivik, R. T. (1979a). Smooth pursuit eye movements and attention in psychiatric patients. *Biological Psychiatry, 14*, 859–879.

Pivik, R. T. (1979b). Target velocity and smooth pursuit eye movements in psychiatric patients. *Psychiatry Research, 1*, 313–323.

Pivik, R. T., Bylsma, F. W., and Cooper, P. M. (1987). The effects of dark adaptation on pursuit tracking dysfunction in psychotics with impaired vestibular suppression. *Progress in Neuro-Psychopharmacology & Biological Psychology, 11,* 259–265.

Ponder, E., and Kennedy, W. P. (1978). On the act of blinking. *Quarterly Journal of Experimental Physiology, 18,* 89–110.

Reischies, F. M., Gaebel, W., Mielewczyk, A., and Frick, K. (1988). Disturbed eye movements guided by visuospatial cues in schizophrenic patients. *Pharmacopsychiatry, 21,* 346–347.

Rosenbaum, D. A. (1982). Hierarchical organization of motor programs. In S. P. Wise (Ed.), *Higher brain functions. Recent explorations of the brain's emergent properties.* New York: Wiley.

Rosenbaum, D. A., Hindorff, V., and Munro, E. M. (1987). Scheduling and programming of rapid finger sequences: Tests and elaborations of the hierarchical editor model. *Journal of Experimental Psychology and Human Perception, 13,* 193–203.

Ross, D. E., Ochs, A. L., Hill, M. R., Goldberg, S. C., Pandurangi, A. K., and Winfrey, C. J. (1988). Erratic eye tracking in schizophrenic patients as revealed by high-resolution techniques. *Biological Psychiatry, 24,* 675–688.

Rubin, L. S. (1974). *The utilization of pupillometry in the differential diagnosis and treatment of psychotic disorders.* New York: Plenum Press.

Rubin, L. S. (1976). Sympathetic-parasympathetic imbalance as a diagnostic concomitant of schizophrenia: Implications of pharmacotherapy. *Research Communications in Psychology and Psychiatry Behavior, 1,* 73–89.

Schmid-Burgk, W., Becker, W., Diekmann, V., Jürgens, R., and Kornhuber, H. H. (1982). Disturbed smooth pursuit and saccadic eye movements in schizophrenia. *Archiv für Psychiatrie und Nervenkrankheiten, 232,* 381–389.

Schmid-Burgk, W., Becker, W., Jürgens, R., and Kornhuber, H. H. (1983). Saccadic eye movements in psychiatric patients. *Neuropsychobiology, 10,* 193–198.

Schneider, R. D., and Grossi, V. (1979). Differences in muscle activity before, during, and after responding in a simple reaction time task: Schizophrenics vs. normals. *Psychiatry Research, 1,* 141–145.

Shagass, C., Roemer, R. A., and Amadeo, M. (1974). Eye tracking performance in psychiatric patients. *Biological Psychiatry, 9,* 245–260.

Shagass, C., Roemer, R. A., and Amadeo, M. (1976). Eye tracking performance and engagement of attention. *Archives of General Psychiatry, 33,* 121–125.

Siever, L. J., Coursey, R. D., Alterman, I., Buchsbaum, M. S., and Murphy, D. L. (1984). Impaired smooth pursuit eye movement: Vulnerability marker for schizotypal personality disorder in a normal volunteer population. *American Journal of Psychiatry, 141,* 1560–1566.

Siever, L. J., Insel, T. R., Hamilton, J., Nurnberger, J., Alterman, I., and Murphy, D. L. (1987). Eye-tracking, attention and amphetamine challenge. *Journal of Psychiatric Research, 21,* 129–135.

Siever, L. J., van Kammen, D. P., Linnoila, M., Alterman, I., Hare, T., and Murphy, D. L. (1986). Smooth pursuit eye movement disorder and its psychobiologic correlates in unmedicated schizophrenics. *Biological Psychiatry, 21,* 1167–1174.

Silverstein, M. L. and Arzt, A. T. (1985). Neuropsychological dysfunction in schizophrenia. Relation to associative thought disorder. *Journal of Nervous and Mental Disease, 173,* 341–346.

Smeraldi, E., Gambini, O., Bellodi, L., Sachetti, E., Vita, A., diRosa, M., Macciardi, F., and Cazzullo, C. L. (1987). Combined measure of smooth pursuit eye movements and ventricle–brain ratio in schizophrenic disorders. *Psychiatry Research, 21,* 293–301.

Smolen, V. F., Murdock, H. R., and Williams, E. J. (1975). Bioavailability analysis of chlorpromazine in humans from pupillometric data. *Journal of Pharmacology and Experimental Therapeutics, 195,* 404–415.

Spohn, H. E., Coyne, L., and Spray, J. (1988). The effect of neuroleptics and tardive dyskinesia on smooth-pursuit eye movement in chronic schizophrenics. *Archives of General Psychiatry*, *45*, 833–840.

Spohn, H. E., Coyne, L., Lacoursiere, R., Mazur, D., and Hayes, K. (1985). Relation of neuroleptic dose and tardive dyskinesia to attention, information-processing and psychophysiology in medicated schizophrenics. *Archives of General Psychiatry*, *42*, 849–859.

Spohn, H. E., Lacoursiere, R. B., Thompson, K., and Coyne, L. (1978). The effect of antipsychotic drug treatment on attention and information processing in chronic schizophrenics. In L. C. Wynne, R. L. Cromwell, and S. Mathysse (Eds.), *The nature of schizophrenia*. New York: Wiley.

Steinhauer, S., and Zubin, J. (1982). Vulnerability to schizophrenia: Information processing in the pupil and event-related potential. In E. Usdin and I. Hanin (Eds.), *Biological markers in psychiatry and neurology*, pp. 371–388. New York: Pergamon Press.

Stevens, J. R. (1978). Eye blink and schizophrenia: Psychosis or tardive dyskinesia? *American Journal of Psychiatry*, *135*, 223–226.

Stilson, D. W., Haseth, K., Schneider, R. J., Walsmith, C. R., Rogers, M. D., and Astrup, C. (1966). Pupillary response to light as an indicator of functional psychoses: A failure to replicate. *Journal of Nervous and Mental Disease*, *143*, 438–442.

Straube, E. R. (1982). Pupillometric, cardiac, and electrodermal reactivity of schizophrenic patients under different stimulus conditions. Abstracts of papers presented at the twenty-second annual meeting of the society for psychophysiological research. *Psychophysiology*, *19*, 589–590.

Straube, E. R., Schied, H. W., Rein, W., and Breyer-Pfaff, U. (1987). Autonomic Nervous System Differences as Predictors of Short-Term Outcome in Schizophrenics. Pharmacopsychiatry, *20*, 105–110.

Szymczewska, J. (1971). Excitability of the vestibular system in schizophrenic patients treated with neuroleptics. *Rosznik Pomorskiej Akaddemii Medyzpei*, *17*, 429–450.

Thaker, G. K., Nguyen, J. A., and Tamminga, C. A. (1989). Saccadic distractability in schizophrenic patients with tardive dyskinesia. *Archives of General Psychiatry*, *46*, 755–756.

Tomer, R., Mintz, M., Levy, A., and Myslobodsky, M. (1981). Smooth pursuit pattern in schizophrenic patients during cognitive task. *Biological Psychiatry*, *16*, 131–144.

Torrey, E. F. (1980). Neurological abnormalities in schizophrenic patients. *Biological Psychiatry*, *15*, 381–388.

van den Bosch, R. J. Rozendaal, N., and Mol, J. M. F. A. (1987). Symptom correlates of eye tracking dysfunction. *Biological Psychiatry*, *22*, 919–921.

Venables, P. H. (1978). Die Psychophysiologie der Schizophrenie. *Der Nervenarzt*, *49*, 625–633.

Vrtunski, P. B., Simpson, D. M., and Meltzer, H. Y. (1989). Voluntary movement dysfunction in schizophrenics. *Biological Psychiatry*, *25*, 529–539.

Vrtunski, P. B., Simpson, D. M., Weiss, K. M., and Davis, G. C. (1986). Abnormalities of fine motor control in schizophrenia. *Psychiatry Research*, *18*, 275–284.

Walker, E. (1981). Attentional and neuromotor functions of schizophrenics, schizoaffectives, and patients with other affective disorders. *Archives of General Psychiatry*, *38*, 1355–1358.

Walker, E., and Shaye, J. (1982). Familial schizophrenia: A predictor of neromotor and attentional abnormalities in schizophrenia. *Archives of General Psychiatry*, *39*, 1153–1156.

Wegner, J. T., Catalano, F., Gibralter, J., and Kane, J. M. (1985). Schizophrenics with tardive dyskinesia. *Archives of General Psychiatry*, *42*, 860–865.

Welsh, M. C., and Pennington, B. F. (1988). Assessing frontal lobe functioning in children: views from developmental psychology. *Developmental Neuropsychology*, *4*, 199–230.

Wertheim, A. H., Van Gelder, P., Lautin, A., Peselow, E., and Cohen, N. (1985). High thresholds for movement perception in schizophrenia may indicate abnormal extraneous noise levels of central vestibular activity. *Biological Psychiatry*, *20*, 1197–1210.

Westphal, A. (1907). Über ein im katatonischen Stupor beobachtetes Pupillenphänomen sowie

Bemerkungen über die Pupillenstarre bei Hysterie. *Deutsche Medizinische Wochenzeitschrift*, *33*, 1080–1084.

Wilder, J. (1958). Modern psychophysiology and the law of initial value. *American Journal of Psychotherapy*, *12*, 199–221.

Woods, B. T., Kinney, D. K., and Yurgelun-Todd, D. (1986). Neurologic abnormalities in schizophrenic patients and their families. I. Comparison of schizophrenic, bipolar, and substance abuse patients and normal controls. *Archives of General Psychiatry*, *43*, 657–663.

Woods, B. T., Yurgelun-Todd, D., and Kinney, D. K. (1987). Relationship of neurological abnormalities in schizophrenics to family psychopathology. *Biological Psychiatry*, *22*, 325–331.

Youssef, H. A., and Waddington, J. L. (1988). Primitive (developmental) reflexes and diffuse cerebral dysfunction in schizophrenia and bipolar affective disorder: Overrepresentation in patients with tardive kinesia. *Biological Psychiatry*, *23*, 791–796.

# Chapter 8

# Anatomical Bases
# for Schizophrenia

The notion of schizophrenia as a disease, inextricably linked with that of neuropathological change, was as much a part of the nosological concept of Kraepelin as of many researchers today. Indeed, with Kraepelin's argument that such changes involved frontal and temporal cortices, we come almost full circle to an idea now in vogue in a number of laboratories (e.g., Zec and Weinberger, 1986).

We shall discuss the evidence here not so much from a comprehensive historical perspective, but from a hierarchical one. What is the evidence for gross anatomical and metabolic change? Are there records of unusually functioning brain regions in schizophrenics? Are there microanatomical changes in schizophrenic brain material? Finally, are there anatomical, psychological, or physiological reasons to suppose there is a functional asymmetry in the brain of schizophrenics that differs from the norm (see Chapter 9)?

## I. *In Vivo* Studies: Cerebral Atrophy and Metabolism

The possibility that a brain lesion lies at the root of schizophrenia implies that one should be able to measure a degree of cerebral atrophy that would result from the loss of neuronal tissue. The presence of such atrophy might be more easy to discern than the loss or decreased density of neuronal tissue determined by processing innumerable sections of brain tissue *postmortem* and comparing the results for a large number of patients to demonstrate specificity. Certainly an indication of atrophy can be obtained from measures of brain weight and volume *postmortem* (cf. Brown *et al.*, 1986). However, *in vivo* indications of atrophy are possible through radiographic measures of the change in the volume of the fluid-filled cerebral ventricles that increase in size with the disappearance of the surrounding cerebral tissue. Of course the question of diagnostic specificity still requires the comparison of a large number of psychiatric and neurological patients.

## A. Pneumoencephalography

The first attempts at pneumoencephalography in schizophrenia were reported by Jacobi and Winkler (1927) and Lempke (1935) in Germany. They were based on the discovery by Dandy (1919) that the cerebral ventricles could be made radiographically visible after the introduction of air. The size of the ventricles could be assessed relatively easily. It was hoped that if cerebral atrophy were present, the increase in ventricle size would be relatively easy to compare among subjects.

The first studies of Jacobi and Winkler indeed reported increased ventricle size in 18 of 19 chronic schizophrenics. Positive findings, though not always so numerous, characterized some 30 studies that followed (Haug, 1962; Asano, 1967). There were a few reports of negative findings in small groups of patients (e.g., Storey, 1966), but these could be explained by the use of neurological controls that also showed atrophy. The study of Huber et al. (1979) in Germany is often cited, since it was both the largest such study and is reasonably representative. Here the ventricles of 190 schizophrenics (age, < 50 yr) were compared with those of 27 control subjects that included a subgroup of 11 with affective psychoses. Wider ventricles were particularly apparent among the so-called defect schizophrenics (i.e., those that would have shown a large proportion of negative symptoms). The result remained significant when only subjects under 40 yr were considered. Thus, age was not a major contributing factor. Atrophy was rarer among those with affective psychoses.

However, these results were skeptically received at the time and later received much technical criticism. For example, the amount of air introduced into the ventricles is critical (and not without danger) and was usually inadequately controlled. It is ironic that more recent tomographic studies qualitatively support many pneumoencephalographic findings.

## B. Computer Tomography

### 1. Principle Findings

In 1976, T. J. Crow's group at the Clinical Research Center, in England, reported the first results of schizophrenics studied with the noninvasive method of computerized axial tomography (CT) (Johnstone et al., 1976). This report was made shortly after the first presentation of the technique by their fellow countryman, Hounsfield (1973).

In origin the technique is simple. X-Ray sources are placed around the head; the relative weakening of the radiation passing through tissues and media of varying density is recorded by receivers on the opposite side. In practice, pictures of brain sections are recorded to obtain maximal dimensions of the different ventricles (Figure 8.1) and, in some studies, of the cortical sulci and

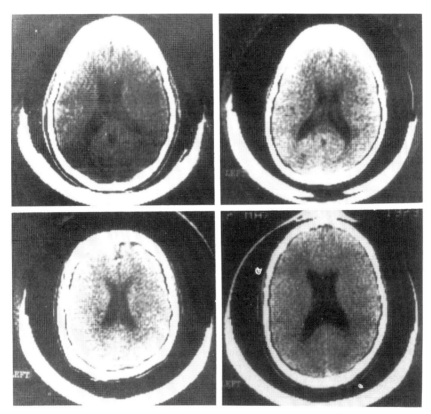

**Figure 8.1** Examples of computed tomographic scans (CT) of schizophreniform patients with large ventricles. Ventricle to brain ratios (VBR) were reported as 10.2 (top left), 12.7 (top right), 10.1 (bottom left) and 14.5 (bottom right) (from Weinberger *et al.*, 1982, © American Medical Association).

fissures (cf. Hounsfield, 1973; Dennert and Andreasen, 1983, for methods). Refinements in the method of computer analysis have been introduced over the years, but there is still controversy about the most reliable basis for ascertaining an increase in ventricle size (e.g., width vs. ventricle–brain ratio (VBR); planimetric, linear, and various hand- or computer-controlled measurement methods; Andreasen *et al.*, 1982a; Jernigan *et al.*, 1982a,b; Reveley, 1985; Raz *et al.*, 1987). Comparing absolute data from several studies remains unreliable (i.e., different CT scanning machines). The most widely accepted criterion for what constitutes an "abnormality" is that the measure deviates by two standard deviations from the norm. (For a critical discussion of research methods and evaluation of the outcome, see Maser and Keith, 1983.)

The general findings from earlier studies seemed to be confirmed from the very first CT study by Johnstone and her colleagues (1976). She found that

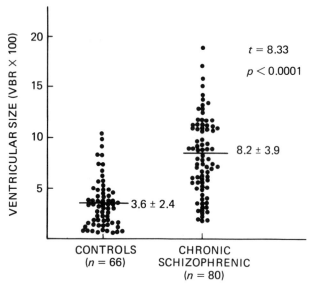

**Figure 8.2**   Mean ventricular size, represented by the bar, shown in terms of the ventricle to brain ratio (VBR) for groups of chronic schizophrenic and healthy subjects (after Weinberger *et al.*, 1979).

planimetric measures of the ventricular circumference of 17 institutionalized schizophrenics showed increases in comparison with 8 age-matched controls. Values for only 3 patients overlapped with the control group. The implicit atrophy correlated with age-related disorientation, poor intellectual performance on the Withers–Hinton test battery, and, in 4 cases, prior leucotomy.

Since this initial report, the majority of the 100 or so published studies of schizophrenia using CT techniques have found evidence for cerebral atrophy in one form or another in some patients (Figure 8.2). Although most of these studies have been carried out in the United States, where the National Institute of Mental Health (NIMH) has been particularly active, we are aware of studies carried out in at least 10 countries on three continents. More than half of these studies found increased lateral ventricle size (e.g., Weinberger *et al.*, 1979a; Tanaka *et al.*, 1981; Frangos and Athanassenas, 1982; Gross *et al.*, 1982; Reveley, 1985). More recently there are increasing numbers of reports of larger third (e.g., Gross *et al.*, 1982; Boronow *et al.*, 1985; Doran *et al.*, 1987) and occasionally larger fourth ventricle size (e.g., Weinberger *et al.*, 1979b). Further, there may be a widening of the cortical sulci (Largen *et al.*, 1984) and the sylvian (Dewan *et al.*, 1983) or interhemispheric (Nyback *et al.*, 1982) fissures. Only a minority of reports describe several measures. In such cases, there may be larger fissures and/or ventricles

(Johnstone *et al.*, 1989). Changes in one measure are not indicative of changes in another (Nyback *et al.*, 1984; Pandurangi *et al.*, 1986). The VBR may increase while the sulci remain normal (Boronow *et al.*, 1985) or vice versa (Largen *et al.*, 1984; McCarley *et al.*, 1989). Even among measures of various gyri, cortical sulci may be normal in subjects in which the sylvian fissure is larger (Pandurangi *et al.*, 1984). However, there are cases where both increased in size (Owen *et al.*, 1988; Rossi *et al.*, 1988). A report on 35 chronic schizophrenics at the NIMH described an increased VBR that correlated with signs of frontal atrophy. This was not true for 26 medical and 31 healthy controls (Doran *et al.*, 1987).

Thus, with or without considering possible methodological faults in one study or another, it is possible to find evidence of atrophy in the brain of some schizophrenics for which the locus may range from the prefrontal cortex to the cerebellum. (For a review, see Andreasen, 1986.) The former region may be relevant, the latter probably less so (Johnstone *et al.*, 1989). Reports of changes in the temporal horn or sylvian fissure are interpreted as reflecting temporal lobe atrophy (e.g., McCarley *et al.*, 1989). Curiously, irrespective of the specific CT measure there is no general agreement on the relative contribution of white or grey matter to the loss of tissue implied by ventricle or sulcal widening. Although for many investigators there is the unwritten assumption that the larger contribution derives from a loss of grey matter, it is more conventional in neurological patients to attribute sulcal widening, for example, to a loss of white matter (LeMay, 1984).

Atrophy was reported in most studies, although occasional studies, sometimes with less severely ill patients (e.g., Jernigan *et al.*, 1982a), have failed to find increased ventricle size (e.g., Gluck *et al.*, 1980; Mundt *et al.*, 1980; Benes *et al.*, 1986). This result in itself is remarkable, since most studies have been concerned with small numbers of patients and are susceptible to type 2 statistical error. However the incidence of atrophy ranges widely from 6% (Andreasen *et al.*, 1982b) to 60% (Golden *et al.*, 1980). Reviewing 16 studies in which the cerebellar vermis was measured, Lohr and Jeste (1986) found some cerebellar atrophy in 18% of scans. The incidence of frontal or cerebellar atrophy and its coincidence with other schizophrenic features may be an important indicator for the understanding of the heterogeneity of schizophrenia.

Let us try briefly to put these findings into context. One-third of schizophrenic patients is likely to show some sort of cerebral atrophy that reflects a diffuse loss of cerebral tissue. How localized the loss can be must still be determined, but it is not a loss in the sense of a focal brain lesion. How large can the loss be? Johnstone *et al.* (1989) found a 16% increase in area of the third ventricle on their scans of schizophrenic patients compared with a wide range of nonschizophrenic subjects. Such an increase in area represents an even larger increase in volume. Weinberger's group at the NIMH found lateral ventricle volume increases of 67% in severe cases (i.e., from 15 to 24 ml or 2–3% of brain volume. A 9-ml increase in ventricle volume is not so different from the report of a 7.8 cm$^3$ decrease in temporal lobe volume. To put these figures in perspective, the volume of a normal amygdala is 1.62 ml; Kelsoe *et al.*, 1988; Suddath *et al.*, 1989).

Now we must consider whether findings of a variable prevalence of atrophy are related to age, medication status, and hospitalization—factors that may confound our interpretation—or, more interestingly, whether they are associated with particular subgroups or symptom pictures. The results are derived from studies that sought differences from matched healthy control populations and others that sought correlations, within their schizophrenic group, between an index of atrophy and other characteristics of their subjects.

## 2. Age, Medication, Hospitalization, and Length of Illness

One of the important questions asked by investigators is whether brain damage in some form that leads to cerebral atrophy is "progressive," reflecting a degenerative process, or "static," reflecting some sort of insult at a given point in time. Secondary to this question is whether the experience or treatment of the patient can enhance or exaggerate the degeneration.

It should not be overlooked that, in the normal healthy population, there is a tendency for lateral ventricle size to increase with age (Reisner *et al.*, 1980). Atrophy may be particularly prevalent in elderly (dementing) psychiatric patients (e.g., Jacoby and Levi, 1980a,b). A tendency for increased size with age in normal subjects may be more marked for the third ventricle.

The apparent increase in size for schizophrenics disappeared when age was controlled in 46 subjects studied by Nyback *et al.* (1984) and among another 32 subjects studied by Pandurangi *et al.* (1988). Nevertheless, atrophy is found in young adults (<30 yr) (Andreasen *et al.*, 1982b; Pandurangi *et al.*, 1986), even in teenagers with a spectrum diagnosis (Schulz *et al.*, 1983a), as well as in older schizophrenics (Weinberger *et al.*, 1979c; Nyback *et al.*, 1982). In the Nyback *et al.* study of 60 patients, measurements (made by raters blind to the diagnosis) included the width of cortical sulci and sylvian and interhemispheric fissures. Increases were independent of age, duration of illness, or hospitalization. However, in Weinberger's study there was a tendency for the measures to increase with age. (This is claimed to be particularly true for frontal signs of atrophy; Doran *et al.*, 1987.) This could also reflect the longer duration of the illness. Nasrallah *et al.* (1986) checked 11 chronic patients 3 yr after their initial scans. Although 4 patients did show some increase, there was no significant increase for the group as a whole. Indirect support for the absence of progressive atrophy comes from a small study by Classen and Fritze (1988) with 16 patients showing a fivefold variation of VBR. The size of the ventricles was unrelated to the age of onset. That some investigators have found increasing atrophy and age to correlate in schizophrenia (Reisner *et al.*, 1980) and others have not (Nyback *et al.*, 1982) underscores a remark made by the latter Swedish group that the variability among the schizophrenic populations studied is so great that it obscures any finer relationship of atrophy to the subject's age.

Tanaka *et al.* (1981) found that VBR correlated positively with the length of illness but not the age of 49 patients (20–60 yr). Such a correlation was also reported in a study of 31 patients (mean age, 30 yr) in New York (Smith *et al.*, 1985a). The length of institutional stay is unlikely to reflect this finding, since 10 physically ill subjects who had been in the hospital as long as 18 schizophrenics had showed no signs of the atrophy found in the psychiatric group (Johnstone *et al.*, 1978).

Could the duration of neuroleptic treatment be relevant? For this same group of schizophrenics, studied by Johnstone, there was no apparent relationship between ventricle size and the amount of neuroleptic treatment received. At the NIMH, Weinberger *et al.* (1982) also claimed that where atrophy occurred it predated medical treatment. In a *postmortem* study of 29 Swedish subjects, Pakkenberg (1987) found no relationship between morphology, ventricle size, and treatment duration.

A number of groups have questioned the relationship of neuroleptic treatment to cerebral atrophy from another perspective. Does the presence of atrophy affect response to neuroleptic treatment? The answer from the NIMH was a definite yes (Weinberger *et al.*, 1980). Based on a small sample of 10 patients, they reported a markedly poorer response to neuroleptic treatment in those with an increased VBR. This reflects the experience of other investigators (e.g., Gattaz *et al.*, 1988). Indeed, some groups have shown that such nonresponders have more negative than positive symptoms (Schulz *et al.*, 1983b; Luchins *et al.*, 1984; review, Goetz and Van Kammen, 1986). A *caveat* must be added to this statement. There are *treatment resistant* subjects with no signs of cerebral atrophy (Smith *et al.*, 1987a) and some such subjects show a clear positive symptomatology (Ota *et al.*, 1987).

Thus, if the incidence of atrophy in schizophrenia does not appear to depend crucially on age or medical treatment, it seems reasonable to ask if it tends to occur more often in a particular subgroup or in association with particular symptoms.

## 3. Schizophrenic Subgroups, Symptoms, and Specificity

*a. Schizophrenic Subgroups*   There seems no doubt that atrophy may occur in acute or chronically ill, young or old schizophrenic patients (Nyback *et al.*, 1982; Weinberger *et al.*, 1982; Luchins and Meltzer, 1986). Further, the lateral ventricle is often larger in patients who show poor premorbid function (Weinberger *et al.*, 1980; Pearlson *et al.*, 1985; Williams *et al.*,

1985), particularly if the subjects show poor social function (Owens *et al.*, 1985), are not able to live independently, have fewer types of relationships (Seidman *et al.*, 1987), or are unable to keep a job (Pearlson *et al.*, 1984). Once again this relationship is not necessary or exclusive and atrophy may not be present in such patients (Andreasen *et al.*, 1982; Nasrallah *et al.*, 1983).

More controversial is the possible association of atrophy with positive or negative symptoms that may occur, respectively, more in the acutely or more in the chronically ill. This idea was first suggested by the neurologist Hughlings-Jackson in the last century. He believed that, whereas negative symptoms derived from a loss of function attributable directly to brain lesions, positive symptoms were the result of the disinhibition of intact areas through damage elsewhere.

The study of Andreasen and colleagues (1982a) in Iowa has been influential in the study of correlates of negative and positive symptoms. They compared 16 patients with ventricles that were larger by at least one standard deviation with 16 patients with smaller ventricles. Patients with larger ventricles showed many negative signs, such as avolition and anhedonia, whereas those with smaller ventricles had Schneiderian first rank symptoms, such as hallucinations, delusions, and bizarre thinking. The factors of affect and formal thought disorder did not distinguish the two groups. Other laboratories have apparently found patients with negative symptoms among their sample with cerebral atrophy (Pearlson *et al.*, 1984, 1985; Williams *et al.*, 1985). In view of the relatively few patients who show negative or positive symptoms alone, a group in Japan has put a different emphasis on these findings (Ota *et al.*, 1987). Their results, based on 25 subjects, showed a correlation between increasing atrophy and the absence of positive, rather than the presence of negative, symptoms.

Since Andreasen's report, many investigators have been unable to find such clear-cut results (e.g., Nasrallah *et al.*, 1983; Luchins *et al.*, 1984; Losonczy *et al.*, 1986; Keilp *et al.*, 1988; Macdonald and Best, 1989). The reasons for this, perhaps the broadest controversy about the relationship of atrophy to schizophrenic features, may lie with the variable etiology of the range of symptoms studied and subsequently lumped as a "negative score". Further, the constellation of (negative or positive) symptoms studied does vary from study to study. Notable here are the factors of affect and thought disorder, which Andreasen found did not correlate with atrophy. These factors can be subdivided in many ways and included or excluded in the symptom scores (cf. *Schizophrenia Bulletin, 11*, No. 3, 1985, Chapters 15 and 16, for a critical review).

In Bonn, Gross *et al.* (1982) found that 25% of their 117 patients (who all had Schneiderian first rank symptoms) showed increased third ventricle size. Indeed, Farmer and colleagues (1987), based in London, tried to classify their patients in various ways and concluded that those with first rank symptoms or

Crow's type 1 illness showed the largest ventricles. Thus, contrary to a popular conception, there is no unequivocal link between the likelihoods of showing negative symptoms and cerebral atrophy.

It may well be that the severity rather than the nature of the symptoms is associated with cerebral atrophy. This is the conclusion of Stahl and colleagues (1988) after looking at 8 severely ill patients. This is the same group that failed to find evidence of atrophy in more mildly ill subjects showing no neurological soft signs (Jernigan *et al.*, 1982a). The team led by Nasrallah (1982) also felt that the correlation with the presence or absence of negative symptoms was less impressive. Instead, they suggested that the degree of atrophy may be more closely associated with other subtypes. Thus, in their sample of 55, hebephrenics tended to have larger ventricles than undifferentiated schizophrenics. The ventricle size of nonparanoid subjects depended on whether they belonged more to the hebephrenic or to the undifferentiated group. Paranoids, not usually regarded as undifferentiated, tended to have larger ventricles. This trend, although supported by Frangos and Athanassenas (1982), was not confirmed in population samples studied by Golden *et al.* (1980) or Boronow *et al.* (1985). However, this feature may be questioned, since the reverse relationship was reported in dementing subjects with paranoid delusions (Jacoby and Levy, 1980a). It is, of course, debatable whether a symptom from one syndrome is comparable with a similar one from another.

*b. Specificity*   The previous discussion raises the question of the specificity of cerebral atrophy. Excepting patients with overt neurological problems (e.g., Pick's disease), do other psychiatric groups show cerebral atrophy? Although Weinberger *et al.* (1982) were definitely of the opinion that the affectively ill ($n = 23$) did not show atrophy, this laboratory soon put out another report (Rieder *et al.* 1983), after studying 19 schizoaffectives and 15 patients with a bipolar disorder, stating that some patients with any of these disorders can show atrophy. This observation was confirmed in the study of 11 schizophrenics at the Clinical Research Centre in England. Schizophrenic ventricles were significantly larger than those of neurotics, but not more than those of affectively ill patients (Johnstone *et al.*, 1981; Owens *et al.*, 1985). In Figure 8.3 we show a similar finding from a comparison of young manics, young chronically ill schizophrenics, and healthy controls (Nasrallah *et al.*, 1982b). The absence of a difference seems particularly apparent if the subjects are aging, affectively ill, or dementing (Jacoby and Levi, 1980a,b).

One should perhaps point out that some patients with completely unrelated and putatively "nonorganic" syndromes can show increased lateral ventricle size. From a sample of 50 anorexics aged 15 to 30 yr, 35 showed ventricles larger than any of the age-matched controls (Krieg *et al.*, 1988). Many showed sulcal changes. Interestingly, the ventricle size decreased slightly after the patients had regained weight.

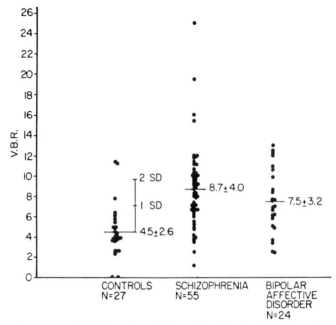

**Figure 8.3**  A sattergram distribution of VBRs for manic, schizophrenic and control subjects. The mean values and standard deviations are shown (from Nasrallah *et al.*, 1982b).

It is clear that there is no consensus about whether cerebral atrophy is more associated with one group of clinical symptoms or another. In the case of schizophrenia, it matters little if the subgroups are called negative, type 1, or hebephrenic. Perhaps the greater incidence of atrophy in those with symptoms of schizophrenia or dementia is related to specific aspects of their performance and cognitive abilities. For this reason, some laboratories have looked for correlates with neurological signs, neurophysiological measures of information processing, neurochemical response, and neuropsychological performance.

## 4. Neuropsychology and Psychophysiology

Unfortunately, detailed psychophysiological studies with CT correlates are not abundant. Thus, schizophrenics whose ventricles or sulci have been accurately assessed by CT techniques have not yet been the subject of many reports on performance of specific tests of cognitive function nor of detailed event-related potential (ERP) studies in information processing paradigms used by psychophysiologists.

It may come as a surprise to some readers that, on standard comprehensive neurological examinations, 50–65% of schizophrenics show signs of central nervous impairment. This incidence compares with the top end of the range for the incidence of CT-measured cerebral atrophy. It certainly distinguishes these patients from the population at large, which shows an incidence of neurological signs of 5%. However, like the increase of ventricle size, it does not separate schizophrenics from some other psychiatric groups (for review, see Heinrichs and Buchanan, 1988).

Undoubtedly part of this high incidence is accounted for by the incidence of abnormal Parkinsonian and dyskinetic movements often seen in medicated schizophrenics. Indeed such abnormal movements are more frequent among those with large cerebral ventricles (Famuyiwa *et al.*, 1979; Owens *et al.*, 1985). However, it is important to try to distinguish between drug- and disease-related movements. Bartels and Themelis (1983) compared 29 patients with moderate to severe tardive dyskinesia with 29 schizophrenics who did not show these symptoms but had received similar long-term phar-macotherapy. In the dyskinetic patients, not only was the third ventricle significantly larger, but so was the distance between the caudate nuclei. The area of the head of the caudate nucleus and the lentiform body on CT scans was smaller in dyskinetics. The distance between the caudate nuclei is relevant, but only relevant for those with motor problems. (For a review, see Johnstone *et al.*, 1989.)

Is there a direct relationship between increased ventricle size and cognitive function? We should note that memory and orienting is impaired in normal subjects with increasing age and ventricle size (Jacoby *et al.*, 1980a,b). Early reports of increased ventricle size in schizophrenics also recorded poor performance on the Withers and Hinton (1971) tests of the sensorium, poor paired associate learning, and a tendency to poorer memory (Johnstone *et al.*, 1976, 1978; see also Famuyiwa *et al.*, 1979).

It seems that tests of general ability and the simple tests set to help measure intelligence (e.g., Wechsler Adult Intelligence Scale, WAIS) are not sensitive enough to show any differential levels of performance between those with and without atrophy (Nyback *et al.*, 1984; Owens *et al.*, 1985; Kolakowska *et al.*, 1985; Houston *et al.*, 1986; Pandurangi *et al.*, 1986). This may not be surprising in view of the small degree of atrophy found in many patients. Sometimes atrophy in schizophrenics has been shown to correlate with digit–symbol and block-design subtest performance (Rieder *et al.*, 1979; Donnelly *et al.*, 1980; Kemali *et al.*, 1986).

Attempts to measure more specific cognitive abilities (e.g., concept forma-tion, trail making, Halstead–Reitan test battery) report a deterioration of cognitive ability that correlates with increased lateral ($n = 23$, Pandurangi *et al.*, 1986; $n = 28$, Keilp *et al.*, 1988) or third ventricle size ($n = 23$, Nyman *et al.*, 1986) or with increased sulcal size ($n = 4$, Rieder *et al.*, 1979). In a much larger study of sulcal widening, Nasrallah *et al.* (1983; $n = 55$) found that such patients showed increased thought disorder and poorer cognitive performance on the mini-mental state exam of Folstein and McHugh (1975). An indication of the strength of the correlation came in an early study from the NIMH (Donnelly *et al.*, 1980), in which they found they were able to predict the performance of 12 of 15 subjects from the CT scan. The strength of the result is weakened by the unfortunate fact that these patients also scored 20 points lower than controls on the total IQ test. For other investigators, such as Gruzelier and colleagues (1988) in London, the relationship was less obvious. Of 28 schizophrenics with CT measures, 10 showed signs of atrophy. There was no relationship between atrophy and performance on digit-span, memory, conditioning, or fluency tests, despite the fact that they could distinguish schizophrenic performance from that of patients with depression or affective psychoses.

Anyone with experience in conducting these sorts of tests may be impressed by the claim of Golden and colleagues (1980) that the performance of 42 schizophrenics (age 21–40 yr) on 8 of 14 subscales of the Luria–Nebraska test battery correlated significantly with increased VBR, namely, on measures of tactile sense, expressive speech (naming and classifying), reading, writing, arithmetic, pathognomonic neurological soft signs, and left and right hemisphere function. (For a full description of the battery, see Golden *et al.*, 1978; see Spiers, 1982, for a critique.) Despite criticism of this battery, it remains of interest that some cognitive abilities (e.g., classification) but not all (e.g., memory) were impaired. However Bilder and colleagues (1988; $n = 56$) found, using a similar battery of tests based on Luria and WAIS scales, that patients without signs of atrophy tended to be more impaired than those showing signs. Again, a simple interpretation of their results is somewhat compromised by the low mean IQ of 83 in the schizophrenic group.

In view of the apparent decline of some cognitive abilities in association with cerebral atrophy and the well-known reduction of evoked-potential amplitude during the performance of tests of attention-related function in schizophrenics, it is a pity that there have been few studies investigating relationships between atrophy and ERPs or the electrodermal orienting response (EDOR). Certainly, patients with cerebral atrophy can show reduced ERP amplitudes (Morihisa and McAnulty, 1985; Romani *et al.*, 1987). A relationship between the atrophy and the function underlying the ERP change was not drawn. Indeed Romani *et al.* (1987) found that only a weak correlation existed between amplitude reduction and atrophy. The preliminary study by McCarley, Faux, and colleagues (1989) in Massachusetts illustrates why a relationship may be difficult to show. They report on 9 chronic schizophrenics who showed varying degrees of atrophy on the majority of some 15 CT measures. Compared with 9 healthy controls, $P_2$ and $P_3$ amplitudes were reduced, but among schizophrenics, amplitudes correlated positively with increasing atrophy and symptom severity (cf. details in Chapter 9).

As part of the continuing analysis of the Copenhagen high risk study (Chapter 12), Cannon *et al.* (1988) reported on the relationship of ventricular enlargement and EDOR in 9 schizophrenics, 10 borderline cases, 15 healthy controls. Hyporesponders were found in orienting, conditioning, and generalization test conditions; hyporesponding was found to correlate with third but not lateral ventricle enlargement, independent of diagnosis. Clearly, neither the nature of the response nor the presence of atrophy seems to be specific to schizophrenia. It is interesting to recall the preponderance of negative symptoms in the group with atrophy and that an association of perinatal problems with the probability of EDOR hyporesponse was reported from this database. (cf. Sections I, B, 3 and I, B, 5).

Some laboratories have found that patients with atrophy tend to show abnormal EEGs. Thus, slow or disorganized EEGs were found in young subjects (28–30 yr) in a sample of 23 studied by Pandurangi *et al.* (1986) in New York. Morihisa and McAnulty (1985) reported that increased VBR (particularly reflecting enlargement in the anterior horn) was associated with a bilateral increased incidence of slow delta activity. Such subjects may not be as common as these studies would make out. Weinberger and Wyatt (1982) could find only 6 of 29 subjects with abnormal EEGs (increased incidence of slow theta waves) that showed evidence of atrophy. A similar if unexpected warning against premature expectations of finding relations between CT results and other physiological functions comes from a study of regional cerebral blood flow from the Karolinska Institute in Stockholm (Wiesel *et al.*, 1987). They found no relationship between the blood flow and the CT parameters they measured in 18 paranoid and hebephrenic schizophrenics.

So one may justifiably ask, apprehensively, if there is any connection between CT parameters and hypothesized changes of monoamine metabolism. This question might be addressed by examining the responsiveness of subjects to the dopamine (DA) blocking properties of neuroleptic agents or by measuring neurotransmitters in body fluids.

An influential report from the NIMH compared 10 schizophrenics with large VBRs and 10 with smaller VBRs (Weinberger *et al.*, 1980). The former were unresponsive to neuroleptics (i.e., DA antagonists). This result is consistent with the hypothesis that hyperdopaminergic function may be more characteristic of patients with type 1 or positive symptoms and without cerebral atrophy. An additional 12 subjects were studied by Jeste *et al.* (1983) for their response to the DA agonist apomorphine (0.01 mg/kg). Supporting Weinberger's results, they found that patients with no atrophy worsened (i.e., putatively hyperdopaminergic) and those with atrophy either showed no change or improved (i.e., symptoms relatively unrelated to DA status). More recent work with larger samples also found that schizophrenics with more CT anomalies were less responsive to typical neuroleptics (Gattaz *et al.*, 1988).

Another result from the NIMH team supports Weinberger's differentiation on the basis of CT results and his attribution of hyperdopaminergic function to those patients with normal scans. Kleinman *et al.* (1984) found that, as a group, 55 schizophrenics showed more eye-blinking than normal healthy subjects. (This behavior has been attributed to DA dysfunction; see Chapter 7.) Neuroleptic treatment, however, only brought about a decrease of blinking in those who showed ventricles of a normal size.

This observation leads us to ask what direct measures of DA metabolism show. We can quite easily summarize the results. Very often a negative correlation is seen between cerebrospinal fluid (CSF) levels of the DA metabolite homovanillic acid (HVA) and measures of cerebral atrophy (data from 221 schizophrenics; Van Kammen *et al.*, 1983, 1984, 1986; Nyback *et al.*, 1984; Oxenstierna *et al.*, 1984; Losonczy *et al.*, 1986; Houston *et al.*, 1986; Doran *et al.*, 1987; $r = -0.9$; Figure 8.4). The implication is that low DA utilization may be more common among those with cerebral atrophy. This suggestion fits with the probability of decreased response of these subjects to neuroleptic treatment.

DBH, dopamine beta hydroxylase, is an enzyme crucial to the synthesis of NA (noradrenaline); subsequently, since NA is a precursor of DA, its activity can affect DA levels. MAO, monoamine oxidase, is one of the enzymes involved in NA and DA catabolism. There is no evidence of a specific correlation between CT measures and plasma DBH or MAO activity (Goetz and Van Kammen, 1986; Pandurangi *et al.*, 1986), although levels of the former enzyme are often low in many schizophrenics, notably in those with increased VBR (e.g., Van Kammen *et al.*, 1983, 1986).

Evidence for changes of metabolism in the other monoaminergic neuro-transmitter, serotonin, are inconsistent with decreases (Potkin *et al.*, 1983; Nyback *et al.*, 1984; Van Kammen *et al.*, 1984; Doran *et al.*, 1987) and no changes (Oxenstierna *et al.*, 1984; Losonczy *et al.*, 1986) in the metabolite being recorded. One study has been concerned with CSF amino acids (Reveley *et al.*, 1987). Measures of glutamate and tyrosine were unremark-able, but their 12 chronic schizophrenic patients showed high levels of glycine, leucine, alanine, and phenylalanine compared with 9 controls. The investigators note that high levels of alanine are typical of patients with degenerative diseases.

## 5. Risk Factors

Three factors that have been linked to an increased risk of developing schizophrenia have also been investigated for an association with cerebral atrophy. The studies involve retrospective analyses. The first analysis con-cerned whether there was a greater incidence of family members suffering from schizophrenia for those schizophrenic subjects showing ventricular

**A. GAS scores and CSF concentrations**

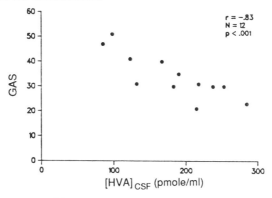

**B. Third ventricle widths and CSF HVA concentrations**

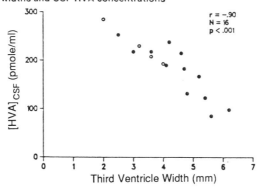

**C. GAS scores and third ventricle widths**

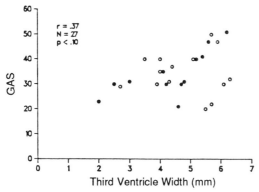

● = Patients with values for all three variables: third ventricle width, HVA, and GAS. ○ = Other patients.

**Figure 8.4** Relationships among Global Assessment Scale scores (GAS), cerebrospinal fluid (CSF), homovanillic acid (HVA), and third ventricle width in chronic schizophrenic patients (from Houston *et al.*, 1986).

enlargement and whether there were signs of atrophy among family members with or without illness.

A study of 12 families in the United States reported that, although the ventricles of the schizophrenic subjects were larger than those of their siblings, there seemed nonetheless to be a familial component in comparison with control families (DeLisi et al., 1986). Most results have provided little support for the existence of such a component.

Reveley et al. (1982), in a study of monozygotic (MZ) twins, found that, for healthy twins and twins discordant for schizophrenia, ventricle size was highly correlated between twin partners ($r = 0.89, 0.87$, respectively). Indeed, the search for family members with schizophrenic illness has tended to show a weaker or stronger relationship of atrophy to the absence of such a family history, (Oxenstierna et al., 1984; Reveley et al., 1984; Turner et al., 1986, $n = 30$; Lewis et al., 1987; Romani et al., 1987). (i.e., schizophrenics without atrophy are more likely to have a family history of schizophrenic illness). In other samples, no CT differences were found among schizophrenics with and without a family history for schizophrenia ($n = 64$, Farmer et al., 1987; Pakkenberg, 1987).

Owen et al. (1989) from the Institute of Psychiatry in London studied 3 groups of 48 families—one containing healthy subjects, one with schizophrenics with a first or second degree relative with psychiatric illness, and one with schizophrenics without such a relative. Both groups of schizophrenics exhibited a similar degree of cerebral atrophy greater than what was shown by the healthy subjects. However, considering the 23 schizophrenics with a family history of schizophrenias separately from the 18 with a family history of affective disturbances showed that the former group had a significantly increased VBR. The result of this study echoes the implication of the DeLisi study just discussed. However, as Owen et al. remark, we must be most careful in the appraisal of this result since many family members will not have lived through or reached the age at which a major psychiatric illness could be expected. This weakness in the design of all such studies will tend to increase the number of subjects incorrectly assigned to a group with a negative family history. This holds true, particularly for the group with cases of affective disturbance in the family, since such disturbances usually first appear in older subjects.

An example of a risk factor that can be independent of familial indications is the presence of complications at the birth of the subject who develops schizophrenia. There is no real discord between the studies reported. Generalizing about birth complications, there is a significant relationship between the frequency of birth complications and the later development of schizophrenia with cerebral atrophy of one form or another (Delisi et al., 1986; Turner et al., 1986; Owen et al., 1988). Owen and colleagues reviewed the birth records for 61 schizophrenics discharged from the Maudsley Hospital in

London over a 4-yr period. They distinguished between "definite" complications (e.g., high or difficult forceps delivery) and equivocal complications (e.g., forceps or other instrumental delivery). They found 8 of 14 with definite complications showed more CT atrophy (including sulci and VBR) than the mean for the groups with and without obstetric complications. This was true for only 6 of 38 subjects without complications at birth. The examples of birth complications we have listed were those most frequently reported in this study, but the relationship seems to exist for a range of perinatal traumata (DeLisi *et al.*, 1986; Turner *et al.*, 1986).

It is important to emphasize a point made by Reveley and colleagues, that most births with these sorts of complications do not lead to psychiatric illness. The point to be made is one of risk. Thus, it is not surprising that a few other groups who have reviewed birth records (among many other factors) failed to find a significant relationship. This result may be partly due to the inadequacy of earlier records, to not making a thorough investigation, and to a type II statistical error due to the small sample size. There is no exclusive relationship between obstetric complications, cerebral atrophy, and schizophrenia. For example, the study from London also reported an association between the high incidence of birth complications and an early onset for schizophrenia. Although teenage schizophrenics can show cerebral atrophy (Schulz *et al.*, 1983a), marked atrophy has also been noted in schizophrenics with a late onset after 44 years of age or more (Rabins *et al.*, 1987, $n = 29$).

Finally, one may ask about the purported relationship between the season of birth and the probability of developing schizophrenia with cerebral atrophy. Such risk studies have scarcely been reported. Sacchetti *et al.* (1985) in Italy, Degreef *et al.* (1988) in New York, and Zipursky and Schulz (1987) in Pittsburgh found that more subjects with cerebral atrophy were born between December or January and March. This concurs with the season when patients with an absence of a genetic or family history for schizophrenia tend to be born (Kinney and Jacobsen, 1978; Shur, 1982). However, no group has studied a sufficient number of subjects to derive a meaningful and significant relationship. (See Chapter 12 for further discussion and criticism of risk studies.)

## C. The Contribution of Magnetic Resonance Imaging to Neuropathological Assessment

The technique of magnetic resonance imaging (known as MRI) has the potential to produce images of the cranium and brain with greater resolution than the CT methods just described. Resolution of both tissue composition and spatial definition may be improved. The principle of MRI rests on sensing the resonance of protons (hydrogen nuclei of water) vibrating in a magnetic field oscillating at various radio frequencies. $T_1$, the spin lattice relaxation time, is a measure of the time taken for the protons to regain equilibrium after a pulse. Solid tissues have short $T_1$s and fluids have long $T_1$s. The $T_1$ values of gray matter are greater than that of white matter.

The potential advantages of MRI are threefold. First, the subject is not exposed to radiation. [This does not mean that all putative risks are eliminated (Adey, 1988).] Second, one can generate three-dimensional pictures in the transverse, sagittal, and coronal planes. However, the third advantage of improved resolution depends very much on the magnetic field strength and imaging technique used. Currently, field strengths from 0.08 to 1.5 tesla are used. The images derived can be $T_1$-weighted by using an inversion recovery technique (30–600 msec). Maximal anatomical resolution would be obtained with 1.5-tesla field strength at 600 msec. $T_2$-weighted images derived from the spin–echo method are more sensitive to tissue change (i.e., pathology highlighted).

The first studies in the mid 1980s from North Carolina and New York concentrated on frontal (Smith *et al.*, 1984) and posterior (Mathew and Partain, 1985) regions of small controlled groups of chronic schizophrenics (spin–echo, 0.3–0.5 tesla, 30 msec). At first no differences were evident from the frontal lobes, subcortices, VBR, or cerebellar regions. In light of concurrent dramatic claims from *postmortem* studies of potential differences in interhemispheric transmission and the size of the corpus callosum (cf. Chapter 9), these studies sought, in particular, *in vivo* evidence for such a putative anomaly. Indeed, the early expanded series from Duke University in North Carolina seemed to show an increased callosal length and larger septal area (Mathew *et al.*, 1985). However, this observation has received very limited support from *postmortem* (Nasrallah *et al.*, 1983) and MRI studies elsewhere [0.5 tesla, inversion recovery, 500–2000 msec, Nasrallah *et al.*, 1986; Rossi *et al.*, 1988 (area decrease); Uematsu and Kaiya, 1988 (increased length anteriorly)].

Meanwhile, the New York group also expanded their controlled series of patients ($n = 29$, Smith *et al.*, 1985b, 1987b; spin–echo and inversion recovery, 30 msec). Although they were able to find VBR increases in some patients, and these values correlated with baseline measurements of negative symptoms such as anergia, they were unable to report significant group differences on linear or area measurements. Similar controlled studies in the United States (Mander *et al.*, 1987) and the United Kingdom (Johnstone *et al.*, 1986; Besson *et al.*, 1987) also reported minimal changes in their chronically ill patients (0.08 tesla, inverse resonance, 600 msec). The former team attributed minor differences in their images to possible changes in the constitution of the blood–brain barrier. The English group could find no differences in the make-up of periventricular structures that were considered likely to contribute to CT measures of the increased ventricular size reported.

However, Besson *et al.* (1987) in Scotland were able to find some evidence for increased ventricle size in 11 of 23 patients. Comparing these subjects with the less severely ill, they found increased $T_1$ measures in the frontal images (i.e., biased for resolution and measurement rather than for changes of density and pathology) to be associated with the presence of more negative symptoms, whereas similar signs in medial and temporal regions were more associated with positive symptoms. Both groups of changes were more significant on the left side of the brain. In addition, the presence of dyskinesias in their patients seemed to be associated with increased $T_1$ in the basal ganglia.

More recently, a series of over 60 patients studied by Andreasen's group in Iowa and Weinberger's group at the NIMH have shown more results comparable with those emerging from CT studies (using 0.5 tesla, inversion recovery, 600 msec). Comparing sagittal and coronal slices in chronic patients, Andreasen *et al.* (1986) found a tendency for smaller crania, cerebra, and frontal regions. Despite presenting their patients with powerful tests of their ability to perform and change mental set (Wisconsin card and Stroop tests), they found no relationship between performance and MRI results. Further, they warned against overinterpretation of the size differences they reported in view of significant differences in the socioeconomic background of their comparison groups. There are indeed many reasons, most quite unrelated to psychopathology, why some individuals may show smaller crania and cerebra. Such individuals have not been found by other groups (e.g., Weinberger *et al.*, 1987).

The subjects at the NIMH continue to prove to be the most organic of the various samples reported by different teams of anatomical investigators. Kelsoe *et al.* (1988) found that sections across the anterior part of the third ventricle and posterior part of the lateral ventricle were, respectively, 73 and 62% larger in their schizophrenic group. Of the 23 subjects, 12 had ventricles larger than any of the 14 healthy controls. Despite this marked finding, the investigators were unable to find any relationship between the anatomical measures and the age, age of onset, or duration of illness of their patients. This team at the NIMH then turned its attention to slices across the temporal lobes (including the hippocampus and amygdala; Suddath *et al.*, 1989). They still used a 0.5-tesla magnet with a 600 msec inversion time, but used a much shorter echo time (30 msec) with computerized image analysis. They replicated their finding of a 67% increase of lateral ventricle size ($\sim 7.8$ cm$^3$) with 17 largely undifferentiated schizophrenics. More intriguingly, they were able to discern a 20% decrease in temporal lobe size ($\sim 18.5$ cm$^3$) which, with the change of methods, was attributable to a grey rather than white matter loss. A similar, but much less distinct, trend was found after comparison with bipolar and healthy subjects in England (Johnstone *et al.*, 1989; cf. Chapter 9). Before attempting to consider the implications of these results for the mechanism of degeneration and its cause, we advise awaiting confirmation or refutation from other research groups using both schizophrenics and subjects with other psychiatric illnesses.

It seems that the results of MRI studies to date have proved disappointing, in view of the expectations in the early 1980s. It is worth asking why this may be so. The NIMH group has pointed out that improved resolution does not necessarily make the borders between structures more distinct. Their estimates of the amygdalohippocampal volume were nearly twice those reported *postmortem*. They also point out what one may realistically hope to measure with current methods. They found an increased mean ventricle size (15.4–24.7 ml) that represented about 1% of the brain volume. *Postmortem* measures (see Section II) of a 20% reduction in amygdala volume represent 0.33 ml ($<0.05\%$ brain volume). For MRI studies, this is both well within the sampling error and unrealistic with present techniques. Clearly, the most recent studies are illustrative of the rapid progress that is being made.

## D. Studies of Regional Cerebral Blood Flow

The history of cerebral blood flow (CBF) measurement goes back to 1948, when Kety and Schmidt published the results of studies of the passage of the relatively inert gas nitrous oxide through the blood stream of schizophrenic patients. From this and subsequent studies (e.g., Hoyer and Oesterreich, 1975), it was deduced that CBF was reduced in patients with nonproductive symptoms but probably normal in others. Cases with catatonic activation and hallucinations sometimes showed increased CBF, but this may have reflected a more general state of activation, as has been seen in other subjects (Kety, 1951). The studies were uncontrolled and the technique was limited. Measures could only be achieved for the whole brain, grey and white matter together.

The application of the same principle to the intracarotid administration of the inert gas xenon as a radioactive isotope ($^{133}$Xe) at once opened the doors for regional tomographic quantitative measures (Ingvar and Franzen, 1974a,b). By the end of the decade, the technique had been simplified to the noninvasive inhalation of xenon, and applied in a number of laboratories around the world (Figure 8.5). The inhalation technique avoids the disadvantage of intracarotid administration since both hemispheres can be studied. This includes areas supplied by the vertebrobasilar vascular bed, which is not reached by intra-carotid injections. There remain a number of problems for assessment (cf. Mathew *et al.*, 1988). Thus, the speed of xenon clearance varies between gray matter (fast) and white matter and the intracranial blood supply (slow). *Gray matter flow* is only approximated by estimation of the initial slope for increasing xenon concentration or an index derived from an exponential analysis of the slopes (Olesen, 1974). The former technique tends to be more sensitive.

**Figure 8.5** Representation of a subject undergoing Xenon Xe 133 inhalation procedure for regional blood flow while doing an automated version of the Wisconsin card sorting test (from Weinberger *et al.*, 1986, © American Medical Association).

Further, only recent studies have attempted to estimate the influence of carbon dioxide levels, which have sometimes been found to account for initial measures of regional CBF changes (e.g., Berman *et al.*, 1986; Weinberger *et al.*, 1986) and sometimes not (Mathew *et al.*, 1988). Thus, comparison of data among studies can be confounded by different estimation techniques. In addition, subject variables such as age (inverse relation to CBF) and sex (higher CBF in women) have been taken into account only in some studies. A further vexing problem for studies of both metabolism and blood flow is the subject state during the tedious procedures necessary for these measures (e.g., high or low arousal).

Of the 25 or so published reports with controls, slightly more than half have found that the mean regional flows for their schizophrenic groups ($n = 6$–60) show an attenuation of the relative hyperfrontal CBF pattern seen in healthy subjects at rest (i.e., there is a decrease in the slope of the gradient between levels of frontal and posterior CBF). This tendency is claimed for adolescents who had never received neuroleptic medication ($\sim$16 yr; Chabrol *et al.*, 1985), older subjects (61 yr; Ingvar and Franzen, 1974b), and remitted patients (Geraud *et al.*, 1987). Although CBF is inversely related to age and illness duration, it does not seem to be related to the age of onset or the presence of schizophrenia in the family (Mathew *et al.*, 1988). A relatively hypofrontal pattern seems likely to occur in chronic patients, whether paranoid, nonparanoid, or undifferentiated (Mathew *et al.*, 1982; Ariel *et al.*, 1983). A more conservative interpretation of these studies that would also account for some of the other results is that, particularly in the early stages (Dousse *et al.*, 1988), a slight but general decrease of CBF stretches from the frontal to the occipital lobes. In contrast to schizophrenics, depressed patients usually show normal CBF patterns, although manics, in the depressed state, can show reduced flow (Gustafson *et al.*, 1981).

Early Swedish studies emphasized the hypofrontal aspect of the fronto-posterior gradient in subjects with negative symptoms of withdrawal and autism (Ingvar and Franzen, 1974a; Franzen and Ingvar, 1975b). This is more evident from measures of initial flow than "gray matter indices." (Unusually, both were reported by Ingvar, 1980; see methods.) The hypofrontal pattern is more clearly seen in the older, more chronically ill patients, but there is an increasing number of reports of the anteroposterior gradient being more influenced by increases of the posterocentral blood flow than by decreases in the anterofrontal regions of the younger subjects more usually studied (Franzen and Ingvar, 1975a; Mathew *et al.*, 1988; cf. PET studies).

Seldom have enough subjects been studied to draw a convincing link to particular symptoms. However, more recently a particularly thorough and large scale study of 108 schizophrenics and age- and sex-matched controls found the thought-disorder symptom cluster to be related to CBF in many cortical regions (Mathew *et al.*, 1988). In fact, the significant feature is their finding that thought disorders correlated inversely with the anteroposterior CBF gradient.

Of the 16 subjects studied by Kurachi *et al.* (1985), 8 were hallucinating and showed increased flow in temporal regions (see previous text on activation in whole brain studies). They used measures of initial slope. Using the gray matter index, Dousse *et al.* (1988) could not replicate this result in their 13 patients with auditory hallucinations. (The problem relates to the sensitivity of the two measures.) However, they did report a decrease in the temporal lobe for the 6 patients with visual hallucinations. The problems involved in comparing these two studies not only involve the different measures, but the location of the scintillation counters. In the latter case, the sites were not ideal for measuring superior temporal flow.

To the extent that cognitive activity, as reflected by learning in several sensory modalities, is reflected by increased frontal flow in normal subjects (Roland, 1982), it is not surprising that low relative frontal CBF has been negatively correlated with ratings for cognitive dysfunction in schizophrenics (Ingvar and Franzen, 1974). The relationship of CBF to cognitive function has been the subject of a particularly influential study from NIMH (Berman *et al.*, 1986; Weinberger *et al.*, 1986).

These authors were not convinced that their subjects (up to 24 chronic schizophrenics) showed CBF differences at rest. Apparent differences disappeared when $CO_2$ levels were considered. The investigators chose to present

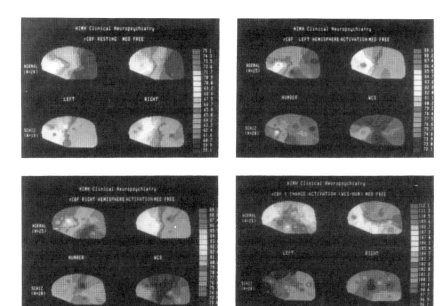

**Figure 8.6** Regional cerebral blood flow (rCBF) maps showing lateral views of the cerebral cortex (frontal on the left, occipital on the right). Note that the scales are not comparable between figures. Med, medication; schiz, schizophrenics; WCS, Wisconsin card-sorting test. *Top left,* Both hemispheres in resting state for normal and for medicated chronic schizophrenics. *Top right/bottom left,* Same subject groups during number matching and Wisconsin card-sorting tasks. *Bottom right,* Percentage change maps (Weinberger *et al.,* 1986, © American Medical Association).

to their patients tasks testing arithmetic abilities, continuous performance (CPTx), electrodermal orienting response, and Wisconsin card-sorting as indicators of effort, vigilance, arousal, and categorical thinking. The striking result was that only the Wisconsin card-sorting task showed a difference. There was an increase of frontal CBF in the control group, but the patients failed to show any increase in frontal flow irrespective of medication status (Figure 8.6). Whereas it may be true that not every subject with frontal brain damage has difficulties on this task and that a number of schizophrenics will show increased frontal flow in this procedure, the result does suggest that there are long-term chronic patients who seem to have biological and psychological signs of poor adaptive function of the frontal lobes. The point is underlined by a report comparing type 1 with type 2 schizophrenics (Guenther *et al.,* 1986). By asking their subjects to squeeze a handle, they obtained an increase of CBF in the contralateral frontal lobe of controls (type 1 and mildly depressed patients). This increase was not obtained in the

severely ill schizophrenic and depressed patients. The absence of frontal
activation may not be a discriminating feature for schizophrenics, but it may
be a pointer to the problem of patients with poor prognosis.

The problem in most *in vivo* CBF studies is that they do reflect cerebral
activation independent of the study situation. Even in studies of subjects at
rest, one can never be sure who is truly relaxed and empty-minded, who is
working out tomorrow's schedule, and who is fantasizing about the previous
evening. These studies are bound to generate heterogeneous findings. The
pattern will only be revealed after many, many subjects have been studied.

# E. Studies of Regional Cerebral Energy Metabolism with Positron Emission Tomography

In the early 1980s, it became possible to try to directly confirm some of the
potentially important and exciting implications of regional CBF studies. The
principle of positron emission tomography (PET), established by Sokoloff *et al.*
(1977), is based on the administration of glucose labeled with isotopes of
fluorine ($^{18}F$) or carbon ($^{11}C$) with a very short half-life. In fact, usually
deoxyglucose is administered. This substance is taken up like glucose, but
since it cannot be metabolized it remains at the uptake site, with its radioactive
label, flagging areas of high metabolic activity. Thus, PET scanners can take
pictures of slices through the brain, as do other brain-imaging techniques,
showing images of the demand for energy in various brain regions. However,
the resolution of the technique is not yet as high as that of other forms of brain
imaging.

It is not surprising, in view of the level of expensive technology required by
PET scanning, that the first teams in this field were those from laboratories with
the greatest resources, namely those at the NIMH in Bethesda, at Brookhaven in
New York, and at the Karolinska Institute in Sweden.

The NIMH group reported on 16 subjects with first rank symptoms
(Buchsbaum *et al.*, 1982, 1984). Reflecting the results of a number of CBF
studies, they found that schizophrenics at rest showed no absolute differences
compared with healthy controls. However, regional comparisons showed a
hypofrontal pattern of metabolism which was caused more by an increased
metabolism in posterior regions than by lowered levels anteriorly, irrespective
of medication status. More recent reports with patients free of medication
and studied under controls of somatosensory stimulation of the right arm
found similar but more specific results, namely, an increased temporal lobe
metabolism in schizophrenics with respect to healthy subjects (DeLisi *et al.*,
1989).

No change (Kishimoto *et al.*, 1987) or decreased rates of temporal lobe metabolism are the more widespread findings, both at rest or under auditory vigilance testing (Wolkin *et al.*, 1985; R. M. Cohen *et al.*, 1987; Gur *et al.*, 1987). With acute patients, Weisel (1985) reported a comparatively low parietal metabolism prior to treatment. In a second test, with patients on sulpiride medication the group found metabolic levels in their patients to rise in parietal and basal ganglia areas. However, although such an increase concurs with the findings of Buchsbaum *et al.* (1987) in the basal ganglia of chronic patients largely treated with typical neuroleptics, the reverse result was reported by a later Swedish study of acute patients using sulpiride (Wik *et al.*, 1989). (Note that the washout period for the NIMH study was 5 weeks, on average, and in some cases only 2 weeks prior to study.) The Swedish study also raised another important consideration in running such "high-tech" studies. The patients and the healthy controls showed some decreases of frontal metabolism on the second run. This result may well reflect the stress—or unhappy state of mind—of patients undergoing to-mographic investigations. This is one of the more important of several factors that render both the comparison of heterogeneous results and the drawing of conclusions about the effects of medication impractical at this time.

The question of the effects of long-term medication was specifically addressed recently by a Canadian group (Szechtman *et al.*, 1988). They compared 5 schizophrenics who had been on neuroleptic treatment for 1 yr with 14 who had been so treated for 4–14 yr. They found a mild nonsignifi-cant attenuation of the cortical metabolic pattern over several years, but a larger increase in the region of the basal ganglia (and thalamus). However, it is difficult to evaluate this report since the cortical pattern referred to was one of hyperfrontal and hypoposterior metabolic activity.

However, light is shed on these results by an intriguing study of 20 chronic schizophrenics, of whom 17 were medicated, in Japan (Kishimoto *et al.*, 1987). Of their patients, 6 showed normal metabolic patterns. These were the 6 with the lowest Brief Psychiatric Rating Scale (BPRS) scores for psycho-pathology. The 6 with the worst scores, all of whom were nonparanoid, showed marked hypofrontal metabolism. The 8 "in-between" subjects showed lower lateralized parietal metabolism related to handedness (see Figure 8.7).

In New York, Farkas *et al.* (1984) were able to confirm the hypofrontal pattern in a more chronically ill group. Indeed, the two subjects with more florid symptoms had metabolic measures at the top end of the range for the group. What is important, however, is that the investigators attempted to exclude patients with evidence of neurological features. All 16 patients had normal CT scans. Of these, 7 had been free of medication for 6 months or more. The fact that this group was not distinctive with respect to regional metabolism led the authors to suggest that the hypofrontal pattern—when present—is a feature of the patient irrespective of symptom severity.

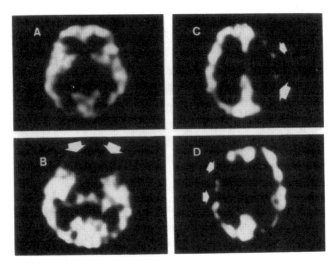

**Figure 8.7**   Positron emission tomograms (PET), illustrating (A) a healthy control subject, (B) a hypofrontal schizophrenic, (C) a hypoparietal schizophrenic, and (D) a hypotemporal schizophrenic (from Kishimoto *et al.*, 1990).

Broadly speaking, regional cerebral metabolic activity tends to confirm the attenuation of the frontal–posterior cortical gradient reported from CBF studies. As in CBF studies, depressed patients seem to show a normal distribution of metabolic rates (Kuhl *et al.*, 1985) unless their symptoms are particularly severe. Then decreases are recorded (Baxter *et al.*, 1985). However, as with most studies of schizophrenics, if the sample is large (i.e., from several laboratories), subjects with different characteristics will be found. In fact Cleghorn *et al.* (1989) recently reported increased frontal and reduced parietal glucose metabolism in 8 never-medicated DSM-III schizophrenic patients. The patients were considered to be more acute (illness less than 2 yr) and were reported to have less neuropsychological impairment than most of the patients of the other studies, although they made more errors on the Wisconsin card-sorting (category) test. Interestingly, the hyperfrontal pattern persisted when retested after 1 yr on neuroleptic medication.

It is difficult to conceive how PET studies could be very easily carried out on schizophrenics performing intellectual tasks. However, one group did run some scans while the healthy subjects were performing tasks requiring abstract reasoning. They found that *higher* metabolic rates were associated with *poorer* task performance (Haier *et al.*, 1988). It is unfortunately difficult to pursue this research direction reliably with the psychiatrically ill. As an alternative, it would be of interest to look for correlations between CBF indicators of state, CT measures of anatomical change and the predominance in the subjects studied of smaller or larger clusters of symptom-features (e.g., alogia or anhedonia versus positive/negative or poor premorbid/good premorbid).

## II. *In Vitro* Studies of Degeneration

Reports of gross or microanatomical changes in schizophrenia, usually derived from *postmortem* dissection, bring with them expectations of reliable results derived from indisputable "hard" material that is on the laboratory bench for all to see. In reality, histological examination is associated with as many methodological problems as any other technique mentioned in this chapter. How was the brain treated *postmortem?* Was there shrinkage? The quality and specificity of stains is as disputable as the diagnosis of schizophrenia in the subjects studied. The questions of which areas and slices to sample and how to interpret minor changes are common to *in vivo* and *in vitro* studies. In the following brief discussion, first we shall consider studies of whole brain and evidence for atrophy and then we shall look at five major subdivisions of the brain; cerebellum, basal ganglia, diencephalon, limbic structures, and, finally, temporal and frontal lobes.

## A. Whole Brain

From the foregoing sections we might be led to believe that an organic pathology of some sort is present in a sizeable minority of schizophrenics. Would we really expect such changes to be evident in whole brain?

The recent result from Andreasen and her colleagues (1986), using MRI techniques, suggests that the answer could be "yes." They reported a trend toward smaller crania and cerebra in their patients. In Sweden, Pakkenberg (1987) reported a trend for a decreased volume (5–6%) and weight (8–9%) in 29 chronic schizophrenics in comparison with normal controls. This result is of the same magnitude as a recent report from England. Brown *et al.* (1986) found that 41 schizophrenic brains were, on average, 6% lighter than those of 29 patients with affective disorder. Even if the trend is slight and the variability large, such a difference at the level of the whole brain represents the loss of a considerable amount of tissue (far more than that in the hippocampus and amygdala combined). It is of the same magnitude as the loss reported for patients with Alzheimer's disease, but less than that for Huntington's chorea.

More importantly, Brown and colleagues (1986) furnished confirmation of the CT evidence for increased lateral ventricle size, despite the problems of working with preserved tissue. In the anterior horn, increases of 19% and in the temporal horn, increases of 97% were reported. Thus it seems reasonable, considering that several techniques have provided results suggesting cerebral atrophy, to look microscopically for the whereabouts of this loss. The presence of neurons with vacuoles (foreign inclusions), fibrils (unusual proteins), and gliosis has been sought as a sign of degeneration and found in widely disparate brain areas over the past 100 yr (e.g., Alzheimer, 1897). By the time of the first International Congress of Neuropathology in Rome (1952), some 250 descriptions of signs of degeneration in schizophrenia had been published (Stevens, 1982). It has proved astonishingly difficult, however, to show a link between atrophy of the brain and signs of degeneration.

In a qualitative analysis of 100 brains, Jellinger (1985) could find no evidence for increased gliosis. Roberts *et al.* (1987) undertook a quantitative study of 18 brains that were known to be atrophied (Brown *et al.*, 1986). They used an immunocytochemical stain for a fibrillary protein that is the product of the astrocytic reaction. Certainly they found gliosis in the periventricular regions where one would expect it from earlier anatomical (Nieto and Escobar, 1972) and CT studies (see previous text), but they reported that in comparison with affective or normal subjects there were no increased levels of gliosis in the 20 limbic and temporal brain areas studied. The absence of any remarkable gliosis in schizophrenic tissue is supported by other studies (Nasrallah *et al.*, 1983). This later report did raise the possibility that subjects with a late onset for the illness show more gliosis than other subjects. The questions remain: Where do the neural changes take place that could be responsible for atrophy, and what are they?

## B. Cerebellum

A few CT studies have implicated cerebellar atrophy (incidence 18%; Lohr and Jeste, 1986). Although individuals have been reported to show disorganization or loss of Purkinje cells (Roizin *et al.*, 1959; Reyes and Gordon, 1981), larger patient samples, indeed the 23 subjects studied by Lohr and Jeste from the Yakovlev collection in the United States, showed no differences of density in the anterior or posterior vermis nor in the size of the cell or nucleus of Purkinje cells.

## C. Basal Ganglia

For the basal ganglia, including the pallidum, there are a number of earlier claims for the presence (Buscaino, 1920) and absence (Nagasaka, 1925) of changes in schizophrenia. More recent and extensive work from Bogerts' group at the Brain Research Institute in Düsseldorf (Germany), much of it on the neuroleptic-free material assembled by the Vogts earlier this century, showed no changes of weight nor signs of degeneration in the various parts of the basal ganglia (Dom *et al.,* 1981; Bogerts *et al.,* 1985). This may seem surprising in view of the high incidence of biochemical changes that occur in some parts of this system, particularly after neuroleptic treatment (Chapters 13, 14). Indeed, in view of the behavioral functions of this system and the particular features of catatonic schizophrenics, one is inclined to view the claim of pallidal anomalies in this group sympathetically (Hopf, 1954). After all, there is reasonable evidence for anomalies in some subjects who show marked tardive dyskinesia (Gross and Kaltenbeck, 1970; Jellinger, 1977), and these subjects are prone to minor infarcts in this region (Kameyama *et al.,* 1975). This latter report may point to the source of the unusual change noted by Early and colleagues (1986) in St. Louis, Missouri. They reported increased blood flow in the globus pallidus on the left side of a small group of patients who had never received neuroleptic medication.

## D. Diencephalon and Limbic System

Apart from a few cases reported by Stevens (1982), there is no compelling evidence for a widespread incidence of thalamic degeneration (Lesch and Bogerts, 1984). However, both these groups have seen a decreased number of interneurons and increased fibrillosis in the pulvinar nucleus of some subjects (Dom *et al.,* 1981). Opinions differ more about the hypothalamus. Surprisingly, despite implications of hypothalamic dysfunction in psychosis (Davison and Bagley, 1969), this area has not been the focus of modern quantitative pathological study. Reports of plaques or gliosis in some subjects have persisted over the years (Dide, 1934; Morgan and Gregory, 1935; Stevens, 1982). Vegetative signs apparent in some patients could have their origin in dysfunction of this part of the diencephalon (cf. Lesch and Bogerts, 1984).

Discussion of the hypothalamus leads figuratively and anatomically into the limbic system. Over the last 60 years, the most persistent reports of pathological changes concern the temporal lobe, in particular, the hippocampus and amygdala that lie within it. It is fair to say that current work confirms, in a general way, the original reports (Josephy, 1923; Watanabe, 1934).

Stevens (1982) found intense gliosis on the surface of the amygdala of 4 subjects. Indeed 18 of her sample of 25 showed some fibrillary gliosis as marked by Holzer's stain. Among cases with organic changes, those with changes in the amygdala have a relatively high incidence (cf. Chapter 9). Bogerts *et al.* (1985) found, on average, that the amygdala decreased 22% in volume in their sample of 13. A still higher incidence of anomalies may be present in the hippocampal complex. [Hippocampal complex: i.e., in septum (Stevens, 1982); in CA 1–4 (Torrey and Peterson, 1974; Falkai and Bogerts, 1986); in entorhinal cortex (Jakob and Beckmann, 1986; Falkai *et al.,* 1988);

dentate gyrus and subiculum (no evidence).] The changes reported, respectively, include septal fibrils, fewer pyramidal cells and perforant fibers, and fewer neurons and abnormal lamination. About 80% of the more than 50 subjects studied were affected in some way.

These results are difficult to completely reconcile with those of a *postmortem* series studied in England (Brown *et al.,* 1986; Roberts *et al.,* 1987), in which no disproportionate signs of degeneration were recorded. However, an 11% decrease in the thickness of the parahippocampal gyrus was recorded. Further, they stated quite specifically that, with the use of their specific immunocytochemical methods, the possibility of other forms of degeneration, perhaps of a type with a more insidious and early onset, cannot be excluded. This is precisely the sort of change that has been the subject of the studies of the Scheibels and their colleagues on the Yakovlev collection (Scheibel and Kovelman, 1981; Kovelman and Scheibel, 1984; Altshuler *et al.,* 1987; Conrad and Scheibel, 1987).

Their basic finding, from the thoroughly studied material of the 8 chronic schizophrenics examined, is that the hippocampal pyramidal layer, though present, is disorganized. The apical dendrites are disoriented. They may be 70–90° out of alignment. This is particularly marked in the anterior regions. Disorder is most apparent at the borders between the different cell areas of Ammons Horn (Figure 8.8). The investigators interpret their results as evidence for a developmental insult, since the cells in the different cell layers

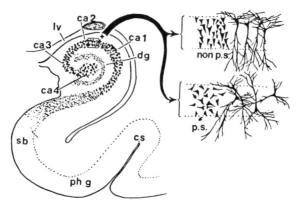

**Figure 8.8**   Schematized coronal section through human ventromedial temporal lobe showing transition from neocortex to archicortex (hippocampal–dentate complex). The close-ups on the right show organized (non p.s.) and disorganized (p.s.) histological patterns as may appear in normal and schizophrenic tissue, respectively. cs, collateral sulcus; phg, parahippocampal gyrus; sb, subiculum; ca 1–4, divisions of the cornu ammonis of the hippocampus; dg, dentate gyrus; lv, lateral ventricle (from Conrad and Scheibel, 1987).

migrate at different periods in the second or third trimester of pregnancy. Whether, of course, the ultimate cause has something to do with seasonal hormonal changes, viral infection, or a genetic problem is quite another question (see Conrad and Scheibel, 1987).

Is there something misleading in this influential series of reports? It is probably not so important to criticize the diagnosis. Recent material in the series was studied by examiners blind to the diagnosis and the authors found a marked increase of disorganization paralleling the severity of psychotic symptoms. A disadvantage which is more difficult to control is that all the schizophrenics had received either a frontal lobectomy or leukotomy. The authors argue that the possibility of transneuronal degenerative changes resulting in this sort of pathological change are unlikely, but it is a possibility that is difficult to eliminate. A great advantage of this particular sample is that they derive from a period before the introduction of neuroleptic therapy; thus, the possibility of pharmacological effects can be dismissed.

## E. Frontal Lobe

Finally, we consider the frontal lobe, for which there is the longest pedigree of reports of pathological change. Some 90 years after Alzheimer (1897) reported a loss of cortical cells in schizophrenia, Benes and colleagues confirmed the finding quantitatively (Benes *et al.,* 1986; Benes and Bird, 1987). Although they used a small sample of 10 chronic schizophrenics, they performed careful multiple regression and classification analyses to rule out the possible influences of age, fixation duration, hypoxia, and medication. Neuronal losses were particularly marked in prefrontal lamina VI, cingulate lamina V, and motor cortex lamina III. The neuronal loss probably extends to the area of the insula and claustrum (Jakob and Beckmann, 1986). As striking as these results are, they pertain to a very small number of individuals. Without much more work, we have no idea in what proportion of schizo-phrenics they occur. Do they represent the exception or the rule for any particular subgroup?

In conclusion, modern studies confirm a degenerative loss or disorganiza-tion of neurons in the neo- and allocortices of the frontal and temporal lobes in some schizophrenics. Former evidence for subcortical gliosis must be judged to be, at the least, a rarer phenomenon. In which schizophrenics are these pathological changes found? Although there is good reason to believe that the severity of symptoms is associated with a more progressive pathology (Conrad and Scheibel, 1987), there is little support for the idea that patients with more negative symptoms (e.g., Crow's type II) are any more vulnerable than those with positive symptoms (Bogerts *et al.,* 1985). Whereas Jakob and Beckmann (1986) found hebephrenics to be more susceptible to limbic damage, Bogerts (1985) found the reverse. One cannot easily associate diagnostic type with vulnerability to damage, let alone with the probability of damage to a particular area, based on current evidence. The refinements of analysis in recent years have not altered the validity of Janice Stevens' (1982) report that "there is no diagnostic pattern."

## III. Suggested Readings

For the reader interested in commentary and review of matters discussed in this chapter, we suggest three rather different recently published points of view by Roberts (1990), Waddington (1990), and Marks and Luchins (1990).

## IV. Summary Statements and Interpretations

### A. Computer Tomography

#### 1. Incidence and Psychopathology

The reported incidence of mild cerebral atrophy measured in schizophrenics with a CT scan is about 30%, but varies considerably (0–60%) with the sample tested. Most studies report a widening of the lateral or third cerebral ventricles. Some reports of atrophy refer to the widening of various fissures and sulci, particularly of the frontal lobe, but rarely to the cerebellum or fourth ventricle. Most studies define atrophy as two standard deviations above the mean of the control population.

Early reports of clear-cut associations with negative symptoms are not confirmed in recent studies. There are also CT findings in patients with positive symptoms (including delusions and hallucinations). However, the prevalence of positive CT findings is higher in chronic populations. Although some studies find a higher incidence of ventricular enlargement in poor premorbid patients, a relationship with poor long-term prognosis is not clear in the absence of long-term follow-up studies. There is evidence that atrophy in schizophrenics may not be progressive, even though it is correlated with age, independent of diagnostic status (i.e., degeneration is certainly not as progressive as in Alzheimer's disease).

There are reports of an increased likelihood of a poor response to neuroleptics in patients with mild cerebral atrophy.

CT findings are not limited to schizophrenia: patients with affective disorder show about the same range of deviations.

It should not be overlooked that reports of atrophy in given patient samples often reflect mild deviations from normal and are statistical in nature. Some authors attempt to explain these findings without regard to their diffuse nature and lack of specificity. Although there are examples of frontal or limbic degeneration, these findings are inconsistently reported from different laboratories and patient populations.

Normally the degree of atrophy recorded in schizophrenics may not be comparable with serious pathologies such as Alzheimer's disease. In most cases, the deviation is a statistical one with large overlapping regions. Some neuroradiologists, therefore, do not consider this truly pathologic (cf. report of a meeting between neuroradiologists and schizophrenia researchers at a NIMH symposium in *Schizophrenia Bulletin, 9* (2); Maser and Keith, 1983). Nevertheless, the volumes of neural tissues involved can be considerable in some cases, and findings of varying degrees of mild to more severe atrophy seem to hint toward a subgroup within the group of schizophrenias. With the aid of other improved brain-imaging techniques, such findings may become increasingly significant for schizophrenia research, and may possibly help clarify the heterogeneity issue. In this context, CT results should be viewed alongside the correlations discussed in subsequent sections and the application of other techniques in the study of the anatomy of schizophrenia. (Of current interest is the putative poor drug response of patients with alterations in the CT.)

## 2. Cognitive and Neuropsychological Correlates

Schizophrenics with signs of atrophy do worse in several neuropsychological tests. The deviations are not large and some studies report no deficits. One correlation with psychophysiological measures is claimed: electrodermal hyporesponse and enlargement of the third ventricle.

Diffuse and mild neuropsychological deficits (e.g., block design, tactile, arithmetic, and paired associate learning tests) are recorded for schizophrenics with diffuse and mild signs of cerebral atrophy.

The association of reduced electrodermal response and a widening of the third ventricle, perhaps indicating adjacent limbic degeneration, should be studied further to assess the relevance of the neuroanatomical specificity (elsewhere, experimental work has implicated limbic involvement). However, one should bear in mind that this was one report on a nonspecific correlation for a nonspecific measure.

## 3. Biochemical Correlates

Signs of cerebral atrophy correlate negatively with levels of dopamine metabolites (e.g., CSF) and less consistently with levels of serotonin metabolites.

These relatively consistent findings are encouraging and plausible if considered with the poor response to neuroleptics, especially in those with negative symptoms. They may help to describe a subgroup within schizophrenia and help to resolve some of the contradictory biochemical findings in Chapter 13.

### 4. Family History

Several early studies report that schizophrenic patients with atrophy are frequently without a family history of psychiatric illness. However, in some studies no relationship between CT findings and family history was found.

Retrospective studies reveal a higher incidence of birth complications in schizophrenics with CT findings.

It is difficult to be conclusive about the relationship between CT results and family history for two methodological reasons. (1) It is often difficult to establish a diagnosis in relatives retrospectively. (2) Many of the relatives in psychiatric comparison groups have not passed through the age of risk, which leads to an underassessment of incidence.

There is a statistical relationship between the incidence of cerebral atrophy and the likelihood of birth complications. It has been claimed recently that the type of atrophy is reflected by a widening of the ventricles and not the sulci (Cannon *et al.*, 1989). This is interpreted as consistent with developmental changes in the second trimester (see *postmortem* studies). Note that this does not imply that birth complications cause schizophrenia but that the vulnerability may increase. Thus it may be just one of several factors increasing the risk of developing schizophrenia. (It should be kept in mind that there are many schizophrenics with no history of obvious perinatal complications and many without obvious cerebral atrophy.)

## B. Magnetic Resonance Imaging (MRI)

Preliminary data from this relatively new technique confirm some but not other data deriving from alternative methods.

## C. Patterns of Cerebral Blood Flow and Cerebral Energy Consumption

The distribution of blood flow and energy consumption (e.g., PET studies) frequently differs from normal, but relative rather than absolute differences are usual. Most authors observe a relative decrease of frontal blood flow in schizophrenics at rest or, in one laboratory, when they perform a conceptual task (Wisconsin card-sorting). The reports refer to chronic and acute patients.

In some cases, metabolic changes are more accurately portrayed as relative increases in posterior regions. In contrast, one team finds a relatively increased frontal glucose metabolism in acute untreated schizophrenics (Cleghorn *et al.*, 1989).

It is not clear if a relative lower frontal or higher posterior activity is the pathognomonic finding. (Caveat: decreased blood flow and increased metabolism may be associated with difficulties in information processing.)

There are two main sorts of associations with reduced frontal activity: One is clinical, the other is cognitive. Patients with reduced frontal flow are more often withdrawn and chronic. One study of the putative cognitive impact of reduced frontal activity showed that prefrontal blood flow was reduced in chronic schizophrenics performing a sorting task. (There were no differences for other cognitive tasks or electrodermal measures.) These results on prefrontal function support those reported in Chapter 2. A putative subgroup with frontal deficits was also mentioned in the hypothesis of Frith and Done (1988; cf. Chapter 7). It may also be the case that the frontal regions are not specifically involved. There are many tasks on which schizophrenics show signs of inadequate cortical activation (whatever region is involved; cf. Chapters 5 and 6). Even on simple tasks such as squeezing a handle there is less contralateral cortical activity than in healthy and depressive controls. The only alternative explanation is that there are particular task–subgroup interactions which are still not sufficiently understood.

## D. Postmortem Studies

### 1. Global Changes (Whole Brain)

Reports of larger ventricles are confirmed.

We would not expect that all schizophrenics can be characterized by signs of cerebral atrophy.

### 2. Regional Changes

Most current evidence points toward alterations in the temporal lobes (e.g., hippocampus, sometimes also amygdala). Some studies report changes in the frontal lobe, but relatively few systematic studies have been carried out on this region. Less consistent are findings relating to other regions.

If we assume that methodological artifacts can be excluded, then two possibilities emerge: schizophrenics or subgroups have a "temporal limbic" disease or the frontal axis is involved. Some evidence for the first explanation comes from epileptic patients with temporal lobe foci who have symptoms reminiscent of schizophrenia. Support for the second idea comes from the cognitive and emotional symptoms of schizophrenia. We cannot decide the answers to these questions on the basis of *postmortem* data alone, for we have little information about how representative the results really are (e.g., bias toward chronic long-term patients dying in state hospitals). The question arises whether the patient with a good prognosis shows the same pattern.

# References

Adey, W. R. (1988). Cell membranes: The electromagnetic environment and cancer promotion. *Neurochemical Research*, *13*, 671–677.

Altshuler, L. L., Conrad, A., Kovelman, J. A., and Scheibel, A. (1987). Hippocampal pyramidal cell orientation in schizophrenia: A controlled neurohistologic study of the Yakovlev collection. *Archives of General Psychiatry*, *44*, 1094–1098.

Alzheimer, A. (1897). Beiträge zur pathologischen Anatomie der Hirnrinde und zur anatomischen Grundlage einiger Psychosen. *Monatsschrift für Psychiatrie und Neurologie*, *2*, 82–120.

Andreasen, N. C. (1986). Cerebral localization: Its relevance to psychiatry. In N. C. Andreasen (Eds.), *Progress in psychiatry*, pp. 1–16. Washington, D.C.: American Psychiatric Press.

Andreasen, N. C., Nasrallah, H. A., Dunn, V., Olson, S. A., Grove, W. M., Erhardt, J. C., Coffman, J. A., and Crossett, J. H. W. (1986). Structural abnormalities in the frontal system in schizophrenia: A magnetic resonance imaging study. *Archives of General Psychiatry*, *43*, 136–144.

Andreasen, N. C., Olsen, S. A., Dennert, J. W., and Smith, M. R. (1982a). Ventricular enlargement in schizophrenia: relationship to positive and negative symptoms. *American Journal of Psychiatry*, *139*, 297–302.

Andreasen, N. C., Smith, M. R., Jacoby, C. G., Dennert, J. W., and Olsen, A. (1982b). Ventricular enlargement in schizophrenia: definition and prevalence. *American Journal of Psychiatry*, *139*, 292–296.

Ariel, R. N., Golden, C. J., Berg, R. A., Quaife, M. A., Dirksen, J. W., Forsell, T., Wilson, J., and Graber, B. (1983). Regional cerebral blood flow in schizophrenics: tests using the xenon XE 133 inhalation method. *Archives of General Psychiatry*, *40*, 258–263.

Asano, N. 91967). Pneumoencephalographic study of schizophrenia. In H. Mitsade (Ed) Clinical/Genetics in psychiatry *Problems in Nosological Classification*, Tokyo: Igaku Shoin.

Bartels, M., and Themelis, J. (1983). Computerized tomography in tardive dyskinesia: Evidence of structural abnormalities in the basal ganglia system. *Archiv für Psychiatrie und Nervenkrankheiten*, *233*, 371–379.

Baxter, L. R., Phelps, M. E., Mazziotta, J. C., Schwartz, J. M., Gerner, R. H., Selin, C. E., Sumida, R. M. (1985). Cerebral metabolic rates for glucose in mood disorders: Studies with positron emission tomography and fluorodeoxyglucose F18. *Archives of General Psychiatry*, *42*, 441–447.

Benes, F. M., and Bird, E. D. (1987). An analysis of the arrangement of neurons in the cingulate cortex of schizophrenic patients. *Archives of General Psychiatry*, *44*, 608–616.

Benes, F. M., Davidson, J., and Bird, E. D. (1986). Quantitative cytoarchitectural studies of the cerebral cortex of schizophrenics. *Archives of General Psychiatry*, *43*, 31–35.

Berman, K. K., Zec, R. F., and Weinberger, D. R. (1986). Physiologic dysfunction of dorsolateral prefrontal cortex in schizophrenia. II. Role of neuroleptic treatment, attention and mental effort. *Archives of General Psychiatry*, *43*, 126–135.

Besson, J. A. O., Corrigan, F. M., Cherryman, G. R., and Smith, F. W. (1987). Nuclear magnetic resonance brain imaging in chronic schizophrenia. *British Journal of Psychiatry*, *150*, 161–163.

Bilder, R. M., Degreef, G., Pandurangi, A. K., Rieder, R. O., Sackheim, H. A., and Mukherjee, S. (1988). Neuropsychological deterioration and CT scan findings in chronic schizophrenia. *Schizophrenia Research*, *1*, 37–45.

Bogerts, B., Meertz, E., and Schonfeldt-Bausch, R. (1985). Basal ganglia and limbic system pathology in schizophrenia: A morphometric study of brain volume and shrinkage. *Archives of General Psychiatry*, *42*, 784–791.

Boronow, J., Pickar, D., Ninan, P. T., Roy, A., Hommer, D., Linnoila, M., and Paul, S. M.

(1985). Atrophy limited to the third ventricle in chronic schizophrenic patients: Report of a controlled series. *Archives of General Psychiatry*, *42*, 266–271.

Brown, R., Colter, N., Corsellis, N., Crow, T. J., Frith, C. D., Jagoe, R., Johnstone, E. C., and Marsh, L. (1986). Post-mortem evidence of structural brain changes in schizophrenia. *Archives of General Psychiatry*, *43*, 36–42.

Buchsbaum, M. S., DeLisi, L. E., Holcomb, H. H., Cappelletti, J., King, A. C., Johnson, J., Hazlett, E., Dowling-Zimmerman, S., Post, R. M., Morihisa, J., Carpenter, W., Cohen, R., Pickar, D., Weinberger, D. R., Margolin, R., and Kessler, R. (1984). Anteroposterior gradients in cerebral glucose use in schizophrenia and affective disorder. *Archives of General Psychiatry*, *41*, 1159–1166.

Buchsbaum, M. S., Ingvar, D. H., Kessler, R., Waters, R. N., Cappelletti, J., Van Kammen, D. P., King, A. C., Johnson, J. L., Manning, R. G., Flynn, R. W., Mann, L. S., Bunney, W. E., and Sokoloff, L. (1982). Cerebral glucography with positron emission tomography: Use in normal subjects and in patients with schizophrenia. *Archives of General Psychiatry*, *39*, 251–259.

Buchsbaum, M. S., Wu, J. C., DeLisi, L. E., Holcomb, H. H., Hazlett, E., Cooper-Langston, K., and Kessler, R. (1987). Positron emission tomography studies of basal ganglia and somatosensory cortex neuroleptic drug effects: Differences between normal controls and schizophrenic patients. *Biological Psychiatry*, *22*, 479–494.

Buscaino, V. M. (1920). Le cause anatoma-patologiche della manifestazione schizophrenica della demenza precoce. *Ricerce Patologica Nervosa Mentale*, *25*, 197–226.

Cannon, T. D., Fuhrmann, M., Mednick, S. A., Machon, R. A., Parnas, J., and Schulsinger, F. (1988). Third ventricle enlargement and reduced electrodermal responsiveness. *Psychophysiology*, *25*, 153–156.

Cannon, T. D., Mednick, S. A., and Parnas, J. (1989). Genetic and perinatal determinants of structural brain deficits in schizophrenia. *Archives of General Psychiatry*, *46*, 883–889.

Chabrol, H., Guell, A., Bes, A., and Moron, P. (1985). Cerebral blood flow in schizophrenic adolescents. *American Journal of Psychiatry*, *143*, 130.

Classen, W., and Fritze, J. (1988). Ventricular size, cognitive and psychomotor performance, and laterality in schizophrenia. *Neuropsychobiology*, *20*, 87–90.

Cleghorn, J. M., Garnett, E. S., Nahmias, C., Firnau, G., Brown, G. M., Kaplan, R., Szechtman, H., and Szechtman, B. (1989). Increased frontal and reduced parietal glucose metabolism in acute untreated schizophrenia. *Psychiatry Research*, *28*, 119–133.

Cohen, R. M., Semple, W. E., Gross, M., Nordahl, T. E., DeLisi, L. E., Holcomb, H. H., King, A. C., Morihisa, J. N., and Pickar, D. (1987). Dysfunction in a prefrontal substrate of sustained attention in schizophrenia. *Life Sciences*, *40*, 2031–2039.

Conrad, A. J., and Scheibel, A. B. (1987). Schizophrenia and the hippocampus: The embryological hypothesis extended. *Schizophrenia Bulletin*, *13*, 577–587.

Dandy, W. E. (1919). Roentgenography of the brain after injection of air into the spinal cord. *Annals of Surgery*, *70*, 397–403.

Davison, K., and Bagley, C. (1969). Schizophrenia-like psychoses associated with organic disorders of the CNS. In R. N. Herrington (Ed.), *Current problem in neuropsychiatry*, pp. 113–184. British Journal of Psychiatry Special Publication No. 4.

Degreef, G., Mukherjee, S., Bilder, R., and Schnur, D. (1988). Season of birth and CT scan findings in schizophrenic patients. *Biological Psychiatry*, *24*, 461–464.

DeLisi, L. E., Goldin, L. R., Hanovit, J. R., Maxwell, E., Kurtz, D., and Gershon, E. S. (1986). A family study of the association of increased ventricular size with schizophrenia. *Archives of General Psychiatry*, *43*, 148–153.

DeLisi, L. E., Buchsbaum, M. S., Holcomb, H. H., Langston, K. C., King, A. C., Kessler, R., Pickar, D., Carpenter, W. T., Morihisa, J. M., Margolin, R., and Weinberger, D. R. (1989).

Increased temporal lobe glucose use in chronic schizophrenic patients. *Biological Psychiatry*, *25*, 835–851.

Dennert, J. W., and Andreasen, N. C. (1983). CT scanning and schizophrenia: A review. *Psychiatric Developments*, *1*, 105–121.

Dewan, M. J., Pandurangi, A. K., Lee, S. H., Ramachandran, T. R., Levy, B. F., Boucher, M., Yozawitz, A., and Major, L. (1983). Central brain morphology in chronic schizophrenic patients: A controlled CT study. *Biological Psychiatry*, *18*, 1133–1140.

Dide, M. M. (1934). Les syndrome hypothalamiques et la dyspsychogenese. *Revue Neurologique*, *6*, 941–943.

Dom, R., de Saedeler, J., Bogerts, B., and Hopf, A. (1981). Quantitative cytometric analysis of basal ganglia in catatonic schizophrenics. In C. Perris, G. Struwe, and B. Jansson (Eds.), *Biological Psychiatry*, pp. 723–726. Amsterdam: Elsevier.

Donnelly, E. F., Weinberger, D. R., Waldman, I. N., and Wyatt, R. J. (1980). Cognitive impairment associated with morphological brain abnormalities on computed tomography in chronic schizophrenic patients. *Journal of Nervous and Mental Disease*, *168*, 305–308.

Doran, A. R., Boronow, J., Weinberger, D. R., Wolkowitz, O. M., Breier, A., and Pickar, D. (1987). Structural brain pathology in schizophrenia revisited: Prefrontal cortex pathology is inversely correlated with cerebrospinal fluid levels of homovanillic acid. *Neuropsychopharmacology*, *1*, 25–32.

Douse, M., Mamo, H., Ponsin, J. C., and Dinh, Y. T. (1988). Cerebral blood flow in schizophrenia. *Experimental Neurology*, *100*, 98–111.

Early, T. S., Reiman, E. M., Raichle, M. E., and Spitznagel, E. L. (1986). Left globus pallidus abnormality in never-medicated patients with schizophrenia. *Proceedings of the National Academy of Sciences, U.S.A.*, *84*, 561–562.

Falkai, P., and Bogerts, B. (1986). Cell loss in the hippocampus of schizophrenics. *European Archives of Psychiatry and Neurological Science*, *236*, 154–161.

Falkai, P., Bogerts, B., and Rozumek, M. (1988). Limbic pathology in schizophrenia: The entorhinal region—a morphometric study. *Biological Psychiatry*, *24*, 515–521.

Famuyiwa, O., Eccleston, D., Donaldson, A. A., and Garside, R. F. (1979). Tardive dyskinesia and dementia. *British Journal of Psychiatry*, *135*, 500–504.

Farkas, T., Wolf, A. P., Jaeger, J., Brodie, J. D., Christman, D. R., and Fowler, J. S. (1984). Regional brain glucose metabolism in chronic schizophrenia: A positron emission transaxial tomographic study. *Archives of General Psychiatry*, *41*, 293–300.

Farmer, A., Jackson, R., McGuffin, P., and Storey, P. (1987). Cerebral ventricular enlargement in chronic schizophrenia: Consistencies and contradictions. *British Journal of Psychiatry*, *150*, 324–330.

Folstein, M. F., and McHugh, P. (1975). Mini-mental state. *Journal of Psychiatric Research*, *1*, 21–89.

Frangos, E., and Athanassenas, G. (1982). Differences in lateral brain ventricular size among various types of chronic schizophrenics: Evidence based on a CT study. *Acta Psychiatrica Scandinavica*, *66*, 459–463.

Franzen, G., and Ingvar, D. H. (1975a). Absence of activation in frontal structures during psychological testing of chronic schizophrenics. *Journal of Neurology, Neurosurgery and Psychiatry*, *38*, 1027–1032.

Franzen, G., and Ingvar, D. H. (1975a). Abnormal distribution of cerebral activity in chronic schizophrenia. *Journal of Psychiatric Research*, *12*, 199–214.

Frith, C. D., and Done, D. J. (1988). Towards a neuropsychology of schizophrenia. *British Journal of Psychiatry*, *153*, 437–443.

Gattaz, W. F., Rost, W., Kohlmeyer, K., Hubner, C., and Gasser, T. (1988). CT scans and neuroleptic response in schizophrenia: A multidimensional approach. *Psychiatry Research*, *26*, 293–303.

Geraud, G., Arne-Bes, M. C., Guell, A., and Bes, A. (1987). Reversibility of hemodynamic hypofrontality in schizophrenia. *Journal of Cerebral Blood Flow and Metabolism, 7*, 9–12.

Gluck, E., Radu, E. W., Mundt, C., and Gerhardt, P. (1980). A computed tomographic trohoc study of chronic schizophrenia. *Neuroradiology, 20*, 167–171.

Goetz, K. L., and Van Kammen, D. P. (1986). Computerized axial tomography scans and subtypes of schizophrenia. *Journal of Nervous and Mental Disease, 174*, 31–41.

Golden, C. J., Hammeke, T. A., and Purisch, A. D. (1978). Diagnostic validity of a neuropsychological battery derived from Luria neuropsychological tests. *Journal of Consulting and Clinical Psychology, 46*, 1258–1265.

Golden, C. J., Moses, J. A., Zelazowski, R., Graber, B., Zatz, L. M., Horvath, T. B., and Berger, P. A. (1980). Cerebral ventricular size and neuropsychological impairment in young chronic schizophrenics: Measurement by the standardized Luria-Nebraska neuropsychological battery. *Archives of General Psychiatry, 37*, 619–623.

Gross, H., and Kaltenbeck, E. (1970). Zur Neuropathologie der persistierenden choreiformen Hyperkinesen unter neuroleptischer Langzeittherapie. *Psihofarmakologija (Zagreb), 2*, 195–204.

Gross, G., Huber, G., and Schüttler, R. (1982). Computerised tomography studies on schizophrenic diseases. *Archiv für Psychiatrie und Nervenkdrankheiten, 231*, 519–526.

Gruzelier, J., Seymour, K., Wilson, L., Jolley, A., and Hirsch, S. (1988). Impairments on neuropsychologic tests of temporohippocampal frontohippocampal functions and word fluency in remitting schizophrenia and affective disorders. *Archives of General Psychiatry, 45*, 623–629.

Guenther, W., Moser, E., Mueller-Spahn, F., Von Oefele, K., Buell, U., and Hippius, H. (1986). Pathological cerebral blood flow during motor function in schizophrenic and endogenous depressed patients. *Biological Psychiatry, 21*, 889–899.

Gur, R. C., Gur, R. E., Obrist, W. D., Skolnick, B. E., and Reivich, M. (1987). The effects of age on regional cerebral blood flow at rest and during cognitive activity. *Archives of General Psychiatry, 44*, 617–621.

Gustafson, L., Risberg, J., and Silfverskiold, P. (1981). Regional cerebral blood flow in organic dementia and affective disorders. *Advances in Biological Psychiatry, 6*, 109–116.

Haier, R. J., Siegel, B., Nuechterlein, K. H., Hazlett, E., Wu, J. C., Pack, J., Browning, H. L., and Buchsbaum, M. S. (1988). Cortical glucose metabolic rate correlates of abstract reasoning and attention studied with positron emission tomography. *Intelligence, 12*, 199–217.

Haug, J. O. (1962). Pneumoencephalographic studies in mental disease. *Acta Psychiatrica Scandinavica, 16 Suppl.* 51–104.

Heinrichs, D. W., and Buchanan, R. W. (1988). Significance and meaning of neurological signs in schizophrenia. *American Journal of Psychiatry, 145*, 11–18.

Hopf, A. (1954). Orientierende Untersuchungen zur Frage pathoanatomischer Veränderungen im Pallidum und Striatum bei Schizophrenie. *Journal für Hirnforschung, 1*, 97–145.

Hounsfield, G. N. (1973). Computerized transverse axial scanning (tomography). Part 1. Description of system. *British Journal of Radiology, 46*, 1016–1022.

Houston, J. P., Maas, J. W., Bowden, C. L., Contreras, S. A., McIntyre, K. L., and Javors, M. A. (1986). Cerebrospinal fluid HVA, central brain atrophy and clinical state in schizophrenia. *Psychiatry Research, 19*, 207–214.

Hoyer, S., and Oesterreich, K. (1975). Blood flow and oxidative metabolism of the brain in patients with schizophrenia. *Psychiatric Clinics of North America, 8*, 304–313.

Hoyer, S., and Oesterreich, K. (1977). Blood flow and metabolism of the brain in the course of acute schizophrenia. *Acta Neurologica Scandinavica, 56, Suppl. 64*, 534–535.

Huber, G., Gross, G., and Schütter, R. (1979). *Schizophrenie: Eine verlaufs- und sozialpsychiatrische Langzeitstudie.* Berlin: Springer.

Huber, G., Gross, G., and Schuettler, R. (1980). Longitudinal studies of schizophrenic patients. *Schizophrenia Bulletin, 6*, 592–605.

Hughlings-Jackson, J. (1931). In J. Taylor (Ed.), *Selected writings*. London: Hodder & Stoughton.

Ingvar, D. H. (1980). Abnormal distribution of cerebral activity in chronic schizophrenia: A neurophysiological interpretation. In C. Baxter and T. Melneckuk (Eds.). *Perspectives in Schizophrenic Research*, 107–125.

Ingvar, D. H., and Franzen, G. (1974a). Abnormalities in cerebral blood flow distribution in patients with chronic schizophrenia. *Acta Psychiatrica Scandinavica, 50*, 425–462.

Ingvar, D. H., and Franzen, G. (1974b). Distribution of cerebral activity in chronic schizophrenia. *Lancet II*, 1484–1486.

Jakob, H., and Beckmann, H. (1986). Prenatal developmental disturbances in the limbic allocortex in schizophrenics. *Journal of Neural Transmission, 65*, 303–326.

Jacobi, W., and Winkler, H. (1927). Encephalographische Studien an chronisch Schizophrenen. *Archiv für Psychiatrie und Nervenkrankheiten, 81*, 299–332.

Jacoby, R. J., and Levy, R. (1980a). Computed tomography in the elderly. 1. Affective disorder. *British Journal of Psychiatry, 136*, 270–275.

Jacoby, R. J., and Levy, R. (1980b). Computed tomography in the elderly. 2. Senile dementia: Diagnosis and functional impairment. *British Journal of Psychiatry, 136*, 256–269.

Jellinger, K. (1977). Neuropathologic findings after neuroleptic long-term therapy. In L. Roizin, H. Shiraki, and N. Grecevic (Eds.). *Neurotoxicology*, 25–42. New York: Raven Press.

Jellinger, K. (1985). Neuromorphological background of pathochemical studies in major psychoses. In H. Beckman and P. Riederer (Eds.), *Pathochemical markers in major psychoses*, pp. 1–23. Heidelberg: Springer.

Jernigan, T. L., Zatz, L. M., Moses, J. A., and Berger, P. A. (1982a). Computed tomography in schizophrenics and normal volunteers. I. Fluid volume. *Archives of General Psychiatry, 39*, 765–770.

Jernigan, T. L., Zatz, L. M., Moses, J. A., and Cardellino, J. P. (1982b). Computed tomography in schizophrenics and normal volunteers. II. Cranial asymmetry. *Archives of General Psychiatry, 39*, 771–773.

Jeste, D. V., Zalcman, S., Weinberger, D. R., Cutler, N. R., Bigelow, L. B., Kleinman, J. E., Rogol, A., and Wyatt, R. J. (1983). Apomorphine response and subtyping of schizophrenia. *Progress in Neuropsychopharmacology and Biological Psychiatry, 7*, 83–88.

Johnstone, E. C., Crow, T. J., Frith, C. D., Husband, J., and Kreel, L. (1976). Cerebroventricular size and cognitive impairment in chronic schizophrenia. *Lancet*, II 924–926.

Johnstone, E. C., Crow, T. J., Frith, C. D., Stevens, M., Kreel, L., and Husband, J. (1978). The dementia of dementia praecox. *Acta Psychiatrica Scandinavica, 57*, 305–324.

Johnstone, E. C., Crow, T. J., Macmillan, J. F., Owens, D. G., Bydder, G. M., and Steiner, R. E. (1986). A magnetic resonance study of early schizophrenia. *Journal of Neurology, Neurosurgery and Psychiatry, 49*, 136–139.

Johnstone, E. C., Owens, D. G. C., Crow, T. J., and Jagoe, R. (1981). A CT study of 188 patients with schizophrenia, affective psychosis and neurotic illness. In C. Perris, G. Struwe, and B. Jansson (Eds.), *Biological Psychiatry*. Amsterdam: Elsevier.

Johnstone, E. C., Owens, D. G. C., Crow, T. J., Frith, C. D., Alexandropolis, K., Bydder, G., and Colter, N. (1989). Temporal lobe structure as determined by nuclear magnetic resonance in schizophrenia and bipolar affective disorder. *Journal of Neurology, Neurosurgery and Psychiatry, 52*, 736–741.

Josephy, H. (1923). Beitraege zur Histopathologie der Dementia praecox. *Zeitschrift für Neurologie, 86*, 391–408.

Kameyama, M., Yamanouchi, H., and Suda, E. (1975). Oral dyskinesia in the aged (in Japanese). *Acta Gerontologica Japonica, 59*, 5–15.

Keilp, J. G., Sweeney, J. A., Jacobsen, P., Solomon, C., Louis, L., Deck, M., Frances, A., and Mann, J. J. (1988). Cognitive impairment in schizophrenia: Specific relations to ventricular size and negative symptomatology. *Biological Psychiatry, 24,* 47–55.

Kelsoe, J. R., Cadet, J. L., Pickar, D., and Weinberger, D. R. (1988). Quantitative neuroanatomy in schizophrenia: A controlled magnetic resonance imaging study. *Archives of General Psychiatry, 45,* 533–541.

Kemali, D., Maj, M., Galderisi, S., Salvati, A., Starace, F., Valente, A., and Pirozzi, R. (1986). Clinical, biological and neuropsychological features associated with lateral ventricular enlargement in DSM-III schizophrenic disorder. *Psychiatry Research, 21,* 137–149.

Kety, S. S. (1951). The theory and application of the exchange of inert gas at the lungs and tissues. *Pharmacology Reviews, 3,* 1–41.

Kety, S. S., and Schmidt, C. F. (1948). The nitrous oxide method for the quantitative determination of cerebral blood flow in man: Theory, procedure and normal values. *Journal of Clinical Investigation, 27,* 476–483.

Kinney, D. K., and Jacobsen, B. (1978). Environmental factors in schizophrenia: New adoption study evidence. In L. C. Wynne, R. L. Cromwell, and S. Mattysse (Eds.), *The nature of schizophrenia: New approaches to research and treatment,* pp. 38–51. New York: Wiley.

Kishimoto, H., Kuwaharra, H., Ohno, S., Takazu, O., Hama, Y., Sato, C., Ishii, T., Nomura, Y., Fujita, H., Miyauchi, T., Matushita, M., Yokoi, S., and Iio, M. (1987). Three subtypes of chronic schizophrenia identified using (11C)-glucose positron emission tomography. *Psychiatry Research, 21,* 285–292.

Kleinman, J. E., Karson, C. N., Weinberger, D. R., Freed, W. J., Berman, K. F., and Wyatt, R. J. (1984). Eye blinking and cerebral ventricular size in chronic schizophrenic patients. *American Journal of Psychiatry, 141,* 1430–1432.

Kolakowska, T., Williams, A. W., Jambor, K., and Ardern, M. (1985). Schizophrenia with good and poor outcome. III. Neurological 'soft' signs, cognitive impairment and their clinical significances. *British Journal of Psychiatry, 146,* 348–357.

Kovelman, J. A., and Scheibel, A. B. (1984). A neurohistological correlate of schizophrenia. *Biological Psychiatry, 19,* 1601–1621.

Krieg, J. C., Pirke, J. M., Lauer, C., and Backmund, H. (1988). Endocrine, metabolic and cranial computed tomographic findings in anorexia nervosa. *Biological Psychiatry, 23,* 377–387.

Kuhl, D. E., Metter, J. E., and Riege, W. H. (1985). Patterns of cerebral glucose utilization in depression, multiple infarct dementia and Alzheimers disease. In L. Sokoloff (Eds.), *Brain imaging and brain function,* pp. 211–226. New York: Raven Press.

Kurachi, M., Kobayashi, K., Matsubara, R., Hiramatsu, H., Yamaguchi, N., Matsuda, H., Maeda, T., and Hisada, K. (1985). Regional cerebral blood flow in schizophrenic disorders. *European Neurology, 24,* 176–181.

Largen, J. W., Smith, R. C., Calderon, N., Baumgartner, R., Lu, R. B., Schoolar, J. C., and Ravichandran, G. K. (1984). Abnormalities of brain structure and density in schizophrenia. *Biological Psychiatry, 19,* 991–1011.

LeMay, M. (1984). Radiologic changes of the aging brain and skull. *American Journal of Neuroradiology, 5,* 269–275.

Lempke, R. (1935). Untersuchungen über die soziale Prognose der Schizophrenie unter besonderer Berücksichtigung des encephalographischen Befundes. *Archiv für Psychiatrie und Nervenkrankheiten, 104,* 89–136.

Lesch, A., and Bogerts, B. (1984). The diencephalon in schizophrenia: Evidence for reduced thickness of the periventricular grey matter. *European Archives of Psychiatry and Neurological Sciences, 234,* 212–219.

Lewis, S. W., Reveley, A. M., Reveley, M. A., Chitkara, B., and Murray, R. M. (1987). The familial-sporadic distinction as a strategy in schizophrenia research. *British Journal of Psychiatry, 151,* 306–313.

Lohr, J. B., and Jeste, D. V. (1986). Cerebellar pathology in schizophrenia? A neuronometric study. *Biological Psychiatry, 21,* 865–875.

Losonczy, M. F., Song, P. S., Mohs, R. C., Mathe, A. A., Davidson, M., Davis, B. M., and Davis, K. L. (1986). Correlates of lateral ventricular size in chronic schizophrenia. II. Biological measures. *Archives of General Psychiatry, 43,* 1113–1118.

Luchins, D. J., Lewine, R. R. J., and Meltzer, H. Y. (1984). Lateral ventricular size, psychopathology an medication response in the psychoses. *Biological Psychiatry, 19,* 29–44.

Luchins, D. J., and Meltzer, H. Y. (1986). A comparison of CT findings in acute and chronic ward schizophrenics. *Psychiatry Research, 17,* 7–14.

Macdonald, H. L., and Best, J. J. K. (1989). The Scottish first episode schizophrenia study. VI. Computerized tomography brain scans in patients and controls. *British Journal of Psychiatry, 154,* 492–498.

Mander, A. J., Whitfield, A., Kean, D. M., Smith, M. A., Douglas, R. H. B., and Kendell, R. E. (1987). Cerebral and brainstem changes after ECT revealed by nuclear magnetic resonance imaging. *British Journal of Psychiatry, 151,* 69–71.

Marks, R. C., and Luchins, D. J. (1990). Relationship between brain imaging findings in schizophrenia and psychopathology. In N. C. Andreasen (Ed.), *Positive and negative symptoms and syndromes,* pp. 89–123. Basel: Karger.

Maser, J. D., and Keith, S. J. (1983). CT scans and schizophrenia report on a workshop. *Schizophrenia Bulletin, 9,* 265–283.

Mathew, R. J., Duncan, G. C., Weinman, M. L., and Barr, D. L. (1982). Regional cerebral blood flow in schizophrenia. *Archives of General Psychiatry, 39,* 1121–1124.

Mathew, R. J., and Partain, C. J. (1985). Midsagittal sections of the cerebellar vermis obtained with magnetic resonance imaging of schizophrenic patients. *American Journal of Psychiatry, 142,* 970–971.

Mathew, R. J., Partain, C. J., Prakash, R., Kulkarni, M. V., Logan, T. P., and Wilson, W. H. (1985). A study of the septum pellucidum and corpus callosum in schizophrenia with MR imaging. *Acta Psychiatrica Scandinavica, 72,* 414–421.

Mathew, R. J., Wilson, W. H., Tant, S. R., Robinson, L., and Prakash, R. (1988). Abnormal resting regional cerebral blood flow patterns and their correlates in schizophrenia. *Archives of General Psychiatry, 45,* 542–549.

McCarley, R. W., Faux, S. F., Shenton, M. W., LeMay, M., Cane, M., Ballinger, R., and Duffy, F. H. (1989). CT abnormalities in schizophrenia: A preliminary study of their correlations with P300/200 electrophysiological features and positive/negative symptoms. *Archives of General Psychiatry, 46,* 698–708.

Morgan, L. O., and Gregory, H. S. (1935). Pathological changes in the tuber cinereum in a group of psychoses. *Journal of Nervous and Mental Disease, 82,* 286–298.

Morihisa, J. M., and McAnulty, G. B. (1985). Structure and tomography in schizophrenia. *Biological Psychiatry, 20,* 3–19.

Mundt, C. H., Radie, W., and Gluck, E. (1980). Computertomographische Untersuchungen der Liquorräume an chronisch shizophrenen Patienten. *Der Nervenarzt, 51,* 743–748.

Nagasaka, G. (1925). Zur Pathologie der extrapyramidalen Zentren bei Schizophrenie. *Arbeiten der Neurologischen Institut, Wien, 27,* 363–396.

Nasrallah, H. A., Jacoby, C. C., McCalley-Whitters, M., and Kuperman, S. (1987a). Cerebral ventricular enlargement in subtypes of chronic schizophrenia. *Archives of General Psychiatry, 39,* 774–777.

Nasrallah, H. A., Kuperman, S., Jacoby, C. G., McCalley-Whitters, M., and Hamra, B. (1983). Clinical correlates of sulcal widening in chronic schizophrenia. *Psychiatry Research, 10,* 237–242.

Nasrallah, H. A., McCalley-Whitters, M., and Jacoby, C. G. (1983b). Cerebral ventricular enlargement in young manic males. A controlled CT study. *Journal of Affective Disorders*, *4*, 15–19.

Nasrallah, H. A., Olson, S. C., McCalley-Whitters, M., Chapman, S., and Jacoby, C. G. (1986). Cerebral ventricular enlargement in schizophrenia: A preliminary follow-up study. *Archives of General Psychiatry*, *43*, 157–159.

Nieto, D., and Escobar, A. (1972). Major psychoses. In J. Minckler (Ed.), *Pathology of the nervous system*, pp. 2654–2665. New York: McGraw-Hill.

Nyback, H., Berggren, B. M., Nyman, H., Sedvall, G., and Wiesel, F. A. (1984). Cerebro-ventricular volume, cerebrospinal fluid monoamine metabolites and intellectual performance in schizophrenic patients. *Catecholamines: Neuropharmacology and Central Nervous System*, New York: Alan Liss.

Nyback, H., Wiesel, F. A., Berggren, B. M., and Hindmarsh, T. (1982). Computed tomography of the brain in patients with acute psychosis and in healthy volunteers. *Acta Psychiatrica Scandinavica*, *65*, 403–414.

Nyman, H., Nyback, H., Wiesel, F. A., Oxenstierna, G., and Schalling, D. (1986). Neuropsy-chological test performance, brain morphological measures and CSF monoamine metabolites in schizophrenic patients. *Acta Psychiatrica Scandinavica*, *74*, 292–301.

Olesen, J. (1974). Cerebral blood flow methods for measurement, regulation, effects of drugs and changes in disease. *Acta Neurologica Scandinavica*, *50*, *Suppl. 57*, 19–30.

Ota, T., Maeshiro, H., Ishido, H., Shimizu, Y., Uchida, R., Toyoshima, R., Ohshima, A., Takazawa, A., Motomura, H., and Noguchi, T. (1987). Treatment resistant chronic psycho-pathology and CT scans in schizophrenia. *Acta Psychiatrica Scandinavica*, *75*, 415–427.

Owen, M. J., Lewis, S. W., and Murray, R. M. (1988). Obstetric complications and schizo-phrenia: A computed tomographic study. *Psychological Medicine*, *18*, 331–339.

Owen, M. J., Lewis, S. W., and Murray, R. M. (1989). Family history and cerebral ventricular enlargement in schizophrenia: A case control study. *The British Journal of Psychiatry*, *154*, 629–634.

Owens, D. G. C., Johnstone, E. C., Crow, T. J., Frith, C. D., Jagoe, J. R., and Kreel, L. (1985). Lateral ventricular size in schizophrenia relationship to the disease process and its clinical manifestations. *Psychological Medicine*, *15*, 27–41.

Oxenstierna, G., Bergstrand, G., Bjerkenstedt, L., Sedvall, G., and Wik, G. (1984). Evidence of disturbed CSF circulation and brain atrophy in cases of schizophrenic psychosis. *The British Journal of Psychiatry*, *144*, 654–661.

Pakkenberg, B. (1987). Post-mortem study of chronic schizophrenic brains. *The British Journal of Psychiatry*, *151*, 744–752.

Pandurangi, A. K., Bilder, R. M., Rieder, R. O., Mukherjee, S., and Hamer, R. M. (1988). Schizophrenic symptoms and deterioration: Relation to computed tomographic findings. *Journal of Nervous and Mental Disease*, *176*, 200–206.

Pandurangi, A. K., Dewan, M. J., Boucher, M., Levy, B., Ramachandran, T., Bartell, K., Blick, P. A., and Major, L. (1986). A comprehensive study of chronic schizophrenic subjects. II. Biological, neuropsychological and clinical correlates of CT abnormality. *Acta Psychiatrica Scandinavica*, *73*, 161–171.

Pandurangi, A. K., Dewan, M. J., Lee, S. H., Ramachandran, T. R., Levy, B. F., Boucher, M., Yozawitz, A., and Major, L. (1984). The ventricular system in chronic schizophrenic patients: A controlled computed tomography study. *The British Journal of Psychiatry*, *144*, 172–176.

Pearlson, G. D., Garbacz, D. J., and Breakey, W. (1984). Lateral ventricular enlargement associated with persistent unemployment and negative symptoms in schizophrenia and bipolar disorder. *Psychiatry Research*, *12*, 1–9.

Pearlson, G. D., Garbacz, D. J., Moberg, P. J., Ahn, H. S., and DePaulo, J. R. (1985). Symptomatic, familial, perinatal and social correlates of computerised axial tomography (CAT) changes in schizophrenics and bipolars. *Journal of Nervous and Mental Disease*, *173*, 42–50.

Potkin, S. G., Weinberger, D. R., Linnoila, M., and Wyatt, R. J. (1983). Low CSF 5-

hydroxyindoleacetic acid in schizophrenic patients with enlarged cerebral ventricles. *American Journal of Psychiatry*, *140*, 21–25.

Rabins, P., Pearlson, G., Jayaram, G., Steele, C., and Tune, L. (1987). Increased ventricle-to-brain ratio in late-onset schizophrenia. *American Journal of Psychiatry*, *144*, 1216–1218.

Raz, S., Raz, N., Weinberger, D. R., Boronow, J., Pickar, D., Bigler, E. D., and Turkheimer, E. (1987). Morphological brain abnormalities in schizophrenia determined by computed tomography: A problem of measurement? *Psychiatry Research*, *22*, 91–98.

Reisner, T., Zeiler, K., and Strobl, G. (1980). Quantitative Erfassung der Seitenventikelbreite im CT—Vergleichswerte einer Normalpopulation. *Fortschritte der Neurologie und Psychiatrie*, *48*, 168–174.

Reveley, A. M., Reveley, M. A., Clifford, C. A., and Murray, R. M. (1982). Cerebral ventricular size in twins discordant for schizophrenia. *Lancet*, *II*, 540–541.

Reveley, A. M., Reveley, M. A., and Murray, R. M. (1984). Cerebral ventricular enlargement in non-genetic schizophrenia: A controlled study. *British Journal of Psychiatry*, *144*, 89–93.

Reveley, M. A. (1985). Ventricular enlargement in schizophrenia: The validity of computerised tomographic findings. *British Journal of Psychiatry*, *147*, 233–240.

Reveley, M. A., De Belleroche, J., Recordati, A., and Hirsch, S. R. (1987). Increased CSF amino acids and ventricular enlargement in schizophrenia: A preliminary study. *Biological Psychiatry*, *22*, 413–420.

Reyes, M. G., and Gordon, A. (1981). Cerebellar vermis in schizophrenia. *Lancet*, *II*, 700–701.

Rieder, R. O., Donnelly, E. F., Herdt, J. R., and Waldman, I. N. (1979). Sulcal prominence in young chronic schizophrenic patients: CT scan findings associated with impairment on neuropsychological tests. *Psychiatry Research*, *1*, 1–8.

Rieder, R. O., Weinberger, D. R., Van Kammen, D. P., and Post, R. M. (1983). Computed tomographic scans in patients with schizophrenia, schizo-affective and bipolar affective disorder. *Archives of General Psychiatry*, *40*, 735–739.

Roberts, G. W., Colter, N., Lofthouse, R., Johnstone, E. C., and Crow, T. J. (1987). Is there gliosis in schizophrenia? Investigation of the temporal lobe. *Biological Psychiatry*, *22*, 1459–1468.

Roberts, G. W. (1990). Schizophrenia: The cellular biology of a functional psychosis. *Trends of Neuroscience*, *13*, 207–211.

Roizin, L., True, C., and Knight, M. (1959). Structural effects of tranquilizers. *Research Publications of the Association for Research in Nervous and Mental Disease*, *17*, 285–324.

Roland, P. E. (1982). Cortical regulation of selective attention in man. A regional cerebral blood flow study. *Journal of Neurophysiology*, *48*, 1059–1078.

Romani, A., Merello, S., Gozzoli, L., Grassi, M., and Cosi, V. (1987). P300 and CT scan in patients with chronic schizophrenia. *The British Journal of Psychiatry*, *151*, 506–513.

Rossi, A., Stratta, P., Galucci, M., Amicarelli, I., Passariello, R., and Casacchia, M. (1988). Standardized magnetic resonance image intensity study in schizophrenia. *Psychiatry Research*, *25*, 223–231.

Sacchetti, E., Vita, A., Ciussani, S., Alciati, A., Conte, G., Pennati, A., Invernizzi, G., and Cazullo, C. L. (1985). Season of birth and cerebral ventricular enlargement in schizophrenia. 14th Collegum Internationale Neuro-Psychopharmacologicum (CINP)—1985 abstracts.

Scheibel, A. B., and Kovelman, J. A. (1981). Disorientation of the hippocampal pyramidal cell and its processes in the schizophrenic patient. *Biological Psychiatry*, *16*, 101–102.

Schulz, S. C., Koller, M. M., Kishore, P. R., Hamer, R. M., Gehl, J. J., and Friedel, R. O. (1983a). Ventricular enlargement in teenage patients with schizophrenia spectrum disorder. *American Journal of Psychiatry*, *140*, 1592–1595.

Schulz, S. C., Sinicrope, P., Kishore, P. R., and Friedel, R. O. (1983b). Treatment response and ventricular brain enlargement in young schizophrenic patients. *Psychopharmacology Bulletin*, *19*, 510–512.

Seidman, L. J., Sokolove, R. L., McElroy, C., Knapp, P. H., and Sabin, T. (1987). Lateral ventricular size and social network differentiation in young, nonchronic schizophrenic patients. *American Journal of Psychiatry*, *144*, 512–514.

Shur, E. (1982). Season of birth in high and low genetic risk schizophrenics. *British Journal of Psychiatry*, *140*, 410–415.

Smith, R. C., Baumgartner, R., and Calderon, M. (1987a). Magnetic resonance imaging studies of the brains of schizophrenic patients. *Psychiatry Research*, *20*, 33–46.

Smith, R. C., Baumgartner, R., Calderon, M., Affas, A., Ravichandran, G. K., and Peters, I. D. (1985a). Magnetic resonance imaging studies of schizophrenia. *Psychopharmacology Bulletin*, *21*, 588–594.

Smith, R. C., Baumgartner, R., Ravichandran, G. K., Largen, J., Calderon, M., Burd, A., and Mauldin, M. (1987b). Cortical atrophy and white matter density in the brains of schizophrenics and clinical response to neuroleptics. *Acta Psychiatrica Scandinavica*, *75*, 11–19.

Smith, R. C., Baumgartner, R., Ravichandran, G. K., Mauldin, M., Burd, A., Vroulis, G., Gordon, J., and Calderon, M. (1985b). Lateral ventricular enlargement and clinical response in schizophrenia. *Psychiatry Research*, *14*, 241–253.

Smith, R. C., Calderon, M., Ravichandran, G. K., Largen, J., Vroulis, G., Shvartsburd, A., Gordon, J., and Schoolar, J. C. (1984). Nuclear magnetic resonance in schizophrenia: A preliminary study. *Psychiatry Research*, *12*, 137–147.

Sokoloff, L., Reivich, M., Kennedy, C., Des Rosiers, M. H., Patlak, C. S., Pettigrew, K. D., Saukurada, O., and Shinohara, M. (1977). The ($^{14}$C)-deoxyglucose method for the measurement of local cerebral glucose utilization theory, procedure and normal values in the conscious and anesthetized albino rat. *Journal of Neurochemistry*, *28*, 897–916.

Spiers, P. A. (1982). The Luria–Nebraska neuropsychological battery revisited: Theory, practice or just practising. *Journal of Consulting and Clinical Psychology*, *2*, 301–306.

Stahl, S. M., Jernigan, T., Pfefferbaum, A., and Zatz, L. (1988). Brain computerized tomography in sub-types of severe chronic schizophrenia. *Psychological Medicine*, *18*, 73–77.

Stevens, J. (1982). Neuropathology of schizophrenia. *Archives of General Psychiatry*, *39*, 1131–1139.

Storey, P. B. (1966). Lumbar air encephalography in chronic schizophrenia: A controlled experiment. *British Journal of Psychiatry*, *112*, 135–144.

Suddath, R. L., Casanova, M. F., Goldberg, T. E., Daniel, D. G., Kelsoe, J. R., and Weiberger, D. R. (1989). Temporal lobe pathology in schizophrenia: A quantitative magnetic resonance imaging study. *American Journal of Psychiatry*, *146*, 464–472.

Szechtman, H., Nahmias, C., Garnett, S., Firnau, G., Brown, G. M., Kaplan, R. D., and Cleghorn, J. M. (1988). Effect of neuroleptics on altered cerebral glucose metabolism in schizophrenia. *Archives of General Psychiatry*, *45*, 523–532.

Tanaka, Y., Hazama, H., Kawahara, R., and Kobayashi, K. (1981). Computerized tomography of the brain in schizophrenic patients: A controlled study. *Acta Psychiatrica Scandinavica*, *63*, 191–197.

Torrey, E. F., and Peterson, M. R. (1974). Schizophrenia and the limbic system. *Lancet*, *II*, 942–946.

Turner, S. W., Toone, B. K., and Brett-Jones, J. R. (1986). Computerised tomographic scan changes in early schizophrenia—Preliminary findings. *Psychological Medicine*, *16*, 219–225.

Uematsu, M., and Kaiya, H. (1988). The morphology of the corpus callosum in schiophrenia: An MRI study. *Schizophrenia Research*, *1*, 391–398.

Van Kammen, D. P., Mann, L. S., Sternberg, P. E., Scheinin, M., Ninan, P. T., Marder, S. R., Van Kammen, W. B., Rieder, R. O., and Linnoila, M. (1983). Dopamine-β-hydroxylase activity and homovanillic acid in spinal fluid of schizophrenics with brain atrophy. *Science*, *220*, 974.

Van Kammen, D. P., Mann, L. S., Sternberg, P. E., Scheinin, M., Ninan, P., Van Kammen,

W. B., and Linnoila, M. (1984). Cortical atrophy and enlarged ventricles associated with low levels of cerebrospinal fluid monoamine metabolites and dopamine beta-hydroxylase activity in schizophrenia. *Neurology and Neurobiology, 8C*, 167–172.

Van Kammen, D. P., Van Kammen, W. B., Mann, L. S., Seppala, T., and Linnoila, M. (1986). Dopamine metabolism in the cerebrospinal fluid of drug-free schizophrenic patients with and without cortical atrophy. *Archives of General Psychiatry, 43*, 978–983.

Waddington, J. L. (1990). Sight and insight: Regional cerebral metabolic activity in schizophrenia visualized by positron emission tomography, and competing neurodevelopmental perspectives. *The British Journal of Psychiatry, 156*, 615–619.

Watanabe, M. (1934). Beitrag zur Histopathologie des Gehirns von Dementia praecox. *Japanese Journal for Internal Medicine, Paediatrics and Psychiatry, 31*, 245–255.

Weinberger, D. R., and Wyatt, R. J. (1982). Brain morphology in schizophrenia: *In vivo* studies. In F. A. Henn and H. A. Nasrallah (Eds.), *Schizophrenia as a brain disease*, pp. 1–48. New York: Oxford University Press.

Weinberger, D. R., Berman, K. F., Iadorola, M., Driesen, N., Karson, C., and Coppola, R. (1987). Hat size in schizophrenia. *Archives of General Psychiatry, 44*, 672.

Weinberger, D. R., Berman, K. F., and Zec, R. F. (1986). Physiologic dysfunction of dorsolateral prefrontal cortex in schizophrenia. I. Regional cerebral blood flow evidence. *Archives of General Psychiatry, 43*, 114–124.

Weinberger, D. R., Bigelow, L. B., Kleinman, J. E., Klein, S. T., Rosenblatt, J. E., and Wyatt, R. J. (1980). Cerebral ventricular enlargement in chronic schizophrenia: An association with poor response to treatment. *Archives of General Psychiatry, 37*, 11–13.

Weinberger, D. R., DeLisi, L. E., Perman, G. P., Targum, S., and Wyatt, R. J. (1982). Computed tomography in schizophreniform disorder and other acute psychiatric disorders. *Archives of General Psychiatry, 39*, 778–783.

Weinberger, D. R., Torrey, E. F., Neophytides, A. N., and Wyatt, R. J. (1979a). Lateral cerebral ventricular enlargement in chronic schizophrenia. *Archives of General Psychiatry, 36*, 735–739.

Weinberger, D. R., Torrey, E. F., Neophytides, A. N., and Wyatt, R. J. (1979b). Structural abnormalities in the cerebral cortex of chronic schizophrenic patients. *Archives of General Psychiatry, 36*, 935–939.

Weinberger, D. R., Torrey, E. F., and Wyatt, R. J. (1979c). Cerebrellar atrophy in chronic schizophrenia. *Lancet, II*, 718–719.

Wiesel, F. A., Wik, G., Sjogren, I., Blomqvist, G., and Greitz, T. (1987a). Altered relationships between metabolic rates of glucose in brain regions of schizophrenic patients. *Acta Psychiatrica Scandinavica, 76*, 642–647.

Wiesel, F. A., Wik, G., Sjogren, I., Blomqvist, G., Greitz, T., and Stone-Elander, S. (1987b). Regional brain glucose metabolism in drug-free schizophrenic patients and clinical correlates. *Acta Psychiatrica Scandinavica, 76*, 628–641.

Wiesel, F. A., Blomqvist, G., Ehrin, E., Greitz, T., Ingvar, D. H., Litton, J., Nilsson, L., Sedvall, G., Stone-Elander, S., Widen, L., and Wik, G. (1985). Brain energy metabolism in schizophrenia studied with ($^{11}$C)-glucose. In T. Greitz, D. Ingvar, and L. Widen (Eds.), *The metabolism of the human brain studied with positron emission tomography*, pp. 485–493. New York: Raven Press.

Wik, G., Wiesel, F. A., Sjogren, I., Blomqvist, G., Greitz, T., and Stone-Elander, S. (1989). Effects of sulpiride and chlorpromazine on regional cerebral glucose metabolism in schizophrenic patients as determined by positron emission tomography. *Psychopharmacology, 97*, 309–318.

Williams, A. O., Reveley, M. A., Kolakowska, T., Ardern, M., and Mandelbrote, B. M. (1985). Schizophrenia with good and poor outcome. II. Cerebral ventricular size and its clinical significance. *British Journal of Psychiatry, 146*, 239–246.

Withers, E., and Hinton, J. (1971). Three forms of the clinical tests of the sensorium and their reliability. *British Journal of Psychiatry*, *119*, 1–81.

Wolkin, A., Jaeger, J., Brodie, J. D., Wolf, A. P., Fowler, J., Rotrosen, J., Gomez-Mont, F., and Cancro, R. (1985). Persistence of cerebral metabolic abnormalities in chronic schizophrenia as determined by positron emission tomography. *American Journal of Psychiatry*, *142*, 564.

Zec, R. F., and Weinberger, D. R. (1986). Brain areas implicated in schizophrenia: A selective overview. In H. A. Nasrallah and D. R. Weinberger (eds.), *Handbook of Schizophrenia, Vol. 1*. pp. 175–206. Amsterdam: Elsevier.

Zipursky, R. B., and Schulz, S. C. (1987). Seasonality of birth and CT findings in schizophrenia. *Biological Psychiatry*, *22*, 1288–1292.

# Chapter 9

# Asymmetric Hemispheric Function

## I. Lateralization of Structure and Function in Healthy Individuals

Asymmetry pervades form and function of the normal healthy human body. Unpaired organs are displaced to one side, the two sides of the face differ, the female breasts and male testicles differ in size between the two sides.

Asymmetrical development in the normal healthy brain is evident from the 16th week of gestation. By the 31st week, the planum temporale has developed on the left side. Surprisingly this is 7–10 days behind the development of the equivalent structure on the right. Gyral and sulcal development in the right cerebrum precedes that in the left. By adulthood, the right frontal and left temporal lobes are usually larger than those lobes on the opposite side. (For reviews, see Bryden, 1982; Bradshaw and Nettleton, 1983; Geschwind and Galaburda, 1985.)

Asymmetries are even more evident with respect to function. For example, most individuals prefer to use their right hand for eating, writing, and social interactions. This implies a specialization for manual skills in the *left* cerebral hemisphere.

More importantly, speech functions are situated in the left hemisphere of approximately 90% of right-handed individuals. With left handers, the function is less clearly lateralized: approximately 40% of this group have speech functions in the left hemisphere. Because of this function, the left hemisphere is considered the dominant hemisphere (in most people). Speech production is a sequential process and, accordingly, another important feature of the left hemisphere is sequential data processing. That means that controlled data processing is largely a feature of the left or dominant hemisphere (cf. Chapter 2).

In contrast, the *right* hemisphere operates more "holistically" and is engaged in Gestalt perception. Indeed a major part of the right hemisphere's special role is the processing of spatial relations. A special feature here is face recognition. Another specialization is musical appreciation. The right or nondominant hemisphere also specializes in the mediation of some aspects of emotion. (For a more detailed analysis, see Bradshaw and Nettleton, 1981; Gainotti, 1983.)

Normally the two hemispheres communicate with each other by way of a large number of neural connections constituting the commissures and corpus callosum. In this way, each side of the brain may know or monitor what is occurring elsewhere. The importance of this ability was demonstrated by Sperry and his group studying the abilities of subjects in whom these connections were broken, but who were otherwise healthy (e.g., Sperry, 1982; Figure 9.1 and 9.2). These figures illustrate that, without the connections between the two hemispheres (or impaired communication between the hemispheres), one side may not know what the other is doing or may have difficulty accounting for the actions of the other half of the brain (e.g., Gazzaniga, 1983).

These experiments demonstrated another important feature of hemispheric specialization. The subject was only aware of the processes going on in the dominant hemisphere. The processes in the nondominant hemisphere only reached awareness if communicated via the corpus callosum to the dominant (usually left) hemisphere. This may have implications for the disturbed consciousness of schizophrenics (i.e., a disturbance in the dominant hemisphere and in the transfer of functions from the nondominant to the dominant hemisphere).

Figure 9.2 demonstrates how some of the functions and their transfer have been tested.

Sperry (1982) studied some of the abilities of patients in whom the most important of the interhemispheric connections, the corpus callosum, had been destroyed. By asking the experimental subject to fixate a point in the middle of the visual field he could present pictures to one half of the field that would be exclusively processed by the opposite hemisphere. Thus, for example, stimulus information in the left visual field would be passed via the optic chiasma to the right occipital cortex for processing (Figure 9.1). In the example shown in Figure 9.2, the right hemisphere "sees" the letter "B"; this was confirmed by the subject correctly selecting the letter "B" from a number of model letters presented to his left hand. However, when asked what letter the subject had seen, he replied, "R." This shows that the information about the letter "B" had not reached the level of consciousness in the left hemisphere.

On another occasion, a picture of a naked woman was shown to the left visual field (right visual hemisphere) of this split-brain patient. The patient chuckled but could not explain why. Of course when the same picture was shown to the opposite (left) hemisphere, the subject was able to talk about what appealed to him in the picture; he was now fully conscious or aware of the picture. These examples show that one is only consciously aware of the processes of the right hemisphere when there is an intact connection between the right and left hemispheres. Most such important information exchanges normally occur over the corpus callosum. Such exchange is impaired if the callosum is damaged.

For 150 years, the complementarity of the hemispheres has been part of the

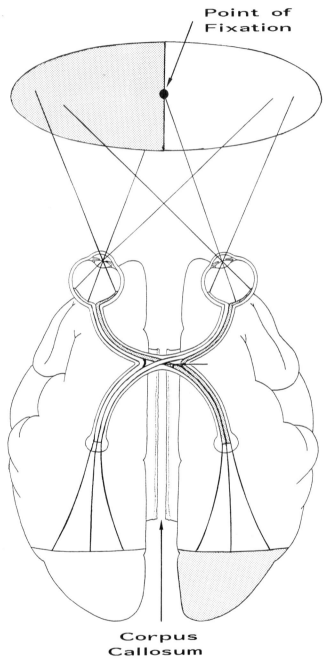

**Figure 9.1**   Schematic illustration of the projection of the left visual field over the optic chiasma to the right visual (occipital) cortex.

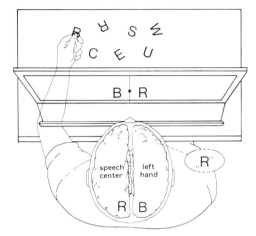

**Figure 9.2**  Illustration of the situation in which split-brain subjects are tested. One can separate the visual field on the screen in front of the subject into left and right sides. The subject is asked to fixate a point in the middle and then find the stimulus seen (e.g., letter 'R') by feeling with his left hand the models that he cannot see. The hand correctly finds the 'B' seen by his right hemisphere but can only verbalize the 'R' seen by his left hemisphere (after Sperry, 1970).

dogma of neuropsychology (Wigan, 1844). However, is the asymmetry of function more rooted in the software or in the hardware? This controversy has been equally long-lived (Dax, 1836). The answer has important implications for the understanding of lateralized function in schizophrenia. Lateral hardware anomalies may be present but may not reflect the schizophrenic condition. There may be conditions that favor both the development of schizophrenia and lateral software anomalies, but the latter need not necessarily concur with the former. Last but not least of the questions facing this area of research is whether an abnormality on one side in fact reflects a change on the other. Does left-sided hypofunction reflect right-sided hyperfunction? Are both present? Or neither? Does the problem lie with the interhemispheric transfer of information? It is not easy to discover the answers. First we must examine apparent empirical differences.

Another important problem is that, even if the function is lateralized, the full display of abilities nearly always requires a functioning complementary hemisphere. Thus, a poor performance does not necessarily mean that only the hemisphere leading in the function is involved (e.g. Gazzaniga, 1983).

We shall refer to the left hemisphere as the "dominant" hemisphere and the right hemisphere as the "nondominant" hemisphere throughout this chapter. Even if this is not always literally the case, in the reports discussed, this situation has usually been established in terms of hand preference.

## II. Neuropsychological Comparisons with Patients Sustaining Left-Sided Damage

If there were unilateral brain damage in schizophrenics, what might be the clinically observable symptoms or neuropsychological impairments? In this section, we look at the performance of some schizophrenics in test situations that produce clear results for patients with lateral brain damage. In the next section we will discuss the evidence for lateral structural changes in schizophrenics.

Extensive left cerebral damage can result in aphasia. Although schizophrenics are not aphasic, their thought disturbance, language difficulties, and impaired abstract and analytical abilities are believed to imply a related dysphasic disturbance (cf. Chapter 2). We can consider the results of Faber *et al.*, (1983). They found that only one of a group of five specialists could accurately discriminate a group 14 schizophrenics from 13 neurologically impaired patients. The most marked differences found between these two groups were poverty of speech, anomia (difficulty finding the right word), and the use of words with private meanings. To some extent, schizophrenics showed less comprehension and were more prone to derailment than aphasics. The difficulty with discrimination was most pronounced for schizophrenics with formal thought disorder.

Fine feature analysis is a characteristic of left hemisphere analytic abilities (Polich, 1984). Aphasics have difficulty performing tasks requiring these abilities (Cohen *et al.*, 1981). On such tasks, that test letter naming and dot counting abilities for stimuli presented to separate visual fields, schizophrenics (particularly nonparanoid subjects) show left-hemispheric impairments (Magaro and Chamral, 1983).

Impairments of verbal comprehension and object naming in brain-damaged subjects were more severe if left hemisphere injuries were inflicted after the age of 5. Thus, the less severe deficit of schizophrenics may be more consistent with an insult at earlier stages of development. It is interesting to note that left brain damage occurring in the perinatal period is associated with increased prevalence of sinistrality (Vargha-Khadem *et al.*, 1985). There are also claims that, in large samples of schizophrenics (e.g., 200, Gur, 1977), there is an increased incidence of left-handedness. Studies of left-handed preferences have produced many conflicting results. In many cases this may be because of the reliance on self-report; one researcher in this field found self-report to be "patently unreliable" (Taylor, 1987). Yet, intriguingly, Andreasen and Olsen (1982) reported CT evidence of increased atrophy in their sinistral schizophrenics. Their dextral patients showed more positive signs and less atrophy. However, we are not aware of subsequent larger studies to follow up the possible associations between cerebral atrophy, hemisphere dominance, and predominance of clinical signs.

Over the last 10 yr, an Italian group from Milan (Scarone *et al.*, 1983,

1987) has accumulated results from patients studied with the short aphasia test (Heinburger and Reitan, 1961) and the quality extinction test (QET; Schwartz *et al.*, 1979). The former examines writing and geometric performance, in errors which reflect left- and right-sided damage, respectively. The latter tests the loss of sensitivity to textures presented to each hand (extinction). Right extinction points to left-sided damage, whereas left extinction is nonspecific. By 1983, they were able to show that about half of their 91 patients showed left extinction and geometric errors in the absence of writing errors (i.e., right parietal dysfunction). Nearly a quarter showed right extinction (i.e., left-sided impairment). In both cases, the incidence was about three times higher than in healthy subjects. More recently they subdivided the group according to sex, age, and diagnosis (now $n = 136$). They reported that, although signs increased with age, chronicity of the illness was the more important factor. Although there were some differences based on sex and diagnosis (e.g., fewer undifferentiated females but more disorganized males showed these signs), the existence of a pattern related to gender or diagnostic group is, as yet, unconvincing.

It may be disappointing to find that some schizophrenics show lateralized dysfunction and others do not, that is, that the impairment may be on the left or the right. This should not be surprising, given the heterogeneity we have come to expect in schizophrenia. Further, the results are differential with respect to hemisphere within the schizophrenic group, let alone in comparison with controls, so generalized deficits cannot explain all the results.

An early attempt to compare the task performance of schizophrenics with that of brain-damaged subjects (Kleist, 1960) was enthusiastically interpreted as illustrating a potential association of psychosis with damage to the left side of the brain. In a computer analysis of the symptoms of 80 subjects with localized brain injury, Davison and Bagley (1969) showed an association of left cerebral damage, particularly to the temporal lobe, with primary delusions and catatonic symptoms. Damage to the temporal lobe, on either side, is particularly likely as a consequence of the development of epilepsy. Unfortunately, this study failed to look for the cardinal features of negative symptomatology. In Canada, Flor-Henry (1969) made a systematic comparison of epileptic subjects, of whom 50 were with and 50 were without schizophreniform symptoms. A left temporal focus was clearly associated with the presence of psychotic features. However, such a clear outcome could not be replicated in the analysis of 62 cases of temporal lobe epilepsy by Shukla and Katiyar (1980). If there are numerous cases of temporal lobe epilepsy with and without psychotic symptoms (Merrin, 1981), one may well question whether it is appropriate or meaningful to select individual symptoms from such cases and equate them implicitly with the fully developed psychotic syndrome (Ulrich, 1979).

However, a later report from Flor-Henry presents an examination of groups of schizophrenic (54) and affectively ill (60) patients (Flor-Henry and Yeudall,

1979). This study claimed a clear distinction between schizophrenics and manic–depressives on tests of ideomotor apraxia, word fluency, and trail-making, but not on constructional apraxia, verbal learning, or the Purdue pegboard tests. The investigators point out that these results indicate similar function for the nondominant hemisphere of the two groups, but differences for the dominant frontal, parietal, and temporal regions. A discriminant function analysis for 69 subjects on 27 neuropsychological tests showed that, whereas both groups had some signs of bilateral dysfunction, schizophrenics showed more dysfunction on the left and manic-depressives showed more on the right.

Elsewhere in Canada, Kolb and Whishaw (1983) applied 14 tests from the range extensively developed by Milner for the characterization of the locus of brain damage to a sample of 30 schizophrenics and matched controls. They confirmed a major impairment of schizophrenic performance on tests sensitive to left temporal lobe damage, but an impairment was equally apparent for tests sensitive to frontal (card-sorting and design fluency) and temporal (paired associate and Wechsler figures) damage bilaterally.

John Gruzelier and colleagues in London also report an interesting attempt to use some of these same tests to distinguish schizophrenic performance from that of patients with affective psychoses, mania, or depression (Gruzelier *et al.*, 1988). However, if one is looking for a foolproof discrimination, one can only be impressed by the heterogeneity of results. On conditioned spatial or nonspatial tests, some schizophrenics performed superiorly and others in-feriorly to other groups. The same was true in letter and semantic fluency tests (but only the affectively ill had bilateral deficits on spatial learning and memory tests). The single clear lateralized differences occurred on Hebb's recurring-digits test. Here the schizophrenic impairment indicated a left hemisphere impairment. Performance was worse in subjects with symptoms of withdrawal. Those with more productive signs tended to show more problems with the block-span memory, implicating more right-sided involvement. In general, this was also the sort of result obtained by the group at the Clinical Research Centre in England (Crow and Stevens, 1978).

We return to further evidence from psychological testing directed at measuring sensory information processing in a later section. Such tests are not usually formally considered representative of neuropsychological signs (Sections VII and VIII below).

## III. Anatomical "Hardware" and "Software" Asymmetries: Brain Imaging Studies

Is there direct evidence for lateralized structural differences in schizophrenic subjects? In view of the mammoth size of the task, microscopic studies of *postmortem* brain tissue from schizophrenic patients have not, for the most part, attempted to compare the two sides of the brain. An exception is the study by Jakob and Beckmann (1986), who restricted themselves to the plane of the amygdala in 13 of their 64 subjects. Of these subjects, 10 showed more lamina pathology and decreased cell numbers on the left side. The hypothesis that the corpus callosum that connects the frontal and temporal lobes of the two hemispheres is physically different in schizophrenics is discussed in Section VIII.

## A. Computer Tomography

When early pneumoencephalographic studies looked for lateralized differences, larger ventricles were apparent on the left side in 25–33% of patients (Haug, 1962; Hunter *et al.*, 1968). In an early and extensive CT study of 79 patients at the NIMH, Luchins *et al.* (1982) found no lateral differences in those showing increased signs of atrophy. The normal asymmetry of larger frontal lobes on the right and a larger temporo-occipital lobe on the left was apparent. Surprisingly, they found that this asymmetry tended to be reversed in patients without signs of atrophy. What makes their report more intriguing is that precisely these patients consistently scored lower verbal than nonverbal IQs (which might indicate poorer left temporal lobe function). Although many studies do not report having looked for correlations with IQs, several have reported the absence of correlations between significant CT changes and total IQ measures (e.g., McCarley *et al.*, 1989).

Most CT studies have concentrated on ventricular size and been unable to note significant lateral differences (e.g. Andreasen *et al.*, 1982; Jernigan *et al.*, 1982), but this may well be attributable to the greater variability recorded from the schizophrenic groups (Nyback *et al.*, 1982). However, two teams comment on the severity of the symptoms shown by individuals with more signs of atrophy on the left (Losonczy *et al.*, 1986) and in the left frontal regions (Golden *et al.*, 1981). Density changes of tissue on the left side that are difficult to interpret have also been reported (Coffman *et al.*, 1984; Burns *et al.*, 1987).

Few investigators have noticed any lateralized changes in sulcal measurements. However, Rossi and colleagues (1988) noted that the size of the sylvian fissure on the left side correlated with larger third ventricle size. Further, it was this measure of increased size of the left sylvian fissure that Nyman *et al.* (1986) found to correlate with cognitive signs of left hemisphere dysfunction. The preliminary report from McCarley *et al.* (1989) found surprisingly marked correlations of sylvian fissure enlargement with the degree of positive or negative symptoms shown. Thus, left sylvian measures correlated with positive symptoms of thought disorder and delusions (>0.73) and right sylvian measures correlated with negative symptoms (e.g., apathy, alogia; >0.64).

It is too soon to draw conclusions. Too few teams have branched out to measure some of the 20 or more variables other than ventricle size that they could measure, and those that have tried to do so have studied an unrepresentative handful of subjects. But useful hypotheses and indications for further study are emerging. Clearly the relationship between indicators of frontal and temporal lobe changes and features associated with types I and II schizophrenia merit close attention.

## B. Magnetic Resonance Imaging

MRI studies support the trend from CT data pointing toward more atrophy on the left side (lateral ventricle; Kelsoe *et al.*, 1988). Indeed, Besson *et al.* (1987) reported that, in comparison with subjects showing relatively mild symptoms, severe negative symptoms were associated more with left frontal and severe positive symptoms with left medial and temporal changes (cf. McCarley *et al.*, 1989).

Clearly, at the level of resolution provided by current CT methods, severe symptoms of schizophrenia can be accompanied by increased pathology on the left side of the brain. This may be more posteriorly located in subjects with verbal and memory problems. Crow (1986) and Johnstone *et al.* (1989), while confirming this trend for their patients at the Clinical Research Centre, suggest more controversially that these are individuals with earlier onset and worse prognosis. As yet there is no unequivocal evidence from other groups to support this hypothesis.

## C. Regional Cerebral Blood Flow

Do studies of regional CBF and metabolism support the idea of a lateralized deficit in schizophrenia? It is clear that asymmetric patterns of CBF are not striking in schizophrenia; they were not observed by Kurachi *et al.* (1985) nor by Mathew *et al.* (1982). A French study of 27 floridly paranoid young patients found slightly decreased flow on the right side, but measures were considerably more variable in their patients than in the controls (Dousse *et al.*, 1988). Further, the reader who is trying to interpret these reports should recall, in the first instance, that there are indications that higher rates of metabolism may be related to impaired function. Second, it should be remembered that the presence of absolute differences (a rare result) may be functionally less important than a relative difference or an asymmetry between the two sides (i.e. a lateralized gradient).

In their extended study of 108 patients, Mathew *et al.* (1988), broadly speaking, confirmed there were no major lateral differences in the resting condition, but in detail they could make a lateralized distinction in their patients on the basis of increased flow in left temporal regions. Recently, increased CBF has been reported even from the left pallidum of never-medicated schizophrenics (Early *et al.*, 1986). However it is doubtful that this result can be generalized. Uytdenhoef *et al.* (1983) saw a not dissimilar pattern to that reported by Mathew in their depressed patients, with low right posterior and higher left frontal flow.

In a matched group of 19 schizophrenics and controls, Gur *et al.* (1985) also found some evidence for increased flow on the left side at rest. In a condition under which activation was brought about by a verbal task, flow increased anteriorly rather than posteriorly, as in controls. On a spatial task, schizophrenics showed less CBF on the right, the side usually activated by such tasks. In a further analysis, with 15 medicated and 19 unmedicated schizophrenics, Gur *et al.* (1989) found that the lateralized changes were more common than the frontal signs and that increased flow and metabolism on the left was related both to the specificity of symptoms to schizophrenics and to their severity.

One problem for the interpretation of these results is that of expectations. Might there be less CBF on one side because of the "lesion," or increased CBF in compensation? For example, Ariel *et al.* (1983) reported lower CBF in left frontal regions in the resting condition.

## D. Positron Emission Tomography

Evidence from PET studies of glucose utilization do not help resolve the issue. Hints of unusual or attenuated asymmetries have been noted in schizophrenic patients (Sheppard *et al.*, 1983; Wolkin *et al.*, 1985), but the results conflict. Possibly an underlying asymmetry is masked by a bilateral frontotemporal reduction of metabolism (perhaps resulting from medication; Wolkin *et al.*, 1985). Yet in just 6 subjects, a tendency for a right-sided temporal increase has been noted (Jernigan *et al.*, 1985). That the evidence is not more marked is surprising, considering the technique is able to resolve the normal asymmetry of glucose uptake in the basal ganglia (L > R, Buchsbaum *et al.*, 1987; Wiesel *et al.*, 1985, 1987a,b; Szechtman *et al.*, 1988). Wolkin and colleagues indeed claimed a slight metabolic increase here.

Consistent with CBF results, a recent analysis of energy metabolism in the temporal lobe found small but significant increases on the left with respect to the right side of the brain in schizophrenics ($n = 21$). Metabolism tended to be higher on both sides than in controls ($n = 19$), who did not show lateralized differences (Delisi *et al.*, 1989). Of further interest is that this increase on the left correlated positively with psychopathology in general, and with the prominence of hallucinations in particular (cf. CBF studies; Chapter 7).

A more clear-cut report comes from a Japanese group (Kishimoto *et al.*, 1987). Of their 20 patients, 8 showed hypoparietal metabolism, but only ipsilateral to their preferred handedness (i.e., consistent with CBF measures:

lower on the right side of right handers). These subjects were not particularly severely ill, nor old, nor ultra-long-term patients. In contrast to the others, they were more paranoid (cf. Dousse *et al.*, 1988; CBF studies). Although the result does offer some support to the CBF studies of Mathew and colleagues, conclusions with respect to locus cannot be drawn until the result is replicated elsewhere.

As yet, it seems that studies of CBF and metabolism for the most part do not provide clear support for the indications for lateralized dysfunction coming from CT and NMR studies. Although the number of reports referring to higher levels on the left side is increasing, the magnitude of the changes is less than impressive and the locus affected varies among the reports (and patients) studied. Certainly we are still a long way from demonstrating changes that discriminate schizophrenic from other psychiatric illnesses. This is not unexpected at a time in the development of the technique in which new ligands are still being tested and the methods of measurement are not uniform.

## IV. The Asymmetrical Localization of Activation and Cognitive Function: Electrophysiological Studies

### A. Electroencephalography

Since EEG recording started to become widely available some 50 years ago, most psychiatric clinics have acquired the capability of recording EEGs. If only every second clinic published a paper each decade, the number of reports from psychiatric patients would be on the order of several thousand. Since it is usual to record EEGs from several sites, most of these studies would have some information about lateralization. It is therefore not easy to select a few studies representative of the broad range of conditions under which subjects have been studied [e.g., at rest (eyes open/closed), with sensory stimulation, with task and motor performance].

Although clinical assessments are still often performed subjectively "by eye," computer controlled spectral measures gradually replaced these methods in research reports between the end of the 1960s and the end of the 1970s. The opinion that was passed on to this new era is illustrated by two studies, a reanalysis of 1494 subjects by Small *et al.* (1979) and of 159 psychiatric patients (27 schizophrenics) by Abrams and Taylor (1979). The latter report found that less than half the schizophrenics showed lateralized abnormalities at rest. These were usually located temporally and could be found on the left or the right side. The former study confirmed that abnormalities could be more often found in organic, neurotic personality, or bipolar affective disorders. Under all conditions, but particularly during activation, left-sided disorders were more frequent in depression and right-sided abnormalities in schizophrenia (DSM I and II).

If we are to believe that a bias for anomalies to appear on one side or the other prevails in particular diagnostic categories, then it must be clear what the normal pattern is. This is *not* clear. The spectral analysis of Rodin *et al.* (1968) reported a higher power in all frequency bands on the right side of normal controls. Giannatrapani and Kayton (1974) found a higher spectral power on the left side of their healthy population. Thus, the EEG of an individual psychiatric patient cannot, with certainty, be said to show a lateralized abnormality with respect to spectral characteristics.

Questions remain whether there is a probability of a lateralized abnormality across the schizophrenic population and whether this can be ascribed to a particular diagnostic category or subgroup. Flor-Henry and Koles (1980) extensively studied an unmedicated population of 53 schizophrenic, 63 depressives, 75 manics, and 60 healthy controls. They examined the data in a number of ways, but concentrated on changes in the alpha band at parietal and temporal sites. As Gruzelier (1983) remarked in his review of lateral asymmetries, it is astonishing how few differences emerged from this study. One of the few results that perhaps permits a generalization was the finding of less coherence between temporal recording sites in schizophrenic and manic patients. Similar findings for alpha and beta bands have been reported from other laboratories (Shaw *et al.*, 1979; Dymond *et al.*, 1980). (Coherence is the degree of synchronization between pairs of signals as a function of frequency). More coherence has been reported for a few schizophrenics in lower frequency theta bands (Weller and Montague, 1979).

At more anterior recording sites, a number of schizophrenics show unusual increases of alpha power (Giannatrapani and Kayton, 1974; Etevenon *et al.*, 1979; Matousek *et al.*, 1981; Shagass *et al.*, 1983), but this could be an artifact resulting from the failure to adequately remove records contaminated with eye movements. (Many schizophrenics blink more than usual.) If this is not done, then the mean alpha spectrum increases (Karson *et al.*, 1988). In general, no differences with respect to healthy controls have been reported often (Fenton *et al.*, 1980; Iacono, 1982; Guenther and Breitling, 1985). The topographic study of Karson and colleagues (1987) at the NIMH also failed to find any significant lateralization in the diffuse increase of slow delta activity they reported from 15 medication-free schizophrenics. (There was a very slight trend for increases in the right frontal and left centroparietal leads.)

Most of this work was conducted on schizophrenics at rest. When the subjects were asked to perform verbal or spatial tasks, the differences in activity between the two hemispheres was often attenuated (Flor-Henry, 1976; Alpert and Martz, 1977; Stevens and Livermore, 1982; Shaw *et al.*, 1983). Indeed, an attenuation of alpha activity on the right side seemed to occur during task performance (Merrin *et al.*, 1986). This may be associated with increased representation of faster frequencies (beta) on the left side. Where present, a lateralization of activity in higher frequency bands was claimed to be more apparent on the left (Flor-Henry, 1969; Coger *et al.*, 1979; Flor-Henry *et al.*, 1979; Dymond *et al.*, 1980; Itil, 1980). This was particularly apparent from temporal records of subjects who showed first rank symptoms (Morstyn *et al.*, 1983a,b; Jutai *et al.*, 1984).

Can the lack of generalizable results be attributed to the mixing of marked differences shown by subgroups of schizophrenics? The numbers of subjects studied have seldom allowed a reasonable division into subgroups. Serafetinides and colleagues (1981) found less of an asymmetry at beta frequencies in subjects with more emotional symptoms (i.e., reduced dominance in the presumably afflicted hemisphere). Indeed, Rodin *et al.* (1968) originally attributed the changes they saw in anhedonic subjects to changes in the right hemisphere. Even the comparison of 5 subjects with negative and 6 with positive symptoms showed predominant beta activity on the right side (Gruzelier *et al.*, 1984). More recently, Gaebel and Ulrich (1988) noted that patients who were more depressed or anxious showed more alpha power on the left. It is not clear to what extent a right-sided increase of activity in patients with negative symptoms is restricted to the beta band; opposite effects have been seen in other bands. Alternatively, different groups interpret their results as increases on one side, when in fact, there is a relative decrease on the other side.

Paranoid subjects were reported to show more and hebephrenics less variability in their EEG records from the left hemisphere (Etevenon *et al.*, 1979). A subsequent comparison of 7 paranoids with 10 residuals, recording from parietal and occipital sites, confirmed a left-sided difference for the paranoid group, with a greater proportion of both the higher and lower frequency bands (Etevenon *et al.*, 1983).

Janice Stevens and colleagues (Stevens *et al.*, 1979; Stevens and Livermore, 1982) made telemetered recordings from parietal and temporal sites in mobile medicated and unmedicated patients. They also found unusual left hemisphere activity in florid paranoids. Their method allowed them to correlate EEG changes with the unplannable occurrence of psychotic symptoms. Hallucinations coincided with increased left-sided slow activity from temporal leads (Figure 9.3.) When they summed the activities recorded during abnormal behavior (e.g., hallucinations, eye movements, and catatonic periods), they found a decline in total power in their schizophrenic group and, in particular, reduced left-sided temporal alpha activity compared with control group patients. (An individual case is illustrated in Figure 9.3.) This compares well with the recent finding that schizophrenic subjects who reported hallucinating during a PET procedure showed reduced metabolism in Wernicke's area in the left hemisphere (Cleghorn and Garnett, 1991). Otherwise, Stevens and colleagues could find no remarkable correlations between

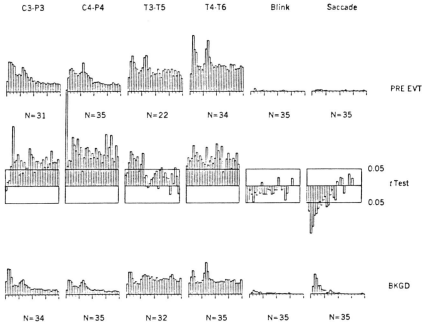

**Figure 9.3**   *Top,* Averaged spectra and blink/saccade intervals calculated during auditory hallucinations in one schizophrenic case. *Bottom,* Similar analysis during periods sampled when the subject was looking at a book (BKGD) without reporting hallucinations. PRE EVT means before hallucinations. T-test bar diagrams illustrate the direction of significance between the conditions for each 2 Hz interval (after Stevens *et al.,* 1979, © American Medical Association).

behavioral activity and EEG measures. During the performance of verbal tasks, there were lateral shifts in alpha activity, as recorded in healthy controls. Unfortunately only 6 subjects were given spatial tasks to perform. They did not show a right-sided alpha block like healthy subjects (i.e., attenuated lateralization).

A number of studies claim that there was no evident effect of neuroleptic treatment, but very few have set out to compare the effects of neuroleptic treatment on EEG lateralization. An early double-blind placebo-controlled study by Serafetinides (1972, 1973) found that when a clinical improvement was associated with treatment, there was an increase of voltage in the left hemisphere. There is a trend for such a lateralization in normal subjects (Sugarman *et al.,* 1973), whereas the opposite effect, an attenuation of normal lateralized frontal EEG patterns, was achieved with amphetamine treatment (Goldstein and Stoltzfus, 1973), which itself can induce a paranoid-like psychosis. By comparing patients on and off medications, a normalization of the EEG in schizophrenics has been confirmed elsewhere (D'Elia *et al.,* 1977; Etevenon *et al.,* 1979; Merrin *et al.,* 1986).

On the whole, EEG studies have not succeeded in demonstrating schizophrenic-specific lateralized differences of activity that can be generalized across subjects. However, there is a tendency toward an attenuation of activity on the right and for increased incidence of variable activity on the left side. For valid statements to be made about any individual, however, several records must be made over a period of time. A large study containing a number of patients in several clearly defined subgroups and the examination of changes relating to several frequency bands at frontal as well as posterior sites during resting and task performance conditions is clearly still required. Methodological issues that should be attended to in such a study (variably reported in the cited literature) include the technique for artifact recognition and removal (e.g., eye movements), the use of variance stabilizing transformations, the size and consistency of the EEG sample taken for analysis, and the medication status of the subjects.

## B. Event-Related Potentials

There are few studies that address the question of whether there are unusual lateralized effects to be seen in the ERPs of schizophrenics and these have, for the most part, yet to produce answers to the most interesting questions. There are two reasons for this, which reflect the number of recording sites and the range of paradigms and potentials that can be recorded in the different modalities. Traditionally the averaging of the EEG after stimulus events to produce ERPs was done with 1–3 electrodes in the midline. Up to the mid-1980s, few laboratories made the effort to record from more than the odd electrode on either side of the midline of the scalp. Only slowly during the 1980s have the methods for rapid assembly of multiple recording sites and the evaluation of the huge amount of data resulting become at all widespread. Considering the dozen components in several sensory modalities that potentially reflect a large range of exogenous and endogenous features, it will take quite some time to assemble the number of reports necessary to enable generalizations to be made about the effects of psychopathology.

The main finding to date seems to be that the side of the brain of healthy subjects principally involved in processing the attributes of the event is no longer dominant in schizophrenics. There is an attenuation of the normal asymmetric distribution of component maxima. This seems to apply to early components related to sensory processing (e.g., somatosensory, <100 msec; Cooper et al., 1985) as well as to later components elicited by attended and nonattended stimuli (visual, auditory, >100 msec; Roemer et al., 1978, 1979; Buchsbaum et al., 1979).

Late ERPs (e.g., $P_3$) are usually maximal on the right in tests using visual stimuli. This lateralization is seen from about 8 years of age (Kurtzberg et al., 1979). Auditory stimuli elicit a maximum on the left. In Boston, Morstyn and colleagues (1983a,b) studied 10 medicated schizophrenics with first rank symptoms on an auditory discrimination. Recording from 20 sites, they showed that the $P_3$ maximum lay relatively posterior (centroparietally) on the left side of healthy subjects but was more anteriorly located toward the right in their schizophrenics. One of the present authors has a similar finding (Oades and Zerbin, 1991). (A similar finding has been reported for the early sensory $P_{50}$ component; Reite *et al.*, 1988.)

We should not forget that the early results from Shagass' group in Philadelphia (Shagass *et al.*, 1980), using visual and auditory stimuli, reported increased variability or decreased stability of ERPs in schizophrenics. They, along with Buchsbaum at the NIMH and Hirsch's group in London, claim evidence for impaired left hemisphere function (Buchsbaum *et al.*, 1979; Connolly *et al.*, 1985; see also, Niwa *et al.*, 1983).

Left-sided anomalies are not restricted to simple sensory stimulation. Kemali and colleagues (1988) in Naples used task-relevant and -irrelevant word stimuli presented centrally or to each hemifield. They found a mild left-sided processing deficit, particularly in schizophrenics with negative symptoms. This is in contrast to the studies just discussed, which noted an association with first rank symptoms.

The incongruity of attenuated lateralization and left-sided dysfunction in several paradigms in which the asymmetry in normal subjects differs may be explicable in terms of the different treatments and presentations of results. Increased variability implies that some ERPs may be larger than normal but, since the latency is also variable, means are likely to be lower than normal. Additional confusion may arise if the mixture of subgroups of schizophrenics brings together different characteristics. For example, the attenuation of laterality is said to be more pronounced in paranoids than in hebephrenics (Maurer and Dierks, 1987).

The sort of studies now needed might be illustrated by the exciting preliminary work of McCarley, Faux, Shenton, and collaborators (1989) at Brockton and Boston. They looked for a relationship between clinical symptoms, CT results, and ERPs elicited on a two-tone oddball task (in which the target for response was the rarer higher tone). As many have found, they saw decreased $P_2$ and $P_3$ amplitude in the schizophrenics in the condition of attending to the target. As fewer have found, but consistent with our previous discussion, the subtraction of waves recorded in the passive recording from the attention condition showed $P_3$ peaks to be shifted to the right in controls but on the left in schizophrenics. More interestingly, although their first sample compared only 9 schizophrenics and 9 healthy controls, they obtained correlations ($\sim 0.7$) between CT results, the type of symptom, and ERPs. Left sylvian fissure enlargement correlated with $P_3$ amplitude at left temporal sites; this, in turn, related to the incidence of positive symptoms (especially thought disorder and delusions). Left sulcal width increased with $P_2$ amplitude at left central sites and negative symptoms. The reader should note the unexpected aspect of the result here. Considering the amplitude was reduced in schizophrenics, among schizophrenics it increased with both clinical and tomographic signs of severity. As yet, it is too soon to know if this report is itself an outlier or has really uncovered an overlooked feature of schizophrenia. The sample was very small. The authors were also candid enough to acknowledge group differences on verbal IQ and socioeconomic background of the subjects. Further, the schizophrenics were medicated (245 chlorpromazine equivalents).

What about the effects of treatment? Neuroleptics may normalize the attenuated asymmetry (Maurer and Dierks, 1987), possibly by raising variability on the previously undisturbed side (Roemer et al., 1978). The effect seen also depends on the class of neuroleptic administered (Mintz et al., 1982). This group, from Tel Aviv, has pointed out an additional and important source of error when attempting to generalize from the results of ERP studies (Tomer et al., 1987). They studied 20 schizophrenics, representing several subgroups, for late visual-flash-evoked responses ($P_3N_4$). Of these patients, 8 showed lateralized dyskinesic or Parkinsonian disturbances. Higher amplitudes were noted contralateral to the side expressing the Parkinsonian symptoms, but lower amplitudes were seen contralateral to the dyskinesic symptoms. [It is relevant to note here that unilateral damage to the dorsolateral frontal cortex (particularly the frontal eye fields) can elicit contralateral akinetic symptoms (Watson et al., 1978).] The authors suggest that their result implicates which hemisphere may be vulnerable to disturbance in a given patient. In turn, this result supports the results discussed earlier (e.g., aphasia), which indicate that either hemisphere may be disturbed in a proportion of schizophrenics. This, in addition to the differential laterality depending on modality and task found in normal subjects, may be responsible for the current confusion in the interpretation of ERP studies.

## C. Electrodermal Orienting Response

The only other electrophysiological measure that could shed light on the problems of asymmetric nervous activity is the EDOR. One of the most intensive series of experiments in this area came from Gruzelier and colleagues in London, (For a review, see Gruzelier, 1983.) In contrast to the attenuation of laterality observed in scalp records, they found that the healthy control group showed no consistent signs of laterality in records from both hands. Fifty responders from a sample of 107 schizophrenics were claimed to show smaller reactions in their left hand (Gruzelier, 1973; Gruzelier and Venables, 1974). Ten patients with largely unipolar depression tended to show lower responses on the right. Opposite asymmetries among chronic schizophrenics and groups of depressive patients were also reported from Mys-lobodsky's laboratory in Israel (Myslobodsky and Horesch, 1978) and from the United States (Schneider, 1983). Neuroleptic treatment reduced this anomaly to the extent that some individuals showed the opposite asymmetry (Gruzelier and Hammond, 1978).

In the view of Gruzelier, the implications for central dysfunction are illustrated from observations of neurological patients (Luria and Homskaya, 1963; unpublished sources). The patients had had the medial or basal parts of the left frontal lobe removed or, in one case, there had been a tumor in this area. The EDOR was lower ipsilaterally.

Although some earlier studies found unspecified asymmetries of the EDOR (e.g., Dykman *et al.*, 1968), most recent reports have not been able to replicate Gruzelier's results in chronic (Tarrier *et al.*, 1978; Bernstein *et al.*, 1981), in acute (Toone *et al.*, 1981) or in remitted (Iacono, 1982) schizo-phrenics. Negative results even came from a former colleague of Gruzelier, Venables (1977), now working in York. Indeed, one of us has also been unable to observe any lateral effects in 54 acute schizophrenics, medicated or unmedicated (24), nor in comparison groups of neurotic and healthy subjects (Straube, 1983). Recent, carefully run studies have both refined recording conditions and extended the number of parameters measured (e.g., controlling for gender, latency, and recovery time). Individual, but no systematic, asymmetries have emerged from most reports. (For a review, see Freixa i Baque *et al.*, 1984.)

Nevertheless, recent reports from London claim that laterality of the EDOR varies with the symptoms. Those with smaller left-sided responses tend to show predominantly negative signs, whereas those with acute, florid symp-toms have higher EDOR amplitude in the left hand (Gruzelier, 1981, 1984; Gruzelier and Manchanda, 1982). However, with a lack of confirmation from elsewhere (Bernstein, 1987) and the absence of recent studies on the EDOR in patients with unilateral brain damage, we must conclude that EDOR studies, as yet, do not contribute to the discussion of the possible site or direction of asymmetric function in the CNS of schizophrenics.

# V. Biochemical Asymmetries

Whether there are neurochemical asymmetries in schizophrenic brain has more than academic consequences. To be sure, more or less dopamine (DA) activity on one side could be of etiological and pathological importance. Should neuroleptics (or other pharmacological agents), then, only affect that side of the brain (or improve the balance by an opposite effect on the other side)?

Further, the study of schizophrenics or their brain tissue assumes an understanding of what the normal asymmetries in the neurochemical system under study are and whether the neuroleptics with which they are usually treated induce asymmetries.

Studies of peripheral biochemical change are not likely to be sources of much information about CNS asymmetry, but signs of cerebral asymmetry could correlate with peripheral measures. This issue has, as yet, scarcely been addressed. However, Nyman and colleagues (1986) in Sweden did examine 23 schizophrenics, free of medication, for CT, neuropsychological, and CSF changes. They recorded increases of size in the third ventricle and left and right sylvian fissures. Wider ventricles correlated with neuropsychological tests sensitive to left hemisphere dysfunction, but there were no correlations between these signs and CSF measures of DA, NA, or 5-HT. It is a pity that the group did not investigate more carefully neurotransmitter metabolism, since levels of the parent monoamine alone are not clearly indicative of the activity of the system.

Investigations of brain tissue *postmortem* are often subject to constraints of availability. It is not always easy to obtain bilateral samples for analysis. Nonetheless, such comparisons have seldom been undertaken. As we have indicated elsewhere (Chapters 13 and 14), there is only one ongoing study that has shown lateral differences peculiar to schizophrenics (Reynolds, 1979, 1983). In material from more than 30 schizophrenics, Reynolds found a left-sided DA increase of over 40% in the amygdala. We cannot be sure whether this change reflected disease or neuroleptic treatment that the subjects surely had received. Reynolds did not report on the treatment history of his subjects. However, we may note that Mackay *et al.* (1982) found no obvious effect of long-term neuroleptic treatment on DA levels in the basal ganglia. Reynolds argued that a putative effect of treatment would be likely, at most, to accentuate an intrinsic asymmetry.

More recently, Reynolds and his colleagues in Nottingham and Toronto reported a 19% increase of $D_2$ binding sites in the right putamen of 16 schizophrenics (Reynolds *et al.*, 1987). In 6 of these, there was a 40% increase on one side; in 5 cases this was the right side. This supports hypotheses enunciated elsewhere for changes of DA metabolism in schizophrenia, and conceivably, in some cases, dysfunction lateralized on opposite sides along the anteroposterior axis (right frontostriate and left temporal systems) (Chapters 6 and 7).

Neuroleptics may also have a lateralized mode of action. The direction of this effect could even be different from that seen in healthy subjects because of cerebral asymmetry in schizophrenia. The issue is complex since healthy subjects probably show a number of neurochemical asymmetries, have an asymmetrical blood delivery system (Deshmukh and Meyer, 1978; Dabbs and Choo, 1980), and separate classes of neuroleptics have different lateralized effects (Tomer *et al.*, 1982).

Consider the following example. The intracarotid administration (i.e., unilateral cerebral supply) of three neuroleptics to rats induced limb abduction ipsilaterally and adduction contralaterally (Fritze, 1984). This may not be surprising because of asymmetries of blood flow (Waziri, 1980), but the pattern of response could be altered if there were unilateral pathological changes of DA activity (cf. Reynolds *et al.*, 1987). Further motor responses do seem to differ between neuroleptics with and without piperazine side chains, as was shown by a study of the effects of 15 antipsychotic agents on eye movements in Myslobodsky's laboratory (Tomer *et al.*, 1982). As we have mentioned when discussing ERPs, the same research group has shown that neural function may vary differentially as a function of Parkinsonian and dyskinesic symptoms, which themselves can appear on the left or the right side. The conclusion is that we do not have enough information on the lateralized effects of neuroleptics on normal and abnormally lateralized cerebral systems.

If there is a lack of detailed information about neurochemical asymmetries in the healthy human brain, there is a wealth of detail from animal studies. This is not the place to delve in detail into the literature, but a few points are pertinent to a balanced consideration of human studies.

Most studies have used the rat, but cats and monkeys have also been investigated. Some 80% of rats exhibit a more-or-less lateralized preference in their behavior as measured by a preferred direction for circling, a preferred direction of choice in a Y maze, or a preferred lever in an operant chamber. Of these rats, 85% prefer the right side (e.g., Castellano *et al.*, 1987). Ipsilateral to the preferred circling direction (which can be to the right or left), there is an increased ratio of $D_1$ to $D_2$ receptors in the basal ganglia (Glick *et al.*, 1988). (This recent report attempts to resolve the plethora of earlier conflicting evidence on the relationship of lateralized DA activity to turning preferences, but it confirms that, across the population, there is in general a 10–12% higher level of $D_1$ and $D_2$ receptors, and possibly of other measures of DA activity, on the left side; cf. Glick *et al.*, 1974; Jerussi and Taylor, 1982; Schneider *et al.*, 1982.) Frontal glucose metabolism is high and the hypothalamus more sensitive to the rewarding effects of electrical self-stimulation contralateral to this behavior preference (Glick *et al.*, 1979, 1980). A mosaic of left–right or right–left asymmetries has also been reported for the GABA, NA, 5-HT, and cholinergic transmitter systems (e.g., Valdes *et al.*, 1981; Starr and Kilpatrick, 1981; Oke *et al.*, 1983).

From these results one should expect some asymmetries, such as those that have been reported for DA and other transmitter systems in animals, in the normal human brain (e.g., Oke *et al.*, 1978, Glick and Ross, 1981; Reynolds *et al.*, 1987). These asymmetries are related to handedness (as in the rat). DA levels are higher on the left and $D_2$ receptors higher on the right. They may be expected to vary with metabolism in the frontal lobes (temporal lobes?) and with the disposition to various mental states.

Haloperidol treatment can alter the DA laterality in the rat (Jerussi and Taylor, 1982) and EEG laterality in humans (Section VIII). Although the high doses of amphetamine used by Glick and colleagues exaggerate behavioral and biochemical lateralization, lower doses attenuate biochemical asymmetry in the rat (Lee *et al.*, 1987) and EEG lateralization in humans (Section VIII). These results are important in view of the parallels between amphetamine-induced and schizophrenic psychoses and their treatment with neuroleptics.

It may be as important, for considerations of the etiology of the psychotic syndrome, that (1) unilateral brain damage, particularly to the dominant side, can affect cognitive (Glick and Cox, 1976), agonistic, and general (Robinson *et al.*, 1980) motor behavior, and unilateral ischemia can result in bilateral changes of monoaminergic activity (Robinson *et al.*, 1980); (2) bilateral frontal damage can exert unilateral effects that depend qualitatively on the side preference (handedness) of the animal (Ross and Glick, 1981); and (3) unilateral damage to homologous cortical regions on either side can exert quantitatively different effects on the DA systems of the two sides (Boyeson and Feeney, 1985).

We have cited evidence to show the numerous permutations and combinations of the possible interactions between treatment and unilateral brain damage and lateralized neurotransmitter systems. These details, these possibilities, *must* be considered in any hypothesis of lateralized dysfunction in schizophrenia.

## VI. Evidence from Motor Functions

### A. Reflexes

Could a change in the speed of neural processing in schizophrenia be shown by the limited number of neurons found in a muscular reflex? The Hoffman reflex was studied in a series of reports by Goode and colleagues (1977, 1980, 1981).

Electrical stimulation of the tibial nerve in the knee (innervating the gastrocnemius and soleus) results in an initial EMG response at 5 msec, followed by a reflex response at 35 msec. The recovery of excitability in the alpha motor afferent from the muscle spindle results in a facilitatory peak at 300 msec followed by a trough. These features can be ascertained by sending a second pulse at intervals varying up to a second after the first stimulation.

Pilot work on 7 schizophrenics by Goode *et al.* (1980) suggested that this effect was lateralized but independent of handedness. With 27 schizophrenic and schizoaffective subjects, tests for cognitive laterality (visual and dichotic) and of the Hoffmann reflex were conducted. The length of the reduction of the poststimulation excitable period correlated negatively with contralateral, usually left hemisphere, impairment ($r = -0.43$). However, this result could not be replicated in the third study ($n = 36$). Goode *et al.* (1981) maintained that the basic effect remained and was more marked with increased quantity and severity of negative symptoms. However, the subjects showed very variable responses. The failure to include healthy or other comparison groups makes it difficult to interpret the data.

## B. Eye Movements

Over 30 yr ago it was postulated that the direction of eye movements might reflect features of central information processing (Teitelbaum, 1954; Day, 1964). Directional preferences were recorded for individuals (Bakan, 1969) and attributed to activation of the contralateral hemisphere (Kinsbourne, 1970). Determinants of the preferred direction include personality traits (Barnat, 1974) and cognitive style (Harnad, 1972; Huang and Byrne, 1978). In response to verbal questions, the eyes move more often to the right and, after emotionally charged questions or those demanding spatial abilities, the eyes tend to move left (Kinsbourne, 1972; Schwartz, 1975). These authors disagreed about whether the reason for the preference was to ease lateral processing or was a result of lateralized processing needs. Either way it was believed to derive from changes in the frontal eye fields. Although the role of this area in eye movement control remains controversial, it does seem that the frontal region is important for scanning and that the closely connected superior colliculus is important for localizing stimuli. Both types of focused and unfocused activity can be inhibited by the substantia nigra. (For a review, see Levin, 1984.) Important for the interpretation of the effects in psychiatric patients is the report from Pardowski *et al.* (1978) that damage to the right side of the brain increases the incidence of eye movements to the right.

In a series of experiments with a range of psychiatric and healthy subjects, Gur (1977, 1978, 1979) recorded eye movements in response to verbal and spatial tasks with and without emotional content. For example, she compared 24 controls with 48 medicated schizophrenics, half of whom were paranoid (1978). Schizophrenics, in the same way as the controls, tended to show eye movements to the right after verbal and to the left after spatial questions. Just as in controls, when the experimenter sat in front of the subject (as opposed to behind), the emotional responses (to the left) were exaggerated. The paranoids showed, in particular, a stronger bias to right-sided movements and increased staring in all conditions. This was interpreted as indicating left-sided activation. Bearing in mind studies of brain damage, it may be more accurate to say that this reflects a right-sided problem. In support, Sandel and Alcorn (1980) reported more left bias in nonparanoid subjects with negative symptoms. This implies a left-sided impairment. Depressed subjects also showed this tendency but manic–depressives and schizoaffectives showed fewer left movements. The report of Gur was confirmed in her laboratory and elsewhere and found to be independent of medication (Schweitzer *et al.*, 1978; Schweitzer, 1979). More recent studies have found neither a normal pattern of lateralized eye movements nor a difference in psychiatric patients to be clearly distinguishable (Marder and Woods, 1987).

Interest in this field (and in the Hoffmann reflex) has fallen off over the last 10 years. Why should this be? More careful studies of eye movements in healthy subjects have sometimes failed to find marked preferences in response to, for example, verbal versus musical problem solving (Saring and Von Cramon, 1980). The earlier studies varied in which eye movements they recorded (e.g., stares, vertical movements), when they recorded them in relation to the question, and how they recorded them. The role of the environment may be crucial. The German study (mentioned above) was carried out in the dark. They found no preferences for the first eye movement, but a slight left preference during the thinking and answering periods if they included saccade measures.

## C. Handedness, Dyskinesias, and Turning

Let us briefly review two types of motor features discussed briefly in the foregoing sections—handedness and dyskinesia.

A large number of studies of handedness (cf. Section II) has produced equivocal results (Nasrallah, 1986; Taylor, 1987). A degree of sinistrality may be represented more in one subgroup of schizophrenia than in another and, thus, contribute to these discrepancies. If such a group exists, it could be the less severely ill or paranoid group (rather than nonparanoids or hebephrenics; Nasrallah *et al.*, 1982). The strongest evidence comes from just such patients in studies that included twins discordant for schizophrenia and handedness (Boklage, 1977; Luchins *et al.*, 1979, 1980). The schizophrenic twin was usually the left-handed one. Of course the opposing idea, that right handers are less susceptible to schizophrenia, should not be inferred. Truly identical monozygotic twins showed a 92% concordance for right-handedness and for schizophrenia. (Mirror-image twins showed a 25% concordance for schizophrenia.) Interestingly, perhaps because the definition of sinistrality seemed to include any degree of deviation from pure right-handedness, the schizoaffective patients were predominantly left-handed. In contrast, the right-handed twin of left-handed patients tended to be depressive.

The identification of the preferred hand may of course represent the extreme of a lateralized change in the psychiatric group. Some patients with right-handed preferences may show the start of other unusual lateralizations. As just one example of this, Merrin (1984) studied hand-grip strength in this same diagnostic group of paranoid schizophrenics. Whereas hand grip correlated with handedness in normal subjects, there was no correlation in the schizophrenic group.

Such an incongruity with respect to normal patterns of lateralization for two or more features has been claimed to be more characteristic of schizophrenics than a dominance change for one of these features (Doty, 1989). This review puts emphasis on a finding by Piran et al. (1982). They reported that, in a sample of 26 schizophrenics, 16 brain-damaged psychotics, and 36 healthy controls, an incongruous laterality such as right-hand but left-eye dominance distinguished 81% of the patients (12% false positives, brain-damaged like schizophrenics, and 27% false negatives, schizophrenics like brain-damaged). Irrespective of the methodological problems of such studies, it might be fair to say that a misclassification of 25% of the subjects was low enough to warrant pursuit of the general hypothesis that there may be lateralized differences of cerebral processing in schizophrenics, but is too high to allow conclusions about the specific measurements made.

Indeed, if one is to draw any conclusions from such studies, it is appropriate, finally, to question the assumption that handedness is necessarily linked to other functions, even the lateralization of speech. Geschwind and Galaburda (1985) speculate that random dominance and even right-sided shifts for speech specialization may be more frequent than supposed. Such variance in the baseline could contribute to the inconsistencies in schizophrenia research.

Dyskinesias may involve limb movements and/or orofacial twitches. They are thought, often but not necessarily, to arise as a consequence of neuroleptic treatment. They appear bilaterally in about half of all cases, but they can appear lateralized to the left or right side. Brain damage in the region of the frontal eye fields, particularly on the left side, can produce contralateral dyskinesia (Section V). One would suppose the prevalence of unilateral dyskinesias to reflect normal lateralized cerebral dominance tendencies, which may vary in a substantial minority of individuals (see previous text). Right-sided dyskinesias, particularly of limb movements, have been reported commonly (Waziri, 1980; Burke et al., 1982; Myslobodsky et al., 1984; Wilson et al., 1984), but a recent detailed study of orofacial movements using ultrasound sensors in 27 schizophrenics without lateralized limb dyskinesias found more left-sided twitches in all cases (Altschuler et al., 1988).

At the other extreme, dystonias involving posture and even circling behavior while walking have been observed in neuroleptic-treated schizophrenics (Corbin et al., 1987) and dementing patients (Ekbom et al., 1972). Rotation to the left and the right was seen in different individuals. (The reader should bear in mind the uneven lateralized effects of different neuroleptic medications.) Indeed, Bracha (1987) found that, while normal individuals turn left as often as they turn right during the course of a day's activity, a group of 10 unmedicated (some never treated) schizophrenics showed a 70% preference for turning left, even though their overall activity was not significantly different. The implications for asymmetries in the frontal lobe–basal ganglia axis and the parallel with animal studies of DA function have been drawn (Section V).

## VII. Evidence from Sensory Information Processing: Vision, Activation, and Visual Attention

Many of the very large number of tests of psychological function have been applied to questions about lateralization of the underlying processes. Only a limited selection can be made here. Three types of study are important: the presentation of visual stimuli to different fields (this section) dichotic auditory discrimination, and tactile processing between the two hands (next section). Such designs permit study of hemispheric function and their interactions.

Visual studies related to lateralized function rely on hemispheric preferences for processing stimuli presented to the contralateral hemi-retina (cf. Figure 9.1 and description of the Sperry experiment).

An early influential study was that of Beaumont and Dimond (1973), who compared the performance of schizophrenics with that of psychiatric and control subjects (12 each) on a test of their ability to match verbal and spatial stimuli presented to the same or opposite visual fields. The schizophrenics made more errors in all conditions: matching words in the left hemisphere, pictures in the right hemisphere, and stimuli across hemispheres. Unfortunately, full details of diagnosis and methods were not reported. Theories of right- or left-lateralized and hemispheric transfer deficits are supported. Perhaps there was a general performance deficit. No relevant control was reported.

Eaton conducted a similar study for her doctoral dissertation on 51 schizophrenics. Later she replicated the main results for 24 medication-free schizophrenics (Eaton, 1979; Eaton *et al.*, 1979). She presented naming tasks and tests of the ability to match form and digits (respectively, left, right, and nonspecific hemispheric specializations). The main result was a slow reaction time on the naming task. Reintroduction of neuroleptic therapy improved not only the impaired naming performance (a presumed left hemisphere function), but also the letter-matching performance, presumably carried out more in the right hemisphere.

At about the same time, Gur (1978) also ran a study of 24 medicated schizophrenics and controls matched for educational and social backgrounds. Subjects had to report on either the position of a dot in a rectangle or the nature of a nonsense syllable, presented to either visual field. The schizophrenics were impaired overall, but did show a right hemisphere advantage for the spatial task, as did the controls. They did not show a left-hemisphere advantage for syllable identification. Further, similar work with 10 schizophrenics revealed not just the absence of the left-hemisphere advantage for verbal stimuli, but an advantage for the right side (Connolly *et al.*, 1983).

However, it may be legitimate here to question whether the different tasks presented had been matched for differing degrees of difficulty (cf. Chapman and Chapman, 1973).

Interpretations of these and reports of similar results (for review, see Taylor, 1987) vary from left-hemisphere impairment (Gruzelier, 1983) to interhemisphere interaction difficulties (Gur, 1978), and do not exclude mild bilateral dysfunction.

Those who prefer the left-hemisphere dysfunction hypothesis should consider the evidence for visual tasks tapping other right-hemisphere specializations (e.g., emotion and attention-related activation).

In normal individuals, the right hemisphere is strongly involved in processing information about faces and, in particular, the emotion they show (Heilman and Valenstein, 1979). A number of studies have shown that schizophrenics from different subgroups are poor in identifying emotions depicted in photographs and on videotapes of faces (Dougherty *et al.*, 1974; Muzekari and Bates, 1977; Cutting, 1981). This feature has even been claimed for the children of a schizophrenic parent (Anthony, 1978). However these reports can be criticized on the grounds of task specificity (the use of verbal reports incurs potential problems beyond those associated with the visual task) and diagnostic specificity (few sub- and comparison groups were used to illustrate the uniqueness of the impairment). However, the study by Cutting is of interest because it points out a deficit in the acutely ill that did not extend to judgments of color or of the age of the subjects portrayed.)

Feinberg and colleagues (1986) obviated some of these problems by asking subjects to match pictures for the emotion illustrated, and to match them independent of the emotional content. They used pictures of similar and dissimilar models of both sexes showing a wide range of expressions. Responses had to be marked in the appropriate "same" or "different" column of a score sheet. They compared 20 chronic schizophrenics and 20 depressed inpatients of the Mt. Sinai Hospital in New York with 20 healthy controls. Schizophrenics were impaired on tests of emotion and identity matching. Depressed subjects scored high errors only on the emotion-matching task (cf. Morrison *et al.*, 1988; Chapter 1).

A report from Heilman's group in Florida using the Posner test of the *covert orienting of attention*[1] has shown no laterality effects in healthy normal

---

[1]Of the several varieties of Posner task applied, we describe elements of the procedure of Posner *et al.* (1988). Subjects must fixate a cross on a monitor throughout the task (i.e., no eye movements). They press a key when they detect a star in a square subtending 1° at 4° to the right or left of the cross. On cued trials (80%), the square brightens 100 msec before the target appears; on 20% of cued trials, the star appears in the opposite square (i.e., miscue condition; intertrial interval, 1100–1800 msec). Measures of reaction time refer to the benefit of cueing with respect to no cue and the cost of miscueing. Arrows or words can be displayed indicating whether response should be made with the hand or finger on the left or the right side (Figure 9.4).

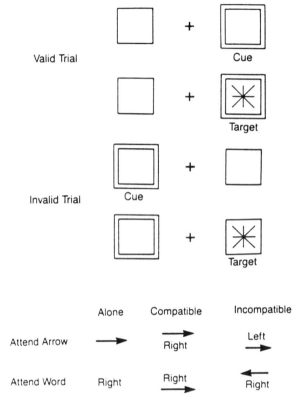

**Figure 9.4** Schematic examples of stimulus conditions that can be presented in the covert visual-orienting task. The subject fixates the cross in the midline. The "cue" condition involves brightening of one of the peripheral boxes. When a "target" (a star) appears on the cued side, then the condition is considered valid; when it appears on the uncued side, it is called invalid. In the arrow–word conflict version of this task, the symbol or word command may appear alone in the midline, together and be compatible, or together and be incompatible (after Posner *et al.*, 1988, © American Medical Association).

subjects, that is, there were no benefits in being cued in one direction or the other about where a target will appear with respect to the costs (reaction-time delays) of incorrect cues.

There are differences favoring right-hemisphere processing if the cue refers to the hand that should be used for response when the target is seen (Verfaellie *et al.*, 1988). Together, the two results have been interpreted as showing right-hemisphere specialization for intention but not for the orienting of attention.

However, compared with conditions with no warnings, warning stimuli in the left visual field can reduce reaction times more than warnings in the right field (Heilman and Van den Abell, 1979). Thus activation, necessary for pursuant selection and processing, is a right hemisphere specialization. This was confirmed independently by Kostandov (1980) using a backward masking procedure (Chapter 2). The advantage for stimuli in the left visual field was not evident in the 14 remitted schizophrenics described in this report.

Recently Posner himself has examined the performance of 12 schizophrenics (DSM-III-R) and 30 healthy controls on his task. For schizophrenics, the speed of detection of the targets to the left and right of the fixation point were slower if the target had been cued. In the absence of a cue or in the presence of a false cue, detection latencies to stimuli in the right field were much longer (Figure 9.5). The longest reaction times on the right came from three subjects who had never received neuroleptics. Sixteen unipolar and bipolar subjects showed left-field (right-hemisphere) impairment.

This fascinating report does not stop with these results. The experimenters noticed that many of the subjects talked to themselves during the task. The

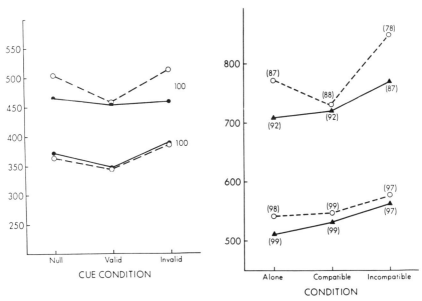

**Figure 9.5** *Left,* Mean reaction times for 12 schizophrenics (upper) and 30 normal subjects (lower) in the spatial covert orienting of attention task as a function of cued condition (no cue, valid, invalid), visual field (left—, right---) at a cue to target interval of 100 ms. *Right;* mean reaction times for ten schizophrenic and 12 normal subjects in the arrow-word conflict task as a function of stimulus condition (alone, compatible, incompatible) and instruction condition (attend arrow, attend word). Mean percent correct is shown in parentheses (after Posner et al., 1988). © American Medical Association.

possibility that this reflected auditory hallucinations and the fact that those with most marked hallucinations performed poorly prompted them to investigate the potential contribution of left-sided activation of the language center to the delay of right-sided detection. Indeed, they found that the performance of controls who had to shadow a story aloud during performance contributed to a right-sided detection delay, but the effect was much weaker than that exhibited by the schizophrenics.

The pattern of detection impairment seemed to reflect left-hemisphere dysfunction, yet in detail it did not match the well-described patterns deriving from damage to the parietal, thalamic, and midbrain centers known to be involved in the orienting of attention from studies in brain-damaged humans and monkeys. Could the effect be due to problems with the left prefrontal cingulate area, implicated in PET studies in the attention to language (Petersen *et al.*, 1988)? The task was repeated with 10 of their patients, with instructions to respond with the left or right (index, middle) finger of the dominant hand, according to the arrows or words displayed (Figure 9.4). Posner already knew the pattern to be expected from patients with left- or right-sided brain damage (they show, respectively, difficulties with the words or the symbols). Individual patients with closed-head injuries, who are also slower to orient to the right, respond poorly if the word conflicts with the arrow. This result was, indeed, also obtained with the schizophrenic group (Figure 9.5). Further, despite the small numbers, there was a significant effect of medication. Neuroleptics impaired performance under the attend-arrow condition and improved performance under the attend-word condition. Preliminary results from the replication with subjects before and after medication confirm the effect for the word condition.

The evidence speaks for a deficit in the schizophrenic group in the ability to coordinate visual location and language involving left-sided anterior regions (e.g., prefrontal cingulate).

## VIII. Evidence from Sensory Information Processing

### A. Auditory Tasks

Dichotic presentations of sounds or verbal stimuli, simultaneously or sequentially to each ear, show that there is usually a right ear advantage (REA) for the processing of this information in normal healthy subjects. This reflects the dominant crossed connection to the speech centers of the left hemisphere. (The neuronal pathway is shown in Figure 9.6; note, as with vision there is a less significant ipsilateral connection.) Left temporal lobe damage reduces overall discriminative performance, but particularly the REA (Schulhoff and Goodglass, 1969; Sparks *et al.*, 1970; Efron *et al.*, 1983). Even right-handed stutterers are said to have less of an REA (Sussman and McNeilage, 1975).

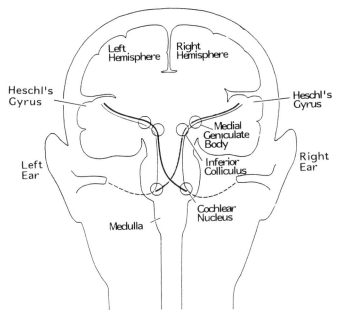

**Figure 9.6** Schematic illustration of the neuronal path from the ears over the inferior colliculus and medial geniculate (thalamus) to the contralateral auditory cortex. The thin line represents the minor ipsilateral pathway.

Auditory thresholds have been examined as a function of frequency, loudness, and length of sound. The main finding of Gruzelier's group in London with chronic schizophrenics was of marked inter- and intraindividual variability over time. Independent of medication or symptom severity, the group could record both an REA and its later disappearance (Gruzelier and Hammond, 1976; 1979; Kugler et al., 1982).

Perhaps the investigators should have looked at whether the patients were hallucinating. An interesting result, reminiscent of one of Posner's findings, comes from Leningrad (Bazhin *et al.*, 1975). This group reported a higher threshold for tones played to the right ear in hallucinating subjects. Paranoids and healthy subjects did not differ (Figure 9.7). [Similarly, a poor perfor-mance on the right side for hallucinating schizophrenics was reported by Alpert *et al.* (1976) using verbal material.] Balogh *et al.* (1979) also found that process-paranoid schizophrenics had difficulties localizing sound sources. The performance was compared with psychiatric and normal controls (12 per group). Sound sources ranged from 0.5° to 4.5° from the midline. This is similar to the attention-orienting movements studied by Posner (see previous section). The schizophrenics were particularly impaired for sounds from the right and when sounds were closer to the midline on the right.

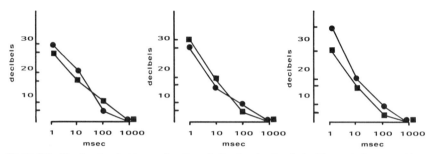

**Figure 9.7**   Hearing thresholds as a function of stimulus duration in healthy controls, paranoid schizophrenics, and schizophrenics with auditory hallucinations (after Bazhin *et al.*, 1985).

Using sounds, syllables, or words, some investigators have found no changes in the REA for schizophrenics compared with controls (Bull and Venables, 1974; Straube and Germer, 1979). This lack of effect is also the considered opinion of Bruder (1983) in reviewing this field of study. Particularly if the stimuli require discrimination of physical stimulus characteristics rather than semantic comprehension (as in story shadowing), some claim to find an exaggerated REA [Lerner *et al.*, 1977; Nachson, 1980; Gruzelier and Hammond, 1980; Walker and McGuire, 1982; Lishman *et al.*, 1978 (males only)]. The importance of the two different task situations is borne out by a study from Wexler (1986) comparing the ability to discriminate tones and fused–rhymed words (different lead consonant, same syllable, binaural overlap). The asymmetry of discrimination of tones was evident in all groups, but on the latter task (with semantic content) asymmetry attenuated or disappeared.

Surprisingly, it seems that if an exaggerated REA is widespread, it appears to be of little use for processing simultaneously presented verbal material (e.g., stories). Whereas recognition for material presented to the right ear may not be impaired, comprehension is; the REA is lost while symptoms persist (Wexler and Heninger, 1979; Yosawitz *et al.*, 1979; Green and Kotenko, 1980; Johnson and Crockett, 1982; Kugler, 1983) and may even be attenuated in children with a schizophrenic parent (Hallett *et al.*, 1986). Indeed, the performance often seems to be slightly impaired bilaterally. When medication has been considered, it appears to reduce the anomalies recorded, particularly in left-hemisphere processing (Gruzelier, 1983).

Some support for an emphasis on comprehension abilities comes from a study carried out in Tokyo (Niwa *et al.*, 1983). Patients were asked to discriminate a target from among 4 frequency-modulated tones presented to both ears. In different sessions (total = 10), subjects directed their attention to one particular side. A thousand stimuli were presented, which illustrates the emphasis on vigilance. The relatively slow reaction time and high number of errors of omission can be regarded as a reflection of a general vigilance deficit. These measures were not related to the ear receiving the stimulus, but the relatively low number of commission errors were more common after right ear presentations.

The variations on the paradigm used in each study are too numerous and complex to be discussed here. Most of these studies show deficient methods with inadequate controls for the physical character of the sounds or words presented and the order of report. They take little account of the state or personality of the subjects tested. One cannot ascribe any particular effect to one diagnostic category. Most theories of lateralization can find a measure of support from individual sets of results. Perhaps more remarkable than the nature of the REA in schizophrenics is the need felt by some authors to comment on the minority of patients showing a left-ear advantage for verbal stimuli (cf. nonhallucinators of Alpert *et al.,* 1976; Lishman *et al.,* 1978; Wexler and Heninger, 1979; Green and Kotenko, 1980). One possible interpretation here is that a subgroup of patients may show more of a right hemisphere involvement (cf. Geschwind and Galaburda, 1985; Section VI).

## B. Tactile Tasks

As in the other sensory modalities, tactile (haptic) information predominantly passes first to the contralateral hemisphere. More than in the other modalities, investigators of haptic information processing have been concerned about the subsequent transfer of this information from one to the other side. Thus, interpretations of results often concern the adequacy of interhemispheric transfer and, by implication, potential dysfunction in the corpus callosum that contains the fibers crossing between the hemispheres.

With one exception (Jones and Miller, 1981), ERP studies do not question the dominance of the contralateral hemisphere (Gulman *et al.,* 1982; Shagass *et al.,* 1983). In contrast, psychological studies, although of heuristic interest, are full of varied methods, inadequate controls for task difficulty (Green, 1978; Weller and Kugler, 1979), and conflicting results. (For a review, see Walker and McGuire, 1982.)

In this paradigm, subjects are usually blindfolded and are given an object in one hand to discriminate or recognize. The crucial test requires intermanual transfer. Can the object be identified with the other hand? Does the speed of recognition change? Some tasks are simple tasks of localization (e.g., Dimond *et al.,* 1980); others measure the number of errors made in recall (e.g., Carr, 1980) or the number of trials to learn a discrimination (Green, 1978). These studies and others purport to show that schizophrenics have problems on the intermanual transfer condition. The impairment is either not lateralized (Dimond *et al.,* 1980) or there is no right-sided advantage, implicating left-hemispheric impairment (Kugler and Henley, 1979; Weller and Kugler, 1979;

Torrey, 1980). In some patients, as in some of the mentioned auditory studies, the deficit was transitory (Dimond *et al.*, 1979). In others, there is no distinction between the performance of schizophrenics and other psychiatric groups (Wade and Taylor, 1984). These findings along with the often-recorded general performance deficit render interpretations in terms of callosal transfer unconvincing (cf. Gruzelier, 1983).

## C. Corpus Callosum

Is the corpus callosum different in schizophrenics? Across these 200 million or so fibers (Sperry, 1982), the cerebral cortices of the two hemispheres communicate (cf. Section I). This represents about 2% of total cortical neurons. The statistic seems to indicate either that the hemispheres can operate relatively independently or that there is much convergence on interhemispheric connections; perhaps both occur to some extent. (Intriguingly there is an absence of direct interhemispheric connections from the amygdala.) Among normal subjects, the size of the corpus callosum can vary by a factor of 2 and that of the anterior commissures by a factor of 7. In development, myelination of callosal fibers may not be complete before the age of 12 yr, and functional maturation may take a few years longer. (For reviews, see Innocenti, 1986; Pandya and Seltzer, 1986; Demeter *et al.*, 1988; Doty, 1989.)

It has been claimed from *postmortem* measures that this fiber bundle is thicker in schizophrenics (Rosenthal and Bigelow, 1972; Bigelow *et al.*, 1983). This could mean increased connectivity through more fibers or increased pathology impairing transfer of information. Although some would claim (see previous paragraphs) that transfer was impaired, Tress *et al.* (1979) have suggested the opposite. They studied the interocular transfer of movement aftereffects. Transfer is absent in subjects with callosal agenesis (a failure of callosal development). Two-thirds of these subjects showed effects in which the difference between ipsi- and contralateral measures was smaller than normal. This slight effect suggests too much rather than too little information transfer.

However, is the callosum reliably bigger? In the initial *postmortem* study, the comparison was between 10 chronic schizophrenics and alcoholic or personality-disturbed patients. This seems hardly the most appropriate comparison group for an increase in size. However, the authors insist, after replication, on an increase in comparison with neurological (13) and other psychiatric subjects (14) in which morphological degeneration seemed unlikely. The increase was more anterior than posterior ($n = 29$). Together with Nasrallah, they found no signs of increased glia nor of increased fibers, but fibrillary gliosis was increased in late onset paranoids in comparison with early onset nonparanoids (Nasrallah *et al.*, 1983). This contradicts an earlier conference report from Nasrallah's laboratory using the same material as

Bigelow *et al.* (1983). Then, using MRI techniques, Nasrallah found, first, smaller anterior quartile (again, a conflict) and smaller relative size in young male schizophrenics (as presented in a conference report), an observation which later was interpreted as increased size in female schizophrenics with respect to normal controls (Nasrallah *et al.*, 1986). It is likely that measures vary considerably with age as well as with the purported age of onset. Although Smith *et al.* (1984) and Rossi (1988) found no differences, a slight increase in callosal length was reported by Mathew *et al.* (1985), particularly anteriorly (Uematsu *et al.*, 1988), with MRI techniques. Although one might not quarrel with individual differences in the corpus callosum, the robustness of an effect specific to schizophrenia surely remains in question.

A recent in-depth MRI study of 12 pairs of monozygotic twins discordant for schizophrenia at the NIMH (Casanova *et al.*, 1990) found no real change of callosal size. Instead, their analysis suggested that in the presence of ventricular enlargement the callosum can acquire a distorted shape. This could explain the heterogeneity of result reported by earlier investigators.

# IX. Suggested Readings

For a comprehensive and insightful survey of normal and unusual aspects of asymmetry of structure and function, the reader should consult the three-part review by Geschwind and Galaburda (1985), which has recently been published in book form (1990). Heilman *et al.* (1986) and Hellige (1990) have also reviewed much of the field, whereas the reviews of Taylor (1987), Flor-Henry (1989), and Doty (1989) specifically consider the feature with respect to schizophrenia.

# X. Summary Statements and Interpretations

## A. Neuropsychological Tests

No clear pattern emerges from neuropsychological tests despite several claims of evidence for specifically left- or right-hemispheric disturbance.

There is limited evidence for subgroup differences in a few studies: It is possible that more withdrawn subjects have more problems with tests demanding more left-hemispheric functions, whereas patients with more productive symptoms have more problems with tests demanding more right-sided functions.

No clear picture arises from the heterogeneous nature of the neuropsychological tests used and from the different subgroups tested. From the more extensive results discussed in Chapters 2–4, it is unlikely that any clear lateralized pattern is applicable for all schizophrenics. They are impaired on verbal tests (left hemisphere) as well as in facial recognition or Gestalt tasks (right hemisphere).

Another general problem is the inference made from the examined function to the lateralization within the brain. The relationship is less stringent than often believed (cf. Gazzaniga, 1983). Without direct evidence from brain studies, no firm claim can be made.

## B. Brain-Imaging Techniques

### 1. CT and NMR

Although the database is small, most studies suggest more alterations on the left side of the brain in schizophrenics. One team reports on subgroup differences: They found more left frontal atrophy in patients with predominant negative symptoms and more left temporal atrophy in those with positive symptoms.

There are too few unequivocal findings to support any general conclusions. Nevertheless, the findings are heuristically interesting. Is there really a subgroup with more left-sided problems? Are the frontal and temporal parts differentially involved in subgroups?

### 2. CBF and PET

There is no clear evidence for deviant lateral activation; some report higher activation on the right and some on the left hemisphere.

In view of potential lateralized neurotransmitter function most studies may be confounded by medication effects.

## C. Brain and Peripheral Electrical Activity

### 1. EEG

EEG anomalies are heterogeneous, can appear on either side (as in other illnesses), and do not indicate which hemisphere shows changed function. Resting EEGs show no clear lateralized spectral differences (e.g., diffuse increase of delta activity). It would be useful to compare subjects with elevated or depressed emotions or clearly productive or nonproductive symptoms during task performance. One possible subgroup difference emerges: Paranoid patients (especially with hallucinations) show increased activation (less alpha) over the left hemisphere (*N.B.*, active hallucinators show unusual CBF at the left side of the brain).

Methodological problems include artifact (eye movement) removal and the amount of EEG sampled. A more general conceptual problem concerns the localization of the deviance. Does changed activity on the one side indicate deviant processing on this side of the brain or the other and can a putative defect on one side lead to changes of the intact hemisphere?

### 2. EP

Most investigators find a left hemisphere deficit, but some report only an attenuation of normal lateralization or no changes. This applies to early as well as middle and late potentials.

Reports of attenuated lateral differences could reflect unilateral, bilateral, or interhemispheric transmission changes. It is therefore not clear what is the basis of a lateralized change in these groups.

Are there subgroup differences of real hemispheric deficits? The issue is controversial: among those reporting a left-sided deficit, some see an association with positive and others with negative symptoms.

### 3. EDOR

There is no unequivocal evidence for a lateralized deficit. Earlier reports of smaller left-hand responses were not confirmed. One study found that with-drawn negative-symptom patients had higher amplitudes on the right hand (left hemisphere) and more active positive-symptom patients had higher left-hand amplitudes.

These subgroup differences need to be replicated.

## D. Dopamine (DA) System

First indications of changes of the DA system in right anterior and left posterior subcortical regions require elaboration and confirmation. A claim for increased *postmortem* levels of DA in the left amygdala needs to be replicated by other teams.

As yet, the range of individual variability and the range of lateralized effects of neuroleptic treatment have been inadequately appreciated and investigated in psychiatric patients.

Animal and human studies suggest that lateralization in the normal DA system may be related to cortical and subcortical mechanisms for mediating the effects of reward.

## E. Motor and Movement Functions: Muscular Reflexes

The few studies show no clear evidence for lateralization.

### 1. Eye Movements

Earlier findings of exaggerated movements to the right in paranoid subjects and a bias to the left in nonparanoid negative-symptom schizophrenics are not confirmed.

A problem with this area of research is that, even in normal subjects, a clearly distinctive lateralized movement does not always occur in response to certain task demands, as might be expected (e.g., left movements in response to spatial tasks and right movements to verbal tasks).

### 2. Handedness

Examination of discordant monozygotic twins reveals a slightly higher incidence of left-handedness in the affected twin, but results from other schizophrenic samples are equivocal.

The twin finding provides additional information to the puzzle of how monozygotic twins can be discordant for schizophrenia. We have discussed reports of a lower birth weight in the affected twin. These results may indicate a disturbance of perinatal development affecting brain development, but a shift in handedness does not explain schizophrenia in general, where no clear pattern emerges for nontwin groups.

## F. Information Processing

### 1. Lateralization—Visual Hemifield Detection

Numerous studies in this field point equally often to a left as well as a right-sided deficit.

There is little evidence for differential subgroup effects to solve these contradictions. One study claims the presence of hallucinations is likely to be accompanied by a deficit in left-hemisphere processing.

### 2. Lateralization—Dichotic Shadowing

Most authors report that the normal right ear advantage for verbal stimuli (left-hemisphere function) is present (even exaggerated) in schizophrenics. Some find that a minority of their patients have a left-side advantage in dichotic tasks. Again, hallucinating subjects may show a biased performance (e.g., a higher threshold for tones presented to the right ear). There is also a report of a higher right-ear omission rate on a target detection task, but the hallucination factor was not controlled.

From these studies in the visual and auditory modality there is not much evidence for a lateralized deficit in schizophrenia as a whole, but there may be lateralization in certain subgroups. The only information at hand concerns schizophrenics with auditory hallucinations. They perform poorly if stimuli are presented to the right ear (left hemisphere).

### 3. Hemispheric Transfer: Tactile Transfer and Corpus Callosum Anatomy

There is no clear evidence for a deficit in hemispheric transfer of tactile information. Reports of changes in the corpus callosum are unconvincing and have been disconfirmed.

# References

Abrams, R., and Taylor, M. A. (1979). Laboratory studies in the validation of psychiatric diagnoses. In J. Gruzelier and P. Flor-Henry (Eds.), *Hemispheric asymmetries of function in psychiatric diagnoses*, pp. 363–373. Amsterdam: Elsevier.

Alpert, M., and Martz, J. (1977). Cognitive views of schizophrenia in light of recent studies of brain asymmetry. In C. Shagass, S. Gershon, and A. Friedhoff (Eds.), *Psychopathology and brain dysfunction*, pp. 1–13. New York: Raven.

Alpert, M., Rubenstein, H., and Kesselman, M. (1976). Asymmetry of information processing in hallucinators and nonhallucinators. *Journal of Nervous and Mental Diseases*, *162*, 258–265.

Altshuler, L. L., Cummings, J. L., Bartzokis, G., Hill, M. A., and May, P. R. A. (1988). Lateral asymmetries of tardive dyskinesia in schizophrenia. *Biological Psychiatry*, *24*, 83–86.

Andreasen, N. C., and Olsen, S. (1982). Negative versus positive schizophrenia. *Archives of General Psychiatry*, *39*, 789–794.

Andreasen, N. C., Olsen, S. A., Dennert, J. W., and Smith, M. R. (1982). Ventricular enlargement in schizophrenia: Relationship to positive and negative symptoms. *American Journal of Psychiatry*, *139*, 297–302.

Anthony, B. (1978). Piagetian egocentrism, empathy, and affect discrimination in children at high risk for psychosis. In E. Anthony (Ed.), *The child in his family*, pp. 359–379. New York: Wiley.

Ariel, R. N., Golden, C. J., Berg, R. A., Quaife, M. A., Dirksen, J. W., Forsell, T., Wilson, J., and Graber, B. (1983). Regional cerebral blood flow in schizophrenics: Tests using the xenon XE 133 inhalation method. *Archives of General Psychiatry*, *40*, 258–263.

Bakan, P. (1969). Hypnotizability, laterality of eye movements and functional brain asymmetry. *Perceptual and Motor Skills*, *28*, 927–932.

Balogh, D. W., Schuck, J. R., and Leventhal, D. B. (1979). A study of schizophrenics' ability to localize the source of a sound. *Journal of Nervous and Mental Diseases*, *167*, 484–487.

Barnat, M. R. (1974). Some personality correlates of the conjugate lateral eye-movement phenomenon. *Journal of Personality Assessment*, *38*, 223–225.

Bazhin, E. F., Wasserman, L. I., and Tonkongii, I. M. (1975). Auditory hallucinations and left temporal lobe pathology. *Neuropsychologia*, *13*, 481–487.

Beaumont, J. G., and Dimond, S. (1973). Brain disconnection and schizophrenia. *British Journal of Psychiatry*, *123*, 661–662.

Bernstein, A., Taylor, K., Starkey, P., Juni, S., Lubowsky, J., and Paley, H. (1981). Bilateral skin conductance, finger pulse volume, and EEG orienting response to tones of differing intensities in chronic schizophrenics and controls. *Journal of Nervous and Mental Disease*, *169*, 513–528.

Bernstein, A. S. (1987). Orienting response research in schizophrenia: Where we have come and where we might go. *Schizophrenia Bulletin, 13*, 623–641.

Besson, J. A. O., Corrigan, F. M., Cherryman, G. R., and Smith, F. W. (1987). Nuclear magnetic resonance brain imaging in chronic schizophrenia. *British Journal of Psychiatry, 150*, 161–163.

Bigelow, L. B., Nasrallah, H. A., and Rauscher, F. P. (1983). Corpus callosum thickness in chronic schizophrenia. *British Journal of Psychiatry, 142*, 284–287.

Boklage, E. C. (1977). Schizophrenia, brain asymmetry development and twinning: Cellular relationship with etiological and possibly prognostic implications. *Biological Psychiatry, 12*, 17–35.

Boyeson, M. G., and Feeney, D. M. (1985). Striatal dopamine after cortical injury. *Experimental Neurology, 89*, 479–483.

Bracha, H. S. (1987). Asymmetric rotational (circling) behavior, a dopamine-related asymmetry: Preliminary findings in unmedicated and never medicated schizophrenic patients. *Biological Psychiatry, 22*, 995–1003.

Bradshaw, J. L., and Nettleton, N. C. (1981). The nature of hemispheric specialization in man. *The Behavioral and Brain Sciences, 4*, 51–92.

Bradshaw, J. L., and Nettleton, N. C. (1983). *Human cerebral asymmetry*. Englewood Cliffs, New Jersey: Prentice-Hall.

Bryden, M. P. (Ed.) (1982). *Laterality: Functional asymmetry in the intact brain*. New York: Academic Press.

Bruder, G. E. (1983). Cerebral laterality and psychopathology: A review of dichotic listening studies. *Schizophrenia Bulletin, 9*, 134–151.

Buchsbaum, M. S., Carpenter, W. T., Fedio, P., Goodwin, F. K., Murphy, D. L., and Post, R. M. (1979). Hemispheric differences in evoked potential enhancement by selective attention to hemiretinally presented stimuli in schizophrenic, affective and post-temporal lobectomy patients. In J. Gruzelier and P. Flor-Henry (Eds.), *Hemisphere asymmetries of function in psychopathology*, pp. 317–328. Amsterdam: Elsevier.

Buchsbaum, M. S., Wu, J. C., DeLisi, L. E., Holcomb, H. H., Hazlett, E., Cooper-Langston, K., and Kessler, R. (1987). Positron emission tomography studies of basal ganglia and somatosensory cortex neuroleptic drug effects: Differences between normal controls and schizophrenic patients. *Biological Psychiatry, 22*, 479–494.

Bull, H. C., and Venables, P. H. (1974). Speech perception in schizophrenia. *British Journal of Psychiatry, 125*, 350–354.

Burke, R. E., Fahn, S., Jankowic, J., Marsden, C. D., Lane, A. E., Gollomp, S., and Heon, J. (1982). Tardive dystonia: Late onset and persistent dystonia caused by antipsychotic drugs. *Neurology, 32*, 1335–1346.

Burns, E. M., Nasrallah, H. A., Kathol, M. H., Kruckeberg, T. W., and Coffman, J. A. (1987). Right versus left hemispheric blood-brain barrier permeability in schizophrenia: A dynamic computed tomographic study. *Psychiatry Research, 22*, 229–241.

Casanova, M. F., Sanders, R. D., Goldberg, T. E., Bigelow, L. B., Christison, G., Torrey, E. F., and Weinberger, D. R. (1990). Morphometry of the corpus callosum in monozygotic twins discordant for schizophrenia: A magnetic resonance imaging study. *Journal of Neurology, Neurosurgery and Psychiatry, 53*, 416–421.

Carr, S. A. (1980). Interhemispheric transfer of sterognostic information in chronic schizo-phrenics. *British Journal of Psychiatry, 136*, 53–58.

Castellano, M. A., Diaz-Palarea, M. D., Rodriguez, M., and Barroso, J. (1987). Lateralization in male rats and dopaminergic system: Evidence of right sided population bias. *Physiology and Behavior, 40*, 607–612.

Chapman, L. J., and Chapman, J. P. (1973). Disordered thought in schizophrenia. In K. M.

Corquodale, G. Lindzey, and K. E. Clark, (Eds.). Englewood Cliffs, New Jersey: Prentice-Hall.

Cleghorn, J. M., and Garnett, E. S. (1991). Patterns of regional brain metabolism during auditory hallucinations *Biological Psychiatry, 29,* 75.

Coffman, J. A., Andreasen, N. C., and Nasrallah, H. A. (1984). Left hemisphere density deficits in chronic schizophrenia. *Biological Psychiatry, 19,* 1237–1247.

Coger, R. W., Dymond, A. M., and Serafetinides, E. A. (1979). Electroencephalographic similarities between chronic alcoholics and chronic, nonparanoid schizophrenics. *Archives of General Psychiatry, 36,* 91–94.

Cohen, R., Woll, G., and Ehrenstein, W. H. (1981). Recognition deficits resulting from focussed attention in aphasia. *Psychological Research, 43,* 391–405.

Connolly, J. F., Gruzelier, J. H., Kleinman, K. M., and Hirsch, S. R. (1983). Visual evoked potentials in schizophrenia: Intensity effects and hemispheric asymmetry. *British Journal of Psychiatry, 142,* 152–155.

Connolly, J. F., Manchanda, R., Gruzelier, J. H., and Hirsch, S. R. (1985). Pathway and hemispheric differences in the event-related potential (ERP) to monaural stimulation: A comparison of schizophrenic patients with normal controls. *Biological Psychiatry, 20,* 293–303.

Corbin, D. O. C., Williams, A. C., and White, A. C. (1987). Tardive dystonia: Which way do schizophrenics twist? *Lancet I,* 268–269.

Cooper, J. E., Andrews, H., and Barber, C. (1985). Stable abnormalities in the lateralization of early cortical somatosensory evoked potentials in schizophrenic patients. *British Journal of Psychiatry, 146,* 585–593.

Crow, T. J. (1986). Left brain, retrotransposons and schizophrenia. *British Medical Journal, 293,* 3–4.

Crow, T. J., and Stevens, M. (1978). Age disorientation in chronic schizophrenia: The nature of cognitive deficit. *British Journal of Psychiatry, 133,* 137–142.

Cutting, J. (1981). Judgment of emotional expression in schizophrenics. *British Journal of Psychiatry, 139,* 1–6.

Dabbs, J. M., and Choo, G. (1980). Left–right carotid blood flow predicts specialized mental ability. *Neuropsychologia, 18,* 711–713.

Davison, K., and Bagley, C. R. (1969). Schizophrenia-like psychoses associated with organic disorders of the central nervous system: A review of the literature. *British Journal of Psychiatry, 4,* 113–184.

Dax, M. (1865). Lesions de la moitie gauche de l'encephale coincidant avec trouble des signes de la pensee. Deuxieme serie (lu a Montpellier en 1836), Gax Hbd.

Day, M. (1964). An eye movement phenomenon relating to attention, thought and anxiety. *Perceptual and Motor Skills, 19,* 443–446.

D'Elia, G., Jacobsson, L., Von Knorring, L., Mattison, B., Mjorndal, T., Oreland, L., Perris, C., and Rapp, W. (1977). Changes in psychopathology in relation to EEG variables and visual averaged evoked responses. *Acta Psychiatrica Scandinavica, 55,* 309–318.

Demeter, S., Ringo, J. L., and Doty, R. W. (1988). Morphometric analysis of the human corpus callosum and anterior commissure. *Human Neurobiology, 6,* 219–226.

Deshmukh, V. D., and Meyer, J. S. (1978). *Noninvasive measurement of regional cerebral blood flow in man.* New York: S. P. Medical & Scientific.

Delisi, L. E., Buchsbaum, M. S., Holcomb, H. H., Langston, K. C., King, A. C., Kessler, R., Pickar, D., Carpenter, W. T., Morihisa, J. M., Margolin, R., and Weinberger, D. R. (1989). Increased temporal lobe glucose use in chronic schizophrenic patients. *Biological Psychiatry, 25,* 835–851.

Dimond, S. J., Scammell, R., Pryce, I. J., Haws, D., and Gray, C. (1980). Some failures of intermanual and cross-lateral transfer in chronic schizophrenia. *Journal of Abnormal Psychology*, *89*, 505–509.

Dimond, S. J., Scammell, R., Pryce, I. J., Huss, D., and Gray, C. (1979). Callosal transfer and left-hand anomia in schizophrenia. *Biological Psychiatry*, *14*, 735–739.

Doty, R. W. (1989). Schizophrenia: A disease of interhemispheric processes at forebrain and brainstem levels? *Behavioural Brain Research*, *34*, 1–33.

Dougherty, F. E., Bartlett, E., and Izard, C. (1974). Responses of schizophrenics to expressions of the fundamental emotions. *Journal of Clinical Psychology*, *30*, 243–246.

Dousse, M., Mamo, H., Ponsin, J. C., and Dinh, Y. T. (1988). Cerebral blood flow in schizophrenia. *Experimental Neurology*, *100*, 98–111.

Dykman, R. A., Reese, W. G., Galbrecht, C. R., Ackerman, P. T., and Sunderman, R. S. (1968). Autonomic response in psychiatric patients. *Annals of the New York Academy of Sciences*, *147*, 237–303.

Dymond, A. M., Coger, R. W., and Serafetinides, E. A. (1980). EEG banding and asymmetry in schizophrenics, alcoholics and controls: An objective comparison. *Research Communications in Psychology, Psychiatry and Behavior*, *5*, 113–122.

Early, T. S., Reiman, E. M., Raichle, M. E., and Spitznagel, E. L. (1986). Left globus pallidus abnormality in never-medicated patients with schizophrenia. *Proceedings of the National Academy of Sciences, U.S.A.*, *84*, 561–562.

Eaton, E. M. (1979). Hemisphere-related visual information processing in acute schizophrenia before and after neuroleptic medication. In J. H. Gruzelier and P. Flor-Henry (Eds.), *Hemisphere asymmetries of Function in psychopathology*, pp. 511–527. Amsterdam: Elsevier.

Eaton, E. M., Busk, J., Maloney, M. P., Sloane, R. B., Whipple, K., and White, K. (1979). Hemispheric dysfunction in schizophrenia. *Psychiatry Research*, *1*, 325–332.

Efron, R., Crandall, P. H., Koss, B., Divenyi, P. L., and Yund, E. W. (1983). Central auditory processing. III. The "cocktail party" effect and anterior temporal lobectomy. *Brain and Language*, *19*, 254–263.

Ekbom, K., Lindholm, H., and Ljungberg, L. (1972). New dystonic syndrome associated with butyrophenone therapy. *Journal of Neurology*, *202*, 94–103.

Etevenon, P., Peron-Magnan, P., Campistron, D., Verdaux, G., and Deniker, P. (1983). Differences in EEG symmetry between patients with schizophrenia. In P. Flor-Henry and J. H. Gruzelier (Eds.), *Laterality and psychopathology*. Amsterdam: Elsevier.

Etevenon, P., Ridoux, P., Rioux, P., Peron-Magnan, P., Verdaux, G., and Deniker, P. (1979). Intra- and interhemispheric EEG differences quantified by spectral analysis. *Acta Psychiatrica Scandinavica*, *60*, 57–68.

Faber, R., Abrams, R., Taylor, M. A., Kasprison, A., Morris, C., and Weisz, R. (1983). Comparison of schizophrenic patients with formal thought disorder and neurologically impaired patients with aphasia. *American Journal of Psychiatry*, *140*, 1348–1351.

Feinberg, T. E., Rifkin, A., Schaffer, C., and Walker, E. (1986). Facial discrimination and emotional recognition in schizophrenia and affective disorders. *Archives of General Psychiatry*, *43*, 276–279.

Fenton, G. W., Fenwick, P. B. C., Dollimore, J., Dunn, T. L., and Hirsch, S. R. (1980). EEG spectral analysis in schizophrenia. *British Journal of Psychiatry*, *136*, 445–455.

Flor-Henry, P. (1969). Psychoses and temporal lobe epilepsy: A controlled investigation. *Epilepsia*, *10*, 363–395.

Flor-Henry, P. (1976). Lateralized temporal-limbic dysfunction and psychopathology. *Annals of the New York Academy of Sciences*, *280*, 777–797.

Flor-Henry, P. (1989). Interhemispheric relationships and depression in schizophrenia in the perspective of cerebral laterality. In R. Williams and J. T. Dalby (Eds.), *Depression in Schizophrenics*, pp. 29–46. New York: Plenum Press.

Flor-Henry, P., and Yeudall, L. T. (1979). Neuropsychological investigation of schizophrenia and manic depressive psychoses. In J. H. Gruzelier and P. Flor-Henry (Eds.), *Hemisphere asymmetries of function in psychopathology*, pp. 341–362. Amsterdam: Elsevier.

Flor-Henry, P., Koles, Z. J., Howarth, B. G., and Burton, L. (1979). Neurophysiological studies of schizophrenia, mania and depression. In J. Gruzelier and P. Flor-Henry (Eds.), *Hemisphere asymmetries of function in psychopathology*, pp. 189–222. Amsterdam: Elsevier.

Flor-Henry, P., and Koles, Z. J. (1980). EEG studies in depression, mania and normals: Evidence for partial shifts of laterality in the affective psychoses. *Advances in Biological Psychiatry, 4*, 21–43.

Freixa i Baque, E., Catteau, M. C., Miossec, Y., and Roy, J. C. (1984). Asymmetry of electrodermal activity: A review. *Biological Psychology, 18*, 219–239.

Fritze, J. (1984). Can neuroleptics influence the function of the brain hemispheres asymmetrically? *Neuropharmacology, 23*, 79–82.

Gaebel, W., and Ulrich, G. (1988). Topographical distribution of absolute alpha power in the EEG and psychopathology in schizophrenic outpatients. *Acta Psychiatrica Scandinavica, 77*, 390–397.

Gainotti, G. (1983). Emotions and hemispheric lateration. Review of the literature. *Encephale, 9*, 345–364.

Gazzaniga, M. S. (1983). Fonctions cognitives de l'hemisphere gauche. *Revue de Neurologie (Paris), 139*, 19–22.

Geschwind, N., and Galaburda, A. M. (1985). Cerebral lateralization: Biological mechanisms, associations, and pathology. 1. A hypothesis and a program for research. *Archives of Neurology, 42*, 428–459.

Giannatrapani, D., and Kayton, L. (1974). Schizophrenia and EEG spectral analysis. *Electroencephalography and Clinical Neurophysiology, 36*, 377–386.

Glick, S. D., and Cox, R. D. (1976). Differential effects of unilateral and bilateral caudate lesions on side preferences and timing behavior in rats. *Journal of Comparative and Physiological Psychology, 90*, 528–535.

Glick, S. D., and Ross, D. A. (1981). Right-sided population bias and lateralization of activity in normal rats. *Brain Research, 205*, 222–225.

Glick, S. D., Jerussi, T. P., Waters, D. H., and Green, J. P. (1974). Amphetamine-induced changes in striatal dopamine and acetylcholine levels and relationship to rotation (circling behavior) in rats. *Biochemical Pharmacology, 23*, 3223–3225.

Glick, S. D., Lyon, R. A., Hinds, P. A., Sowek, C., and Titeler, M. (1988). Correlated asymmetries in striatal $D_1$ and $D_2$ binding: Relationship to apomorphine-induced rotation. *Brain Research, 455*, 43–48.

Glick, S. D., Meibach, R. C., Cox, R. D., and Maayani, S. (1979). Multiple and interrelated functional asymmetries in rat brain. *Life Sciences, 25*, 395–400.

Glick, S. D., Weaver, L. M., and Meibach, R. C. (1980). Lateralization of reward in rats: Differences in reinforcing thresholds. *Science, 207*, 1093–1095.

Golden, C. J., Graber, B., Coffman, J., Berg, R. A., Newlin, D. B., and Bloch, S. (1981). Structural brain deficits in schizophrenia: Identification by computed tomographic scan density measurements. *Archives of General Psychiatry, 38*, 1014–1017.

Goldstein, L., and Stoltzfuss, N. W. (1973). Psychoactive drug-induced changes of interhemispheric EEG amplitude relationships. *Agents and Actions, 3*, 124–132.

Goode, D. J., Glenn, S., Manning, A. A., and Middleton, J. F. (1980). Lateral asymmetry of the Hoffman reflex: Relation to cortical laterality. *Journal of Neurology, Neurosurgery and Psychiatry, 43*, 831–835.

Goode, D. J., Manning, A. A., and Middleton, J. F. (1981). Cortical laterality and asymmetry of the Hoffman reflex in psychiatric patients. *Biological Psychiatry, 16*, 1137–1157.

Goode, D. J., Meltzer, H. Y., Mazura, T. A., and Crayton, J. W. (1977). Physiologic abnormalities of the neuromuscular system on psychosis. *Schizophrenia Bulletin, 3*, 121–132.

Green, J. P. (1978). Defective interhemispheric transfer in schizophrenia. *Journal of Abnormal Psychology, 87,* 472–480.

Green, P., and Kotenko, V. (1980). Superior speech comprehension in schizophrenics under monaural versus binaural listening conditions. *Journal of Abnormal Psychology, 89,* 399–408.

Gruzelier, J. H. (1973). Bilateral asymmetry of skin conductance orienting activity and levels in schizophrenia. *Biological Psychology, 1,* 21–41.

Gruzelier, J. H. (1981). Hemispheric imbalances masquerading as paranoid and non-paranoid syndromes. *Schizophrenia Bulletin, 7,* 662–673.

Gruzelier, J. H. (1983). A critical assessment and integration of lateral asymmetries in schizophrenia. In M. S. Myslobodsky (Ed.), *Hemisyndromes: Psychobiology, neurology and psychiatry,* pp. 265–326. New York: Academic Press.

Gruzelier, J. H. (1984). Hemispheric imbalance in schizophrenia. *International Journal of Psychophysiology, 1,* 227–240.

Gruzelier, J. H., and Hammond, N. V. (1976). Schizophrenia: A dominant hemisphere temporal-limbic disorder? *Research Communications in Psychology, Psychiatry and Behavior, 1,* 33–72.

Gruzelier, J. H., and Hammond, N. V. (1978). The effect of chlorpromazine upon psycho-physiological endocrine and information processing measures in schizophrenia. *Journal of Psychiatric Research, 14,* 167–182.

Gruzelier, J. H., and Hammond, N. V. (1979). Gains, losses and lateral differences in hearing of schizophrenic patients. *The British Journal of Psychology, 70,* 319–330.

Gruzelier, J. H., and Hammond, N. V. (1980). Lateralized deficits and drug influences on the dichotic listening of schizophrenic patients. *Biological Psychiatry, 15,* 759–779.

Gruzelier, J., and Manchanda, R. (1982). The syndrome of schizophrenia: Relations between electrodermal response, lateral asymmetries and clinical ratings. *British Journal of Psychiatry, 141,* 488–495.

Gruzelier, J., and Venables, P. (1974). Bimodality and lateral asymmetry of skin conductance orienting activity in schizophrenics: Replication and evidence of lateral asymmetry in patients with depression and disorders of personality. *Biological Psychiatry, 8,* 55–73.

Gruzelier, J., Jutai, J. W., Connolly, J. F., and Hirsch, S. R. (1984). Cerebral asymmetries in unmedicated schizophrenic patients in EEG spectra and their relation to clinical and autonomic parameters. *Advances in Biological Psychiatry, 15,* 12–19.

Gruzelier, J., Seymour, K., Wilson, L., Jolley, A., and Hirsch, S. (1988). Impairments on neuropsychologic tests of temporohippocampal and frontohippocampal functions and word fluency in remitting schizophrenia and affective disorders. *Archives of General Psychiatry, 45,* 623–629.

Guenther, W., and Breitling, D. (1988). Predominant sensorimotor area left hemisphere dysfunction in schizophrenia measured by brain electrical activity mapping. *Biological Psychiatry, 20,* 515–532.

Gulmann, N. C., Wildschiodtz, G., and Orbaek, K. (1982). Alteration of interhemispheric conduction through corpus callosum in chronic schizophrenia. *Biological Psychiatry, 17,* 585–594.

Gur, R. E. (1977). Motoric laterality imbalance in schizophrenia: A possible concomitant of left hemisphere dysfunction. *Archives of General Psychiatry, 34,* 33–37.

Gur, R. E. (1978). Left hemisphere dysfunction and left hemisphere over activation in schizophrenia. *Journal of Abnormal Psychology, 87,* 226–238.

Gur, R. E. (1979). Cognitive concomitants of hemispheric dysfunction in schizophrenia. *Archives of General Psychiatry, 36,* 269–274.

Gur, R. E., Resnick, S. M., and Gur, R. C. (1989). Laterality and frontality of cerebral blood flow and metabolism in schizophrenia: Relationship to symptom specificity. *Psychiatry Research, 27,* 325–334.

Gur, R. E., Gur, R. C., Skolnick, B. C., Caroff, S., Obrist, W. D., Resnick, S., and Reivich, M. (1985). Brain function in psychiatric disorders. III. Regional cerebral blood flow in unmedicated schizophrenics. *Archives of General Psychiatry, 42*, 329–334.

Hallett, S., Quinn, D., and Hewitt, J. (1986). Defective interhemispheric integration and anomalous language lateralization in children at risk for schizophrenia. *Journal of Nervous and Mental Diseases, 174*, 418–427.

Harnad, S. (1972). Creativity, lateral saccades and the non-dominant hemisphere. *Perceptual and Motor Skills, 34*, 653–654.

Haug, J. O. (1962). Pneumoencephalographic studies in mental disease. *Acta Psychiatrica Scandinavica, 16 Suppl.*, 51–104.

Heilman, K. M., Bowers, D., Valenstein, E. S., and Watson, R. T. (1986). The right hemisphere: Neuropsychological functions. *Journal of Neurosurgery, 64*, 693–704.

Heilman, K. M., and Valenstein, E. (1979). *Clinical neuropsychology.* New York: Oxford University Press.

Heilman, K. M., and Van Den Abell, T. (1979). Right hemispheric dominance for mediating cerebral activation. *Neuropsychologia, 17*, 315–321.

Heinburger, R. F., and Reitan, R. M. (1961). Easily administered written test for lateralising brain lesions. *Journal of Neurosurgery, 18*, 301–312.

Hellige, J. B. (1990). Hemispheric asymmetry. *Annual Review of Psychology, 41*, 55–80.

Huang, M., and Byrne, B. (1978). Cognitive style and lateral eye movements. *British Journal of Psychology, 69*, 85–90.

Hunter, R., Jones, M., and Cooper, F. (1968). Modified lumbar air encephalography in the investigation of long-stay patients. *Journal of Neurological Sciences, 6*, 593–596.

Iacono, W. (1982). Bilateral electrodermal habituation–dishabituation and resting EEG in remitted schizophrenics. *Journal of Nervous and Mental Disease, 170*, 91–101.

Innocenti, G. M. (1986). General organization of callosal connections in the cerebral cortex. In E. G. Jones and A. Peters (Eds.), *Cerebral cortex*, Vol. 5, pp. 191–253. New York: Plenum Press.

Itil, T. M. (1980). Computer-analyzed electroencephalogram to predict the therapeutic outcome in schizophrenia. In C. Baxter and T. Melnechuk (Eds.), *Perspectives in schizophrenia research*, pp. 61–75. New York: Raven Press.

Jakob, H., and Beckmann, H. (1986). Prenatal developmental disturbances in the limbic allocortex in schizophrenics. *Journal of Neural Transmission, 65*, 303–326.

Jernigan, T. L., Sargent, T., Pfefferbaum, A., Kusubov, N., and Stahl, S. M. (1985). 18-Fluorodeoxyglucose PET in schizophrenia. *Psychiatry Research, 16*, 317.

Jernigan, T. L., Zatz, L. M., Moses, J. A., and Cardellino, J. P. (1982). Computed tomography in schizophrenics and normal volunteers. II. Cranial asymmetry. *Archives of General Psychiatry, 39*, 771–773.

Jerussi, T. P., and Taylor, C. A. (1982). Bilateral asymmetry in striatal dopamine metabolism: Implications for pharmacotherapy of schizophrenia. *Brain Research, 246*, 71–75.

Johnson, O., and Crockett, D. (1982). Changes in perceptual asymmetries with clinical improvement of depression and schizophrenia. *Journal of Abnormal Psychology, 91*, 45–54.

Johnstone, E. C., Owens, D. G. C., Crow, T. J., Frith, C. D., Alexandropolis, K., Bydder, G., and Colter, N. (1989). Temporal lobe structure as determined by nuclear magnetic resonance in schizophrenia and bipolar affective disorder. *Journal of Neurology, Neurosurgery and Psychiatry, 52*, 736–741.

Jones, G. H., and Miller, J. J. (1981). Functional tests of the corpus callosum in schizophrenia. *British Journal of Psychiatry, 139*, 553–557.

Jutai, J. W., Gruzelier, J. H., Connolly, J. F., Manchanda, R., and Hirsch, S. R. (1984). Schizophrenia and spectral analysis of the visual evoked potential. *British Journal of Psychiatry, 145*, 496–501.

Karson, C. N., Coppola, R., and Daniel, D. G. (1988). Alpha frequency in schizophrenia: An association with enlarged cerebral ventricles. *American Journal of Psychiatry, 145*, 861–864.

Karson, C. N., Coppola, R., Morihisa, J. D., and Weinberger, D. R. (1987). Computed electroencephalographic activity mapping in schizophrenia: The resting state reconsidered. *Archives of General Psychiatry, 44*, 514–517.

Kelsoe, J. R., Cadet, J. L., Pickar, D., and Weinberger, D. R. (1988). Quantitative neuroanatomy in schizophrenia: A controlled magnetic resonance imaging study. *Archives of General Psychiatry, 45*, 533–541.

Kemali, D., Galderisi, S., Maj, M., Mucci, A., Cesarelli, N., and D'Ambra, L. (1988). Event-related potentials in schizophrenic patients: Clinical and neurophysiological correlates. *Research Communications in Psychology, Psychiatry and Behavior, 13*, 3–16.

Kinsbourne, M. (1970). Cerebral basis of lateral asymmetries in attention. *Acta Psychologica, 33*, 193–201.

Kinsbourne, M. (1972). Eye and head turning indicates cerebral lateralization. *Science, 176*, 539–541.

Kishimoto, H., Kuwaharra, H., Ohno, S., Takazu, O., Hama, Y., Sato, C., Ishii, T., Nomura, Y., Fujita, H., Miyauchi, T., Matushita, M., Yokoi, S., and Iio, M. (1987). Three subtypes of chronic schizophrenia identified using ($^{11}$C)-glucose positron emission tomography. *Psychiatry Research, 21*, 285–292.

Kleist, K. (1960). Schizophrenic symptoms and cerebral pathology. *Journal of Mental Science, 106*, 246–255.

Kolb, B., and Whishaw, I. Q. (1983). Performance of schizophrenic patients on tests sensitive to left or right frontal, temporal, or parietal function in neurological patients. *Journal of Nervous and Mental Diseases, 171*, 435–443.

Kostandov, E. A. (1980). Asymmetry of visual perception and interhemispheric interaction. *Neuroscience Behavior and Physiology, 10*, 36–47.

Kugler, B. T. (1983). Auditory processing in schizophrenic patients. In P. Flor-Henry and J. H. Gruzelier (Eds.), *Laterality and psychopathology*. Amsterdam: Elsevier.

Kugler, B. T., Caudrey, D. J., and Gruzelier, J. H. (1982). Bilateral auditory acuity of schizophrenic patients: Effects of repeated testing, time of day and medication. *Psychological Medicine, 12*, 775–781.

Kugler, B. T., and Henley, S. H. A. (1979). Laterality effects in the tactile modality in schizophrenia. In J. H. Gruzelier and P. Flor-Henry (eds.), *Hemisphere asymmetries of function in psychopathology*, pp. 475–489. Amsterdam: Elsevier.

Kurachi, M., Kobayashi, K., Matsubara, R., Hiramatsu, H., Yamaguchi, N., Matsuda, H., Maeda, T., and Hisada, K. (1985). Regional cerebral blood flow in schizophrenic disorders. *European Neurology, 24*, 176–181.

Kurtzberg, D., Vaughan, H. G., and Kreuzer, J. (1979). Task-related cortical potentials in children. *Progress in Clinical Neurophysiology, 6*, 216–223.

Lee, E. H. Y., Huang, S. L., and Chai, C. Y. (1987). Association between the behavioral and neurochemical effects of amphetamine: Hemispheric asymmetry study. *Life Sciences, 40*, 1431–1437.

Lerner, J., Nachson, I., and Carmon, A. (1977). Responses of paranoid and nonparanoid schizophrenics in a dichotic listening task. *Journal of Nervous and Mental Diseases, 164*, 247–252.

Levin, S. (1984). Frontal lobe dysfunction in schizophrenia. I. Eye movement impairments. *Journal of Psychiatric Research, 18*, 27–55.

Lishman, W. A., Toone, B. K., Colbourne, C. J., McMeekan, E. R. L., and Mance, R. M. (1978). Dichotic listening in psychotic patients. *British Journal of Psychiatry, 132*, 333–341.

Losonczy, M. F., Song, P. S., Mohs, R. C., Mathe, A. A., Davidson, M., Davis, B. M., and

Davis, K. L. (1986). Correlates of lateral ventricular size in chronic schizophrenia. II. Biological measures. *Archives of General Psychiatry, 43,* 1113–1118.

Luchins, D. J., Weinberger, D. R., and Wyatt, R. J. (1979). Anomalous lateralization associated with a milder form of schizophrenia. *American Journal of Psychiatry, 136,* 1598–1599.

Luchins, D., Pollin, W., and Wyatt, R. J. (1980). Laterality in monozygotic schizophrenic twins: An alternative hypothesis. *Biological Psychiatry, 15,* 87–93.

Luchins, D. J., Weinberger, D. R., and Wyatt, R. J. (1982). Schizophrenia and cerebral asymmetry detected by computed tomography. *American Journal of Psychiatry, 139,* 753–757.

Luria, A. R., and Homskaya, E. D. (1963). Le trouble de role regulateur du langage au course des lesions au lobe frontal. *Neuropsychologia, 1,* 9–26.

Mackay, A. V. P., Iversen, L. L., Rossor, M., Spokes, E., Bird, E., Arregui, A., Creese, I., and Snyder, S. H. (1982). Increased brain dopamine and dopamine receptors in schizophrenia. *Archives of General Psychiatry, 31,* 991–997.

Magaro, P. A., and Chamral, D. L. (1983). Information processing and lateralization in schizophrenia. *Biological Psychiatry, 18,* 29–44.

Marder, L., and Woods, D. J. (1987). Left hemispheric overactivation in schizophrenia: Relationship to clockwise circling. *Psychiatry Research, 20,* 215–220.

Mathew, R. J., Duncan, G. C., Weinman, M. L., and Barr, D. L. (1982). Regional cerebral blood flow in schizophrenia. *Archives of General Psychiatry, 39,* 1121–1124.

Mathew, R. J., Partain, C. J., Prakash, R., Kulkarni, M. V., Logan, T. P., and Wilson, W. H. (1985). A study of the septum pellucidum and corpus callosum in schizophrenia with MR imaging. *Acta Psychiatrica Scandinavica, 72,* 414–421.

Mathew, R. J., Wilson, W. H., Tant, S. R., Robinson, L., and Prakash, R. (1988). Abnormal resting regional cerebral blood flow patterns and their correlates in schizophrenia. *Archives of General Psychiatry, 45,* 542–549.

Matousek, M., Capone, C., and Okawa, M. (1981). Measurement of interhemispheral differences as a diagnostic tool in psychiatry. *Advances in Biological Psychiatry, 6,* 76–80.

Maurer, K., and Dierks, T. (1987). Brain mapping—Topographische Darstellung des EEGs und der evozierten Potentiale in Psychiatrie und Neurologie. *Zeitschrift für Elektroencephalographie, Elektromyographie und verwandte Gebiete, 18,* 4–12.

McCarley, R. W., Faux, S. F., Shenton, M. W., LeMay, M., Cane, M., Ballinger, R., and Duffy, F. H. (1989). CT abnormalities in schizophrenia: A preliminary study of their correlations with P300/200 electrophysiological features and positive/negative symptoms. *Archives of General Psychiatry, 46,* 698–708.

Merrin, E. L. (1981). Schizophrenia and brain asymmetry: An evaluation of evidence for dominant lobe dysfunction. *Journal of Nervous and Mental Diseases, 169,* 405–416.

Merrin, E. L. (1984). Motor and sighting dominance in schizophrenia and affective disorder: Evidence for right-hand grip strength prominence in paranoid schizophrenia and bipolar illness. *British Journal of Psychiatry, 146,* 539–544.

Merrin, E. L., Fein, G., Floyd, T. C., and Yingling, C. D. (1986). EEG asymmetry in schizophrenic patients before and during neuroleptic treatment. *Biological Psychiatry, 21,* 455–464.

Mintz, M., Tomer, R., and Myslobodsky, M. S. (1982). Neuroleptic-induced lateral asymmetry of visual evoked potentials in schizophrenia. *Biological Psychiatry, 17,* 815–828.

Morrison, R. L., Bellack, A. S., and Mueser, K. T. (1988). Deficits in facial-affect recognition and schizophrenia. *Schizophrenia Bulletin, 14,* 67–83.

Morstyn, R., Duffy, F. H., and McCarley, R. W. (1983a). Altered topography of EEG spectral content in schizophrenia. *Electroencephalography and Clinical Neurophysiology, 56,* 263–271.

Morstyn, R., Duffy, F. H., and McCarley, R. W. (1983b). Altered P300 topography in schizophrenia. *Archives of General Psychiatry, 40,* 729–734.

Muzekari, L. H., and Bates, M. E. (1977). Judgment of emotion among chronic schizophrenics. *Journal of Clinical Psychology, 33*, 662–666.

Myslobodsky, M. S., Holden, T., and Saudler, R. (1984). Asymmetry of abnormal involuntary movements: a prevalence study. *Biological Psychiatry, 9*, 623–628.

Myslobodsky, M. S., and Horesch, N. (1978). Bilateral electrodermal activity in depressed patients. *Biological Psychology, 6*, 111–120.

Nachson, I. (1980). Hemispheric dysfunctioning in schizophrenia. *Journal of Nervous and Mental Diseases, 168*, 241–242.

Nasrallah, H. A. (1986). Is schizophrenia a left hemisphere disease? In N. C. Andreasen (Eds.), *Progress in psychiatry*, pp. 53–74. Washington, D.C.: American Psychiatric Press.

Nasrallah, H. A., McCalley-Whitters, M., Bigelow, L. B., and Rauscher, F. P. (1983). A histological study of the corpus callosum in chronic schizophrenia. *Psychiatry Research, 8*, 251–260.

Nasrallah, H. A., McCalley-Whitters, M., and Kuperman, S. (1982). Neurological differences between paranoid and non-paranoid schizophrenia. I. Sensory and motoric lateralization. *Journal of Clinical Psychiatry, 43*, 305–306.

Nasrallah, H. A., Olson, S. C., McCalley-Whitters, M., Chapman, S., and Jacoby, C. G. (1986). Cerebral ventricular enlargement in schizophrenia: A preliminary follow-up study. *Archives of General Psychiatry, 43*, 157–159.

Niwa, S. I., Hiramatsu, K. I., Kameyama, T., Saitoh, O., Itoh, K., and Utenia, H. (1983). Left hemisphere's inability to sustain attention over extended time periods in schizophrenics. *British Journal of Psychiatry, 142*, 477–481.

Nyback, H., Wiesel, F. A., Berggren, B. M., and Hindmarsh, T. (1982). Computed tomography of the brain in patients with acute psychosis and in healthy volunteers. *Acta Psychiatrica Scandinavica, 65*, 403–414.

Nyman, H., Nyback, H., Wiesel, F. A., Oxenstierna, G., and Schalling, D. (1986). Neuropsychological test performance, brain morphological measures and CSF monoamine metabolites in schizophrenic patients. *Acta Psychiatrica Scandinavica, 74*, 292–301.

Oades, R. D., and Zerbin, D. (1991). Signs of differential stimulus processing problems: a comment on event-related potentials in young schizophrenic and autistic subjects. In C. Eggers (Ed.). Schizophrenia and youth. Heidelberg: Springer-Verlag.

Oke, A., Keller, R., Mefford, I., and Adams, R. N. (1978). Lateralization of norepinephrine in human thalamus. *Science, 200*, 1411–1413.

Oke, A., Skolnick, J., and Adams, R. N. (1983). Catecholamine distribution patterns in rat thalamus. *Brain Research, 269*, 180–183.

Pandya, D. N., and Seltzer, B. (1986). The topography of commissural fibers. In F. Lepore, M. Pito, and H. H. Jasper (Eds.), *Two hemispheres—one brain, functions of the corpus callosum*, pp. 44–73. New York: Liss.

Pardowski, W., Bricker, B., Zaretsky, H., and Alba, A. (1978). The effect of unilateral brain damage on the appearance of question-induced CLEM reactions. *Cortex, 14*, 420–430.

Petersen, S. E., Fox, P. T., Posner, M. I., Mintun, M., and Raichle, M. E. (1988). Positron emission tomographic studies of the cortical anatomy of single-word processing. *Nature (London), 331*, 585–589.

Piran, N., Bigler, E. D., and Cohen, D. (1982). Motoric laterality and eye dominance suggest unique pattern of cerebral organization in schizophrenia. *Archives of General Psychiatry, 39*, 1006–1010.

Polich, J. (1984). Hemispheric patterns in visual search. *Brain and Cognition, 3*, 128–139.

Posner, M. I., Peterson, M. I., Fox, P. T., and Raichle, M. E. (1988). Localization of cognitive operations in the human brain. *Science, 240*, 1627–1631.

Reite, M., Teale, P., Zimmerman, J., Davis, K., Whalen, J., and Edrich, J. (1988). Source origin of a 50-msec latency auditory evoked field component in young schizophrenic men. *Biological Psychiatry*, *24*, 495–506.

Reynolds, G. P. (1979). Post-mortem neurochemical studies in schizophrenia. In H. Haefner, W. F. Gattaz, and W. Janzarik (Eds.), *Search for the causes of schizophrenia*, pp. 236–240. Heidelberg: Springer-Verlag.

Reynolds, G. P. (1983). Increased concentrations and lateral asymmetry of amygdala dopamine in schizophrenia. *Nature (London)* 306/Dec 8 527–529.

Reynolds, G. P., Czudek, C., Bzowej, N., and Seeman, P. (1987). Dopamine receptor asymmetry in schizophrenia. *Lancet*, I 979.

Robinson, R. G., Shoemaker, W. J., and Schlumpf, M. (1980). Time course in changes of catecholamines following right hemispheric cerebral infarction in the rat. *Brain Research*, *181*, 202–208.

Rodin, E., Grisell, J., and Gottlieb, J. (1968). Some electrographic differences between chronic schizophrenic patients and normal subjects. In J. Wortis (Eds.), *Recent advances in biological psychiatry*. New York: Plenum Press.

Roemer, R. A., Shagass, C., Straumanis, J. J., and Amadeo, M. (1978). Pattern evoked potential measurements suggesting lateralized hemispheric dysfunction in chronic schizophrenia. *Biological Psychiatry*, *13*, 185–192.

Roemer, R. A., Shagass, C., Straumanis, J. J., and Amadeo, M. (1979). Somatosensory and auditory evoked potential studies of functional differences between the cerebral hemispheres in psychosis. *Biological Psychiatry*, *14*, 357–372.

Rosenthal, R., and Bigelow, L. B. (1972). Quantitative brain measurements in chronic schizophrenia. *British Journal of Psychiatry*, *121*, 259–264.

Ross, D. A., and Glick, S. D. (1981). Lateralized effects of bilateral frontal cortex lesions in rats. *Brain Research*, *210*, 379–382.

Rossi, A., Stratta, P., Galucci, M., Amicarelli, I., Passariello, R., and Casacchia, M. (1988). Standardized magnetic resonance image intensity study in schizophrenia. *Psychiatry Research*, *25*, 223–231.

Sandel, A., and Alcorn, J. D. (1980). Individual hemisphericity and maladaptive behaviors. *Journal of Abnormal Psychology*, *89*, 514–517.

Saring, W., and Von Cramon, D. (1980). Is there an interaction between cognitive activity and lateral eye movements? *Neuropsychologia*, *18*, 591–596.

Scarone, S., Cazzullo, C. L., and Gambini, O. (1987). Asymmetry of lateralized hemispheric functions in schizophrenia: Influence of clinical and epidemiological characteristics in quality extinction test performance. *British Journal of Psychiatry*, *151*, 15–17.

Scarone, S., Gambini, O., and Pieri, E. (1983). Dominant hemisphere dysfunction in chronic schizophrenia: Schwartz test and short aphasia screening test. In P. Flor-Henry and J. H. Gruzelier (Eds.), *Laterality and psychopathology*. Amsterdam: Elsevier.

Schneider, S. J. (1983). Multiple measures of hemisphere dysfunction in schizophrenia and depression. *Psychological Medicine*, *13*, 287–297.

Schneider, L. H., Murphy, R. B., and Coons, E. E. (1982). Lateralization of striatal dopamine ($D_2$) receptors in normal rats. *Neuroscience Letters*, *33*, 281–284.

Schulhoff, C., and Goodglass, H. (1969). Dichotic listening, side of brain injury and cerebral dominance. *Neuropsychologia*, *7*, 149–160.

Schwartz, G. E. (1975). Right hemisphere lateralization for emotion in the human brain: Interactions with cognition. *Science*, *190*, 286–288.

Schwartz, A. S., Marchok, P. L., Kreinick, C. J., and Flynn, R. E. (1979). The asymmetric lateralization of tactile extinction in patients with unilateral cerebral dysfunction. *Brain*, *102*, 669–684.

Schweitzer, L. (1979). Differences of cerebral lateralization among schizophrenic and depressed patients. *Biological Psychiatry*, *14*, 721–731.

Schweitzer, L., Becker, E., and Welsh, H. (1978). Abnormalities of cerebral lateralization in schizophrenic patients. *Archives of General Psychiatry, 35*, 982–985.

Serafetinides, E. A. (1972). Laterality and voltage in the EEG of psychiatric patients. *Diseases of the Nervous System, 33*, 622–623.

Serafetinides, E. A. (1973). Voltage laterality in the EEG of psychiatric patients. *Diseases of the Nervous System, 34*, 190–191.

Serafetinides, E. A., Coger, R. W., Martin, J., and Dymond, A. M. (1981). Schizophrenic symptomatology and cerebral dominance patterns: A comparison of EEG, AER and BPRS measures. *Comprehensive Psychiatry, 22*, 218–225.

Shagass, C., Roemer, R. A., and Straumanis, J. J. (1980). Deviant topography of sensory evoked potentials in psychosis. *Advances in Biological Psychiatry, 4*, 94–101.

Shagass, C., Josiassen, R. C., Roemer, R. A., Straumanis, J. J., and Stepner, S. M. (1983). Failure to replicate evoked potential observature suggesting corpus callosum dysfunction in schizophrenia. *British Journal of Psychiatry, 142*, 471–476.

Shaw, J. C., Brooks, S., Colter, N., and O'Connor, K. P. (1979). A comparison of schizophrenic and neurotic patients using EEG power and coherence spectra. In J. Gruzelier and P. Flor-Henry (Eds.), *Hemisphere asymmetries of function in psychopathology*, pp. 257–284. Amsterdam: Elsevier.

Shaw, J. C., Colter, N., and Resek, G. (1983). EEG coherence, lateral preference and schizophrenia. *Psychological Medicine, 13*, 299–306.

Sheppard, G., Gruzelier, J., Manchanda, R., Hirsch, S. R., Wise, R., Franchowiak, R., and Jones, T. (1983). 15-O positron emission tomographic scanning in predominantly never treated acute schizophrenic patients. *Lancet, II*, 148–1152.

Shukla, G. D., and Katiyar, B. C. (1980). Psychiatric disorders in temporal lobe epilepsy. *British Journal of Psychiatry, 137*, 181–182.

Small, J. G., Sharpley, P. H., Milstein, V., and Small, I. F. (1979). Research diagnostic criteria and EEG findings in hospitalised schizophrenic patients. In J. Obiols, C. Ballus, E. Gonzalez-Monelus, and J. Pujol (Eds.), *Biological psychiatry today*. Amsterdam: Elsevier.

Smith, R. C., Calderon, M., Ravichandran, G. K., Largen, J., Vroulis, G., Shvartsburd, A., Gordon, J., and Schoolar, J. C. (1984). Nuclear magnetic resonance in schizophrenia: A preliminary study. *Psychiatry Research, 12*, 137–147.

Sparks, R., Goodglass, H., and Nickel, B. (1970). Ipsilateral versus contralateral extinction in dichotic listening resulting from hemispheric lesions. *Cortex, 6*, 249–260.

Sperry, R. W. (1970). Perception in the absence of the neocortical commissures. In D. A. Hamburg, K. H. Pribram and A. J. Stunkard (Eds.). *Perception and its disorders*. Baltimore: Waverly Press, Inc.

Sperry, R. W. (1982). Forebrain commissurotomy and conscious awareness. In J. Orbach (Ed.), *Neuropsychology after Lashley*. Hillsdale, New Jersey: Erlbaum.

Starr, M. S., and Kilpatrick, I. C. (1981). Bilateral asymmetry in brain GABA function? *Neuroscience Letters, 25*, 167–172.

Stevens, J. R., and Livermore, A. (1982). Telemetered EEG in schizophrenia: Spectral analysis during abnormal behaviour episodes. *Journal of Neurology, Neurosurgery and Psychiatry, 45*, 385–395.

Stevens, J. R., Bigelow, L., Denney, D., Lipkin, J., Livermore, A. H., Rauscher, F., and Wyatt, R. J. (1979). Telemetered EEG–EOG during psychotic behaviors of schizophrenia. *Archives of General Psychiatry, 36*, 251–262.

Straube, E. R. (1983). *Psychophysiologische Untersuchung Schizophrener. Reaktivität des autonomen Nervensystems unter besonderer Berücksichtigung der elektrodermalen Orientierungsreaktion*. Tübingen: Habilitationsschrift.

Straube, E. R., and Germer, C. K. (1979). Dichotic shadowing and selective attention to word meaning in schizophrenia. *Journal of Abnormal Psychology, 88*, 346–353.

Sugarman, A. A., Goldstein, L., Marjerrison, G., and Stoltzfuss, N. (1973). Recent research in EEG amplitude analysis. *Diseases of the Nervous System*, *34*, 162–166.

Sussman, H. M., and MacNeilage, P. F. (1975). Studies of hemispheric specialization for speech production. *Brain and Language*, *2*, 131–151.

Szechtman, H., Nahmias, C., Garnett, S., Firnau, G., Brown, G. M., Kaplan, R. D., and Cleghorn, J. M. (1988). Effect of neuroleptics on altered cerebral glucose metabolism in schizophrenia. *Archives of General Psychiatry*, *45*, 523–532.

Tarrier, N., Cooke, E., and Lader, M. (1978). Electrodermal and heart rate measurement in chronic and partially remitted schizophrenic patients. *Acta Psychiatrica Scandinavica*, *57*, 369–376.

Taylor, P. J. (1987). Hemispheric lateralization and schizophrenia. In H. Helmchen and F. A. Henn (Eds.), *Biological perspectives of schizophrenia*, pp. 213–236. New York: Wiley.

Teitelbaum, H. (1954). Spontaneous rhythmic ocular movements. Their possible relationship to mental activity. *Neurology*, *4*, 350–354.

Tomer, R., Mintz, M., and Myslobodsky, M. S. (1982). Left hemisphere hyperactivity in schizophrenia: Abnormality inherent to psychosis or neuroleptic side-effects? *Psychopharmacology*, *77*, 168–170.

Tomer, R., Mintz, M., Kempler, S., and Sigal, M. (1987). Lateralized neuroleptic-induced side effects are associated with asymmetric visual evoked potentials. *Psychiatry Research*, *22*, 311–318.

Toone, B. K., Cooke, E., and Lader, M. H. (1981). Electrodermal activity in the affective disorders and schizophrenia. *Psychological Medicine*, 497–508.

Torrey, E. F. (1980). Neurological abnormalities in schizophrenic patients. *Biological Psychiatry*, *15*, 381–388.

Tress, K. H., Kugler, B. T. and Caudrey, D. J. (1979). Interhemispheric integration in schizophrenia. In J. Gruzelier and P. Flor-Henry (Eds.). *Hemisphere asymmetries of function in psychopathology*. Amsterdam: Elsevier.

Uematsu, M., and Kaiya, H. (1988). The morphology of the corpus callosum in schizophrenia: An MRI study. *Schizophrenia Research*, *1*, 391–398.

Ulrich, G. (1979). Der Lateralitätsaspekt in der psychiatrischen Forschung. *Fortschritte der Neurologie-Psychiatrie*, *47*, 418–430.

Uytdenhoef, P., Portelange, P., Jacquy, J., Charles, G., Linkowski, P., and Mendlewicz, J. (1983). Regional cerebral blood flow and lateralized hemispheric dysfunction in depression. *British Journal of Psychiatry*, *143*, 128–132.

Valdes, J. J., Mactututus, C. F., Cory, R. N., and Cameron, W. R. (1981). Localization of norepinenphrine, serotonin and choline uptake into hippocampal synaptosomes of sinistral rats. *Physiology and Behavior*, *27*, 381–383.

Vargha-Khadem, F., O'Gorman, A. M., and Watters, G. V. (1985). Aphasia and handedness in relation to hemispheric side, age at injury and severity of cerebral lesion in childhood. *Brain*, *108*, 677–696.

Venables, P. H. (1977). The electrodermal psychophysiology of schizophrenics and children at risk for schizophrenia: Controversies and developments. *Schizophrenia Bulletin*, *3*, 28–48.

Verfaellie, M., Bowers, D., and Heilman, K. M. (1988). Hemispheric asymmetries in mediating intention, but not selective attention. *Neuropsychologia*, *26*, 521–531.

Wade, J. B., and Taylor, M. A. (1984). Interhemispheric transfer in schizophrenia and affective disorder. *Biological Psychiatry*, *19*, 107–111.

Walker, E., and McGuire, M. (1982). Intra- and interhemispheric information processing in schizophrenia. *Psychology Bulletin*, *92*, 701–725.

Watson, R. T., Miller, B. D., and Heilman, K. M. (1978). Non-sensory neglect. *Annals of Neurology*, *3*, 505–508.

Waziri, R. (1980). Lateralization of neuroleptic induced dyskinesia indicates pharmacological asymmetry in the brains. *Psychopharmacology*, *68*, 51–53.

Weller, M., and Kugler, B. T. (1979). Tactile discrimination in schizophrenia and affective psychoses. In J. H. Gruzelier and P. Flor-Henry (Eds.), *Hemisphere asymmetries of function in psychopathology*, pp. 463–474. Amsterdam: Elsevier.

Weller, M., and Montague, J. D. (1979). Electroencephalographic coherence in schizophrenia: A preliminary study. In J. Gruzelier and P. Flor-Henry (Eds.), *Hemisphere asymmetries of function in psychopathology*, pp. 285–292. Amsterdam: Elsevier.

Wexler, B. E. (1986). Alterations in cerebral laterality during acute psychotic illnesses. *British Journal of Psychiatry*, *149*, 202–209.

Wexler, B. E., and Heninger, G. R. (1979). Alterations in cerebral laterality during acute psychotic illnesses. *Archives of General Psychiatry*, *36*, 278–284.

Wiesel, F. A., Wik, G., Sjogren, I., Blomqvist, G., and Greitz, T. (1987a). Altered relationships between metabolic rates of glucose in brain regions of schizophrenic patients. *Acta Psychiatrica Scandinavica*, *76*, 642–647.

Wiesel, F. A., Wik, G., Sjogren, I., Blomqvist, G., Greitz, T., and Stone-Elander, S. (1987b). Regional brain glucose metabolism in drug-free schizophrenic patients and clinical correlates. *Acta Psychiatrica Scandinavica*, *76*, 628–641.

Wiesel, F. A., Blomqvist, G., Ehrin, E., Greitz, T., Ingvar, D. H., Litton, J., Nilsson, L., Sedvall, G., Stone-Elander, S., Widen, L., and Wik, G. (1985). Brain energy metabolism in schizophrenia studied with ($^{11}$C)-glucose. In T. Greitz, D. Ingvar, and L. Widen (Eds.), *The metabolism of the human brain studied with positron emission tomography*, pp. 485–493. New York: Raven Press.

Wigan, A. L. (1985). The duality of the mind (reprint). In J. Bogen (Ed.), *A new view of insanity: The duality of the mind proved by the structure, functions and diseases of the brain and by the phenomena of mental derangement, as shown to be essential to moral responsibility*, (original, 1844) London: Longman. Simon: Malibu, California.

Wilson, R. L., Waziri, R., Nasrallah, H. A., and Whitters, M. M. (1984). The lateralization of tardive dyskinesia. *Biological Psychiatry*, *19*, 629–635.

Wolkin, A., Jaeger, J., Brodie, J. D., Wolf, A. P., Fowler, J., Rotrosen, J., Gomez-Mont, F., and Cancro, R. (1985). Persistence of cerebral metabolic abnormalities in chronic schizophrenia as determined by positron emission tomography. *American Journal of Psychiatry*, *142*, 564.

Yosawitz, A., Bruder, G., Sutton, S., Sharpe, L., Gurlanx, B., Heiss, J., and Costa, L. (1979). Dichotic perception: Evidence for right hemisphere dysfunction in affective psychosis. *British Journal of Psychiatry*, *135*, 224–237.

# PART V

# Inheritance versus Environment

Whether and to what extent schizophrenia is inherited is simultaneously one of the more important and one of the more difficult issues for investigators to address. The area of schizophrenia research that tackles this question is one that is often characterized by a number of nonscientific opinions.

Two factors contribute to this bias and distortion. The first is the widespread opinion that it is more human to claim that psychological deviations arise through an unfortunate constellation of environmental influences than through a genetic disposition. The second factor indirectly arises from the first: many people believe that the possibility of a genetic cause implies the probability that most forms of therapy will be hopeless. The response to this is as follows:

These opinions are based on three misunderstandings. (1) Even in illnesses with a known genetic basis, therapy can alleviate the symptoms to a great extent. (2) Prejudice hinders the objective approach necessary in the search for the best therapy. It is necessary to consider *all* the factors that may play a role in the illness. (3) Even when genetic disturbance, the more-or-less marked influence of the environment in modulating behavior, as seen in nearly all cases known, is not excluded. Indeed, the resultant experience has given rise to diathesis/stress or vulnerability/stress models of the origin of the anomalous behavioral outcome in order to consider the interaction between genetic disposition and environmental factors.

In Chapter 10 the evidence for a genetic disposition underlying the behavioral patterns subsumed in the term schizophrenia will be discussed. In Chapter 11, the evidence will be considered concerning a role of environmental stress in the development of schizophrenia. Chapter 12 discusses a special feature: whether certain behavioral and neuropsychological characteristics in children born to a schizophrenic parent or found in the normal population are related to similar features found in schizophrenics and whether these features are high risk indicators.

# Chapter 10

# Genetic Studies

## I. Is Schizophrenia Inherited?

### A. Familial Aggregation of Schizophrenia

A schizophrenic is more likely than a nonschizophrenic to have a blood relation who is also schizophrenic. All research reports agree on this point (e.g., Gottesman and Shields, 1982; Frangos *et al.*, 1985; Kendler *et al.*, 1985; Winokur *et al.*, 1985; McGue *et al.*, 1986). The risk of a first degree relative developing schizophrenia is about 10 times higher than that of a relative of a nonschizophrenic subject (see Table 10.1). (The risk for someone without close relatives with schizophrenia is approximately 0.85%; see also Chapter 1.)

It should be emphasized that about 90% of schizophrenics have no schizophrenic parents, brothers, or sisters (Gottesman and Shields, 1982; McGue and Gottesman, 1989). However, the probability that the monozygotic (MZ) twin of a schizophrenic also suffers in some degree from schizophrenia is higher than that of the twin that comes from another egg and does not share 100% of the genetic material [i.e., dizygotic (DZ); Table 10.1].

It appears that schizophrenia has a genetic component, but that inheritance may not follow classical Mendelian rules, with dominant and recessive genes for the major features, as for example, Huntington's chorea does. However, other illnesses pose problems similar to those encountered in the study of schizophrenia. There are many illnesses with a psychiatric and/or somatic character in which the hereditary mechanism is poorly understood. For example, the incidence of diabetes mellitus is also higher in the families of those who have the illness but, like schizophrenia, it seems to have a relatively low penetrance. The expression of the phenotype is apparently affected by other factors, since not all of the carriers of the relevant genes succumb to the illness.

Not just the incidence of schizophrenia, but also the incidence for subgroups and for specific symptoms, has been investigated. In earlier reports there seemed to be an increased incidence (concordance) for the symptoms of traditional subgroups in the kindred or twins studied (Fischer *et al.*, 1969;

**Table 10.1** Rates of Definite Schizophrenia
among Relatives of Schizophrenics[a]

| Familial relationship | n | % Affected |
|---|---|---|
| Offspring of two schizophrenics | 134 | 37 |
| Offspring of one schizophrenic | 1678 | 9 |
| Siblings | 7523 | 7 |
| Grandchildren | 739 | 3 |
| Monozygotic twins | 106 | 44 |
| First cousins | 1600 | 2 |
| Dizygotic twins | 149 | 12 |
| Spouses | 399 | 1 |

[a] Adapted from McGue and Gottesman, 1989.

Pollin *et al.*, 1969; Diebold *et al.*, 1977; Kallman, cited in Gottesman and
Shields, 1982). However, more recent studies (e.g., Kendler *et al.*, 1988) and
a critical review (McGuffin *et al.*, 1987) have questioned these reports.

Even if the question of whether prominent symptom patterns have a genetic
basis is disregarded, the reader should be cautioned against assuming that
there is enough evidence from family studies alone to understand the genetic
influence in schizophrenia, since the putative genetic and the putative environmental influences cannot be separated. If, for example, a child is raised by a
mentally disturbed parent, then the poor milieu and a negative influence on
the development of the child may theoretically also cause a mental handicap.

It may also be noted that, in most cases, the psychiatrists who were
retrospectively attempting to establish diagnoses were often not blind to the
type of family to which the subjects belonged. Bias favoring achievement of a
positive result for the investigation(s) may be involved (see the difficulties in
carrying out diagnoses, Chapter 1).

## B. Twin Studies

When searching for semiquantitative information on the degree of influence
exerted by hereditary and environmental factors in the etiology of schizophrenia,
the measures of concordance from twin studies are the appropriate gauge. If
genetic inheritance has a decisive influence, then MZ twins who share the same
genetic material should show a far greater incidence of schizophrenia when one
of them is schizophrenic than DZ twins. (If dominant genes were involved, the
incidence in the MZ twin should approach 100% whereas that in the DZ twin
would be about 50%.)

As can be seen in Table 10.1, the incidence rates of concordance are
considerably lower than would be expected from a straightforward Medelian

**Table 10.2** Effects of Diagnostic Criteria on Twin Concordance for Schizophrenia[a]

|                          | Monozygotic        | Dizygotic   | MZ:DZ |
|--------------------------|--------------------|-------------|-------|
| Chart diagnoses          | 10/24 (42)[b]      | 3/33  (9)   | 4.6   |
| Consensus of six judges  | 11/22 (50)         | 3/33  (9)   | 5.5   |
| Broad criteria (Meehl)   | 14/24 (58)         | 8/33 (24)   | 2.4   |
| Narrow criteria (Birley) | 3/15 (20)          | 3/22 (14)   | 1.5   |

[a]From Gottesman and Schields, 1982.
[b]Numbers in parentheses indicate percentages.

of inheritance. Because of the relatively numerous twin studies carried out, we must select and summarize the information. (For more complete discussions of both results and criticism of methods, see Jackson, 1960; Zerbin-Rüdin, 1972; Neale and Oltmanns, 1980; Gottesman and Shields, 1982; McGuffin *et al.*, 1984; Gottesman *et al.*, 1987; Kringlen, 1987; McGue and Gottesman, 1989.) The more recent studies attempt to consider the criticism of Jackson (1960), among others, of the methods formerly used.

The study of Gottesman and Shields (1982) at the Maudsley Hospital in London shall serve as an example for genetic research with twins. In this study, the selection and diagnosis of the subjects was carefully carried out: six evaluators blind to the zygosity of the subjects were employed. (The authors exerted much effort establishing the zygosity of their subjects. This was not as easy as it might appear and was treated relatively generously in earlier studies.) The degree of concordance depends on the diagnosis, but no matter what diagnostic scheme was used, or how narrowly or generously the criteria were applied, the concordance for schizophrenia was higher with the MZ than with the DZ twins in all cases. On the basis of the judgment of the six evaluators, the concordance was 50% for MZ and 9% for DZ twins (see Table 10.2; Gottesman and Shields, 1982).

The data are in good agreement with concordance rates derived from other more recent studies. However, older studies reported higher concordances. If justifiable criticisms of the methods are disregarded, one of the reasons for this higher concordance is most likely to be the inclusion of subjects with widely varying degrees of illness (i.e., the severity of the illness of the index twin also plays a role in the concordance rates). Relevant here is the re-analysis of an earlier study reported by Gottesman and Shields (1982) in their review. When this group of twins was divided into severely and mildly ill groups, the concordance rates for MZ twins were 75 and 17%, respectively. (The total concordance, without taking the severity of symptoms into account, was 46% for MZ and 14% for DZ twins.)

It is interesting to compare these results with those of Kendler and Robinette (1983) based on the twin register of the American Academy of Sciences. (Earlier reports from this database came from Pollin and colleagues; see Chapter 11.) From a base of 16,000 twins, 590 pairs had two or at least one schizophrenic twin. The concordance rate for schizophrenia was 31% for MZ and 6.5% for DZ twins. This concordance can be compared with that for diabetes mellitus, 19 versus 8%, and that for high blood pressure, 26 versus 11%. These concordance values are lower than those found in the Maudsley study, but do confirm the more general experience that concordance rates tend to be higher when the subjects are taken from a purely clinical background, than from the population at large. Once again, selection factors can be seen to play a role. It is also relevant that after Kendler and Robinette divided their population according to the severity of the illnesses, higher concordance rates were found in the more severely ill, which confirms the findings of Gottesman and Shields (1982).

Of course radical proponents of the influence of environmental factors still object to interpretations of these findings in terms of a genetic component in the transmission of schizophrenia. Some suggest that monozygocity and the necessary similarity of looks and behavior incur problems in the development of the "ego" and of the individual's identity, which are precisely the problems that these psychoanalysts suggest are uppermost in the anomalous development leading to schizophrenia (cf. Arieti, 1955). However, contrary to this argument, it should be noted that the incidence of schizophrenia in samples of MZ-twin probands or DZ-twin probands is no higher than in nontwin samples (Gottesman and Shields, 1982).

In order to counter the criticism of the "environmentalists," the development of MZ twins who were separated immediately after birth and grew up apart must be followed. This is a very rare circumstance. The numbers of cases available do not allow a statistically significant conclusion to be drawn. Evidence from 7 MZ twins (all separated in early childhood) speaks against interpretations that consider an identity problem the cause of the higher concordance rates in MZ twins: 5 of these twins were concordant for schizophrenia (see review and personal observations of Kringlen, 1987).

## C. Adoption Studies

Adoption studies provide a useful complementary paradigm for investigating the contribution of hereditary and environmental factors in the development of schizophrenia. If there is a hereditary component, there is an increased likelihood of a child of a schizophrenic patient to develop schizophrenia after adoption into a healthy family. The comparison is drawn with children of healthy parents adopted into healthy families. The control and index groups discussed here were carefully matched according to the relevant demographic features.

Several adoption studies have been carried out in Denmark, where there is a particularly comprehensive register of psychiatric illnesses. These studies have mostly been instigated by workers at the National Institutes of Mental Health (NIMH) (e.g., Rosenthal *et al.*, 1968, 1971, who searched the register for schizophrenic patients who had given their children up for adoption, and Kety *et al.*, 1975, 1978, who started with registered adopted probands who had developed schizophrenia). An earlier comprehensive study was carried out by Heston (1966) in the United States with a procedure similar to that adopted by Rosenthal.

The principal finding of the studies of Heston, Rosenthal, and colleagues was that a higher proportion of the children of schizophrenic biological parents than of the children of parents with no recorded illness who were adopted into healthy families eventually developed a schizophrenia-like illness. Some of the individuals concerned were adopted at an early age (i.e., <1 yr). For example, in the study of Heston (1966), 5 (11%) of the 47 adopted offspring of schizophrenic mothers became schizophrenic. None of the children in the control group became schizophrenic. Interestingly, Heston reported that not only schizophrenia, but also "sociopathy, neurosis, and mental deficiency," even greater artistic gifts were more frequent in the index group than in the control group.

The Danish–American study (Rosenthal *et al.*, 1968) and, more recently, a Finnish adoption study (Tienari *et al.*, 1985) reported lower frequencies than Heston (1966). However, cases with schizophrenia were still higher in the index group than in the control group. For example, Rosenthal *et al.* recorded a definitive schizophrenia in 6% of the adopted offspring deriving from a parent with schizophrenia ($n = 52$). This point is emphasized by the reanalysis of their results by Lowing *et al.* (1983). Using more modern diagnostic criteria, only 3% could be diagnosed as schizophrenic (DSM-III). However, as in the Heston study, the authors noted a higher incidence of milder psychiatric problems, especially schizotypal personality disorder, in the index offspring than in the control group. (This finding will be discussed in more detail in a subsequent section.)

It could therefore be claimed that modern diagnostic criteria uncover a lower incidence of fully developed schizophrenia in offspring of schizophrenic patients adopted into healthy families than the earlier studies (see also Tienari *et al.*, 1985, and subsequent text). The reported incidences are slightly lower than those expected from reports in which the offspring was reared by a schizophrenic biological parent and not by a healthy nonbiological parent. In the former case, 10% of the offspring were expected to be affected. This discrepancy permits consideration of the possible role of differences in the familial milieu (i.e., high risk offspring reared by a disturbed or by a healthy person).

This was the starting point for an additional project in Denmark by the

NIMH team. Wender *et al.* (1974) wanted to know what the influence of the adoptive father or mother on the adopted child might be. They searched in the Danish registers for those cases in which the adopting parent eventually became schizophrenic after adopting a child from healthy biological parents. (Compared with the previous design, this is the reverse procedure. Adopting schizophrenic *parents*, not the offspring of schizophrenic biological parents, formed the index group. This procedure is called a *cross-fostering* design.)

The result was that no more deviance was observed in the children of healthy biological parents (raised by a schizophrenic parent; *n* = 28) than in those children raised by healthy parents (*n* = 79). [For more details of the design and the results in this and the other two Danish–American adoption studies, the reader is referred to Gottesman and Shields (1982) who gave an extensive review of the field.] The unavoidable weakness of the study by Wender *et al.* (1974) is that there is no information about the nature of the interaction between the adopting parents and the child, since it is based on retrospective, if blind, analysis of case register data.

Indeed, these results did arouse controversy. Prominent in the debate over the validity of the conclusions have been Lidz and Blatt (1983) at Yale University, who maintained that environmental factors had played a much larger role than had been admitted. They argued that factors such as the age at adoption, the size of the family, and the age of illness onset were not considered. They further criticized that the inclusion of schizophrenia-like illnesses, such as borderline and spectrum diagnoses, may make the picture less rather than more clear. (Other problems include the small number of children appropriate for study and the even smaller number that might be expected to develop schizophrenia.) Thus, in their opinion, evidence from which to attempt to distinguish between genetic and environmental contributions to the development of schizophrenia is limited.

The Finnish team of Tienari and colleagues (1985) also criticized the results of the Danish–American adoption studies, which they felt had not considered sufficiently the different familial environments encountered by the adopted children. This factor can be seen in their own exhaustive study of the fate of 91 children adopted from schizophrenic mothers and 91 control children adopted from healthy mothers. Nevertheless, as in the Danish–American study, they found that more children of schizophrenic mothers developed schizophrenia or schizophrenia-like illnesses. Tienari *et al.* (1985) reported six (7%) schizophrenic cases in the index group and one (1%) psychotic proband in the control group. From 128 (133) matched pairs examined in a later re-analysis (Tienari *et al.,* 1989, 1991), there was no further incidence of illness in the control group, but three cases of paranoia and one of manic–depression had developed in the index group.

However, additional findings from Tienari *et al.* (1991) concerning the role of the family environment are of considerable relevance for a theory of gene–

**Table 10.3**  Demonstration of the Putative Gene/Environment Interaction in Adopted Offspring of Schizophrenic or Healthy Biological Mothers as a Function of the Family Atmosphere in the Adoptive Family[a]

| Offspring | Family atmosphere | | |
|---|---|---|---|
| | Healthy | Disturbed | Severely disturbed |
| Schizophrenic biological mother ($n = 133$) | | | |
| Healthy | 33 | 10 | 4 |
| Neurotic | 7 | 8 | 9 |
| Psychotic/Personality Disorder/Borderline | 3 | 8 | 20 |
| Nonschizophrenic biological mother ($n = 131$) | | | |
| Healthy | 31 | 15 | 5 |
| Neurotic | 12 | 13 | 11 |
| Psychotic/Personality Disorder/Borderline | 2 | 5 | 7 |

[a]Percentage of offspring with or without a disturbance in the different family groups. Adapted from Tienari et al., 1990.

environment interactions in schizophrenia. In contrast to the Danish–American adoption studies, they examined the family members themselves and recorded their patterns of interactions. They found more disturbed offspring in the more disturbed family environments (independent of the index status of the offspring). However, they also found that the likelihood of a severe disturbance (including schizophrenia) was greater if the offspring of a schizophrenic mother was brought up in an adoptive family with a disturbed family atmosphere (compared with the offspring of the control group who did not have the same risk status). From the index group, 20% of the offspring brought up in a disturbed adoptive family developed a severe character disorder or worse, whereas only 7% of the control group received the same rating (Table 10.3). These results appear to show the joint effects of genetic vulnerability and family environment (Tienari et al., 1991).

Naturally, Tienari and colleagues (1985, 1989, 1991) asked whether the disturbed family situation could have arisen through the adoption of the potentially psychotic child. However, since similar disturbances of the interactions between members of the family also occurred with the adoption of children from healthy parents, the authors doubt if this was the primary cause. Furthermore, they compared the incidence of clear clinical cases of schizophrenia in children who came directly from the biological parents or came indirectly by way of an institution. The incidence was higher in the latter case. Thus, Tienari *et al.* (1985, 1991) concluded that although a genetic predisposition played a role, unfavorable environmental conditions were important for the development of a complete schizophrenic illness. From this evidence, one might also argue that a "good" family environment can exert a protective effect (Tienari *et al.*, 1985, 1991; Gottesman *et al.*, 1987). However all these comments must be regarded as tentative; the conclusions may yet be strengthened or weakened. Not all subjects in these studies had reached the critical age for the development of schizophrenia.

## II. Patterns of Disturbance in First-Degree Relatives of Schizophrenics

### A. Offspring of Monozygotic Twins Discordant for Schizophrenia

Even if the results described so far are accepted as indicative of a heritable component in schizophrenia, it may explain only a part of the variance. At least 50% of the MZ twins with a schizophrenic parent are discordant for the illness. However, it is possible that those who do not develop schizophrenia are carriers. Factors may be present that suppress the release of the symptoms, as suggested earlier (i.e., the threshold for expression of the illness is not exceeded). This interpretation is supported by the conclusions of an elegant study by Fischer (1971, 1973) in Denmark.

Fischer studied the children of the nonschizophrenic twin partners of MZ twin pairs in which the other twin was schizophrenic ($n = 25$). In this group, she found a 13% incidence of schizophrenia. A recent re-analysis of the same material by Gottesman (now in Charlottesville, Virginia) and Bertelsen from Aarhus, Denmark (1989) confirms these findings (17% with a schizophrenic or schizophrenic-like psychosis; ICD diagnosis). This percentage is astonishingly close to that expected from a genetic model if one parent was schizophrenic (Figure 10.1; i.e., healthy twins with the same genetic complement as the schizophrenic partners seem to be carriers). In the offspring of the schizophrenic MZ twin, schizophrenia occurred with about the same incidence (16%) as in the offspring of the schizophrenic DZ twins (18%). The offspring of nonschizophrenic DZ twins had a much lower incidence of schizophrenia (3%; Figure 10.1).

Kringlen (1987) reported similar findings with 155 offspring of discordant MZ and DZ twins. There were 13% schizophrenic offspring in the former group and 3% in the latter. From such results it seems that, although schizophrenia cannot be attributed to genetic factors alone, an increased risk of developing schizophrenia must be genetically transmitted, even if one of the twins does not show a schizophrenia phenotype.

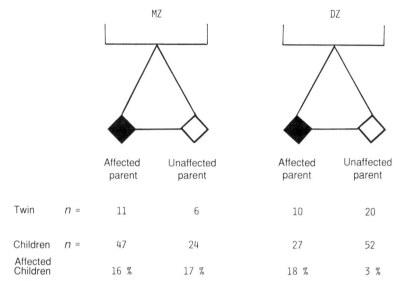

| | | Affected parent | Unaffected parent | Affected parent | Unaffected parent |
|---|---|---|---|---|---|
| Twin | n = | 11 | 6 | 10 | 20 |
| Children | n = | 47 | 24 | 27 | 52 |
| Affected Children | | 16 % | 17 % | 18 % | 3 % |

**Figure 10.1** Schematic illustration of the number of offspring of members of dizygotic (DZ) and monozygotic (MZ) twin pairs who developed schizophrenia as a function of whether their parent was the healthy or ill member of the twin pair (after Propping, 1989).

## B. Disturbances in Nonschizophrenic Relatives of Schizophrenics

It is rather important to provide a little more background at this time. The present concern is the mental health of the nonschizophrenic subjects. As mentioned briefly earlier, it is known from more detailed analyses that many of the discordant nonschizophrenic members of MZ twins are not necessarily completely mentally normal. (All too often the data presented in tables are crude and oversimplified. Subjects who do not develop schizophrenia may be classed along with healthy subjects when, in fact, a category of non-schizophrenic would be more appropriate.) Using data from several reports, Table 10.4 shows that schizoid disturbances (as far as they were recorded as such) and other psychiatric disturbances are relatively frequent among discordant twins. This does not mean that the evaluators did not find completely normal subjects among the partners of MZ twins that are schizophrenic. However, from the results described earlier, it would be expected that, if disturbed, the nonschizophrenic partners would show a less severe form of a (perhaps) schizophrenia-like personality disturbance.

Let us now return to the adoption studies. One of the earlier investigations (Rosenthal *et al.*, 1968, 1971) reported that many of the offspring adopted

**Table 10.4**  Pairwise Monozygotic Rates for Schizophrenia/
Questionable Schizophrenia, Schizoid, Other Psychiatric
Conditions, and Normality in Some Schizophrenic Twin Studies[a,b]

| Study | *n* | S (%) | Si (%) | P (%) | N (%) |
|---|---|---|---|---|---|
| Luxenburger | 14 | 72 | 14 | — | 14 |
| Rosanoff *et al.* | 41 | 61 | — | 7 | 32 |
| Kallmann | 174 | 69 | 21 | 5 | 5 |
| Slater | 37 | 64 | — | 14 | 22 |
| Kringlen | 45 | 38 | — | 29 | 33 |
| Fischer | 21 | 48 | 5 | 5 | 43 |
| Gottesman & Shields | 22 | 50 | 9 | 18 | 23 |

[a]From Gottesman and Shields, 1982.
[b]S, schizophrenia/questionable schizophrenia; Si, schizoid; P, other psychiatric conditions; N, normal.

from their biological parents could be given a *spectrum diagnosis,* that is, mental disturbances were recorded that could be ascribed to schizophrenia and the periphery of a conventional diagnosis of schizophrenia (e.g., personality disorders with mild schizophrenia-like features). From the index group, 32% of adopted offspring without schizophrenic parents were given a spectrum diagnosis; from the control group, the figure was 16%. Since these diagnoses were somewhat vague, the outcome of this study was criticized (e.g., Lidz *et al.,* 1981). Lowing *et al.* (1983) from the NIMH re-analyzed the material, as already reported. Both analyses were carried out blind to the status of the offspring of the probands. Lowing *et al.* (1983) then used DSM-III criteria. There was some change in the diagnosis of the parents, but the higher incidence of spectrum subjects was confirmed. They diagnosed only one case of schizophrenia (2.5%), but 38% of the index group and 13% of the control group were considered spectrum cases. Within the spectrum diagnosis, schizotypal and schizoid personality disorders had the highest frequency (Table 10.5). This was also true if only the adopted offspring of chronic schizophrenics were considered.

The incidence of borderline cases and borderline personality disturbances (DSM-III) did not distinguish the two groups reanalyzed by Lowing and colleagues. Kendler and Gruenenberg (1984) also found, in their reanalysis of another Danish–American adoption study, an increased incidence of DSM-III-defined spectrum personality disturbances (rated blind) among the biological parents of the adopted children that eventually developed schizophrenia. Prominent were schizotypal and paranoid personality disorders, but not borderline cases.

Kendler and Gruenberg used the material of Kety *et al.* (1975) who were

**Table 10.5**  Reanalysis of the Rosenthal *et al.* (1968, 1971) Adoption Study by Lowing *et al.* (1983)

| DSM III diagnosis | Adopted offspring | |
|---|---|---|
| | Schizophrenic biological parent (*n* = 39) | Nonschizophrenic biological parent (*n* = 39) |
| Schizophrenia | 1 | 0 |
| Spectrum personality disorder[a] | 14 | 5 |
| No spectrum disorder | 24 | 34 |

[a]Schizotypal personality disorder, schizoid personality disorder, borderline personality disorder, and "mixed spectrum".

interested in adopted offspring with schizophrenia (from the Danish register) and in the rate of schizophrenia in the biological *parents* of these children. [The so-called "Kety strategy" represented the third Danish adoption study of the NIMH, along with the "conventional strategy" of the study of Rosenthal *et al.* (1968, 1971) and the "cross-fostering strategy" of Wender *et al.*, 1974.]

This argument will now be extended to a large-scale study of the incidence of spectrum personality disturbances in first degree relatives of unequivocally diagnosed chronic schizophrenics (Baron *et al.*, 1983, 1987). This study was run by the New York Psychiatric Institute at two major hospitals. It found a significantly higher incidence of spectrum personality disturbances in 376 first degree relatives of 90 schizophrenics (RDC; DSM-III) than in a control group of 346 first degree relatives of 90 nonschizophrenics.

In detail, Baron found a schizotypal personality disturbance in 15% of the first degree relatives of the schizophrenics but in only 2% of the control relatives. Paranoid personality disturbances and chronic schizophrenia were less frequent than schizotypal traits among the relatives of the schizophrenics, but were still significantly more frequent than in the controls, with incidences of 7% and 6%, respectively. Kendler and colleagues (1984) from another clinic in New York presented similar results in a study of first degree relatives. Coryell and Zimmerman (1989) found no differences, but the diagnoses of the relatives were mostly attained through telephone interviews, which may be a disadvantage. Schulz *et al.* (1986) in Pittsburgh wanted to know whether the incidence of schizophrenia or schizotypal disturbances was higher among the first degree relatives of patients with a schizotypal personality disturbance. They obtained negative results. Unfortunately there were several weaknesses in the study. In particular, the experimental group used was too small (*n* = 22), and only 44 relatives were investigated. If the incidence is considered, it may be expected from the previous studies that the use of small groups extremely reduces the chance of finding subjects with schizotypal or schizophrenic symptoms. Therefore, little weight can be placed on these negative results.

The reasons for classifying the spectrum diagnosis under the DSM largely arose from the adoption studies (particularly those of Rosenthal and colleagues). Unfortunately, it provides no clear broadly accepted definition. However, most of the authors cited included schizotypal, paranoid, or schizoid personality disorders. Borderline personality disorder seemed to be less frequent in first degree relatives of schizophrenics, but no definitive answer can yet be given. Some of the personality disorders defined in the DSM-III-R do overlap. (See Gottesman, 1987, for an extensive discussion.)

Relevant to whether a narrow or broad definition of the illness relates to the putative common genetic element is a study by Gottesman, now at the University of Virginia. This American–English study (Farmer et al., 1987) revealed that the inclusion of schizotypal personality disturbances, atypical psychoses, and mood-incongruent delusions along with definitive cases of schizophrenia markedly increased concordance values for MZ over DZ twins. They calculated the concordance rates for a number of diagnostic constellations, but this particular constellation of diagnoses showed the largest difference between MZ and DZ twins. The other extreme shows that if a very narrow definition of schizophrenia is used (e.g., Abrams and Taylor, 1983, Chicago), extremely few schizophrenic patients are reported from the families of these schizophrenics.

In summary, it can be said that there is an increased incidence of schizophrenic spectrum personality disturbances that are genetically in some way related to schizophrenia among the first degree relatives of schizophrenics (e.g., schizotypal, schizoid, paranoid, and probably other psychotic disturbances such a atypical psychosis, mood-incongruent delusions, and schizoaffective disorder). Remarkable, though, is the absence in all studies of reports of (DSM-III-R) borderline personality disturbances among the relatives of schizophrenic patients. This is in contrast to prior expectations (see review by Schied, 1990).

These findings could form part of a working hypothesis for current research, to facilitate the assembly of new symptom constellations from an empirical base for studies of the nature of genetic transmission in schizophrenia (cf. Morey, 1988).

## III. Genetic Models and Genetic Analysis

### A. Single Major Locus Models

From the data discussed earlier, it seems evident that the classic Mendelian single major locus models cannot adequately explain the observations (i.e., one dominant or recessive gene). In other words, it is unlikely that a direct pathway from the genotype to the phenotype exists. For example, not all the twin partners of affected MZ twins are schizophrenic themselves. They must, however, transmit "something" in their genetic material, since more offspring of the unaffected become ill than would be expected if no transmission had occurred.

Several authors have therefore proposed that a dominant or recessive single gene with reduced penetrance may explain the data. Debray and colleagues (1979) from France ran likelihood estimates for 12 different potential genetic models of transmission, including single major locus models with low penetrance. Their data were based on 1333 individuals from 25 families with a schizophrenic member, covering 4 generations. The authors were not able to decide among several models, since they obtained similar likelihood estimates, but they were able to conclude that modified (low penetrance) single major locus models were untenable (later confirmed by Tsuang *et al.* 1982, and others; see reviews by Faraone *et al.*, 1988; McGue and Gottesman, 1989; see Crow, 1990, for a continuation of the argument for a single locus in a modified form).

## B. Polygenic Models

Polygenic models propose that several genes found at several loci may explain the pattern of transmission in schizophrenia. There are three main reasons to propose this alternative: (1) different degrees of severity of schizophrenia may be better explained by differences in the number of loci responsible (additive effects) than by single major locus models; (2) the puzzling heterogeneity may be better explained by different genes (i.e., by different combinations of genes in different schizophrenic patients); or (3) schizophrenia may be the result of the interaction of several genes. Also, (4) the fact that the rate of schizophrenia in the population is constant despite the reduced rate of reproduction of schizophrenic patients cannot be explained by single major locus models.

There have been several studies performed so far, but no clear support has become evident for the one or the other variant two-locus model, several-locus model, and so on. (See reviews by Gottesman and Shields, 1982; Faraone *et al.*, 1988.)

## C. Multifactorial Models

A multifactorial model assumes that the phenotype is the result of a combination of genetic transmission *and* environmental influences. A multifactorial model was first proposed by Gottesman and Shields (1967) for the mode of transmission in schizophrenia, but such models have been applied earlier to account for other nonstraightforward familial distributions of (psycho)somatic illnesses, such as high blood pressure, allergies, and diabetes

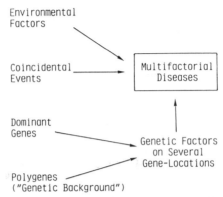

**Figure 10.2**  Schematic illustration of the multifactorial model. Several genes (most likely a dominant gene and its genetic background) as well as environmental factors contribute to the "multifactorial" illness (after Propping, 1989).

mellitus. In the case of schizophrenia, it is suggested that all individuals have some unobservable liability or predisposition to develop the illness. The model assumes that the mode of transmission is polygenic; therefore the arguments given previously also apply here. The main advantage is that the model also considers environmental factors (Figure 10.2). Another special feature is that a normal distribution of the predisposition in the general population is assumed. The appearance of the illness is seen as the crossing of a threshold. The model also accounts for spectrum personality disorders (second threshold) (see Baron, 1986a,b, 1987; Figure 10.3).

There are several old "goodness-of-fit" calculations that have yielded

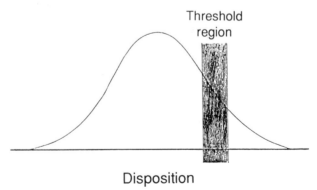

**Figure 10.3**  Gaussian distribution of the disposition to illness in the population (i.e., the subclinical spectrum or threshold region). The illness is overt in the area to the right (after Propping, 1989).

mixed results (cf. Matthysse and Kidd, 1976; review by Gottesman and Shields, 1982). More recent analyses incorporate the two-threshold assumption (i.e., different degrees of the expression of the phenotype from schizoid personality disorder to schizophrenia) and use path analysis in order to disentangle the effects of genetic and environmental factors. Several studies were again initiated by Gottesman and co-workers (see Rao *et al.*, 1981; McGue *et al.*, 1983, 1987) using all information available from several Western European family and twin databases. The results of the "goodness-of-fit" calculations for these data were all similar, favoring the assumption of a multifactorial model and rejecting single major locus models. The authors also concluded that genetic factors accounted for most of the variance (about 60%) but that environmental factors were also important, just to a lesser degree (see review by Faraone *et al.*, 1988, for more details).

## D. Mixed Models

A variant of the multifactorial model is the mixed model. The mixed model assumes that a major locus gene exists with a polygenic background and environmental factors (see Figure 10.2). The model therefore takes into account the heterogeneity and the similarity of the phenotype. Carter and Chung (1980) were not able to find support for a mixed model, but they only used hospital diagnoses to calculate the "goodness-of-fit" with the data from 507 siblings. Baron (1987) also included spectrum disorders in his analysis, using diagnoses based on a standardized interview (79 chronic schizophrenics and their first degree relatives). The result of this study was discussed already. Baron (1987) found that a single recessive major locus makes the largest contribution to the transmission of the liability (63%). In the model, there was also a statistical likelihood for a polygenic influence, but it was considerably lower (20%). The contribution of environmental effects (random and common sibling environment) to the variance in liability was estimated to be 17%.

   In summary, both mixed and polyfactorial models can be supported to some extent. Thus, as yet, no clear decision can be made about which mode of transmission is the most likely, although single major locus models can probably be rejected (see also McGue and Gottesman, 1989). A problem for these mathematical models and the "goodness-of-fit" estimations is that they depend on the reliability of the diagnosis and, more critically, on the concept of schizophrenia. Therefore, no definitive answers can be expected from this type of calculation. If a researcher decides to include only hospitalized schizophrenic patients, or even only DSM-III-R defined chronic schizophrenic patients, he or she gets a different picture of the mode of transmission than the researcher who believes that spectrum disorders, including schizoid or paranoid personality traits, belong to the genetic concept of schizophrenia.

Another problem is, then, to define the borders of the spectrum (see the comprehensive discussion of this problem by Gottesman *et al.*, 1987). Since it is not clear what the appropriate phenotype for analysis should be in schizophrenia research, we must await more precisely defined biological or genetic markers. (These markers will be discussed in the next section.)

## E. Molecular Genetic Approaches

Three recent studies conducted by teams from London (Sherrington *et al.*, 1988), Edinburgh (St. Clair *et al.*, 1989), and Yale (Kennedy *et al.*, 1988) have not waited for improved diagnosis and recognition of schizophrenia, but plunged into the material from well-known pedigrees with the newer techniques of molecular biology. Sherrington and colleagues claimed to have demonstrated that the inheritance of a disposition to psychiatric disorders belonging to the schizophrenia spectrum can be associated with genetic material on chromosome 5. The latter two studies, with negative results, have shown that not all cases of schizophrenia can be so explained. How did this all come about?

Three conditions were necessary: the availability of pedigrees providing psychiatric information and genetic material, the methods for locating the genetic fragments responsible, and a sign of where to look among the vast library of genes available.

The analysis of large family clans will be considered first. Sherrington *et al.* (1988) studied two British and five Icelandic pedigrees covering three generations. The Icelandic families were those described by Karlsson (1982, 1988). This database of 104 persons included 39 cases of schizophrenia, 5 with schizoid disturbances, and a further 10 cases of disorders including phobias, anxiety, and depression. Kennedy *et al.* (1988) searched northern Swedish pedigrees. This material covers 157 persons in seven branches. They were able to diagnose 31 cases of schizophrenia and found 50 unaffected subjects. St. Clair *et al.* used the same phenotypic descriptions as the London group, with 15 families in Scotland. Of 166 members whose DNA was examined, 75 had some mental disturbance; for 44 this was schizophrenia, and, for a further 5 cases, a psychosis or spectrum personality was determined.

We will now discuss the methods. Basically, these tools involve the use of restriction enzymes to identify places at which the different genomes vary. When following the inheritance of parts of a chromosome through a family, one can use the variations of the sequences of DNA as genetic markers. These variations become visible when they disrupt the recognition site for a restriction enzyme. The sequences of DNA marked by these sites are called restriction fragment length polymorphisms (RFLPs). Among the thousands of such sequences already known in humans, it has been possible to track RFLPs that pass from generation to generation with a disease (e.g., Huntington's chorea, manic depression; Egeland *et al.*, 1987[1]). It can be concluded that the genes contributing to the disease lie in a chromosomal region near the RFLP.

Why did these groups look at chromosome 5? The sign was provided by a case reported by Bassett *et al.* (1988). The case concerned an uncle and nephew who were both schizophrenic and had certain unusual facial features in common. They both carried an extra copy of the region known as 5q11–13 translocated to chromosome 1. (Additionally, at the time it was thought that the glucocorticoid receptor was encoded near the 5q region. Disturbance of glucocorticoid metabolism can give rise to psychoses. This locus has since been shown not to be as close as originally thought.)

Sherrington *et al.* (1988) reported finding strong concordance with a putative dominant character predisposing to schizophrenia. The concordance has been improved by including the other psychiatric illnesses, but in view of the relatively inadequate information provided by the individuals concerned, this finding must be treated with reserve. The transmission of schizophrenia and of the genetic markers was $10^{6.49}$-fold more likely if they were genetically linked than unlinked (i.e., the relatively high lod score of 6.49 speaks in favor of a single gene locus[2]). Two features, one in the design and the other in the methods, must qualify this result. There was a deliberately biased sampling of families for signs of genes with a high penetrance. This was deemed a necessary design feature to increase the likelihood of finding what their methods could detect, namely, a single gene locus. However it is difficult to believe that the lod score increased when they broadened the diagnostic criteria to include various depressive illnesses. Family, twin, and adoption studies have not provided evidence for a genetic link between these two types of psychiatric disturbance (e.g., Loranger, 1981).

However, reasonable criticism can also be made of the reports of negative results (Byerley *et al.*, 1989). The pedigree studied by Kennedy *et al.* (1988)

---

[1]They reported evidence that a locus on the short arm of chromosome 11 conferred susceptibility for a manic–depressive illness in an Amish kindred. This is close to the region coding for tyrosine hydroxylase, the rat-limiting enzyme for catecholamine synthesis (however, as yet, no linkage studies for these two loci have been reported). Furthermore, manic–depressive illnesses are heterogeneous: the link with site 11p has been excluded in three Icelandic and four American families. X-linked dominant transmission has been implicated in some European and Jewish families (see Byerley *et al.*, 1989). Indeed, a subsequent extension of the Amish pedigree has questioned the significance of the original results (Kelsoe *et al.*, 1989).

[2]The "lod" score or "log of the odds" refers to the usual parametric statistic for assessing the strength of a linkage. The conventional threshold for acceptance of linkage is 3.0, whereas that for rejection of a linkage between a polymorphic test marker and a particular disease locus is $-2.0$. For example, in 1990 the status of combined studies on a marker for Huntington's disease on the short arm of chromosome 4 was 87.7 at a recombination frequency of 0.04; in contrast, for the 11p marker for bipolar affective disorder, the lod score has decreased from 4.08 in the original study to $-9.3$ after subsequent additional investigations.

may prove to be an exceptional case. There is reason to suppose that it is also demonstrating segregation for mental retardation. This adds considerable complexity to the analysis. Although the report of St. Clair *et al.* is laudable for its attempt to test several hypotheses for the linkage of different syndromes, their basic assumption of an autosomal dominant mode for inheritance is unlikely. Byerley is not alone in suggesting that a recessive mode is more likely (see previous section).

What might the combined results mean? It seems that schizophrenia may rarely be linked to defects in an unknown gene on chromosome 5. It may be a dominant gene, the inheritance of which leads to the inheritance of a susceptibility to schizophrenia. However, carriers do not necessarily develop schizophrenia. It has not been shown that a chromosome 5 defect is sufficient for the development of schizophrenia nor that all schizophrenia develops from this or any other gene. Using five RFLPs, Kennedy *et al.* found no evidence of a link between chromosome 5 and schizophrenia, but noted that a demonstration of the heterogeneity of schizophrenia would require finding another genetic locus (Lander, 1988).[3] Striking in the results of Sherrington *et al.* (1988) is that apparently several subtypes of schizophrenia may have a common genetic source. Again, the suggestion is that the etiology does not match the results of current diagnostic practices. Future studies should aim to attain more psychiatric and genetic information from more members. This information should be combined with recently developed genetic maps to demonstrate linkage. Such techniques could already be applied to other behavioral and physiological markers correlating with schizophrenia (e.g., pursuit eye movements, sensitivity to amphetamine; Lander, 1988; see also Chapter 7, and especially Holzman *et al.* 1988).

# IV. Suggested Readings

The reader interested in making a more detailed assessment of inheritance of schizophrenia may read the following publications: Gottesman and Shields, 1982; McGuffin and Sturt, 1986; Andrew *et al.*, 1987; Gottesman *et al.*, 1987; Gershon *et al.*, 1987; Faraone *et al.*, 1988; Holzmann *et al.*, 1988; Crow, 1990; and the review of the Dahlem conference in Helmchen and Henn, 1987.

---

[3]There are at least two other reports of features with an increased incidence in small groups of schizophrenics, the origin of which has been traced to a locus on chromosome 19 (19p13) (see discussion in Byerley *et al.*, 1989). It should not be overlooked that there may be a number of genetic defects necessary for the expression of the phenotype. It may be a combination of all or only some of these that is sufficient for the illness to appear.

# V. Summary Statements and Interpretations

## A. Monozygotic (MZ) and Dizygotic (DZ) Twin Studies

The rate of schizophrenia is higher in MZ than in DZ twins. The concordance is generally less than 50%, but is higher if one of the twins is severely ill.

The numbers speak for a genetic contribution, but are far lower than those expected for a straightforward dominant–recessive model of inheritance.

## B. Adoption Studies

The adopted (index) offspring of schizophrenic parents are at higher risk for developing schizophrenia than control children. However, the incidence of schizophrenia is lower than in children living with the affected parent. In some adoption studies, schizophrenia is rare, but spectrum personality disorder (e.g., schizotypal personality disorder) is more frequent.

These results demonstrate that both the genetic disposition and the environment play a role in the development of schizophrenia.

## C. First-Degree Relatives of Schizophrenics

About 15% of the relatives of schizophrenics have personality disorders which have some similarity with schizophrenia (i.e., schizotypal personality disorder and other spectrum features).

A common heritable factor seems to be the basis of both the fully developed illness and the spectrum personality disorder. There may be at least two influences that determine the severity of the expression as spectrum or fully developed schizophrenia: environmental stress and the degree of genetic load (reflected, for example, by the number of afflicted relatives; Odegaard, 1972, in Propping, 1989). The phenotype is the product of a genetic/environment interaction but the genetic predisposition seems to be the necessary condition. Birth complications and slight cortical atrophy seem to play the same unfavorable role as aversive environmental influences (see Chapters 8 and 12). Another possibility is that of a phenocopy, if the same putative pathognomonic area is afflicted by atrophic processes.

## D. Mechanisms of Inheritance

The exact mode of inheritance is not clear, although most researchers exclude at least the possibility of a single major locus gene. Psychiatric genetics today favor polyfactorial or mixed models (i.e., this is the result of most mathematical likelihood estimations when comparing the model with the appearance of schizophrenia or spectrum disorders in pedigrees).

The polyfactorial model assumes that several genes are responsible for schizophrenia and the additional influence of the environment result in the crossing of a second threshold. The appearance of spectrum disorders is being considered as the crossing of an initial threshold. In general, it is suggested that the liability or the disposition to develop the illness is distributed continuously in the population (Gaussian distribution). The mixed model assumes that, in addition to the factors involved in the polyfactorial mode of transmission, a single major gene locus is responsible.

The mixed and polyfactorial models seem to be plausible with respect to the fact that the phenotype is heterogeneous, the illness can appear without family history of schizophrenia, and schizophrenia does not die out despite the fact that schizophrenic patients have fewer offspring than healthy persons. However, the exact proof for one or the other model is difficult to present because of the variable nature of and the difficulty defining the borders of the various expressions of the phenotype in the general population, from mild spectrum features to severe breakdown.

## E. Molecular Genetics

A recent claim that the genetic locus is on chromosome 5 is not supported by several other studies.

It is theoretically possible, as discussed earlier, that more than one locus is required to bring about a sufficient liability for developing schizophrenia. If so, a search for a single locus would only make sense if the existence and contribution of a major gene could be assumed. Information pertinent to a decision between the alternatives is not available.

## References

Abrams, R., and Taylor, M. A. (1983). The genetics of schizophrenia: A reassessment using modern criteria. *American Journal of Psychiatry*, *140*, 171–175.

Andrew, B., Watt, D. C., Gillespie, C., and Chapel, H. (1987). A study of genetic linkage in schizophrenia. *Psychological Medicine*, *17*, 363–370.

Arieti, S. (1955). Interpretation of schizophrenia. New York: Brunner.

Baron, M. (1982). Genetic models of schizophrenia. *Acta Psychiatrics Scandinavica*, *65*, 263.

Baron, M. (1986a). Genetics of schizophrenia: I. Familial patterns and mode of inheritance. *Society of Biological Psychiatry*, *21*, 1051–1066.

Baron, M. (1986b). Genetics of schizophrenia: II. Vulnerability traits and gene markers. *Society of Biological Psychiatry*, *21*, 1189–1211.

Baron, M. (1987). Genetic models and the transmission of schizophrenia. In H. Häfner, W. F. Gattaz and W. Janzarik (Eds.). *Search for the causes of schizophrenia*. Berlin: Springer.

Baron, M., Gruen, R., Asnis, L., and Kane, J. (1983). Familial relatedness of schizophrenia and schizotypal states. *American Journal of Psychiatry*, *140*, 1437–1442.

Baron, M., Gruen, R., Rainer, J. D., Kane, J., Asnis, L., and Lord, S. (1985). A family study of schizophrenic and normal control probands: Implications for the spectrum concept of schizophrenia. *American Journal of Psychiatry*, *142*, 447–454.

Basset, A. S., Jones, B. D., McGillivray, B. C. and Pantzar, J. T. (1988). Partial trisomy chromosome 5 cosegregating with schizophrenia. *Lancet*, *1*, 799–800.

Byerley, W., Mellon, C., O'Connell, P., Lalouel, J.-M., Nakamura, Y., Leppert, M. and White, R. (1989). Mapping genes for manic-depression and schizophrenia with DNA markers. *Trends in Neurosciences*, *12*, 46–48.

Carter, C. L., and Chung, C. S. (1980). Segregating analysis of schizophrenia under a mixed genetic model. *Human Heredity*, *30*, 350.

Coryell, W. H., and Zimmerman, M. (1989). Personality disorder in the families of depressed, schizophrenic, and never-ill probands. *American Journal of Psychiatry*, *146*, 496–502.

Crow, T. J. (1990). Nature of the genetic contribution to psychotic illness—a continuum viewpoint. *Acta Psychiatrica Scandinavica*, *81*, 401–408.

Debray, Q., Coillard, V., and Stewart, J. (1979). Schizophrenia: A study of genetic models. *Human Heredity*, *29*, 27–36.

Diebold, K., Arnold, E., and Pfaff, W. (1977). Statistische Untersuchungen zur Symptomatik und Syndromatik von 120 endogen psychotischen Elter- Kind- und Geschwisterpaaren. *Fortschr. d.Neurologie, Psychiat. u.ihrer Grenzgeb*, *45*, 349–364.

Egeland, J. A., Gerhard, D. S., Pauls, D. L., Sussex, J. N., Kidd, K. K., Allen, C. R., Hostetter, A. M., and Housman, D. E. (1987). Bipolar affective disorders linked to DNA markers on chromosome 11. *Nature*, *325*, 783–787.

Faraone, S. V., Lyons, M. J., and Tsuang, M. T. (1988). Mathematical models of genetic transmission. In M. T. Tsuang, J. C. Simpson (Eds.), *Handbook of schizophrenia, Vol. 3: Nosology, epidemiology and genetics*. (pp. 501–530). Amsterdam: Elsevier.

Farmer, A. E., McGuffin, P., and Gottesman, I. I. (1987). Twin concordance for DSM-III schizophrenia. *Archives of General Psychiatry*, *44*, 634–644.

Fischer, M. (1971). Psychoses in the offspring of schizophrenic monozygotic twins and their normal co-twins. *British Journal of Psychiatry*, *118*, 43–52.

Fischer, M. (1973). Genetic and environmental factors in schizophrenia. *Acta Psychiatrics Scandinavica*, Suppl. 238.

Fischer, M., Harvald, B., and Hauge, M. (1969). A Danish twin-study of schizophrenia. *British Journal of Psychiatry*, *115*, 981–990.

Frangos, E., Athanassenas, G., Tsitourides, S., Katsanou, N., and Alexandrakou, P. (1985). Prevalence of DSM-III schizophrenia among the first-degree relatives of schizophrenic probands. *Acta Psychiatrics Scandinavica*, *72*, 382–386.

Gershon, E. S., Merril, C. R., Goldin, L. R., DeLisi, L. E., Berrettini, W. H., and Nurnberger, J. I., Jr. (1987). The role of molecular genetics in psychiatry. *Biological Psychiatry*, *22*, 1388–1405.

Gottesman, I. I., and Bertelsen, A. (1989). Confirming unexpressed genotypes for schizophrenia. *Archives of General Psychiatry*, *46*, 867–872.

Gottesman, I. I., McGuffin, P., and Farmer, A. E. (1987). Clinical genetics as clues to the "real" genetics of schizophrenia. *Schizophrenia Bulletin*, *13*, 23–47.

Gottesman, I. I., and Shields, J. A. (1967). A polygenic theory of schizophrenia. *Proceedings in North Atlantic Academic Sciences*, *58*, 199–205.

Gottesman, I. I., and Shields, J. (1982). *Schizophrenia: The epigenetic puzzle*. Cambridge: Cambridge University Press.

Helmchen, H., and Henn, A. (Eds.) (1987). *Biological perspectives of schizophrenia. Dahlem workshop reports*. New York: Wiley.

Heston, L. L. (1966). Psychiatric disorders in foster home reared children of schizophrenic mothers. *British Journal of Psychiatry*, *112*, 819–825.

Holzman, P. S., Kringlen, E., Mattysse, S., Flanagan, S. D., Lipton, R. B., Cramer, G., Levin,

S., Lange, K., and Levy, D. L. (1988). A single dominant gene can account for eye tracking dysfunction and schizophrenia in offspring of discordant twins. *Archiv of General Psychiatry*, *45*, 641–647.

Jackson, D. D. (1960). A critique of the literature on the genetics of schizophrenia. In D. D. Jackson (Ed.), *The study of schizophrenia*. New York: Basic Books.

Karlsson, J. L. (1982). Family transmission of schizophrenia: A review and synthesis. *British Journal of Psychiatry*, *140*, 600–606.

Karlsson, J. L. (1988). Partly dominant transmission of schizophrenia in Iceland. *British Journal of Psychiatry*, *152*, 324–329.

Kelsoe, J. R., Ginns, E. I., Egeland, J. A., Gerhard, D. S., Goldstein, A. M., Bale, S. J., Pauls, D. L., Long, R. T., Kidd, K. K., Conte, G., and Housman, D. E. (1989). Re-evaluation of the linkage relationship between chromosome lip loci and the gene for bipolar affective disorder in the old order Amish. *Nature*, *342*, 238–243.

Kendler, K. S., and Gruenberg, A. M. (1984). An independent analysis of the Danish adoption study of schizophrenia. *Archives of General Psychiatry*, *41*, 555–564.

Kendler, K. S., Gruenberg, A. M., and Tsuang, M. T. (1985). Psychiatric illness in first-degree relatives of schizophrenic and surgical control patients. *Archives of General Psychiatry*, *42*, 770–779.

Kendler, K. S., Gruenberg, A. M., and Tsuang, M. T. (1988). A family study of the subtypes of schizophrenia. *American Journal of Psychiatry*, *145*, 57–62.

Kendler, K. S. and Robinette, C. D. (1983). Schizophrenia in the National Academy of Sciences-National Research Council Twin Registry: A 16-year update. *American Journal of Psychiatry*, *140*, 1551–1563.

Kendler, K. S., Masterson, C. C., Ungaro, R., and Davis, K. L. (1984). A family history study of schizophrenia-related personality disorders. *American Journal of Psychiatry*, *141*, 424–427.

Kennedy, J. L., Guiffra, L. A., Moises, H. W., Cavalli-Sforzas, L. L., Pakstis, A. J., Kidd, J. R., Castiglione, C. M., Sjogren, B., Wetterberg, L., and Kidd, K. K. (1988). Evidence against linkage of schizophrenia to markers on chromosome 5 in a north Swedish pedigree. *Nature*, *336*, 167–170.

Kety, S. S., Rosenthal, D., Wender, P. H., Schulsinger, F., and Jacobsen, B. (1975). Mental illness in the biological and adoptive families of adopted individuals who have become schizophrenic: A preliminary report based on psychiatric interviews. In R. R. Fieve, D. Rosenthal, H. Brill (Eds.), *Genetic research in psychiatry*. Baltimore: Johns Hopkins University Press.

Kety, S. S., Rosenthal, D., Wender, P. H., Schulsinger, F., Jacobsen, B. (1978). The biological and adoptive families of adopted individuals who become schizophrenic: Prevalence of mental illness and other characteristics. In L. C. Wynne, R. L. Cromwell, S. Matthysse (Eds.), *The nature of schizophrenia*. New York: Wiley.

Kringlen, E. (1987). Contribution of genetic studies on schizophrenia. In H. Häfner, W. F. Gattaz, W. Janzarik (Eds.), *Search for the causes of schizophrenia*. Berlin: Springer.

Lander, E. S. (1988). Splitting schizophrenia. *Nature*, *336*, 105–106.

Lidz, T., and Blatt, S. (1983). Critique of the Danish-American studies of the biological and adoptive relatives of adoptees who became schizophrenic. *American Journal of Psychiatry*, *140*, 426–434.

Lidz, T., Blatt, S., Cook, B. (1981). Critique of the Danish-American studies of the adopted-away offspring of schizophrenic parents. *American Journal of Psychiatry*, *138*, 1063–1068.

Loranger, A. W. (1981). Genetic independence of manic-depression and schizophrenia. *Acta Psychiatrics Scandinavica*, *63*, 444–452.

Lowing, P. A., Mirsky, A. F., and Pereira, R. (1983). The inheritance of schizophrenia spectrum disorders: A reanalysis of the Danish adoptee study data. *American Journal of Psychiatry*, *140*, 1167–1171.

Matthysse, S. W., and Kidd, K. K. (1976). Estimating the genetic contribution to schizophrenia. *American Journal of Psychiatry, 133*, 185–191.

McGue, M., Gottesman, I., and Rao, D. C. (1983). The transmission of schizophrenia under a multifactorial threshold model. *American Journal of Human Genetics, 35*, 1161.

McGue, M., and Gottesman, I. I. (1989). Genetic linkage in schizophrenia: perspectives from genetic epidemiology. *Schizophrenia Bulletin, 15*, 453–464.

McGue, M., Gottesman, I. I., and Rao, D. C. (1986). The analysis of schizophrenia family data. *Behavior Genetics, 16*, 75–87.

McGue, M., Gottesman, I. I., and Rao, D. C. (1987). Resolving genetic models for the transmission of schizophrenia. *Genetics and Epidemiology, 2*, 99.

McGuffin, P., Farmer, A., and Gottesman, I. I. (1987). Is there really a split in schizophrenia? *British Journal of Psychiatry, 150*, 581–592.

McGuffin, P., Farmer, A. E., Gottesman, I. I., Murray, R. M., and Reveley, A. M. (1984). Twin concordance for operationally defined schizophrenia. *Archives of General Psychiatry, 41*, 541–545.

McGuffin, P., and Sturt, E. (1986). Genetic markers in schizophrenia. *Human Heredity, 36*, 65–88.

Morey, L. C. (1988). The categorical representation of personality disorder: A cluster analysis of DSM-III-R personality features. *Journal of Abnormal Psychology, 97*, 314–321.

Neale, J. M., and Oltmanns, T. F. (1980). *Schizophrenia*. New York: John Wiley & Sons.

Odegaard, O. (1972). The multifactorial theory of inheritance in predisposition of schizophrenia. In A. K. Kaplan (Ed.), *Genetic factors in schizophrenia.* (pp. 256–275). Springfield, Illinois: Charles C. Thomas.

Pollin, W., Allen, M. G., Hoffer, A., Stabenau, J. R., and Huber, Z. (1969). Psychopathology in 15,909 pairs of veteran twins. *American Journal of Psychiatry, 7*, 597–609.

Propping, P. (1989). *Psychiatrische Genetik. Befunde und Konzepte.* Berlin: Springer.

Rao, D. C., Marton, N. E., Gottesman, I. I., and Lew, R. (1981). Path analysis of qualitative data on pairs of relatives: Application to schizophrenia. *Human Heredity, 31*, 325–333.

Rosenthal, D., Wender, P. H., Kety, S. S., Schulsinger, F., Welner, J., and Oatergaard, L. (1968). Schizophrenics' offspring reared in adoptive homes. In D. Rosenthal, S. S. Kety (Eds.), *The transmission of schizophrenia.* New York: Pergamon Press.

Rosenthal, D., Wender, P. H., Kety, S. S., Welner, J., and Schulsinger, F. (1971). The adopted away offspring of schizophrenics. *American Journal of Psychiatry, 128*, 307–311.

Schied, H.-W. (1990). Psychiatric concepts and therapy. In E. R. Straube, K. Hahlweg (Eds.), *Schizophrenia: Concepts, Vulnerability, and Intervention.* Berlin: Springer.

Schulz, P. M., Schulz, S. C., Goldberg, S. C., Ettigi, P., Resnick, R. J., and Friedel, R. O. (1986). Diagnoses of the relatives of schizotypal outpatients. *Journal of Nervous and Mental Disease, 174*, 457–463.

Sherrington, R., Brynjolfsson, J., Petursson, H., Potter, M., Dudleston, K., Barraclough, B., Wasmuth, J., Dobbs, M., and Gurling, H. (1988). Localization of a susceptibility locus for schizophrenia on chromosome 5. *Nature, 336*, 164–167.

St. Clair, D., Blackwood, D., Muir, W., Baillie, D., Hubbard, A., Wright, A., and Evans, H. J. (1989). No linkage of chromosome 5q11-q13 markers to schizophrenia in Scottish families. *Nature, 339*, 305–309.

Tienari, P., Kaleva, M., Lahti, I., Laksy, K., Moring, J., Naarala, M., Sorri, A., Wahlberg K-E., and Wynne, L. (1991). Adoption studies on schizophrenia. *In: C., Eggers (ed.): Schizophrenia and youth. Berlin: Springer Verlag.*

Tienari, P., Lahti, I., Sorri, A., Naarala, M., Moring, J., and Wahlberg, K. E., (1989). The Finnish adoptive family study of schizophrenia: Possible joint effects of genetic vulnerability and family environment. *British Journal of Psychiatry, 155*, Suppl. 5, 29–32.

Tienari, P., Sorri, A., Lahti, I., Naarala, M., Wahlberg, K.-E., Rönkkö, T. Pohjola, J., and

Moring, J. (1985). The Finnish adoptive family study of schizophrenia. *The Yale Journal of Biology and Medicine*, *58*, 227–237.

Tsuang, M. T., Bucher, K. D., and Fleming, J. A. (1982). Testing the monogenetic theory of schizophrenia: An application of segregation analysis to blind family study data. *British Journal of Psychiatry*, *140*, 595.

Wender, P. H., Rosenthal, D., Kety, S. S., Schulsinger, F., and Welner, J. (1974). Crossfostering: A research strategy for clarifying the role of genetic and experiential factors in the etiology of schizophrenia. *Archives of General Psychiatry*, *30*, 121–128.

Winokur, G., Scharfetter, C., and Angst, J. (1985). A family study of psychotic symptomatology in schizophrenia, schizoaffective disorder, unipolar depression, and bipolar disorder. *European Archives of Psychiatry and Neurological Sciences*, *234*, 295–298.

Zerbin-Rüdin, E. (1972). Genetic research and the theory of schizophrenia. *International Journal of Mental Health*, *1*, 42–62.

# Chapter 11

# Environmental Influences
# and the Origin
# of Schizophrenia

## I. Studies of Monozygotic Twins Discordant for Schizophrenia

If one assumes that schizophrenia can have some genetic basis (see Chapter 10), then one may ask what protects the healthy monozygotic (MZ) twin from the illness affecting the other twin? After all, about 50% of MZ twins are discordant for schizophrenia. Since most of these genetically identical twins grow up under similar psychosocial conditions, only subtle differences in the events and environmental conditions experienced by the discordant twin can be expected.

However, as discussed in the previous chapter, the differences in the mental status of those who are and are not ill is seldom as large as the statistics based on clinically apparent syndromes would seem to indicate (e.g., Gottesman and Shields, 1982).

In a recent review of six twin studies, Kringlen (1987) showed that an average of 32% of the twins of definite schizophrenics were themselves definitely schizophrenic, 17% had milder schizophrenia spectrum disorders, and 21% had neurotic-like disorders. Only 30% could be considered normal.

Not enough is known about the developmental differences and the possibly decisive influences that force the vulnerable individual from a personality disturbance to psychosis. One of the difficulties in studying this question is the retrospective nature usually used for investigation. The individual becomes the subject of study only after a twin develops schizophrenia. Until now there has been only one prospective study, organized by the National Institutes of Mental Health (NIMH). In this case, a large sample of twins has been observed since the 1960s. The main question asked in this study concerned the origin of the developmental disturbances rather than the origin of schizophrenia itself. The investigators recorded birth conditions, childhood development, familial interactions, and various biochemical parameters.

One factor that distinguished MZ twins was birth condition. The lighter of the pair of MZ twins at birth was the one more likely to develop schizophrenia (Belmaker *et al.*, 1974). (It should be noted that, in many cases, weight differences were very small.) One indirect deduction from this is that the twin who has experienced a less favorable intrauterine environment is more vulnerable to unfavorable environmental conditions. If there were also a genetic predisposition to schizophrenia in this individual, then the threshold for development of the illness could be expected to be lower. However, the role of low birth weight in the later development of psychiatric illness is not acknowledged by all authors (e.g., Wahl, 1976; Gottesman and Shields, 1982).

There is agreement between the results of the NIMH study and other studies on the nature of the premorbid personality. From an analysis of the interactions between the two twins, the NIMH group reported that the one who was the more submissive was the one who was more likely to develop schizophrenia. Kringlen (1987) also noted that the twin who was more dependent and submissive was the one more likely to become schizophrenic. However, this does not clarify whether such submissiveness is the result of an already psychobiologically weak system or, independent of this, an early symptom of schizophrenia. Some would see the latter alternative as supportive of what psychoanalysts call a core symptom of schizophrenia, namely, the weak "ego" (Federn, 1953; Scharfetter, 1983).

In conclusion, there is not much information on the factors that contribute to the discordance found in MZ twins.

## II. Poor Living Conditions and Socioeconomic Status

In the 1930s, Brugger (cited in Häfner, 1972) analyzed the admissions to the psychiatric hospitals of two German provinces, Thüringen and Upper Bavaria. He found that schizophrenics most often came from the lower economic classes (in terms of employment). Could some unfavorable aspect of the living conditions contribute to the development of schizophrenia? At about the same time, Faris and Dunham (1939) found somewhat similar results relating to the bleak low-income areas of large cities in the United States. They collected data on newly registered patients from hospitals in and around Chicago from 1922 to 1934 (these included private institutions in order to avoid bias). The analysis showed that a relatively high proportion of schizophrenics came from districts in which the lower social classes lived rather than from those with a higher standard of living. Thus, there were relatively more admissions for schizophrenia from the low-income areas of central Chicago than from apartment areas on the periphery or from single houses in the residential suburbs. (Of 100,000 inhabitants, 700 schizophrenics came from "poor" living areas and 322 came from "good" areas; Figure 11.1). Interestingly,

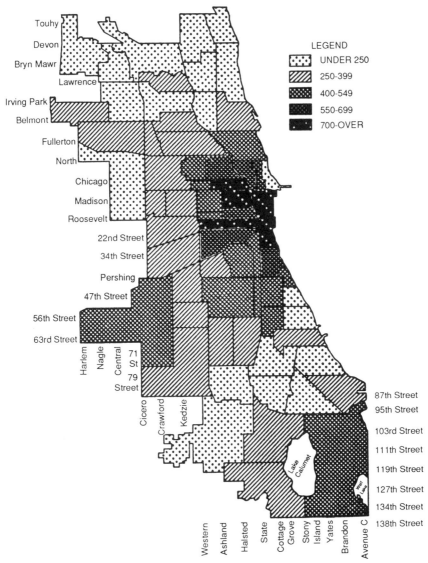

**Figure 11.1** Distribution of the incidence of schizophrenia per 100,000 adult population in various urban zones in Chicago, 1922–1931 (from Faris and Dunham, 1939, in Neale and Oltmanns, 1980).

Faris and Dunham could find no increased incidence of manic–depressive illnesses in the poor, nor in those from any particular area of Chicago.

These results naturally elicited much interest and criticism. Numerous attempts to replicate them were initiated. A relatively increased incidence of schizophrenia from areas with poor living conditions or from the lower economic classes has been confirmed to a large extent by Rowitz and Levy (1968) for Chicago in the U.S., Häfner *et al.* (1969) for Mannheim, Germany and Bagley *et al.* (1973) for Brighton, England. Klussman and Angermeyer (1987) reviewed 27 reports on this theme and conducted their own study in Hamburg, Germany. They claimed to find an inverse relationship for the affective psychoses (i.e., the percentage of blue-collar workers is somewhat lower in affective psychoses when compared with white-collar workers). Others did not find such an inverse relationship but confirmed that patients with an affective disorder did not show the same low class bias as schizophrenics. (For a review, see Klusmann and Angermeyer, 1987.)

It should be emphasized that, without further information, an increased incidence of schizophrenia among those living in lower socioeconomic circumstances does not imply anything about the direction of causality (Rabkin, 1980). Two possibilities are (1) *the environmental hypothesis,* which postulates that the more difficult living conditions in lower economic strata contribute to the development of schizophrenia; and (2) *the social selection* or *social drift hypothesis,* which predicts that schizophrenia or the development of premorbid symptoms hinders the attainment of an adequate socioeconomic status. In other words one would expect a movement (if any) down the social ladder due to the mentally and socially disabling circumstances of the premorbid or morbid features of schizophrenia (Cochrane, 1983).

Is there an indication of whether an environmental or a social hypothesis is the more likely explanation? If the difficult conditions facing the inhabitants of low-income areas should be contributory or even decisive for the development of schizophrenia, then the proportion of African-Americans and Caucasians in low-income areas that become ill should be similar. The data of Faris and Dunham (1939) show that this is not the case. In fact, Caucasians from the slums were overrepresented in the admissions to the psychiatric hospitals, and the frequency of admissions of African-Americans was proportional. This implies, excluding the possibility of racial or cultural differences (e.g., genetic vulnerability), that the Caucasian schizophrenics were showing social drift and that other factors may have been relevant for the African-American population. There is much evidence against a differential genetic vulnerability between races (see Sartorius *et al.,* 1974; Chapters 1 and 14).

Evidence against a specific influence of living conditions in the development of schizophrenia is that, with the possible exception of affective disturbances, there is an increased proportion of patients with other psychiatric diagnoses among the lower socioeconomic classes [e.g., Hollingshead and Redlich, 1958, New Haven; Dilling and Weyerer, 1978, Upper Bavaria (new project)].

A nonspecific relationship between schizophrenia and social class or living conditions may mean that social disintegration, unemployment, poverty, and the absence of socioeconomic opportunity are not the primary causes of schizophrenia. However, stress arising from such conditions may well contribute to the lowering of the threshold for mental illness, particularly for schizophrenia (see Section III). Furthermore, poverty in all or any of its meanings will certainly be an unfavorable factor for the long-term development of the illness (Dohrenwend *et al.*, 1987).

The social drift hypothesis suggests that the handicaps of a schizophrenic illness can bring about downward movement through the socioeconomic strata. A distinction should be made here between two different assumptions. First, downward drift may take place after the onset of the illness (e.g., in employment) and is known as intragenerational movement. A second possibility is that, before onset, during the premorbid period, the developing schizophrenic no longer attains the socioeconomic status of his parents(s); this is called intergenerational movement (i.e., a drop in social status with respect to that of previous generations).

Evidence exists for both effects. Not surprisingly, many researchers have found that when schizophrenics have had several clinical admissions, they are no longer able to achieve high professional or social goals or even reattain their premorbid level (intragenerational movement; e.g., Giel *et al.*, 1987).

However, several systematic studies also found that there was a downward drift relative to the socioeconomic status of the father (intergenerational movement). These investigations found that before onset of the illness the social status of the son was, in many cases, already less than that of his father. For example, Goldberg and Morrison (1963) from the United Kingdom and Dunham *et al.* (1966) from the United States found that although the educational level attained matched that expected from the social level of the parents, the professional performance seen later was significantly lower when compared with that of control groups, even before the onset of clear clinical symptoms. Whereas the majority of reports confirm these results, the reader should note that there are exceptions (e.g., Neale and Oltmanns, 1980; Giel *et al.*, 1987).

A number of sociological factors could interfere with the reliability of longitudinal studies of relatively small selected populations. One factor that could give rise to discrepant results is the point in time chosen for the study. Downward trends would not be unusual in times of economic crisis. Turner and Wagonfeld (1967) attempted to take this into consideration. They compared the professional development of schizophrenic patients before the onset of illness with the general socioeconomic trends shown in a district of the state of New York. Once again, they confirmed that in the premorbid phase their patients had drifted downward from their fathers' level more than comparable groups in the society. This study also confirmed that a greater percentage of their patients had come from the lower social classes.

The American and Danish investigators who conducted adoption studies in the 1960s (Chapter 10) re-analyzed their results in light of the drift hypothesis. Children adopted from a schizophrenic parent did not attain a vocational level comparable with a control group of adopted children originating from families with no elevated genetic risk for schizophrenia. The difference between these two groups of adopted children is not easily explained by the different socioeconomic environment of their adoptive parents nor by the socioeconomic differences between the groups of their biological parents (cited in Neale and Oltmanns, 1980). Wender *et al.* (1973) came to a similar conclusion when re-analyzing the data of Heston (1966).

Silverton and Mednick (1984) also analyzed their high risk prospective data for evidence of social drift. They compared the socioeconomic mobility of the offspring of women who eventually developed a schizophrenic illness with that of offspring of those who did not. They noted intergenerational downward mobility only in the former group. The latter group, who did not develop schizophrenia, were comparable in socioeconomic status to the control group. Once again the findings could not be explained by differences in the social class of the parents (cf. Chapter 12).

## III. Aversive Experience

### A. Methods and Theoretical Background: Commentary

To begin with, three rather different basic questions should be addressed. First, do difficult living circumstances exert a specific formative influence on the development of schizophrenia?

If the nature of the living conditions is formative, then the character of such circumstances should be directly linked to the appearance of schizophrenia. It is theoretically conceivable that a particular type of upbringing or associated experiences would facilitate the appearance of typical schizophrenic symptoms. If such a link could be demonstrated, the conclusion could be made that there was a specific connection between the style of upbringing or related experiences and the incidence of schizophrenic symptoms.

Should it turn out that there is no connection between the content of the experience and the character of the symptoms, then the possibility of a more general or formal connection between the two should be sought. That is, we are asking if quantitative aspects of the aversive experience (e.g., intensity or frequency) can lead cumulatively to the development of one of the worst psychiatric illnesses, namely, schizophrenia.

If, however, the specific role of the environment cannot be confirmed, since it may be discovered that the same experiences occur in other psychiatric disturbances as well, it is still not possible to conclude that environmental conditions are irrelevant. Difficult environmental conditions can still play a decisive and provocative role. They may not cause or "form" schizophrenia, but they may trigger its onset and influence its course.

The next important point for the evaluation of environmental effects is the question of whether an event is independent of the effects of the illness on the environment. People with severe psychiatric illness can create considerable turmoil in their social environment and thus cause many dependent aversive responses. Schizophrenics are particularly prone to evaluate events differently from others. Consider the premorbid period, when some schizophrenics are already showing marked psychosocial deficits. The future patient can bring about events unfavorable enough to have a trigger function. Feedback from the situation can disturb the balance sufficiently to bring about the catastrophe. For example, the future patient who considers himself spied on by his colleagues at work may respond in such an aggressive way that he is fired from his workplace. Emotional difficulties experienced by schizophrenics can lead to the breakup of long-established friendships.

Another problem is the retrospective nature of most reports on environmental stresses experienced before onset of the illness. Reports on rather trivial events can take on extraordinary significance after the breakdown has occurred. Both patients and relatives may therefore show a strong tendency toward giving the event(s) a particular meaning. For example, a relative may recount that an increased work load was responsible for what followed.

A biasing of reports is a major problem for retrospective studies on people who are already ill (see critical discussion by Tennant, 1985). To reduce the impact of this sort of error, a number of researchers attempt to assess only the independent events, that is, those that are independent of the effects of the illness (e.g., the death of a loved one).

Finally, it is necessary to differentiate whether particular events occur during the premorbid phase or during the phase of remission (see Kendler's 1985 reply to Tennant). An already labile system may react to events differently from one that does not yet show the same degree of lability (i.e., the same event may have a different effect on the patient when he has not yet experienced the illness compared with when he has just recovered from a severe breakdown).

Working backward through the themes discussed in the previous section, the first question is whether certain life events occur more frequently among schizophrenics than among healthy controls, thus approaching the question of whether these events may exert a role in provoking the illness. Later, the more pretentious question will be raised concerning whether unfavorable events could exert a specific and formative influence on the origin of schizophrenia.

## B. Life Events

### 1. A Provocative Role? Comparison with Healthy Controls

The life events that researchers consider range from extreme situations—such as the aversive experiences on the battlefield or during natural disasters—to events encountered by most people—such as the birth of a child, marriage, divorce, death of a loved one, loss of work, and occasional extreme work loads.

Life events play some role in the origin of schizophrenia. This is the message derived from a careful study by Brown and Birley (1968) at the

Maudsley Hospital and Institute of Psychiatry in London. In particular, they reported that schizophrenics experienced more independent life events than healthy control subjects. An increase in the incidence of such events was found in 60% of the schizophrenic patients shortly before their admission to the clinic. Similar findings were reported by Jacobs and Myers (1976) and Gruen and Baron (1984) in the United States, Canton and Fraccon (1985) in Italy, and Al Khani *et al.* (1986) in Saudi Arabia. (For a review, see Rabkin, 1980.)

Other researchers at the Maudsley Hospital and Institute of Psychiatry also found a coincidence of life events with an early relapse (Leff *et al.*, 1973). The results are even more convincing because they were observations in a prospective study. However, as already discussed, life events occurring after the appearance of the illness, as opposed to before onset, may have a different quality for the patient. Nevertheless, it is possible to conclude that life events play a role in the onset and course of schizophrenia. However, these studies do not broach the question of whether the events were specific for the illness.

## 2. A Specific Role in Schizophrenia? Comparison with Psychiatric Controls

With only one exception, none of the studies that have brought a careful methodological approach to the issue have found that life events are more frequent in the premorbid phase of schizophrenia than in any other psychiatric illness (see subsequent text). The exception was the study by Chung *et al.* (1986) in Australia. The increased incidence was only found in a group with schizophreniform disturbances (DSM-III diagnosis) when compared to healthy subjects and hypomanic patients.

Leff and Vaughn (1980) found no difference in the number of independent life events experienced by schizophrenic and depressed patients at the Maudsley Hospital. Indeed, others, such as Ambelas (1987) in England, found that manic patients had experienced more life events than schizophrenics. Furthermore, Dohrenwend *et al.* (1987) in the United States found that depressed patients had been subjected to more independent life events than schizophrenics. Earlier work also showing that the schizophrenic premorbid experience of life events is not special was reviewed by Tennant (1985).

Thus, although life events play no specific role in the development of schizophrenia, they should not be underestimated for their often important trigger function.

## 3. Do Aversive Experiences and Living Conditions Exert a Formative Influence on the Expression of Schizophrenia?

Based on the results reported in the previous section, the expected answer to this question is "no," especially considering that the life events that are subjected to study are relatively short-term and fairly common types of experiences (e.g., moving to another city, divorce, exam). However, it is still possible to suppose that especially intense, chronic, stressful, or threatening events could be more specifically connected with the development of a severe psychiatric breakdown (i.e., specific formal and formative relationship).

Relevant to this thesis (although not in favor of it) is the account by Tennant (1985) of some studies made during World War II purporting to show that extreme events experienced in battle were not more likely to lead to the development of schizophrenia than that of other psychiatric illnesses. Cutting (1985) discussed several studies that reviewed the incidence of the experience of a war-time concentration camp in the life histories of psychiatric patients. He mentioned Ettinger's follow-up study on 3000 patients in Israel who were former concentration camp inmates. No particular increase of schizophrenia was reported in this group.

It would thus seem that experiencing some extremely intense and threatening situations is not necessarily associated with an increased likelihood of developing what is arguably the severest of functional psychoses.

However, the question of whether the content of potentially formative influences (e.g., in childhood and development) could lay down the path for the development of schizophrenia still has not been answered. This will be discussed in the next section.

The concluding comments here are directed to the putative role of differences in genetic loading for schizophrenia. It is conceivable that stressful experiences might well elicit different responses from those with a high or low genetic risk for schizophrenia. Gruen and Baron (1984) at the New York Psychiatric Institute asked whether there was an interaction between familial incidence of schizophrenia and experiences of severe stress. The authors recorded severe stressful life events (e.g., jail, marital separation, bankruptcy) in 15% of the 52 patients before the onset of schizophrenia. However, there was no statistically significant interaction between the occurrence of stressful life events and the incidence of schizophrenia or spectrum disorders in the patients' families.

## IV. Interactions in the Family

### A. Deviant Parental Interactions as a Formative Influence: Historical Perspective

The subtle complex of relationships that putatively contributes to a schizophrenic breakdown may be poorly reflected by counting the life events or estimating the quality of living conditions. Furthermore, the decisive experience may not occur in adolescence or adulthood, but in childhood. How can the significant events in the development of a schizophrenic be demonstrated? To show that some events are "noxious" probably requires a finer analysis than has been attempted as yet.

Many psychiatrists and clinical psychologists have tried to detect the supposedly unique childhood conditions and family relationships of those who became schizophrenic. In particular, psychoanalytical theorists set out to show that there is a direct connection between childhood experiences and the origin of schizophrenia (e.g., Alanen, 1968). The more conventional claims that biological vulnerability interacts with the environment (e.g., Arieti, 1971) have been expressed more radically by others, who claim that the role of the mother is decisive (e.g., the existence of "schizophrenogenic mothers;" Fromm-Reichmann, 1948) or that the childhood experience of the schizophrenic is a constant "training in irrationality" (Lidz, 1973).

Bateson *et al.* (1956) promulgated the idea that the simultaneous receipt of positive and negative messages in different modes from parents (often mothers) may have a strong formative influence on the personality and the early development of schizophrenic features; this is known as the "double bind." These parents may, for example, encourage a certain behavior verbally but show a negative facial expression at the same time or at the time the child has started to respond. The child is thus "trapped;" there is no way to escape since the different possibilities for response have no clear valence. These authors seek support for their theories through extensive case descriptions of familial interactions rather than through quantitative analysis, because they claim that such analyses do not do justice to the subtle networks in the families. We shall not delve into the details of psychodynamic family theory since we are addressing empirical research in this book. However, for the popular concept of the double bind, attempts have been made to develop methods of studying the basic assumption in order to provide statistically based support for the theory. Unfortunately, this undertaking failed (Ringuette and Kennedy, 1966; Schuham, 1967). Later, Sluzki and Ransom (1976) concluded that double bind communication is not a specific feature of the mother of a schizophrenic patient; it can be observed to some extent in all families.

Another "statistical" approach to the family relationship problem was implemented by Schofield and Balian (1959). These authors interviewed 170 schizophrenics about their mothers. There were no differences between the responses of the schizophrenics and those of the healthy control group for most topics that were discussed. Only 10% of the schizophrenics reported two features (dominance and overprotection) not mentioned by the healthy probands. The specificity is unclear, since no psychiatric control group was interviewed and, as mentioned elsewhere, there are problems with retrospective studies that can lead to a considerable bias in the results.

Waring and Ricks (1965) and Ricks and Berry (1970) tried to avoid relying on subjective records of past experience during their studies in the United States. They checked the mental health files of children who were admitted to the Judge Baker Clinic in Boston. (These files included extensive information about the family atmosphere as well as marital adjustment of the parents of schizophrenics.) Approximately 12 years later, they identified 100 persons who had developed a schizophrenic illness. They selected a control group of persons matched for age, sex, and social class who did not develop a psychiatric disturbance but had also been a patient in the same clinic as a child.

With respect to the marital adjustment of the parents, they characterized a feature called "emotional divorce" (i.e., sleeping in different rooms, little interaction, mutual withdrawal, covert hostility, estrangement, and distrust between the couple). This feature was predictive for cases of chronic schizophrenia. Furthermore, in these cases, the family was significantly more often characterized as a "symbiotic union" in the premorbid period (i.e.) there was an overly close relationship between one parent and one child, to the exclusion of the other parent). Another group of schizophrenics, who had already been released at the time of the follow-up, had been openly rejected as a child significantly more often than those in the control group. In general, all the family environments of the schizophrenics were considered to be disordered in the premorbid period, whereas only about half the families of the control group (without a psychiatric disturbance) were judged on a blind assessment to be disturbed.

Remarkable in this study was the finding that a high proportion of the parents of those children who later developed schizophrenia showed a schizoid personality disturbance (15%) or psychotic features (28%). This raises the question of whether poor marital adjustment can be considered independent of the high incidence of psychiatric disturbance shown by the parents of children who eventually became schizophrenic.

Let us briefly summarize the deviations found in the children who eventually developed a schizophrenic illness, even though this is not the subject of this section. A complex pattern was found, the main features of which were withdrawal, low self-esteem, neurological impairments, and low social adjustment. This pattern most clearly discriminated the male children who became chronic schizophrenic adults from the control group. Both sexes of the index group differed in a number of measures of emotional responsiveness from the control group; they showed more anxiety, were more vulnerable, and had a higher feeling of self-isolation, alienation, and unreality.

These findings are surely fascinating, but it should be pointed out that one cannot decide at this time between environmental (parental behavior) or genetic contributions to the behavior observed in the child and the development of schizophrenia. Was the behavior of the parents alone enough to cause turmoil in the children, was there a genetic predisposition, or, more likely, did the interaction of both cause the disturbance? A problem with this study was that only those children with emotional problems were selected. To what extent can the result be generalized? For methodological reasons, it is not justified to assume that all families with a child who eventually develops schizophrenia show disturbed marital adjustment and other deviant behavior.

The advantage of a study conducted by Robins (1966) was that the author did not rely on psychiatric files but based his findings on intensive interviews of children and parents at the St. Louis Child Guidance Center. The other advantage of the study was that it included a matched control group and that the comparison was made with a group of children who eventually developed sociopathic symptoms. Of 526 children interviewed, 463 were followed into adulthood. A schizophrenic illness was diagnosed in 26 (6%) of the index children. Male children of the index group showed more disturbances as children. Both sexes (of preschizophrenics) were found to be more depressed and showed more worry and dependency than both control groups. No large differences were found with respect to parental features. The fathers of the schizophrenics were often more antisocial than the fathers of non-schizophrenics in the matched normal control group, but this aspect did not differ from children who became antisocial themselves.

In the 1950s and 1960s, other investigators tried to recreate and observe family interactions in a laboratory or clinic situation, usually in the case of a child who had already become ill. The interactions studied mainly concerned either the approach of the family members to solving a problem suggested by the therapist or their attitude toward certain routine situations (e.g., Strodtbeck, 1951; 1954; Fontana, 1966; Reiss, 1967; Mishler and Waxler, 1968; see Neale and Oltmanns, 1980, for a critical review).

Briefly, such studies found that families with a healthy child worked together to solve problems, but families with a son already in the poor premorbid phase of a developing psychosis showed the mother and son usually building an alliance; the father was excluded from most interactions. Many authors saw in this observation a confirmation of Lidz's thesis, which says that a schism in the family is an important etiological component of schizophrenia (similar to the "symbiotic union" between one parent and the preschizophrenic child, as reported in the Boston study). The pattern was different in the case of a schizophrenic daughter. She was usually excluded from discussion, even ignored. As Neale and Oltmanns (1980) emphasize, it is difficult to evaluate these parental attitudes with respect to the etiology of schizophrenia, particularly since it is not clear whether the attitudes developed before or after the onset of the psychiatric problem in their child. Whatever the etiology, the presence of a disturbed pattern of interactions certainly does not have a beneficial effect on the development of the adolescent at risk.

## B. Communication Deviance in Parents: A Formative Influence?

Researchers who investigate the disturbance of communication or deviant cognitive style shown by parents of schizophrenics have a rather different goal. They ask whether certain patterns of parental communications can lead to the cognitive disturbances described for children that eventually become schizophrenic (i.e., they do not investigate the broad range of parental behavior).

The work of Wynne and colleagues (initially at the NIMH, now at the University of Rochester) has had an influence on the theory that environmental factors are important for the stimulation of schizophrenia. At an early stage of their studies, they evaluated both the Rorschach and Thematic Aperception Test (TAT; H. A. Murray) protocols carried out with the parents of schizophrenics (Singer and Wynne, 1963a, 1965b). The authors claimed that they could correctly (and blindly) distinguish more than 80% of the protocols of the parents of schizophrenics from those of the healthy controls. For example, it was said to be typical that the descriptions of the TAT or Rorschach pictures were not grouped around a common thematic focus. Adequate clues were often not distributed throughout the communication, which therefore did not allow the investigator to decode the meaning. The implicit assumption here is that deviant thought processes are reflected in deviant communication and that this type of communication will have an effect on the child who eventually becomes mentally ill (see also Sass *et al.,* 1984).

A study conducted at the Institute for Psychiatry in London by Hirsch and Leff (1975) tried to replicate the Wynne and Singer investigation. They found that deviant communication can be observed in the parents of schizophrenics, but less frequently than the earlier studies had indicated; nevertheless, it was significantly more frequent than in healthy controls. The authors attributed the quantitative difference between their results and those of Wynne and colleagues to the selection of subjects for study, since the psychiatrists in the area surrounding the NIMH were sending Wynne many parents of schizophrenics in whom they had noted an odd style of communication (i.e., the psychiatrists were informed of the purpose of the NIMH study!).

A further report from Wynne's group again aroused much interest (Wynne *et al.,* 1976). They replicated their own findings but also claimed that even foster parents showed deviant communication, implying that it existed independent of a putative genetic disposition. Singer, a member of the research team in this investigation, had the responsibility of evaluating the protocols taken from the parents of children who were later to develop schizophrenia and to review protocols taken from parents who were to adopt a child that later developed schizophrenia. (There was also a control group of parents who raised children who did not develop any psychiatric problems.) Singer was not told the origin of the protocols. To the surprise of all concerned, Singer was able, with considerable accuracy, to predict from the protocols which parents would eventually have a schizophrenic in the family. This included those parents who were not the biological parents of the child they raised. However, Häfner (1986) pointed out that the protocols for the three experimental groups were made out in three different forms of handwriting, so that it is not clear whether that evaluation was as blind as was claimed.

Despite these methodological reservations, the reliability of the results should not be rejected out of hand. The presence of a psychotic child may be indicated by a disturbed parental pattern of communication. Whether this indicates a specific formative influence or a response to a disturbed family member cannot be determined from this study (e.g., comments by Wynne *et al.*, 1976).

Of course, deviant responses on Rorschach or TAT protocols are not going to elucidate the development of schizophrenia completely. Other aspects of this sample of parents had already been investigated by Zahn (1968) and Wender *et al.* (1968), also working at the NIMH. Zahn found that the biological parents of children that became ill made significantly more deviant associations as measured by the Kent–Rosanoff test (Chapters 1 and 2). However, Wynne *et al.* (1976) later reported that word-association deviance was not correlated with Rorschach-communication deviance. Wender *et al.* (1968) had already analyzed the psychopathology ratings. They observed significantly more psychopathology in the group of biological (but not adoptive) parents. Thus, one could speculate that the deviance of the adoptive parents is related to the stress of raising a deviant child and that of the biological parents is related to the biological (genetic) basis of the illness (but see subsequent text).

Later on, Wynne (1981) reported results from another NIMH group that was unable to reproduce his (adoption group) findings. This led Wynne to specify more closely what conclusions could be drawn from the NIMH studies (see also Sass *et al.*, 1984). Wynne (1981) reported that a recognizable form of disorganized communication was observable among the biological parents who had a schizophrenic son or daughter with formal thought disorder. This type of communication was infrequent among the biological parents of paranoid schizophrenics without formal thought disorder. Wynne again warned against the simplified conclusions that there is enough evidence to assume that the ultimate cause of schizophrenia is solely environmental or solely genetic. The group added that the direction of causality between illness and communication style could not be deduced from this sort of study. In addition, they called for long-term prospective studies observing the interaction before the onset of severe pathology (see discussion of the Goldstein project).

Another problem with these studies of communication deviance is that the direct communication between parents and their children was not systematically analyzed and compared with the communication-deviance measures. Liem (1974) tried to fill this gap. In his study, a youngster and parent were given the sort of communication task that B. Cohen has often used (Chapter 2). The complex design required that every participant communicated with one participant from each group (the groups consisted of parents of schizo-phrenic and nonschizophrenic youngsters and their respective offspring). Suffice it to say that deviant (direct) communication was found only in the schizophrenics and not in the parents.

Finally, let us consider the only prospective study that has been carried out in this field to date. M. Goldstein and colleagues at the University of California at Los Angeles (UCLA) studied deviant communication (and affective style) in more than 50 sets of parents who came to the psychological advisory center at UCLA because of the difficulties they were having with the rearing of their children. (The project started over 20 years ago. The method to assess communication deviance was broadly similar to that used by Wynne and modified by Jones, 1977. The assessment of the affective style was quite similar to the modern concept of "expressed emotion;" see next section.) In 1985 and 1987, Goldstein summarized the results of the original study and the follow-up that occurred 15 years later when the children had become adults ($n = 54$). Indeed, in comparison with parents whose children developed other psychiatric problems or no psychiatric disturbances, an increased incidence of deviant communication was evident among the parents whose children later developed disturbances in the schizophrenia spectrum [$n = 15$; i.e., schizo-phrenia ($n = 4$), schizotypal personality disorder, schizoid personality disor-der, paranoid personality disorder, borderline personality disorder ($n = 10$)]. The diagnostic status was assessed by independent blind DSM–III diagnoses (see further discussion of the project in Chapter 12 and Table 12.7).

The relationship between the total spectrum outcome and the evidence for communication deviance in the parents 15 years earlier is outlined in Table 11.1. The numbers were too low to differentiate between the outcome of broad and narrow spectrum disorders, but there was some evidence for a

**Table 11.1**  Degree of Communication Deviance of Parents as Predictor of Psychiatric Outcome of the Offspring 15 Years Later

| Communication deviance of the parent | Offspring | | |
|---|---|---|---|
| | No mental illness | Other mental illness | Schizophrenia spectrum |
| Low | 8 | 3 | 1 |
| Intermediate | 3 | 12 | 4 |
| High | 3 | 7 | 10 |

[a]Data compiled according to the results of Goldstein, 1987, $n = 51$.

stronger relationship between severe communication deviance and the total spectrum disorder group compared with the control groups. Among the data presented, it cannot be overlooked that many of the parents of children who eventually showed some sort of psychiatric problem (other than the schizophrenia spectrum) had also shown moderate to marked deviant communication 15 years earlier. However, Goldstein (1985, 1987) pointed out that if the measures of deviant communication were combined with those for the so-called negative affective style, there was a clearer association with the later development of schizophrenia or spectrum diagnoses in their children.

## C. High Expressed Emotion as a Trigger for Early Relapse

In the 1950s, Brown and colleagues at the Institute for Psychiatry in London observed that the relapse rate of young schizophrenics 6 months after their release was higher if they went to stay with their parents than if they lived alone or with a sibling (Brown et al., 1958; Brown, 1959). Brown's group investigated whether the difference made evident by this categorization of living conditions was associated with residual psychopathology. On the basis of 156 patients who had spent a relatively long period in the hospital, they found that this was not so. Curiously, among the group that lived with their parents, those who had working mothers showed fewer relapses. This led Brown's group to the supposition that the nature and frequency of face-to-face contact in the family had provoked the relapse.

In order to examine what might cause the provocation, Brown and colleagues developed a questionnaire known as the Camberwell Family Interview (CFI). The interview is conducted with a key relative; questions are asked regarding how the illness started, the daily schedule in the household, the behavior of the patient over the last 3 months, work-sharing in the house, joint activities, and familial interactions. The idea behind the assessment is to solicit the real feelings and attitudes toward the patient by talking about the daily experiences in the house.

The protocol records the number of positive and negative critical comments, the nature of the attitude (warm or hostile), and the nature of the emotional involvement (e.g., self-sacrifice, overprotection, extreme compassion, or states of high emotional agitation) shown by the member of the family who interacts most with the patient. The interview is usually carried out when the patient is still in the clinic. Considerable drawbacks of the assessment are that it is time-consuming and requires well-trained evaluators (since assessment is not only based on the semantic content but also on the speed and emphasis of the voice). A new development is a shortened version of the CFI with 5-min speech samples (cf. Gottschalk et al., 1988).

A relative can in principle be any person who has close contact with the patient, who probably has to live with and take care of the patient, and may take the role of a "key person." In most of the studies discussed, the patients were relatively young and the relatives or key persons were usually the parents.

Brown *et al.* (1962) found that the number of critical (negative) comments and the intensity of the emotional involvement of the member of the family concerned was significantly correlated with the incidence of relapse in the patient within the next 9 months. In other words, this procedure enabled a prognosis to be made on the basis of the critical attitude and emotional response of the person most closely relating to the patient. This is a remarkable claim, since it would seem possible to spotlight the amount of stress faced by a given patient without recourse to a retrospective evaluation of the case history. The research team of Vaughn and Leff (1976) at the same institute was able to replicate this report. From this point on, the decisive combination of predictors, namely, the frequency of critical comments and the degree of emotional overinvolvement, became known as *high expressed emotion (EE)*.

High-EE relatives tend to react irritably toward the patient, doubt how genuine the illness is, and allow the sick member of the family relatively little autonomy. They are less tolerant of the patient's reduced capabilities and impaired social adaptability. In contrast, low-EE relatives are more tolerant, relaxed, and express some understanding for the difficulties and wishes of the patient (e.g., to withdraw at times). Barrowclough *et al.,* (1987) demonstrated that the knowledge of high-EE relatives about schizophrenia is significantly less than that of low-EE relatives.

Examples of *critical comments* are:

1. "I really cannot stand the way he behaves at meals."
2. "I was just totally disgusted with him. He does nothing. *I* am working pretty hard and try to get ahead."
3. "He *deliberately* tried to irritate me."

Examples of *emotional overinvolvement* are:

1. "I call him every two hours to find out what happens or what is going on."
2. "But I could never leave him out of my sight."
   (Both statements are from a seemingly overprotective mother concerning her adult son.)
3. "He was so beautiful, the most beautiful child. He gave me a lot of joy and mostly heartache. My broken heart! He was so beautiful!"
4. "He didn't need too much, if he did need something mum was always there, lets face it. . . ."
5. "I feel great guilt that he is in the hospital. I think I could cure him better than the doctors do."

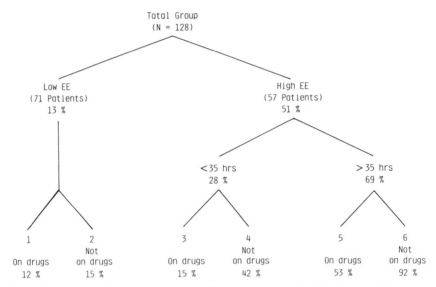

**Figure 11.2**  Results of a prospective study of short-term outcome in schizophrenia. Relapse rates of former patients 9 mo after discharge. Effect of expressed emotion (EE) of a key person in the household and of maintenance medication (after Vaughn and Leff, 1976).

Of course there are other factors that influence the latency to relapse. These include the frequency of the contact between the persons concerned and whether the patient continues to take the prescribed medication. If these factors occur together (i.e., high-EE face-to-face contact exceeding 35 hr per week and neglect to take medication, 92% of patients experience a relapse within 9 mo of release. On the other hand, if the patient enters a low-EE environment in which emotional engagement is not too high and critical comments are infrequent, the incidence of relapse falls to 13%. In the latter case, the role of medication seems to be less significant, since the relapse rate does not fall any further in low-EE situations in which it is certain that medication is still being taken (Figure 11.2).

The role of continued medication should not be overlooked. If patients in high-EE families continue to take medication, but do not have too many hours of contact, relapse rates approach those recorded from low-EE households. Indeed, even if the number of hours of contact is high (> 35 hr/week), continued medication lowers the rate of relapse. Continued treatment with neuroleptics seems to provide protection against the effects of a highly emotive member of the family (Vaughn and Leff, 1981; Leff and Vaughn, 1985). However, neuroleptics fail if the stress is extreme. If life events and high-EE coincide, then even neuroleptic treatment can do little to protect against relapse (Leff *et al.*, 1983).

It is interesting to note that, among patients from low-EE households, there is an increased incidence of independent stressful life events in the period shortly before admission (Vaughn and Leff, 1976). However, as already discussed, even though this factor cannot be said to be a specific trigger for schizophrenia, its contribution complicates the assessment of the CFI results.

In the meantime, a number of studies more-or-less confirm the original findings on factors provoking relapses in Western and other cultures (e.g., Moline *et al.*, 1985; Vaughn *et al.*, 1984; Strachan *et al.*, 1986 in the United States; Karno *et al.*, 1987 with Mexicans in California; McCreadie and Robinson, 1987, in Scotland; Wig *et al.*, 1987 in India; see review, Kuipers and Bebbington, 1988; Table 11.2).

However, as always in schizophrenia research, there are some studies that raise the problem of the extent to which the results can be generalized, although the vast majority of the studies support the EE concept. For example, MacMillan *et al.* (1986), reporting work in North London by the Crow and Johnstone group, have found results that are more equivocal about the role of EE. The study reported on 77 patients released after the first episode of schizophrenia. Although MacMillan and colleagues found a significantly lower relapse rate from low-EE than high-EE families (about 39 as opposed to 63%) in their 2-yr follow-up, a more detailed analysis revealed less impressive numbers. Their patients were also participating in a trial of prophylactic medication. When the data were controlled for the effect of placebo and length of preadmission illness (both of which were related to a poor outcome), the significance of the effect of EE was lost.

This report gave rise to criticism of some points of methodology (Leff and Vaughn, 1986) and assumptions made in the analysis, since more patients in low-EE than high-EE households received active medication (Kuipers and Bebbington, 1988). Goldstein's group in Los Angeles (Mintz *et al.*, 1987) re-analyzed the results in a number of ways, taking the drug effect into consideration. In the worst case, there was a trend for EE to predict outcome; in the best, there was a significant effect. The latter result matches the experience of Nuechterlein *et al.* (1986) on mostly first-episode patients wholly maintained on a fixed dose of neuroleptic.

Another negative finding came from Hamburg (Dulz and Hand, 1986); this group did not find any difference between the relapse rates of patients coming from high- or low-EE households. However, Vaughn (1986) pointed out that not all these patients returned to their relatives after discharge from the hospital. This may explain, in part, the discrepant findings. Straube *et al.* (1989) reported a tendency in the expected direction, but stated that other potential predictors of the 2-yr outcome (e.g., psychophysiological and information-processing measures) were more closely related to short-term outcome (as assessed by a multiple-regression analysis). Parker *et al.* (1988) also corroborated that EE alone did not predict outcome, but a combination of

**Table 11.2** Outcome of 14 EE studies[a,b]

| Reference | Location | Subjects (N) | Episode | Followup | Relapse rate High EE (%) | Relapse rate Low EE (%) |
|---|---|---|---|---|---|---|
| Brown et al. (1962)[c] | South London | 97 (male) | All | 1 yr | 56 | 21 |
| Brown et al. (1972) | South London | 101 | All | 9 mo | 58 | 16 |
| Vaughn and Leff (1976) | South London | 37 | All | 9 mo | 50 | 12 |
| Leff and Vaughn (1981)[d] | South London | 36 | All | 2 yr | 62 | 20 |
| Vaughn et al. (1984) | Los Angeles | 54 | All | 9 mo | 56 | 17 |
| Moline et al. (1985)[e] | Chicago | 24 | All | 1 yr | 91 | 31 |
| Dulz and Hand (1986)[f] | Hamburg | 46 | All | 9 mo | 58 | 65 |
| MacMillan et al. (1986) | North London | 67 | First | 2 yr | 63 | 39 |
| Nuechterlein et al. (1986)[g] | Los Angeles | 26 | All | 1 yr | 37 | 0 |
| Karno et al. (1987) | Southern California | 44 | All | 9 mo | 59 | 26 |
| Leff et al. (1987) | Chandigarh, India | 76 | First | 1 yr | 33 | 14 |
| Tarrier et al. (1988)[h] | Salford, England | 48 | All | 9 mo | 48 | 21 |
| Vaughn (personal communication) | Sydney, Australia | 87 | All | 9 mo | 52 | 23 |
| Rostworowska (personal communication) | Cracow, Poland | 36 | All | 16 mo | 60 | 9 |

[a]From Kuipers and Bebbington, 1988.

[b]Although McCreadie and Robinson (1987) showed some support for an effect of EE, their study was retrospective.

[c]Their measure of 'emotional over-involvement' was the prototype of EE.

[d]Follow-up of same patients as Vaughn and Leff (1976).

[e]Nonstandard criteria for high EE.

[f]An unknown number of subjects were not living with their EE-rated relatives.

[g]All patients on fixed-dose fluphenazine.

[h]Patients receiving standard care with or without education in the authors' intervention program.

EE status with other factors (e.g., poor premorbid course) was linked with early relapse. McCreadie and Phillips (1988) could not confirm the influence of EE in a group of relatively well-integrated former schizophrenic patients.

From these studies it seems that the EE effect may possibly be obscured by other variables, which should be taken into account in further studies.

1. EE status is not the only variable that influences the postdischarge course. Other factors include medication compliance, life events, or frequency of face-to-face contact (see previous text).
2. The impact of high EE could be less on well-stabilized patients than on more vulnerable patients with a poor premorbid course (see previous text). Differences in psychophysiological reactivity irrespective of EE may play a role (see previous text; Tarrier and Barrowclough, 1987). Duration of the illness may also be a factor; for example, a lower relapse rate was observed after the first admission than after subsequent admissions (33 vs 69%; Leff and Brown, 1977).
3. Thus, it follows that EE status may not always be independent of patient characteristics. In fact, Miklowitz *et al.* (1983) in the United States did show that the relatives (parents) with emotional overinvolvement (i.e., one component of the total high-EE pattern) more frequently had schizophrenic patients in their household with more severe residual symptoms or fewer psychosocial capabilities. (This seems to indicate that when a greater degree of helplessness is shown by the patient a more protective attitude is elicited from the relative, but this may not always be so.)
4. Unfortunately, the attitude of the patient was ignored in nearly all EE studies. Warner and Atkinson (1988) showed that patients who perceived their parents positively tended to experience a milder course. Strachan *et al.* (1989) found that differences in the patients' coping style played a role.
5. The EE status of the key relative can change during the follow-up period. A spontaneous decrease during the 9-month follow-up period has been observed by several authors (Brown *et al.*, 1972; Dulz and Hand, 1986; Hogarty *et al.*, 1986; Tarrier *et al.*, 1989). An upward EE trend may even be observed in some relatives (Tarrier *et al.*, 1988). The coping style in the families can also change over time (e.g., Birchwood *et al.*, 1990).
6. Gender may also play a role. Goldstein and Kreisman (1988) reported that sons were sent to the hospital when they were ill more often than were daughters. Hogarty (1985) even claimed that EE is only predictive of relapse in men.
7. No universal definition of relapse exists. Some use "symptom relapse," while others use readmission to the clinic as the criterion. The reasons for readmission can vary widely among patients.
8. Finally, those who use the CFI need careful training. Since the method is now widespread, evaluation criteria and training experience may differ

considerably from evaluator to evaluator. A method is needed that is less dependent on the background of experience and training.

At this point it may be useful to ask whether the report of the key relative really reflects what is happening in the home (i.e., does the CFI carried out in the clinic with the key person but without the patient reflect the relevant features of the key person's interactions with the patient?). Several studies now exist that tackle this question in various ways. The concordant findings are that the CFI is a fairly reliable predictor of the interaction actually observed in the laboratory or at home between key person and patient (Kuipers, 1979; Miklowitz *et al.*, 1984; Strachan *et al.*, 1986; Hahlweg *et al.*, 1987).

Another way to demonstrate the impact of the EE measure on the patient is to record the physiological response during a confrontation with a high-EE relative. Tarrier and colleagues (1979; Tarrier and Barrowclough, 1987) at the Institute of Psychiatry in London measured the electrodermal responsiveness of remitted patients in the presence of low- and high-EE relatives. The differential emotional stress elicited was evident from the variations of spontaneous electrodermal fluctuations recorded. The presence of low-EE

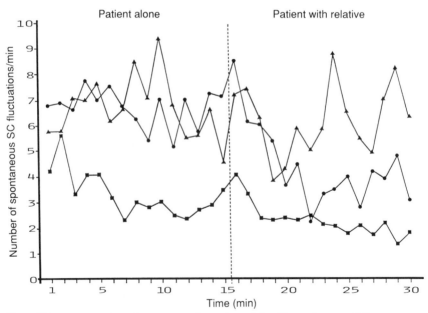

**Figure 11.3**  Mean number of spontaneous fluctuations of the skin conductance (SC) or (electrodermal) response over time in a schizophrenic as a function of the presence or absence of a relative (after Tarrier *et al.*, 1979).

relatives induced a lower level of electrodermal activation than did the presence of relatives with high EE. It should be noted that the electrodermal level recorded before the relatives came into the laboratory did not discriminate among patients (cf. Figure 11.3). Sturgeon *et al.* reported similar findings (1981; 1984).

In view of the theoretical impact of the results, it is unfortunate that neither group recorded what really happened in the interactions between the patient and the low- and high-EE relatives. This would have been desirable, not only to confirm the expected high-EE content of the conversation, but also to show that the electrodermal results were not artifacts arising from changed patterns of breathing and speaking "provoked" by the high-EE relative.

It may be noted that the effect of high EE on this measure is not limited to the schizophrenic in remission but has also been recorded in disturbed adolescents who were regarded as at risk for schizophrenic spectrum disorder (Valone *et al.*, 1984).

An additional finding, although peripheral to the EE concept, is of heuristic importance: the tendency to show higher ANS arousal remained elevated for some patients over months, even when the level of EE fell due to social intervention (Leff *et al.*, 1982). Thus, this may indicate a vulnerability marker independent of the immediate influence of EE [see similar findings from case reports by Tarrier and Barrowclough (1987), and in Chapters 6 and 14].

Considered as a whole, these results are seductive. High EE seems to be an important part of the mechanism initiating relapse, which in turn seems to be reflected by a psychophysiological indicator of vulnerability in the patient. Additional, but indirect, evidence supporting the assumption that the EE status of a key relative is important for the postdischarge course of illness comes from intervention studies (Chapter 13). Several studies show that a reduction of high EE through intervention with the key relative leads to a significant decrease in the relapse rate.

However, care must be taken before ascribing the direction of causality, and particularly before interpreting these findings as significant and formative for the origin of schizophrenia itself. First, it was noted that schizophrenics do not come only from high-EE households. Second, the provocation of a relapse through high EE is not specific to schizophrenia. Relapses also have been shown to be provoked more by high-EE than by low-EE situations in neurotic–depressive patients (Vaughn and Leff, 1976) and in patients with other types of affective disorders (Hooley *et al.*, 1986; Miklowitz *et al.*, 1988; Hooley and Teasdale, 1989). Positive feedback from both sides probably produces a vicious circle between the features of the illness and the environment.

Nevertheless, the high-EE status of a key person seems to be a relevant, although unspecific, noxious event that fairly reliably predicts a poor short-term course of the illness in most studies completed to date.

## V. Suggested Readings

Early studies on the role of family factors and parental style on the eventual development of schizophrenia are reviewed in detail by Neale and Oltmanns (1980). Brown *et al.* (1962) give one of the first descriptions of the EE factor as a cause of relapse. Leff and Vaughn (1985) give the most comprehensive survey of EE research, and Kuipers and Bebbington (1988) present the latest review of EE research and its contribution to early relapse. Dohrenwend, one of the most influential researchers in the field of life-event research, surveys the field, reports on his groups new findings, and comments critically on earlier conclusions (Dohrenwend *et al.*, 1987).

We also suggest the original research report of the adoption study of Tienari and co-workers (1985), since it is the most comprehensive and most detailed analysis of gene–environment interaction, that is, of its contribution to the etiology of the psychological disturbances and the schizophrenic illness.

## VI. Summary Statements and Interpretations

### A. Differences between Twins

The eventually affected twin usually has a slightly lower birth weight than the unaffected one. Other differences concern the type of postnatal social interaction (e.g., the eventually affected twin is often the more submissive of the two during childhood).

These results show that little is known about the origin of the discordance in MZ twins. Perinatal factors may play a role in the crossing of the threshold for expression of the illness. This supports findings reported earlier as well as those to be discussed in Chapter 12. Is the submissive behavior of the twin that will become affected a consequence of a "weaker nervous system" brought about by unfavorable perinatal conditions? We can only speculate that this might be the case, since there is little direct evidence (see the association of sulcal widening, low birth weight, and the development of schizophrenia in nontwins; Cannon *et al.*, 1989; Chapters 7–9).

### B. Social Drift

Schizophrenics are admitted more frequently from inner city areas, areas with poor living conditions, or both.

Most test results suggest that the reason for this is a downward social drift and not the living conditions in these areas, but poor living conditions may aggravate an already labile state. Premorbid difficulties, characteristic of a high proportion of schizophrenics, hinder adequate school and job performance.

## C. Life Events

Independent life events are no more frequent in the premorbid phase of schizophrenia than in other psychiatric disturbances. An increased incidence of schizophrenia is not associated with conditions of extreme stress.

Life events can certainly have a provocative influence, but they are not formative and hence do not cause schizophrenia.

## D. Family Interaction

### 1. Disturbed Family Atmosphere

The family environment of children who eventually become schizophrenic is disturbed more often than that of control probands. This finding is the result of large scale prospective studies. However, deviant personality traits close to schizophrenia spectrum personality disorders are very often reported in the parents themselves. These reports do not discuss whether or how these deviant personalities are responsible for the disturbed family atmosphere.

Both factors may contribute: the family atmosphere and the potential genetic load of a schizophrenia spectrum personality disorder in one of the parents.

### 2. Communication and Thought Disorder in the Parents

Slightly deviant thought processes can be observed in parents of schizophrenics.

The direction of causality is not clear in these findings, which, with one exception, do not come from prospective studies. Does the stress of rearing a schizophrenic child provoke the disturbed communication, or is deviant communication formative for schizophrenia? The only prospective study (Goldstein, UCLA) provides somewhat equivocal findings. The appearance of a schizophrenia spectrum disorder was associated with deviant communication, a so-called negative affective style in the parents, and a family history of severe psychiatric disturbances (see also Chapter 12). However, the type of communication was not correlated with the finding of heritability. Thus, two independent factors may contribute. Although heuristically interesting, these findings leave some unsolved questions. How representative was the sample? Why are unaffected nonschizophrenic siblings not influenced by the deviant style of communication of the parents?

### 3. High Expressed Emotion (EE) and Relapse

Many studies clearly show that a negative and overinvolved emotional style in a key relative can provoke an early relapse. Several studies show that high EE is not the only factor related to relapse; the most important other factors among these is the compliance to medication. Therapy studies show that relapse rates can also be reduced by changing high EE to low EE. The EE factor is not specific to schizophrenia: High EE provokes relapse in other psychiatric disturbances such as affective disorders.

With the current popularity of the EE concept, it is often overlooked that EE is only one, albeit important, factor related to early relapse. Uncontrolled elements in these studies include the presence or absence of a social net as well as of life events. The possibility of these putative intervening variables resulting in some of the negative findings reported is discussed in the text. Future research should take account of such factors.

# References

Al Khani, M. A. F., Bebbington, P. E., Watson, J. P., and House, F. (1986). Life events and schizophrenia: A Saudi Arabian study. *British Journal of Psychiatry, 148*, 12–22.

Alanen, Y. O. (1968). From the mothers of schizophrenic patients to interactional family dynamics. In D. Rosenthal, S. S. Kety (Eds.), *The Transmission of Schizophrenia.* Oxford: Pergamon Press.

Ambelas, A. (1987). Life events and mania. A special relationship? *British Journal of Psychiatry, 150*, 235–240.

Arieti, S. (1971). Schizophrenia. *American Journal of Psychiatry, 128*, 348–350.

Bagley, C., Jacobson, S., and Palmer, C. (1973). Social structure and the ecological distribution of mental illness, suicide, and delinquency. *Psychological Medicine, 3*, 177–187.

Barrowclough, C., Tarrier, N., Watts, S., Vaughn, C., Bamrah, J. S., and Freeman, H. L. (1987). Assessing the functional value of relatives' knowledge about schizophrenia: a preliminary report. *British Journal of Psychiatry, 151*, 1–8.

Bateson, G., Jackson, D. D., Haley, J., and Weakland, J. H. (1956). Toward a theory of schizophrenia. *Behavioral Science, 1*, 251–264.

Belmaker, R., Pollin, W., Wyatt, R. J., and Cohen, S. (1974). A follow-up of monocygotic twins discordant for schizophrenia. *Archives of General Psychiatry, 30*, 219–222.

Birchwood, M., and Cochrane, R. (1990). Families coping with schizophrenia: Coping styles, their origins and correlates. *Psychological Medicine, 2014*, 857–865.

Brown, G. W. (1959). Experiences of discharged chronic schizophrenic mental hospital patients in various types of living groups. *Milbank Memorial Foundation Quarterly, 37*, 105–131.

Brown, G. W., and Birley, J. L. T. (1968). Crises and life changes and the onset of schizophrenia. *Journal of Health and Social Behavior, 9*, 203–214.

Brown, G. W., Birley, J. L. T., and Wing, J. K. (1972). Influence of family life on the course of schizophrenic disorders: replication. *British Journal of Psychiatry, 121*, 241–258.

Brown, G. W., Carstairs, G. M., and Topping, G. (1958). Post-hospital adjustment of chronic mental patients. *Lancet, 2*, 685–689.

Brown, G. W., Monck, E. M., Carstairs, G. M., and Wing, J. K. (1962). Influence of family life on the course of schizophrenic illness. *British Journal of Preventive and Social Medicine, 16*, 55–68.

Cannon, T. D., Mednick, S. A., and Parnas, J. (1989). Genetic and perinatal determinants of structural brain deficits in schizophrenia. *Archives of General Psychiatry, 46*, 883–889.

Canton, G., and Fraccon, I. G. (1985). Life events and schizophrenia. A replication. *Acta Psychiatrica Scandinavica, 71*, 211–216.

Chung, R. K., Langeluddecke, P., and Tennant, C. (1986). Threatening life events in the onset of schizophrenia, schizophreniform psychosis and hypomania. *British Journal of Psychiatry, 148*, 680–685.

Cochrane, R. (1983). *The social creation of mental illness.* Essex: Longman.

Cutting, J. (1985). *The psychology of schizophrenia.* Edinburgh: Churchill Livingstone.

Dilling, H., and Weyerer, S. (1978). *Epidemiologie psychischer Störungen und psychiatrische Versorgung.* München: Urban & Schwarzenberg.

Dohrenwend, B. P., Shrout, P. E., Link, B. G., and Skodol, A. E. (1987). Social and psychological risk factors for episodes of schizophrenia. In H. Häfner, W. F. Gattaz, W. Janzarik (Eds.), *Search for the causes of schizophrenia.* Berlin: Springer.

Dulz, B., and Hand, I. (1986). Short-term relapse in young schizophrenics: can it be predicted and affected by family (CFI), patient, and treatment variables? An experimental study. In M. J. Goldstein, I. Hand, and K. Hahlweg (Eds.), *Treatment of Schizophrenia: Family Assessment and Intervention* (pp. 59–75). Berlin: Springer.

Dunham, H. W., Phillips, P. and Srinivasan, B. (1966). A research note on diagnosed mental illness and social class. *American Sociological Review, 31*, 223–227.

Faris, R. E. L., and Dunham, H. W. (1939). *Mental disorders in urban areas: An ecological study of schizophrenia and other psychoses.* Chicago: University of Chicago Press.

Federn, P. (1953). *Ego psychology and the psychoses.* Edit. and with an introduction by E. Weiss. London: Imago Publishing.

Fontana, A. F. (1966). Familial etiology of schizophrenia: Is a scientific methodology possible? *Psychological Bulletin, 66*, 214–227.

Fromm-Reichmann, F. (1948). Notes on the development of treatment of schizophrenics by psychoanalytic psychotherapy. *Psychiatry, II*, 263–273.

Giel, R., Wiersma, D., and DeJong, A. (1987). The issue of social class and schizophrenia in the Netherlands. In M. C. Angermeyer (Ed.), *From social class to social stress.* Berlin: Springer.

Goldberg, E. M., and Morrison, S. L. (1963). Schizophrenia and social class. *British Journal of Psychiatry, 109*, 785–802.

Goldstein, J. M., and Kreisman, D. (1988). Gender, family environment and schizophrenia. *Psychological Medicine, 18*, 861–872.

Goldstein, M. J. (1985). Family factors that antedate the onset of schizophrenia and related disorders: The results of a fifteen year prospective longitudinal study. *Acta Psychiatrics Scandinavica, 71*, 7–18.

Goldstein, M. J. (1987). The UCLA high-risk project. *Schizophrenia Bulletin, 13*, 505–514.

Gottesman, I. I., and Shields, J. (1982). Schizophrenia: The epigenetic puzzle. Cambridge: Cambridge University Press.

Gottschalk, L. A., Falloon, I. R. H., Marder, S. S., Lebell, M. B., Gift, T. E., and Wynne, L. C. (1988). The prediction of relapse of schizophrenic patients using emotional data obtained from their relatives. *Psychiatry Research, 25*, 261–276.

Gruen, R., and Baron, M. (1984). Stressful life events and schizophrenia. *Neuropsychobiology, 12*, 206–208.

Häfner, H. (1972). Der Einfluß von Umweltfaktoren auf die Disposition zur Schizophrenie. *Fortschritte der Medizin, 90.* Jg., 217–220.

Häfner, H. (1986). Personal communication.

Häfner, H., Reimann, H., Immich, H., and Martini, H. (1969). Inzidenz seelischer Erkrankungen in Mannheim 1965. *Social Psychiatry, 4*, 126–135.

Hahlweg, K., Nuechterlein, K. H., Goldstein, M. J., Magana, A., Doane, J. A., Snyder, K. S., and Mintz, J. (1987). Parental-expressed emotion and intrafamilial communication behavior. In K. Hahlweg, M. J. Goldstein (Eds.), *Understanding major mental disorder. The contribution of family interaction research.* (pp. 156–175). New York: Family Process Press.

Heston, L. L. (1966). Psychiatric disorders in foster home reared children of schizophrenic mothers. *British Journal of Psychiatry, 112*, 819–825.

Hirsch, S. R., and Leff, J. P. (1975). Abnormalities in parents of schizophrenics. Maudsley Monograph No. 22. London: Oxford University Press.

Hogarty, G. E. (1985). Expressed emotion and schizophrenic relapse: implications from the Pittsburgh Study. In M. Alpert (Ed.), *Controversies in schizophrenia.* (pp. 354–365). New York: Guilford Press.

Hogarty, G. E., Anderson, C. N., Reis, D. J., Kornblith, S. J., Greenwald, D. P., Javna, C. D., and Madonia, M. J. (1986). Family psychoeducation, social skills training, and maintenance chemotherapy in the aftercare treatment of schizophrenia. I. One-year effects of a controlled study on relapse and expressed emotion. *Archives of General Psychiatry, 43,* 633–642.

Hollingshead, A. B., and Redlich, F. C. (1958). *Social class and mental illness.* New York: John Wiley & Sons.

Hooley, J. M., Orley, J., and Teasdale, J. D. (1986). Levels of expressed emotions and relapse in depressed patients. *British Journal of Psychiatry, 148,* 642–647.

Hooley, J. M., and Teasdale, J. D. (1989). Predictors of relapse in unipolar depressives: expressed emotion, marital distress, and perceived criticism. *Journal of Abnormal Psychology, 98,* 229–235.

Jacobs, S., and Meyers, J. (1976). Recent life events and acute schizophrenic psychosis: A controlled study. *Journal of Nervous and Mental Disease, 162,* 75–87.

Jones, J. E. (1977). Patterns of transactional style deviance in the TAT's of parents of schizophrenics. *Family Process, 16,* 327–337.

Karno, M., Jenkins, J. H., De la Selva, A., Santana, F., Telles, C., Lopez, S., and Mintz, J. (1987). Expressed emotion and schizophrenic outcome among Mexican-American families. *Journal of Nervous and Mental Disease, 175,* 143–1551.

Kendler, K. S. (1985). Commentary by K. S. Kendler. In C. C. Tennant. Stress and Schizophrenia: A Review. *Integrative Psychiatry, 3,* 255–256.

Klusmann, D., and Angermeyer, M. C. (1987). Urban ecology and psychiatric admission rates: Results from a study in the city of Hamburg. In M. C. Angermeyer (Ed.), *From social class to social stress.* Berlin: Springer.

Kringlen, E. (1987). Contribution of genetic studies on schizophrenia. In H. Häfner, W. F. Gattaz, W. Janzarik (Eds.), *Search for the causes of schizophrenia.* Berlin: Springer.

Kuipers, L. (1979). Expressed Emotion: A review. *British Journal of Social and Clinical Psychology, 18,* 237–243.

Kuipers, L., and Bebbington, P. (1988). Expressed emotion research in schizophrenia: theoretical and clinical implications. *Psychological Medicine, 18,* 893–909.

Leff, J., Hirsch, S. R., Rhode, P., Gaind, R., and Stevens, B. C. (1973). Life events and maintenance. Therapy in schizophrenic relapse. *British Journal of Psychiatry, 123,* 659–660.

Leff, J., Kuipers, L., Berkowitz, R., Vaughn, C., and Sturgeon, D. (1983). Life events, relatives' expressed emotion and maintenance neuroleptics in schizophrenic relapse. *Psychological Medicine, 13,* 799–806.

Leff, J., and Vaughn, C. (1980). The interaction of life events and relatives' expressed emotion in schizophrenia and depressive neurosis. *British Journal of Psychiatry, 136,* 146–153.

Leff, J., and Vaughn, C. (1986). Correspondence. First episodes of schizophrenia. *British Journal of Psychiatry, 148,* 215–219.

Leff, J. P., and Brown, G. W. (1977). Family and social factors in the course of schizophrenia. *British Journal of Psychiatry, 130,* 417–420.

Leff, J. P., Kuipers, L., Berkowitz, R., Eberlein-Fries, R., and Sturgeon, D. (1982). A controlled trial of social intervention in schizophrenic families. *British Journal of Psychiatry, 141,* 121–134.

Leff, J., and Vaughn, C. (1985). *Expressed emotion in families. Its significance for mental illness.* New York: The Guilford Press.

Lidz, T. (1973). *The origin and treatment of schizophrenic disorders.* New York: Basic Books.

Liem, J. H. (1974). Effects of verbal communications of parents and children: A comparison of normal and schizophrenic families. *Journal of Consulting and Clinical Psychology, 42*, 438–450.

MacMillan, J. F., Gold, A., Crow, T. J., Johnson, A. L., and Johnstone, E. C. (1986). Expressed emotion and relapse. *British Journal of Psychiatry, 148*, 133–143.

McCreadie, R. G., and Phillips, K. (1988). The Nithsdale schizrenia survey. VII. Does relatives' high expressed emotion predict relapse? *British Journal of Psychiatry, 152*, 477–481.

McCreadie, R. G., and Robinson, A. D. T. (1987). The Nithsdale schizophrenia survey. VI. Relatives' expressed emotion: Prevalence, patterns, and clinical assessment. *British Journal of Psychiatry, 150*, 640–644.

Miklowitz, D. J., Goldstein, M. J., Falloon, I. R., and Doane, J. A. (1984). Interactional correlates of expressed emotion in the families of schizophrenics. *British Journal of Psychiatry, 144*, 482–487.

Miklowitz, D. J., Goldstein, M. J., and Falloon, I. R. H. (1983). Premorbid and symptomatic characteristics of schizophrenics from families with high and low levels of expressed emotion. *Journal of Abnormal Psychology, 92*, 359–367.

Miklowitz, D. J., Goldstein, M. J., Nuechterlein, K. H., Snyder, K. S., and Mintz, J. (1988). Family factors and the course of bipolar affective disorder. *Archives of General Psychiatry, 45*, 225–231.

Mintz, J., Mintz, L., and Goldstein, M. (1987). Expressed emotion and relapse in first episodes of schizophrenia. A rejoinder to MacMillan *et al.* (1986). *British Journal of Psychiatry, 151*, 314–320.

Mishler, E. G., and Waxler, N. E. (1968). Interaction in families: An experimental study of family processes and schizophrenia. New York: Wiley.

Moline, R. A., Singh, S., Morris, A., and Meltzer, H. Y. (1985). Family expressed emotion and relapse in schizophrenia in 24 urban American patients. *The American Journal of Psychiatry and Supplementation, 142*, 1078–1081.

Neale, J. M., and Oltmanns, T. F. (1980). Schizophrenia. New York: John Wiley & Sons.

Nuechterlein, K. H., Snyder, K. H., Dawson, M. E., Rappe, S., Gitlin, S., and Fogelson, D. (1986). Expressed emotion, fixed dose fluphenazine decanoate maintenance and relapse in recent onset schizophrenia. *Psychopharmacological Bulletin, 22*, 633–639.

Parker, G., Johnston, P., and Hayward, L. (1988). Parental expressed emotion as a predictor of schizophrenic relapse. *Archives of General Psychiatry, 45*, 806–813.

Rabkin, J. G. (1980). Stressful live events and schizophrenia: A review of the research literature. *Psychological Bulletin, 87*, 408–425.

Reiss, D. (1967). Individual thinking and family interaction: II. A study of pattern recognition and hypothesis testing in families of normals, character disorders, and schizophrenics. *Journal of Psychiatric Research, 5*, 193–211.

Ricks, D. F., and Berry, J. C. (1970). Family and symptom patterns that precede schizophrenia. In M. Roff, D. Ricks (Eds.), *Life history research in psychopathology*. Minneapolis: University of Minnesota Press.

Ringuette, E., and Kennedy, T. (1966). An experimental study of the double-bind hypothesis. *Journal of Abnormal Psychology, 71*, 136–141.

Robins, L. N. (1966). *Deviant children grow up*. Baltimore: Williams & Wilkins.

Rowitz, L., and Levy, L. (1968). Ecological analysis of treated mental disorders in Chicago. *Archives of General Psychiatry, 19*, 571–579.

Sartorius, N., Shapiro, R. and Jablensky, A. (1974). The International Pilot Study of Schizophrenia. *Schizophrenia Bulletin, 1*, 21–34.

Sass, L. A., Gunderson, J. G., Thaler Singer, M., and Wynne, L. C. (1984). Parental communication deviance and forms of thinking in male schizophrenic offspring. *Journal of Nervous and Mental Disease, 172*, 513–520.

Scharfetter, C. (1983). Schizophrene Menschen. Psychopathologie, Verlauf, Forschungszugänge, Therapiegrundsätze. München: Urban & Schwarzenberg.

Schofield, W., and Balian, L. (1959). A comparative study of the personal histories of schizophrenic and nonpsychiatric patients. *Journal of Abnormal and Social Psychology, 59,* 216–225.

Schuham, A. L. (1967). The double-bind hypothesis a decade later. *Psychological Bulletin, 68,* 409.

Silverton, S., and Mednick, S. (1984). Class drift and schizophrenia. *Acta Psychiatrica Scandinavica, 70,* 304–309.

Singer, M. T., and Wynne, L. C. (1963). Differentiating characteristics of parents of childhood schizophrenics, childhood neurotics and young adult schizophrenics. *American Journal of Psychiatry, 120,* 234–243.

Singer, M. T., and Wynne, L. C. (1965a). Thought disorder and family relations of schizophrenics: III. Methodology using projective techniques. *Archives of General Psychiatry, 12,* 187–200.

Singer, M. T., and Wynne, L. C. (1965b). Thought disorder and family relations of schizophrenics: IV. Results and implications. *Archives of General Psychiatry, 12,* 201–212.

Sluzki, C. E., and Ransom, D. C. (1976). Double bind: The foundation of the communicational approach to the family. New York: Grune & Stratton.

Strachan, A. M., Leff, J. P., Goldstein, M. J., Doane, J. A., and Burtt, C. (1986). Emotional attitudes and direct communication in the families of schizophrenics: A cross-national replication. *British Journal of Psychiatry, 149,* 279–287.

Strachan, A. M., Feingold, D., Goldstein, M. J., Miklowitz, D. J., and Nuechterlein, K. H. (1989). Is expressed emotion an index of transactional process? II. The patient's coping style. *Family Process, 28,* 1–13.

Straube, E. R., Wagner, W., Foerster, K., Heimann, H. (1989). Findings significant with respect to short- and medium-term outcome in schizophrenia—a preliminary report. *Progress in Neuropsychopharmacology & Biol. Psych, 13,* 185–179.

Strodtbeck, F. (1951). Husband–wife interaction over revealed differences. *American Sociological Review, 16,* 468–473.

Strodtbeck, F. (1954). The family as a three-person-group. *American Sociological Review, 19,* 23–29.

Sturgeon, D., Kuipers, L., Berkowitz, R., Turpin, G., and Leff, J. (1981). Psychophysiological responses of schizophrenic patients to high and low expressed emotion relative. *British Journal of Psychiatry, 138,* 40–45.

Sturgeon, D., Turpin, G., Kuipers, L., Berkowitz, R., and Leff, J. (1984). Psychophysiological responses of schizophrenic patients to high and low expressed emotion relatives: A follow-up study. *British Journal of Psychiatry, 145,* 62–69.

Tarrier, N., and Barrowclough, C. (1987). A longitudinal psychophysiological assessment of a schizophrenic patient in relation to the expressed emotion of his relatives. *Behavior Psychotherapy, 15,* 45–57.

Tarrier, N., Barrowclough, C., Porceddu, K., and Watts, S. (1988). The assessment of psychophysiological reactivity to the expressed emotion of the relatives of schizophrenic patients. *British Journal of Psychiatry, 152,* 618–624.

Tarrier, N., Barrowclough, C., Vaughn, C., Bamrah, J. S., Porceddu, K., Watts, S., and Freeman, H. (1989). The community management of schizophrenia: a controlled trial of a behavioral intervention with families to reduce relapse. *British Journal of Psychiatry, 154,* 625–628.

Tarrier, N., Vaughn, C., Lader, M. H., and Leff, J. P. (1979). Bodily reactions to people and events in schizophrenics. *Archives of General Psychiatry, 36,* 311–315.

Tennant, C. C. (1985). Stress and schizophrenia: A review. *Integr. Psychiatry, 3,* 248–261.

Tienari, P., Sorri, A., Lahti, I., Naarala, M., Wahlberg, K-E., Ronkko, T., Pohjola, J., and Moring, J. (1985). The Finnish adoptive family study of schizophrenia. *Yale Journal of Biological Medicine, 58,* 227.

Turner, R. J., and Wagonfeld, M. O. (1967). Occupational mobility and schizophrenia: An assessment of the social causation and social selection hypotheses. *American Sociological Review, 32,* 104–113.

Valone, K., Goldstein, M. J., and Norton, J. P. (1984). Parental expressed emotion and psychophysiological reactivity in an adolescent sample at risk for schizophrenia spectrum disorders. *Journal of Abnormal Psychology, 93,* 448–457.

Vaughn, C. E. (1986). Pattern of emotional response in the families of schizophrenic patients. In M. J. Goldstein, E. Hand and K. Halweg (Eds.). *Treatment of Schizophrenia: Family Assessment and Intervention.* Berlin: Springer.

Vaughn, C. E., and Leff, J. P. (1976). The influence of family and social factors on the course of psychiatric illness. *British Journal of Psychiatry, 129,* 125–137.

Vaughn, C. E., and Leff, J. P. (1981). Patterns of emotional response in relatives of schizophrenic patients. *Schizophrenia Bulletin, 7,* 43–57.

Vaughn, C. E., Snyder, K. S., Jones, S., Freeman, W. B., and Falloon, I. R. H. (1984). Family factors in schizophrenic relapse. *Archives of General Psychiatry, 41,* 1169–1177.

Wahl, O. F. (1976). Monozygotic twins discordant for schizophrenia: A review. *Psychological Bulletin, 83,* 91–106.

Waring, M., and Ricks, D. (1965). Family patterns of children who became adult schizophrenics. *Journal of Nervous and Mental Disease, 140,* 351–365.

Warner, R., and Atkinson, M. (1988). The relationship between schizophrenic patient's perceptions of their parents and the course of their illness. *British Journal of Psychiatry, 153,* 344–353.

Wender, P. H., Rosenthal, D., and Kety, S. S. (1968). A psychiatric assessment of the adoptive parents of schizophrenics. In D. Rosenthal and S. S. Kety (Eds.), *The transmission of schizophrenia.* New York: Pergamon.

Wender, P. H., Rosenthal, D., Kety, S. S., Schulsinger, F., and Weiner, J. (1973). Social class and psychopathology in adoptees: A natural experimental method for separating the roles of genetic and experiental factors. *Archives of General Psychiatry, 28,* 318–325.

Wig, N. N., Menon, D. K., Bedi, H., Ghosh, A., Kuipers, L., Leff, J., Korten, A., Day, R., Sartorius, N., Ernberg, G., and Jablensky, A. (1987). Expressed emotion and schizophrenia in North India. I. Cross-cultural transfer of ratings of relatives' expressed emotion. *British Journal of Psychiatry, 151,* 156–173.

Wynne, L. C. (1981). Current concepts about schizophrenics and family relationships. *Journal of Nervous and Mental Disease, 169,* 82–89.

Wynne, L. C., Thaler Singer, M., and Toohey, M. L. (1976). Communication of the adoptive parents of schizophrenics. In J. Jorstad and E. Ugelstad (Eds.), *Schizophrenia 75. Psychotherapy, family studies, research.* Oslo: Universitetsforlaget.

Zahn, T. P. (1968). Word association in adoptive and biological parents of schizophrenics. *Archives of Dermatology, 19,* 501–503.

# Chapter 12

# Populations at High Risk
# for Schizophrenia

## I. Introduction

Research into the nature of the factors that constitute a high risk for schizophrenia is undoubtedly one of the prime strategies for the study of schizophrenia. Above all, in this kind of investigation the sources of error inherent in already severely ill samples can be avoided. (We refer particularly to the difficulty of discriminating a schizophrenia-specific deficit from a general impairment due to general consequences of the illness; cf. Chapters 2, 3, and 4.)

Risk studies try to uncover (1) marker variables for the genetic basis of the illness in nonschizophrenic relatives of schizophrenics and (2) predictor variables for the development of psychosis in hypothetically prepsychotic subjects. The ultimate purpose is to identify features that can be tackled by preventative or therapeutic strategies.

The following three sections represent the three major ways in which risk factors can be investigated.

The studies described in Section II investigate the characteristics of the offspring of a schizophrenic mother or father before the age of a possible onset of the psychosis. The features seen in the index but not the control group are then treated as candidates for biological and behavioral markers of the illness. The methodological disadvantage is, however, that living with a schizophrenic parent could provide an unfavorable environment for the child: environmental and hereditary factors are therefore difficult to disentangle.

Section III describes potentially fruitful high-risk studies that follow the mental health of children up to and through the age at which illness is likely to occur. Through a longitudinal investigation, insight into the behavioral precursors or environmental determinants of schizophrenia is sought. The characteristics of the child or adolescent who eventually develops schizophrenia are compared with those of children who remain nonpsychotic through the age of risk ($\sim$ 25 yr) in order to uncover potential predictors of the later illness. A disadvantage of this type of study is its length. The researcher will have to wait

10–20 yr on average, before he or she can classify childhood or adolescent data according to the outcome.

Section IV discusses that individuals from the general population can be selected if they show personality or, conceivably, biological characteristics similar to those shown by schizophrenics. The disadvantage of such studies is that large samples must be recruited to obtain statistically meaningful results, since less than 1% of the population is at risk for schizophrenia (i.e., a sample of more than 2000 subjects is needed). This disadvantage is in addition to other problems incurred by a long-term follow-up study. The methodological advantage is, however, that this type of study is more representative than is studying children of schizophrenic parents, since only about 10% of schizophrenics have a schizophrenic parent (cf. methodology discussion, Lewine *et al.*, 1981). Of course some researchers try to avoid the sample-size problem by studying youngsters with emotional and behavioral problems. Goldstein (1987) showed that the probability that individuals in such a group would develop schizophrenia was up to 7 times higher than that of an unselected control group from the general population. (Yet again one may ask if this group is representative. We do not know enough about the proportion of schizophrenics who have behavioral problems in their youth.)

## II. Features in Children of Schizophrenic Parents

At present there are longitudinal studies of school-age children with a schizophrenic parent being conducted at at least 10 centers. The 8 studies of which we are aware that have a sample size larger than 20 are shown in Table 12.1.

### A. The Mednick–Schulsinger Study

One of the earliest prospective studies with an appropriately large sample was that initiated by the psychologist and physician Sarnoff Mednick and the psychiatrist Fini Schulsinger in Copenhagen. Their study became the model for those that followed. For this reason, and because the children have now reached the critical age of young adults, we shall discuss the Mednick–Schulsinger study in more detail than the others.

The Mednick–Schulsinger study started in 1962 with 207 children of mothers with severe chronic schizophrenia and 104 healthy mothers. This selection was made before the era of research diagnostic criteria. Schizophrenic mothers were included in the study only when two experienced psychiatrists were absolutely certain of the diagnosis. Care was given to matching the groups on a wide range of factors (e.g., age, where they grew up and lived).

**Table 12.1** Overview of the Larger ($n > 20$) Current Longitudinal Investigations of School-Age Children at High Risk for Schizophrenia with at Least One Schizophrenic Parent

| Project center | Principal investigators | Study started | High risk group | | | Control healthy parents | Group psychiatric parents |
| --- | --- | --- | --- | --- | --- | --- | --- |
| | | | Schizophrenic parent | Age | Risk group (n) | | |
| Copenhagen, Denmark[b] | Mednick, Schulsinger | 1962 | Mother | 9–20 yr | 207 | + | – |
| New York, New York | Erlenmeyer, Kimling | 1971 | Father, mother, both | 7–12 yr | 63 | + | + |
| Stony Brook, New York | Weintraub, Neale | 1971 | Father, mother | 6–16 yr | 57 | + | + |
| Minneapolis, Minnesota | Garmezy, Neuchterlein | 1971 | Mother | 10–14 yr | 24 | + | + |
| Rochester, New York[b] | Wynne, Cromwell, Klein, Salzmann | 1972 | Mother, father | 4, 7, or 10 yr | 42 | – | + |
| Jerusalem, Israel[b] | Rosenthal, Nagler, Mirsky | 1987 | Mother, father | 8–15 yr | 50 | + | – |
| St. Louis, Missouri | Anthony | 1966 | Mother, father, both | 6–12 yr | 94 | + | + |
| Pittsburgh, Pennsylvania | Schachter | 1968 | Mother | 3–4 mo | 14 | + | – |
| | | | | 6–16 yr | 29 | + | – |

[a]Compiled after Garmezy, 1974; Rieder, 1979; Watt *et al.*, 1984; Erlenmeyer-Kimling and Cornblatt, 1984. Excluded from the table but referred to in the text are the following studies ($n < 20$): Asarnow/Steffy (Waterloo, Canada), 9 adopted children; Grunebaum (Boston, Massachusetts), 13 children with birth complications or perinatal neurophysiological anomalies; Fish (New York, New York), $n = 12$; McNeil/Kaij (Sweden), $n = 13$.

[b]These projects also studied birth complications and neurological signs.

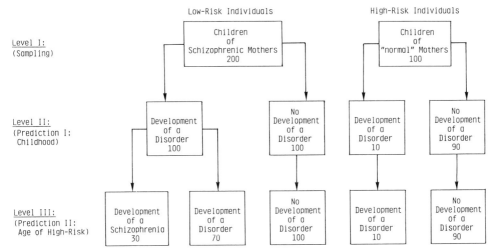

**Figure 12.1** Design and predictions of the Danish and North American high risk project (after Mednick and Schulsinger, 1968).

The children were studied with measures of personality, for social competence, for cognitive performance, and for psychophysiological reactivity. The one major drawback of the study was the large age variation at the first investigation (9–20 yr). The design of the study is shown in Figure 12.1.

Ten years after the initial investigation, 173 members of the high-risk group were restudied (e.g., John *et al.*, 1982; Mednick *et al.*, 1984, 1987). In the index group (aged 18–30 yr), 15 were found to be schizophrenic by at least two of the three diagnostic procedures. There was only one clear case of schizophrenia in the control group. These values of 9 and 1%, respectively, are both remarkably close to the expected incidence within the two groups.

## B. Perinatal Complications

In the Mednick–Schulsinger study, there were no particular differences between healthy and schizophrenic mothers in the course of their pregnancies nor in the difficulties they experienced at birth (Table 12.2; Parnas *et al.*, 1982). Similarly, the study carried out in Israel reported no differences in the incidence of complications at birth (Marcus *et al.*, 1984).

Rieder and colleagues from the National Institutes of Mental Health (NIMH) report on an interim assessment of a nationwide study of still-births in a population of 58,000. In families in which neither parent was psychiatrically ill, the incidence of still-birth was 3.8% If one or the other parent was schizophrenic, the rate was twice as high (7.5%). (When the diagnosis was not clearcut or there was a spectrum diagnosis, the proportion of still-births at 3.3% was no different from that in the general healthy population.)

**Table 12.2** Incidence of Perinatal Complications in Mothers Who Were Schizophrenic, "Borderline" Schizophrenic, or Had No Psychiatric Disturbance[a,b]

| Nature of perinatal complication | S (N = 12) n | (%) | bl-S (N = 25) n | (%) | C (N = 33) n | (%) |
|---|---|---|---|---|---|---|
| Eklampsia | 0 | (0) | 0 | (0) | 1 | (3) |
| Previous fetal loss | 0 | (0) | 0 | (0) | 1 | (3) |
| Premature rupture of membrane | 1 | (8) | 1 | (4) | 9 | (23) |
| Abnormal fetal position | 3 | (25) | 0 | (0) | 0 | (0) |
| Narrow pelvis | 0 | (0) | 0 | (0) | 1 | (3) |
| Pelvis contractions during delivery | 1 | (8) | 0 | (0) | 1 | (3) |
| Bleeding after delivery | 0 | (0) | 1 | (4) | 1 | (3) |
| Asphyxia | 1 | (8) | 0 | (0) | 2 | (5) |
| Umbilical cord complication | 2 | (17) | 0 | (0) | 1 | (3) |
| Primary uterine intertia | 0 | (0) | 0 | (0) | 1 | (3) |
| Secondary uterine inertia | 1 | (8) | 0 | (0) | 1 | (3) |
| Forceps used | 2 | (17) | 0 | (0) | 1 | (3) |
| Caesarian section | 0 | (0) | 0 | (0) | 1 | (3) |
| Signs of prematurity >2500 g | 2 | (17) | 1 | (4) | 2 | (5) |
| Signs of prematurity <2500 g | 0 | (0) | 1 | (4) | 3 | (8) |
| Placental abnormality | 1 | (8) | 2 | (8) | 1 | (3) |
| Labor >24 hr | 2 | (17) | 2 | (8) | 3 | (8) |
| Labor >48 hr | 1 | (8) | 1 | (4) | 3 | (8) |

[a] After Parnas et al., 1982.
[b] S, Schizophrenic; bl-S, borderline schizophrenic, now termed schizophrenia spectrum personality disorder; C, no psychiatric disturbance.

Wrede, Mednick, and colleagues (1980) obtained equal-sized samples of healthy and schizophrenic mothers ($n = 192$) from the birth records in Helsinki between 1960 and 1964. They found significantly more pregnancy and birth complications in the group of schizophrenic mothers. In up to 12% of births to chronic schizophrenic mothers, the doctors and midwives described the health of the child as not satisfactory. In the control group, the rate did not exceed 4%. The diagnosis of the mother cannot have had a direct influence on the rating by the obstetricians, because in most cases the mother became ill after the birth. (However, this does not preclude the possibility that premorbid signs played a role; see subsequent discussion.)

Unfortunately, another factor emerges that could well have influenced the results. The mothers who became schizophrenic came from a lower socioeconomic class than the healthy controls. This could have led to less-than-satisfactory health care in the pre- and neonatal periods. This suggestion receives indirect support from a study by Chalmers (1983). In a prospective report, this author found a potential connection between the incidence of pregnancy and birth complications and a range of psychosocial influences such as educational level and the attitude toward pregnancy. Further, preschizophrenic mothers were prone to take more medication in pregnancy, which may have influenced the number of complications. This could be the case even with the preschizophrenic mothers in the study of Wrede *et al.* (1980). They might have had premorbid signs during pregnancy and birth, which may have influenced the number of complications.

A further problem for the evaluation of this study is the heterogeneous category of birth and pregnancy complications. This term includes such items as "unusual mental state of the mother," "mother too thin or too large," "mother under the influence of medication at the time of birth," and "poor health of the mother" (Wrede *et al.*, 1980). Some of these complications therefore might not be independent of the mental health of the mother, even if she was not overtly psychotic at the time of pregnancy and child delivery.

From such considerations, one cannot exclude the possibility that the increased incidence of complications has something to do with the premorbid characteristics of the mothers before they developed the full schizophrenic syndrome. However, it may be more correct here to refer to a nonspecific psychiatric state of the mother, since no other psychiatric group was studied for control purposes. Indeed, reviews of the literature on perinatal complications conclude that, in the majority of studies, there was no clustering of problems specific to groups of schizophrenic mothers when compared with control groups that included mothers with other psychiatric diagnosis (cf. McNeil and Kaij, 1978; Marcuse and Cornblatt, 1986). However, if the birth protocols of those children who eventually developed schizophrenia were compared with those of children who did not develop schizophrenia, the picture becomes quite different (see Section III).

## C. Delay and Disturbance of Sensorimotor Development

Mednick and Schulsinger (1965) observed no sign of either developmental delay or any unusual neurological signs in the offspring of the schizophrenic mothers. In contrast, in a small group of high-risk children in New York ($n = 12$), Fish and Dixon (1978) found some developmental delay and slight disturbance of neurointegration. For example, they reported decreased nystagmus and motor coordination that was not appropriate for the age group. However, the changes were transitory and apparently improved later in development.

Positive results from neurological tests in the Minnesota high-risk group were recorded by Hanson and colleagues (1976). On tests of motor, visual, and auditory coordination, Marcus *et al.* (1984) found an increased incidence of disturbances in their Israeli study. In particular, using normalized rating scales and blind assessment, they found evidence of delayed sensorimotor development. Negative reports derive from studies of small groups in which the mother often was asked retrospectively about the development of her children. Their conclusions are therefore less reliable (cf. the reviews of McNeil and Kaij, 1978; Marcuse and Cornblatt, 1986).

## D. Emotionality and Social Competence

In the Danish study, teachers were given a questionnaire about the behavior of children at school. The analysis showed that the high-risk children were more difficult than those in the low-risk group. Children of schizophrenic mothers were described as more "nervous," more easily disturbed or excitable, and more withdrawn than the low-risk children (Mednick and Schulsinger, 1965).

The social workers in the Danish study reported that the high-risk children lived under more difficult conditions at home. There were more difficulties in the relationship between parents and in that between parent and child. However, since the social workers were informed of the status of the mother, their reports could be biased. Indeed, since many teachers also knew about the psychiatric problems of the mother, it is better to suspend judgment of their analysis until enough time has passed to assess whether or not particular individuals in the high-risk group developed schizophrenia.

Disturbed school behavior in children (age, 7–15 yr) of parents with a psychiatric disorder, but not necessarily a diagnosis of schizophrenia, was reported in a study run by Weintraub and Cromwell at Stony Brook University (New York). The advantage of this study was the inclusion of a group of children with depressive parents in addition to those from schizophrenic and healthy families. The analysis of both the teachers' questionnaire and the judgments of the class at school clearly showed that deviant behavior was present in the offspring of parents who were schizophrenic, but to the same degree as in those of parents with unipolar and bipolar affective disorders. A number of these children were, of course, receiving treatment for their emotional or behavioral difficulties, but the nature of the treatment did not differentiate between offspring with parents suffering from a schizophrenic or affective disorder (Weintraub 1987).

The high-risk study run by Rosenthal from the NIMH in cooperation with colleagues in Israel unfortunately included no psychiatric control group. They found that the high-risk children were more distractable than children from healthy families. This study, at least, had the advantage that the raters and teachers were blind to the psychiatric status of the mothers (Sohlberg and Yaniv, 1985).

However, another project in New York run by Wynne and colleagues at the University of Rochester used a healthy and a depressive control group (see review of Garmezy, 1978). Further, the teachers who received the question-naire had no information on the status of the parents. They found no difference among the children deriving from any of these groups, but in a more detailed analysis they compared children of parents with nuclear schizophrenia with those of parents with a more diffuse and broader schizophrenic syndrome. The former group showed significantly less social competence (Fisher *et al.*, 1980).

A preliminary analysis of a subgroup in the high-risk study of Erlenmeyer-Kimling showed that such children showed less emotional stability than children of healthy or psychiatric parents (control groups). The teachers in this study were questioned retrospectively, but were not aware of the status of the children (Watt *et al.*, 1984). This is the only study that reports a specific deficit (i.e., comparing the children of the index group with the children of a psychiatric control group), but the data are preliminary, since not all children have been examined.

## E. Thought Disorder and Information Processing

Of the several tests reported in the Mednick–Schulsinger study (1965), the result of one pointed to the poorer performance of high-risk children. In the Kent–Rosanoff test, the children showed significantly more deviant associations and a longer response latency in comparison with a group at low risk. Associative disturbances may therefore be related to the characteristic symptoms of adult schizophrenics (cf. Chapter 2). However, the deviations were very mild, were only present in *some* of their children, and were compromised by a statistical problem. (The authors did not adapt the statistical significance to correct for multiple chi$^2$ testing). Yet a re-analysis performed after the children had reached the age of risk sheds some light on the validity of the findings; the incidence of deviant associations correlated with the later appearance of thought disorder among those becoming schizophrenic (Parnas and Sohnlsinger, 1986).

The Stony Brook project also presented evidence that mild forms of language and thought disturbance already exist in high-risk children. From an analysis of tape recordings of the spontaneous speech of the children, they found that those at high risk produced less speech and that the individual ideas expressed were inadequately related to each other. This made it difficult for the listener to find out what the children really had in mind. However, these changes were not large enough to justify the full diagnosis of thought disturbance (Weintraub, 1987). This provides indirect support for the result of Mednick and Schulsinger (1965).

Nuechterlein (1983) ran a carefully prepared investigation of high-risk children as part of the Minnesota project (see Garmezy, 1974). He examined the signal detection performance of children on several versions of the continuous performance test (CPT; Chapter 4). In the CPT, a rapid sequence (lasting 3–10 min) of single letters, digits, or playing cards is displayed on a screen. The subject must respond (press a button) when he or she sees a predesignated target. The main requirement of this kind of test is that of sustained attention. Nuechterlein also used versions of the CPT with perceptually degraded (blurred) digits or playing cards. The tests were run three times, and measures of motivation, fearfulness, and emotionality were also recorded. In addition to the group at high risk for schizophrenia, he investigated the performance of (1) hyperactive children, (2) children of normal mothers, and (3) children of nonpsychotic mothers with mild psychological disturbances. (The presence of a group of hyperactive children is particularly welcome in view of their problems with sustained attention.) Further, the schizophrenic parents were divided into three groups: (1) those with a diagnosis of pure schizophrenia, (2) those with a schizoaffective diagnosis, and (3) those with a schizotypal personality disturbance (DSM-III).

The main result of this exhaustive series of tests follows. Compared with all the other groups, children (age, 9–16 yr) of mothers with "pure schizophrenia" or a schizotypal personality detected fewer targets than those in the other groups [i.e., showed lower measures of sensitivity ($d'$) but no change of response criterion (beta)]. However, only the test with degraded stimuli alone discriminated the high-risk children from children of healthy mothers. (In contrast, hyperactive children showed a decreased response criterion, but better detection performance compared with the groups at risk for schizophrenia, reflecting their impulsiveness and tendency to risk a response when required to decide if the stimulus was a target.)

Consistent with Nuechterlein's findings are those from Erlenmeyer-Kimling and Cornblatt (1978) and Cornblatt and Erlenmeyer-Kimling (1985) at the New York Institute of Psychiatry. They used a version of the CPT adapted for children (age, 7–12 yr) of a schizophrenic parent. The CPT consisted of a succession of two double-digit stimuli. Recorded voices were played simultaneously to provide distraction. With further minor variations in the task, poorer CPT performance has been recorded for small groups of high-risk children in a number of reports (Herman *et al.*, 1977; Wood and Cook, 1979; Steffy *et al.*, 1984).

In contrast to this result, it seems that a simple CPT (e.g., the target is a "7" in a series of digits) does not seem to be demanding enough to reveal deficits (e.g., with one group of foster high-risk children and one of young adults with a schizotypal personality disturbance; Asarnow *et al.*, 1978; Section IV). This observation is further supported by the results of Grunebaum *et al.* (1974, 1978). The authors tested children (age 5–6 yr) with the nondegraded CPT. Children of schizophrenic mothers did not differ in their CPT performance from those of mothers with affective disorders. Both performed worse than children of healthy mothers.

A difficult figure discrimination or distracting versions of the CPT seem to tap specific deficits in children at risk for developing schizophrenia.

Another test that is claimed to discriminate between adult schizophrenics and controls is the span-of-apprehension test. The subject is presented tachistoscopally with a target letter along with an array of irrelevant letters (see discussion in Chapter 4). When used with foster children born to schizophrenic mothers, there is some evidence for an impairment of recognition accuracy (Asarnow *et. al.*, 1978). However, this was not confirmed by Harvey *et al.* (1985) from the Stony Brook project, who compared the index with various control groups, including children of mothers with affective disorder. Asarnow *et al.* (1985) suggested that the inclusion of more severely ill mothers and the presentation of targets at the periphery of the field (i.e., in a nonfoveal position) in their study may explain the discrepancy.

Wagener *et al.* (1986) ran a study comparing the performance of the mothers with that of their schizophrenic offspring ($n = 25$), and found a relationship between the performance of the two groups on both the span-of-apprehension and communication-deviance tests of Cohen (see Chapter 4).

It is interesting that only one small group of children has been studied with other prominent selective attention tasks such as the dichotic listening (shadowing) task used in several studies with adult schizophrenics. Asarnow *et al.* (1978) asked the subjects to write down a series of digits presented to one ear while ignoring digits presented to the other ear and found only a marginally significant tendency for high-risk children to make more intrusion errors in their task. It is of interest to note that Spring *et al.* (1980) also found that siblings of schizophrenics showed subtle differences from normal controls in a dichotic listening task using verbal material. The siblings showed more intrusions from the irrelevant channel when the responses were analyzed at the phoneme levels, but showed no gross differences at the whole word level. The Stroop test was not found to discriminate between groups. (For both studies, see Chapter 4.)

Harvey *et al.* (1981) examined a subsample of the risk group from the Stony Brook project with the digit-span task (5–6 digits were presented auditorily for immediate recall). (It is not clear from the report if the subsample was representative of the whole group at risk.) With this version of the digit-span task, no differences were found. Even when irrelevant digits, read by a voice of the opposite sex, were interspersed with the relevant ones, the overall performance of the children of parents with either schizophrenia or unipolar affective disorder dropped well below that of the healthy controls. (Both tasks with and without distraction were matched for task difficulty, which means that the distraction task had fewer items.)

Erlenmeyer-Kimling and Cornblatt (1978) from the New York project found that high-risk children had more problems recalling a long series of digits. When distraction was introduced, the same result was found as in the Stony Brook project (i.e., the group differences disappeared), but the task was not matched for difficulty.

However, the Stony Brook study went further and looked for a specific effect of the serial position of the digits on recall (Harvey *et al.*, 1981).

Normally, significant positions within the material facilitate recall. As can be seen in Figure 12.2, the first digits and the last digits were more easily remembered by all subjects. The former is called the *primacy effect* and the latter the *recency effect*. From research in cognitive psychology with healthy subjects it is believed that the primacy effect expresses mental organization and active rehearsal whereas the recency effect expresses the more automatic storage in the sensory buffer store (Chapter 3).

Curiously only the children of a schizophrenic parent showed a weakening of the primacy effect under distraction with irrelevant stimuli (Figures 12.2 and 12.3). Such a finding is comparable to findings with adult schizophrenics (Oltmanns *et al.*, 1978; Chapter 3). It should be stressed here that these tasks were matched for difficulty. Harvey *et al.* (1981) interpret these findings as indicating a disruption of rehearsal by distracting stimuli; the second irrelevant message may hinder an adequate organization of the material in the short-term store.

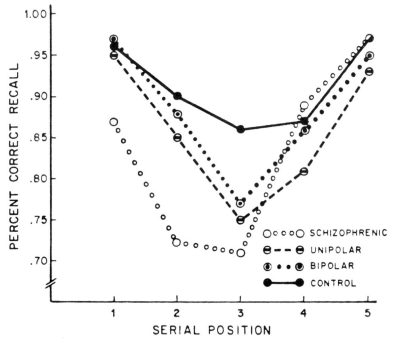

**Figure 12.2**  The proportion of digits correctly recalled as a function of their serial position in high risk subjects and controls. Digits were presented under a distraction condition. The groups studied consisted of children of schizophrenic, unipolar and bipolar depressive, and normal healthy subjects (Harvey *et al.*, 1981).

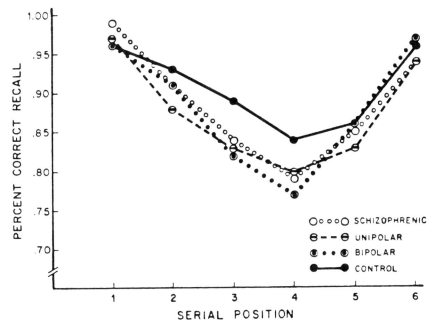

**Figure 12.3**  Proportion of digits correctly recalled as a function of their serial position in high risk subjects and controls. Digits were presented under a nondistraction condition. The groups studied consisted of children of schizophrenic, unipolar and bipolar depressive, and normal healthy subjects (Harvey *et al.*, 1981).

In light of these findings it is remarkable that, in other areas of perceptual and sensory motor tasks for which deviations can be demonstrated in actively schizophrenic patients, no clearly deviant performance can be found in high-risk children when compared with adequate control groups:

Tasks for which many studies report adult schizophrenic patients to be deviant include the reaction-time (RT) task. In particular we refer to the cross-modality shift and the crossover RT tasks. (Deficits with the former, however, do not seem to be specific to adult schizophrenics; cf. Section V.)

The Minnesota study reported distinctly slower simple RTs but no crossover effect in high-risk children compared with the low-risk groups (Marcus, 1972; Garmozy, 1974). The form of test was similar to that showing crossover in schizophrenic adults (Shakow, 1962). Surprisingly, Marcus was unable to improve performance by offering material incentives for success, but this study suffered from the absence of a psychiatric comparison group.

However, other research teams have found that the slowing of the RT in high-risk groups was not a reliable discriminator among groups (e.g., Asarnow *et al.*, 1978). Indeed, neither simple RT nor RT modality-shift effects could be shown in the same children that demonstrated CPT impairments in the Minnesota project (Phipps-Yonas, 1984). Only with a choice RT task, with 10 alternative stimuli to attend to, were Wood and Cook (1979) able to demonstrate poorer performance in siblings of schizophrenics than in normal controls. This study must be repeated since the role of task difficulty and specificity was not clarified.

A number of task- and subject-related factors might contribute to the variable incidence of slowed simple RTs in high-risk groups, apart from those passed on from the biological parent. Indeed, this is the implication of a cross-fostering report from Rosenthal's group (Van Dyke et al., 1975). They found that adults that had been reared with a schizophrenic parent showed a slow RT, irrespective of whether a biological parent had been diagnosed with schizophrenia. The RTs of adult schizophrenics did not depend on whether schizophrenia was common in the family. The authors therefore assumed that unfavorable rearing conditions may have caused the slowing in RT.

This finding draws our attention to the general methodological problem discussed in the introduction. "Nature/nurture" effects cannot be separated if no control group of offspring from a parent with a similar severe mental disorder has been tested. Not all the projects compiled in Table 12.1 examined an appropriate comparison group, that is, children that were at risk for other severe psychiatric disorders. (The Israeli and Danish projects had no psychiatric control group, i.e., no offspring of a parent with a non-schizophrenic psychiatric diagnosis.) The other large scale projects that we have often mentioned, from New York, Stony Brook, and Minnesota, had adequate psychiatric controls.

## F. Intelligence Quotients

In the Danish study, the IQ of the high-risk group was slightly but not significantly lower than that of the low-risk group (Walker et al., 1981). The same overall result emerged from the long-term study in Israel (Sohlberg and Yani, 1985). In detailed analysis, they found that the offspring of schizophrenic parents were poorer on the arithmetic subtest of the Wechsler battery and showed noticeably poorer abilities to concentrate in class. Since there was no psychiatric control group, it is not wise to attribute these weaknesses specifically to children at high risk for schizophrenia.

The high-risk project from St. Louis included children of parents who had a psychiatric or physical illness or who had no illness. They reported no significant difference in IQ among any of the groups. It is interesting to note that the stability of values on retest was lowest for the children of parents with schizophrenic and schizoaffective diagnoses (Worland et al., 1982).

In the New York study by Erlenmeyer-Kimling, the high-risk children had an IQ equivalent to that of the population at large (mean IQ,105). The fact that the control children had a significantly higher IQ can probably be attributed to a weakness in the design (i.e., original selection procedure: Watt *et al.,* 1984). (Note, however, that in the other tests by this group discussed previously, samples were matched for IQ and other relevant factors.)

## G. Psychophysiological Measures of Reactivity

### 1. High Risk Children

Mednick and Schulsinger (1965) recorded both electrodermal and cardiovascular indices of the reactivity of the autonomic nervous system (ANS). Unfortunately, as yet, only an analysis of the former has been published (Venables, 1987; Venables personal communication). The basal electrodermal conductance level during the resting phase and the amplitude of response to a series of mild tone stimuli (54 dB; 1000 Hz) was found to be higher in the high-risk children. A large response was present when the tone was an unconditioned or a conditioned stimulus preceding a loud stressful tone (95 dB). As for adult schizophrenics, the time to regain the initial levels of electrodermal activity (i.e., the recovery time) was much shorter in the high-risk group of children.

A small number of high-risk (12) and low-risk (30) children from the Rochester project was also studied in this paradigm. Using tones of medium intensity (75 dB; 1000 Hz), they found that high-risk children gave larger responses, but not significantly so. However, in the conditioning phase, which was similar to that of the Danish study, there were differences. After a long warning tone (8 sec, 57 dB) came a loud burst of white noise (95 dB). The high-risk children responded much more strongly to the conditioned tone (Salzman and Klein, 1978). Further, the baseline level of arousal, although no different in the first half, was much higher in the second half of the experiment. In contrast to the Danish study, they found no difference in recovery time.

Autonomic reactivity has even been investigated in babies newly born to schizophrenic mothers (Schachter *et al.,* 1975). The three groups of mothers were either certainly schizophrenic, not schizophrenic, or not schizophrenic with a first degree relative with schizophrenia. Clicks were played back to the babies while they slept and their electrocardiographic response (ECG) was recorded. The offspring (age, 3–4 mo) of the schizophrenic mothers showed an acceleration of the ECG in response to the click compared with the controls. Surprisingly, the acceleration correlated with the dose of neuroleptics administered to the mother. Two interpretations of these results seem possible. First, the ECG acceleration was influenced by neuroleptic-induced changes in the uterine environment. Second, if the size of the neuroleptic dose is any reflection of the severity of psychosis, perhaps the baby's response is a genetic marker for the schizophrenic condition. As yet, there have been no systematic studies of the effects of neuroleptics received during pregnancy on cardiovascular function in infants. It cannot be excluded that neuroleptics increase heart rate, since some studies have reported this effect, but results are contradictory or inconclusive (cf. Chapter 5). Thus, it remains questionable if the claimed effect can be generalized to the newborn as an aftereffect of the neuroleptic treatment of the mother.

In contrast to these three studies, others have reported no changes of autonomic reactivity in high-risk children, whether in New York City (Erlen-meyer-Kimling *et al.*, 1974), St. Louis (Janes and Stern, 1976; Janes *et al.*, 1978), or Israel (Kugelmass *et al.*, 1985). The New York City result prompted Mednick (1978) to re-analyze the Danish results.

Mednick noticed that there were demographic differences present in the American and Danish studies. In the latter, there were fewer children from orderly or intact families. He now took into consideration whether there was a broken home, a frequently absent parent, or an institutional upbringing. The autonomic reactivity proved to be significantly larger in high-risk children from a broken home than in those brought up in an intact family. The amplitude was larger and the latency shorter. For control children, the status of the home made no difference (Figure 12.4). It would seem that a negative family background could enable an otherwise latent genetic risk for schizophrenia to exert an overt effect on autonomic measures of reactivity.

It is interesting to note here that, with respect to electrodermal reactivity, a relationship between a negative environment and a genetic predisposition has been revealed. This is strikingly parallel to what the same measure shows in adult schizophrenics released on remission into the charge of a relative with high expressed emotion (EE). In this case, a high electrodermal activity to the presence of a high-EE relative, perhaps indicative of stress, seems to be a predictor of early relapse (cf. Chapter 11).

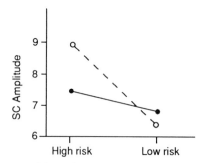

**Figure 12.4** Skin conductance (SC) or electrodermal (EDOR) amplitude of response to neutral stimuli in children at high and low risk for schizophrenia based on whether they came from an intact (●) or a broken (○) home (after Mednick, 1978).

However, one aspect of the electrodermal studies remains remarkable and unexpected: the well-documented group of adult schizophrenic electrodermal nonresponders (i.e., showing no orienting response to neutral stimuli; Chapter 5) seems to be underrepresented in high-risk samples, although not completely absent (Mednick, 1990, personal communication).

There have been only a few investigations of the EEG or event-related potentials (ERPs) of high-risk children.

The New York group claimed, in their first report, that a reduced $P_{300}$ amplitude of the visual ERP characterized the (schizophrenic) high-risk group (Friedman *et al.*, 1979, 1982). Unfortunately, this claim was not confirmed in a follow-up analysis (Erlenmeyer-Kimling and Cornblatt, 1987). Later, they reported that only the children of the affective-disordered parent showed a significantly lower $N_{100}$ in an auditory oddball paradigm (Friedman *et al.*, 1988).

Itil and colleagues (1974) obtained records from a small number of the Danish children in the Mednick–Schulsinger study. They claimed to see some minor EEG and ERP changes (e.g., more high-frequency beta EEG activity and shorter latency auditory ERPs in the high-risk group). However, the opposite finding with respect to the ERP latency was observed in a small German sample ($n = 12$, 9–16 yr). The research team of Kornhuber in Ulm saw longer $N_{200}$ and $P_{300}$ latencies to target stimuli in the high-risk children compared with a matched low-risk group. The authors used an auditory oddball paradigm and interpreted their finding in terms of "slowed target classification" by the high-risk children (Schreiber *et al.*, 1989).

## 2. Adopted Offspring of Schizophrenic Parents and Monozygotic Twins Discordant for Schizophrenia

David Rosenthal, then director of the psychology and psychopathology section of the NIMH, initiated an adoption study in Denmark that has already figured in our previous discussion and in Chapter 11. The research protocol, including records of autonomic reactivity, was similar to that of the Mednick–Schulsinger investigation and took place in the same laboratory and research hospital in Copenhagen, the Kommune Hospitalet (Van Dyke *et al.*, 1974). The main result was that even children with a biological parent with schizophrenia who are brought up in a healthy family (not living in a household with a schizophrenic) showed an overall stronger electrodermal response to the various stimuli than did adopted controls.

Another way to tackle the questions of whether electrodermal responses provide an indication of inherited or environmental influences is to study monozygotic (MZ) twins who are discordant for schizophrenia. This study was attempted by Zahn and colleagues in the United States (using the twin material of Pollin *et al.*, 1969; cf. Chapter 10). For the duration of the extensive biochemical and psychological investigation, the twins lived with their families for 2 weeks in the clinical center at the NIMH. Skin conductance and heart rate were recorded over 4 sessions during a rest period, while doing arithmetical problems, under cold pressure, and while performing reaction-time and word-association tests (Zahn, 1977).

A slightly but not significantly higher level of arousal during the rest period was found in the healthy discordant twin than in the healthy control twins with no schizophrenic sibling.

More interesting were the results obtained when the demands were higher (e.g., task stress). In these situations, the discordant healthy twin showed a larger electrodermal response amplitude than the healthy control twins. The sick twins however showed distinctly attenuated responses compared with the healthy discordant partners; thus, the results are similar to those reported in chronic long-term patients (Chapter 5). As discussed previously and in contrast to this, the dominant pattern in young nonschizophrenic high-risk persons (children of schizophrenic mothers or discordant siblings of MZ schizophrenic twins) is that of increased electrodermal activity.

## III. Putative Predictors for the Development of Schizophrenia: Longitudinal Studies of the Children of Schizophrenic Parents

### A. Incidence of Schizophrenia in High Risk Groups

The early projects in Denmark and Israel have been running long enough for the subjects to reach the age when they might be expected to develop schizophrenia. In the former study, a clinical interview was conducted 10 yr after the initial investigation, and in the latter 14 yr after (Mednick et al., 1987; Mirsky et al., 1985).

The results of these interviews (Table 12.3 and 12.4) show that 9 and 11% of the subjects, respectively, became schizophrenic. This incidence, along with the 1% incidence in the control group, is remarkably close to the expected incidence. Unfortunately, it must be pointed out that the psychiatrist who conducted the interviews in the Danish study was not blind to the risk status of his subjects. Thus, bias may be the reason, in part, that an astonishing proportion of the high-risk subjects were judged to be psychiatrically disturbed, as the authors themselves observed. This criticism is not applicable to the Israeli study, in which the diagnosis was made blind and according to DSM-III criteria.

A remarkable finding in the Israeli project was the high incidence of other psychiatric illnesses in the high-risk group (50 vs 7% in the control group). This suggests that interviewer bias may not have been wholly responsible for the similar finding in the Danish study. The bias seems most apparent in the

**Table 12.3**  Psychiatric Diagnoses of the Offspring of Schizophrenic Mothers and Controls in the Danish Study after 10 Years[a,b]

| Diagnostic category | Offspring of schizophrenic mother ($n = 173$) | | Offspring of non-schizophrenic mother ($n = 91$) | |
|---|---|---|---|---|
| | $n$ | % | $n$ | % |
| Schizophrenia | 15 | 9 | 1 | 1 |
| Spectrum disorder[c] | 55 | 32 | 4 | 4 |
| Psychopathy | 5 | 3 | 4 | 4 |
| Neurosis | 30 | 17 | 33 | 36 |
| Other personality disorder | 22 | 13 | 9 | 10 |
| Other nonspecific diagnosis | 21 | 12 | 13 | 15 |
| No psychiatric disturbance | 25 | 14 | 27 | 30 |

[a] Adapted from Mednick et al., 1987.
[b] Risk group age: 19–30 yr.
[c] Originally known as borderline schizophrenia, after DSM III it is now termed a spectrum diagnosis (Mednick et al., 1987; Parnas et al., 1990). The group includes schizotypal, schizoid, and paranoid personality disorders (Mednick et al., 1987).

**Table 12.4**  Psychiatric Diagnoses of the Offspring of a Schizophrenic Father or Mother and Controls in the Israeli Project after 14 Years[a,b]

| DSM III category | Offspring of schizophrenic parent ($n = 46$) | | Offspring of non-schizophrenic parent ($n = 44$) | |
|---|---|---|---|---|
| | $n$ | % | $n$ | % |
| Schizophrenia | 5 | 11 | 0 | 0 |
| Spectrum disorder | 4 | 9 | 0 | 0 |
| Typical affective disorder | 6 | 13 | 0 | 0 |
| Atypical affective disorder | 4 | 9 | 1 | 2 |
| Other diagnoses | 4 | 9 | 3 | 7 |
| No diagnosis | 23 | 50 | 40 | 91 |

[a] Adapted from Mirsky et al., 1985.
[b] Risk group age: 22–29 yr.

high proportion (32%) of personality disorders from the so-called spectrum diagnosis of schizophrenia. The Israel study revealed only 9% of subjects with a spectrum diagnosis.[1] Here the relatively high proportion of affective disturbances is noticeable. In response to this, the authors checked on the diagnosis of the parents, but could find no explanation (Mirsky et al., 1985). On the basis of previously mentioned studies, one would not expect a clustering of affective disorders in the relatives of schizophrenics.

Can investigators who always have emphasized the role of the environment claim from the evidence presented that merely living with a schizophrenic parent is stressful enough to trigger schizophrenia or, indeed, any psychiatric disturbance? One condition suggests that this is not the case. In the Israel project, half the children in both the high-risk and control groups were raised in a kibbutz. This condition implies that the children were raised with other children and had reduced contact with their own parents. The results therefore rebuff those who favor a dominant role for the family environment and were a surprise to the authors themselves. (One of these authors was, in fact, a leader of the kibbutz movement and largely responsible for the development of the educational program in the kibbutz system.) A range of anomalies, not including schizophrenia, was found to be more clustered in the high-risk than in the low-risk groups when both were raised in the kibbutz, as well as being more clustered than in the group raised by their own parents in town. It is perhaps equally surprising that living with a schizophrenic mother or father seemed in no way to increase the likelihood of schizophrenia or any other psychiatric disturbance. Naturally the authors also looked for any other destabilizing factors peculiar to the kibbutz situation (e.g., terrorism and similar threats). Despite careful analysis, they were unable to discover anything significant (Mirsky et al., 1985).

The central question of any risk study is naturally what the characteristics of the precursors are that will eventually lead to schizophrenia. As yet, an answer can only be proposed on the basis of the Danish study. Relevant data from the other projects are not available. Only some of the probands in the New York City and Stony Brook projects have reached the critical age. At this stage, the authors were only able to point out that more psychiatric abnormalities were present in the high-risk groups than among the offspring of healthy parents (Stony Brook, Weintraub, 1987; New York Psychiatric Institute, Erlenmeyer-Kimling and Cornblatt, 1987). Although the probands in the Israel project have reached the critical age, the number of affected individuals ($n = 5$) is too small for statistical analysis (Table 12.4).

---

[1] A spectrum diagnosis means that schizophrenia or schizophrenialike symptoms are present. The latter are rated as a personality disturbance, rarely requiring treatment. Different meanings are attributed to the term (Kendler et al., 1981). It usually includes schizophrenia, schizotypal, and sometimes schizoid and paranoid personality disturbance but rarely borderline personality disorder as defined in DSM-III-R; Chapter 10).

Therefore, again, in these following sections, the analyses and findings of the Danish project serve as the leitmotiv. Other relevant studies are related to them.

The reader should now note that the comparison is run *within* the risk group. In contrast to the previous sections, the premorbid features of the eventually schizophrenic group ($n = 15$) are compared with those of the children at risk who are still nonschizophrenic (and are even without a spectrum personality disorder).

## B. Perinatal Complications

The authors of the Danish study present evidence for a significant increase in the incidence of birth complications in the subjects that have become schizophrenic. Parnas *et al.* (1982) found that, even in the borderline schizophrenic group (now defined as schizotypal; Parnas *et al.*, 1990), the incidence of complications at birth was relatively higher than in the high-risk subjects who had not yet developed schizophrenia. We have described the meaning of birth complications as used by these authors in Section II and Table 12.2. These birth-complication findings should be interpreted with caution, since there is reason to doubt that the measure is independent of the mental health status of the mother (Section II). However, the fact that subjects with positive and others with negative psychiatric findings both belonged to the high-risk group weakens one point of criticism, namely, that there was a bias in the diagnosis: the higher incidence of those with a current schizophrenia or spectrum diagnosis could not be related to the mothers' diagnosis since both types of offspring had schizophrenic mothers. This still leaves the question of whether the severity of the mothers' illness was the same in both groups.

Of additional interest, Parnas *et al.* (1990) reported that even among patients with a spectrum diagnosis, one could distinguish between the individuals who became schizophrenic and the ones who developed a schizotypal personality disorder. The former had a higher incidence of complications at birth (see Table 12.5). Of course, one cannot say that this necessarily had an influence on the development of schizophrenia. As has already been indicated, one could postulate that the mothers of those who became schizophrenic were themselves more severely ill than the mothers of those who became schizotypal, although the authors do not address this issue in their discussion. However, it is possible from their analysis to say that the mothers of those who developed schizophrenia had developed their illness earlier than the mothers whose offspring remained healthy. These mothers might then have had an unfavorable prodromal phase or might have already been ill when the birth occurred. This is corroborated by another analysis of the Danish high-risk sample (Jorgensen *et al.*, 1987). The authors report that

**Table 12.5**  Mean Score on a Perinatal Complication Scale in Children Who Eventually Developed a Schizophrenia or a Spectrum Personality Disorder (Schizotypal Personality Disorder) Compared with the Ratings of the Control Group[a,b]

| | Perinatal complications | | |
|---|---|---|---|
| | Schizophrenia | Schizotypal personality disorder | No mental illness |
| Frequency score | 1.50 (1.38) | 0.40 (0.76) | 0.85 (1.09)[c] |
| Severity score | 1.08 (0.90) | 0.40 (0.71) | 0.72 (0.83)[c] |

[a] After Parnas *et al.*, 1990.
[b] Results are given as means with standard deviation in parentheses.
[c] Significant difference between children with schizophrenia and children with schizotypal personality disorder.

more schizophrenics were born to younger nonparanoid schizophrenic mothers. The higher rate of birth complications reported in this group may therefore be a consequence of the higher likelihood that, during pregnancy, prodromal-illness-related factors may have caused more self-neglect in this group. This point should be clarified in further analysis. Thus, perinatal complications may be a factor secondary to the early onset of schizophrenia and, perhaps, more severe illness of the mother.

From these results (and the methodological problems discussed earlier and in Section II), it is difficult to reach a conclusion about the contribution of perinatal complications to the eventual development of schizophrenia (Talovik *et al.*, 1980). Whatever the final conclusion, it is clear from the review of Gottesman and Shields (1982) that perinatal complications cannot be the primary cause leading to schizophrenia. If such problems have an influence on the development of schizophrenia, then it must be as a loading factor in conjunction or interaction with a genetic risk that reduces the threshold for the illness or with other noxious exogenous effects (e.g., growing up in an institution).

Schulsinger *et al.* (1987) found a combination of perinatal complications and institutional rearing significantly more often in those who became schizophrenic than in those who were diagnosed with a schizotypal personality disorder. The assumption of the authors that "schizophrenia may be considered as a complicated form of schizotypal personality disorder" (p. 431) is intriguing. However, the methodological problems are the same as before. Is the higher rate of institutionalization of those who became schizophrenic independent of the severity and frequency of the mother's illness? (For reviews, consult Lewis, 1989; Lyon *et al.*, 1989).

It may be of interest to note here that the research group of Nasrallah at the Ohio State University found, in two studies, a lower incidence of family history of schizophrenia in those with records of perinatal complications (Wilcox and Nasrallah, 1987; Schwarzkopf *et al.*, 1989). In the Danish low-risk sample, perinatal complications occurred as often as in the general population (Mednick and Silverton, 1988). Thus, there seems to be neither a special genetic link between schizophrenia and perinatal complications (or a specific type of complication) nor a primary causal role for perinatal complications.

However, if perinatal complications are not the primary cause, what is their role in "nongenetic" schizophrenias? The fact that perinatal complications are a rather common phenomenon, not necessarily followed by schizophrenia, can only signify that the correlation between schizophrenia and perinatal complications in some persons is mediated by a third factor (inheritance or environment?). A superficial look at the results of the Nasrallah group would suggest that this factor is an environmental factor. Since we have seen that the environment alone does not seem to cause schizophrenia, this explanation alone is rather unlikely. Therefore, the combination or interaction of "borderline" genetic load (no schizophrenic phenotype in the relatives) with environmental and perinatal insult may have caused the effect in the "nongenetic" sample. (For further discussion of this problem, see also McNeil, 1988; Chapter 16.)

This argument refutes the suggestion that perinatal complications are only an epiphenomenon of an increased severity of symptoms or an earlier breakdown of the schizophrenic mother (as discussed previously). Thus, perinatal complications may be relevant but are not the only factors in the concert of noxious events that may decide the final outcome.

## C. Cerebral Atrophy

In the Danish study, computer tomography (CT) measures showed a slightly greater widening of the cerebral ventricles in those developing schizophrenia than in those developing a schizotypal personality. Measures from healthy controls were intermediate between these two groups (Parnas *et al.*, 1990). Although Owen *et al.* (1988) and others (e.g., review by Murray *et al.*, 1988) reported a coincidence of birth complications and cerebral atrophy in a retrospective analysis with adult schizophrenics, there was apparently no correlation between the CT results and records of birth complications in the Danish data. A correlation of CT-measured atrophy with birth weight was recorded (Silverton *et al.*, 1985). Unfortunately, CT scans were taken only from a proportion of the subjects who had developed schizophrenia ($n = 7$). It is not known if the sample was representative of the group as a whole.

# D. Season of Birth

Very early in the history of schizophrenia research, Tramer (1928) and Huntington (1938) observed that an unusual proportion of psychotics (reported as suffering from dementia praecox or schizophrenia, respectively) were born in the winter months in the northern hemisphere. More recently, some authors have questioned the methodology and statistics of such studies (e.g., Lewis and Griffin, 1981; Lewis, 1989) and others could not replicate them (e.g., Shur, 1982). However, the overall conclusion from over 30 studies, some comparing samples of 20,000 births in the schizophrenic and general population, is that proportionately more schizophrenics are born in the late winter months than other members of the population (e.g., Hare and Moran, 1981; Zipursky and Schulz, 1987; review by Häfner et al., 1987). The emphasis on the term "winter months" is borne out by studies from Australia, which reported a peak for schizophrenic births in the June–November period, the austral winter and early spring period (e.g., Jones and Frei, 1979).

The reason for this putative relationship is unclear. Some investigators have suggested that the higher incidence of infectious diseases at that time may play a role. It is then assumed that this leads to a higher risk for perinatal complications during the winter months (cf. review by Eaton, 1985). A correlation between winter birth and larger ventricles in adult schizophrenics as reported by Degreef et al. (1988) may be considered by some to be indirect support. Mednick et al. (1988) investigated possible links between influenza epidemics and schizophrenia in Finland. They found indications of an influenza epidemic during the second trimester of fetal development of future schizophrenics. However, the inference is statistical. The analysis of the perinatal period was retrospective and the authors had no information about whether the mothers of the schizophrenics had indeed caught influenza during the critical period of their pregnancy.

In the Danish project, 7 of the 15 schizophrenics from the high-risk group were born between January and March (i.e., 46%). Only 25% of the healthy high-risk subjects were born in this quarter, which is consistent with a relatively even distribution of births through the year (Parnas et al., 1982).

The analysis has gone further to show another surprising facet of birth statistics (Machón et al., 1983). Compared with the healthy subjects, more of the schizophrenics were born both in the winter months and in a large town. In other words, there was a cluster among the schizophrenics of births in winter in a city. (The city refers to greater Copenhagen as opposed to elsewhere in Denmark.) The authors speculated that there was a connection here that referred to the increased likelihood of viral infection at this time of year and that infection was more easily spread in highly populated areas. Unless one includes data on birth complications, there is no evidence that the mothers or the children suffered more than expected from such illnesses.

Later, the Danish–American group reported a correlation between (urban) winter birth and the incidence of perinatal complications (Machón *et al.*, 1987). Whether the correlation was an artifact or whether support from other studies for a more straightforward explanation will emerge is, for the moment, an open question. One also should not overlook the fact that the numbers were very small: thus, the findings cannot be generalized. (See also important critical discussions of the methods of these studies by Lewis, 1989.)

## E. Psychosocial Factors

We have discussed several lines of evidence that would support the role of negative environmental influences in the expression of the basic genetic loading for schizophrenia, leading to the fully developed illness. The Danish high-risk children who eventually became schizophrenic were, for example, more often brought up in institutions away from home, compared with those that remained healthy or even those that developed a schizotypal problem (see previous text). In contrast, examination of the incidence of an institutional upbringing in children who did not have a schizophrenic parent shows no relationship with the eventual development of psychiatric problems (Parnas *et al.*, 1985, 1990).

One supposes that only children predisposed to develop schizophrenia are likely to have the threshold for its expression lowered by an institutional upbringing. Even in this case, though, one cannot be sure that it was not the early-onset (or possibly also the more frequent and more severe) illness of the mother that necessitated the child being taken into care. Therefore, putative environmental or heritable factors (e.g., higher genetic loading for children with a mother who is more severely ill) cannot easily be differentiated in this type of study.

The same type of criticism applies to the analysis of the childrens' relationships with their parents in the Danish study (Burman *et al.*, 1987). These relationships were rated less satisfactory for children who developed schizophrenia than for the group developing a schizotypal problem. The implication, could be that the more difficult premorbid phase of the offspring who eventually developed schizophrenia is responsible for the greater turmoil in the relationship, adding to the problems of living with an early onset mother.

Thus, although the ratings by Burman and colleagues (1987) were done prospectively, it is not clear whether the schizophrenia of the offspring could have been caused (1) by the early-onset severe type of schizophrenia of the mother, (2) by environmental stress lowering the threshold for schizophrenia, or (3) by a more severe premorbid phase of the offspring, which in turn led to increasingly problematical relationships with the parents. This again illustrates the difficulty of separating cause and effect in questions dealing with complex psychobiological systems in various environments, each with a relatively unknown noxious potential.

## F. School Behavior—Behavioral Precursors

The analysis of the protocols run by the teachers in the Danish study are illuminating (John *et al.*, 1982). Remarkably, the observations made 10 yr prior to the illness allow one to differentiate between those who did and those who did not become schizophrenic. There can have been no bias in the teachers' judgment since we are discussing children who had schizophrenic mothers. Those who became ill were described as "lonely and withdrawn" (Table 12.6). Furthermore, a difference was observed with respect to gender. Girls who eventually became ill were more "nervous" than those who remained healthy. Boys who became ill were observed to be more easily "excitable" or "irritable" and showed "longer-lasting emotional reactions." Further, they tended to disturb the class more frequently with "inappropriate behavior." Indeed, it is astonishing that the teachers commented more often that these children (and not the others) would develop emotional and psychotic problems.

Both Parnas *et al.* (1982) in Denmark and Fish (1982, 1987) in the United States reported that many of those who later developed schizophrenia were remarkably quiet and "passive" as babies (e.g., underactivity, hypotonia, lack of crying). It is not clear if these individuals were withdrawn later at school, as in the Danish study. However, Fish noted a strong relationship between passivity and a later development of more negative symptoms and blunted affect. Parnas and Schulsinger (1986) found that the incidence of deviant

**Table 12.6** Characteristics That Differentiate Children That Become Schizophrenic from Those That Do Not When Both Come from a High Risk Group with a Schizophrenic Mother[a,b]

| Boys | Girls |
|------|-------|
| Lonely and withdrawn | Lonely and withdrawn |
| | Nervous |
| Long-lasting emotional reactions | |
| Easily aroused | |
| Irritable | |
| Disturbing/inappropriate class behavior | |

[a]From John *et al.*, 1982.

[b]Only items from the teachers' questionnaire that were significant (chi$^2$ test) are shown.

associations when tested as a child or adolescent correlated with the appearance of thought disorder in those who developed the full picture of the illness later.

Less dramatic differences were recorded between the children who became schizotypal (called borderline cases at the time) and those who remained healthy. The former group was rather withdrawn and lonely, and was not accepted by the class as a whole. The girls were more "nervous," but they were also more active and showed "longer-lasting emotional reactions" (Parnas *et al.*, 1982).

These findings dealing with the question of possible behavioral precursors of schizophrenia are certainly important and of interest. However, as Parker and Asher (1987) pointed out in their review, the question of a specific relationship to certain syndromes still needs much further clarification.

## G. Electrodermal Activity: Relation to Other Predictors

Mednick *et al.* (1987) and Rieder (1979) reported that the eventual development of schizophrenia correlated with higher electrodermal activity recorded in childhood, but only in males and not in females. Further, as in Zahn's (1977) twin study, electrodermal activity in response to neutral and conditioned stimuli in turn correlated with the previous occurrence of complications during pregnancy and birth.

It is difficult to offer a satisfactory explanation for these results. Obviously, electrodermal excitability can be influenced by a range of negative environmental factors. The point is made by the increased electrodermal arousal in high-risk children coming from a family that has not remained intact. The results also imply, however, that a predisposition for schizophrenia is a necessary condition for increased electrodermal excitability in the children investigated. It is this which, at least in the male subjects studied, is related to the eventual development of schizophrenia.

## IV. Putative High-Risk Markers in the General Population

This area of high-risk research must be considered separately from that in the children of schizophrenics (cf. Introduction). Here, in contrast, high risk is assessed on the basis of specific characteristics of the children and young adults under study.

## A. The Mauritius Project

In the year in which Mauritius gained independence, the chief psychiatrist of the islands, Dr. Raman, suggested to the World Health Organization (WHO) that a program designed to investigate and to improve mental health in Mauritius should be set up. WHO arranged for Dr. Schulsinger from Copenhagen to visit the islands. The consequence was that after the Danish project, a closely related study was started in Mauritius.

From initial investigations carried out on all 1800 children from two districts of Mauritius, a group of 200 were selected. In contrast to the Danish study, subjects were divided into groups according to their psychological rather than their genetic risk. Children were defined as "at risk" if they showed autonomic hyperreactivity on measures of their electrodermal response ($n = 99$) or if they were electrodermal nonresponders ($n = 37$). The remaining children were controls ($n = 66$; cf. Chapter 5). [The electrodermal method used stimuli for orienting and conditioning almost identical to those of the Danish study (Section II.)] In addition the children were observed in a standardized play situation. At the time of the first investigation in 1972/1973, the children were 3 yr old. After that, half the children attended kindergarten and half did not. Follow-up studies were conducted at ages 9 and 11.5 yr.

The most interesting results appeared at age 11.5, when the smooth pursuit eye movements (SPEM) were recorded. They found that children who were electrodermal hyperresponders and who had a low IQ showed deviant SPEM and, in particular, abnormal saccades. The abnormality parallels that shown by adult schizophrenics, who also showed a relationship between electrodermal hyperresponse and SPEM (Chapter 7). Whether these subjects will develop schizophrenia, of course, is not known at this time. One will have to wait another 10–20 yr to know whether unusual psychophysiological reactivity is a marker for the eventual appearance of schizophrenia (Bell *et al.*, 1975; Schulsinger *et al.*, 1975; Venables, 1977, 1987, personal communication).

## B. The Chapman Questionnaires

The well-known schizophrenia research team led by Loren J. and Jean P. Chapman of the University of Wisconsin developed questionnaires at the end of the 1970s about personality deviations. The rating scales related to "physical anhedonia," "perceptual aberration," and "impulsive nonconformity" (Chapman *et al.*, 1978; Chapman and Chapman, 1978, 1987). The aim was to test the authors' hypothesis (explicit in the names of the scales) about characteristics found in the general population that might constitute an increased risk for the development of a psychosis.

On what were the rating scales based? Responses indicating agreement or disagreement were required to the following types of statements: from the perceptual aberration scale, "I sometimes have the feeling that a part of my body no longer belongs to me;" from the anhedonia scale, "One type of food tastes much like another;" or from the nonconformist scale, "Normally I react first and later think about it."

At first the relationship of the features tested to schizophrenia was indeed hypothetical. Only a proportion of patients with clinical manifestations of schizophrenia score higher on these scales (Chapman *et al.*, 1978; Chapman and Chapman, 1978). According to Schuck *et al.* (1984), a marked anhedonia is not specific to schizophrenia. It is equally likely to be found in several groups of discharged psychiatric patients. Unfortunately, these latter authors did not check the scales of perceptual aberration and impulsive nonconformity.

Some of the indications of a putative risk for schizophrenia are of a very indirect nature. For example, the authors' reasoning concerns a relationship between high scores on the perceptual aberration scale and communication deviance measured with the Cohen test in nonschizophrenic subjects (Martin and Chapman, 1982). The inference is that, since communication deviations were found also in schizophrenic patients (cf. Chapter 2), the high scores in the perceptual rating scale are markers of the risk for schizophrenia in nonpsychiatric populations.

Simons and colleagues (1982) studied a group of students selected for their high scores on the perceptual aberration and anhedonia scales. Surprisingly, in contrast to the reports of studies of high-risk children, they showed a crossover reaction-time effect reminiscent of that found in adult schizophrenics. The effect was particularly marked in those who scored highest on the perceptual aberration scale.

Psychophysiological abnormalities have been recorded for subjects scoring high on the anhedonia and perceptual aberration scales. For example, a more marked postimperative negative variation (PINV) and a reduced somatosensory $P_{400}$ were reported by a German group in Tübingen (Lutzenberger *et al.*, 1981; Rockstroh *et al.*, 1982) and by Shagass' group in Philadelphia (Josiassen *et al.*, 1985). However, the specificity of these findings for schizophrenia is questionable. Such recordings have also been made with other patient groups (e.g., depressives).

Bernstein and Riedel (1987) in New York noted a reduced orienting reaction on both electrodermal and cardiovascular measures (as in some schizophrenics) in persons with high scores for anhedonia and perceptual aberration. As in schizophrenics, responses normalized as task demands increased (cf. Chapter 5).

In a later study, Simons followed another course. In a manner similar to the Mauritius project, autonomic components of the orienting reaction were treated as independent variables (Simons *et al.*, 1983). They observed that electrodermal nonresponders in a population of college students (who remained nonresponders when the test was repeated) showed significantly higher values on a whole series of scales, compared with those showing normal electrodermal responses [e.g., the schizoid subscale of the Minnesota multi-phasic personality inventory (MMPI) compiled by Golden and Meehl (1979), the ego-strength scale of Baron (1953), the sensation-seeking scale of Zucker-man (1979), and Chapman's perceptual aberration scale, but not the physical anhedonia scale].

Raine and Venables (1984) at York confirmed the relationship between electrodermal nonresponse and schizoid personality deviations in adolescents who had been rated by their teachers as antisocial in a classroom context. (Schizoid personalities were defined in terms of high scores on the psychot-icism scale of Eysenck and Eysenck, 1975.)

That there should be a relationship to psychosis from two types of measure as different as electrodermal nonresponse and perceptual aberration or schizoid tendencies is certainly intriguing. Obviously it would be rather important to follow through with this study to see if the high schizoid or perceptual aberration scores have any value as predictors for the later development of schizophrenia in these subjects. The important question remains whether the behavioral deviations and the psychophysiological anomalies simply reflect similar but milder (schizophrenic) symptoms in those who will never become schizophrenic or whether they are actual predictors of the eventual develop-ment of schizophrenia?

Relevant to the eventual answers to these questions is a recent intensive study by Chapman and Chapman (1987). In addition to the scales just mentioned, they added one on "magical ideation." (An example of a statement requiring comment is, "I believe I am able to learn to read the thoughts of others any time I want.") They took these 4 scales to 3500 college students, aged about 18. The analysis was continued in depth only for those students who deviated from the mean by two standard deviations or more on at least one of the scales. This gave a study group of 469 students (13%), who were given a structured clinical interview [schedules for affective disorders and schizophrenia (SADS), lifetime version, of Spitzer and Endicott (1977)] supplemented with additional questions about psychotic-like and schizotypal symptoms.

The results showed that the students ($n = 159$) who scored high on both the perceptual aberration and the magical ideation scales (known as the Per–Mag scales) showed most psychopathological abnormalities reminiscent of schizophrenia on interview. When these students were again examined after 2 yr, these abnormalities were more advanced. Indeed, 22% had sought professional help for their problems. Three probands already showed clear psychiatric symptoms—paranoid, schizophrenic, and bipolar affective disor-der—and the latter two were already inpatients.

Considering the large size of the sample studied, the incidence of schizo-phrenia was very low. Yet at an age of about 18 yr, the students had barely reached the critical age for developing schizophrenia. The Chapmans expect that more cases in the Per–Mag group will soon develop schizophrenia. (The next follow-up study will have occurred 4 yr after initial testing.)

## C. Cognition and Information Processing: Schizotypal Adolescents

Indirect evidence that the high-risk children discussed in Section II may have been showing subthreshold cognitive features related to the putative core deficit of schizophrenics comes from a quite different type of study, namely, that of the information processing of basically nonpsychiatric populations with personality features reminiscent of schizophrenia. Nuechterlein and Dawson (1984) at UCLA examined college students with elevated ratings on the 2-7-8 profile of the MMPI. They described these subjects as having a schizotypal personality, although the features would not have been defined as such by the DSM-III-R. Compared with a group with no elevations on any subscale and a second group with raised scores on other subscales, the schizotypal students detected fewer targets and registered a lower $d'$ (sensitivity) on the degraded stimulus CPT.

The possibility of a biological factor correlating with the impairments of these groups was investigated by Buchsbaum et al. (1978). They studied a group of individuals with low platelet monoamine oxidase (MAO) and serum dopamine beta hydroxylase (DBH,: cf. Chapters 13 and 14). They made more CPT errors of commission than a group with low MAO but raised DBH. However, low levels of MAO are found only in a proportion of individuals, and these may show a wide range of psychiatric problems apart from schizophrenia.

Other aspects of information processing have been studied with a backward masking paradigm. If a visual pattern succeeds a briefly presented letter with too short an interval, the registration of the pattern interferes with the identification of the letter. A much longer interval between the two stimuli is required for the identification of the letter by American college students with a 2-7-8 MMPI profile (Steronko and Woods, 1978; Merritt and Balogh, 1986) or in DSM-III-defined schizotypal subjects with respect to patients with borderline personality or depressive disorders (Saccuzzo and Schubert, 1981; Braff, 1981; see review by Balogh and Merritt, 1987, and Chapter 4 for more details).

Another report that points to a possible impairment of information processing in young adults with 2-7-8 profiles was that of Asarnow et al. (1983), who demonstrated impaired target-selection accuracy on the span-of-apprehension task in these subjects (cf. similar findings in high-risk children; Section II).

## D. UCLA High Risk Project

Over 20 yr ago, Michael Goldstein's team started an investigation of 64 children and adolescents whose parents had sought help from the psychologi-

Table 12.7  Psychiatric Diagnoses of Young Adults Who Were Behaviorally Deviant as Youngsters[a,b]

| Diagnosis | n | % |
|---|---|---|
| Major depression | 6 | 11 |
| Schizophrenia | 4 | 7 |
| Personality disorders | } 5 | 2 } 9 |
|   Schizotypal | 1 | |
|   Schizoid | 3 } 15 | 6 } 28 |
|   Paranoid | 1 | 2 |
|   Borderline | 6 | 11 |
| Mixed | 6 | 11 |
| Antisocial/drug abuse | 11 | 20 |
| No psychiatric disturbance | 16 | 30 |
| Total | 54 | 100 |

[a] Adapted from Goldstein, 1987.

[b] Mean age when behaviorally deviant, 16.5 yr; mean age when diagnosed as adult, 31.5 yr.

cal advisory service at the University of California at Los Angeles. We already discussed the family communication and affective style aspects of the study in Chapter 11, and we described electrodermal activity findings from the family interaction sessions in Chapter 5.

We will, therefore, now concentrate on features of the adolescents that might be putative predictors of schizophrenia spectrum disorder. Fifteen years after the initial interviews, 5 (9%) of the 54 remaining subjects had a diagnosis in the narrow spectrum and 15 (28%) probands were diagnosed as belonging to the broad spectrum (Table 12.7 and Chapter 11).

Considering the initial interests of the authors, it is notable that there were many cases of major depressive disorder (11%). Assessment of the youngsters, blind to the nature of the problem of the proband or family, showed that only a relatively small proportion (30%) were without any notable psychiatric features. It should be stressed that none of the subjects showed any psychotic or borderline features when initially tested, although all had shown behavioral or emotional problems.

Goldstein (1987) did not discuss how representative this rather specially selected group might be, yet originally they said they were interested in factors leading to the development of schizophrenia. In order to try to bring out the type of conflict that might be a precursor to schizophrenia, they divided the final group of subjects according to 4 types of problems of the adolescents: (1) antisocial and aggressive behavior; (2) overt and active conflict with one of the parents; (3) passive or negative attitude; and (4) withdrawal or social isolation (cf. Goldstein et al., 1968). The authors hypothesized, at the first assessment, that groups 2 and 4 belonged together and that adolescents in these groups were likely to become schizophrenic. In the follow-up analysis, however, there proved to be no relationship between a particular group and a particular outcome. This negative result remained even after taking into account the breadth of the spectrum diagnosis (Goldstein, 1987).

As discussed in the previous chapter, the family interaction seems to have had a decisive influence. However, Goldstein (1987) also showed that a combination of deviance in the parents and a higher genetic load indicated by increased psychiatric problems (schizophrenia but also nonspecific) in the first- and second-degree relatives increased the risk to develop a narrow spectrum in the probands.

# V. Suggested Readings

The theme of Volume 13 (3) (1987) of the *Schizophrenia Bulletin* is high-risk research. The latest accounts of most of the high-risk studies (which define risk as having a schizophrenic parent) are given: the Danish project, the Israel project, the Stony Brook project, and the New York City Project. The new results from alternative risk models such as the project of the Chapmans and the UCLA project (Goldstein and co-workers) are also presented. The *Schizophrenia Bulletin* issue also includes a chapter on methodological considerations. Volume 11 (1) of the 1985 *Schizophrenia Bulletin* presents a more detailed discussion of the Israel project. Nuechterlein and Zaucha (1990) compare in their survey the information-processing deficits of actively symptomatic schizophrenics with that of subjects at high risk.

# VI. Summary Statements and Interpretations

## A. Potential Risk Factors—Differences between Risk and Nonrisk Groups

### 1. Perinatal Complications

Reports of more perinatal complications in birth records of subjects born to schizophrenic mothers (in some studies, also fathers) exist but are not confirmed by all authors.

Factors that might contribute to an increase of perinatal complications include disturbances already present, even during the premorbid phase of the mothers (e.g., self-neglect, medication, attitude to pregnancy, less health care). Birth and pregnancy complications—in addition to other factors—may raise the vulnerability in some subjects (see next section). However, since perinatal complication is an ubiquitous phenomenon and since reports of perinatal complications are not found in the majority of the patients, perinatal complications cannot be considered a dominant factor in the formation of the illness.

## 2. Neuromotor Signs

Small disturbances of sensorimotor coordination are recorded for some children at risk for developing schizophrenia. One study discusses retarded development of these functions as a possible cause of the observed increase with respect to controls, but not all authors observe neuromotor disturbances in high-risk children.

Despite conflicting findings, evidence for an association gains some support from studies of adult schizophrenics in whom a relatively robust relationship between motor coordination problems and thought disorder are reported.

## 3. Emotional Stability/Social Competence

There are more difficulties reported in children of schizophrenics, but in studies with adequate control groups no differences between children of schizophrenics and children of parents with affective disorder can be detected.

This means that children of schizophrenics have considerably more problems than children of healthy parents but this is a nonspecific factor.

## 4. Information Processing

Deviant information processing in high-risk children shows some similarities to disturbances shown by adult schizophrenics.

Thought processes are mildly disturbed (e.g., deviant associations, lack of referential cues between the ideas expressed). They have problems in detecting relevant signals among irrelevant items (span of apprehension) or when the signal is difficult to identify in a vigilance task (degraded stimuli). Externally presented structure is less effectively used to assist recall performance (e.g., the position of items in a digit-span task) but only in the presence of distracting task-irrelevant digits.

No specific problems for high-risk children are reported on reaction-time tasks.

Children of schizophrenics seem to have problems organizing and stabilizing internal stimulus traces in the presence of irrelevant stimuli. This is most clearly shown in the digit-span task, since the distraction and nondistraction versions were matched for task difficulty.

Children of schizophrenics show no overall recall deficit under distraction, but no primacy (position) advantage as seen in the control groups. (Primacy implies that the items undergo internal organization in order to improve performance.)

The results of the span of apprehension and degraded CPT can be criticized since the distraction or degraded stimuli made the task more difficult. An impairment may only show that children of schizophrenics have more problems with more difficult tasks, perhaps because they may live under more stressful family conditions. It is reasonable to question the role of poor family environments (e.g., living with a schizophrenic parent) in the poor performance under more difficult tasks conditions, since the adoption study of Kringlen and co-workers (Chapter 11) showed that the children at risk who live in the most stressful family conditions are the most disturbed. This factor should be controlled in future information processing studies.

Nevertheless, some similarities with adult schizophrenic performance deficits do exist, although the tests criticized for task difficulty did not always compare schizophrenics with adequate controls.

The lack of a differential effect in the realm of RT performance is surprising in view of the wealth of results from adult schizophrenics. Since Cromwell's group reports a deficit in the first degree relatives of schizophrenics with the Steffy procedure (embedded version of the crossover paradigm), one might speculate that the age (i.e., stage of development) of the children may play a role. Information-processing characteristics depend on development, be they normal or abnormal (cf. perception of serial redundancies in the Steffy procedure).

## 5. IQ

There is no general lowering of intellectual processes in high-risk children, but some perform poorly on certain subtests.

These findings contrast with reports of lower IQ in some adult schizophrenics (e.g., chronic patients with cerebral atrophy). Since only averages are reported in high-risk studies, the possibility of subgroups with a low IQ cannot be excluded.

## 6. Skin Conductance Activity

Some studies report higher electrodermal reactivity to neutral and demanding stimuli, but others find no differences. In contrast to adult schizophrenics, electrodermal nonresponse is underrepresented in children at risk for schizophrenia.

Environmental stress factors may explain the differences between adults and children. In the presence of unfavorable environmental factors, a rise of electrodermal reactivity is found in those at risk but not in a nonrisk control group. Perhaps an interaction of genetic risk and stress factors provokes higher electrodermal reactivity (cf. results of the Kringlen group on the additive effects of high genetic load and poor family environment). This interaction should be checked in future studies.

Confirmation of electrodermal activity increases in schizophrenics in the presence of a high-EE relative would also point to the role of environmental stress in shaping psychophysiological reactivity—at least in high-risk individuals and in young more acutely ill schizophrenics (cf. Chapters 6 and 11).

Since higher or normal reactivity is the dominant finding in non-symptomatic high-risk subjects one could postulate that a shift toward reduced responsiveness occurs during the illness, perhaps as a protective mechanism (cf. lower reactivity in ill adult MZ twins).

A report of a correlation between increased electrodermal activity and the incidence of birth complications requires confirmation, but it could reflect an interaction between certain types of exogenous insult and a genetic vulnerability.

### 7. Electroencephalogram (EEG) and Evoked Potentials (EP)

EEG and EP studies of high-risk children are rare. Reports of differences are equivocal and inconsistent (e.g., shorter or longer EP latencies). The absence of clear $P_{300}$ findings in high-risk children contrasts with $P_{300}$ reductions in adult schizophrenics.

Again age effects probably play a role here, since $P_{300}$ disorders are found in adult symptom-free siblings of schizophrenics (cf. Chapter 6). Since $P_{300}$ amplitude reduction is observed in several psychiatrically ill adult populations (where adequate control groups were tested), and in autistic children (Oades *et al.*, 1988; Courchesne *et al.*, 1989) suggests that $P_{300}$ differences may emerge in future high-risk studies under adequate task conditions (Chapter 6).

## B. Putative Predictors of the Breakdown—Differences between Children Who Eventually Develop Schizophrenia and Those Who Do Not

### 1. Perinatal Complications, CT Findings, and Season of Birth

A bias toward more perinatal complications, more CT findings, and more late winter births for those children who eventually developed the illness was recorded in the Danish project.

Although all these factors were reported for schizophrenics from other nonrisk studies, they cannot be considered as the ultimate cause in most of the patients. First, there are methodological limitations to the studies as discussed earlier and in more detail in the text. Second, only a subgroup of schizophrenics is born in winter (putative viral infection) and only a subgroup has cerebral atrophy and/or perinatal complications.

Nevertheless, the findings are heuristically valuable. They possibly point to one of the "noxious" factors involved in the lowering of the disease threshold. We refer here to a diathesis–stress model in which the stress might not be environmental but of somatic origin (e.g., an acquired cerebral weakness through unfavorable perinatal conditions). Not all who are putative genetic carriers develop schizophrenia. However the occurrence of somatic insults like perinatal complications may explain why in some persons a schizophrenic breakdown occurs although these individuals have the same genetic risk as the other group of high-risk children who remain healthy or develop only a schizotypal personality disorder.

## 2. Psychosocial factors

Those who eventually develop schizophrenia are likely to have experienced unfavorable environmental conditions.

High-risk studies of environmental factors (e.g., living with a schizophrenic parent) are easily confounded with genetic factors. This hinders an assessment of environmental contributions. Many of the factors rated as environmental contributions. Many of the factors rated as environmental may in reality be genetic. Thus, unfavorable child-rearing conditions could be due to the higher severity of the illness of the parent. The more severe and earlier breakdown of the offspring could result from a higher genetic load, more turmoil at home, or more frequent hospitalization of the parent.

However, the threshold-lowering effect of a poor family climate is, for example, evident in the adoption study of Tienari and co-workers (Chapters 10 and 11). Poor family climate raises the likelihood of a psychiatric breakdown in general, but to a higher degree in those who are putative genetic carriers, that is, adopted from a schizophrenic parent.

## 3. Behavioral Precursors (School Behavior)

Children of schizophrenics who become ill show more emotional and behavioral problems of adaptation at school. One report claims a link between passivity in childhood and the development of negative symptoms. Boys at risk may be more excitable and irritable, yet more lonely and withdrawn (the Danish project).

These data suggest that for many the problems of adapting to the demands of society start long before the actual disease develops.

## 4. Skin Conductance Activity

Higher electrodermal reactivity may relate to the eventual breakdown in males but not in females (the Danish project).

There is no obvious explanation for this claim. Considering related results already presented, it would be worth knowing what the role of the amount of stress experienced may be and to what extent this is gender related. Could this finding reflect differences in the age of onset of psychosis (which is usually earlier in males)?

General comments concerning this type of risk study. It should be kept in mind that most of the data come from only one—the Danish—project. We have to wait until the children in the other projects pass through the age of risk in order to base our judgment on more solid data.

## C. Putative Risk Indicators in the General Population

Conclusive statements on the relationship of particular features (discussed in this section) to the development of schizophrenia are premature, because either the few studies were of a cross-sectional nature or, in the longitudinal studies, not all subjects have passed through the age of risk.

There are a few similarities in the patterns of experimental task performance between probands showing some risk-related features and symptomatic patients.

Schizotypal adolescents (MMPI or DSM ratings) show poor performance on the degraded CPT, on backward masking, and on the span-of-apprehension task (cf. critical discussion of these tests given earlier). Mauritius project: electrodermal hyperresponders show poor SPEM (cf. Chapter 7). Those with high perceptual aberration scores (Chapman scale) often show electrodermal nonresponse, reduced $P_{300}$, and cross-over effects. Schizoid traits and weak ratings of ego function may relate to electrodermal nonresponse.

There are some findings that suggest that high perceptual aberration and magical thinking assessed by the Chapman scales predicts psychotic problems, but the follow up period is, as yet, too short to be definitive.

Irrespective of the predictive aspect, it is interesting that similar patterns of disturbances—similar to schizophrenia—exist in the general population. This is important for the concept of schizophrenia, even if not all of these subjects develop schizophrenia. This would be unlikely since a higher proportion of subjects shows schizophrenia-related signs than statistically-speaking is at risk (i.e., <1% of the population). For example, about 5–6% have deviant ratings on the perceptual aberration and magic-thinking rating scales. This means that schizophrenia-related personality traits and behavioral and experimental features exist in the general population (continuously distributed/Gaussian distribution), which in turn might explain the appearance of schizophrenia in pedigrees without schizophrenic family members. Schizophrenia may result when there is a combination of subthreshold genetic load and a certain amount of environmental stress (including perinatal insult).

# References

Anthony, E. J. (1969). A clinical evaluation of children with psychotic parents. *American Journal of Psychiatry, 126*, 177–184.

Asarnow, R. F., Nuechterlein, K. H., and Marder, S. R. (1983). Span of apprehension performance, neuropsychological functioning, and indices of psychosis-proneness. *Journal of Nervous and Mental Disease, 171*, 662–669.

Asarnow, R. F., Steffy, R., and Waldman, I. (1985). Comment on Harvey, Weintraub, and Neale: Span of apprehension deficits in children vulnerable to psychopathology. *Journal of Abnormal Psychology, 94*, 414–417.

Asarnow, R. F., Steffy, R. A., MacCrimmon, D. J., and Cleghorn, J. M. (1978). An attentional assessment of foster children at risk for schizophrenia. In L. C. Wynne, R. L. Cromwell, S. Matthysse (Eds.), *The nature of schizophrenia*. New York: John Wiley & Sons.

Balogh, D. W., and Merritt, R. D. (1987). Visual masking and the schizophrenia spectrum: Interfacing clinical and experimental methods. *Schizophrenia Bulletin, 13*, 679–698.

Baron, F. (1953). An ego strength scale which predicts response to psychotherapy. *Journal of Consulting Psychology, 17*, 327–333.

Bell, B., Mednick, S. A., Raman, A. C., Schulsinger, F., Sutton-Smith, B., and Venables, P. H. (1975). A longitudinal psychophysiological study of three-year-old Mauritian children: Preliminary report. *Developmental Medicine and Child Neurology, 17*, 320–324.

Bernstein, A. S., and Riedel, J. A. (1987). Psychophysiological response patterns in college students with high physical anhedonia: Scores appear to reflect schizotypy rather than depression. *Biological Psychiatry, 22*, 829–847.

Braff, D. L. (1981). Impaired speed of information processing in nonmedicated schizotypal patients. *Schizophrenia Bulletin, 7*, 499–508.

Buchsbaum, M. S., Murphy, D. L., Coursey, R.D., Lake, C. R., and Zeigler, M. G. (1978). Platelet monoamine oxidase, plasma dopamine-beta-hydroxylase and attention in a "biochemical high risk" sample. *Journal of Psychiatric Research, 14*, 215–224.

Burman, B., Mednick, S. A., Machon, R. A., Parnas, J., Schulsinger, F. (1987). Children at high-risk for schizophrenia: Parent and offspring perceptions of family relationships. *Journal of Abnormal Psychology, 96*, 364–366.

Chalmers, B. (1983). Psychosocial factors and obstetric complications. *Psychological Medicine, 13*, 333–339.

Chapman, L. J., and Chapman, J. P. (1978). Revised scale for physical anhedonia. Unpublished manuscript. University of Wisconsin.

Chapman, L. J., and Chapman, J. P. (1987). The search for symptoms predictive of schizophrenia. *Schizophrenia Bulletin, 13*, 497–503.

Chapman, L. J., Chapman, J. P., and Raulin, M. C. (1978). Body image aberration in schizophrenia. *Journal of Abnormal Psychology, 87*, 399–407.

Cohen, B. D. (1978). Referent communication disturbances in schizophrenia. In S. Schwartz (Ed.), *Language and cognition in schizophrenia*. Hillsdale, NJ: Lawrence Erlbaum Ass.

Cornblatt, B., and Erlenmeyer-Kimling, L. (1985). Global attentional deviance as a marker of risk for schizophrenia: Specificity and predictive validity. *Journal of Abnormal Psychology, 94*, 470–486.

Courchesne, E., Lincoln, A. J., Yeung-Courchesne, R., Elmasian, R., and Grillon, C. (1989). Pathophysiologic findings in nonretarded autism and receptive developmental language disorder. *Journal of Autism and Developmental Disorder, 19*, 1–17.

Degreef, G., Mukherjee, S., Bilder, R., and Schnur, D. (1988). Season of birth and CT scan findings in schizophrenic patients. *Biological Psychiatry, 24*, 461–464.

Eaton, W. W. (1985). Epidemiology of schizophrenia. *Epidemiologic Reviews, 7*, 105–126.

Erlenmeyer-Kimling, L., and Cornblatt, B. (1978). Attentional measures in a study of children at high-risk for schizophrenia. *Journal of Psychiatric Research, 14,* 93–98.

Erlenmeyer-Kimling, L., and Cornblatt, B. (1984). Kinder schizophrener Eltern: Die Untersuchung psychobiologischer Merkmale. In H.-C. Steinhausen (Ed.), *Risikokinder. Ergebnisse der Kinderpsychiatrie und -psychologie.* Stuttgart: Kohlhammer.

Erlenmeyer-Kimling, L., and Cornblatt, B. (1987). The New York High-Risk-Project: A Followup report. *Schizophrenia Bulletin, 13,* 451–461.

Erlenmeyer-Kimling, L., Friedman, D., Cornblatt, B. and Jacobsen, R. (1985). Electrodermal recovery data on children of schizophrenic parents. *Psychiatry Research, 14,* 149–161.

Erlenmeyer-Kimling, L., and Rainier, J. D. (1973). "Progress report." National Institute of Mental Health, Bethesda, Maryland.

Eysenck, H. J., and Eysenck, S. G. B. (1975). Manual of the Eysenck Personality Questionnaire: Adult version and childrens' version. London: University of London Press.

Fish, B. (1982). Attempts at intervention with high-risk children, from infancy on. In M. J. Goldstein (Ed.). *Preventive Intervention in Schizophrenia: Are we ready?* Washington, DC: Superintendent of Documents, U. S. Government Printing Office.

Fish, B. (1987). Infant predictors of the longitudinal course of schizophrenic development. *Schizophrenia Bulletin, 13,* 395–410.

Fish, B., and Dixon, W. J. (1978). Vestibular hyporeactivity in infants at risk for schizophrenia. *Archives of General Psychiatry, 35,* 963–971.

Fisher, L., Harder, D. W., and Kokes, R. F. (1980). Child competence and psychiatric risk. III. Comparisons based on diagnosis of hospitalized parent. *Journal of Nervous and Mental Disease, 168,* 338–342.

Friedman, D., Cornblatt, B., Vaughn, H., Jr., and Erlenmeyer-Kimling, L. (1988). Auditory event-related potentials in children at risk for schizophrenia: The complete initial sample. *Psychiatry Research, 26,* 203–221.

Friedman, D., Vaughn, H. G., Jr., and Erlenmeyer-Kimling, L. (1979). Event-related potential investigations in children at high risk for schizophrenia. In D. Lehmann, E. Callaway (Eds.), *Event-related potentials in man: Application and problems.* New York: Plenum Press.

Friedman, D., Vaughn, H. G., Jr., and Erlenmeyer-Kimling, L. (1982). Cognitive brain potentials in children at risk for schizophrenia: Preliminary findings. *Schizophrenia Bulletin, 8,* 514–531.

Garmezy, N. (1974). Children at risk: the search for the antecedents of schizophrenia. Part II: ongoing research programs, issues, and interventions. *Schizophrenia Bulletin, Issue 9,* 55–125.

Garmezy, N. (1978). Current status of a sample of the other high-risk research programs. In Wynne, L. C., Cromwell, R. L., Matthysse, S. (Eds.). The nature of schizophrenia. New York: Wiley.

Golden, R. R., and Meehl, P. E. (1979). Detection of the schizoid taxon with MMPI indicators. *Journal of Abnormal Psychology, 88,* 217–233.

Goldstein, M. J. (1987). The UCLA high-risk project. *Schizophrenia Bulletin, 13,* 505–514.

Goldstein, M. J., Judd, L. L., Rodnick, E. H., Alkire, A., and Gould, E. (1968). A method for studying social influence and coping patterns within families of disturbed adolescents. *Journal of Nervous and Mental Disease, 147,* 233–251.

Gottesman, I. I., and Shield, J. (1982). Schizophrenia: The epigenetic puzzle. Cambridge: Cambridge University Press.

Grunebaum, H., Cohler, B. J., Kaufmann, C., Gallant, D. (1978). Children of depressed and schizophrenic mothers. *Child Psychiatry & Human Development, 8,* 219–228.

Grunebaum, H., Weiss, J. L., Gallant, D., and Cohler, B. J. (1974). Attention in young children of psychotic mothers. *American Journal of Psychiatry, 131,* 887–891.

Häfner, H., Haas, S., Pfeifer-Kurda, M., Eichhorn, S., and Michitsuji, S. (1987). Abnormal seasonality of schizophrenic birth. A specific finding? *European Archives of Psychiatry and Neurological Sciences, 236*, 333–342.

Hanson, D., Gottesman, I. I., and Heston, L. L. (1976). Some possible childhood indicators of adult schizophrenia inferred from children of schizophrenics. *British Journal of Psychiatry, 129*,142–154.

Hare, E., and Moran, P. (1981). A relation between seasonal temperature and the birth rate of schizophrenic patients. *Acta Psychiatrica Scandinavica, 63*, 396–405.

Harvey, P., Winters, K., Weintraub, S., and Neale, J. M. (1981). Distractibility in children vulnerable to psychopathology. *Journal of Abnormal Psychology, 90*, 298–304.

Harvey, P. D., Weintraub, S., and Neale, J. M. (1985). Span of apprehension deficits in children vulnerable to psychopathology: A failure to replicate. *Journal of Abnormal Psychology, 94*, 410–413.

Herman, J., Mirsky, A. F., Ricks, N. C., and Gallant, D. (1977). Behavioral and electrographic measures of attention in children at risk for schizophrenia. *Journal of Abnormal Psychology, 86*, 27–33.

Huntington, E. (1938). Season of birth. Its relation to human abilities. New York: Wiley.

Itil, T. M., Hsu, W., Saletu, B., and Mednick, S. (1974). Computer EEG auditory evoked potential investigations in children at high risk for schizophrenia. *American Journal of Psychiatry, 131*, 892–900.

Janes, C. L., Hesselbrock, V., and Stern, J. A. (1978). Parental psychopathology, age, and race as related to electrodermal activity of children. *Psychophysiology, 15*, 24–34.

Janes, C. L., and Stern, J. A. (1976). Electrodermal response configuration as a function of rated psychopathology in children. *Journal of Nervous and Mental Disease, 162*, 184–194.

John, R. S., Mednick, S. A., and Schulsinger, F. (1982). Teacher reports as a predictor of schizophrenia and borderline schizophrenia: A bayesian decision analysis. *Journal of Abnormal Psychology, 91*, 399–413.

Jones, I. H., and Frei, D. (1979). Seasonal births in schizophrenia. A southern hemisphere study using matched pairs. *Acta Psychiatrics Scandinavica, 59*, 164–172.

Jorgensen, A., Teasdale, T. W., Parnas, J., Schulsinger, F., Schulsinger, and H., Mednick, S. A. (1987). The Copenhagen high-risk project. The diagnosis of maternal schizophrenia and its relation to offspring diagnosis. *British Journal of Psychiatry, 151*, 753–757.

Josiassen, R. C., Shagass, C., Roemer, R. A., and Straumanis, J. J. (1985). Attention-related effects on somatosensory evoked potentials in college students at high risk for psychopathology. *Journal of Abnormal Psychology, 94*, 507–518.

Kendler, K. S., Gruenberg, A. M., and Strauss, J. S. (1981). An independent analysis of the Copenhagen sample of the Danish adoption study of schizophrenia. III. The relationship between paranoid psychosis (delusional disorder) and the schizophrenia spectrum disorders. *Archives of General Psychiatry, 38*, 985–987.

Kugelmass, S., Marcus, J., and Schmuell, J. (1985). Psychophysiological reactivity in high-risk children. *Schizophrenia Bulletin, 11*, 66–73.

Lewine, R. R. J., Watt, N. F., and Grubb, T. W. (1981). High-risk-for-schizophrenia-research: Sampling bias and its implications. *Schizophrenia Bulletin, 7*, 273–280.

Lewis, M. S., and Griffin, P. A. (1981). An explanation for the season of birth effect in schizophrenia and certain other diseases. *Psychological Bulletin, 89*, 589–596.

Lewis, S. W. (1989). Congenital risk factors for schizophrenia. *Psychological Medicine, 19*, 5–13.

Lutzenberger, W., Elbert, T., Rockstroh, B., Birbaumer, N., and Stegagno, L. (1981). Slow cortical potentials in subjects with high or low scores on a questionnaire measuring physical anhedonia and body image distortion. *Psychophysiology, 18*, 371–380.

Lyon, M., Barr, C. E., Cannon, T. D., Mednick, S. A., and Shore, D. (1989). Fetal neural development and schizophrenia. *Schizophrenia Bulletin, 15*, 149–161.

Machón, R. A., Mednick, S. A., and Schulsinger, F. (1983). The interaction of seasonality, place of birth, genetic risk and subsequent schizophrenia in a high risk sample. *British Journal of Psychiatry, 143*, 383–388.

Machón, R. A., Mednick, S. A., and Schulsinger, F. (1987). Seasonality, birth complications and schizophrenia in a high risk sample. *British Journal of Psychiatry, 151*, 122–124.

Marcus, J., Auerbach, J., Wilkinson, L., and Burack, C. M. (1984). Infants at risk for schizophrenia: The Jerusalem infant development study. In N. F. Watt, E. J. Anthony, L. C. Wynne, and J. E. Rolf (Eds.), *Children at risk for schizophrenia*. Cambridge: Cambridge University Press.

Marcus, L. M. (1972). Studies of attention in children vulnerable to schizophrenia. Unpublished doctoral dissertation. University of Minnesota.

Marcuse, Y., and Cornblatt, B. (1986). Children at high risk for schizophrenia: Predictions from infancy to childhood functioning. In L. Erlenmeyer-Kimling, N. E. Miller (Eds.), *Life-span research on the prediction of psychopathology*. Hillsdale, NJ: Erlbaum Assoc.

Martin, E. M., and Chapman, L. J. (1982). Communication effectiveness in psychosis-prone college students. *Journal of Abnormal Psychology, 91*, 420–425.

McNeil, T. F. (1988). Obstetric factors and perinatal injuries. In M. T. Tsuang, J. C. Simpson (Eds.), *Handbook of schizophrenia, Vol. 3: Nosology, Epidemiology and Genetics.* (pp. 319–344). Amsterdam: Elsevier.

McNeil, T. F., and Kaij, L. (1978). Obstetric factors in the development of schizophrenia: Complications in the births of preschizophrenics and in reproductions by schizophrenic parents. In L. C. Wynne, R. L. Cromwell, and S. Matthysse (Eds.), *The nature of schizophrenia*. New York: Wiley.

Mednick, S. A. (1978). Berkson's fallacy and high-risk research. In L. C. Wynne, R. L. Cromwell, and S. Matthysse (Eds.), *The nature of schizophrenia*. New York: Wiley.

Mednick, S. A. (1990). Personal communication.

Mednick, S. A., Cudeck, R., Griffith, J. J., Talovic, S. A., and Schulsinger, F. (1984). The Danish-high-risk-project: Recent methods and findings. In N. F. Watt, E. J. Anthony, L. C. Wynne, J. E. Rolf (Eds.), *Children at risk for schizophrenia*. Cambridge: Cambridge University Press.

Mednick, S. A., Machon, R. A., Huttunen, M. O., and Bonett, D. (1988). Adult schizophrenia following prenatal exposure to an influenza epidemic. *Archives of General Psychiatry, 45*, 189–192.

Mednick, S. A., Parnas, J., and Schulsinger, F. (1987). The Copenhagen high-risk project, 1962–1986. *Schizophrenia Bulletin, 13*, 485–495.

Mednick, S. A., and Schulsinger, F. (1965). A longitudinal study of children with a high risk for schizophrenia: A preliminary report. In S. G. Vandenberg (Ed.), *Methods and goals in human behavior genetics*. New York: Academic Press.

Mednick, S. A., and Schulsinger, F. (1968). Some premorbid characteristics related to breakdown in children with schizophrenic mothers. In D. Rosenthal and S. S. Kety (Eds.), *The transmission of schizophrenia*. New York: Elmsford.

Mednick, S. A., and Silverton, L. (1988). High-risk studies of the etiology of schizophrenia. In M. T. Tsuang and J. C. Simpson (Eds.), *Handbook of schizophrenia, Vol. 3: Nosology, Epidemiology and Genetics.* (pp. 543–562). Amsterdam: Elsevier.

Merrit, R. D., and Balogh, D. W. (1984). The use of backward masking paradigm to assess the visual information processing of schizotypics: A reevaluation of Steronko and Woods. *Journal of Nervous and Mental Disease, 172*, 216–224.

Mirsky, A. (1985). Addendum: Bringing the Israeli high-risk study to completion. *Schizophrenia Bulletin, 11*, 30.

Mirsky, A. F., Silberman, E. K., Latz, A., and Nagler, S. (1985). Adult outcome of high-risk children: Differential effects of town and kibbutz rearing. *Schizophrenia Bulletin, 11*, 150–154.

Murray, R. M., Reveley, A. M., and Lewis, S. W. (1988). Family history, obstetric complications and cerebral abnormality in schizophrenia. In M. T. Tsuang and J. C. Simpson (Eds.), *Handbook of Schizophrenia, Vol. 3: Nosology, Epidemiology and Genetics.* (pp. 563–577). Amsterdam: Elsevier.

Nagler, S. (1985). Overall design and methodology of the Israeli high-risk study. *Schizophrenia Bulletin, 11*, 31–37.

Nuechterlein, K. H. (1983). Signal detection in vigilance tasks and behavioral attributes among offspring of schizophrenic mothers and among hyperactive children. *Journal of Abnormal Psychology, 92*, 4–28.

Nuechterlein, K. H., and Dawson, M. E. (1984). Information processing and attentional functioning in the developmental course of schizophrenic disorders. *Schizophrenia Bulletin, 10*, 160–203.

Nuechterlein, K. H., and Zaucha, K. M. (1990). Similarities between information-processing abnormalities of actively symptomatic schizophrenic patients and high-risk children. In E. R. Straube and K. Hahlweg (Eds.), *Schizophrenia. Concepts, Vulnerability, and Intervention.* (pp. 77–96). Berlin: Springer.

Oades, R. D., Walker, M. K., Geffen, L. B., and Stern, L. M. (1988). Event-related potentials in autistic and healthy children on an auditory choice reaction time task. *International Journal of Psychophysiology, 6*, 25–37.

Oltmanns, T. F. (1978). Selective attention in schizophrenia and manic psychoses: The effect of distraction on information processing. *Journal of Abnormal Psychology, 87*, 212–225.

Oltmanns, T. F., Weintraub, S., Stone, A. A., and Neale, J. M. (1978). Cognitive slippage in children vulnerable to schizophrenia. *Journal of Abnormal Child Psychology, 6*, 237–245.

Owen, M. J., Lewis, S. W., and Murray, R. M. (1988). Obstetric complications and schizophrenia: A computed tomographic study. *Psychological Medicine, 18*, 331–339.

Parker, J. G., and Asher, S. R. (1987). Peer relations and later personal adjustment: Are low-accepted children at risk? *Psychological Bulletin, 102*, 357–389.

Parnas, J., Schulsinger, F., and Mednick, S. A. (1990). The Copenhagen high-risk study. Major psychopathological and etiological findings. In E. R. Straube and K. Hahlweg (Eds.), *Schizophrenia. Concepts, Vulnerability, and Intervention.* (pp. 45–56). Berlin: Springer.

Parnas, J., Schulsinger, F., Teasdale, T. W., Schulsinger, H., Feldman, P. M., and Mednick, S. A. (1982). Perinatal complications and clinical outcome within the schizophrenia spectrum. *British Journal of Psychiatry, 140*, 416–420.

Parnas, J., and Schulsinger, H. (1986). Continuity of formal thought disorder from childhood to adulthood in a high-risk sample. *Acta Psychiatrica Scandinavica, 74*, 246–251.

Parnas, J., Teasdale, T. W., and Schulsinger, H. (1985). Institutional rearing and diagnostic outcome in children of schizophrenic mothers: A prospective high-risk study. *Archives of General Psychiatry, 42*, 762–769.

Phipps-Yonas, S. (1984). Visual and auditory reaction time in children vulnerable to psychopathology. In N. F. Watt, E. J. Anthony, L. C. Wynne, and J. E. Rolf (Eds.), *Children at risk for schizophrenia.* Cambridge: Cambridge University Press.

Pollin, W., Allen, M. G., Hoffer, A., Stabenau, J. R., and Huber, Z. (1969). Psychopathology in 15,909 pairs of veteran twins. *American Journal of Psychiatry, 7*, 597–609.

Raine, A., and Venables, P. H. (1984). Electrodermal nonresponding, antisocial behavior, and schizoid tendencies in adolescents. *Psychophysiology, 21*, 424–433.

Rieder, R. O. (1979). Children at risk. In L. Bellak (Ed.), *Disorders of the Schizophrenic Syndrome.* New York: Basic Books.

Rieder, Ro. O., Rosenthal, D., Wender, P., and Blumenthal, H. (1975). The offspring of schizophrenics. Fetal and neonatal deaths. *Archives of General Psychiatry, 32*, 200–211.

Rockstroh, B., Elbert, T., Birbaumer, N., and Lutzenberger, W. (1982). Slow brain potentials and behavior. Baltimore: Urban & Schwarzenberg.

Rosenthal, D. (1971). A program of research on heredity in schizophrenia. *Behavioral Science,* *16*, 191–201.

Saccuzzo, D. P., and Schubert, D. L. (1981). Backward masking as a measure of slow processing in schizophrenia spectrum disorders. *Journal of Abnormal Psychology, 90*, 305–312.

Salzman, L. F., and Klein, R. H. (1978). Habituation and conditioning of electrodermal responses in high risk children. *Schizophrenia Bulletin, 4*, 210–222.

Schachter, J., Kerr, J., Lachin, J. M., and Faer, M. (1975). Newborn offspring of a schizophrenic parent: Cardiac reactivity to auditory stimuli. *Psychophysiology, 12*, 483–492.

Schreiber, H., Stolz, G., Rothmeier, J., Kornhuber, H. H., and Born, J. (1989). Prolonged latencies of the N2 and P3 of the auditory event-related potential in children at risk for schizophrenia. *European Archives of Psychiatry and Neurological Sciences, 238*, 185–188.

Schuck, J., Leventhal, D., Rothstein, H., and Irizarry, V. (1984). Physical anhedonia and schizophrenia. *Journal of Abnormal Psychology, 93*, 342–344.

Schulsinger, F., Mednick, S. A., Venables, P. H., Raman, A. C., and Bell, B. (1975). Early detection and prevention of mental illness: The Mauritius project. *Neuropsychobiology, 1*, 166–179.

Schulsinger, F., Parnas, J., Mednick, S., Teasdale, T. W., and Schulsinger, H. (1987). Heredity-environment interaction and schizophrenia. *Journal of Psychiatric Research, 212*, 431–436.

Schwarzkopf, S. B., Nasrallah, H. A., Olson, S. C., Coffman, J. A., and McLaughlin, J. A. (1989). Perinatal complications and genetic loading in schizophrenia: Preliminary findings. *Psychiatry Research, 27*, 233–239.

Shakow, D. (1962). Segmental set. *Archives of General Psychiatry, 6*, 1–2.

Shur, E. (1982). Season of birth in high and low genetic risk schizophrenics. *British Journal of Psychiatry, 140*, 410–415.

Silverton, L., Finello, K. M., Mednick, S. A., and Schulsinger, F. (1985). Low birth weight and ventricular enlargement in a high-risk sample. *Journal of Abnormal Psychology, 94*, 405–409.

Simons, R. F., Losito, B. D., Rose, S. C., and MacMillan, F. W. (1983). Electrodermal nonresponding among college undergraduates: Temporal stability, situational specifity, and relationship to heart rate change. *Psychophysiology, 20*, 498–505.

Simons, R. F., McMillan III, F. W., and Ireland, F. B. (1982). Reaction-time crossover in preselected schizotypic subjects. *Journal of Abnormal Psychology, 91*, 414–419.

Sohlberg, S. C., and Yaniv, S. (1985). Social adjustment and cognitive performance of high-risk children. *Schizophrenia Bulletin, 11*, 61–65.

Spitzer, R. L., and Endicott, J. (1972). Schedule for affective disorders and schizophrenia—Lifetime Version (SADS-L). New York: New York State Psychiatric Institute.

Spitzer, R. L., and Endicott, J. (1977). *Schedule for Affective Disorders and Schizophrenia-Lifetime Version (SADS-L).* (3rd ed.). New York: New York State Psychiatric Institute, Biometrics Research.

Spring, B. (1980). Shift of attention in schizophrenics, siblings of schizophrenics, and depressed patients. *Journal of Nervous and Mental Disease, 168*, 133–139.

Steffy, R. A., Asarnow, R. F., Asarnow, J. R., MacCrimmon, D. J., and Cleghorn, J. M. (1984). The McMaster-Waterloo high-risk project: Multifaceted strategy for high-risk research. In N. F. Watt, E. J. Anthony, L. C. Wynne, and J. E. Rolf (Eds.), *Children at Risk for Schizophrenia*. Cambridge: Cambridge University Press.

Steronko, R. J., and Woods, D. J. (1978). Impairment in early stages of visual information processing in nonpsychotic schizotypic individuals. *Journal of Abnormal Psychology, 87*, 481–490.

Talovic, S. A., Mednick, S. A., Schulsinger, F., and Falloon, I. R. H. (1980). Schizophrenia in high-risk subjects: Prognostic maternal characteristics. *Journal of Abnormal Psychology, 89*, 501–504.

Tramer, T. (1928). Über die biologische Bedeutung des Geburtsmonats für die Psycho-seerkrankung. *Schweizer Archiv für Neurologie und Psychiatrie, 24*, 17–24.

Van Dyke, J. L., Rosenthal, D., and Rasmussen, P. V. (1974). Electrodermal functioning in adopted-away offspring of schizophrenics. *Journal of Psychiatric Research, 10*, 199–215.

Van Dyke, J. L., Rosenthal, D., and Rasmussen, P. V. (1975). Schizophrenia: Effects of inheritance and rearing on reaction time. *Canadian Journal of Behavioral Science, 7*, 223–236.

Venables, P. H. (1977). The electrodermal psychophysiology of schizophrenics and children at risk for schizophrenia: Controversies and developments. *Schizophrenia Bulletin, 3*, 28–48.

Venables, P. H. (1987). Personal communication.

Wagener, D. K., Hogarty, G. E., Goldstein, M. J., Asarnow, R. F., and Browne, A. (1986). Information processing and communication deviance in schizophrenic patients and their mothers. *Psychiatry Research, 18*, 365–377.

Walker, E., Hoppes, E., Emory, E., Mednick, S. A., and Schulsinger, F. (1981). Environmental factors related to schizophrenia in psychophysiologically labile high-risk males. *Journal of Abnormal Psychology, 4*, 313–320.

Watt, N. F., Grubb, T. W., and Erlenmeyer-Kimling, L. (1984). Social, emotional, and intellectual behavior at school among children at high-risk for schizophrenia. In N. F. Watt, E. J. Anthony, L. C. Wynne, and J. E. Rolf (Eds.) *Children at risk for schizophrenia.* Cambridge: Cambridge University Press.

Weintraub, S. (1987). Risk factors in schizophrenia: The Stony Brook high-risk project. *Schizophrenia Bulletin, 13*, 439–450.

Weintraub, S., and Neale, J. M. (1984). Social behavior of children at risk for schizophrenia. In N. F. Watt, E. J. Anthony, L. C.Wynne, and J. E. Rolf (Eds.) *Children at risk for schizophrenia.* Cambridge: Cambridge University Press.

Wilcox, J., and Nasrallah, H. A. (1987). Perinatal distress and prognosis of psychotic illness. *Neuropsychobiology, 17*, 173–175.

Wilcox, J. A., and Nasrallah, H. A. (1987). Perinatal insult as a risk factor in paranoid and nonparanoid schizophrenia. *Psychopathology, 20*, 285–287.

Wood, R. L., and Cook, M. (1979). Attentional deficit in the siblings of schizophrenics. *Psychological Medicine, 9*, 465–467.

Worland, J., Weeks, D. G., Weiner, S. M., and Schechtman, J. (1982). Longitudinal, prospective evaluations of intelligence in children at risk. *Schizophrenia Bulletin, 8*, 135–141.

Wrede, G., Mednick, S. A., Huttunen, M. O., and Nilsson, C. G. (1980). Pregnancy and delivery complications in the births of an unselected series of Finnish children with schizophrenic mothers. *Acta Psychiatrica Scandinavica, 62*, 369–381.

Zahn, T. P. (1977). Autonomic nervous system characteristics possibly related to a genetic predisposition to schizophrenia. *Schizophrenia Bulletin, 3*, 49–60.

Zipursky, R. B., and Schulz, S. C. (1987). Seasonality of birth and CT findings in schizophrenia. *Biological Psychiatry, 22*, 1288–1292.

Zuckerman, M. (1979). *Sensation seeking: Beyond the optimal level of arousal.* Hillsdale, New York: Erlbaum.

# PART VI

# Neurotransmission, Therapy, and Investigations on Long-Term Outcome

# Chapter 13

# Neurotransmission, Pharmacotherapy, and Psychotherapy

## I. Neurotransmitter Systems

### A. Introduction: The Dopamine Hypothesis

In France, in 1952, Delay, Deniker, and Harl discovered that many schizophrenics responded positively to pharmacological treatment with neuroleptics. This provided a major boost for the study of chemical neurotransmission and biochemical dysfunction in mental illness (Davis, 1985). However, it was not until the early 1960s that changes of catecholaminergic transmission, in particular transmission involving dopamine, were related to the mechanisms of action of neuroleptic treatment.

The major biochemical effect shared by all neuroleptics (e.g., haloperidol, chlorpromazine, fluphenazine) is their ability to block postsynaptic dopamine (DA) receptors. Using positron emission tomography (PET), a team from the Karolinska Institute in Stockholm was recently able to demonstrate, *in vivo,* that members of all classes of neuroleptic do bind to DA receptors, occupying 65–84% of the sites available (Farde *et al.,* 1988, as measured in the putamen). (The calculation was made by comparison with the binding of [$^{11}$C-]raclopride in drug-naive subjects. This neuroleptic is one of the most specific ligands available for the DA binding site known as the $D_2$ receptor.) Broadly speaking, the degree to which neuroleptics exert such anti-dopaminergic effects (i.e., postsynaptic blocking) correlates with their clinical efficacy (Figure 13.1). The correlation is one of the foundations of the dopamine hypothesis of schizophrenia, which was first proposed in Europe in the 1960s (Van Rossum, 1966) and was then promulgated in the early 1970s in the United States by Horn and Snyder (1971), Stevens (1973), and Snyder (1976).

Simply stated, the DA hypothesis suggests that there may be an increase of DA neurotransmission in the illness. Superficially, the correlation between

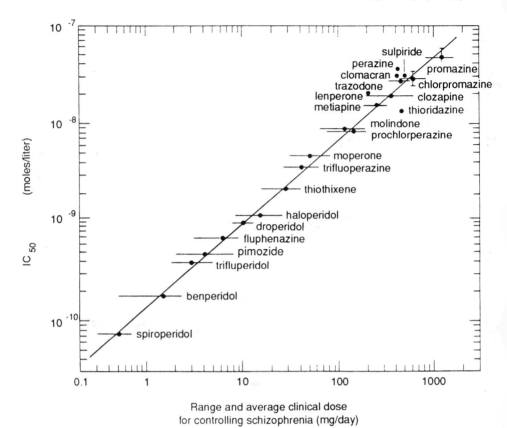

**Figure 13.1**   The clinical doses of neuroleptics (abscissa) correlate with their *in vitro* concentrations for blocking dopamine $D_2$ receptors (ordinate). The $IC_{50}$ value is the neuroleptic concentration which blocks 50% of the binding of tritiated haloperidol to $D_2$ receptors (after Seeman *et al.*, 1986).

clinical efficacy and binding looks very impressive. However, it should be noted that the accuracy and consistency with which clinical efficacy is assessed (i.e., by the observation of behavioral changes scored on a rating scale) is of a rather different order of magnitude than the quantitative assessment of binding. Furthermore, it should not be entirely overlooked that some neuroleptics also show a similar but less marked blocking effect on the noradrenergic (NA) system (e.g., Iversen, 1986).

## B. The Dopamine Systems

Figure 13.2 illustrates the synthesis of DA in neuronal terminals, its release into the synaptic cleft, and the receptor site for continued transmission on the

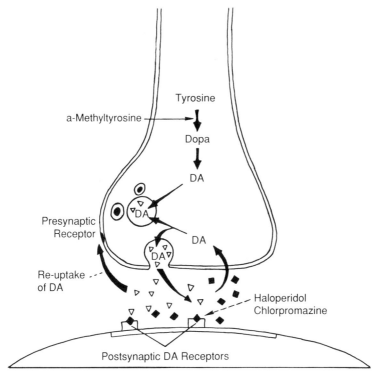

**Figure 13.2** Schematic illustration of the synthetic pathway for the neurotransmitter dopamine (DA) from its precursor molecules within the presynaptic bouton. Release of DA from storage vesicles into the synaptic cleft and binding with the postsynaptic receptor are also shown. Neuroleptics such as haloperidol can block this binding; unused DA may then be taken up at sites on the presynaptic membrane where it may exert negative feedback on DA synthesis.

postsynaptic neuronal element. The usual mode of action of neuroleptics is believed to occur when they bind to this site and block further neurotransmission. DA that is not bound to the postsynaptic element can bind to presynaptic sites on the terminal (re-uptake) and exert negative feedback on the synthesis and release of DA. These sites are also available for neuroleptic binding. The occurrence of presynaptic binding has been determined after treatment of animals with low doses of neuroleptics, but the effects are usually regarded as subordinate to those found at postsynaptic sites after normal doses. The distribution of synthesis- and release-regulating autoreceptors varies between different DA projection systems (Kilts *et al.*, 1987; see subsequent text).

All neuroleptics produce some degree of antipsychotic or sedative action, or both, in most schizophrenic patients. Any neuroleptic substance has several simultaneous effects on central nervous function. These effects depend, in part, on the function of the brain area affected (e.g., hypothalamus or cortex) and, in part, on the detailed nature of the neuroleptic's binding action (e.g., membrane binding site and affinity of binding; see Section II). Some of these effects are important for treatment (e.g., antipsychotic effects), but others are unwanted (e.g., side-effects, changes of hormonal secretion, dyskinesias). The range of effects is different for each class of neuroleptic (e.g., "typical" butyrophenones as opposed to "atypical" dibenzodiazepines; see subsequent text). In order to understand what neuroleptics do, it is important first to realize that there are several DA projection systems in the brain.

Most DA is found either in hypothalamic systems that influence the release of hormones from the pituitary or in systems projecting from the midbrain. Fibers from the midbrain nuclei, in particular the substantia nigra (SN) and the ventral tegmental area (VTA), ascend for the most part to influence motor, motivational, and cognitive function in the forebrain (Oades and Halliday, 1987). There are three major relevant pathways from the DA nuclei of the midbrain. They are the *mesostriatal* or *nigrostriatal* (to the neostriatum of the basal ganglia), *mesolimbic* (to the subcortical parts of the limbic system), and *mesocortical* (to the whole human cerebral cortex, but especially motor, frontal, and association areas) pathways (Gaspar *et al.*, 1989). These are illustrated in the simplified scheme of Figure 13.3. Neuroleptics influence DA activity in all these pathways to a degree that depends on the type of neuroleptic (e.g., "atypical" or "typical" neuroleptic) and the type and configuration of receptors found in each terminal (and cell body) region (e.g., $D_1$ and $D_2$ receptors).

There are two main types of DA receptor known as the $D_1$ and $D_2$ binding sites (Kebabian and Calne, 1979). Stimulation of $D_1$ sites usually enhances activity of adenylate cyclase.

This enzyme is linked to the production of cyclic adenosine monophosphate (cAMP) in the postsynaptic neuron. The activation of this second messenger sets the sequence of events in motion that lead to the propagation of neural impulses. Stimulation of $D_2$ receptors usually either inhibits this activation (e.g., in the neostriatum; Seeman, 1980) or has no effect (e.g., some mesolimbic sites such as the Nucleus accumbens; Stoof and Verheijden, 1986). Stimulation at $D_2$ sites activates the guanine rather than the adenosine nucleotide.

Classical or typical neuroleptics exert their major effect in DA systems at $D_2$ binding sites (for further details, see Bradley, 1986). However, it should be noted that some neuroleptic effects, for example, sedation, may also involve non-DA actions (e.g., at alpha noradrenergic receptors).

Typical neuroleptics (e.g., haloperidol) influence motor aspects of behavior, mostly in the neostriatum (caudate and putamen nuclei), which receives major input from the SN and most parts of the limbic and neocortices. These input regions also contain $D_2$ receptors. By influencing transmission in this system,

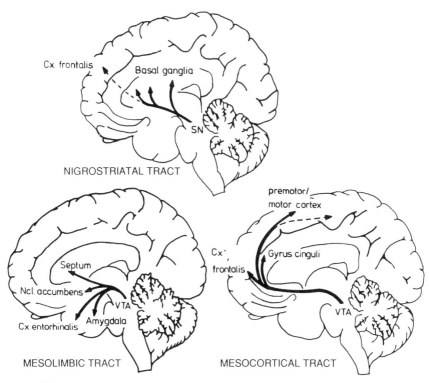

**Figure 13.3** A schematic lateral view of the brain to illustrate the dopamine (DA) pathways ascending from the substantia nigra (SN; nigrostriatal tract, *top*) and from the ventrotegmental area in the midbrain (VTA; mesolimbic tract, *lower left;* mesocortical tract, *lower right*). Ncl, nucleus; Cx, cortex (U. Schall).

neuroleptic treatment can give rise to movement disorders and Parkinson-like symptoms. These may consist of reduced spontaneous movements, rigidity, tremor, dyskinesia, and a poverty of expression. The cause is presumed to be related to the reduction of DA activity in this extrapyramidal motor system. It may be noted that in Parkinson's disease there is a primary loss of nigrostriatal DA neurons. The remaining neurons show an increase in activity (e.g., turnover rate of DA) in an attempt to compensate for this loss. In schizophrenics with motor problems or dyskinesia, a similar tendency for low brain levels of DA and higher cerebrospinal fluid (CSF) levels of its metabolite homovanillic acid (HVA) have been recorded (Kornhuber *et al.*, 1989; Lu *et al.*, 1989). This indirectly implies that there is an increase of DA turnover in the synapses of these patients.

A note of caution should be added at this juncture. It is widely accepted that DA pathways do not mediate specific functions, in the behavioral sense.

Rather, DA activity affects the processing of information in DA projection areas by modulating other neuronal systems. For example, studies of motor function in monkeys, carried out by Evarts (1984) at the National Institutes of Mental Health (NIMH) in Bethesda, Maryland, show that DA is not released during the execution of motor movements. Instead, the slow release of DA is recorded during the preparatory phase preceding specific intentional movements. The release and effect of DA is measurable on a time scale of minutes rather than seconds or fractions of a second.

Again, a note of caution should be extended regarding the involvement of DA systems in the hypothalamus and the retina. Neither is believed to play a major role in schizophrenia, but an anomalously functioning DA system in schizophrenia, as well as neuroleptic treatment, is likely to modify DA-influenced activities in the hypothalamus and retina. Thus, there is evidence of a change of sensitivity in the hypothalamic DA system from the hormonal secretion patterns in some schizophrenics. Challenges with DA agonists can lead to increases of plasma growth hormone and decreased plasma prolactin (Zemlan et al., 1985). Psychopathology has been claimed to be inversely correlated with prolactin levels in schizophrenics who do not show marked cerebral atrophy (Johnstone et al., 1977; Kleinman et al., 1982). In a similar vein, changes in the role of retinal DA in the process of adaptation to changing levels of illumination have been reported in some schizophrenics (Granger, 19957).

In contrast to the effects of neuroleptics on motor behavior, it is not at all clear which structure(s) or system(s) is responsible for their antipsychotic effect. Insofar as atypical neuroleptics (e.g., clozapine) do not usually involve motor side-effects, it is assumed that the relevant site(s) lie in the mesolimbic or mesocortical projection systems that have their origin in the VTA. Relevant mesolimbic structures include the N. accumbens, septum, and entorhinal cortex. These regions appear to be important for the initiation of behavior (Robbins and Everett, 1982) and DA activity here will modulate switching between opposing behavioral tendencies (Oades, 1985). The amygdala and orbitofrontal cortex are involved in mediating motivational aspects of the organization of behavior (Fuster, 1980). The mesocortical DA projection areas of the frontal and temporal cortices (Foote and Morrison, 1987) are clearly important for the integration of information and the planning of behavioral patterns at a high level (Luria, 1978; Streitfeld, 1980). Qualitatively speaking, many of these functions are more-or-less impaired in schizophrenia, and the function of all these regions is likely to be affected by neuroleptic treatment. The degree to which these functions are impaired in individuals or groups of schizophrenics and the relative effects of different neuroleptics on the function of each area varies. The therapeutic implications make this a most important topic for further research in the laboratory.

## C. Dopamine-Related Changes in Schizophrenia

### 1. Theory and Methods

The discovery of the "antidopaminergic" effect of neuroleptics naturally led to the expectation of increased DA activity in one form or another in the central nervous system (CNS) of schizophrenics. Many find support for this expectation in the psychotomimetic properties of substances that enhance DA levels (Snyder, 1973; Robinson and Becker, 1986). (Examples include the administration of the precursor L-DOPA; amphetamine, which stimulates DA release; and disulfiram, which inhibits the conversion of DA to NA.)

However, it should not be forgotten that some object to the DA hypothesis on the grounds of the therapeutic lag. Whereas neuroleptics can alter levels of DA activity on the first day of treatment, a clinical improvement may take 10–50 days to be appreciable. This objection is an important one and requires a brief reply. The initial reaction of a DA neuron to the blockade of postsynaptic receptors with a neuroleptic is to release more DA in compensation. At first, there is an acute increase in metabolism (i.e., HVA levels increase). With the continuing presence of a typical neuroleptic, there are three coincidental events: HVA levels (as measured in the plasma of neuroleptic-sensitive individuals) decrease; depolarization block of SN neuronal activity spreads to the VTA; and a therapeutic clinical response develops (in relation to HVA levels). Hence, the therapeutic lag may be explained by the time needed for a neuroleptic to reduce significantly both VTA neuronal firing and DA metabolism. It should be emphasized that these are coincidences; the correlations are not direct evidence for the interdependence of the sequence of events following neuroleptic administration (see review by Hand *et al.*, 1987).

Next, the potential basis for the DA hypothesis should be examined. There are two major ways in which "overactivity" could occur. First, there could be an increase of DA levels, DA metabolism, or turnover. Second, there could be an increased number of DA binding sites (called $B_{max}$) or, conceivably, changes of their affinity for DA (called $K_d$). The result would be a proportionately larger postsynaptic effect than normal. (In detail, other possibilities are feasible but have received scant attention; for example, autoreceptor hyposensitivity or changes of second messenger activity in the postsynaptic element.)

The relevant techniques to examine these possibilities—namely, radioenzymatic assays, high pressure liquid chromatography, and various measures of the binding of radioactive ligands to DA receptors—gradually became available between the late 1960s and the late 1970s. A proportion of neurotransmitter excess and of the major DA metabolite HVA is transported to the CSF. Thus, samples of CSF might be expected to provide an indirect indication of major central changes. (For a warning against comparing CSF and ventricular measures levels too closely, see Gjerris *et al.*, 1988.) Certainly samples of CSF

HVA more closely resemble central nervous activity than samples from the plasma or urine, where about 75% of HVA is derived from the periphery (Kopin, 1985). (For these reasons, one should be cautious when interpreting measures reported from plasma or urine, but it is hoped that their accuracy may be improved by current attempts to block peripheral monoamine oxidase (MAO) with agents such as debrisoquin.)

One further warning should be added before the reader looks at the results of CSF studies. It is unusual for investigators to report the dates that their samples were taken. It seems that in both healthy subjects and those with psychiatric disorders, CSF samples taken in the summer (e.g., May) often show monoamine metabolite levels that are higher than those taken in winter (e.g., December). The difference in HVA levels can amount to 50% (Brewerton *et al.*, 1988; Csernansky *et al.*, 1988). This is a potentially powerful source of variation that may well have contributed to the number of inconclusive results reported from various laboratories.

To date, binding studies are performed *postmortem*. These studies involve many unavoidable potentially confounding variables such as the cause and time of death, hypoxia, the time prior to extraction, the treatment of the tissue during analysis (e.g., washout of excess medication), and the properties of the ligand used. However, as yet, the only alternative is the *in vivo* visualization of radioactive ligand binding with PET. Although this and related imaging techniques provide a great hope for the future, at present they are both very expensive and lack sufficient resolution to be very useful.

## 2. Results

A number of laboratories have measured CSF levels of HVA in acute and chronic schizophrenics and failed to find significant differences with respect to manic, depressed, or healthy populations (Persson and Roos, 1969; Rimon *et al.*, 1971; Bowers, 1973; Post *et al.*, 1975; Gerner *et al.*, 1984). Of course, after treatment, when DA receptors are blocked (which may continue for weeks after neuroleptic withdrawal), there can be higher CSF levels of DA and HVA reflecting released unbound DA and its metabolism to HVA. This is illustrated in studies of Gattaz *et al.* (1983) from the Mannheim Mental Health Research Institute, Germany, (Figure 13.4). HVA levels usually fall after withdrawal of neuroleptic treatment (see also Bagdy *et al.*, 1985). In confirmation of the authors' interpretation of the results, increased HVA has been reported in the cortex of medicated but not unmedicated schizophrenics (Bacopoulos *et al.*, 1979) and to be particularly restricted to the frontal cortex (Reynolds and Czudek, personal communication).

In contrast to these results, a few recent studies have reported small decreases of HVA (and DA) in CSF samples (Van Kammen *et al.*, 1983; Lindström, 1985). The decreases seem to be prevalent in patients showing

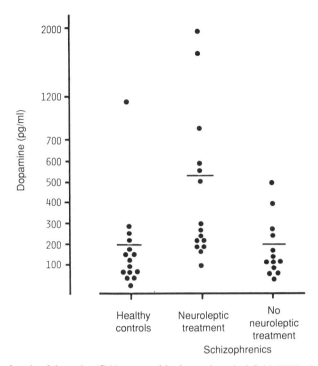

**Figure 13.4**  Levels of dopamine (DA) measured in the cerebrospinal fluid (CSF) of healthy subjects and schizophrenics before and after medication (after Gattaz *et al.*, 1983).

defect symptoms and slight signs of cerebral atrophy (Losonczy *et al.*, 1986; Van Kammen *et al.*, 1986). These changes may reflect small alterations of receptor sensitivity (Pearlson and Coyle, 1983) that will be discussed subsequently. Whether such putative changes result from chronicity of symptoms or chronicity of neuroleptic treatment, or are only to be found in a restricted subgroup of patients, remains an open question. Clearly, studies of CSF samples have not obtained results that unequivocally support the hypothesis that DA systems are abnormally active in schizophrenia as a whole. What about the possibility of changes specific to their illness in definable subgroups of schizophrenics?

Preliminary results do suggest the working hypothesis that negative symptoms and cerebral atrophy are more likely to be associated with low DA activity, and vice versa (see Chapter 8). Yet the heterogeneity of results found in other psychiatric groups does not encourage trying to discriminate the schizophrenic response on the basis of CSF measures alone. Manic patients show either no change or higher levels of HVA than healthy controls; depressives show either no change or lower than normal CSF HVA levels (Post *et al.*, 1980; Gerner *et al.*, 1984; Davis *et al.*, 1988).

Most early reports of slight changes in the levels of neurotransmitter or metabolites found in *postmortem* analyses of brain tissue (e.g., Bird *et al.*, 1979; Crow *et al.*, 1979; Farley *et al.*, 1980) have not been confirmed. Modest increases of utilization have been found in the basal ganglia and related limbic regions (Farley *et al.*, 1977; Toru *et al.*, 1982; Bridge *et al.*, 1985, 1987), but this has not been consistent. (Utilization is an indirect measure of transmitter activity and usually refers to the ratio of levels of metabolite(s) to transmitter.) The only apparently reproducible finding, in over 30 elderly chronic subjects studied by Reynolds (1983, Reynolds *et al.*, 1987), was of an increased level of DA in the amygdala on the left side of the brain. Levels were two-thirds higher than on the right side, a change that was not reflected in other markers of DA function (except for HVA) and was not found in the hippocampus, N. accumbens, neostriatum, or neocortex. Unlike the neostriatum, where there is a slightly higher level of DA binding on the right side of healthy subjects, there is no normal laterality of DA function evident in the amygdala. (See previous section for binding methods; see also section in Chapter 8 on laterality.)

It is interesting to note a possible link between increased DA levels and reduced cerebral glucose metabolism. From a study using PET (Chapter 8), Wiesel *et al.* (1987) reported increased glucose metabolism in the left amygdala of healthy controls and paranoid subjects but increased metabolism in the right amygdala in hebephrenics. In caution, it should first be noted that Reynolds' subjects were not young, and Wiesel's hebephrenics had the more chronic course and a longer history of neuroleptic therapy than the paranoid patients.

Haberland and Hetey (1987) recently reported increases ($\sim 250\%$) of high affinity uptake of DA and NA in synaptosomes from the N. accumbens and neostriatum but not from the frontal cortex of schizophrenics. This was a careful study in which material was only taken from patients with first rank Schneiderian symptoms (Crow's type I syndrome; Chapter 1). The increase was independent of whether subjects had received neuroleptics in the previous year ($n = 6$ v 6). Furthermore, they claimed that DA release was also decreased after physiological stimulation (with potassium). Unfortunately, Czudek and Reynolds (1989) were unable to find binding changes at the presynaptic DA site using a new ligand (GBR 12935).

Nonetheless, such results would be compatible with small increases of DA and decreases of HVA in brain tissue (reported earlier), which in turn could lead to compensatory increases of DA receptors. This interpretation is based on the expectation that an increase in the measurable pool of DA means that it is not being actively used for transmission. This argument receives support from decreased HVA levels, since this metabolite reflects postsynaptic activity. When overall DA neurotransmission is low or lower than might be expected, conditions are appropriate for an increase in the number of postsynaptic receptors. Such an increase may be viewed as a homeostatic response to reinstate former higher levels of neurotransmission.

Next, *postmortem* studies of DA binding sites will be considered.

"Schizophrenia breakthrough claimed: scientists find 'sites of craziness' " (*Los Angeles Times*, Nov. 9, 1977)

Looking at the results some 10–15 yr later, can it be said that the jubilation was justified? The proposal of the DA hypothesis certainly initiated a feverish round of studies in the late 1970s. Numerous reports emerged from the major centers at the NIMH in Bethesda, Maryland, (R. Wyatt); the National Centre for Nervous, Mental, and Muscular Disorders in Tokyo (M. Toru); and cooperative work both in England between the Clinical Research Centre at Harrow (T. Crow) and Addenbrooke's Hospital in Cambridge (L. Iversen, E. Bird, G. Reynolds) and between the Clarke Institute of Psychiatry in Toronto, Canada (P. Seeman) and the Neurobiology (K. Jellinger, P. Riederer) and Biochemical Pharmacology (O. Hornykiewicz ) Institutes in Vienna. Cooperation is continuing between these investigators, although many have moved to new addresses and the number of collaborators has increased.

In contrast to CSF studies, an increase of central DA receptors was shown by binding studies in numerous laboratories (Crow *et al.,* 1978, 1979; Lee and Seeman, 1978, 1980; Owen *et al.,* 1978; Reisine *et al.,* 1980; Reynolds *et al.,* 1981; Mita *et al.,* 1986). The main regions studied came from the basal ganglia (i.e., nuclei caudatus, putamen, accumbens, substantia nigra; Owen *et al.,* 1984). The increase was approximately 40% and was based on at least 142 subjects. However, it should be emphasized that a considerable overlap was seen between the amount of binding shown in healthy subjects and schizophrenic patients.

However, apart from the methodological problems already raised, these studies were concerned with a very limited range of brain regions from patients who had been treated with neuroleptics for years. This presents at least four problems: (1) not every DA area may be overactive (some may be underactive); (2) there has been disagreement on the precise localization of the N. accumbens (is the septum or other related region involved?); (3) long-term blockade of neurotransmission with neuroleptics clearly leads to the development of increased numbers of DA receptors in animals (e.g., Clow *et al.,* 1980) and humans (e.g., Mackay *et al.,* 1982); and (4) long-term medical treatment and institutionalization may lead to differential trophic effects (e.g., lateralized and region-specific changes, reduction of neurons, increase of glia, disorganization of neuronal elements, and the resulting changes in the distribution and affinity of receptors; see Chapter 4).

The questions of regional specificity and increased binding after treatment still have not been addressed satisfactorily. Although there are reports suggestive of increased binding elsewhere in the brain (e.g., frontal cortex), the results may be questioned on the basis of the specificity of the substances (ligands) for DA binding sites and medication (see Bennett *et al.*, 1979; Whitaker *et al.*, 1981). The meaning of receptor increases in a few patients that were unmedicated for a year (e.g., Crow *et al.*, 1978, 1979) or after withdrawal of treatment for a few weeks is questionable in view of reports of no increases in small groups of unmedicated patients (Reynolds *et al.*, 1981; Mackay *et al.*, 1982) and the long-term changes that remain following the withdrawal of neuroleptic treatment in animals (e.g., Clow *et al.*, 1980; Owen *et al.*, 1980).

It must be emphasized that there is no doubt that many schizophrenics show an increased number of $D_2$-type DA binding sites. What has not been clearly established is that this increase is related causally to the illness (or some symptoms) independent of treatment after illness onset. This having been said, there are three reasons why it can be argued that some schizophrenics (possibly a subgroup) may show an increased number of $D_2$ sites related to the illness and why this effect should be considered.

First, Crow and colleagues (e.g., Cross *et al.*, 1983), who have conducted extensive analyses at the Clinical Research Centre in Harrow, claim that there is a positive relationship between psychotic symptoms and an increased density of DA receptors in patients who have not received neuroleptic medication ($n = 14$; $r = 0.7$). They further reported that patients with Huntington's chorea, treated with doses of neuroleptics similar to those used for schizophrenics, show a much lower increase in the number of binding sites than would be expected from a comparison with animal studies (i.e., 25% increase).

This brings the discussion to the second reason. The 25% increase just mentioned relates to the lower of two modes of binding reported from an extensive study of brain material collected from four countries by Seeman and his colleagues in Toronto (Seeman *et al.*, 1987; Figure 13.5). The second mode of binding refers to a 2.3-fold increase of DA-binding density in the nuclei of the caudate, putamen, and accumbens. Material from both modes had similar binding affinities, suggestive of similar medication dosages *premortem* and adequate washing of the tissue in the analysis. The 25% increase of binding was found in 27 caudate and 14 accumbens nuclei; the degree of increase matches that seen in neuroleptic treated patients with Alzheimer's and Huntington's diseases (Figure 13.5). A 130% increase of binding was found in 24 caudate and 17 accumbens nuclei and seems to be unique to schizophrenic tissue.

The third reason refers to use of the technique of the future, namely, brain imaging of binding *in vivo*. Using PET to give tomographic images of the distribution of a radioactively labeled $D_2$ ligand (methylspiperone) in the brain, Wong and colleagues (1986) at the John Hopkins Medical Institutions

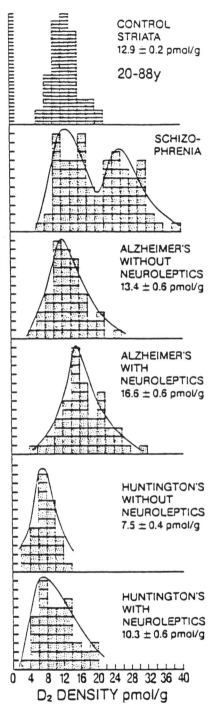

**Figure 13.5** A comparison of dopamine $D_2$ densities in control and diseased striata from neuroleptic patients. Each rectangle indicates one striatum. The striata from schizophrenics showed a bimodal distribution of $D_2$ densities at 14 and 26 pmol/g (after Seeman *et al.*, 1987).

**Table 13.1** PET Studies of Neuroleptic Binding in Neostriatum of Normal Subjects and Schizophrenic Patients[a]

| Reference | Subjects[b] | n | Age (yr) | B max |
|---|---|---|---|---|
| Farde et al., 1986 | C | 4 | — | 14 ± 2 |
| Wong et al., 1986a,b | C | 4 | — | 9 ± 1 |
| | C | 11 | (24) | 17 ± 3 |
| | S, drug-naive | 10 | (31) | 42 ± 5 |
| | S, drug-treated | 5 | (27) | 43 ± 5 |
| Farde et al., 1987 | C | 14 | (29) | 25 ± 6 |
| | S, drug-naive | 15 | (24) | 25 ± 7 |
| Martinot et al., 1989, | C | 12 | (29) | 2.05 ± 0.2[c] |
| 1990 | S, never drug-treated | 9 | | |
| | S, 1 hr drug-free | 3 | (29) | 2.08 ± 0.3[c] |

[a]After Andreasen et al., 1988.

[b]C, normal; S, schizophrenic; mean ages are given for combined index and comparison groups.

[c]Striatum/cerebellum ratio: long half-life of ligand prevented partial saturation plot to determine B max.

in Baltimore reported increased $D_2$ binding in the neostriatum of a few neuroleptic-naive subjects (see Table 13.1). Their values for the density of $D_2$ binding match those of Seeman and colleagues (1987). However, care must be exercised before accepting these results. The group from the Karolinska Institute in Sweden (Farde et al., 1987) found high levels of binding in their PET studies, using raclopride, in both controls and schizophrenics. A group in Paris found that six patients with acute exacerbations showed approximately 20% more binding, using the ligand bromospiperone, than the chronic patients (Martinot et al., 1989). Given the diversity of methodology used by these groups, the occurrence of discrepant results is not surprising (see workshop discussion in Andreasen et al., 1988; see also Table 13.1). Further, studies to replicate and refine the methods in these initial studies are anticipated.

It remains to be seen if increased $D_2$ binding really is characteristic of acute schizophrenics (when neuroleptic therapy is most likely to be beneficial) or whether it is perhaps related to another subgroup. The problem is illustrated by a recent report on material from 27 schizophrenics (Kornhuber et al., 1989). Increased numbers of $D_2$ binding sites were found in the 18 patients treated with neuroleptics in the previous 3 months but not in the 9 who had been free of medication during the same period. The authors could not clearly relate the difference to the presence of positive symptoms since these were shown by the medicated subjects.

What about the $D_1$ binding site? If DA systems are altered in (some)

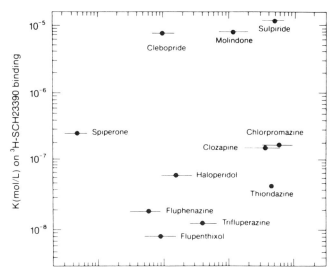

**Figure 13.6** Correlation between log affinities for the dopamine $D_1$ ligand SCH23390 and the log clinical potencies of phenothiazines and neuroleptics of a similar structure (correlation between actual $K_i$ and dose was $r = 0.95$, $p < 0.001$) (after Seeman *et al.*, 1986; see also Hess *et al.*, 1987).

schizophrenics, then, *a priori*, some changes of function might be expected at the level of both receptor types. Behavioral pharmacological studies strongly support the idea that the complete expression of DA function involves $D_1$–$D_2$ interactions—$D_1$ receptor activation may "enable" $D_2$-mediated function (Clark and White, 1987). As can be seen from the clinical efficacy of typical neuroleptics (Figure 13.6), the $D_1$ site is only modestly implicated; thus, on this basis, the evidence for the involvement of $D_1$ sites in schizophrenia is weaker than that for the $D_2$ sites. However, it is intriguing to note that the ability of atypical neuroleptics to displace the binding of a specific $D_1$ antagonist (SCH 23390) shows a rank order of potency roughly paralleling their clinical potency (Andersen *et al.*, 1986). Indeed the search for potential changes of $D_1$ binding in schizophrenia has been limited because $D_1$-specific ligands only became available in the mid-1980s.

Early studies of adenylate cyclase activity, part of the second messenger system at $D_1$ receptor sites, and the first attempt to measure the binding of the antagonist SCH 23390 proved inconclusive (Carenzi *et al.*, 1975; Cross *et al.*, 1981; Memo *et al.*, 1983; Pimoule *et al.*, 1985). However, the transatlantic cooperation between the laboratories mentioned earlier has enabled more than 25 brains to be analyzed for $D_1$ binding. At levels of 19 pmol/g in the striatum, there is absolutely no difference compared with Alzheimer patients, L-DOPA-treated Parkinson's patients, or age-matched healthy controls

(Seeman *et al.*, 1987). The question of binding outside the basal ganglia remains open for the moment.

A group from the University of California at San Diego (Hess *et al.*, 1987) recently claimed that there was a decrease of the number of striatal $D_1$ sites but an increase of their affinity ($n = 8$). However, this was not confirmed in a study of 14 patients in England (Reynolds and Czudek, 1988). [The long-term treatment of animals with conventional neuroleptics can induce a decrease of $D_1$ receptor sensitivity (Jenner *et al.*, 1985; Ryan-Jastrow and Gnegy, 1989)].

Apart from the major binding sites, there remain many aspects of DA neurotransmission to be investigated. The first obvious possibility is that the synthetic enzyme (tyrosine hydroxylase), the enzyme responsible for converting DA to NA (dopamine beta hydroxylase) and the enzymes responsible for the metabolism of DA (monoamine oxidase and catechol-O-methyltransferase) show different levels of activity. Although the activity of these enzymes in the cerebral tissue of schizophrenics has not been widely studied, the reports available suggest that there are no changes (McGeer and McGeer, 1977; Cross *et al.*, 1978; Crow *et al.*, 1979; Toru *et al.*, 1982).

Other possibilities for changes in the mechanisms of DA transmission include enhanced coupling of DA receptor activation to second messengers and the nature of the interchange between sites of high and low affinity for DA (and ligands), particularly at $D_2$ binding sites. It remains equivocal whether the postsynaptic receptor normally operates in a high- or low-affinity state; evidence exists for both possibilities (Seeman, 1987). It is conceivable that the high-affinity state is usual, but in schizophrenia the proportion is higher, the mechanisms for their desensitization to low-affinity states are impaired, or both.

Finally, as a cautionary comment, it should not be forgotten that the DA hypothesis arose out of the relationship between the therapeutic and binding properties of neuroleptics. Twenty years ago there appeared to be a relationship between anticholinergic and therapeutic effects in the treatment of Parkinson's patients. We now know that this was a red herring and that the predominant problem was DA deficiency, which impaired the inhibition of postsynaptic cholinergic neurons.

## D. A Role for Noradrenaline

DA may not be the only transmitter with a putatively impaired function in some schizophrenics. There is some evidence that the other catecholamine with a widespread distribution in the central nervous system, namely noradrenaline (NA) (Moore and Bloom, 1978), may function anomalously in some patients (Hornykiewicz, 1982; Van Kammen and Antelman, 1984). As with DA the reasoning starts with the pharmacological effects of some therapeutic agents. A range of neuroleptics (e.g., chlorpromazine, clozapine) antagonize NA function to a greater or lesser extent (Peroutka and Snyder, 1980).

A few *postmortem* studies have noted a modest increase of levels of NA or of its metabolites in closely related limbic nuclei (e.g., N. accumbens, septum; Farley *et al.*, 1978; Crow *et al.*, 1979; Kleinman *et al.*, 1983). However, these results have not been consistently confirmed (Iversen *et al.*, 1983). More consistently, raised levels of NA have been found in the CSF, but without changes of its metabolite (Gomes *et al.*, 1980; Sternberg *et al.*, 1981; Kemali *et al.*, 1982). Small increases of the NA metabolite MHPG (3,4-methoxy-hydroxy-phenylglycol) are sometimes seen in patients on admission, in parallel with increased sympathetic activity (Swahn and Sedvall, 1988). However, these changes may quickly disappear following treatment. These heterogeneous results show that it remains unclear whether NA changes are a result of the schizophrenic condition or are effects of medication (Gattaz *et al.*, 1983). (Many of the patients in these studies had been free of medication for a mere 15 days. This is a very short period with respect to the persistence of effects after years of neuroleptic treatment.)

Indirect evidence suggesting that levels of NA activity remain unchanged in the schizophrenic condition comes from reports that levels of the enzyme required to convert DA to NA, dopamine beta hydroxylase (DBH), are usually not different between schizophrenics and healthy controls, but are lower in those with a good prognosis who respond to neuroleptic treatment (Sternberg *et al.*, 1982; 1983). DBH levels remain remarkably consistent and independent of mental state or treatment.

Van Kammen and colleagues have raised the question of whether NA (or DA) levels might reflect the state of the individual patients (e.g., agitation) rather than representing any basic enduring neurochemical disturbance that could be regarded as a trait of schizophrenia (Van Kammen and Antelman, 1984; Van Kammen *et al.*, 1985). After all, there are changes of NA activity between the states of mania and depression in patients with affective disorder (metabolism is higher in manic phases; Post *et al.*, 1980; Gerner *et al.*, 1984). The infamous lack of consistency in repeated NA analyses suggests that the data do not provide a sound basis for generalizations on the effects of illness. NA levels may reflect mental state (e.g., arousal, stress), time of day, or a number of other factors.

Nevertheless, changes of markers for NA activity have been found in a range of schizophrenics. However, it is of interest that chronic paranoid subjects predominate, showing quantitatively larger changes whether they be of limbic levels of NA (Farley *et al.*, 1978), of its metabolite (Kleinman *et al.*, 1983), or of CSF NA (Lake *et al.*, 1980).

Van Kammen found that patients on neuroleptic treatment who deteriorate after a challenge with amphetamine will deteriorate on withdrawal of the neuroleptic. Those who do not deteriorate tend not to relapse on withdrawal of treatment (*n* = 50; review by Angrist and Van Kammen, 1984).

Administration of amphetamine does not only promote psychosis but also increases CSF levels of NA and DA (Perlow *et al.*, 1980). Psychosis can be aggravated by promoting synaptic NA activity (e.g., imipramine, yohimbine; Glazer et al., 1987) or improved if NA availability is reduced (e.g., clonidine; Hornykiewicz, 1982). However, $\alpha$-NA receptors are not clearly elevated (platelet sites; Kafka and Van Kammen, 1983) and antagonists (e.g., phenoxybenzamine) are without therapeutic effect. The $\alpha$-2 inhibitory agonist, clonidine, was found to be as useful as neuroleptic therapy in a few (paranoid) schizophrenics in a double-blind study (Freedman et al., 1982; Van Kammen et al., 1989). Using a relatively high dose (0.8 mg/d), a mild improvement of negative and positive features as well as of some cognitive problems was reported. Treatment was also associated with marked decreases of blood pressure and heart rate.

Four of five double-blind studies report that propranolol, which is an antagonist at the $\beta$-NA binding site, can have a mild therapeutic effect. It is better than placebo, but not as effective as haloperidol; it may be useful as an adjunct to neuroleptic therapy (Lindstrom and Persson, 1980; Yorkston et al., 1981; Peet et al., 1981; Pugh et al., 1983; Manchanda and Hirsch, 1986). Peet et al. (1981a,b) is of the view that pharmacokinetic interactions between propranolol and neuroleptics are responsible for an enhanced efficacy of neuroleptic treatment. However, production of a second messenger (cAMP), through adenylate cyclase activity, is associated with the $\beta$ receptor. Such activity tends to be low in schizophrenics but is restored by propranolol treatment. Thus there may be a basis for the mild therapeutic affects of $\beta$ blockade (Kafka and Van Kammen, 1983).

It seems reasonable to conclude that NA function may be mildly disturbed in many schizophrenics. In some cases this may be exaggerated by the state of the individual. However, if there is a change of DA activity, either as a result of the illness or through medication, then alterations of NA level are likely to be a consequence (i.e., changes of NA levels are likely to be either secondary or iatrogenic in nature). This would be expected from pharmacological (Tassin et al., 1982) and behavioral (Oades et al., 1986) studies of the nature of DA–NA interactions in animals. Metabolism of both transmitters is regionally highly sensitive to various forms of stress (Herman et al., 1982). It may be appropriate to draw analogies with Parkinsonism and presenile dementia. In these illnesses, the primary motor and cognitive deficits seem to be largely attributable to deficiencies of DA and acetylcholine, respectively. However, in the advanced stages there are deficits of NA activity in both cases. Thus, in schizophrenia there may also be a limited role for NA treatment restricted to some symptoms of cognitive dysfunction.

## E. Neurotransmission Problems in Other Biogenic Amine Systems

In view of the widespread interactions between neurotransmitters and the numerous side-effects of antipsychotic medication, it is not surprising that there are reports of possible anomalous function for almost all neurotransmitters and mechanisms of neurotransmission in schizophrenia.

Prior to the 1970s it was popular to consider a serotonergic dysfunction in schizophrenia, largely because of the serotonergic action of a number of hallucinogenic compounds. Since the mid-1960s, there have been more than 20 reports published on the levels of the serotonergic metabolite 5-hydroxyindoleacetic acid (5-HIAA) in the CSF. Most researchers found that schizophrenics showed no significant differences (Potkin *et al.*, 1983; Losonczy *et al.*, 1986). This is emphasized by the negative finding of Lindstrom (1985) with patients free of medication.

However, following a few early reports of lower than normal levels of 5-HIAA, it emerges from more recent investigations that two features of schizophrenic patients may increase the likelihood that decreased levels are found in the CSF. An unequivocal increase of cerebral ventricle size, revealed by computer tomography (implying the presence of cerebral atrophy) is likely to be associated with reduced levels of 5-HIAA (Potkin *et al.*, 1983; Nyback *et al.*, 1983; Losonczy *et al.*, 1986; see also Chapter 8). Also, a demonstrated suicidal tendency may also be associated with low levels of 5-HIAA (Banki *et al.*, 1984; Ninan *et al.*, 1984). There are conflicting data on this point, and the result could not be replicated in all laboratories (Roy *et al.*, 1985). Indeed, a *postmortem* study that included schizophrenics who had committed suicide actually showed increases of serotonin and 5-HIAA in some regions (Korpi *et al.*, 1986). Consequently, the reader should realize that data from such patients should not be considered when making generalizations about the role of serotonin metabolism in schizophrenia. In general, no abnormalities have emerged in the serotonin or kynurenine metabolic pathways of schizophrenics (e.g., Joseph *et al.*, 1979).

*Postmortem* studies of brain tissue from a few schizophrenics have suggested that serotonin levels may be higher than usual in the basal ganglia, but there are conflicting data for the hypothalamus (Crow *et al.*, 1979; Winblad *et al.*, 1979; Farley *et al.*, 1980). More recent suggestions of changes in some of the binding sites in the frontal cortex have also resulted in inconclusive or negative results (Bennett *et al.*, 1979; Whitaker *et al.*, 1981; Reynolds *et al.*, 1983; Mita *et al.*, 1986).

The therapeutic potential of agents that reduce the availability of serotonin or block its postsynaptic action have occasionally been studied. (For a review see Bleich *et al.*, 1988.) Although some improvement of negative symptoms is reported, the efficacy of such agents in treating the cognitive problems of schizophrenics is inferior to that of conventional neuroleptics. It remains equivocal whether these results mean anything more than that serotonergic activity may be secondarily associated with the occurrence of a restricted subset of symptoms. They do not illuminate the etiology of the illness. As mentioned in connection with studies of NA, it should not be overlooked that changes of DA activity, whether brought about by the illness or its treatment, can have major effects on serotonergic activity and function (e.g., Stachowiak *et al.*, 1984).

Glutamate (Kim *et al.*, 1980) and gamma-amino-butyrate (GABA; Garbutt and Van Kammen, 1983) transmission have also been proposed to be deficient in schizophrenia. Pathways using both these transmitters are extremely widespread and numerous in the brain. In many areas, neurons using these transmitters are directly afferent (e.g., excitatory glutamate) or efferent (e.g., inhibitory GABA) to DA neurons. Furthermore, the GABA agonist muscimol is hallucinogenic. Neither therapeutic nor analytic studies have provided conclusive evidence in support of these proposals (Garbutt and Van Kammen, 1983; Korpi *et al.*, 1987). Certainly results from some laboratories have reported increased levels of glutamate that may even correlate with decreases of GABA in brain areas such as the neostriatum, thalamus, and cortex (e.g., Kutay *et al.*, 1989). However, occasional positive reports have proved difficult to replicate; this is very likely attributable to a host of methodological problems in the rapid and reliable assessment of amino acids *postmortem* (Perry *et al.*, 1989).

Recently, in view of increasing evidence of structural disturbance to the frontal and temporal lobes in some schizophrenics (Chapters 8 and 16), interest has increased in the study of binding sites for the amino acid transmitters in these areas. A group from Manchester reported decreased binding of a ligand for GABA uptake sites (nipecotic acid) bilaterally in the amygdala and hippocampus and in the left polar temporal lobe of 22 schizophrenics compared with an equal number of healthy controls (Simpson *et al.*, 1989). Another British group has claimed a reduction of glutamate uptake in the left polar temporal region (Deakin *et al.*, 1989). Deakin and co-workers also reported increases bilaterally in orbitofrontal regions (using aspartate as a ligand). This area is closely connected with the prefrontal and frontal eye field regions where Nishikawa *et al.* (1983) originally found increases in 12 schizophrenics using kainate as a ligand. This group from Japan reported that the changes did not correlate with the length of time the patients had been free of medication or even their length of illness. Using yet another ligand (MK-801), a German group from Würzburg (Kornhuber *et al.*, 1989) found increases in the putamen and a tendency for increases in prefrontal, amygdaloid, and hippocampal regions.

It is very difficult to draw any firm conclusions from these five studies, especially since the methods were different and a different ligand was used in each study. Furthermore, the transmitter system under study is extremely complex. One not only has to take into account binding sites of different affinity and their presynaptic and postsynaptic loci, but also that the glutamate system has three types of receptors [named after their best known ligands N-methyl-D-aspartate (NMDA), kainate, and quisqualate]. However, there is no direct conflict between these studies. In addition, they do point to differential changes of innervation in temporal–limbic versus frontal lobe structures.

Furthermore, it should be noted that these and other transmitters sometimes show anomalous activity in schizophrenics as a result of a chain effect with a causal origin elsewhere in other transmitter systems (Oades, 1982). This seems even more plausible in light of the evidence implicating DA function and the location in some brain areas of glutamate and GABA receptors on elements of DA neurons.

Finally, it would be foolish to overlook the fact that there may be widespread changes of membrane factors or second messengers affecting release and transmission in more than one transmitter system. It has already been suggested that this is an under investigated area (cf. Smythies, 1984). The changes of cAMP production described earlier may provide just one such indicator.

## F. Neuropeptides—Problems of the Present, Studies for the Future

Over the past 10 years, there have been great advances made in the methodology for determining the levels and the binding of peptides in the CNS (e.g., immunohistochemistry and immunocytochemistry). These peptides basically consist of 3–33 amino acid residues joined together in a chain. They are "neuropeptides," which means that there is considerable evidence that they are released at nerve terminals as agents of chemical neurotransmission in much the same way as the more conventional transmitters that have already been discussed.

Some reports of apparent neuropeptide abnormalities associated with schizophrenia are therefore worth noting. Caution is necessary in considering these reports, since most findings still require adequate confirmation. This field of study is not mature enough for generalization. Even if some of these reports are confirmed, great methodological difficulties need to be overcome in order to manipulate the metabolism of molecules that, for the most part, do not cross the blood–brain barrier. Considered here are three groups of these peptides: (1) the family of endorphins (the body's *endo*genous substances with mor*phine*-like properties); (2) peptides known to be associated with the VTA–DA system (ventral tegmental area of the midbrain); and (3) peptides not directly associated with the VTA–DA system.

Changes of central endorphin activity have been proposed to explain (1) the positive Schneiderian symptoms of hallucinations and illusions; and (2) the reduced pain sensitivity frequently shown by patients with blunted negative symptoms. There have been many studies of endorphin-like material in plasma, urine, and CSF. It is necessary to re-emphasize that no clear relationship has been established between central nervous and CSF levels and those found in urine and plasma. Furthermore, results are heterogeneous as a result of methodological differences (authors have even obtained different results with different methods on the same patients).

As might be expected from a decrease of pain sensitivity, higher CSF levels of endorphin-like activity have been reported. This holds true more for acute than for chronic patients, since neuroleptic treatment tends to lower β-endorphin levels (and thus masks the true situation). Unfortunately, extreme cases of pain insensitivity have seldom been singled out for intensive study.

However, with regard to the other main proposal, it seems that for about 25–30% of patients studied ($n = 200$), treatment with the opioid antagonist naloxone could reduce hallucinations. In contrast, administration of β-endorphin usually exacerbates psychotic symptoms. (For a review, see Van Ree and De Wied, 1981; Verhoeven et al., 1986.[1]) However, the usefulness of naloxone for reducing other psychotic symptoms remains in doubt. A recent study organized by the World Health Organization (WHO) found a marked reduction of psychotic symptoms after 4 days of treatment with 0.3 mg/kg/d of naloxone. (There were 43 schizophrenic patients distributed among six centers around the world.) Surprisingly, placebo administration produced an equally large reduction. Each center reported at least one patient for whom naloxone produced a marked and differential therapeutic response (Pickar et al., 1989). It is unknown whether higher doses would be more useful. (Doses of 10 mg were used in these reports to reduce hallucinations.) Furthermore, the question of the mechanisms by which placebos can work is raised once again (cf. *New York Times,* April 3, 1979: "Placebos work, but survey shows widespread misuse!").

Thus, clearly, opioid anomalies are likely for a minority of patients. However, it is not known if these are primary dysfunctions or a result of a change downstream from the primary dysfunction. In general, there is no indication to drop neuroleptic treatment and substitute opioid antagonist therapy.

There have been comparatively few postmortem studies of opioids in schizophrenics. There is little indication of abnormal central nervous levels or binding of endorphin-like material (Lightman et al., 1979). Levels of met-enkephalin (a widely distributed neurotransmitter-like fragment of β-endorphin with 5 amino acid residues) are reported unchanged or perhaps mildly decreased in chronic paranoid subjects (Kleinman et al., 1983). This may be of interest in view of claims from a number of fields of study that the

---

[1]This article also reviews a controversial series of open and double-blind trials of endorphin fragments that have neuroleptic but no opioid properties (des-tyrosine and des-enkephalin gamma endorphins). The original reasoning for this was based on a putative anomalous endorphin metabolism. The results show a modest improvement in half of the subjects with positive symptoms who were relatively neuroleptic resistant and in 24 of 87 subjects with a range of symptoms from a number of studies by different groups. Confirmation of the role of neuroleptics rather than the existence of an opioid metabolic anomaly would seem to be indicated.

function of the amygdaloid region is impaired. In a preliminary study, one group has claimed that met-enkephalin levels are decreased in samples of the amygdala (Carruthers *et al.*, 1984). However, none of these reports have ruled out an effect of neuroleptic treatment.

Perhaps a dozen or more neuropeptides appear to influence, or be influenced by, DA activity in regions innervated by the VTA projection system. However, apart from the opioids, only two thus far have been clearly demonstrated to be associated with the VTA origin of DA pathways. These are *cholecystokinin* (CCK) and *neurotensin* (NT). Both fulfill many physiological criteria for neurotransmitters and can be co-localized with DA in VTA neurons.

The reason for investigating CCK began with animal experiments. Chronic administration of CCK with an implanted osmotic pump results in a decrease of firing of DA cells, specifically in the VTA and not the SN (White and Wang, 1985). This suggests the possibility of DA hyperactivity resulting from a CCK deficiency. Is there evidence for a deficiency of this neuromodulator?

The Belgian group that discovered CCK in the brain (Lotstra *et al.*, 1985) reported decreased levels of this peptide in the CSF of patients suffering from schizophrenia and Parkinsonism but not from depression. The decrease was markedly less in those patients that had recently been treated with neuroleptics. This latter finding may also account for divergent reports from a group in California (Gerner and Yamada, 1982; Gerner *et al.*, 1985).

*Postmortem* studies by the British groups associated with Crow and Bloom report modest decreases of both the level and amount of binding of CCK in the brain (amygdala, hippocampus, and temporal and frontal cortex of 10 regions studied). Unusual for anatomical studies, the changes of the amount of CCK roughly correspond to changes of binding. The limbic changes were associated with type 2 symptoms (i.e., the more chronic and negative symptoms), but the cortical changes were related more to type 1 features that are more common in acutely ill patients with productive symptoms (Farmery *et al.*, 1985; Ferrier *et al.*, 1985; Roberts *et al.*, 1983). Changes in both the cortex and basal ganglia are seen in patients with Huntington's chorea; no changes are seen in dementing patients.

There have been a number of clinical trials of the efficacy of CCK-related peptides. The results have been singularly unconvincing. In view of the difficulty of administering long-chain peptides (avoiding the digestive system) to reach the brain in quantities high enough for the very small fraction to cross the blood–brain barrier against potentially toxic substances, these failures are not surprising (discussion in Freeman and Chiodo, 1988).

A group in North Carolina has made particularly intensive studies of the physiology, pharmacology, and distribution of NT. First, during animal experiments, they found that NT exerts certain neuroleptic-like properties; second, they reported a modest increase of NT levels in one of seven regions studied in the brains of schizophrenics—part of the frontal cortex (Nemeroff *et al.*, 1983). They also reported a lower removal of NT into the CSF in nonhebephrenic patients, which was normalized after neuroleptic treatment (Widerlov *et al.*, 1982). Confirmation of abnormal levels of NT has been reported in acute and chronic patients ($n = 76$; Lindstrom *et al.*, 1988) but has not always been forthcoming (e.g., Bissette *et al.*, 1986). The variability is possibly a function of medication or short periods (e.g., 2 weeks) free of medication. It would be very difficult to demonstrate meaningful changes of NT parameters in the brain or CSF independent of the effects of neuroleptic treatment, which itself has been shown to be able to double the number of NT receptors in the tissue of schizophrenics (Uhl and Kuhar, 1984).

Of the other peptides studied, a decrease of somatostatin has been found in parts of the frontal cortex and hippocampus (Nemeroff *et al.*, 1983; Roberts *et al.*, 1983). However, no changes of somatostatin or of neuropeptide Y were found in a range of subcortical regions taken from schizophrenic brain tissue (Beal *et al.*, 1987). Claims of decreases of thyrotropin (cortex), bombesin (CSF), and increases of substance P (hippocampus) and vasoactive intestinal peptide (amygdala) require confirmation. Angiotensin-related peptides appear unaltered (review by Post *et al.*, 1982).

On the whole, CSF measures of peptide excretion have not shed much light on putative peptide anomalies. However, it is a welcome advance in *postmortem* studies of the brain that a number of different regions have been studied by several groups.

## II. Neuroleptic Effects on Psychopathology, Experimental Symptoms, and the Prediction of Therapeutic Success

### A. Acute Effects on Psychopathology

The most dramatic effect of neuroleptic therapy in the acute stage is the reduction of productive or positive symptoms (e.g., Schneiderian first rank symptoms of delusions, hallucinations, and thought disturbance; Chapter 1). In addition, neuroleptics lower excitability and tension through their sedative effects. As useful as their reduction is the prevention of the reappearance of these symptoms in remitted patients (Hirsch, 1986).

An improvement of clinical symptoms can occur after a few days or, more often, after a few of weeks of treatment. By 1980, Davis and co-workers were able to review over 200 double-blind studies demonstrating the efficacy of neuroleptics with respect to placebo. The results show such an advantage for neuroleptic treatment that this form of pharmacotherapy cannot be dispensed with, especially in the acute stage of treatment of schizophrenia.

Yet the degree to which symptoms can improve with neuroleptic treatment

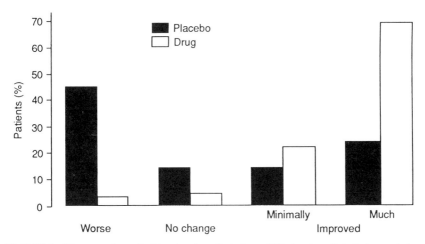

**Figure 13.7** The percentage of schizophrenic patients ($n = 344$) showing clinical change during a multicenter placebo-controlled study of neuroleptic treatment (after Cole *et al.*, 1964, and Davis *et al.*, 1980).

varies considerably. Seldom do all symptoms of schizophrenia disappear. Indeed there is a subgroup of schizophrenic patients that shows very little response to neuroleptic therapy (see Section II, B). For example, considering 68 admissions for schizophrenia, Garver and colleagues (1984) found a 60% improvement for 13 patients in 5–6 days and for 45 patients in 2–7 weeks, but 10 patients did not reach the goal of 60% improvement.

The effect of neuroleptic therapy was impressively demonstrated by a multicenter placebo-controlled study conducted under the guidance of the NIMH in Bethesda, Maryland (cf. Figure 13.7; Cole *et al.*, 1964). The 50 authors of this study investigated the effects of several neuroleptics in 344 new patients in nine clinics. The patients (age, 16–45 yr), who had been in the hospital up to 1 yr prior to the trial, were diagnosed with the most rigorous criteria available at the time. In the neuroleptic phase of the trial, almost no deterioration was noted. Despite improvements in 25% of the sample in the placebo phase (i.e., "spontaneous improvement"), it is remarkable that 75% of patients treated with neuroleptics showed a marked improvement. However, several patients (approximately 23%) showed only a marginal improvement or, in a few cases, no improvement at all. The lack of response in some patients cannot easily be attributed to prescription of the wrong neuroleptic—three different types were used. (Of course, the presence of a group showing spontaneous improvement in the short-term was not unexpected. Such a phenomenon has been regularly observed since the time of Kraepelin.)

The general conclusions from the study by Cole and colleagues (1964) are

**Table 13.2**  Antipsychotic Potency and Sedation of Neuroleptics
at Average Effective Antipsychotic Dosage[a,b]

| Group | Name | Antipsychotic potency | Sedation quotient |
|---|---|---|---|
| Phenothiazine | | | |
| Aliphatic | Chlorpromazine | + | + + + + |
| Piperidine | Thioridazine | + | + + + |
| Piperazine | Trifluoperazine | + + + | + + |
| Piperazine | Fluphenazine | + + + + | + + |
| Butyrophenone | Haloperidol | + + + + | + + |
| Diphenylbutylperidine | Pimozide | + + + + | + |

[a]From Hirsch, 1986.
[b]Relative strengths: low +; high + + + +.

still representative of those of most of the studies that followed (reviews by Norman *et al.*, 1986; Kane, 1987; Jain *et al.*, 1988; Schied, 1990, namely,

1. neuroleptic therapy cannot be dispensed with since the majority of patients show some improvement after treatment;
2. the therapeutic response is heterogeneous, and a minority of patients do not benefit from treatment;
3. there is no sound basis on which to recommend a specific neuroleptic agent for a specific patient.

This last item emphasizes an unfortunate feature of the numerous studies that followed that of Cole *et al.* (1964). They unanimously confirm that it is impossible to describe the type of psychopathology (or subgroups of patients) that predicts a favorable outcome for a given form of treatment (Goldberg *et al.*, 1972; Hollister *et al.*, 1974; Lehmann, 1975; May and Goldberg, 1978; Rappaport *et al.*, 1978; Davis *et al.*, 1980; Csermansky *et al.*, 1985). The question of prognosis will be returned to in more detail later.

If the choice of the right medication cannot be made on the basis of the differences between the dominant symptoms shown by each patient, what guides the choice of treatment in practice? All too often the clinician can only be guided by the differences of antipsychotic potency and the severity of sedative effects shown by different preparations (Table 13.2). In some cases, the clinician can draw on experience from earlier treatments.

## B. Neuroleptic Dose and Plasma Levels

A deficient therapeutic response may result for four very different reasons; each of these should be considered when a less than optimal response is present.

1. The neuroleptic does not affect the yet unknown biological basis of the patient's symptoms (i.e., the patient is a nonresponder).
2. The dose may not be sufficient.
3. There may be individual differences in the bioavailability of the drug (plasma level).
4. Neuroleptic side-effects may mask the therapeutic effect.

What can be achieved by changing the dose? In general, for patients that do not respond to neuroleptics administered in the normal moderate dose range (examples presented later), little will be achieved by changing to a very high dose regime (for comparisons of high and standard doses, see Quitkin *et al.*, 1975; McCreadie and McDonald, 1977; Bjorndahl *et al.*, 1980; Davis *et al.*, 1980; Donlon *et al.*, 1980; Neborsky *et al.*, 1981; Donaldson *et al.*, 1983; Winter *et al.*, 1984; Shostak *et al.*, 1987). However, in highly agitated (psychotic) patients, an initially high dose may be helpful to hinder psychotic development, to ensure that the patient does not damage him or herself or the environment, and to prepare the patient for psychotherapy (cf. Schied, 1990).

In order to check for possible differences in the bioavailability of the drug, several investigators assessed blood plasma level. However, levels of neuroleptic in the plasma (usually haloperidol in published reports) are unfortunately not linearly related to the clinically effective dose. Reviewing 18 studies in which the plasma level was measured, Kane (1987) stated that although some authors reported no correlation with clinical effect, some found a curvilinear relationship. In the case of a curvilinear relationship, the best therapeutic dose lies approximately in the middle range of the plasma levels measured (e.g., Breyer-Pfaff *et al.*, 1983). This middle range of the curve is known as the therapeutic window. Unfortunately, this window varies not only with the particular dose but also with the individual patient. Some examples of plasma concentrations, speaking very generally, are as follows (Jain *et al.*, 1988):

| | |
|---|---|
| Chlorpromazine | 30.0–300 ng/ml |
| Haloperidol | 5.0–15 ng/ml |
| Fluphenazine | 0.2–3 ng/ml |

The results of plasma analysis are seldom used in the daily routine of clinics for adjusting pharmacotherapy to the optimum dose. The clinician is often more concerned with reducing overt side-effects of neuroleptic treatment; this will be discussed in the next section.

## C. Side-Effects of Neuroleptic Treatment

The most frequent side-effects of the antidopaminergic (neuroleptic) treatment are various forms of motor dysfunction. They are historically known as

**Table 13.3**  Relative Frequency of Extrapyramidal Syndromes
in Patients Receiving Neuroleptic Drugs[a]

| Drug | Number of patients taking the drug | Patients with extrapyramidal syndromes | |
| --- | --- | --- | --- |
| | | Number | % |
| Chlorpromazine | 1500 | 525 | 35 |
| Trifluopromazine | 325 | 117 | 36 |
| Thiopropazate | 300 | 132 | 44 |
| Prochlorperazine | 350 | 115 | 43 |
| Perphenazine | 900 | 324 | 36 |
| Trifluoperazine | 200 | 120 | 60 |
| Fluphenazine | 200 | 104 | 52 |

[a]From Marsden *et al.*, 1986.

extrapyramidal symptoms, since they are believed to be mediated, in part, by
the basal ganglia (striatum, pallidum). This region is involved in the execution
of motor functions and receives a major dopaminergic input from the
substantia nigra. However, it should not be overlooked that there are other
parts of the extrapyramidal system (e.g., the red nucleus, cerebellum) and that
the expression of basal ganglia function does depend on the corticospinal
pyramidal tract.

Extrapyramidal symptoms are more likely to be pronounced after patients
have been treated with typical neuroleptics (e.g., butyrophenones) and if the
patients has received a high dose. They may occur after shorter or longer
periods of treatment. In Table 13.3 it can be seen that the incidence of
extrapyramidal symptoms after treatment with any of several neuroleptics is
35–60%. However, it is also important to note that there are differences not
only between different drugs but also between different patients.

The main extrapyramidal symptoms are *akinesia*, acute *dystonia*, *akathisia*,
and *Parkinsonism*.

Akinesia, albeit in a mild form, may occur after treatment with almost any
neuroleptic. It is often the only such symptom that occurs. Characteristic of
akinesia is an empty facial expression and reduced swinging of the arms when
walking or gesticulating when talking. Movements tend to be slow and can
therefore be confused with the sedative effects of treatment.

In contrast, acute dystonia is much more rare (2–20%; Marsden *et al.*,
1986; Norman *et al.*, 1986). It often appears during the first 72 hours of
treatment and consists mainly of spasms.

Akathisia is a bit more common (> 20%; Marsden *et al.*, 1986). It is
characterized by increased restlessness; the patient is unable to sit still or to
keep his limbs still.

Parkinsonism is sometimes known as pseudoparkinsonism since the condition is merely similar to that shown by Parkinson's patients. This condition occurs with a frequency of approximately 15% (Marsden *et al.*, 1986) and consists of tremor, a slowing of movement, rigidity, salivation, and often a mask-like facial expression.

Other nonextrapyramidal effects can include hypotension and tachycardia. Here, the incidence varies between neuroleptic agents. There may also be dermatological changes and altered visual or endocrine function, but these are rare complications.

Anticholinergic drugs are used in the treatment of drug-induced extrapyramidal symptoms. However, some neuroleptics, such as chlorpromazine and thioridazine, have anticholinergic effects as well as the antidopaminergic effects.

In addition, as mentioned earlier, there are long-term side-effects. These, known as *tardive dyskinesias,* also consist of unusual movements. The movements are uncontrolled and mainly center on the face, mouth, and tongue. In animals they can be elicited by stimulation of the $D_1$ receptor. $D_2$ stimulation can exert a permissive effect on the expression of dyskinesias. It is estimated that 25% of all cases develop tardive dyskinesias (Spohn and Strauss, 1989). These side effects are untreatable but "ironically, can be suppressed by the very neuroleptic medications that give rise to it" (Spohn and Strauss, 1989, p. 368). [Further details on tardive dyskinesia are reviewed by Goetz *et al.* (1986). The reader is also referred to reviews of side-effects in general by Marsden *et al.* (1986) and Norman *et al.* (1986).]

## D. Maintenance Therapy: Relapse Protection

There are no sure signs to show which patient may require long-term neuroleptic treatment. However, general guidelines for a good prognosis include satisfactory performance at work, adaptive social abilities, and a low incidence of psychopathological signs before or between episodes. It should be reiterated that this is only a "rule of thumb." There are no sound prognostic features for guiding long-term medication. Despite the tentative nature of these observations, it must be said that the protective properties of continued neuroleptic treatment cannot be dispensed with after the drama of the first psychotic episode has faded (cf. Chapter 11). Naturally, after a reasonably good course, an attempt should be made to reduce, if not eliminate, medication. However, this is only possible with good knowledge and intensive observation of the patient. Attempts to reduce or stop medication must be accompanied by intensive psychotherapeutic support in one form or another (cf. Schied, 1990).

If patients are no longer on medication, about two-thirds may be expected to relapse after 9–12 months, even after a full remission has been recorded.

**Table 13.4** Maintenance Pharmacotherapy in Schizophrenia[a,b]

| Reference | $n$ | Treatment | Relapse (%) | Dropout rate (%) |
|---|---|---|---|---|
| Treatment period: 9 or 12 mo | | | | |
| Hirsch *et al.*, 1973 | 81 | ID | 8 | 9 |
| | | PBO | 66 | |
| Hogarty *et al.*, 1973 | 374 | Drug | 31 | 8 |
| | | PBO | 68 | |
| Kane *et al.*, 1983 | 163 | ID dose | | |
| | | low | 56 | 10 |
| | | intermedate | 24 | |
| | | standard | 14 | |
| Rifkin *et al.*, 1977 | 73 | ID + oral | 5 | 11 |
| | | PBO | 75 | |
| Treatment period: 2 yr | | | | |
| Hogarty *et al.*, 1974 | 360 | Drug | 48 | 8 |
| | | PBO | 80 | |
| Crow *et al.*, 1986 | 120 | Drug | 58 | 11 |
| | | PBO | 70 | |
| Hogarty *et al.*, 1979 | 105 | Oral | 55 | 13 |
| | | ID | 69 | |

[a] Abbreviated version of table compiled by Kane, 1987. Only studies with $n > 70$ and a dropout rate lower than $n = 15$ are included in the table.

[b] PBO, placebo; oral, daily oral administration of neuroleptics; drug, daily administration of neuroleptics; ID, injection of depot (long-action) neuroleptics.

This estimate is based on six large-scale studies with a fairly low-drop-out rate. In contrast only approximately 10% of patients relapse if maintained on depot medication, but this rate may reach 30% after daily oral medication (cf. Table 13.4). [This table, derived from Kane (1987), was originally based on 21 studies, here reduced to include only those with large samples ($n > 70$) and low drop-out rates (n < 15).]

However it can be seen from Table 13.4 that the 2-yr prognosis still is not good, even after taking patients treated with depot medication into consideration. The large scale study of Crow *et al.* (1986) in the United Kingdom reported a 58% relapse rate with daily oral medication. Hogarty *et al.* (1979) in the United States found a relapse rate of 48% with depot medication. As Hirsch (1986) has remarked, it may be that the course of schizophrenia beyond a year is less influenced by neuroleptic treatment. It is possible that, in time, the natural course of the illness overcomes the influence of the medication or that psychosocial factors eventually overcome the protection provided by neuroleptics (as shown in Chapter 12). Thus, additional nonpharmacological support (e.g., family intervention) helps to reduce relapse rates further over a 2-yr period. For example, the relapse rate was only 33% for patients with behavioral intervention in the family, compared with a 59% relapse rate in the control group (Tarrier *et al.*, 1989). This point will be returned to in Section III.

# E. Effects on Experimental Symptoms

Some of the effects that neuroleptics can have on the behavioral, cognitive, and psychophysiological responsiveness of schizophrenics have already been discussed in Chapter 2–6, yet it should be stressed that neuroleptics do not affect all patterns of performance of all subgroups of schizophrenics in the same manner. The likelihood of subgroup differences has been ignored by most researchers. Indeed, only a small proportion of the range of information processing abilities that have been examined in schizophrenia also have been the subject of investigations of the effects of dopaminergic (or cholinergic) medication.

Neuroleptic treatments are sometimes reported to improve performance on reaction-time (RT) tasks (e.g., Schooler and Goldberg, 1972; Spohn *et al.*, 1977), yet an electromyographic (EMG) study specifically aimed at studying peripheral and central contributions to RTs in healthy and schizophrenic subjects claimed there was no contribution of medication to the slowed responsiveness of schizophrenics (Schneider and Grossi, 1979). Thus, it may be no surprise to see that Spohn and Coyne (1988) were unable to replicate the improvements they had previously reported. There were no effects either on simple RT or on the effects of crossover. None of these studies reported the quantity of anticholinergic medication given or the number of subjects receiving such treatment. (The reader will recall that voluntary muscle receives a cholinergic innervation.) Furthermore, Nuechterlein (1977) pointed out that if there is a generally poor response to neuroleptic treatment then there is no RT improvement. Clinical response to neuroleptic treatment remained unreported in these studies.

Similarly, on tests of sustained attention (e.g., *continuous performance test,* CPT), neuroleptic treatment is reported to improve or to not affect performance (Zahn and Carpenter, 1978; Erickson *et al.*, 1984). In a recent study designed to compare the performance of schizophrenic, depressive, and healthy subjects on a difficult version of the CPT, Cornblatt *et al.* (1989) claimed there was no effect of medication on either of the two psychiatric groups. This seems difficult to believe in view of the range of medications used, their effects on information processing in other paradigms, and their range of side-effects (e.g., sedation). A charitable interpretation would suggest that, across the group as a whole, individual improvements and impairments were cancelled out.

To clarify the point of view represented here, one may contrast the recent claims for an improvement and an impairment with medication. Oades *et al.*

(1990) studied a group of adolescent schizophrenics stabilized on neuroleptic medication with a simpler and a more difficult version of the CPT. The schizophrenics showed no differences on the signal-detection measure of judgment (beta) with respect to neurotic or healthy controls, but the measure of sensitivity ($d'$) was impaired. Measures of judgment were strongly correlated with neuroleptic dose, which here implies that treatment helped to normalize this factor. In contrast Harvey and colleagues (1990) at the Mt. Sinai Hospital in New York compared the CPT performance of schizophrenics who were free of medication for at least 3 weeks with a group receiving a standard dose of haloperidol and benztropine. The medicated group tended to show a poorer hit rate and level of sensitivity. However there is an immediately apparent difference between these two reports. The former studied patients stabilized on a range of neuroleptic doses; the latter used a single dose for all subjects without knowing if they would show a clinical response. Indeed that the medicated and unmedicated groups showed a similar degree of psychopathology points to the absence of response in many of their subjects.

Of considerable interest is that Harvey *et al.* also looked at the performance of their subjects on a *backward visual masking* task (see Chapter 4). The medicated patients made fewer detections and showed a longer critical stimulus duration. This result, of course, contrasts with that of Braff and Saccuzzo (1982), but the Californian group emphasized that in neuroleptic-responsive subjects there can be an improved performance on backward masking.

On the *span-of-apprehension* task, target detection can improve on medication in the full-report version of the test (Spohn *et al.*, 1977). Marder *et al.* (1984) saw an improvement on the partial-report version as long as the patients showed a concomitant improvement of conceptual disorganization as assessed by the Brief Psychiatric Rating Scale (BPRS). Perhaps the helpful effect of neuroleptic medication was due to suppressing distraction by the irrelevant digits.

Indeed, when distractability is a problem, it may well be positively influenced by neuroleptic treatment. An example is provided by the *digit-span* task used by Strauss *et al.* (1985). They looked at the degree of distraction as an indicator of selective information-processing ability in an effort to determine whether neuroleptic treatment improved performance. The subject was asked to repeat, in the correct order, a series of digits that had just been played on a tape recorder. In the distraction condition, irrelevant items were included along with the digits. The authors studied 28 stabilized chronic schizophrenic patients and found a negative correlation ($r = -.48$) between distractability and the plasma level of the relevant neuroleptic. Assuming there is a relationship between the level of neuroleptic measured with a radioreceptor assay and the level of neuroleptic activity, then with increased biological

**Table 13.5**  Relationship between Psychological Variables, Psychopathology, and Blood Plasma Level of Neuroleptics and Anticholinergic Drugs in 28 Chronic Schizophrenics

| Psychopathology and effects of neuroleptics | Correlation with psychological variables | |
| --- | --- | --- |
| | Reaction time | Distractability |
| PSE total score | .27 | −.10 |
| Blood plasma level of neuroleptics | .02 | −.84[b] |
| Blood plasma level of anticholinergics | −.17 | .26 |
| Extrapyramidal side-effects | .55[c] | −.02 |

[a] After Strauss *et al.*, 1985.
[b] p < .01.
[c] p < .001.

activity of the drug there was a reduction of distractability (Table 13.5). However, this conclusion is not without other problems. The authors did not measure the performance before medication; furthermore, the performance recorded did not take the severity of illness into account. If this had been the case, then higher doses would be expected to be reflected by increased plasma levels—a relationship that we know is not linear. This in turn would indicate rather improbably that the more severely ill could concentrate better. However, as can be seen in Table 13.5, there was no relationship between symptoms assessed by the present-state examination and distractibility. Curiously, no relationship was found between reaction time and neuroleptic levels, although this measure did correlate with the severity of extrapyramidal symptoms. This does not contradict the results of Schooler, Goldberg, and Spohn described earlier, since these authors did not measure plasma levels of medication.

Finally, it is interesting to note that there was no relationship between the levels of anticholinergic drugs administered to control extrapyramidal symptoms and either reaction time or distractability. It is unfortunate that the Strauss *et al.* study was not placebo controlled and that the study had no pre–post design. Oltmanns *et al.* (1978) reported that taking patients off medication can lead to increased distractability in the digit-span task, thus supporting the interpretation of the data from Strauss *et al.*, 1985.

In each of the cases described before, conflicting results have been reported for the performance of schizophrenics. However in each example these conflicts seem to be at least partially resolved if one regards separately patients known to respond clinically to neuroleptics and those who do not. Thus, at the experimental level, each shows promise as an indicator of the short-term responsiveness of the patient. Nevertheless, neuroleptic therapy does not necessarily improve all cognitive abilities (e.g., not the performance on proverb and digit-symbol tests; Spohn *et al.*, 1978). Indeed, improvements of conceptual or thought disturbance, helpful for the performance of some laboratory tests, may not be reflected in measures of total psychopathology (Marder *et al.*, 1984). Indeed, even for the potentially "good" test responder there is probably an appropriate dose range. Spohn *et al.* (1985) reported that increasing the dose can lead to a worsening of smooth pursuit eye movements, reaction time, and span-of-apprehension performance. These authors also raise the unforseeable complication of side-effects turning up in the subjects. These could easily hinder the performance under test.

## F. Latent Inhibition and Conditioned Blocking (Learned Inattention)

Latent inhibition refers to the normal ability of healthy subjects to be slow to learn that a given stimulus has consequences or associations after multiple previous presentations of the stimulus with no consequences ("pre-exposure"). It belongs to a class of tests of "learned inattention." Normal psychology holds latent inhibition to reflect a loss of stimulus salience or a reduction of attention to the preexposed stimulus (Mackintosh, 1975). Amphetamine treatment leads to a loss, whereas haloperidol treatment can enhance latent inhibition in animals (Weiner *et al.*, 1990).

In conditioned blocking, prior learning about one stimulus blocks the ability to attend to a second stimulus (with the same consequences) when the two form a compound during subsequent learning.

Since amphetamine stimulates the release of catecholamine neurotransmitters and can elicit paranoid symptoms in humans, it is of interest to see how schizophrenics respond on tests of learned inattention and if neuroleptics influence their response.

The absence of latent inhibition in a group of newly admitted acutely ill schizophrenics and its presence in more chronic patients *and* healthy subjects was demonstrated with auditory stimuli by Baruch, Hemsley, and Gray (1988) at the Institute of Psychiatry in London. These authors also showed that the absence of latent inhibition was more apparent in the more severely ill and that the facility for latent inhibition returned to normal in the newly admitted group later during a subchronic phase of their illness.

However, putatively confounding factors prevent an unequivocal interpretation in terms of accelerated learning of the associations of the stimulus in the acutely ill group. These include matching according to the nature of the pathology and medication. It may be relevant to define the pathology more closely; however the level of medication might be crucial. The theory holds that higher dopamine activity is responsible. Recently, Gray has discounted a direct effect of neuroleptic treatment here on the grounds of further, as yet unpublished work (Gray *et al.*, 1991). However, as he also suggested that dopamine transmission played a role in the subjects' performance, it seems likely that their results support our argument: where neuroleptics induce a positive clinical response they may also induce a normalization of learned inattention.

This contention is also supported by the work of one of the authors on conditioned blocking with visual stimuli in adolescent subjects (e.g., Oades *et al.*, 1991). Here, while normal blocking could be found in a subject from any of the groups studied (paranoid and nonparanoid schizophrenics, obsessive–compulsive, and healthy subjects), it was usually reduced in nonparanoid schizophrenics. Reduced blocking was usually associated with high dopamine utilization measured in urine samples. The claim that is relevant here is not the unexpected one, that nonparanoids have high dopamine activity, but that patients with paranoid features were responding positively to neuroleptic treatment in terms of clinical symptoms, dopamine activity, and blocking performance.

Future work with this paradigm might consider comparing schizophrenics with creative subjects who tend to be able to think divergently. Divergent thinking could be associated with reduced blocking and higher dopamine activity (Oades, unpublished results with students). If so, then what is the biological concomitant of the ability to control or inhibit the unwanted cognitive consequences of high dopamine activity—the element that seems to be poorly developed in acutely ill schizophrenics? Neuroleptic treatment would be likely to restrict both the desirable and less desirable abilities.

## G. Atypical Neuroleptics, Dopamine Agonists, and the Search for Alternatives to the "Classical" Neuroleptics

According to the multicenter study by Cole and colleagues (1964), one-fourth of the patients treated for 6 weeks with conventional neuroleptics did not show marked improvement (see Figure 13.7). Hogarty (1979) reported that nearly half of his patients relapsed within 2 yr, despite continued depot treatment. Thus, the search for alternative or complementary forms of treatment continues. Of particular interest are psychopharmacological agents that are more effective on the mesolimbic (mesocortical) systems than in the basal ganglia (e.g., striatum). The atypical neuroleptics seem to fulfill this requirement, since they are associated with a low incidence of extrapyramidal side effects presumed to arise from neostriatal activity.

There are two groups of atypical neuroleptics (review by Tamminga, 1983). The first contains the substituted benzamides, such as sulpiride, tiapride, and raclopride. Sulpiride is nonetheless a very effective $D_2$ receptor blocking agent (Seeman, 1980). As an antipsychotic, it is effective up to 1600 mg/day, particularly in acutely decompensated schizophrenics (Mielke *et al.*, 1977).

Unwanted side-effects in some patients include the disruption of hormonal levels (e.g., prolactin and growth hormone).

One example of sulpiride's use emerges from recent indications of mildly decreased levels of creatinine (an important energy source for muscle tissue) in schizophrenic CSF (Niklasson and Agren, 1984; Swahn and Sedvall, 1988). Levels returned to normal more reliably after sulpiride than after chlorpromazine treatment.

The best-known member of the second group is clozapine, a di-benzodiazepine derivative. As with other neuroleptics, clozapine blocks postsynaptic DA $D_2$ receptors and perhaps more pertinently, the $D_1$ receptor (Farde et al., 1988). Furthermore, it also shows an interesting array of effects, interfering with cholinergic (muscarinic), noradrenergic, serotonergic, and histaminergic binding (Burki, 1980). Clozapine is undoubtedly effective in the mesolimbic and mesocortical DA system arising from the VTA. Neurophysiological recordings show that, after treatment of animals with therapeutically relevant doses, there is a depolarization block in the VTA but not in the substantia nigra. DA release, measured in vivo, is reduced in mesolimbic areas but not in the neostriatum (Grace and Bunney, 1986; Lane and Blaha, 1986; Hand et al., 1987). Typical neuroleptics, such as haloperidol, affect both systems.

Clozapine was first shown to be effective in an open trial by Gross and Langner (1966) in Vienna. This was replicated in controlled trials by Angst et al. (1971) and Gerlach et al. (1973) in Switzerland and Germany, respectively. Clozapine is indispensable for patients who are unresponsive to treatment with typical neuroleptics such as chlorpromazine and haloperidol. Recent studies confirm the usefulness of clozapine in comparison with typical neuroleptics, particularly in managing thought disorder, hostility, suspiciousness, and negative features (e.g., Claghorn et al., 1987). A decided advantage of clozapine lies with the near-absence of extrapyramidal side-effects, but other side-effects do occur (e.g., drowsiness, salivation, hypotension, and hyperthermia). The issue was initially clouded by a number of deaths following treatment as a result of agranulocytosis, and the drug was consequently withdrawn from the market. In Europe, and recently in the United States, however, it is again possible to prescribe the drug to patients that are unresponsive to conventional neuroleptics, but only in a clinical context where continued medical supervision is available. (With weekly white cell counts, the danger of agranulocytosis can be avoided. The sensitive period for the development of agranulocytosis is from the second to the sixth month of treatment. The incidence is about 1% after clozapine, compared to 0.01–0.1% after chlorpromazine.)

Various alternative strategies for restricting DA activity have been attempted without impressive success. Inhibition of DA synthesis with α-methyl-p-tyrosine has been used as one such strategy. Alone, there was no treatment benefit and there were considerable clinical problems (Gershon *et al.*, 1967). Others have found a mild enhancement of the therapeutic effect of neuroleptics when administered together (e.g., Carlsson *et al.*, 1972, 1973).

Low doses of DA agonists can stimulate presynaptic receptors and reduce DA release. However, attempts to use apomorphine and some ergot drugs have met with variable and unreliable effects (review by Tamminga, 1983). In view of the possibility that some VTA projection areas may show DA hypofunction in patients with negative symptoms, it is interesting that some relief may be achieved by co-administration of the DA precursor L-DOPA with neuroleptics. Reviewing six open and four controlled trials, Meltzer *et al.* (1986) maintained that the improvement was greater in chronic schizophrenics with a short duration of illness. As with the studies on amphetamine (see Chapter 14), this form of therapeutic regime is still at the stage of experimental investigation.

In Section I, it was mentioned that NA dysfunction could complicate the picture for some schizophrenics. Alpha adrenergic agents may be helpful for a small group of patients, and beta blockers such as propranolol can enhance the therapeutic effects of haloperidol or chlorpromazine if administered together. Although the D isomer has fewer side-effects, the racemate at a dose of 1–2 g/day is more effective. This adjunct can be useful if patients are particularly irritable or show mania-related symptoms (Gruzelier and Yorkston, 1979; Möller *et al.*, 1979; Lindstrom and Persson, 1980).

An unusual and controversial alternative form of treatment is the administration of high doses of benzodiazepines. Improvements have been recorded in a few individual cases (Beckmann and Haas, 1980; Haas *et al.*, 1982; Nestoros, 1982; Lungjaerde, 1982; Astrup and Vatten, 1984; Gramsch *et al.*, 1984; Weizman *et al.*, 1984). These improvements usually take the form of less anxiety, but improvement of confusion and unusual thought content have also been recorded. Benzodiazepines interact with one of the GABA receptor sites. However, since the GABA system is widely distributed from midbrain to forebrain and motor to sensory system, an approach via the GABA system is unlikely to prove helpful, at least from the current theoretical standpoint. Attempts at therapy using GABA agonists and antagonists have been singularly unproductive (Tamminga, 1983). However, the benzodiazepines are a large family of substances. Recent open studies of novel triazobenzodiazepines (e.g., alprazolam, 5–7 mg) reported significant improvements in the negative symptoms of the majority of patients (Csernansky *et al.*, 1984; Wolkowitz *et al.*, 1986).

The wide range of therapeutic activity discussed in this chapter could be considered an indicator of the heterogeneity of the problems labeled as schizophrenia. A pessimistic point of view would be that all the types of pharmacotherapy tried, thus far, have been aimed at factors peripheral to the central problem of schizophrenia. A more charitable opinion points out that there are a number of neurotransmitter systems functionally more-or-less closely connected with each other (e.g., opioids–GABA–DA–acetylcholine; Oades, 1982). Pharmacotherapy has been aimed at only some of the more accessible features of the activity of a few of the potential links in this chain or net of interactions. As yet, the location of the dysfunction researchers are trying to remedy remains unclear. Each new attempt at pharmacotherapy is at best an intelligent guess, limited by the refinement of the tools available for delivery of the drug and for the appropriate assessment of its effects.

## III. Predictors of the Short-Term Course of Schizophrenia

### A. Psychopathology

Since the response of schizophrenics to neuroleptics is heterogeneous, it would be easy to suppose that the reason for this lies with the heterogeneous assembly of symptoms that can be shown by the different subgroups.

It is, for example, widely agreed in clinical practice that patients with positive or productive symptoms have a better prognosis. However, this has been very difficult to prove from empirical studies, especially since there are all too many exceptions (cf. Goldberg, 1985). Breier and colleagues (1987) from the NIMH recently studied (double-blind placebo controlled) 19 young chronic schizophrenics with mainly positive or negative symptoms. Patients with both sets of symptom showed similar patterns of exacerbation and reduction during treatment and neuroleptic withdrawal. Straube et al. (1988) examined positive and negative symptoms in 45 unmedicated patients, but did not see any relationship to the course of the illness improvement within 4 weeks of treatment with a standardized neuroleptic regimen.

Numerous other studies have tried to define similar or other symptoms or syndromes as predictors of differential drug response or spontaneous recovery. The exercise has not been successful, thus confirming the negative result of the first large-scale study by Cole et al., (1964; cf. Goldberg et al., 1972; Lehmann, 1975; May and Goldberg, 1978; Rappaport et al., 1978; Davis et al., 1980; Buckley, 1982; Csernansky et al., 1985). After reviewing the relevant literature, Davis stated, "Our inability to predict which patients will respond to antipsychotic medication reflects a significant gap in our existing knowledge" (Davis et al., 1980, p. 75). Similarly Kane (1987): "There are no well-established predictors of antipsychotic drug response during an acute episode or exacerbation" (p. 131).

The long-term course (5 or more years), in contrast to the short-term development or the response to neuroleptics, seems more closely related to the dominant pattern of symptoms presented in the initial phase of the illness (see Chapter 14).

## B. Premorbid Adjustment

Another clinical rule is that an acute onset (i.e., good premorbid adaptation) is a predictor for a favorable short-term outcome. At the NIMH, Marder *et al.* (1979) reported a connection between premorbid status and spontaneous improvement in their 22 patients over the 30-day study period. Furthermore, using a number of rating scales to assess the premorbid phase, it was possible to make a reasonable prediction about the likely outcome of neuroleptic therapy (see also Evans *et al.*, 1972; Carpenter and Heinrich, 1981). However, in the just mentioned predictive study, Straube *et al.* (1988) found no relationship between premorbid development (on the Strauss–Carpenter and Phillips scales) and neuroleptic response. Möller *et al.* (1985), in a more comprehensive study with 130 inpatients, checked 21 possible predictors (symptoms and premorbid development). Although the highest correlation was found between premorbid adjustment (assessed with the Strauss–Carpenter scale) and clinical course, this accounted for only about 10% of the variance.

## C. Test Dose–Clinical Response

A very different approach was pursued by May and colleagues (1976a,b,c, 1978) at the Camarillo Hospital in California. They claimed that the subjective (dysphoric) reaction shown by schizophrenics to a single dose of neuroleptic significantly predicted the outcome of a 4-week course of medication. This has since been confirmed by several groups. These reports suggest that, after a single test dose, the change of thought disturbance [even the total change measured on the Global Assessment Scale (GAS)] can also predict the outcome in the short-term (Hogan *et al.*, 1985; Awad and Hogan, 1988; Gaebel *et al.*, 1988; Straube *et al.*, 1988).

## D. Cognitive Variables

The Camarillo group of May and colleagues (1976c) was able to record a remarkable correlation ($r = 0.67$) between sustained attention disturbance measured by the CPT in unmedicated patients and favorable response to chlorpromazine during the following 4-week treatment period. The better drug response (i.e., 4 weeks of haloperidol) in patients who complained of attention disturbances when unmedicated was also found by Straube *et al.* (1988, 1989) in Tübingen.

Another variable that has been studied in this context is reaction time (RT). Several authors have reported that initial RTs correlate negatively with eventual therapeutic success. Simple RTs carried most of the predictive variance (Cancro *et al.*, 1971; Zahn, *et al.*, 1981). However, Straube *et al.* (1988) could find no such correlation. Furthermore, the RT crossover deviation of schizophrenics was not related to outcome (Zahn *et al.*, 1981).

## E. Test Dose—Amphetamine Response

Van Kammen and his colleagues, formerly at the NIMH and now at Pittsburgh, followed an interesting line of research relating as much to the success of neuroleptic therapy as to the putative underlying DA abnormality (Van Kammen et al., 1982a,b,c). In a double-blind procedure, they studied the acute effects of amphetamine (which promotes the release of catecholamines, e.g., DA and NA; cf. Section I). Of the 45 patients tested, 13 showed definite improvement. Deterioration was seen in 18 patients. This group showed elevated CSF levels of NA metabolites and seemed to be particularly sensitive to stress. (There were no differences in the levels of DA and HVA recorded.) Most interesting was that the deterioration was predictive of relapse on withdrawal of neuroleptic therapy. The first of these two modes of response would not be predicted by the hypothesis of DA overactivity in schizophrenia. However, another group has reported that negative symptoms partially improved after amphetamine administration to patients showing both positive and negative features (Angrist et al., 1982). (For discussion of the possibility of DA hypofunction, particularly in the mesocortical areas of patients showing defect symptoms, see Section I.)

A similar result was reported from the wide-ranging study of the Swedish group of Cesarec and Nyman (1985). They added an average of 33 mg of amphetamine to the neuroleptic dose administered to 48 schizophrenics who had been ill for 10 yr. Work efficiency improved markedly in half the group, and 32 showed considerable symptom relief. Worsening only occurred in the absence of neuroleptics. Of interest regarding an earlier comment, when improvements occurred they were also seen on tests of selective information processing including the continuous-performance, digit-symbol, and reaction-time tests.

## F. Plasma Levels of Homovanillic Acid

Before a clinician sets about finding the optimum dose of a given neuroleptic, it is important to determine if the individual patient is likely to respond at all to the neuroleptic of choice. Here plasma measures of the DA metabolite HVA can be useful, especially because they have become a relatively simple procedure to use since the availability of modern chromatographic techniques. HVA levels rise in the acute phase of DA receptor blockade and fall as metabolism and transmission decrease (see Section I). The initial peak that can be measured in the plasma reflects a contribution of HVA of central origin (Davidson et al., 1987). All neuroleptics produce this increase, albeit to varying degrees (e.g., sulpiride produces the smallest and chlorpromazine the largest peak; Kendler and Davis, 1984). Neuroleptic responders tend to have higher plasma levels of HVA than do nonresponders (Bowers et al., 1980; Pickar et al., 1984; Chang et al., 1988). Patients with more severe symptoms have higher HVA levels. More importantly, there may be an immediate rise (50%; Davila *et al.*, 1988), followed by a fall often below pretreatment levels (Chang *et al.*, 1988). In summary, the height of the peak and the depth of the fall over the first 10 days of treatment are predictive of a positive therapeutic response (see also Friedhoff, 1986).

## G. Computer Tomography

Recent computer tomographic (CT) studies report an incidence of schizophrenia of approximately 30% for patients with some signs of cerebral atrophy. Statistically speaking, these patients are less likely to respond positively to neuroleptic treatment (Weinberger *et al.*, 1980; Schulz *et al.*, 1983; Pandurangi *et al.*, 1984, cf. Chapter 7).

## H. Autonomic Nervous System Reactivity

Measures of autonomic nervous system (ANS) reactivity have also been tested in prospective studies. The paradigm common to these studies was the measurement of the electrodermal orienting response (EDOR) to a neutral stimulus (cf. Chapter 5). Frith *et al.* (1979) in the United Kingdom, Zahn *et al.* (1981) in the United States, Cesarec and Nyman (1985) in Sweden, and Straube *et al.* (1987, 1988) in Germany showed that early habituation of unmedicated patients to the orienting stimuli predicted a positive drug response. Frith was even able to obtain this result in a placebo group. However, in more demanding situations using RT and arithmetic tests, the group with a good prognosis showed a better adapted rise in cardiac and electrodermal activity than the group that did not improve clinically with neuroleptic treatment (Zahn *et al.*, 1981).

Thus patients who are likely to be poor responders to neuroleptic therapy also show poorly adapted autonomic responses; relatively speaking, the overreact to neutral stimuli and underreact to demanding task situations.

Schneider (1982) in New York, however, found the opposite to be true. EDOR nonresponders reacted unsatisfactorily to 6 months of neuroleptic treatment. The Uppsala group of Öhman in Sweden also found that EDOR nonresponders had a poorer prognosis for social and professional function measured after 1 yr (Ohlund *et al.*, 1987). (Nonresponse is more common in chronic schizophrenics.)

Can the roots for this discrepancy lie in the nature of the patient or in the time period allowed for determining the prognosis? The reports of the studies led by Frith, Zahn, and Straube were restricted to new admissions and concerned prognoses over 4–12 weeks. The prognosis period was much longer for the study by Ohlund *et al.* (1987), even though acute schizophrenics were used as subjects. Frith's study was concerned with patients showing positive symptoms whereas Schneider studied chronic patients with more negative signs. In view of the differences, it is obvious that the issue cannot be resolved without a study comparing acute *and* chronic patients with positive *and* negative symptoms using different time periods for prognosis.

## IV. Psychotherapy

There are several reasons to attempt a program of psychotherapy in addition to pharmacological treatment of schizophrenic patients.

1. The beneficial effects of neuroleptics do not go far enough or last long enough and do not affect all patients.
2. An attempt should be made to accelerate the process of rehabilitation with other therapeutic measures.
3. In all cases, but especially when the illness is taking on a long-term chronic course, an attempt should be made to make a life outside the clinic possible, and at the highest functional level possible.

This review will concentrate largely on controlled studies of analytic, milieu, or sociotherapies. The reader who is interested in a wide-ranging review of case studies involving individual, usually psychodynamic, psycho-therapeutic approaches should consult Gomes-Schwartz (1984).

## A. Milieu and Psychodynamic Therapies

After World War II, an increasing interest in the effect of the social environment on the functional psychoses resulted in the consideration of the institutional milieu as a treatment factor. Vaglum *et al.* (1985) defines *milieu therapy* as "creating a social setting and a set of patient and staff activities which would promote specific, beneficial emotional and learning experiences for the patients" (p. 349). Therapy is practiced in the patient community. Conflicts and problems are discussed on ward meetings with the patients and there is less of a hierarchical structure on the ward. Unfortunately, therapeutic teams from each institution reported using different sets of activities; this may well have contributed to contradictory results, as pointed out by Valgum *et al.* (1985).

May (1968), at the Camarillo State Hospital in California, decided to examine the effect of different therapeutic approaches in schizophrenia. He compared the results of four treatment regimes: (1) neuroleptic therapy alone; (2) milieu therapy alone; (3) the combination of the two therapeutic regimes; and (4) electroconvulsive treatment (ECT). He studied over 200 newly registered patients who had had a history of less than 2 yr of hospitalization.

Psychotherapy consisted of at least two contact hours per week; ECT was given three times a week. Milieu therapy consisted of the usual therapeutic measures carried out on the wards (e.g., occupational therapy, contact with social workers, and so on). Medication was individually adjusted with respect to the type of neuroleptic and the dose.

The clear and surprising result of this wide-ranging study was that neuroleptic and ECT procedures produced much more improvement than psychotherapy in terms of a number of criteria (e.g., symptoms, length of stay). Judging from the criterion of discharge rate, there were no group differences. The combination of medication and psychotherapy was not more successful than medication alone. Even at the follow-up 5 years later, psychotherapy could not be shown to produce better results (May, 1976, 1981). Not surprisingly, weaknesses in the study have been criticized (e.g., the therapeutic program was relatively unstructured, the therapists had had variable experience and were not regularly supervised). The influence of the therapist's individual motivation, involvement, and interest in the outcome of a particular form of therapy cannot be overlooked.

The advantage of a highly structured *psychodynamically* oriented therapeutic program conducted by a highly motivated team is perhaps illustrated by the study of Carpenter *et al.* (1977) from the NIMH. This, however, was not a controlled comparative study. Patients were administered neuroleptics when it was considered necessary, and success was not measured against other therapeutic procedures. Nonetheless, the 73 patients were reported to show a notable improvement.

This contrasts with the results obtained by the team of Grinspoon *et al.* (1972) over a 2-yr observation period. Their controlled study could find no material change in a group of chronic schizophrenics undergoing psychodynamically oriented therapy. Slightly better results were achieved by the patients undergoing a combination of psychotherapy and pharmacotherapy. Unfortunately, no direct comparison was made with neuroleptic therapy alone. Although this study was conducted with therapists experienced in psychoanalytic methods, no differences were found between the two approaches (psychotherapy and pharmacotherapy) at 3- and 5-yr follow-ups.

A similar study of chronic schizophrenics treated by therapists with a psychoanalytic orientation found a slight improvement in those receiving psychotherapy over those on regimes of combined medication and psychotherapy or neuroleptic treatment alone (Karon and Van den Bos, 1972). However this difference disappeared after 2 yr.

It is important to note that most studies have been based on relatively small sample sizes. In addition, the psychodynamic program differed in most studies from ordinary psychoanalytic therapy since it was not of the "radical revealing" type; the schizophrenic patient would be destabilized by this kind of therapy.

The conflicting results of the psychodynamically oriented therapies inspired an American team to conduct a large-scale study with 95 patients from three Boston clinics (Gunderson *et al.*, 1984; Stanton *et al.*, 1984). Two forms of psychotherapy were practiced by experienced therapists who were convinced of the value of that form of therapy (i.e., highly motivated teams). As Stanton remarked, "we selected only therapists with a commitment and experience with one of the two forms of treatment" (Stanton *et al.*, 1984, p. 531.) Patients in both groups received neuroleptic treatment. (Preliminary results are available, but the full report is not expected until later in the 1990s.

Initially, it is useful to consider the two types of psychotherapy studied as examples of the regimes available. The first relates to the normal clinical treatment of schizophrenia. As reflected by its name, *reality-adaptive support- ive psychotherapy* (RAS), the emphasis in on the management of actual problems. Disturbances are regarded as symptoms of the illness rather than deviations of personality or development. The therapy is directorial, that is, advice and hints are given to assist psychological and behavioral adjustment. Patients are seen once a week.

The second form of therapy is strongly psychoanalytic in orientation and is called the *expressive inside-oriented* (EIO) regime. The problems of the patient with perception of reality, with personal relations, and adjustment to his or her environment are analyzed using the framework of the relationship between the therapist and the patient as a model. Connections are sought between patients' current problems and past experiences. Psychotic difficulties are seen as problems in the development of the patients' personality. Inner experiences of patients are explored in order to shed light on the dynamics of their conflicts and fantasies. Symbolic content is sought in the patients' hallucinations, delusions, and secret desires, but some aspects of psycho- analytic treatment such as the making of free associations or regressive transfer, are avoided. However, the method is much more time consuming than RAS therapy; the patient on EIO therapy undergoes an average of three times as many sessions.

Early results of this study showed that both therapeutic forms could bring about changes, albeit in different areas of function; however, they did not completely confirm the authors' expectation of a net advantage for EIO therapy. Certainly the EIO therapists reported significant improvement of the patients' ego functions according to several rating scales, on which particular therapeutic emphasis had been laid. There were improvements in the percep- tion of reality and the ability to control emotions and impulses. More importantly, they were able to build up a better understanding of their psychotic nature, as well as being able to understand and express themselves better.

In contrast, patients from the RAS group had improved job prospects and were able to keep a job longer or show other indices of productive activity.

Considering the much greater effort put into the EIO form of therapy, it is perhaps surprising that its success was not more marked. Another important consideration is that the patients also are required to remain in the clinic longer with this type of therapy. The question that remains to be answered by this continuing study is whether the marginal benefits of EIO are worth the effort and cost.

It is important to emphasize that, in all cases in the Boston study, neuroleptics were administered; even in Carpenter's study they were given when it was considered necessary. No study has clearly shown that it is therapeutically responsible to dispense with neuroleptics completely. In view of the increased investment of personnel and therapeutic effort, it is questionable, even for the sake of a study, whether the inclusion of a medication-free period is realistic or indeed can even be recommended for a normal clinical setting.

## B. Cognitive Therapy

A new program for training cognitive and social abilities, based on the assumption that cognitive dysfunction represents a fundamental disturbance in schizophrenia, has recently been gaining recognition in central Europe (Brenner et al., 1990) and the United States (Spaulding, 1986). These programs seem to fulfill the requirements for a new and more specific form of psychotherapy set out by Leff (1975). The European program was initially developed by Brenner at the Central Institute for Mental Health at Mannheim (West Germany) before he moved to Bern (Switzerland).

The program attempts to help schizophrenics re-acquire their former cognitive and social abilities. It is a promising new field in which there are a number of reports of success. However, currently only two controlled studies have been published (Mussgay and Olbrich, 1988; Brenner et al., 1990). In this program, the cognitive ability to differentiate the semantic meaning of various concepts is practiced (e.g., definitions, categorization, levels of explanation, comprehension, similar, opposite, and abstract meanings, and so on). Particular emphasis is placed on improving the perception and recognition of the relevant aspects with perceptual material as well as different social contexts. The patients practice role playing, learn how to judge situations appropriately, improve communication skills in a variety of contexts, and learn to understand and manage their own behavior and problems. In practice, five subprograms are usually presented to groups of 5–7 patients: (1) differentiation of cognitive concepts; (2) perceptual discrimination training (e.g., selective attention); (3) improvement of communication; (4) training in improving different social abilities; and (5) problem-solving skills.

Brenner et al. (1990) compared a group of chronic schizophrenics undergoing cognitive training with another group receiving a nonspecific occupational therapy program. The study lasted 12 weeks, involving five meetings a week. The results of the long-term follow-up are still not available but a short-term considerable improvement of symptoms was seen in the group with cognitive training. However, it is not possible to conclude whether the success was due to the cognitive component of the training or to social therapy components.

For just such reasons, Mussgay and Olbrich (1988) attempted to eliminate social therapy components. With a small group of 15 young patients, they offered training in stimulus selection, logical thinking, concept construction, visuomotor coordination, and verbal and visual memory. The control group was offered creative occupation with painting and modeling. Some improvement was noted in both groups, with the cognitive group showing significant improvement on two of six measures. How long this improvement lasted (e.g., after release) has not been reported.

## C. Relapse Prevention

### 1. Social Therapy

Apart from basic cognitive problems, there are a number of handicaps that a schizophrenic faces when trying to return to society (e.g., withdrawal, inadequate performance in social groups, oversensitivity, false interpretation of signals in partnerships, inadequate self-presentation).

Most social therapy programs attempt, through role playing, to improve the patient's abilities in three areas of function: (1) the role of "receiver" in social interactions; (2) the evaluation of a social situation; and (3) the role of the "transmitter" of an appropriate response (cf. Wallace et al., 1980). With acute patients, an attempt is made to promote social and professional integration; with chronic patients, the aim is to improve the quality of life within the constraints of long-term support measures conducted by the clinic.

There are many reports on such programs but, with few exceptions (e.g., Finch and Wallace, 1977; Stein and Test, 1978), they concern uncontrolled short-term studies that too often do not report any information on the status of medication. In addition, the investigators do not report how long the achieved effects lasted nor whether the effect could be generalized to other areas of function in which the patient is deficient.

Perhaps the most thorough controlled study in this area was that of Hogarty and colleagues (1974) on 374 patients discharged from three hospitals in Maryland. These researchers compared the effects of social therapy with respect to the patient's setting under three conditions: (1) social therapy combined with neuroleptic treatment, (2) social therapy with placebo, and (3) neuroleptic or placebo treatment without social therapy. Social therapy was used in an attempt to improve the quality of interpersonal relationships; improve the ability to look after their appearance; teach them to avoid isolation; and offer support in financial matters, job-searching, and household management. The authors called their procedure *major role therapy* (MRT) in view of the aim to provide support when the patient faces the demands of the different roles to be played in society. Their results showed that, with neuroleptic maintenance therapy, fewer patients returned to the clinic. However, the social therapy program had no significant influence on the rate of relapse. This result was unchanged at 1- and 2-yr follow-up intervals (Hogarty and Goldberg, 1973; Hogarty *et al.,* 1974, 1979). In retrospect, Hogarty *et al.* (1975) suggest that their negative result might have been due to factors that they did not control, such as the interactions found in the family (cf. "high emotion;" Chapter 11; Leff and Vaughn, 1985).

For such reasons, Wallace and Liberman (1985) chose to conduct a controlled study of a mixed strategy consisting of a combination of social skills and family therapy. Before describing their results, an explanation of the *social skills training* (SST) is necessary.

By means of role playing, SST attempts to teach the patient skills necessary for picking up cues in social situations (receiving skills), as well as how to interpret them, how to weigh the various possible responses, and not to forget the potential consequences (processing skills). Furthermore, the patient receives practice in expressing the chosen response, verbally or with gesticulations, in a clear and unmistakable form (sending skills). Ambivalent and emotionally loaded situations are avoided.

The SST program is directive, highly structured, and subdivided into small monitorable steps. Highly structured procedures seem to be important for training schizophrenics. Programs incorporating such features can be differentiated from other forms of therapy. "In many respects it is more similar to programs for teaching motor skills (such as tennis, playing a musical instrument, or speaking a foreign language) than to traditional psycho-therapeutic interventions" (Morrison and Bellak, 1984, p. 256).

Wallace and Liberman (1985) from the Camarillo State Hospital and the University of California at Los Angeles compared the efficacy of SST with that of *holistic health therapy* (HHT). HHT aims to improve the tone of physical and mental health through activities such as jogging, yoga, meditation, and discussions on how to cope with stress and how to develop goals in life. The patients were all young and had had several previous admissions. They came from homes with relatives that scored high on scales recording expressed emotion (e.g., the Camberwell Family Interviews; Chapter 11). They were put on an optimal stabilized neuroleptic dose regime (matched between groups) and offered intensive therapy (6 hr/day for 9 mo). Both groups also received family therapy that included the patient. The emphasis and content of this family therapy differed between the two groups. In the SST group, family therapy was aimed at improving social communication abilities. In the HHT group the emphasis was on mental health, overcoming mental problems, and developing insight into familial problems.

**Table 13.6**  Mean Proportion of Correct Answers by SST
and HHT Subjects to Receiving and Processing Questions
in the Role Play Test of Social Competence[a,b]

| Group | Pretreatment | Posttreatment | 9-month followup |
|-------|--------------|---------------|------------------|
| SST   | 0.59         | 0.76          | 0.77             |
| HHT   | 0.58         | 0.62          | 0.58             |

[a]Wallace and Liberman, 1985.
[b]SST, social skills training; HHT, holistic health therapy.

The results show that patients from the SST group were more capable in real interactions and more able to generalize the social skills they had acquired. However, in terms of the incidence of the relapse of symptoms requiring in-patient treatment, the dramatic difference between the two groups that the authors had expected did not appear, although blind assessment showed that the SST group had fewer relapses through the 9-months and 2-yr follow-up stage (Table 13.6).

The reasons for this disappointment could simply be a type 2 statistical error due to small subject groups. More difficult to assess is the role of the family therapy (which *both* groups received) and the degree of compliance achieved with orally administered medication. In the following section, it will be shown that family intervention programs lead to consistent positive results for relapse prevention. With regard to treatment compliance, it is noted that the relapse rate approached that found for placebo. This suggests that, at least at the 2-yr follow-up, many patients were not regularly taking their medication. As Leff (1975) has pointed out, the success of sociotherapy does depend on continued neuroleptic treatment.

## 2. Therapy with Family Involvement

The aims of Langsley and colleagues (1968) at the University of Colorado were to reduce tension, to manage crises in the family, and thus to reduce the rate of relapse. The program involved telephone consultations and up to six sessions a week either at the clinic or at home. In a controlled investigation, Langsley's group studied the efficacy of this crisis management program for 150 families and compared this with 150 families who were managed in the usual way. By following both groups for over 18 months, they were clearly able to prevent relapses with their crisis plan and thereafter to reduce the incidence of relapse. Unfortunately, they did not report on possible differences that may have arisen out of different rates of compliance with neuroleptic treatment between the more and the less improved groups. Compliance may well have been higher in the group receiving the more intensive contact.

More recent work from UCLA (Goldstein *et al.*, 1978; Goldstein and Kopeikin, 1981) showed that crisis management that included the family could reduce the rate of relapse (Table 13.7; Figure 13.8). (In this study as with those following, patients remained on depot medication; the relative advantages of neuroleptic treatment are no longer questioned and the problem of compliance is avoided.) They compared the efficacy or combined social and family therapy (once a week) with the usual form of psychosocial care available in the clinic. The content of the intervention program concentrated on the nature of the illness, the role of stress, and possible problem-solving strategies for present or potential conflicts arising from the patient living with the family. By using the criterion of relapse over the following 6 months, the combined social and family therapy proved to be clearly superior (Figure 13.8). Unfortunately the period of therapy studied was extremely short (6 weeks). In addition to this, better results were obtained with those study patients receiving high doses of medication. It is therefore not surprising to learn that at follow-up 3–6 yr after remission, there was no further difference between the two groups (Goldstein and Kopeikin, 1981).

More stable effects in the long-term can be achieved by longer and more intensive family intervention programs. Just such an example is the 1–2-yr "psychoeducation" program of Hogarty and Anderson from Pittsburgh (Anderson *et al.*, 1986). Hogarty *et al.* (1986) presumed that many of the conflicts and much of the stress that former patients experience are due to ignorance of the family about the illness. The family often feels helpless or reacts emotionally in the face of changes that are difficult to comprehend (e.g., hallucinations, withdrawal, paranoia, reduced performance, and inadequate behavior). Much of the patient's behavior resulting from the illness is perceived as deliberate misbehavior.

In the Pittsburgh program, a number of families came together to hear about the symptoms of the illness and how, with the use of examples, they could respond to many of the consequences. Anderson and colleagues found that just by having the families meet and realize that others had similar problems, they achieved considerable relief. Since many of the families had truly isolated themselves, as a defensive reaction to the unwanted situation, the therapists expressly asked them to build up a network offering reciprocal help. The families were shown the importance of the administration of depot neuroleptics. It was suggested that schizophrenia was best regarded as a form of handicap. Overly high expectations for the outcome of treatment were reduced to a realistic level.

The efficacy of this form of family psychoeducation was compared with (1) an SST program without family intervention (similar to that of Wallace and Liberman, 1985); (2) a combination of the two procedures; and (3) a control group, to which these programs were not offered. In all cases, patients received depot neuroleptic treatment (see Figure 13.8).

**Table 13.7** Recent Family Therapy Programs with Schizophrenia[a]

| Study | Comparison groups | Timing of treatment | Place of meetings | Patients (n) | Mean age | 1st admissions (%) |
|---|---|---|---|---|---|---|
| Goldstein et al., 1978 | 2 × 2 factorial: low and medium drug dose + family crisis therapy or not | 6 weekly family meetings | Clinic | 96 | 23 | 69 |
| Hogarty et al., 1986 | 2 × 2 factorial: relative education and structural family therapy or not; + social skills training or not | Twice a week during hospitalization: every 2 or 3 wks thereafter (for 1 yr) | Clinic | 103 | 27 | 23 |
| Leff et al., 1982, 1985 | Relative education + group versus standard aftercare | 18 biweekly relatives' groups + 6 family meetings (average) | Group at clinic; family at home | 24 | 35 | 30 |
| Tarrier et al., 1988 | 2 × 2 factorial: two forms of intensive interventions versus two forms of control therapy | 13 sessions | Clinic | 83 | 35 | 30 |
| Falloon et al., 1982, 1985; Falloon and Liberman, 1985 | Family education + behavioral family therapy versus individual case management | Weekly for 3 mo, biweekly for 3 mo, monthly for 3 mo | Home | 36 | 25 | 36 |

[a]Compiled in part from Strachan, 1986.

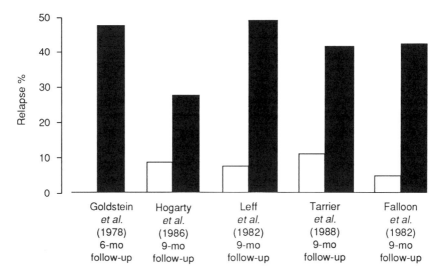

**Figure 13.8** A cross-study comparison of the incidence of relapse after family intervention programs (open bars) and no family intervention (solid bars) reported by various authors on a 6–9 mo follow-up of schizophrenic patients. Compiled in part from Strachan (1986).

There was a much lower rate of relapse over the first year in the group receiving family therapy (19%) when compared with the group receiving no family intervention (41%). Better yet was the combination of family intervention with SST—a relapse rate of 0%! SST alone, much like family therapy alone, had a relapse rate of 21% (Hogarty *et al.*, 1986). (In Figure 13.8, the rate for 9 mo is given to facilitate comparison with other studies.)

After the important role of high expressed emotion (EE) in the family was appreciated by Leff, Vaughn, and colleagues (1982, 1983, 1985), it was natural to attempt to overcome the critical stance and overemotional reactions of the relatives of schizophrenic patients. The London program consisted of three stages completed over a period of 4.5 months: (1) four lectures on the important aspects, causes, symptoms, and possible course of the illness (conducted with the individual family members at home); (2) meeting of high- and low-EE family members (in order for high-EE individuals to learn to recognize and correct their style of interaction); (3) inclusion of the patient in the group in which the dynamics of interactions were made apparent and false types of interaction were pointed out (this last phase was relatively unstructured so that needs and problems could be sufficiently articulated and discussed). However, since low-EE families had little to learn, by the time they reached stage 2 they tended to stay away from the program; thus, only the results for the high-EE group are given in Figure 13.8.

Comparison of family groups receiving the usual therapeutic advice with this newer structured form of intervention showed a clear benefit for the latter over the following 9 months (relapse rate, 50% vs 8%; Figure 13.8). The relationship was maintained after 2 yr (78 vs 20%). The groups were small (N = 12) in comparison with Hogarty's study. It is therefore difficult to make generalizations.

The intensive education program of Tarrier, Barrowclough, Vaughn, and colleagues (1988) from Manchester was also successful. Their program included (1) information about schizophrenia; (2) stress management and practice of the appropriate style of interaction with the former patient; and (3) goal planning for the relative and the patient. This intensive program lasted for 13 sessions; its success was compared with a short educational program (2 sessions) and the routine care program. In addition, medication compliance was checked with plasma analyses. The relapse rate was clearly lower than in those groups receiving only the routine treatment (Figure 13.8). Dividing the families according to high- and low-EE characteristics by the Camberwell family interview criteria showed, for patients coming from a high-EE house-hold, a significantly lower relapse rate (12%) with the intensive behavioral intervention than with the short educational program (43% relapses). (In the low-EE groups, the effect of the intervention programs did not differ.) On the side of the high-EE relatives, there was a distinct lowering of the EE status, especially according to the feature of criticism. After 2 yr there was still a significant difference between the two groups (Tarrier et al., 1989).

For some time, behaviorally oriented family therapy has been conducted by the groups of Liberman (Camarillo and UCLA) and Falloon (now at Buckingham) (Falloon et al., 1982, 1984; Falloon and Liberman, 1983). The therapy was conducted in the home of the former patient, and, in contrast to the other programs, the patient was included from the very beginning. The program provided information regarding what is known about the cause, course, and treatment of schizophrenia. In order to come to terms with conflicts and the stress that can arise, instruction was given on ways of solving problems. Methods to improve communication, both with family members and with those outside the family, were practiced. In the final phase, the success and failure of earlier intentions were discussed and analyzed. For 3 months there were weekly sessions; meetings were then held every second week over the next 3 months. The program could be conducted less intensively if this was considered necessary.

This study differed from the others mentioned since patients were not maintained on depot neuroleptic but stabilized on the lowest possible oral dose. Compliance was checked. Falloon et al. (1978) believed that too much neuroleptic for too long would interfere with the development of the patient's social abilities.

This program was both structured and intense. The relatives often made written records of the steps taken, and the therapist often gave the family some homework to write. In this way, Falloon and colleagues tried to arrive at a strategy that all members of the family had contributed to, that all felt able to carry out, and that was appropriate to the needs of each member of the family.

The authors compared the relapse rate for this program with an individual support program carried out over the same period after 9 and 24 months. After 9 months, only 6% from the family program compared with 44% from the individual program relapsed, whereas, after 24 months, there was an 83% rate of relapse for the comparison group, and only 17% showed a relapse from the intensive program (Falloon *et al.,* 1978; Figure 13.8).

From this impressive series of results there can remain little doubt about the general efficacy of family intervention programs. It should be emphasized, however, that the rate of relapse is only one criterion of success. There are many other important factors about the condition of the patient after discharge from the hospital that should be measured and reported (e.g., symptom reduction, satisfaction with life, success with vocational and social integration). Some of these factors have been the subject of study. However, since it is not possible to effectively discuss them all here, the interested reader is referred to Falloon *et al.,* (1990).

# V. Suggested Readings

For basic neuroanatomic background, read *Principles of Neuroscience* (Kandell and Schwarz, 1985); for in depth neurochemistry, *Basic Neurochemistry* (Siegel, 1989).

Anatomy relating to schizophrenia is reviewed in *Brain Areas Implicated in Schizophrenia: A Selective Overview* (Zec and Weinberger, 1986). Brain structures, transmitter systems, peptides, and information processing are discussed in the review and hypothesis put forward by Gray *et al.* (1991). Recent discussions of neuropsychology, neurotransmission, and treatment are covered in *Schizophrenia: Scientific Progress* (Schulz and Tamminga, 1989).

For pharmacotherapy, clinical pharmacology, and related biochemistry, a standard text is edited by Bradley and Hirsch (1986); see also Kane (1987) for a review of the treatment effects that includes a survey on depot maintenance treatment. The reader who is interested in the effects of electroconvulsive therapy (ECT) (an area not covered in this volume) is referred to Brandon *et al.* (1985), one of the rare descriptions of a controlled ECT study.

Psychotherapy, including psychodynamic approaches, are discussed in several contributions in the textbook edited by Bellack (1984). Falloon *et al.* (1990) give a survey on the method and the effects of family intervention programs; see also Anderson *et al.* (1986).

## VI. Summary Statements and Interpretations

## A. Dopamine

Antidopaminergic drugs reduce schizophrenic symptoms. Dopamine (DA) is a neurotransmitter within three subsystems originating in the brainstem: (1) the nigrostriatal system, projecting from the sustantia nigra mainly to the neo-striatum; (2) the mesolimbic system projecting from the ventral tegmental area (VTA) mainly to the subcortical parts of the limbic system; (3) the mesocortical system, projecting from the VTA to the neocortices (including frontal, motor, and temporal areas). (Separate DA systems also exist in the hypothalamus, thalamus, and retina.)

It is not clear whether DA is primarily involved in schizophrenia despite the reduction of schizophrenic symptoms by DA antagonists (i.e., neuroleptics). First, psychotic symptoms are not eliminated by neuroleptic treatment. Second, there is evidence for overactivity and underactivity of DA in schizophrenics, some of whom do not respond to neuroleptic treatment. Third, neuroleptic efficacy can be accounted for if DA systems are considered as links mediating some of the relevant functions, but the cause lies earlier or later in the chain of neural connections (Oades, 1982).

It is nevertheless interesting that areas that may hypothetically be critical for schizophrenic dysfunction receive a DA innervation [e.g., septum and adjacent areas, temporal and frontal lobes are responsible for initiation and switching between responses, planning and monitoring of behavior, concep-tual data processing, data integration (frontal lobes), attaching motivational and emotional attributes to events, and matching of new events with stored representations of events (limbic structures)].

### 1. Brain Imaging (PET) and Cerebrospinal Fluid (CSF) Findings

It is too early to draw firm conclusions from the few, largely negative, PET studies on DA receptor binding in the brain. CSF measures of DA metabolism reflect the influence of neuroleptic treatment.

Schizophrenics with mainly negative symptoms or with cerebral atrophy often show a reduction of the main DA metabolite HVA.

The possibility of a subgroup showing reduced DA metabolism raises a testable hypothesis.

### 2. Postmortem Analysis of Brain Tissue

More DA binding sites (at least 25%) are found in schizophrenic than in healthy subcortical brain areas as a result of chronic neuroleptic treatment. (Similar increases are seen in humans and animals after chronic neuroleptic treatment.) Increases of approximately 130% are reported from about half the samples analyzed by a multicenter study. Material from the few never-treated patients available shows an increased density of DA receptors, but negative results are seldom given prominence.

Most results concern the striatum and nucleus accumbens. One group reports increased DA levels in the left amygdala, but since few regions have been analyzed as yet, no definite conclusion about deviant *regional* DA activity can be given.

Illness-related changes in DA activity remain controversial. It is exceptional to find *postmortem* material from never-treated schizophrenics. Chronic neuroleptic treatment induces, through mechanisms attempting to compensate for blocked DA activity, an increase in DA receptors that persists for a long time after the withdrawal of treatment. Thus the only indications for changed DA activity in schizophrenia come from the report of a second mode of increased binding, which is nevertheless higher than that found in other psychiatric patients chronically treated with neuroleptics, and the lateral increase of DA levels in the amygdala that awaits confirmation from other laboratories.

Judging from the results of animal studies, second messengers involved in regulating transmission or other transmitters in the chain (e.g., glutamate) may play an important role in mediating schizophrenic symptoms.

## B. Other Transmitters

### 1. Monoamines

Some neuroleptics affect NA activity. However plausibly some symptoms can be accounted for by NA activity changes, there is no consistent direct support for deviant NA function (e.g., *postmortem* studies).

It is likely that some change of NA metabolism in schizophrenics is state-dependent and reflects stress or agitation.

Changes of DA and serotonin (5-HT) are often closely associated. Yet, despite occasional reports of receptor changes postmortem (e.g., decreased 5-HT-2 sites in cortex), specific changes of 5-HT markers have not been widely found.

Diminished responsivity of 5-HT systems (e.g., accompanying negative symptoms) may be associated with similar DA changes.

### 2. Amino Acids: Glutamate and GABA

There are conflicting reports of increased glutamate, reduced GABA levels, and glutamate receptor changes.

Neurotransmitter systems using these amino acids are widespread anatomically and may hypothetically be important in areas of function relevant to schizophrenia research. Thus, a priori changes of markers for amino acids are likely in cases showing CNS atrophy.

However, there are methodological difficulties in measuring their levels in *postmortem* tissue. Increases, no changes, and decreases of one or another of the three types of glutamate receptor are reported.

### 3. Neuropeptides

Changes of endorphin activity may be of secondary importance, contributing to some subgroup features (e.g., pain sensitivity changes). Evidence comes more from treatment effects than from brain tissue or CSF analysis. Cholecystokinin, often co-localized in DA neurons, is claimed to be mildly decreased in limbic and neocortical regions, paralleling DA decreases and chronic negative symptoms. (Changes are also found in other illnesses associated with changed DA activity, such as Parkinsonism.) Evidence regarding other neuropeptides is equivocal.

## C. Effects of Neuroleptics

Neuroleptics usually have a more clear-cut effect on positive symptoms. However, negative symptoms can also be improved, but it is impossible to predict the success of neuroleptic therapy from the clinical symptom picture of an individual patient.

Generally, about 75% of the patients show a marked improvement within 6 weeks of therapy with neuroleptics.

The concept of negative and positive symptoms may be too global to allow a more precise prediction of neuroleptic success. Predictive success can improve with some more precisely defined experimental symptoms (see subsequent text).

### 1. Neuroleptic Dose and Plasma Level

Doses in the middle range of chlorpromazine equivalents are generally more effective than "mega-doses" (i.e., "mega-doses" are not effective in those who do not respond to the standard dose range).

The plasma level of neuroleptics (assumed to be an indicator of the bioavailability of the drug) is not linearly related to clinical effect. It is evident from some studies that the plasma level in the middle range—the so-called therapeutic window—indicates the degree of therapeutic success.

### 3. Side Effects

The most prominent side-effects are alterations of motor function (e.g., akathisia, pseudo-Parkinsonism, and so on). (Note that sedative side-effects may actually be clinically desirable.)

It remains unclear if the neuroleptic-induced motor effects (via striatal mechanisms) are informative about the antipsychotic effect of the neuroleptics. Some believe that the striatum itself has cognitive (filter) functions.

### 2. Neuroleptics and Relapse Prevention

About two-thirds of patients relapse within a year if they are no longer taking medication after discharge. If the patient regularly receives a long-acting depot injection, then the relapse rate is reduced to about 10% over 1 yr. However, the relapse rate rises again for longer periods, even under depot medication.

These findings show that neuroleptics have a protective effect, but that over longer periods, perhaps as a result of the cumulative effects of stress, they can no longer hinder relapse. This situation calls for additional therapeutic measures (see subsequent text).

### 3. Effect of Neuroleptics on Experimental Symptoms

If there is a good clinical response to neuroleptic treatment then simple reaction time and distractibility are reduced, and sustained attention (CPT performance) and information processing is generally enhanced. Reports of no changes in test performance (e.g., reaction time) may reflect a similar absence of clinical response to treatment. Improvements on tests of conceptual thinking follow closely the clinical impression of improvement.

Mixed results in various reports may also reflect subgroup differences and drug-response differences (e.g., experience of sedative effects).

The reduction of distractability is heuristically interesting. One study records a negative correlation between the plasma level of the drug and distractability. The amount of distractability or of poor CPT performance is predictive of a positive response to neuroleptics (next section). In chapter 4, a study was discussed reporting that a subgroup of untreated paranoid patients had selective attention problems in a signal detection task. In contrast to the nonparanoid group, the attention disorder was reduced after medication. It seems that a drug-responsive subgroup of schizophrenics with certain positive symptoms are characterized by disturbed selective attention. Furthermore, one may speculate that these patients may show a distinct pattern of biochemical deviations related to the antidopaminergic effect of neuroleptics.

## C. Experimental Symptoms as Predictors of Short-Term Outcome

### 1. Psychopathology and Premorbid Adjustment

The prediction of short-term outcome after 1–3 mo of hospital treatment by psychopathological predictors is uncertain. Although not found in all studies, poor premorbid adjustment often seems indicative of poor treatment response.

The latter follows the principle that "like predicts like," the past course predicts the course that follows.

The poor prognostic value of the type of psychopathology, including the broad concept of positive and negative symptoms, is puzzling. (The latter was found to have predictive value by some, but not all, authors.) Psychopathological phenomena are the end result of a multitude of endogenous, developmental, and environmental influences. They may therefore only poorly and indirectly indicate the neurobiological aspects of the illness affected by neuroleptic treatment.

## 2. Test Dose

There are convincing results showing that the response to a single dose of a neuroleptic (or several over 2 or more days) predicts short-term outcome over 4 weeks.

From a biological perspective, this suggests an immediate treatment effect (although the total effect on psychopathology is not reached for several weeks).

It is surprising that the test-dose method is not more routinely used in the clinic. Early information on low drug response could be compensated for by an earlier start with alternative and additional therapeutic strategies (e.g., cognitive and social skills training; see subsequent text).

## 3. Experimental Symptoms

Poor neuroleptic response is often found in schizophrenics with fewer problems with sustained attention (CPT), lower distractability (rating scales), or, controversially, with a slower reaction time (see previous discussion), and in patients with cerebral atrophy.

Some researchers report higher skin conductance levels to nondemanding or orienting stimuli in those who eventually do not improve under neuroleptic therapy. Exceptions are seen in those who already show a chronic course when tested.

These predictors were assessed with different groups of patients. Nonetheless, it is possible to try to generalize about the characteristics of the neuroleptic nonresponder. This type of patient probably has a poor premorbid course, larger cerebral ventricles than average, a higher skin conductance level (and probably stronger responses to innocuous tones), is less distracted by irrelevant stimuli in selective attention tasks, performs better on sustained attention tasks, and perhaps shows slower reaction times.

These findings suggest again that there are at least two different types of patients that cannot be differentiated by symptom ratings.

### 4. Alternative Neuroleptic Therapy

The search for alternative pharmacological treatment aims to find substances that (1) produce fewer extrapyramidal side-effects but nevertheless interact with DA systems; (2) have more pronounced effects on other transmitter systems (e.g., NA, GABA, or glutamate); or (3) aim at those subgroups in which the DA system is believed not to be overactivated (see previous discussion).

The only practical alternatives to typical neuroleptics on the market are dibenzodiazepine derivatives (e.g., clozapine). Clozapine can clearly produce marked antipsychotic and minimal extrapyramidal side-effects. This is probably due to stronger effects on the mesolimbic and mesocortical than on the nigrostriatal DA system, as a result of inducing a depolarization block limited to the VTA. The anticholinergic effects of clozapine may also help limit unwanted side-effects.

## D. Psychotherapy

### 1. Milieu, Psychodynamic, and Cognitive Therapies

Any psychotherapy additional to neuroleptic therapy shows some success. This holds true for milieu as well as psychoanalytically oriented therapy. Most authors, however, are reluctant to use standard analytic techniques in order to avoid inducing emotional turmoil in the patient. In a well-staffed, well-trained, and highly motivated therapeutic setting, even the neuroleptic dose can be reduced.

More recently, alternative and more specific intervention methods are being installed with considerable success in several clinics. These approaches are based on the assumption that certain cognitive disturbances are central to the illness (i.e., an attempt is made to reduce the perceptual, language, and thought disturbances with these programs). Most programs also aim to reduce the emotional and social handicaps of the patients. Most of these programs start on the ward when the patients remit after an acute breakdown or are stabilized on neuroleptic therapy in the case of a chronic course.

Although every intensive program administered in addition to medication and adapted to the needs of schizophrenic patients has some success, cognitive training programs have the advantage of being less staff-intensive, less time-consuming, and can even be conducted by nurses on the ward after a short training period.

### 2. Programs Specifically Aimed at Social Handicaps and Emotional Vulnerability

Although some well-designed programs result in progress with social skills, there is much evidence that programs including the family are more effective.

When schizophrenic patients return home from the hospital, their high emotional vulnerability, their residual psychopathology, and their poor psychosocial adaptations present considerable problems for them and the family. Informing the family about the illness and handicaps of the remitting patient can reduce both the tensions in the family and the relapse rate. Modern family intervention programs aim to reduce the "high expressed emotion" style of a key family member, since this is one of the important factors contributing to early relapse (cf. Chapter 11). Such programs are very successful.

However, there is no information on the outcome of these interventions over a period in excess of 2 yr. It is not known whether these programs can really change the long-term course of the illness. Since relapse rates rise considerably after 2 yr, even with optimal administration of long-acting neuroleptics, the need for additional programs that can be shown to help the long-term course is urgent.

# References

Anden, N.E., and Stock, G. (1973). Effect of clozapine on the turnover of dopamine in the corpus striatum and limbic system. *Journal of Pharmacy and Pharmacology, 25*, 346–348.

Andersen, P. H., Nielsen, E. B., Gronvald, F. C., and Braestrup, C. (1986). Some atypical neuroleptics inhibit ($^3$H)-SCH 23390 binding *in vivo*. *European Journal of Pharmacology, 120*, 143–144.

Anderson, C. M., Reiss, D. J., and Hogarty, G. E. (1986). *Schizophrenia and the family*. New York: Guilford Press.

Andreasen, N. C., Carson, R., Diksic, M., Evans, A., Farde, L., Gjedde, A., Hakim, A., Lal, S., Nair, N., Sedvall, G., Tune, L., and Wong, D. (1988). Workshop on schizophrenia, PET and dopamine $D_2$ receptors in the human neostriatum. *Schizophrenia Bulletin, 14*, 471–484.

Angrist, B., and Van Kammen, D. P. (1984). CNS stimulants as tools in the study of schizophrenia. *Trends in Neurosciences, 7*, 388–390.

Angrist, B., Peselow, E., Rubinstein, M., Corwin, J., and Rotrosen, J. (1982). Partial improvement in negative schizophrenic symptoms after amphetamine. *Psychopharmacology, 78*, 128–130.

Angst, J., Bente, D., Berner, P., Heimann, H., Helmchen, H., and Hippius, H. (1971). Das klinische Wirkungsbild von Clozapin. *Pharmacopsychiatrie, 4*, 201–214.

Astrup, C., and Vatten, L. (1984). Effect of the benzodiazepine derivative estazolam in schizophrenia. *Biological Psychiatry, 19*, 85–88.

Awad, A. G., and Hogan, T. P. (1988). Diagnostic criteria as a predictor of drug response in schizophrenia. *Medical Science Research, 614*, 199–200.

Bacopoulos, N. G., Spokes, E. G., Bird, E. D., and Roth, R. H. (1979). Antipsychotic drug action in schizophrenic patients: Effects on cortical dopamine metabolism after long-term treatment. *Science, 205*, 1405–1407.

Bagdy, G., Perenyi, A., Frecska, E., Revai, K., Papp, Z., and Fekete, M. I. K. (1985). Decrease in dopamine, its metabolites and noradrenaline in cerebrospinal fluid of schizophrenic patients after withdrawal of long-term neuroleptic treatment. *Psychopharmacology, 85*, 62–64.

Banki, C. M., Arato, M., Papp, Z., and Kurcz, M. (1984). Cerebrospinal fluid amine metabolites and neuroendocrine changes in psychoses and suicide. In E. Usdin, A. Carlsson, and A.

Dahlstrom (Eds.) *Catecholamines: Neuropharmacology and central nervous system—Therapeutic aspects*, pp. 153–157. New York: Liss.

Beal, M. F., Svendsen, C. N., Bird, E. D., and Martin, J. B. (1987). Somatostatin and neuropeptide Y are unaltered in schizophrenia. *Neurochemical Pathology, 6*, 169–176.

Beckmann, H., and Haas, S. (1980). High dose diazepam in schizophrenia. *Psychopharmacology, 71*, 79–82.

Beckmann, H., Waldmeier, P., Lauber, J., and Gattaz, W. F. (1983). Phenylethylamine and monoamine metabolites in CSF of schizophrenics: Effects of neuroleptic treatment. *Journal of Neural Transmission, 57*, 103–110.

Bellak, L. (1984). *the broad scope of ego function assessment*. In L. Bellak and L. A. Goldsmith (Eds.). New York: Wiley.

Bennett, J. P., Enna, S. J., Bylund, D. B., Gillin, J. C., Wyatt, R. J., and Snyder, S. H. (1979). Neurotransmitter receptors in the frontal cortex of schizophrenics. *Archives of General Psychiatry, 36*, 927–934.

Bird, E. D., Crow, T. J., Iversen, L. L., Longden, A., Mackay, A. V. P., Riley, G. J., and Spokes, E. G. (1979). Dopamine and homovanillic acid concentrations in the post-mortem brain in schizophrenia. *Journal of Physiology (London), 293*, 36–37.

Bird, E. D., Spokes, E. G., and Iversen, L. L. (1979a). Increased dopamine concentration in limbic areas of brain from patients dying with schizophrenia. *Brain, 102*, 347–360.

Bird, E. D., Spokes, E. G., and Iversen, L. L. (1979b). Brain norepinephrine and dopamine in schizophrenia. *Science, 204*, 93–94.

Bissette, G., Nemeroff, C. B., and Mackay, A. V. P. (1986). Peptides in schizophrenia. *Progress in Brain Research, 66*, 161–174.

Bjorndal, N., Bjerre, M., Gerlach, J., Kristjansen, P., Magelund, G., Oestrich, I. H., and Wachrems, J. (1980). High dosage haloperidol therapy in chronic schizophrenic patients: A double-blind study of clinical response, side effects, serum haloperidol and serum prolactin. *Psychopharmacology, 67*, 17–23.

Bleich, A., Brown, S., Kahn, R., and Van Praag, H. (1988). The role of serotonin in schizophrenia. *Schizophrenia Bulletin, 14*, 297–315.

Bowers, M. B., Heninger, G. R., and Sternberg, D. (1980). Clinical processes and central dopaminergic activity in psychotic disorders. *Communications in Psychopharmacology, 4*, 177–183.

Bowers, M. B. (1973). 5-Hydroxyindoleactic acid (5-HIAA) and homovanillic acid (HVA) following probenecid in acute psychotic patients treated with phenothiazines. *Psychopharmacologia, 28*, 309–318.

Bradley, P. B., and Hirsch, S. R. (Eds.) (1986). *The psychopharmacology and treatment of schizophrenia*. Oxford: Oxford University Press.

Bradley, P. B. (1986). Pharmacology of antipsychotic drugs. In P. B. Bradley and S. R. Hirsch (Eds.), *The psychopharmacology and treatment of schizophrenia*. Oxford: Oxford University Press.

Braff, D. L., and Saccuzzo, D. P. (1982). Effect of antipsychotic medication on speed of information processing in schizophrenic patients. *American Journal of Psychiatry, 139*, 1127–1130.

Brandon, S., Cowley, P., McDonald, C., Neville, P., Palmer, R., and Wellstood-Eason, S. (1985). Leicester ECT trial: Results in schizophrenia. *British Journal of Psychiatry, 146*, 177–183.

Breier, A., Wolkowitz, O. M., Doran, A. R., Roy, A., Boronow, J., Hommer, D. W., and Pickar, D. (1987). Neuroleptic responsivity of negative and positive symptoms in schizophrenia. *American Journal of Psychiatry, 144*, 1549–1555.

Brenner, H. D., Kraemer, S., Hermanutz, M., and Hodel, B. (1990). Cognitive treatment in schizophrenia. In E. R. Straube and K. Hahlweg, (Eds.), *Schizophrenia: Concepts, vulnerability and intervention*. Berlin: Springer.

Brewerton, T. D., Berrettini, W. H., Nurnberger, J. I., and Linnoila, M. (1988). Analysis of seasonal fluctuations of CSF monoamine metabolites and neuropeptides in normal controls: Findings with 5-HIAA and HVA. *Psychiatry Research, 23*, 257.

Breyer-Pfaff, U., Brinkschulte, M., Rein, W., Schied, H-W., and Straube, E. (1983). Prediction and evaluation criteria in perazine therapy of acute schizophrenics—Pharmacokinetic data. *Pharmacopsychiatry, 16*, 160–165.

Bridge, T. P., Kleinman, J. E., Karoum, F., and Wyatt, R. J. (1985). Postmortem central catecholamines and antemortem cognitive impairment in elderly schizophrenics and controls. *Neuropsychobiology, 14*, 57–61.

Bridge, T. P., Kleinman, J. E., Soldo, B. J., and Karoum, F. (1987). Central catecholamines, cognitive impairment and affective state in elderly schizophrenics and controls. *Biological Psychiatry, 22*, 139–147.

Buchsbaum, M. S., Coursey, R. D., and Murphy, D. L. (1980). Schizophrenia and platelet monoamine oxidase: Research strategies. *Schizophrenia Bulletin, 6*, 375–384.

Buckley, P. (1982). Identifying schizophrenic patients who should not receive medication. *Schizophrenia Bulletin, 8*, 429–432.

Burki, H. R. (1980). Inhibition of ($^3$H)-clozapine binding in rate brain after oral administration of neuroleptics. *Life Sciences, 26*, 2187–2193.

Cancro, R., Sutton, S., Kerr, J., and Sugerman, A. (1971). Reaction time and prognosis in acute schizophrenia. *Journal of Nervous and Mental Disease, 153*, 351–359.

Carenzi, A., Gillin, J. C., Guidotti, A., Schwartz, M. A., Trabucchi, M., and Wyatt, R. J. (1975). Dopamine sensitive adenyl cyclase in human caudate nucleus. *Archives of General Psychiatry, 32*, 1056–1059.

Carlsson, A., Persson, T., Roos, B. E., and Walinder, J. (1972). Potentiation of phenothiazines by alpha-methyltyrosine in treatment of chronic schizophrenia. *Journal of Neural Transmission, 33*, 83–90.

Carlsson, A., Roos, B. E., Walinder, J., and Skott, A. (1973). Further studies on the mechanism of antipsychotic action: Potentiation by alpha-methyltyrosine of thioridazine effects in chronic schizophrenics. *Journal of Neural Transmission, 34*, 125–132.

Carpenter, W. T., and Heinrich, D. W. (1981). Treatment-relevant subtypes of schizophrenia. *Journal of Nervous and Mental Disease, 169*, 113–119.

Carpenter, W. T., McGlashan, T. H., and Strauss, J. S. (1977). The treatment of acute schizophrenia without drugs: An investigation of some current assumptions. *American Journal of Psychiatry, 134*, 14–20.

Carruthers, R., Dawbarn, D., de Quidt, M., Emson, P. C., Hunter, J., and Reynolds, G. P. (1984). Changes in the neuropeptide content of amygdala in schizophrenia. *British Journal of Pharmacology, 81*, 190.

Cesarec, Z., and Nyman, A. K. (1985). Differential response to amphetamine in schizophrenia. *Acta Psychiatrica Scandinavica, 71*, 523–538.

Chang, W. H., Chen, T. Y., Lee, C. F., Hung, J. C., Hu, W. H., and Yeh, E. K. (1988). Plasma homovanillic acid levels and subtyping of schizophrenia. *Psychiatry Research, 23*, 239–244.

Claghorn, J., Honigfeld, G., Abuzzahab, F. S., Wang, R., Steinbrook, R., Tuason, V., and Klerman, G. (1987). The risks and benefits of clozapine versus chlorpromazine. *Journal of Clinical Psychopharmacology, 7*, 377–384.

Clark, D., and White, F. J. (1987). $D_1$ dopamine receptor—The search for a function: A critical evaluation of the $D_1/D_2$ dopamine receptor classification and its functional implications. *Synapse, 1*, 347–388.

Clow, A., Theodorou, A., Jenner, P., and Marsden, C. D. (1980). Changes in rat striatal dopamine turnover and receptor activity during one year's neuroleptic administration. *European Journal of Pharmacology, 63*, 135–144.

Cole, J. O., Klerman, G. L., and Goldberg, S. C. (1964). Phenothiazine treatment in acute schizophrenia. *Archives of General Psychiatry, 10*, 246–261.

Cornblatt, B. A., Lenzenweger, M. F., and Erlenmeyer-Kimbling, L. (1989). The continuous performance test, identical pairs version. II. Contrasting attentional profiles in schizophrenic depressed patients. *Psychiatry Research, 29*, 65–85.

Cross, A. J., Crow, T. J., Ferrier, I. N., Johnstone, E. C., McCreadie, R. M., Owen, F., Owens, F. G. C., and Poulter, M. (1983). Dopamine receptor changes in schizophrenia in relation to the disease process and movement disorder. *Journal of Neural Transmission, Suppl. 18*, 265–272.

Cross, A. J., Crow, T. J., Killpack, W. S., Longden, A., Owen, F., and Riley, G. J. (1978). The activities of brain dopamine-β-hydroxylase and catechol-*O*-methyl transferase in schizophrenics and controls. *Psychopharmacology, 59*, 117–121.

Cross, A. J., Crow, T. J., Longden, A., Owen, F., Poulter, M., and Riley, G. J. (1978). Evidence for increased dopamine receptor sensitivity in post-mortem brains from patients with schizophrenia. *Journal of Physiology (London), 280*, 37.

Cross, A. J., Crow, T. J., and Owen, F. (1981). (³H)-Flupenthixol binding in post-mortem brain of schizophrenics: Evidence for a selective increase in dopamine D₂ receptors. *Psychopharmacology, 74*, 122–124.

Crow, T. J., Baker, H. F., Cross, A. J., Joseph, M. H., Lofthouse, R., Longden, A., Owen, F., Riley, G. J., Glover, V., and Killpack, W. S. (1979). Monoamine mechanisms in chronic schizophrenia, post-mortem neurochemical findings. *British Journal of Psychiatry, 134*, 249–256.

Crow, T. J., Johnstone, E. C., Longden, A. J., and Owen, F. (1978). Dopaminergic mechanisms in schizophrenia: The antipsychotic effect and the disease process. *Life Sciences, 23*, 563–568.

Crow, T. J., McMillan, J. F., Johnson, A. L., and Johnstone, E. C. (1986). The Northwick Park study of first episodes of schizophrenia. II. A randomized controlled trial of prophylactic neuroleptic treatment. *British Journal of Psychiatry, 148*, 120–127.

Csernansky, J. G., Faull, K. F., and Pfefferbaum, A. (1988). Seasonal changes of CSF monoamine metabolites in psychiatric patients: What is the source? *Psychiatry Research, 25*, 361–363.

Csernansky, J. G., Lombrozo, L., Gulevich, G. D., and Hollister, L. (1984). Treatment of negative schizophrenic symptoms with alprazolam: A preliminary open-label study. *Journal of Clinical Psychopharmacology, 4*, 349–352.

Csernansky, J. G., Kaplan, J., and Hollister, L. E. (1985). Problems in classifications of schizophrenics as neuroleptic responders and nonresponders. *Journal of Nervous and Mental Disease, 173*, 325–331.

Czudek, C., and Reynolds, G. P. (1989). (³H)-GBR 12935 binding to the dopamine uptake site in post-mortem brain tissue in schizophrenia. *Journal of Neural Transmission, 77*, 227–230.

Davidson, M., Giordani, A. B., Mohs, R. C., Horvath, T. B., Davis, B. M., Powchik, P., and Avis, K. L., (1987). Short-term haloperidol administration acutely elevates human plasma homovanillic acid concentration. *Archives of General Psychiatry, 44*, 189–190.

Davila, R., Manero, E., Zumarraga, M., Ania, I., Schweitzer, J. W., and Friedhoff, A. J. (1988). Plasma homovanillic acid as a predictor of response to neuroleptics. *Archives of General Psychiatry, 45*, 564–567.

Davis, G. C., and Bunney, W. E. (1980). Psychopathology and endorphins. In E. Costa and M. Trabucchi (Eds.), *Neural peptides and neural communication*, pp. 455–463. New York: Raven Press.

Davis, G. C., Buchsbaum, M. S., and Bunney, W. E. (1980). Alterations of evoked potentials link research in attention dysfunction to peptide response symptoms of schizophrenia. In E. Costa and M. Trabucchi (Eds.), *Neural peptides and neural communication*, pp. 473–487. New York: Raven Press.

Davis, J. M. (1985). Antipsychotic drugs. In H. I. Kaplan and B. J. Sadock (Eds.), *Comprehensive textbook of psychiatry*, 4th ed., Vol. 2, pp. 481–513. London: Williams and Wilkins.

Davis, J. M., Koslow, S. H., Gibbons, R. D., Maas, J. W., Bowden, C. L., Casper, R., Hanin, I., Javaid, J. I., Chang, S. S., and Stokes, P. E. (1988). Cerebrospinal fluid and urinary biogenic amines in depressed patients and healthy controls. *Archives of General Psychiatry, 45*, 705–717.

Davis, K. L., Davidson, M., Mohs, R. C., and Kendler, K. S. (1985). Plasma homovanillic acid concentration and the severity of schizophrenic illness. *Science, 227*, 1601–1602.

Davis, J. M., Schaffer, C. B., Killian, G. A., Kinard, C., and Chan, C. (1980). Important issues in the drug treatment of schizophrenia. *Schizophrenia Bulletin, 6*, 70–87.

Deakin, J. F., Slater, P., Simpson, M. D., Gilchrist, A. C., Skan, W. J., Royston, M. C., Reynolds, G. P., and Cross, A. J. (1989). Frontal cortical and left temporal glutamatergic dysfunction in schizophrenia. *Journal of Neurochemistry, 52*, 1781–1786.

Delay, J., Deniker, P., and Harl, J-M. (1952). Traitement des etats d'excitation et d'agitation par une methode medicamenteuse derivees de l'hibernotherapie. *Annales de Medicinale Psychologie, 110*, 267–273.

Donaldson, S. R., Gelenberg, A. J., and Baldessarini, R. J. (1983). The pharmacologic treatment of schizophrenia: A progress report. *Schizophrenia Bulletin, 9*, 504–527.

Donlon, P. T., Hopkin, J. T., Tupin, J. P., Wicks, J. J., Wahba, M., and Meadows, A. (1980). Haloperidol for acute schizophrenic patients: An evaluation of 3 oral regimens. *Archives of General Psychiatry, 37*, 691–695.

Erickson, W. D., Yellin, A. M., Hopwood, J. H., Realmuto, G. M., and Greenberg, L. M. (1984). The effect of neuroleptics on attention in adolescent schizophrenics. *Biological Psychiatry, 19*, 745–753.

Evans, J. R., Rodnick, E. H., Goldstein, J. J., and Judd, L. L. (1972). Premorbid adjustment, phenothiazine treatment, and remission in acute schizophrenics. *Archives of General Psychiatry, 27*, 486–490.

Evarts, E. V. (1984). *Movement, mood and memory: Linked functions in the mammalian brain.* The G. Burroughs Mider Lecture. National Institute of Health, Bethesda, Maryland.

Falloon, I. R. H., Boyd, J. L., and McGill, C. W. (1984). *Family care of schizophrenia.* New York: The Guilford Press.

Falloon, I. R. H., Boyd, J. L., McGill, C. W., Razani, J., Moos, H. B., and Gilderman, A. M. (1982). Family management in the prevention of exacerbations of schizophrenia: A controlled study. *New England Journal of Medicine, 306*, 1437–1440.

Falloon, I. R. H., Hahlweg, K., and Tarrier, N. (1990). Family interventions in the community management of schizophrenia. Methods and results. In E. R. Straube and K. Hahlweg (Eds.), *Schizophrenia: Concepts, vulnerability and intervention.* Berlin: Springer.

Falloon, I. R. H., and Liberman, R. P. (1983). Behavior family interventions in the management of chronic schizophrenia. In W. R. McFarlane (Ed.), *Family therapy in schizophrenia.* New York: Guilford Press.

Falloon, I. R. H., Watt, D. C., and Shepard, M. (1978). The social outcome of patients in a trial of long-term continuation therapy in schizophrenia: Pimozide vs. fluphenazine. *Psychological Medicine, 8*, 265–274.

Farde, L., Hall, H., Ehrin, E., and Sedvall, G. (1986). Quantitative analysis of $D_2$ dopamine receptor binding in the living human brain by PET. *Science, 231*, 258–261.

Farde, L., Wiesel, F. A., Hall, H., Halldin, C., Stone-Elander, S., and Sedvall, G. (1987). No $D_2$ receptor increase in PET study of schizophrenia. *Archives of General Psychiatry, 44*, 671–672.

Farde, L., Wiesel, F. A., Halldin, C., and Sedvall, G. (1988). Central $D_2$-dopamine receptor occupancy in schizophrenic patients treated with antipsychotic drugs. *Archives of General Psychiatry, 45*, 71–76.

Farley, I. J., Price, K. S., and Hornykiewicz, O. (1977). Dopamine in the limbic regions of the human brain: Normal and abnormal. *Advances in Biochemical Psychopharmacology, 16*, 57–64.

Farley, I. J., Price, K. S., McCullough, E., Deck, J. H. N., Hordynski, W., and Hornykiewicz, O. (1978). Norepinephrine in chronic paranoid schizophrenia: Above normal levels in limbic forebrain. *Science, 200*, 456–458.

Farley, I. J., Shannak, K. S., and Hornykiewicz, O. (1980). Brain monoamine changes in chronic paranoid schizophrenia ad their possible relation to increased dopamine receptor sensitivity. In G. Pepeu, M. J. Kuhar, and S. J. Enna (Eds.), *Receptors for neurotransmitters and peptide hormones*, pp. 427–433. New York: Raven Press.

Farmery, S. M., Owen, F., Poulter, M., and Crow, T. J. (1985). Reduced high affinity cholecystokinin in hippocampus and frontal cortex of schizophrenic patients. *Life Science, 36*, 473–477.

Ferrier, I. N., Crow, T. J., Farmery, S. M., Roberts, G. W., Owen, F., Adrian, T. E., and Bloom, S. R. (1985). Reduced cholecystokinin levels in the limbic lobe in schizophrenia: A marker for pathology underlying the defect state? *Annals of the New York Academy of Sciences, 448*, 495–506.

Finch, B. E., and Wallace, C. J. (1977). Successful interpersonal skills training with schizophrenic inpatients. *Journal of Consulting and Clinical Psychology, 45*, 885–890.

Foote, S. L., and Morrison, J. H. (1987). Extrathalamic modulation of cortical function. *Annual Review of Neuroscience, 10*, 67–95.

Freedman, R., Kirch, D., Bell, J., Adler, L. E., Pecevich, M., Pachtman, E., and Denver, P. (1982). Clonidine treatment of schizophrenia: Double blind comparison to placebo and neuroleptic drugs. *Acta Psychiatrica Scandinavica, 65*, 35–45.

Freeman, A. S., and Chiodo, L. A. (1988). Electrophysiological effects of cholecystokinin octapeptide on identified rat nigrostriatal dopaminergic neurons. *Brain Research, 439 1–2*, 266–274.

Friedhoff, A. J. (1986). Dopamine as a mediator of a central stabilizing system: Comments on "the current status of the dopamine hypothesis of schizophrenia." *Neuropsychopharmacology, 1*, 189–191.

Frith, C., Stevens, M., Johnstone, E., and Crow, T. (1979). Skin conductance responsivity during acute episodes of schizophrenia as a predictor of symptomatic improvement. *Psychological Medicine, 9*, 101–106.

Fuster, J. M. (Ed.) (1980). *The prefrontal cortex*. New York: Raven Press.

Gaebel, W., Pietzcker, A., Ulrich, G., and Müller-Oerlinghausen, B. (1988). Predictors of neuroleptic treatment response in acute schizophrenia: Results of a treatment study with perazine. *Pharmacopsychiatry, 21*, 384–386.

Garbutt, J. C., and Van Kammen, D. P. (1983). The interaction between GABA and dopamine: Implications for schizophrenia. *Schizophrenia Bulletin, 9*, 336–353.

Garver, D. L., Zemlan, F., Hirschowitz, J., Hitzeman, R., and Mavroidis, M. L. (1984). Dopamine and non-dopamine psychoses. *Psychopharmacology, 84*, 138–140.

Gaspar, P., Berger, B., Febvret, A., Vigny, A., and Henry, J. P. (1989). Catecholamine innervation of the human cerebral cortex as revealed by comparative immunohistochemistry of tyrosine hydroxylase and dopamine-beta-hydroxylase. *The Journal of Comparative Neurology, 279*, 249–271.

Gattaz, W. F., Riederer, P., Reynolds, G., Gattaz, D., and Beckmann, H. (1983). Dopamine and noradrenaline in the cerebrospinal fluid of schizophrenic patients. *Psychiatry Research, 8*, 243–250.

Gerlach, J., Koppelhus, P., Helweg, E., and Monrad, A. (1973). Clozapine and haloperidol in a single blind crossover trial. Treatment of schizophrenia: Therapeutic and biochemical aspects. *Acta Psychiatrica Scandinavica, 50*, 410–424.

Gerner, R. H., and Yamada, T. (1982). Altered neuropeptide concentrations in cerebrospinal fluid of psychiatric patients. *Brain Research, 238*, 298–302.

Gerner, R. H., Fairbanks, L., Anderson, G. M., Young, J. G., Cheinin, M., Linnoila, M., Hare, T. A., Shaywitz, B. A., and Cohen, D. J. (1984). CSF neurochemistry in depressed manic and schizophrenic patients compared with that of normal controls. *American Journal of Psychiatry, 141*, 1533–1540.

Gerner, R. H., Van Kammen, D. P., and Ninan, P. T. (1985). Cerebrospinal fluid cholecystokinin, bombesin and somatostatin in schizophrenia and normals. *Progress in Neuropsychopharmacology and Biological Psychiatry, 9*, 73–82.

Gershon, S., Heikimian, L., Floyd, A., and Hollister, L. (1967). Methyl-*p*-tyrosine in schizophrenia. *Psychopharmacologia, 11*, 189–194.

Gjerris, A., Gjerris, F., Sorensen, P. S., Sorensen, E. B., Christensen, N. J., Fahrenkrug, J., and Rehfeld, J. F. (1980). Do concentrations of neurotransmitters measured in lumbar cerebrospinal fluid reflect the concentration at brain level? *Acta Neurochirurgica (Wien), 91*, 55–59.

Glazer, W. M., Charney, D. S., and Heninger, G. R. (1987). Noradrenergic function in schizophrenia. *Archives of General Psychiatry, 44*, 898–904.

Goetz, C. G., Tanner, C. M., and Klawans, H. L. (1986). Tardive dyskinesia: Clinical and pharmacologic studies. In G. D. Burrows, T. R. Norman, and G. Rubinstein (Eds.), *Handbook of studies on schizophrenia, Part 2. Management and research.* Amsterdam: Elsevier.

Goldberg, S. C. (1985). Negative and deficit symptoms in schizophrenia do respond to neuroleptics. *Schizophrenia Bulletin, 11*, 453–456.

Goldberg, S. C., Frosch, W. A., Drossman, A. K., Schooler, N. R., and Johnson, G. F.S. (1972). Prediction of response to phenothiazines in schizophrenia. *Archives of General Psychiatry, 26*, 367–373.

Goldstein, M. J., and Kopeikin, H. S. (1981). Short- and longterm effects of combining drug and family therapy. In M. J. Goldstein (Ed.), *New developments in interventions with families of schizophrenics.* San Francisco: Jossey-Bass.

Goldstein, M. J., Rodnick, E. H., Evans, J. R., May, P. R. A., and Steinberg, M. R. (1978). Drug and family therapy in the aftercare of acute schizophrenics. *Archives of General Psychiatry, 35*, 1169–1177.

Gomes, U. C. R., Shanley, B. C., Potgieter, L., and Roux, J. T. (1980). Noradrenergic overactivity in chronic schizophrenia: Evidence based on cerebrospinal fluid noradrenaline and cyclic nucleotide concentrations. *British Journal of Psychiatry, 137*, 346–351.

Gomes-Schwartz, B. (1984). Individual psychotherapy of schizophrenia. In A. S. Bellack (Ed.), *Schizophrenia. Treatment, management, and rehabilitation.* New York: Grune & Stratton.

Grace, A. A., and Bunney, B. S. (1986). Induction of depolarization block in midbrain dopamine neurons by repeated administration of haloperidol: Analysis using *in vivo* intracellular recording. *Journal of Pharmacology and Experimental Therapeutics, 238*, 1092–1100.

Gramsch, C., Emrich, H. M., John, S., Beckmann, H., Zaudig, M., and Zerssen, D. (1984). The effect of neuroleptic treatment and of high dosage diazepam therapy on β-endorphin immunoreactivity in plasma of schizophrenic patients. *Journal of Neural Transmission, 59*, 133–141.

Granger, G. W. (1957). Night vision and psychiatric disorders: A review of experimental studies. *Journal of Mental Science, 103*, 48–79.

Gray, J. A., Feldon, J. , Rawlins, J. N. P., Hemsley, D. R., and Smith, A. D. (1991). The neuropsychology of schizophrenia. *The Behavioral and Brain Sciences, 14*, 1–84.

Grinspoon, L., Ewalt, J. R., and Shader, R. I. (1972). *Schizophrenia: Pharmacotherapy and psychotherapy.* Baltimore: Williams & Wilkins.

Gross, H., and Langner, E. (1966). Das Wirkungsprofil eines chemisch neuartigen Breitbandneuroleptikums der Dibenzodiazepingruppe. *Wiener Medizinischer Wochenschrift, 116*, 814–819.

Gruzelier, J. H., and Yorkston, N. J. (1979). Propranolol and schizophrenia: Objective evidence of efficacy. In G. Hemmings (Ed.), *Biological bases of schizophrenia*, pp. 127–146. Lancaster: MTP Press.

Gunderson, J. G., Frank, A. F., Katz, H. M., Vannicelli, M. L., Frosch, J. P., and Knapp, P. H. (1984). Effects of psychotherapy in schizophrenia. II. Comparative outcome of two forms of treatment. *Schizophrenia Bulletin, 10*, 564–598.

Haas, S., Emrich, H. M., and Beckmann, H. (1982). Analgesic and euphoric effects of high dose diazepam in schizophrenia. *Neuropsychobiology, 8*, 123–128.

Haberland, N., and Hetey, L. (1987). Studies in postmortem dopamine uptake. II. Alterations of the synaptosomal catecholamine uptake in postmortem brain regions in schizophrenia. *Journal of Neural Transmission, 68*, 303–313.

Hand, T. H., Hu, X-T., and Wang, R. Y. (1987). Differential effects of typical and atypical antipsychotic drugs on the activity of dopamine neurons and their postsynaptic target cells. In L. A. Chiodo and A. S. Freeman (Eds.), *Neurophysiology of dopaminergic systems—current status and clinical perspectives*, Lakeshore: Lakeshore Publishers.

Harvey, P. D., Keefe, R. S. E., Moskowitz, J., Putnam, K. M., Mohs, R. C., and Davis, K. L. (1990). Attentional markers of vulnerability to schizophrenia: Performance of medicated and unmedicated patients and normals. *Psychiatry Research, 33*, 179–188.

Herman, J. P., Guilloneau, D., Dantzer, R., Scatton, B., Semerdjian-Rouquier, C., and Le Moal, M. (1982). Differential effects of inescapable footshocks and of stimuli previously paired with inescapable footshocks on dopamine turnover in cortical and limbic areas of the rat. *Life Sciences, 30*, 2207–2214.

Hess, E. J., Bracha, S., Kleinman, J. E., and Creese, I. (1987). Dopamine receptor sub-type imbalance in schizophrenia. *Life Sciences, 40*, 1487–1497.

Hirsch, S. R. (1986). Clinical treatment of schizophrenia. In P. B. Bradley and S. R. Hirsch (Eds.), *The psychopharmacology and treatment of schizophrenia*. Oxford: Oxford University Press.

Hirsch, S. R. (1986). Influence of social experience and environment on the course of schizophrenia. In P. B. Bradley and S. R. Hirsch (Eds.), The psychopharmacology and treatment of schizophrenia. Oxford: Oxford University Press.

Hirsch, S. R., Gaind, R., Rohde, P. D., Stevens, B. C., and Wing, J. K (1973). Outpatient maintenance of chronic schizophrenic patients with long-acting fluphenazine: Double-blind placebo trial. *British Medical Journal, 1*, 633–637.

Hogan, T. P., Award, A. G., and Eastwood, M. R. (1985). Early subjective response and prediction of outcome to neuroleptic drug therapy in schizophrenia. *Canadian Journal of Psychiatry, 30*, 246–248.

Hogarty, G. E., and Goldberg, S. C. (1973). Drug and sociotherapy in the aftercare of schizophrenic patients. One year relapse rates. *Archives of General Psychiatry, 28*, 54–64.

Hogarty, G. E., Anderson, C. M., Reiss, D. J., Kornblith, S. J., Greenwald, D. P., Javna, C. D., and Madonia, M. J. (1986). Family psycho-education, social skills training and maintenance chemotherapy in the aftercare treatment of schizophrenia. I. One year effects of a controlled study on relapse and expressed emotion. *Archives of General Psychiatry, 43*, 633–642.

Hogarty, G. E., Goldberg, S. C., and Schooler, N. R. (1975). Drugs and sociotherapy in the aftercare of schizophrenia: A review. In M. Greenblatt (Ed.), *Drugs in combination with other therapies*. New York: Grune & Stratton.

Hogarty, G. E., Goldberg, S. C., Schooler, N. R., Ulrich, R. F., and the Collaborative Study Group. (1974). Drug and sociotherapy in the aftercare of schizophrenic patients. II. Two-year relapse rates. *Archives of General Psychiatry, 31*, 603–608.

Hogarty, G. E., Schooler, N. R., Ulrich, R. F., Mussare, F., Ferro, P., and Herron, E. (1979). Fluphenazine and social therapy in the aftercare of schizophrenic patients: Relapse analyses of a two-year controlled study of fluphenazine hydrochloride. *Archives of General Psychiatry, 36*, 1283–1294.

Hollister, L. E., Overall, J. E., Kimbell, I., Jr., and Pokorny, A. (1974). Specific indications for different classes of phenothiazines. *Archives of General Psychiatry, 30*, 94–99.

Horn, A. S., and Snyder, S. H. (1971). Chlorpromazine and dopamine: conformational similarities that correlate with the antischizophrenic activity of phenothiazine drugs. *Proceedings of the National Academy of Sciences, U.S.A., 68*, 2325–2328.

Hornykiewicz, O. (1982). Brain catecholamine in schizophrenia—A good case for noradrenaline. *Nature (London), 299*, 484–486.

Iversen, L. L., Reynolds, G. P., and Snyder, S. H. (1983). Pathophysiology of schizophrenia— Causal role for dopamine or noradrenaline? *Nature (London), 305*, 377.

Iversen, S. D. (1986). Animal models of schizophrenia. In P. B. Bradley and S. R. Hirsch (Eds.), *The psychopharmacology and treatment of schizophrenia*. Oxford: Oxford University Press.

Jain, A. K., Kelwala, S., and Gershon, S. (1988). Antipsychotic drugs in schizophrenia: Current issues. *International Clinical Psychopharmacology, 3*, 1–30.

Jenner, P., Rupniak, N. M. J., and Marsden, C. D. (1985). Differential alteration of striatal $D_1$ and $D_2$ receptors induced by the long-term administration of haloperidol, sulpiride or clozapine to rats. In D. E. Casy, T. N. Chase, A. V. Christensen, and J. Gerlach (Eds.), *Dyskinesia— Research and treatment*. Berlin: Springer-Verlag.

Johnstone, E., Crow, T. J., and Mashiter, K. (1977). Anterior pituitary hormone secretion in schizophrenia—An approach to neurohumoral mechanisms. *Psychological Medicine, 7*, 223–228.

Joseph, M. H., Baker, M. F., Crow, T. J., Riley, G. J., and Risby, D. (1979). Brain tryptophan metabolism in schizophrenia: a post-mortem study of metabolism on the serotonin and kynurenine pathways in schizophrenic and control subjects. *Psychopharmacology, 62*, 279–285.

Kafka, M. S., and Van Kammen, D. P. (1983). A-adrenergic receptor function in schizophrenia: Receptor number, cyclic adenosine monophosphate production, adenylate cyclase activity and effect of drugs. *Archives of General Psychiatry, 40*, 264–270.

Kandel, E. R., and Schwarz, J. C. (1985). *Principles of neural science*, 2d ed. Amsterdam: Elsevier.

Kane, J. M. (1987). Treatment of schizophrenia. *Schizophrenia Bulletin, 13*, 133–156.

Kane, J. M., Rifkin, A., Woerner, M., Reardon, G., Sarantakos, S., Schiebel, D., and Ramos-Lorenzi, J. (1983). Low dose neuroleptic treatment of outpatient schizophrenics. I. Preliminary results for relapse rates. *Archieves of General Psychiatry, 40*, 893–896.

Karon, B. P., and Van den Bos, G. R. (1972). The consequences of psychotherapy for schizophrenic patients. *Psychotherapy, Theory, Research, and Practice, 9*, 111–120.

Kebabian, J. W., and Calne, B. (1979). Multiple receptors for dopamine. *Nature (London), 277*, 93–96.

Kemali, D., Del Vecchio, M., and Maj, M. (1982). Increased noradrenaline levels in CSF and plasma of schizophrenic patients. *Biological Psychiatry, 17*, 711–718.

Kendler, K. S., and Davis, K. L. (1984). Acute and chronic effects of neuroleptic drugs on plasma and brain homovanillic acid in the rat. *Psychiatry Research, 13*, 51–58.

Kilts, C. D., Anderson, C. M., Ely, T. D., and Nishita, J. K. (1987). Absence of synthesis-modulating nerve terminal autoreceptors on mesoamygdaloid and other mesolimbic dopamine neuronal populations. *Journal of Neuroscience, 7*, 3961–3975.

Kim, J. S., Kornhuber, H. H., Holzmueller, B., Schmid-Burgk, T., Mergner, T., and Krzepinski, G. (1980). Reduction of cerebrospinal fluid glutamic acid in Huntington's chorea and in schizophrenic patients. *Archiv für Psychiatrie und Nervenkrankheiten, 228*, 7–10.

Kim, J. S., Kornhuber, H. H., Schmid-Burck, W., and Holzmueller, B. (1980). Low cerebrospinal fluid glutamate in schizophrenic patients and a new hypothesis of schizophrenia. *Neuroscience Letters, 20,* 379–382.

Kleinman, J. E., Iadorola, M., Govoni, S., Hong, J., Gillin, J. C., and Wyatt, R. J. (1983). Post-mortem measurements of neuropeptides in human brain. *Psychopharmacology Bulletin, 19,* 375–377.

Kleinman, J. E., Weinberger, D. R., Rogol, A. D., Bigelow, L. A., Klein, S. T., Gillin, J. C., and Wyatt, R. J. (1982). Plasma prolactin concentrations and psychopathology in chronic schizophrenia. *Archives of General Psychiatry, 39,* 655–657.

Kopin, I. J. (1985). Catecholamine metabolism: Basic aspects and clinical significance. *Pharmacological Reviews, 37,* 333–364.

Kornhuber, J., Riederer, P., Reynolds, G. P., Beckmann, H., Jellinger, K., and Gabriel, E. (1989). ($^3$H)-Spiperone binding sites in post-mortem brains from schizophrenic patients: Relationship to neuroleptic drug treatment, abnormal movements, and positive symptoms. *Journal of Neural Transmission, 75,* 1–10.

Korpi, E. R., Kaufmann, C. A., Marnela, K. M., and Weinberger, D. R. (1987). Cerebrospinal fluid amino acid concentrations in chronic schizophrenia. *Psychiatry Research, 20,* 337–345.

Korpi, E. R., Kleinman, J. E., Goodman, S. I., Phillips, I., Delisi, L. E., Linnoila, M., and Wyatt, R. J. (1986). Serotonin and 5-hydroxyindole acetic acid in the brains of suicide victims: Comparison in chronic schizophrenic patients with suicide as a cause of death. *Archives of General Psychiatry, 43,* 594–600.

Korpi, E. R., Kleinman, J. E., Goodman, S. I., and Wyatt, R. J. (1987). Neurotransmitter amino acids in post-mortem brains of chronic schizophrenics. *Psychiatry Research, 22,* 291–301.

Kutay, F. Z., Pogun, S., Hariri, N. I., Peker, G., and Erlacin, S. (1989). Free amino acid level determinations in normal and schizophrenic brain. *Progress in Neuropsychopharmacology and Biological Psychiatry, 12,* 1–13.

Lake, C. R., Sternberg, D. E., Van Kammen, D. P., Ballenger, J. C., Ziegler, M. G., Post, R. M., Kopin, I. J., and Bunney, W. E. (1980). Schizophrenia: Elevated cerebrospinal fluid norepinephrine. *Science, 207,* 331–333.

Lane, R. F., and Blaha, C. D. (1986). Electrochemistry *in vivo:* Application to CNS pharmacology. *Annals of the New York Academy of Science, 473,* 42–63.

Langsley, D., Machotka, R., and Flomenhaft, K. (1968). Family crisis therapy. Results and implications. *Family Process, 7,* 145–158.

Lee, T., and Seeman, P. (1980). Elevation of brain neuroleptic/dopamine receptors in schizophrenia. *American Journal of Psychiatry, 137,* 191–197.

Lee, T., Seeman, P., Tourtelotte, W. W., Farley, I. J., and Hornykiewicz, O. (1978). Binding of ($^3$H)-neuroleptics and ($^3$H)-apomorphine in schizophrenic brains. *Nature (London), 274,* 897–900.

Leff, J. (1975). Die Kombination von psychiatrischer Pharmakotherapie mit Soziotherapie. *Der Nervenarzt, 50,* 501–509.

Leff, J., and Vaughn, C. (1985). *Expressed emotion in families. Its significance for mental illness.* New York: The Guilford Press.

Leff, J. P, Kuipers, L., Berkowitz, R., Eberlein-Fries, R., and Sturgeon, D. (1982). A controlled trial of social intervention in the families of schizophrenics patients. *The British Journal of Psychiatry, 141,* 121–134.

Leff, J. P., Kuipers, L., Berkowitz, R., Eberlein-Fries, R., and Sturgeon, D. (1983). Social intervention in the families of schizophrenics: Addendum. *British Journal of Psychiatry, 142,* 313.

Leff, J. P., Kuipers, L., Berkowitz, R., and Sturgeon, D. A. (1985). A controlled trial of social intervention in the families of schizophrenic patients: Two year follow-up. *British Journal of Psychiatry, 146,* 594–600.

Lehmann, H. E. (1975). Psychopharmacological treatment of schizophrenia. *Schizophrenia Bulletin, 13*, 27–45.

Lightman, S. L., Spokes, E. G., Sagnella, G. A., Gordon, D., and Bird, E. D. (1979). Distribution of β-endorphin in normal and schizophrenic human brains. *European Journal of Clinical Investigation, 9*, 377–379.

Lindstrom, L. H., and Persson, E. (1980). Propranolol in chronic schizophrenia: A controlled study in neuroleptic-treated patients. *British Journal of Psychiatry, 137*, 126–130.

Lindstrom, L. H. (1985). Low HVA and normal 5-HIAA CSF levels in drug-free schizophrenic patients compared to healthy volunteers: Correlations to symptomatology and family history. *Psychiatry Research, 14*, 265–273.

Lindstrom, L. H., Widerlov, E., Bisette, G., and Nemeroff, C. B. (1988). Reduced CSF neurotensin concentration in drug-free schizophrenic patients. *Schizophrenia Research, 1*, 55–59.

Losonczy, M. F., Song, P. S., Mohs, R. C., Mathe, A. A., Davidson, M. , Davis, B. M., and Davis, K. L. (1986). Correlates of lateral ventricular size in chronic schizophrenics. II. Biological measures. *Archives of General Psychiatry, 43*, 1113–1118.

Lotstra, F., Verbanck, P. M. P., Gilles, C., Mendlewicz, J., and Vanderhaeghen, J. J. (1985). Reduced cholecystokinin levels in cerebrospinal fluid of parkinsonian and schizophrenic patients. *Annals of the New York Academy of Sciences, 448*, 507–517.

Lu, R. B., Ko, H. C., Lin, W. L., Lin, Y. T., and Ho, S. L. (1989). SF neurochemical study of tardive dyskinesia. *Biological Psychiatry, 25*, 717–724.

Lungjaerde, O. (1982). Effect of the benzodiapzepine derivative estazolam in patients with auditory hallucinations. *Acta Psychiatrica Scandinavica, 65*, 339–354.

Luria, A. R. (1978). *The working brain. An introduction to neuropsychology.* New York: Penguin Press.

Mackay, A. V. P., Iversen, L. L., Rossor, M., Spokes, E., Bird, E., Arregui, A., Creese, I., and Snyder, S. H. (1982). Increased brain dopamine and dopamine receptors in schizophrenia. *Archives of General Psychiatry, 31*, 991–997.

Manchanda, R., and Hirsch, S. R. (1986). Does propranolol have an antipsychotic effect? A placebo controlled study in acute schizophrenia. *British Journal of Psychiatry, 148*, 701–707.

Marder, S. R., Asarnow, R. F., and van Putten, T. (1984). Information processing and neuroleptic response in acute and stabilized schizophrenic patients. *Psychiatry Research, 13*, 41–49.

Marder, S. R., van Kammen, D. P., Docherty, J. P., Rayner, J., and Bunney, W. E. (1979). Predicting drug-free improvement in schizophrenic psychosis. *Archives of General Psychiatry, 36*, 1080–1085.

Marsden, C. D., Mindham, R. H. S., and Mackay, A. V. P. (1986). Extrapyramidal movement disorders produced by antipsychotic drugs. In P. B. Bradley and S. R. Hirsch (Eds.), *The psychopharmacology and treatment of schizophrenia.* Oxford: Oxford University Press.

Martinot, J. L., Peron-Magnan, P., Huret, J. D., Mazoyer, B. M., Baron, J.C., Boulenger, J. P., Loc'h, C., Maziere, B., Caillard, V., Loo, H., and Syrota, A. (1990). Striatal D2 dopaminergic receptors assessed with positron emission tomography and (76Br)-bro-mospiperone in untreated schizophrenic patients. *The American Journal of Psychiatry, 147*, 44–50.

Martinot, J. L., Huret, J. D., Peron-Magnan, P., Mazoyer, B. M., Baron, J. C., Caillard, V., Syrota, A., and Loo, H. (1989). Striatal $D_2$ dopaminergic receptor status ascertained in vivo by positron emission tomography and [76]-Br-bromospiperone in untreated schizophrenics. *Psychiatry Research, 29*, 357–358.

May, P. R. A. (1968). *Treatment of schizophrenia: A comparative study of five treatment methods.* New York: Science House.

May, P. R. A., and Goldberg, S. C. (1978). Prediction of schizophrenic patients' response to pharmacotherapy. In M. A. Lipton, A. DiMascio, and K. F. Killam (Eds.), *Psychopharmacology: A generation of progress*. New York: Raven Press.

May, P. R. A., Tuma, H., and Dixon, W. J. (1976a). Schizophrenia—A follow-up study of results of treatment. I. Design and other problems. *Archives of General Psychiatry, 33*, 474–478.

May, P. R. A., Tuma, H., and Dixon, W. J. (1981). Schizophrenia—A follow-up study of the results of five forms of treatment. *Archives of General Psychiatry, 38*, 776–784.

May, P. R. A., Tuma, H., Yale, C., Potepan, P., and Dixon, W. J. (1976b). Schizophrenia—A follow-up study of results of treatment. II. Hospital stay over two to five years. *Archive of General Psychiatry, 33*, 481–486.

May, P. R. A., van Putten, T., Yale, C., Potepan, P., Jender, D. J., Fairchild, M. D., Goldstein, M. J., and Dixon, W. J. (1976). Predicting individual responses to drug treatment in schizophrenia: A Test-Dose Model. *Journal of Nervous and Mental Disease, 162*, 177–183.

McCreadie, R. G., and MacDonald, I. M. (1977). High dosage haloperidol in chronic schizophrenia. *British Journal of Psychiatry, 131*, 310–316.

McGeer, P. L., and McGeer, E.G. (1977). Possible changes in striatal and limbic cholinergic systems in schizophrenia. *Archives of General Psychiatry, 34*, 1319–1323.

Meltzer, H. Y., Sommers, A. A., and Luchins, D. J. (1986). The effect of neuroleptics and other psychotropic drugs on negative symptoms in schizophrenia. *Journal of Clinical Psychopharmacology, 6*, 329–338.

Memo, M., Kleinman, J. E., and Hanbauer, I. (1983). Coupling of dopamine $D_1$ recognition sites with adenylate cyclase in nuclei accumbens and caudatus of schizophrenics. *Science, 221*, 1304–1307.

Mielke, D. H., Gallant, D. M., Roniger, J. J., Kessler, C., and Kessler, R. L. (1977). Sulpiride: Evaluation of antipsychotic activity in schizophrenic patients. *Diseases of the Nervous System, 38*, 569–571.

Mita, T., Hanada, S., Nishino, N., Kuno, T., Nakai, H., Yamadori, T., Mizoi, Y., and Tanaka, C. (1986). Decreased serotonin $S_2$ and increased dopamine $D_2$ receptors in chronic schizophrenics. *Biological Psychiatry, 21*, 1407–1414.

Möller, H-J., v. Zerssen, D., Emrich, H. M., Kissling, W., Cording, C., Schietsch, H. J., and Riedel, E. (1979). Action of *d*-propranolol in manic psychoses. *Archiv der Psychiatrie und Nervenkrankheiten, 227*, 301–317.

Möller, H. J., Scharl, W., and von Zerssen, D. (1985). Can the result of neuroleptic treatment be predicted? An empirical investigation on schizophrenic inpatients. *Pharmacopsychiatry, 18*, 52–53.

Moore, R. Y., and Bloom, F. E. (1978). Central catecholamine neuron systems: Anatomy and physiology of the dopamine system. *Annual Reviews of Neuroscience, 1*, 129–169.

Morrison, R. L., and Bellack, A. S. (1984). Social skills training. In A. S. Bellack (Ed.), *Schizophrenia. Treatment, management, and rehabilitation*. New York: Grune & Stratton.

Mussgay, L., and Olbrich, R. (1988). Trainingsprogramme in der Behandlung kognitiver Defizite Schizophrener. *Zeitschrift für Klinische Psychologie, 17*, 341–353.

Neborsky, R., Jankowsky, D., Munson, E., and Depry, D. (1981). Rapid treatment of acute psychotic symptoms with high and low dose haloperidol: Behavioral considerations. *Archives of General Psychiatry, 38*, 195–199.

Nemeroff, C. B., Youngblood, W. W., Manberg, P., Prange, A. J., and Kizer, J. S. (1983). Regional brain concentrations of neuropeptides in Huntington's chorea and schizophrenia. *Science, 221*, 972–975.

Nestoros, J. N., Suranyi-Cadotte, B. E., Spees, R.C., Schwartz, G., and Nair, N. P. V. (1982). Diazepam in high-doses is effective in schizophrenia. *Progress in Neuro-psychopharmacology and Biological Psychology, 6*, 513–516.

Niklasson, F., and Agren, H. (1984). Brain energy metabolism and blood–brain barrier permeability in depressive patients: Analyses of creatine, creatinine, urate and albumin in CSF and blood. *Biological Psychiatry, 19*, 1183–1203.

Ninan, P. T., Van Kammen, D. P., Scheinin, M., Linnoila, M., Bunney, W. E., and Goodwin, F. K. (1984). CSF-5-hydroxyindoleacetic acid levels in suicidal schizophrenic patients. *American Journal of Psychiatry, 141*, 566–569.

Nishikawa, T., Takashima, N., and Toru, N. (1983). Increased ($^3$H)kainic acid binding in the prefrontal cortex in schizophrenia. *Neuroscience Letters, 40*, 245–250.

Norman, T. R., Judd, F. K., Marriott, P. F., and Burrows, G. D. (1986). Pharmacotherapy of schizophrenia: Clinical aspects. In G. D. Burrows, T. R. Norman, and G. Rubinstein (Eds.), *Handbook of studies on schizophrenia. Part 2. Management and research.* Amsterdam: Elsevier.

Nuechterlein, K. H., (1977). Reaction time and attention in schizophrenia: A critical evaluation of the data and theories. *Schizophrenia Bulletin, 3*, 373–428.

Nyback, H., Berggren, B. M., Hindmarsh, T., Sedvall, G., and Wiesel, F. A. (1983). Cerobroventricular size and cerebrospinal fluid monoamine metabolites in schizophrenic patients and healthy volunteers. *Psychiatry Research, 9*, 301–308.

Oades, R. D. (Ed.) (1982). *Attention and schizophrenia: Neurobiological bases.* London: Pitman Press.

Oades, R. D. (1985). The role of noradrenaline in tuning and dopamine in switching between signals in the CNS. *Neuroscience and Biobehavioral Reviews, 9*, 261–283.

Oades, R. D., and Halliday, G. M. (1987). The ventral tegmental (A 10) system. Neurobiology I. Anatomy and connectivity. *Brain Research Reviews, 12*, 117–165.

Oades, R. D., Bunk, D., Roepcke, B., and Eggers, C. (1990). Continuous performance errors: Dopaminergic effects in medicated schizophrenic and hyperkinetic patients? *European Journal of Neuroscience, Suppl. 3*, 309.

Oades, R. D., Taghzouti, K., Rivet, J. M., and Le Moal, M. (1986). Locomotor activity in relation to dopamine and noradrenaline in the nucleus accumbens, septal and frontal areas: A 6-hydroxydopamine study. *Neuropsychobiology, 16*, 37–42.

Oades, R., Kulisch, E., Schall, U. and Eggers, C. (1991). Use of redundant information in psychotic patients: a dopaminergic role in conditioning blocking? *Biological Psychiatry, 29*, 665.

Ohlund, L., Alm, T., Lindström, L., Wieselgren, I. M., Öst, L. G., and Öhman, A. (1987). *Electrodermal nonresponding in schizophrenics: Relationship to social outcome.* Presented at the 27th Annual Meeting of Society for Psychophysiological Research, Amsterdam.

Oltmanns, T. F., Ohayon, J., and Neale, J. M. (1978). The effect of anti-psychotic medication and diagnostic criteria on distractibility in schizophrenia. *Journal of Psychiatric Research, 14*, 81–91.

Owen, F., Cross, A. J., Crow, T. J., Longden, A., Poulter, M., and Riley, G. J. (1978). Increased dopamine-receptor sensitivity in schizophrenia. *Lancet*, 223–226.

Owen, F., Cross, A. J., Waddington, J. L., Poulter, M., Gamble S. J., and Crow, T. J. (1980). Dopamine-mediated behaviour and ($^3$H)-spiperone binding to striatal membranes in rats after nine months haloperidol administration. *Life Sciences, 26*, 55–59.

Owen, R., Owen, F., Poulter, F., and Crow, T. J. (1984). Dopamine D$_2$ receptors in substantia nigra in schizophrenia. *Brain Research, 299*, 152–154.

Pandurangi, A. K., Dewan, M. J., Lee, S. H., Ramachandran, T. R., Levy, B. F., Boucher, M., Yozawitz, A., and Major, L. (1984). The ventricular system in chronic schizophrenic patients: A controlled computed tomography study. *British Journal of Psychiatry, 144*, 172–176.

Pandurangi, A. K., Goldberg, S. C., Brink, D. D., Hill, M. H., Gulati, A. N., and Hamer, R. M. (1989). Amphetamine challenge test, response to treatment, and lateral ventricle size in schizophrenia. *Biological Psychiatry, 25*, 207–214.

Pearlson, G., and Coyle, J. T. (1983). The dopamine hypothesis and schizophrenia. In J. T.

Coyle and S. T. Enna (Eds.), *Neuroleptics: Neurochemical, behavioral and clinical perspectives*, pp. 297–324. New York: Raven Press.

Peet, M., Bethell, M. S., Coates, A., Khamnee, A. K., Hall, P., Cooper, S. J., King, D. J., and Yates, R. A. (1981a). Propanolol in schizophrenia. I. Comparison of propanolol, chlorpromazine and placebo. *British Journal of Psychiatry, 139*, 105–111.

Peet, M., Middlemiss, D. N., and Yates, R. A. (1981b). Propanolol in schizophrenia. II. Clinical and biochemical aspects of combining propanolol with chlorpromazine. *British Journal of Psychiatry, 138*, 112–117.

Perlow, M. J., Chiueh, C. C., Lake, C. R., and Wyatt, R. J. (1980). Increased dopamine and norepinephrine concentrations in primate CSF following amphetamine and phenylethylamine administration. *Brain Research, 186*, 469–473.

Peroutka, S. J., and Snyder, S. H. (1980). Relation of neuroleptic drug effects at brain dopamine, serotonin, alpha-adrenergic and histamine receptors to clinical potency. *American Journal of Psychiatry, 137*, 518–522.

Perry, T. L., Hansen, S., and Jones, K. (1989). Schizophrenia, tardive dyskinesia and brain GABA. *Biological Psychiatry, 25*, 200–206.

Persson, T., and Roos, B. E. (1969). Acid metabolites from monoamines in CSF of chronic schizophrenics. *British Journal of Psychiatry, 115*, 95–98.

Pickar, D., Bunney, W. E., Douillet, P., Sethi, B. B., Sharma, M., Vartanian, M. E., Lideman, R. P., Naber, D., Leibl, K., Yamashita, I., Koyama, T., Verhoeven, W. M. A., Vartanian, F., Morozov, P. V., and Khac, T. N. (1989). Repeated naloxone administration in schizophrenia: A phase II World Health Organization Study. *Biological Psychiatry, 25*, 440–448.

Pickar, D., Labarca, R., Linnoila, M., Roy, A., Hommer, D., Everett, D., and Paul, S. M. (1984). Neuroleptic-induced decrease in plasma homovanillic acid and antipsychotic activity in schizophrenic patients. *Science, 225*, 954–957.

Pimoule, C., Schoemaker, H., Reynolds, G. P., and Langer, S. Z. (1985). ($^3$H)Sch 23390 labelled $D_1$ dopamine receptors are unchanged in schizophrenia and Parkinson's disease. *European Journal of Pharmacology, 11*, 235–237.

Post, R. M., Ballenger, J. C., and Goodwin, F. K. (1980). Cerebrospinal fluid studies of neurotransmitter function in manic and depressive illness. In J. H. Wood (Eds.), *Neurobiology of cerebrospinal fluid*. New York: Plenum Press.

Post, R. M., Gold, P., Rubinow, D. R., Ballenger, J. C., Bunney, W. E., and Goodwin, F. K. (1982). Peptides in the cerebrospinal fluid of neuropsychiatric patients: An approach to central nervous system peptide function. *Life Sciences, 31*, 1–15.

Post, R. M., Fink, E., Carpenter, W. T., and Goodwin, F. K. (1975). Cerebrospinal fluid amine metabolites in acute schizophrenia. *Archives of General Psychiatry, 32*, 1063–1069.

Potkin, S. G., Weinberger, D. R., Linnoila, M., and Wyatt, R. J. (1983). Low CSF 5-hydroxyindoleacetic acid in schizophrenic patients with enlarged cerebral ventricles. *American Journal of Psychiatry, 140*, 21–25.

Pugh, C. R., Steinert, J., and Priest, R. G. (1983). Propranolol in schizophrenia: A double blind, placebo controlled trial of propranolol as an adjunct to neuroleptic medication. *British Journal of Psychiatry, 143*, 151–155.

Quitkin, A. F., Rifkin, A., and Klein, D. F. (1975). Very high doses vs standard dosage fluphenazine in schizophrenia. *Archives of General Psychiatry, 32*, 1276–1281.

Rappaport, M., Hopkins, H. K., Hall, K., Belleza, T., and Silverman, J. (1978). Are there schizophrenics for whom drugs may be unnecessary or contraindicated? *International Pharmacopsychiatry, 13*, 100–111.

Reisine, T. D., Rossor, M., Spokes, E., Iversen, L. L., and Yamamura, H. I. (1980). Opiate and neuroleptic receptor alterations in human schizophrenic brain tissue. In G. Pepeu, M. J. Kuhar, and S. J. Enna (Eds.), *Receptors for neurotransmitters and peptide hormones*, pp. 443–450. New York: Raven Press.

Reynolds, G. P. (1983). Increased concentrations and lateral asymmetry of amygdala dopamine in schizophrenia. *Nature (London), 305*, 527–529.

Reynolds, G. P. (1979). Post-mortem neurochemical studies in schizophrenia. In H. Haefner, W. F. Gattaz, and W. Janzarik (Eds.), *Search for the causes of schizophrenia*, pp. 236–240. Heidelberg: Springer.

Reynolds, G. P., Czudek, C., Bzowej, N., and Seeman, P. (1987). Dopamine receptor asymmetry in schizophrenia. *Lancet*, 979.

Reynolds, G. P., and Czudek, C. (1988). Status of the dopaminergic system in post mortem brain in schizophrenia. *Psychopharmacology Bulletin, 24*, 345–347.

Reynolds, G. P., Riederer, P., Jellinger, K., and Gabriel, E. (1981). Dopamine receptors and schizophrenia: The neuroleptic drug problem. *Neuropharmacology, 20*, 1319–1320.

Reynolds, G. P., Rossor, M. N., and Iversen, L. L. (1983). Preliminary studies of human cortical 5-HT2 receptors and their involvement in schizophrenia and neuroleptic drug action. *Journal of neural Transmission, Suppl. 18*, 273–277.

Rimon, R., Roos, B. E., Rakkolainen, V., and Alanen, Y. (1971). The content of 5-HIAA and HVA in the CSF of patients with acute schizophrenia. *Journal of Psychosomatic Research, 15*, 375–378.

Robbins, T. W., and Everett, B. J. (1982). Functional studies of the central catecholamines. *International Review of Neurobiology, 23*, 245–365.

Roberts, G. W., Ferrier, I. N., Lee, Y., Crow, T. J., Johnstone, E. C., Owens, D. G. C., Bacarese-Hamilton, A. J., McGregor, C., O'Shaughnessy, D., Polak, J. M., and Bloom, S. R. (1983). Peptides, the limbic lobe, and schizophrenia. *Brain Research, 288*, 199–211.

Rifkin, A., Quitkin, F., Rabiner, C. J., and Klein, D. F. (1977). Fluphenazine decanoate, fluphenazine hydrochloride given orally, and placebo in remitted schizophrenics. *Archives of General Psychiatry, 34*, 43–47.

Robinson, T. E., and Becker, J. B. (1986). Enduring changes in brain and behavior produced by chronic amphetamine administration: A review and evaluation of animal models of amphetamine psychosis. *Brain Research Reviews, 11*, 157–198.

Roy, A., Ninan, P., Mazonson, A., Pickar, D., Van Kammen, D. P., Linnoila, M., and Paul, S. M. (1985). CSF metabolites in chronic schizophrenic patients who attempt suicide. *Psychological Medicine, 15*, 335–340.

Ryan-Jastrow, T., and Gnegy, M. E. (1989). Castration blocks chronic sulpiride-induced desensitization of striatal $D_1$ receptor-stimulated adenylate cyclase activity in male rats. *The Journal of Pharmacology and Experimental Therapeutics, 248*, 626–631.

Schied, H. W. (1990). Psychiatric concepts and therapy. In E. R. Straube, and K. Hahlweg (Eds.), *Schizophrenia. Concepts, vulnerability, and intervention*. Berlin: Springer.

Schneider, R. D., and Grossi, V. (1979). Differences in muscle activity before, during, and after responding in a simple reaction time task: Schizophrenics vs. normals. *Psychiatry Research, 1*, 141–145.

Schneider, S. J. (1982). Electrodermal activity and therapeutic response to neuroleptic treatment in chronic schizophrenic in-patients. *Psychological Medicine, 12*, 607–613.

Schooler, N. R., and Goldberg, S. C. (1972). Performance tests in a study of phenothiazines in schizophrenia: Caveats and conclusions. *Psychopharmacologia, 24*, 81–98.

Schulz, S. C., Sinicrope, P., Killer, M., Kishore, P., and Friedel, R. O. (1983). Treatment response and ventricular brain ratio in young schizophrenic patients. *Psychopharmacological Bulletin, 19*, 510–512.

Schulz, S. C., and Tamminga, C. (1989). *Schizophrenia. Scientific Progress*. Oxford: Oxford University Press.

Seeman, P. (1986). Dopamine/neuroleptic receptors in schizophrenia. In G. D. Burrows, T. R. Norman, and G. Rubinstein (Eds.). *Handbook on Studies of schizophrenia, Part 2*, Amsterdam: Elsevier.

Seeman, P. (1987). Dopamine receptors and the dopamine hypothesis of schizophrenia. *Synapse, 1*, 133–152.

Seeman, P. (1980). Brain dopamine receptors. *Pharmacological Reviews, 32*, 229–313.

Seeman, P., Bzowej, N., Guan, H. C., Bergeron, C., Reynolds, G. P., Bird, E. D., Riederer, P., Jellinger, K., and Tourtellotte, W. W. (1987). Human brain $D_1$ and $D_2$ dopamine receptors in schizophrenia, Alzheimer's, Parkinson's and Huntington's diseases. *Neuropsychopharmacology, 1*, 5–15.

Shostak, M., Perel, J. M., Stiller, R. L., Wyman, W., and Curran, E. (1987). Plasma haloperidol and clinical response: A role for reduced haloperidol in antipsychotic activity. *Journal of Clinical Psychopharmacology, 7*, 394–400.

Siegel, G. J. (1989). *Basic Neurochemistry.* (4rh Ed.) New York: Raven Press.

Simpson, M. D. C., Slater, P., Deakin, J. F. W., Royston, M. C., and Skan, W. J. (1989). Reduced GABA uptake sites in the temporal lobe in schizophrenia. *Neuroscience Letters, 107*, 211–215.

Smythies, J. R. (1984). The transmethylation hypotheses of schizophrenia reevaluated. *Trends in Neurosciences, 4*, 45–47.

Snyder, S. H. (1973). Amphetamine psychosis: A "model" schizophrenia mediated by catecholamincs. *American Journal of Psychiatry, 130*, 61–67.

Snyder, S. H. (1976). The dopamine hypothesis of schizophrenia: Focus on the dopamine receptor. *American Journal of Psychiatry, 133*, 197–202.

Spaulding, W. (1986). Assessment of adult-onset pervasive behavior disorders. In A. Ciminero, K. Calhoun, and H. Adams (Eds.), *Handbook of behavioral assessment*, 2d ed. New York: Wiley.

Spohn, H. E., and Strauss, M. E. (1989). Relation of neuroleptic and anticholinergic medication to cognitive functions in schizophrenia. *Journal of Abnormal Psychology, 98*, 367–380.

Spohn, H. E., Coyne, L., Lacoursiere, R., Mazur, D., and Hayes, K. (1985). Relation of neuroleptic dose and tardive dyskinesia to attention, information-processing and psychophysiology in medicated schizophrenics. *Archives of General Psychiatry, 42*, 849–859.

Spohn, H. E., Lacoursiere, R. B., Thompson, K., and Coyne, L. (1977). Phenothiazine effects on psychological and psychophysiological dysfunction in chronic schizophrenics. *Archives of General Psychiatry, 34*, 633–644.

Spohn, H. E., Lacoursiere, R. B., Thompson, K., and Coyne, L. (1978). The effects of antipsychotic drug treatment on attention and information processing in chronic schizophrenics. In L. C. Wynne, R. L. Cromwell, and S. Matthysse (Eds.), *The nature of schizophrenia. New approaches to research and treatment.* New York: Wiley.

Spohn, H. E., and Coyne, L. (1988). *The effect of neuroleptics on reaction time.* Presented at the meeting of the Society for Research in Psychopathology, Boston, Massachusetts.

Stachowiak, M. K., Bruno, J. P., Snyder, A. M., Stricker, E. M., and Zigmond, M. J. (1984). Apparent sprouting of striatal serotonergic terminals after dopamine-depleting brain lesions in neonatal rats. *Brain Research, 291*, 164–167.

Stanton, A. H., Gunderson, J. G., Knapp, P. H., Frank, A. F., Vannicelli, M. L., Schnitzer, R., and Rosenthal, R. (1984). Effects of psychotherapy in schizophrenia. I. Design and implementation of a controlled study. *Schizophrenia Bulletin, 10*, 520–551.

Stein, L. I., and Test, M. A. (1978). *Alternatives to mental hospital treatment.* New York: Plenum.

Sternberg, D. E., Charney, D. S., Heninger, G. R., Leckman, J. F., Hafstad, K. M., and Landis, H. (1982). Impaired presynaptic regulation of norepinephrine in schizophrenia: Effects of clonidine in schizophrenic patients and normal controls. *Archives of General Psychiatry, 39*, 285–289.

Sternberg, D. E., van Kammen, D. P., Lake, C. R., Ballenger, J. C., Marder, S. R., and Bunney, W. E., Jr. (1981). The effect of primozide on CSF norepinephrine in schizophrenia. *American Journal of Psychiatry, 138*, 1045–1050.

Sternberg, D. E., van Kammen, D. P., Lerner, P., Ballenger, J. C., Marder, S. R., Post, R. M., and Bunney, W. E. (1983). CSF dopamine B-hydroxylase in schizophrenia: Low activity associated with good prognosis and good response to neuroleptic treatment. *Archives of General Psychiatry, 40,* 743–747.

Sternberg, D. E., van Kammen, D. P., Lerner, P., and Bunney, W. E. (1982). Schizophrenia: Dopamine β-hydroxylase activity and treatment response. *Science, 216,* 1423–1425.

Stevens, J. R. (1973). An anatomy of schizophrenia. *Archives of General Psychiatry, 29,* 177–189.

Stoof, J. C., and Verheijden, P. F. H. M. (1986). $D_2$ receptor stimulation inhibits cyclic AMP formation brought by $D_1$ receptor stimulation in rat neostriatum but not nucleus accumbens. *European Journal of Pharmacology, 129,* 205–206.

Strachan, A. M. (1986). Family Intervention for the Rehabilitation of Schizophrenia: Toward Protection and Coping. *Schizophrenia Bulletin, 12,* 678–698.

Strachan, A. M., Leff, J. P., Goldstein, M. J., Doane, J. A., and Burtt, C. (1986). Emotional attitudes and direct communication in the families of schizophrenics: A crossnational replication. *The British Journal of Psychiatry, 149,* 279–287.

Straube, E. R., Schied, H. W., Rein, W., and Breyer-Pfaff, U. (1987). Autonomic nervous system differences as predictors of short-term outcome in schizophrenics. *Pharmacopsychiatry, 20,* 105–110.

Straube, E., Wagner, W., Foerster, K., and Heimann, H. (1989). Findings significant with respect to short- and medium-term outcome in schizophrenia—A preliminary report. *Progress in Neuro-psychopharmacology and Biological Psychiatry, 13,* 185–197.

Straube, E., Wagner, W., Schied, H. W., Rein, W., and Foerster, K. (1988). Indikatoren der Therapieresponse. In H. Helmchen, H. Hippius, and R. Tölle (Eds.), *Therapie mit Neuroleptika—Perazin,* pp. 172–178. Stuttgart: Thieme.

Strauss, M. E., Lew, M. F., Coyle, J. T., and Tune, M. D. (1985). Psychopharmacologic and clinical correlates of attention in chronic schizophrenia. *American Journal of Psychiatry, 142,* 497–499.

Strauss, M. E., Reynolds, K. S., Jayaram, G., and Tune, L. E. (1990). Effects of anticholinergic medication on memory in schizophrenia. *Schizophrenia Research, 3,* 127–129.

Streitfeld, B. D. (1980). The fiber connections of the temporal lobe with emphasis on the Rhesus monkey. *International Journal of Neuroscience, 11,* 51–71.

Swahn, C. G., and Sedvall, G. (1988). CSF creatinine in schizophrenia. *Biological Psychiatry, 23,* 586–594.

Tamminga, C. A. (1983). Atypical neuroleptics and novel antipsychotic drugs. In J. T. Coyle and S. T. Enna (Eds.), *Neuroleptics: Neurochemical behavioral and clinical perspectives,* pp. 281–295. New York: Raven Press.

Tarrier, N., Barrowclough, C., Vaughn, C., Bamrah, J. S., Porceddu, K., Watts, S., and Freeman, H. (1988). The community management of schizophrenia: A controlled trial of a behavioral intervention with families to reduce relapse. *British Journal of Psychiatry, 153,* 532–542.

Tarrier, N., Barrowclough, C., Vaughn, C., Bamrah, J. S., Porceddu, K., Watts, S., and Freeman, H. (1989). Community management of schizophrenia. A two-year follow-up of a behavioural intervention with families. *British Journal of Psychiatry, 154,* 625–628.

Tassin, J. P., Simon, H., Herve, D., Blanc, G., Le Moal, M., Glowinski, J., and Bockaert, J. (1982). Non-dopaminergic fibres may regulate dopamine-sensitive adenylate cyclase in the prefrontal cortex and nucleus accumbens. *Nature (London), 295,* 696–698.

Toru, M., Nishikawa, T., Mataga, N., and Takashima, M. (1982). Dopamine metabolism increases in post-mortem schizophrenic basal ganglia. *Journal of Neural Transmission, 54,* 181–191.

Uhl, G. R., and Kuhar, M. J. (1984). Chronic neuroleptic treatment enhances neurotensin receptor binding in human and rat substantia nigra. *Nature (London), 309,* 350–352.

Vaglum, P., Friis, S., and Karterud, S. (1985). Why are the results of milieu therapy for schizophrenic patients contradictory? An analysis based on four empirical studies. *The Yale Journal of Biology and Medicine, 58*, 349–361.

Van Kammen, D. P., and Antelman, S. (1984). Impaired noradrenergic neurotransmission in schizophrenia? *Life Sciences, 34*, 1403–1413.

Van Kammen, D. P., and Schulz, S. C. (1985). *d*-Amphetamine raises cortisol levels in schizophrenic patients with and without chronic naltrexone pretreatment. *Journal of Neural Transmission, 64*, 35–43.

Van Kammen, D. P., Docherty, J. P., and Bunney, W. E. (1982a). Prediction of early relapse after pimozide discontinuation by response to *d*-amphetamine during pimozide treatment. *Biological Psychiatry, 17*, 233–242.

Van Kammen, D. P., Docherty, J. P., Marder, S. R., Rayner, J. N., and Bunney, W. E. (1982b). Long-term pimozide pretreatment differentially affects behavioral responses to dextroamphetamine in schizophrenia. *Archives of General Psychiatry, 39*, 275–281.

Van Kammen, D. P., Mann, L. S., Sternberg, D. E., Scheinin, M., Ninan, P. T., Marder, S. R., Van Kammen, W. P., Rieder, R. O., and Linnoila, M. (1983). Dopamine beta hydroxylase activity and homovanillic acid in spinal fluid of schizophrenics with brain atrophy. *Science, 220*, 974–977.

Van Kammen, D. P., Peters, J. L., Van Kammen, W. B., Rosen, J., Yao, J. K., McAdam, D., and Linnoila, M. (1989). Clonidine treatment of schizophrenia: Can we predict treatment response? *Psychiatry Research, 27*, 297–311.

Van Kammen, D. P., Peters, J., Van Kammen, W. B., Nugent, A., Goetz, K. L., Yao, J., and Linnoila, M. (1989). CSF norepinephrine in schizophrenia is elevated prior to relapse after haloperidol withdrawal. *Biological Psychiatry, 26*, 176–188.

Van Kammen, D. P., Rosen, J., Peters, J., Fields, R., and Van Kammen, W. B. (1985). Are there state-dependent markers in schizophrenia? *Psychopharmacology Bulletin, 21*, 497–502.

Van Kammen, D. P., Sternberg, D. E., Hare, T. A., Waters, R. N., and Bunney, W. E. (1982c). CSF levels of γ-aminobutyric acid in schizophrenia. *Archives of General Psychiatry, 39*, 91–97.

Van Kammen, D. P., Van Kammen, W. B., Mann, L. S., Seppala, T., and Linnoila, M. (1986). Dopamine metabolism in the cerebrospinal fluid of drug-free schizophrenic patients with and without cortical atrophy. *Archives of General Psychiatry, 43*, 978–983.

Van Ree, J. M., and De Wied, D. (1981). Endorphins in schizophrenia. *Neuropharmacology, 20*, 1271–1277.

Van Rossum, J. M. (1966). The significance of dopamine receptor blockade for the mechanism of action of neuroleptic drugs. *Archives Internationales de Pharmacodynamie et de Therapie, 160*, 492–494.

Verhoeven, W. M. A., Van Ree, J. M., and De Wied, D. (1986). Neuroleptic-like peptides in schizophrenia. In G. D. Burrows, T. R. Norman, and G. Rubinstein (Eds.), *Handbook of studies of schizophrenia, Part 2*, pp. 253–274.

Wallace, C. J., and Liberman, R. P. (1985). Social skills training for patients with schizophrenia: A controlled clinical trial. *Psychiatry Research, 15*, 239–247.

Wallace, C. J., Nelson, C. J., Liberman, R. P., Aitchison, R. A., Lukoff, D., Elder, J. P., and Ferris, C. (1980). A review and critique of social skills training with schizophrenic patients. *Schizophrenia Bulletin, 6*, 42–63.

Weinberger, D. R., Bigelow, L. B., and Kleinman, J. E. (1980). Cerebral ventricular enlargement in chronic schizophrenia: An association with poor response to treatment. *Archives of General Psychiatry, 17*, 22–23.

Weiner, I. (1990). Neural substrates of latent inhibition: the switching model. *Psychological Bulletin, 108*, 442–461.

Weizman, A., Tyano, S., Wijsenbeek, H., and David, M. B. (1984). High dose diazepam treatment and its effect on prolactin secretion in adolescent schizophrenic patients. *Psychopharmacology, 82*, 382–385.

Whitaker, P. M., Crow, T. J., and Ferrier, I. N. (1981). Tritiated LSD binding in frontal cortex in schizophrenia. *Archives of General Psychiatry, 38*, 278–280.

White, F. J., and Wang, R. Y. (1985). Effects of chronic treatment with cholecystokinin on midbrain dopamine neurons. *Annals of the New York Academy of Sciences, 448*, 682–684.

Widerlov, E., Lindstrom, L. H., Besev, G., Manberg, P., Nemeroff, C. B., Breese, G. R., Kizer, J. S., and Prange, A. J. (1982). Subnormal CSF levels of neurotensin in a sub-group of schizophrenic patients: Normalization after neuroleptic treatment. *American Journal of Psychiatry, 139*, 1122–1126.

Wiesel, F. A., Wik, G., Sjogren, I., Blomqvist, G., and Greitz, T. (1987). Altered relationships between metabolic rates of glucose in brain regions of schizophrenic patients. *Acta Psychiatrica Scandinavica, 76*, 642–647.

Wiesel, F. A., Wik, G., Sjogren, I., Blomqvist, G., Greitz, T., and Stone-Elander, S. (1987). Regional brain glucose metabolism in drug free schizophrenic patients and clinical correlates. *Acta Psychiatrica Scandinavica, 76*, 628–641.

Winblad, B., Bucht, G., Gottfries, C. G., and Roos, B. E. (1979). Monoamines and monoamine metabolites in brains from demented schizophrenics. *Acta Psychiatrica Scandinavica, 60*, 17–28.

Winter, M., Lehmann, E., and Scholz, O. B. (1984). Effects of high and low dosage of haloperidol on the brain in relation to schizophrenic thought disorder. *Pharmacopsychiatrie, 12*, 115–121.

Wolkowitz, O. M., Pickar, D., Doran, A. R., Breier, A., Tarell, J., and Paul, S. M. (1986). Combination alprazolam-neuroleptic treatment of the positive and negative symptoms of schizophrenia. *American Journal of Psychiatry, 143*, 85–87.

Wong, D. F., Gjedde, A., Wagner, H. N. Jr., Dannals, R. F., Douglass, K. H., Link, J. M., and Kuhar, M. J. (1986a). Quantification of neuroreceptors in the living human brain: II. Inhibition studies of receptor density and affinity. *Journal of Cerebral Blood Flow and Metabolism, 6*, 147–153.

Wong, D. F., Wagner, H. N., Tune, L. E., Dannals, R. F., Pearlson, G. D., Links, J. M., Tamminga, C. A., Brousolle, E. P., Ravert, H. T., Wilson, A. A., Toung, J. K. T., Malat, J., Williams, J. A., O'Tuama, L. A., Snyder, S. H., Kuhar, M. J., and Gjedde, A. (1986b). Positron emission tomography reveals elevated dopamine $D_2$ receptors in drug naive schizophrenics. *Science, 234*, 1558–1562.

Yorkston, J. J., Weller, M. D., Gruzelier, J. H., and Hirsch, S. R. (1981). DH-propanolol and chloropromazine following admission for schizophrenia. *Acta Psychiatrica Scandinavica, 63*, 13–27.

Zahn, T. P., Rappaport, J. L., and Thompson, C. L. (1981). Autonomic effects of dextroamphetamine in normal men: Implications for hyperactivity and schizophrenia. *Psychiatry Research, 4*, 39–47.

Zahn, T. P., and Carpenter, W. T. (1978). Effects of short-term outcome and clinical improvement on reaction time in acute schizophrenia. *Journal of Psychiatric Research, 14*, 59–68.

Zec, R. F. and Weinberger, D. R. (1986). The neurology of schizophrenia. In H. A. Nasrallah and D. R. Weinberger (Eds.). *Handbook of Schizophrenia, Vol. 1*. Amsterdam: Elsevier.

Zemlan, F. P., Hitzeman, R. J., Hirschowitz, J., and Garver, D. L. (1985). Down-regulation of central dopamine receptors in schizophrenia. *American Journal of Psychiatry, 142*, 1334–1337.

# Chapter 14

# Long-Term Course
# of Schizophrenia and
# Its Predictability

## I. Types of Schizophrenic Course and Final Outcome

The emphasis in this chapter is on the long-term developmental course of the schizophrenic illness (i.e., > 20 yr). All too often the course over shorter periods presents surprising and unforeseeable changes. This may be one of the reasons for the difficult prediction of shorter term courses (Winokur *et al.*, 1985). Furthermore, this chapter will concentrate on those studies in which there has been a detailed analysis of the characteristics of the temporal course, the factors that aid prediction of development, and the differential nature of the final outcome.

## A. Recovery and Later Forms of Schizophrenic Illness

In the earlier half of the century, most people were of the opinion that schizophrenia was an illness that had a poor long-term prognosis. Fortunately, through the comprehensive long-term studies of four research groups, this view has been modified. These studies were conducted by M. Bleuler (1972) in Zürich, Ciompi and Müller (1976) in Lausanne, Huber and colleagues (1979) in Bonn, and Tsuang and colleagues in Iowa (Tsuang and Dempsey, 1979; Tsuang *et al.*, 1979, 1981; Tsuang, 1982; cf. recent general review by Ciompi, 1988). The development of the illness in approximately 200 to 500 patients (per study) was followed, on the average, for 20 to 40 yr, usually after first admission to the respective clinic (Table 14.1).

It is difficult to compare the four studies, since different methods were used in each, yet the major conclusions of all the studies show an astonishing degree of agreement. If the methodological problems are left aside for a moment (cf. Angst, 1988; McGlashan *et al.*, 1988), it can be seen that about one-fourth of all subjects show a complete recovery and that a slightly higher proportion are left with mild residual symptoms. Less than half of the patients

**Table 14.1**  Comparison of the Essential Methodological Features of Four Large-Scale Studies of Long-Term Outcome[a]

| | Principal investigators | | | |
|---|---|---|---|---|
| | Bleuler, 1972 | Ciompi and Müller, 1976 | Huber et al., 1979 | Tsuang et al., 1979 |
| Diagnostic criteria: | E. and M. Bleuler | E. and M. Bleuler | E. and M. Bleuler, Schneider | Feighner, Schneider, DSM III |
| n: | 208 | 287 | 502 | 200 |
| Location: | Zürich | Lausanne | Bonn | Iowa City |
| Follow-up period: | 22 yr | 37 yr | 24 yr | 33 yr |
| Further selection criteria: | One or more admissions | Only first admissions | One and more admissions | One and more admissions |
| Control group: | No | No | No | Yes |
| Method of assessment at follow-up: | Personal knowledge of patient for whole follow-up period | Interview with patient | Interview with patient | Interview with patient or with relative |
| Method of assessment of intitial diagnosis: | Personal notes | Case record | Case record | Case record |

[a] After Ciompi, 1981, and Tsuang et al., 1979.

in the European studies and slightly more than half in the Iowa study were left with a moderate to severe chronic residual syndrome (Table 14.2).

The main results of these projects have been confirmed in other studies for which less comprehensive analyses are available or where shorter follow-up periods were analyzed: Marinow (1981) in Bulgaria, Sternberg (1981) in Moscow, Watts et al. (1983) in England, Dube et al. (1984) in India, McGlashan (1986) in the United States, Ogawa et al. (1987) in Japan, Harding (1988) and Harding et al. (1989) in the United States, and Munk-Jorgensen and Mortensen (1989) in Denmark.

Of course, the validity and comparability of these data depend on the definition of the patient group, that is, the diagnostic criteria. The European projects used Bleulerian and Schneiderian criteria, and the Iowa study used Feighner criteria at first and later used the DSM-III criteria (cf. detailed discussion by Angst, 1988).

The Feighner criteria, similar to DSM-III, require that the symptoms have been evident for 6 months prior to the first formal diagnosis (i.e., only chronic schizophrenics receive a diagnosis). Indeed, the report of Tsuang and Fleming (1987) confirmed these suspicions: the patients who fulfilled Feighner's criteria had a worse outcome in all areas of function than those who

**Table 14.2**  Outcome at Follow-up of Four Large-Scale Projects:
Three European and One North American[a]

| Psychopathology rating | European projects | | | Psychopathology rating | North American project |
|---|---|---|---|---|---|
| | Bleuler (%) | Ciompi and Müller (%) | Huber *et al.* (%) | | Tsuang and Dempsy (%) |
| No symptoms | 20 | 29 | 26 | Good | 20 |
| Mild | 33 | 24 | 31 | Fair | 26 |
| Medium | 24 | 26 | 29 | Poor | 54 |
| Severe | 24 | 20 | 14 | | |

[a]Results of a global psychopathology rating on a four-point scale after Ciompi, 1981, for the European studies, and result of psychopathology rating on a three-point scale after Tsuang and Dempsey, 1979, for the North American project.

were recorded as schizophrenic in the case notes and who did not fulfill the research criteria. These latter patients were called "atypical schizophrenics" by the Iowa group. A re-analysis of the atypical group according to DSM-III criteria showed that the diagnoses could be categorized as schizoaffective, schizophreniform, and atypical psychotic disturbances (Buda *et al.*, 1988).

However, the results of Harding (1988) from the Vermont Longitudinal Research Project do not agree with this. Harding and co-workers examined 269 DSM-III-defined patients within the framework of a longitudinal project over about 23 yr. Harding (1988) even observed a higher percentage of fully recovered or only mildly impaired probands than the European authors, although their sample selection was targeted to "backward, very disabled, long-stay patients" (cf. Harding's discussion and comparison of their findings with the three large-scale European studies for details; Harding, 1988). This does not mean that the sampling procedure or the characteristics of the sample are irrelevant, but it does suggest that an unequivocal diagnosis of schizophrenia implicates certain similar heterogeneous patterns of outcome, with a certain amount of recovery (approximately 20–30%) and a certain number of severe chronic cases remaining after more than 20 yr of illness (approximately 15–25%).

However, long-term follow-up studies conducted in non-Western societies report milder courses for schizophrenia (cf. Lin and Kleinman, 1988). The WHO field research center in Agra, India, followed the course of 46 schizophrenics for 13–14 yr and observed full recovery in 59% of their former schizophrenic probands (Dube *et al.*, 1984). Recovery was, among other things, defined as an absence of psychiatric problems that would interfere with day-to-day activities. Nevertheless, 13% of the patients were still schizophrenic and most of the remaining 29% still showed residual symptoms. Aside from the just-mentioned problems of comparability and the shorter duration of the follow-up, the data suggested that the "natural" course of schizophrenia is not so natural. This in turn spurred some therapists to try specially adapted long-term programs for the chronic schizophrenics (cf. Ciompi, 1988).

## B. Nonspecific Symptoms at the Follow-up

The authors of the European studies emphasize that a considerable proportion of the probands who remain ill no longer show specific symptoms of schizophrenia at the long-term follow-up (Ciompi, 1981). The detailed analysis from Huber's group in Bonn illustrates this point (Huber *et al.*, 1979). At the end of a 21-yr course average, 55% of the patients no longer showed typical schizophrenic symptoms. Instead, the most obvious symptoms were a lack of drive and energy and a feeling of general insufficiency; they were easily exhausted and rather sensitive. In detail, it is interesting to note that the subjective complaints of those patients who had predominantly nonspecific symptoms were most commonly concerning cognitive disturbances, followed by complaints about a general exhaustion, not feeling well, being too excitable and irritable, and having a lower tolerance to stress along with reduced coping abilities.

It is remarkable that even the probands who do *not* show any psychiatric disorder (considered healthy at follow-up) showed some weaknesses of cognitive test performance that discriminated them from healthy controls. Huber *et al.* (1979) noted that the speed of performance and accuracy of stimulus selection for this group on a test of sustained attention (concentration test) were markedly lower than the norm. The performance of the fully remitted subjects was scarcely any different from the rest of the group's patients, whether or not they had specific or nonspecific symptoms. On the verbal sections of the Wechsler intelligence test, the values for this group were uniformly in the lower half of the normal range; on performance subtests, they showed a number of weaknesses (Huber *et al.*, 1979).

## C. Cerebral Atrophy (Pneumoencephalography)

Huber conducted one of the pioneering *in vivo* tests of structural change in the brain of schizophrenics (Huber, 1957). He made pneumoencephalic recordings (for details, see Chapter 8), since computer tomography (CT) was not available at that time. Huber recorded from a subgroup of patients (57 from a total of 502). Of 18 fully remitted patients, 4 (22%) showed signs of some structural changes, yet of 39 patients with residual symptoms, 20 (51%) showed similar signs. An increase in the size of the third ventricle was the most common feature found. If this finding is extended to the whole group with and without symptoms, then 42% showed some cerebral atrophy.

Later on in their report, Huber *et al.* included borderline findings in the category of pathological results. This led them to conclude that 82% of the nonremitted patients showed some morphological changes in the brain. This is in great excess of findings from CT studies of schizophrenics (Chapter 8). Current estimates of the incidence of cerebral atrophy in the schizophrenic population in general are about 30%. This indicates that Huber's more conservative estimate of 42% of schizophrenic probands with cerebral changes is not too far from the frequencies reported with modern CT scans. The association between structural changes and poor long-term outcome also corroborates modern findings concerning short-term outcome.

An advantage of this study was that patients over 60 yr of age were not studied in order to exclude nonspecific effects of old age. Disadvantages were that the lack of control group and that the analysis was not performed blind to the nature of the groups (see Chapter 8 for other methodological problems of pneumoencephalography).

## D. Psychosocial Condition at Follow-up

In the Iowa study, the psychosocial and psychopathological outcome of the patients was compared with various control groups (Tsuang *et al.*, 1979; Table 14.3). (For reasons of clarity, data has been omitted for the schizoaffective group. Here the number of cases was small and values lay mostly between those with affective and those with schizophrenic psychoses.) The burden imparted by a schizophrenic psychosis is impressively demonstrated. Particularly clear are the data on the differences between the long-term development of symptoms in schizophrenics and in those with a manic–depressive illness. Twice as many manics and three times as many depressive patients as schizophrenics were free of symptoms at the final investigation. Schizophrenics also appeared disadvantaged in psychosocial areas of function. Compared with manics and depressives, only half as many schizophrenics achieved a "good" occupational status and less than one-third had a "good" marital status at the follow-up assessment.

There are no easily comparable data from the European projects available, but if the ability of a patient to obtain a job is used as a criterion, then the proportion with a poor outcome in the European studies approaches that of the Iowa group (i.e., approximately 50%).

## E. Mortality and Somatic Illness

In the Iowa study—in which subjects were followed for about 30 yr—schizophrenics had a higher mortality than average for the rest of the population. For every 1 person dying in the normal population, 1.68 died in the schizophrenic group. The values for the other psychiatric group were

**Table 14.3**  Social and Living Conditions and Psychopathological Status
at the Follow-up Assessment of Schizophrenics Compared with Manics, Depressives,
and a Matched Control Group of Healthy Subjects[a]

| | Diagnostic group[b] | | | |
| | S (n = 186) (%) | M (n = 86) (%) | D (n = 212) (%) | C (n = 144) (%) |
| Condition | | | | |
|---|---|---|---|---|
| Marital status[c] | | | | |
| Good | 21 | 70 | 81 | 89 |
| Fair | 12 | 8 | 9 | 6 |
| Poor | 67 | 22 | 9 | 5 |
| Residential status | | | | |
| Good | 34 | 69 | 70 | 89 |
| Fair | 48 | 17 | 18 | 10 |
| Poor | 18 | 14 | 12 | 1 |
| Occupational status | | | | |
| Good | 35 | 67 | 67 | 88 |
| Fair | 8 | 8 | 16 | 10 |
| Poor | 58 | 24 | 17 | 2 |
| Psychopathological status | | | | |
| Good | 20 | 50 | 61 | 85 |
| Fair | 26 | 21 | 18 | 11 |
| Poor | 54 | 29 | 22 | 4 |

[a] After Tsuang et al., 1979, and Tsuang and Fleming, 1987.
[b] S, schizophrenics; M, manics; D, depressives; C, healthy controls.
[c] Status definitions are as follows. Marital: good, married/widowed; fair, divorced, separated; poor, single.
Residential: good, own home or living with relatives; fair, nursing or county home; poor, mental hospital.
Occupational: good, employed/housewife/retired; fair, unable to work due to physical incapacity; poor, unable to
work due to mental incapacity. Psychopathological: good, no symptoms; fair, presence of some symptoms; poor,
presence of incapacitating symptoms.

about the same. The data from Ciompi and Müller (1976) support this result
for the schizophrenic but here the other psychiatric groups studied had
similarly high mortality rates.

With regard to the mode of death, the Iowa group reported an increased
incidence of suicide as well as of infective and circulatory causes (Buda *et
al.*, 1988). However, since the mode of death was not compared between
groups of psychiatric patients, these findings may not be specific.

Remarkable among the data of the Swiss studies was the scarcity of the
incidence of malignant tumors (Bleuler, 1972; Ciompi and Müller, 1976).
However, observing the subgroups making up the schizophrenic population,
Ciompi and Müller found that catatonics showed a higher incidence than other
subgroups. These results could not be confirmed in Bonn or Iowa (Huber *et
al.*, 1979; Buda *et al.*, 1988) but are reflected by numerous reports on the
reduced incidence of cancers among schizophrenics (review, Masterson and

O'Shea, 1984). As yet, it is possible to only speculate about the underlying cause. Suggestions range from changes in the immune system (e.g., Fudenberg *et al.*, 1984) to a putatively protective effect of neuroleptic treatment (e.g., Mortensen, 1987; Ravn, 1988).

In regard to the incidence of other illnesses, there are reports of a reduced incidence of myasthenia gravis (Gittelson and Richardson, 1973) and rheumatic arthritis in schizophrenia (e.g., Eaton, 1985; Harris, 1988). Indeed, Harris was of the opinion that the evidence is stronger for a reduced incidence of rheumatic arthritis than for cancer. However, no sign of this was evident in the long-term studies discussed here.

These are heuristically interesting findings. They should be carefully checked and followed up, since there certainly are links between immune function, bodily defense mechanisms, and the metabolism of substances involved in neurotransmission. The presence of schizophrenic symptoms may be incompatible with some of these interactions (cf. Oades, 1982, p. 212). However, current information is insufficient for the drawing of any conclusions.

## F. Different Types of Course

As is all too evident from clinical experience, an enormous variety of developmental courses can be encountered in schizophrenia; Huber *et al.* (1979) recorded at least 72 (!) types. This heterogeneity was reduced to four types by Bleuler (1972), to eight sequences by Ciompi and Müller (1976; Ciompi, 1988), and to 12 forms by Huber *et al.* (1979). (The Iowa study has not yet reported on the types of course.) Harding (1988) evaluated her findings in accord with the types of course proposed by Ciompi and Müller (1976). The graphic representation of the courses and their relative frequencies found in the Lausanne project (Ciompi, 1988) and in the Vermont project (Harding, 1988) can be seen in Figure 14.1.

As can be seen in Figure 14.1, there are two dominant types found in the Lausanne project: one-fourth of the patients have an acute onset and an undulating course with complete or partial recovery. Nearly one-fourth show a poor premorbid phase, slow progression toward the illness, and a more simple chronic course. These types are somewhat rare in the Vermont data. More common are cases with a "chronic" onset and undulating course (38%) or those showing phases alternating between acute episodes and recovery (27%). (This also illustrates the unexpectedly better outcome of the more chronic group in the Vermont project.) It seems that in the Vermont sample these types are somewhat overrepresented, since all three European studies confirm that in most cases a chronic onset is followed by a more chronic course and an acute onset with a more undulating course (see subsequent text). This confirms the "rule" that one type of course predicts the next, or as

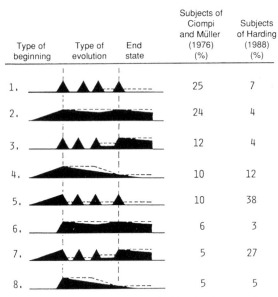

**Figure 14.1**  Schematic illustration of eight types of schizophrenia course in terms of their long-term evolution and the proportion of subjects showing each type in the studies of Ciompi and Müller (1976) and Harding (1988). Dotted lines represent variations of the same evolutionary type.

McGlashan (1988) expresses it, "like predicts like." However, even in the European sample, unexpected "atypical" courses can be observed: 12% of the Lausanne sample started with an acute onset and later showed an undulating course. Cloninger *et al.* (1985) from the St. Louis follow-up study (follow-up after 6–12 yr) found that an even higher percentage of their DSM-III-defined sample showed this unexpected course: 38% had an acute undulating course to begin with but a chronic schizophrenia with poor functioning at the follow-up. These findings show that the "like-predicts-like" rule is a rule of thumb, with many exceptions. This indicates that in an individual case, nearly each type of course and each type of outcome can be expected.

# II. Potential Predictors of Long-Term Outcome in Schizophrenia

## A. Type of Onset

Despite the exceptions just mentioned, the European studies all show that a long poor premorbid phase is likely to be associated with a poor long-term outcome, irrespective of the type of course. [The original data of Bleuler (1972) in this respect showed only a trend. Statistical significance was attained with the addition of more subjects later.] The results from Huber *et al.* (1979) are even more extreme. No patient with a poor premorbid course showed a spontaneous remission later. Ciompi and Müller (1976) found that approximately 60% of those with a poor premorbid course had a poor outcome. McGlashan (1986) from the respected Chestnut Lodge Clinic in Rockville, Maryland, confirmed this relationship for a shorter follow-up period of an average of 15 yr in a sample defined by DSM-III.

Indeed the review of Harrow and Westermayer (1987) also confirms this conclusion. It should be kept in mind, however, as in the previous section, that the relationship is a statistical one: even after an acute onset, unfavorable courses of illness can develop. From the results reviewed by Harrow and Westermayer (1987) and the data of Tsuang and Fleming (1987), it should be noted that a favorable development of the course of illness may still be observed in 20–25% of the so-called process schizophrenics. Klorman *et al.* (1977) interestingly concluded from their data that premorbid functioning has its strongest impact in the earlier stage of the illness. Only later do other factors become more prominent predictors of the long-term outcome (cf. short-term prediction in Chapter 13).

## B. Premorbid Personality Characteristics

The European studies focused especially on the incidence of premorbid schizoid features. The two Swiss studies found no association between such features and outcome (Bleuler, 1972; Ciompi and Müller, 1976). One reason for this may be that it is very difficult to assess the patient's personality type before onset of the illness using case notes. However, the German study in Bonn examined nearly twice as many patients as either of the Swiss studies and thus was perhaps able to detect the more striking or blatant patterns in the case notes. Huber *et al.* (1979) found a group who could be characterized as having been (in premorbid stages) "sensitive" and "inhibited" and another group with poor interpersonal relations and somewhat schizoid features. More patients from the former group experienced a complete remission. It was more usual for patients from the latter group to show residual symptoms (schizo-phrenic symptoms or lasting nonspecific features) that lasted, on average, 24 yr through to the follow-up. Indeed, several earlier North American studies support the conclusion that premorbid "schizoid" features predict an un-favorable outcome (Vaillant, 1962; Stephens *et al.*, 1966; Stephens, 1978). Along with the findings of Angst *et al.* (1985; discussed later), these results seem to be compatible with another feature reported to predict outcome in the Chestnut Lodge sample: McGlashan (1986) observed that patients who were characterized as "loners" in the premorbid phase had a poor outcome.

It is useful to set aside the question of prognosis for a moment and ask what sort of premorbid personality features were typical of the schizophrenics studied by Huber and colleagues. Of 301 patients for whom data were available, 28% (*n* = 83) showed "schizoid" features or had contact problems, sensitivity was shown by 22% (*n* = 67), and, in a further 16% these features were linked to depressive characteristics. Other features accounted for 10% of the group (Huber *et al.*, 1979). A problem for the evaluation of these data is that they were obtained retrospectively from the case notes.

In contrast, Angst and colleagues in Zurich (1985) conducted a prospective study of 6300 military conscripts using the Freiburg Personality Inventory. After 10 years, 25 had become schizophrenic. Compared with 479 controls, these turned out to have been more introverted and less social in the premorbid phase. Interestingly, in contrast to the expectations of the researchers, they did not find that the factor of "emotional lability" differentiated between the groups. Although this study has the advantage of having been conducted prospectively, it has the disadvantage of having examined a selected group of 19-year-old subjects who were psychiatrically unremarkable at the time they were examined. Thus it is possible that, among those subjects with an early onset of psychiatric problems, other features might emerge.

The Chestnut Lodge project found that chronic patients, who could be described as showing severe obsessive symptoms at the first assessment (21 of 163), had an unfavorable long-term global course (Fenton and McGlashan, 1986). Although this project had to rely on case notes, as did the other studies, it had the advantage of having very detailed records available, since it is a well-staffed private hospital with a primarily psychodynamic orientation, but a rigorous scientific approach. The methodological disadvantage was that the patients had a higher than average socioeconomic status than patients from "ordinary" hospitals. However, as a marginal note, it should be stated that status does not seem to reduce the likelihood of experiencing a serious long-term illness, since 41% of their patients were defined as continuously incapacitated at follow-up (McGlashan, 1988).

## C. Symptoms at First Admission

With regard to the wide range of symptoms shown at the first assessment, most studies found that only a very limited number can be considered possible predictors. The studies from Bonn and Lausanne both found a statistical, if not very impressive, correlation between the early appearance of auditory hallucinations and an unfavorable course (Huber *et al.*, 1979; Ciompi and Müller, 1976). The Iowa study found a similar relationship for both auditory and visual hallucinations, and the course over the next 30–40 yr (Tsuang, 1986). In 60% of the poor-outcome patients, auditory hallucinations were present. In 33% of this group, visual hallucinations were present at the first assessment. The Chestnut Lodge study reported a relatively high correlation (*r*

= 0.47) between the incidence of hallucinations at the initial assessment and poor outcome when examining 47 of their patients (Fenton and McGlashan, 1986).

Munk-Jorgensen and Mortensen (1989) in Denmark followed up 53 patients after 12 yr and found the presence of Schneiderian symptoms (e.g., auditory hallucinations and delusions) to be predictive of poor outcome. This was confirmed by a German group with a sample from the Cologne University Psychiatric Clinic ($n = 97$). Besides Schneiderian first rank symptoms, single items such as (mood-incongruent) auditory hallucinations, (mood-incongruent) delusions, and thought incoherence were found to be associated with a higher severity of residual symptoms 10 years later (Marneros et al., 1989a,b; Steinmeier et al., 1989).

The reports of congruent findings from several different studies are rather impressive. It seems as though the presence of at least auditory hallucinations, but probably also of delusions, at first assessment defines a core deficit with poor prognosis.

Most of the other items studied as putative prognostic indicators have not proved of value, or at least the value was not confirmed by other groups. One may assume from the many statistical tests and correlations run in these studies that some of the so-called significant results arose by chance [e.g., for the 50 variables checked by Tsuang (1986) one suspects a type 1 error]. Fenton and McGlashan (1986) avoided this source of error by evaluating their data by means of a multiple regression analysis. They found in addition to the prognostic indicators just mentioned, that depressive features were significantly related to good outcome; this corroborated findings from earlier studies (Vaillant, 1962, 1964a,b; Stephens et al., 1966; Stephens, 1978).

Just one further symptom seems to emerge as a relatively reliable predictor of outcome, at least in the short- and mid-term, namely, the "flattening of affect." This is the result of several 5-yr follow-up studies (Carpenter et al., 1978; Knight et al., 1979; Möller et al., 1984; Jonnsson and Nyman, 1984) and for the 13-yr follow-up of Munk-Jorgensen and Mortensen (1989), yet in the long-term this feature seems not to be so clearly related to outcome. Only Ciompi and Müller (1976) reported that the presence of affective withdrawal and abulia (reduction of volitional acts) at the first assessment was correlated with an unfavorable course in the long-term. Thus, while flattening of affect may be an indicator of the problems the clinician will face in the short-term, it does not form a basis for a clear long-term prognosis.

## D. Subgroups of Schizophrenics

Catatonic schizophrenics in Bonn and Lausanne tended to have a milder outcome than other subgroups. In Bonn, Huber et al. (1979) reported that as

many as 44% of the catatonics actually experienced a spontaneous remission.
(This outcome was twice as good as for the rest of the patients.) In Lausanne,
Ciompi and Müller (1976) found a marked improvement in 46 of 62 catatonic
patients. This is at odds with the result of an American study (Bland and Orn,
1980). However, catatonic symptoms in this study were defined differently
than those in the European studies. The other studies from Europe and Iowa
(cf. Kendler *et al.*, 1984) do not agree that there are any other syndromes or
subgroups to be conclusively correlated with a particular outcome. (For
example, the finding of a better outcome of paranoid schizophrenics in the
Iowa sample was not supported by other groups; Kendler *et al.*, 1984.)

## E. Diagnostic Criteria

DSM-III or Feighner-defined schizophrenics tend to have a poorer outcome
than those diagnosed without the requirement that the symptoms must have
been present for 6 mo (Tsuang and Fleming, 1987), as mentioned earlier. The
three major European studies agree that an acute and abrupt onset of illness
is, in fact, a favorable sign for the long-term development and prognosis.
However, as also mentioned, this is not always the case (McGlashan, 1986;
Harding, 1988). Even acute onset patients can have poor outcome and, when
judged by the development of their symptoms and their outcome, they may
definitely be regarded as schizophrenic.

No further details will be discussed here, since the issue of the nature of the
onset was discussed in a previous section (cf. the extensive and excellent review
of the field by McGlashan, 1988.)

Since even narrow criteria do not define a homogeneous type of outcome,
McGlashan (1988) concluded that the results of "long-term follow-up studies
reviewed here support a broad definition of schizophrenia" (p. 538). The
author also argued against the widely held view that schizophrenia with a
good outcome is in reality an affective disorder. The results reviewed here
support the work of McGlashan (1988).

## F. Gender

Some studies report a milder course for female patients. Huber *et al.* (1979)
from the Bonn study observed more remissions in female than in male
schizophrenics, but the other Lausanne study (Ciompi, 1980) revealed no
relationship. Bleuler (1972) observed an interaction with environmental factors
which will be discussed subsequently.

The finding of a marginally better course and outcome in females is
supported by two studies, one with a shorter 10-yr observation period
(Marneros *et al.*, 1989b), the other arising from the Iowa project (Goldstein,

1988; Goldstein and Link, 1988; Goldstein *et al.*, 1989). Based on up to 161 male and 171 female schizophrenics originally admitted to the Iowa Psychopathic Hospital between 1934 and 1944, the authors found slight differences throughout the patients' histories. Female probands showed (1) a lower likelihood of a poor premorbid period (46% of females, 54% of males); (2) later peak onset (53% male, 32% female before 25 years of age); (3) higher likelihood of schizophrenia in first-degree relatives (female 5.3%, male 2.3%); (4) fewer readmissions (10% recovery for females, 5% for males at the 5-yr follow-up); (5) a more probable affective course or better social function (males showed more negative symptoms and a lack of abilities; e.g., marriage/employment in 48% vs 26% of males); and (6) after 30 yr, 67% of females (vs 78% of males) were regarded as severely ill (see also similar observations by McGlashan and Bardenstein, 1990).

## G. Family History of Schizophrenia

All three European studies failed to find any relevance of the presence or absence of a family history with schizophrenia to the eventual long-term remission from psychopathological or social symptoms. Only Huber *et al.* (1979) reported a marginal paradoxical relationship in which the more the probands had affected relatives, the less schizophrenia-specific their symptoms were at follow-up. McGlashan (1986), however, did find a statistically significant positive correlation between family loading for schizophrenia and poor long-term outcome.

## H. Similarity of Course in the Patient and the Relatives

Only Bleuler (1972) also (personally) examined the relatives of the patients. For these reasons, only Bleuler was in a position to compare the course of illness of his patients with that of the relatives. He found a striking similarity between the courses shown by his patients and those shown by the patients' relatives. However, this was restricted to one aspect of the outcome. In those of his patients who experienced a full remission, no relative showed a severe outcome. For 14 fully remitted patients, there were 14 fully remitted relatives and 4 who retained a mild pathological condition. Other courses were not observed in this group.

At first these figures appear astonishing. However, it should not be overlooked that the actual numbers were small and that, where other outcomes were evident among the patients, there were also quite contrary courses to be found among the relatives. Furthermore, Bleuler's results should not be overgeneralized.

## I. Psychosocial Factors

Disturbed family situations in the premorbid phase of the illness (e.g., a broken home, divorce, death of a parent, or living in a community institution) appeared not to play a role in the long-term course of the patients in the Swiss studies (Bleuler, 1972; Ciompi and Müller, 1976). Huber *et al.* (1979) found merely a negative but nonsignificant trend for their female patients. Bleuler did note that female patients came more often from broken homes, but he could not show that the early separation of the parents had any influence on the final outcome.

However, Bleuler observed that his female patients had experienced twice as many emotional life events as the male patients (e.g., death, separation from partners, and so on). He noted that there was a correlation with a worsening of the psychosis during that time period. Such experiences were associated with either a new episode or an exacerbation of the illness for 58 of 108 women, but only for 16 of 100 men. However, such emotionally charged experiences played an insignificant role in the long-term course (as mentioned previously).

Interestingly, the Chestnut Lodge findings seem to support such a view. McGlashan (1986) reported that a difficult family situation played a role in the development of the course of the illness in the midterm. The multiple regression analysis indicated a significant role for signs of "overinvolvement" and for the forming of "coalitions against the patient" (cf. similar results, Chapter 11). However, over an average 15-yr course, neither of these factors played a significant role. This does not mean that social influences do not play a role in the long-term development of schizophrenia (cf. Ciompi, 1988). The better long-term outcome in non-Western cultures (cf. Lin and Kleinman, 1988) represents an interaction between the still unknown "natural" course and other factors. However, the putative interaction of these factors may play a different role at different stages of the development of the illness.

## III. Suggested Readings

The 1988, Vol. *14* (*4*), issue of the *Schizophrenia Bulletin* (1988) deals with long-term outcome studies. Contributions discuss the European and North American long-term studies, questions methodology, and discusses type of course in schizophrenia. In the same year, Ciompi gave an integrative review and discussion of the heterogeneous outcome considering the results of the more prominent long-term studies. McGlashan and Bardenstein (1990) discuss the evidence for a better outcome in female schizophrenic patients from their own results compared with the findings in the literature. Lin and Kleinman (1988) review the evidence (and conflicting results) for the hypothesis of a better outcome in "non-Western" societies.

## IV. Summary Statements and Interpretations

## A. Situation at the Long-Term Follow-up Assessment

### 1. Symptoms

A full remission occurs in about 25% of the schizophrenic patients, about 25–33% have mild residual symptoms, and about 50% have moderate to severe residual symptoms at follow-up assessments 20–40 yr after the first examination. Most studies concern first admission patients. In the late phase of the illness, nonspecific symptoms are more frequent (approximately 50% of patients) than in earlier phases: These symptoms are negative and nonproductive in nature.

Schizophrenia has no uniform course. It is not a progressively deteriorating illness in all cases. Even if DSM-III criteria are applied at the first assessment, which biases the selection toward chronic cases, then about 20 to 25% of patients remit in the long-term. However, in general, more patients defined by the DSM as schizophreniform had a better outcome (i.e., more DSM-III schizophrenics had a poor outcome at follow-up).

Despite small variations arising from sample definition, the results of studies in Europe and North America are surprisingly similar. Does this then represent the "natural course" of schizophrenia? Reports of milder outcomes in non-Western countries (even where methodological problems were minor, e.g., the second WHO study) raise doubts. Perhaps "cultural" influences play a larger role than is widely believed. Factors that may influence the course include expectations at work, stresses incurred by adopting some social roles, attitudes toward social deviance, existence of a social network (is there a niche for the mentally handicapped in society?), the degree of tolerance, and the nature of family interactions (cf. lower rates of EE relatives in Indian and Mexican families; Leff, 1989).

However, this does not mean that severe outcome and long-term schizophrenic illness do not occur in these countries. Since the incidence (lifetime prevalence) of schizophrenia is about the same in all countries, it cannot be assumed that the difference in the social climate hinders the appearance of the illness or that the stressful climate in Western highly industrialized societies is responsible for the occurrence of schizophrenia. In short, the fact that someone becomes schizophrenic cannot be avoided by a change of the social circumstances in which the person lives, but the eventual course of the illness seem to depend on these circumstances.

Little is known about why social factors exert such different influences on triggering and on the later course. However, it might be speculated that societies interact differently with the already handicapped and that, therefore, there is much room for change and the further development of psychosocial activities to ameliorate the long-term course of the illness.

### 2. Psychosocial Adaptability

In spite of some persistent symptoms, 30–50% of schizophrenics are capable of rehabilitation in society (the proportion varies with the criteria used). Nonetheless, by comparison with other psychiatric illnesses, schizophrenics retain the most severe long-term deficits in social and employment spheres of activity.

These findings impressively illustrate the severe cognitive and emotional handicaps in schizophrenia and the problems former patients have in our societies.

### 3. Mortality and Somatic Diseases

The mortality rate is no higher in schizophrenia than in other psychiatric illnesses. In general, the mortality rates for the psychiatrically ill are higher than those for the general population. There is evidence that fewer schizophrenics suffer from rheumatic arthritis, cancer, and myasthenia gravis. The latter two are not confirmed by all investigators.

The reasons for the putative protection from certain illnesses provided by schizophrenia are not known. It is tempting to speculate that a change in neuroimmune systems occurs in schizophrenia. Some claim that there are links to changes in the metabolism of neurotransmitters and second messengers (e.g., prostaglandins). The possibility that neuroleptic treatment may influence the occurrence of the somatic diseases mentioned (e.g., cancer) has been considered, but reduced cancer rates are not seen by all researchers.

## B. Predictors of the Long-Term Course

### 1. Premorbid Abnormalities

Poor premorbid psychosocial adaptation and schizoid personality features are often, but not always, signs of an unfavorable course.

It should be kept in mind that this is a statistical statement probability. There are still many patients (see text) who had a good premorbid phase and have an unfavorable long-term course, and vice versa.

The presence of schizoid traits in the premorbid course of the illness supports the claim that schizoid or schizotypal personality disorders and schizophrenia are linked phenomena (Chapter 10). The poor prognosis of those who already show these traits in the premorbid phase may point to the existence of a more severe disease in these subjects.

### 2. Symptoms and Prognosis

The early appearance of auditory hallucinations predicts an unfavorable long-term course (in some studies also visual hallucinations). Flattened affect is unfavorable for the short- and midterm course, but its connection with a long-term course remains equivocal.

The well-documented role of hallucinations as a predictor of poor outcome is the most challenging result of the long-term studies. It challenges the concept that type I positive-symptom or first-rank-symptom schizophrenia, in all of which hallucinations are prominent, indicates a favorable outcome (Chapter 1).

These results have the important implication that concepts of positive and negative symptoms, or both, need to change. For example, 60% of patients with a poor outcome start with a typical positive symptom (hallucinations) and end with negative symptoms (e.g., studies of Tsuang's group). The same applies to positive symptoms like paranoia (cf. text). This means that in many cases different groups of outcome are not characterized by such global categories as positive and negative symptoms. These two types of symptom may only reflect different states. Although it has been seen that positive and negative schizophrenics are often characterized by different experimental task performance, the clinical findings here indicate that the positive–negative feature alone does not distinguish two diseases among the schizophrenias. Only with additional information on biological activity or cognitive performance can a decision be made whether a patient belongs to one or another putative subgroup or even to different groups of diseases.

### 3. Traditional Subgroups as Predictors

As yet, the only indication is that catatonics tend to have a better prognosis than other groups.

No additional information exists on what makes the catatonic group so different. It can only be speculated that the dominance of motor symptoms may indicate that different brain regions are affected, which for unknown reasons are linked with a higher chance for complete remission.

### 4. Family History and Prognosis

It is equivocal whether genetic factors are relevant for prognosis. (Only one study reported the hypothetically expected link between family history and poor outcome.)

This finding is surprising, but may only show that it is difficult to assess the family history correctly when one must rely on case reports of variable quality.

### 5. Stressful Experiences and Living Conditions

The short-term development of psychoses and stressful experiences are clearly related, but it remains unclear what role these experiences have in the long-term development of the illness.

The same argument applies here as in previous sections. However, one of the authors of the long-term studies (Manfred Bleuler) followed his patients personally and saw a clear influence of life events on the course of the illness, at least in his female patients. However, he denies that the overall long-term course is different. McGlashan saw a relationship between unfavorable familial atmosphere and poor outcome, but also only for the midterm outcome. This contradicts findings from non-Western less industrialized countries. It may be that a psychosocial climate more favorable for the mentally handicapped is more significant than the occurrence of a life event (e.g., loss of a relative, loss of the job), occurrences that may have a similar incidence in both cultures.

# References

Angst, J. (1988). European long-term follow-up studies of schizophrenia. *Schizophrenia Bulletin, 14,* 501–513.

Angst, J., Isele, R., Scharfetter, C. H., and Scheidegger, P. Zur prämorbiden Persönlichkeit Schizophrener. *Schweizische Archiv Neurologie Neurochirurgie und Psychiatrie, 136,* 45–53.

Bland, R. C., and Orn, H. (1980). Prediction of long-term outcome from presenting symptoms in schizophrenia. *Journal of Clinical Psychiatry, 41,* 85–88.

Bleuler, M. (1972). *Die schizophrenen Geistesstörungen im Lichte langjähriger Kranken- und Familiengeschichten.* Stuttgart: Thieme.

Bleuler, M., Huber, G., Gross, G., and Schüttler, R. (1976). Der langfristige Verlauf schizophrener Psychosen. Gemeinsame Ergebnisse zweier Untersuchungen. *Der Nervenarzt, 47,* 477–481.

Buda, M., Tsuang, M. T., and Fleming, J. A. (1988). Causes of death in DSM-III schizophrenics and other psychotics. *Archives of General Psychiatry, 45,* 283–285.

Cannon-Spoor, H. E., Potkin, S. G., and Wyatt, R. J. (1982). Measurement of premorbid adjustment in chronic schizophrenia. *Schizophrenia Bulletin, 8,* 470–484.

Carpenter, W. T., Bartko, J. J., Strauss, J. S., and Hawk, A. B. (1978). Signs and symptoms as predictors of outcome: A report from the international pilot study of schizophrenia. *American Journal of Psychiatry, 135,* 940–945.

Ciompi, L. (1980). Ist die chronische Schizophrenie ein Artefakt?—Argumente und Gegenargumente. *Fortschritte der Neurologie, Psychiatrie, und ihrer Grenzgebiete, 48,* 237–248.

Ciompi, L. (1981). Neues zur Schizophrenie im Lichte jüngerer Langzeituntersuchungen. In G. Huber (Ed.), *Schizophrenie. Stand und Entwicklungstendenzen der Forschung.* Stuttgart: Schattauer.

Ciompi, L. (1985). Aging and schizophrenic psychosis. *Acta Psychiatria Scandinavica, 71,* 93–105.

Ciompi, L. (1988). Learning from outcome studies: Toward a comprehensive biological–psychosocial understanding of schizophrenia. *Schizophrenia Research, 1,* 373–384.

Ciompi, L., and Müller, C. (1976). *Lebensweg und Alter der Schizophrenen. Eine katamnestische Langzeitstudie bis ins Senium.* Berlin: Springer.

Cloninger, C. R., Martin, R. L., Guze, S. B., and Clayton, P. J. (1985). Diagnosis and prognosis in schizophrenia. *Archives of General Psychiatry, 42,* 15–25.

Dube, K. C., Kumar, N., and Dube, S. (1984). Long term course and outcome of the Agra cases in the International Pilot Study of Schizophrenia. *Acta Psychiatrica Scandinavica, 70,* 170–179.

Eaton, W. W. (1985). Epidemiology of schizophrenia. *Epidemiologic Reviews*, *7*, 105–126.

Fenton, W. S., and McGlashan, T. H. (1986). The prognostic significance of obsessive–compulsive symptoms in schizophrenia. *American Journal of Psychiatry*, *143*, 437–441.

Fudenberg, H. H., Whitten, H. D., Chou, Y. K., Arnaud, P., Shums, A. A., and Khansari, N. K. (1984). Sigma receptors and autoimmune mechanisms in schizophrenia: Preliminary findings and hypotheses. *Biomedicine & Pharmacotherapy*, *38*, 285–290.

Gittelson, N. L., and Richardson, T. D. E. (1973). Myasthenia gravis and schizophrenia: A rare combination. *British Journal of Psychiatry*, *122*, 343–344.

Goldstein, J. M. (1988). Gender differences in the course of schizophrenia. *American Journal of Psychiatry*, *145*, 684–689.

Goldstein, J. M., and Link, B. G. (1988). Gender and the expression of schizophrenia. *Journal of Psychiatric Research*, *22*, 141–155.

Goldstein, J. M., Tsuang, M. T., and Faraone, S. V. (1989). Gender and schizophrenia: Implications for understanding the heterogeneity of the illness. *Psychiatry Research*, *28*, 243–253.

Harding, C. M. (1988). Course types in schizophrenia: An analysis of European and American studies. *Schizophrenia Bulletin*, *14*, 633–643.

Harding, C. M., McCormick, R. V., Strauss, J. S., Ashikaga, T., and Brooks, G. W. (1987). *Computerized life chart methods to map domains of function and illustrate patterns of interactions in the long-term course trajectories of patients who once met criteria for DSM-III schizophrenia*. Presented at the Schizophrenia Conference, Bern.

Harding, C. M., McCormick, R. V., Strauss, J. S., Ashikaga, T., and Brooks, G. W. (1989). Computerized life chart methods to map domains of function and illustrate patterns of interactions in the long term course trajectories of patients who once met the criteria for DSM-III schizophrenia. *British Journal of Psychiatry*, *155*, *Suppl. 5*, 100–106.

Harris, A. E. (1988). Physical disease and schizophrenia. *Schizophrenia Bulletin*, *14*, 85–96.

Harrow, M., and Westermeyer, J. F. (1987). Process-reactive dimension and outcome for narrow concepts of schizophrenia. *Schizophrenia Bulletin*, *13*, 361–368.

Helzer, J. E., Kendell, R. E., and Brockington, I. F. (1983). Contribution of the six-month criterion to the predictive validity of the DSM-III definition of schizophrenia. *Archives of General Psychiatry*, *40*, 1277–1280.

Huber, G. (1957). *Pneumoencephalographische und psychopathologische Bilder bei endogenen Psychosen*. Berlin: Springer.

Huber, G., Gross, G., and Schüttler, R. (1979). *Schizophrenie. Eine verlaufs- und sozialpsychiatrische Langzeitstudie*. Berlin: Springer.

Huber, G., Gross, G., and Schuettler, R. (1980). Longitudinal studies of schizophrenic patients. *Schizophrenia Bulletin*, *6*, 592–605.

Jonsson, H., and Nyman, A. K. (1984). Prediction of outcome in schizophrenia. *Acta Psychiatrica Scandinavica*, *69*, 274–291.

Kendler, K. S., Gruenberg, A. M., and Tsuang, M. T. (1984). Outcome of schizophrenic subtypes defined by four diagnostic systems. *Archives of General Psychiatry*, *41*, 149–154.

Klorman, R., Strauss, J. S., and Kokes, R. F. (1977). Premorbid adjustment in schizophrenia. Part III. The relationship of demographic and diagnostic factors to measures of premorbid adjustment in schizophrenia. *Schizophrenia Bulletin*, *3*, 214–225.

Knight, R. A., Roff, J. D., Barrnett, J., and Moss, J. L. (1979). Concurrent and predictive validity of thought disorder and affectivity: A 22-year follow-up of acute schizophrenics. *Journal of Abnormal Psychology*, *88*, 1–12.

Kraepelin, E. (1909). *Psychiatrie: Ein Lehrbuch für Studierende und Ärzte*, Vol. 1. Leipzig: Barth.

Leff, J. (1989). Environmental personality interaction in the course of schizophrenia. 2nd Symposium: Search for the causes of schizophrenia. Heidelberg.

Lin, K-M., and Kleinman, A. M. (1988). Psychopathology and clinical course of schizophrenia: A cross-cultural perspective. *Schizophrenia Bulletin*, *14*, 555–567.

Loyd, D., Simpson, J. C., and Tsuang, M. T. (1985). Are there sex-differences in the long-term outcome of schizophrenia? Comparisons with mania, depression, and surgical controls. *Journal of Nervous and Mental Disease*, *173*, 643–649.

Marinow, A. (1981). Über Verlauf, Ausgang und Prognose bei Schizophrenen. In G. Huber (Ed.), *Schizophrenie. Stand und Entwicklungstendenzen der Forschung*, pp. 135–149. Stuttgart: Schattauer.

Marneros, A., Deister, A., Rohde, A., Steinmeyer, E. M., and Jünemann, H. (1989a). Long-term outcome of schizoaffective and schizophrenic disorders: A comparative study. I. Definitions, methods, psychopathological and social outcome. *European Archives of Psychiatry and Neurological Sciences*, 238, 118–125.

Marneros, A., Steinmeyer, E. M., Deister, A., Rohde, A., and Jünemann, H. (1989b). Long-term outcome of schizoaffective and schizophrenic disorders: A comparative study. III. Social consequences. *European Archives of Psychiatry and Neurological Sciences*, *238*, 135–139.

Masterson, E., and O'Shea, B. (1984). Smoking and malignancy in schizophrenia. *British Journal of Psychiatry*, *145*, 429–432.

McGlashan, T. H. (1986). Predictors of shorter-, medium-, and longer-term outcome in schizophrenia. *American Journal of Psychiatry*, *143*, 50–55.

McGlashan, T. H. (1988). A selective review of recent North American long-term followup studies of schizophrenia. *Schizophrenia Bulletin*, *14*, 515–542.

McGlashan, T. H., and Bardenstein, K. K. (1990). Gender differences in affective, schizoaffective, and schizophrenic disorders. *Schizoiphrenia Bulletin*, *16*, 319–329.

McGlashan, T. H., Carpenter, W. T., Jr., and Bartko, J. J. (1988). Issues of design and methodology in long-term followup studies. *Schizophrenia Bulletin*, *14*, 569–574.

Möller, H. J., Scharl, W., and von Zerssen, D. (1984). Strauss–Carpenter Skala: Überprüfung ihres prognostischen Wertes für das 5-Jahres-"Outcome" schizophrener Patienten. *European Archives of Psychiatry and Neurological Sciences*, *234*, 112–117.

Mortensen, P. B. (1987). Neuroleptic treatment and other factors modifying cancer risk in schizophrenic patients. *Acta Psychiatrica Scandinavica*, *75*, 585–590.

Munk-Jorgensen, P., and Mortensen, P. B. (1989). Schizophrenia: A 13-year follow-up. *Acta Psychiatrica Scandinavica*, *79*, 391–399.

Oades, R. D. (1982). *Attention and schizophrenia: Neurobiological bases.* London: Pitman.

Ogawa, K., Miya, M., Watarai, A., Nakazawa, M., Yuasa, S., and Utena, H. (1987). A long-term follow-up study of schizophrenia in Japan—With special reference to the course of social adjustment. *British Journal of Psychiatry*, *151*, 758–765.

Ravn, J. (1988). Neuroleptic treatment and other factors modifying cancer risk in schizophrenic patients. *Acta Psychiatrica Scandinavica*, *76*, 605.

Steinmeyer, E. M., Marneros, A., Deister, A., Rohde, A., and Jünemann, H. (1989). Long-term outcome of schizoaffective and schizophrenic disorders: A comparative study. II. Causal–analytical investigations. *European Archives of Psychiatry and Neurological Sciences*, *238*, 126–134.

Stephens, J. H. (1978). Long-term prognosis and follow-up in schizophrenia. *Schizophrenia Bulletin*, *4*, 25–47.

Stephens, J. H., Astrup, C., and Mangrum, J. C. (1966). Prognostic factors in recovered and deteriorated schizophrenics. *American Journal of Psychiatry*, *122*, 1116–1121.

Sternberg, E. (1981). Verlaufsgesetzlichkeiten der Schizophrenie im Lichte von Langzeituntersuchungen bis ins Senium. In G. Huber (Ed.), *Schizophrenie. Stand und Entwicklungstendenzen der Forschung*, pp. 251–262. Stuttgart: Schattauer.

Tsuang, M. T. (1982). Long-term outcome in schizophrenia. *Trends in NeuroScience*, *5*, 203–207.

Tsuang, M. T. (1986). Predictors of poor and good outcome in schizophrenia. In L. Erlenmeyer-Kimling and N. E. Miller (Eds.), *Life-span research on the prediction of psychopathology.* Hillsdale, New Jersey: Erlbaum.

Tsuang, M. T., and Dempsey, M. (1979). Long-term outcome of major psychoses. II. Schizoaffective disorder compared with schizophrenia, affective disorders, and a surgical control group. *Archives of General Psychiatry, 36,* 1302–1304.

Tsuang, M. T., and Fleming, J. A. (1987). Long-term outcome of schizophrenia and other psychoses. In H. Häfner, W. F. Gattaz, and W. Janzarik (Eds.), *Search for the causes of schizophrenia.* Berlin: Springer.

Tsuang, M. T., Woolson, R. F., and Fleming, J. A. (1979). Long-term outcome of major psychoses. I. Schizophrenia and affective disorders compared with psychiatrically symptom-free surgical conditions. *Archives of General Psychiatry, 36,* 1295–1301.

Tsuang, M. T., Woolson, R. F., and Simpson, J. C. (1981). An evaluation of the Feighner criteria for schizophrenia and affective disorders using long-term outcome data. *Psychological Medicine, 11,* 281–287.

Vaillant, G. E. (1962). The prediction of recovery in schizophrenia. *Journal of Nervous and Mental Disease, 135,* 534–542.

Vaillant, G. E. (1964a). An historical review of the remitting schizophrenics. *Journal of Nervous and Mental Diseases, 138,* 48–56.

Vaillant, G. E. (1964b). Prospective prediction of schizophrenic remission. *Archives of General Psychiatry, 11,* 509–518.

Watt, N. P. (1978). Patterns of childhood social development in adult schizophrenia. *Archives of General Psychiatry, 35,* 160–165.

Watts, D. C., Katz, K., and Sheperd, M. (1983). The natural history of schizophrenia: A 5-year prospective follow-up of a standardized clinical and social assessment. *Psychological Medicine, 13,* 663–670.

Winokur, G., Scharfetter, C., and Angst, J. (1985). Stability of psychotic symptomatology (delusions, hallucinations), affective syndromes, and schizophrenic symptoms (thought disorder, incongruent affect) over episodes in remitting psychoses. *European Archives of Psychiatry and Neurological Sciences, 234,* 303–307.

# PART VII

# Integration of the Empirical Results and Theoretical Views

# Chapter 15

# Influential Theories on the Nature of Schizophrenic Symptoms—Old and New

## I. Breakdown of Response Hierarchies and Dominant Response Bias

One of the early influential hypotheses was based on behavior theory then dominating contemporary psychology. Broen and Storms in 1966 claimed that schizophrenic symptoms and experimental performance could be explained as a collapse of the hierarchy of response strengths. An example illustrates what they meant by "response strength." The response "black" to the stimulus "white" is more probable than the response "bicycle," since these stimuli appear together more often in the developmental learning history of each individual; thus, "black" has a greater response strength than "bicycle."

These authors suggested that normal hierarchies of response strength were less differentiated in schizophrenics as a result of increased anxiety and, therefore, increased arousal. Arousal was seen as the source of the physiological activity responsible for a given response strength. If general arousal was high, then the differences between response strengths was reduced. In the opinion of Broen and Storms, this explained the inadequate behavior of the schizophrenics, for example, their inadequate verbal responses.

The numerous problems with this theory can be summarized under three headings: first, anxiety is merely a nonspecific symptom of schizophrenia; second, there is little evidence for a generally increased arousal in schizophrenia (cf. the phenomenon of electrodermal nonresponse); and third, modern psycholinguistics has refuted the idea that speech production can be explained by stringing together speech elements according to response strength or the strength of associations (cf. Chapter 2).

In contrast, Chapman and Chapman (1973) suggested that schizophrenics showed a more pronounced bias toward the dominant meaning of words. The authors showed that this preference becomes evident when a "nondominant" response is appropriate. As related in Chapter 2, such response limitations are characteristic of only a subgroup of schizophrenics who are chronically ill. The suggestion of Chapman and Chapman is not appropriate for schizophrenics who show disorganized response patterns, that is, who process and respond to irrelevant (i.e., nondominant) features.

## II. Set Theory

The reaction times of schizophrenics are faster with regular than with irregular preparatory intervals up to about 6 sec, but beyond this they become faster with irregular than with regular intervals. Normal controls are always quicker with regular preparatory intervals; thus, the difference between schizophrenics and normals is most striking at the long intervals (cf. Chapter 4). This observation provided a major stimulus to Shakow's theory (1962), who started his extensive reaction-time work as early as 1924 at the Worcester State Hospital in Massachusetts. The problem to solve was why schizophrenics do not make use of the regularity of the long intervals. Shakow suggested that the major mental process or set is not stable enough to last until the signal comes. Further, Shakow assumed that minor or "segmental" sets, and therefore irrelevant aspects of a situation, intrude into the mental processes.

Bleuler (1911) expounded the idea that a loss of goal represented the forsaking of a direction of thought for an inappropriate associative sequence of ideas. Interestingly, Chapman and Chapman (1973) drew our attention to the fact that this principle is rather similar to Shakow's hypothesis. Indeed, as can be seen in Chapter 2, schizophrenics often respond in object-classification tasks, or while interpreting sentences, with metaphorical meanings to single items or with details irrelevant to the paramount concepts presented. Typically, schizophrenics cannot see the forest for the trees, as Shakow puts it.

## III. Serial or Parallel Processing Dysfunction

Based on the separation of information processing into automatic and controlled modes (Schneider and Shiffrin, 1977), Callaway and Naghdi (1982) proposed that schizophrenics are deficient in controlled serial processing. Automatic parallel processing is said to be intact.

It is certainly true that schizophrenics have problems in serial processing (e.g., in semantic tasks) but, as will be discussed later, they fail also in certain automatic processing tasks, for example, Gestalt perception. Knight (1984), after reviewing the literature, is of the opinion that "some deficiency in perceptual schema formation in automaticity, or in the holistic stage of processing," may be the basis of schizophrenic deviant performance. This is an interesting hypothesis, but one certainly cannot reduce the schizophrenic cognitive deficit either to the automatic stage of processing alone or to stages of controlled processing only (Chapter 4). The common denominator may be a specific deficit at both levels (cf. Chapter 16).

# IV. Attentional Theories

The supposition that the disturbance of schizophrenic function can be explained in terms of attention has evoked wide interest and, expressed in this general form, experimental support.

From the start of the century, attentional disturbances were viewed as prominent symptoms of schizophrenia (Bleuler, 1911; Kraepelin, 1913), yet both Bleuler and Kraepelin emphasized that this was but one of many symptoms.

Only toward the end of the 1950s, following the ideas and theory put forward by the British experimental psychologist Broadbent (1958), did broad-based, experimental investigations of schizophrenic attention-related phenomena really get going. (It should be noted that Broadbent was only concerned with normal information processing.) Following Broadbent's explanation of selective attention in terms of the filtering of information, it was suggested that the function of this filter was disturbed in schizophrenia (Payne et al., 1959; McGhie and Chapman, 1961). Broadbent's filter "selected" stimuli according to stimulus set (physical features such as color). However, the experimental evidence (discussed in Chapter 4) shows that the findings are not unequivocal. It is doubtful, if the tasks are properly matched for task difficulty, that the problem of schizophrenics really can be explained by a disturbance at the level of stimulus-driven information processing alone, that is, selection by physical cues. (Exceptions and the possible explanations will be discussed in Chapter 16.)

Since even in the domain of normal cognitive psychology the stimulus set theory did not cover all phenomena encountered in the field of perception, Broadbent (1971) extended his theory to a second mechanism called response set. (Selection guided by "response set" occurs, for example, in specific dichotic listening paradigms in which the subject has to respond only to stimuli that belong to a certain category whereas, under stimulus set conditions, the subject has to listen only to a certain source irrespective of the content. A similar, and recently more often applied, division of information processing that is now used by several researchers is that of stimulus-driven and concept-driven.) Again, this new theory by Broadbent was influential for schizophrenia research (e.g., Hemsley and Zawada, 1976). Hemsley and co-workers in the United Kingdom showed that schizophrenics had more problems with the selection by content than did control groups in a dichotic listening experiment. Unfortunately, this was not compared to a stimulus set condition. (Later Hemsley modified his theoretical position somewhat; see Chapter 16).

The concept of "overinclusive thinking," after the observations of Cameron in the 1930s and 1940s, touches on a variant of attention theory and gave rise to numerous studies (see Chapter 2). Overinclusive thinking means that the schizophrenic attends too much to the peripheral elements of a task and that, as a consequence, the categories selected are too broad. Although the concept may remain descriptively useful at the clinical level of observation, it has proved, mainly in its several extensions, too difficult to test experimentally.

However, the idea of overinclusive thinking was, from a heuristic point of view, very fruitful and led to experiments that brought out the idea of two essentially opposite types of attentional deficit among schizophrenics. In one deficit, attention span is too broad and inclusive, allowing a flood of relatively unselected information to influence central cognitive processes, particularly in the acutely ill schizophrenic (overinclusion). The opposite type of information processing may be characterized by a reduced range of stimuli to which attention is allocated. This seems to be seen particularly in the chronically ill schizophrenic in whom negative symptoms dominate (cf. Venables, 1964). These studies, whatever their interpretation, draw our attention to the fact that differences in information processing between subgroups of schizophrenics exist.

Somewhat similar to the latter observation of a reduced range of attention is the hypothesis of two researchers from California. Nuechterlein and Dawson (1984) assume that the available processing capacity for task-relevant cognitive operations is reduced in schizophrenia and fundamental to the illness. This hypothesis is again based on the division of cognitive operations into automatic and controlled processes (Schneider and Shiffrin 1977), especially a variant of this by Kahneman (1973). The principal difference between automatic processing and controlled processing is the demand on processing capacity in the latter (cf. a more extensive discussion in Chapters 2–4). Kahneman's variant of this theory is that, in contrast to the earlier "bottleneck" theories of attention (e.g., filter theory of Broadbent), the available "space" in the processing channel is less decisive than for the amount of processing capacity allocated to a given set of stimuli. In other words, attention to a given stimulus or event varies in accordance with the amount of processing capacity. Therefore, selective attention processing as a part of controlled data processing requires "effort."

A fundamental methodological problem for the study of controlled processes in schizophrenia research is that tasks which need more processing capacity are generally more difficult ones. Severely ill psychiatric patients, whatever their illness, tend to perform poorly on more difficult tasks (Chapter 2, Introduction). Nevertheless, Nuechterlein and Dawson (1984) claim that the schizophrenic deficit on the degraded stimulus version of the continuous performance test (CPT) is specific and a vulnerability marker. Indeed, an impairment is also found in the children of schizophrenics, and could thus be a candidate for a biological marker of schizophrenia (cf. Chapter 12). However, it is just as plausible that such children are merely suffering from more stress than most comparison groups (caused by living with a schizophrenic father or mother) and for this reason alone show an impairment on difficult tasks. Aware of this possibility, Nuechterlein and Dawson argue that the impairment still remains specific, even if the comparison groups are as appropriate as possible (e.g., children of depressive parents and hyperactive children).

Dawson and Nuechterlein (1984) also argue that a reduction of attentional capacity is seen in the electrodermal nonresponse to orienting stimuli. This may indeed be so, and the argument cannot be refuted by the task-difficulty statement. However, this brings us to the problem of whether the attention allocation problem is specific and can be generalized to the total group of schizophrenics, since (1) electrodermal nonresponse is confined to a subgroup with predominantly negative symptoms and (2) electrodermal nonresponse can also be found in depressive patients and in other persons with psychological disturbances.

In an extension of this hypothesis, Nuechterlein and Dawson (1984) say that the reduction of available processing capacity may be caused by the failure of different underlying mechanisms. (1) The pool of processing capacity may be normal, but not enough capacity is allocated to the task. (2) The pool is normal, but more capacity is allocated to irrelevant aspects of the task. (3) Automatic tasks are processed within the controlled processing high-capacity system. (4) The total pool of processing capacity is smaller in schizophrenics.

In their extensive review of the literature, Nuechterlein and Dawson (1984) do not give examples of which kind of "subdeficit" is involved in which kind of deviant schizophrenic performance. Instead they propose further research.

However, from the available literature it is hard to see how the capacity hypothesis is involved in all tasks in which schizophrenics fail. The schizophrenic patient has, for example, problems detecting the adequate emotional expression in faces. The demand on controlled processing capacity is low in such a task. In addition, there are tasks in which schizophrenics use controlled processing instead of automatic holistic (Gestalt) strategies but do not fail, as was shown in the experiment of Schwartz-Place and Gilmore (1980). This looks like the type 3 deficit of Nuechterlein and Dawson (1984) but, contrary to the prediction, the schizophrenics perform relatively better than controls (cf. Chapter 4).

In conclusion, inappropriate or reduced allocation of processing resources may describe correctly some of the failures in schizophrenics or possibly, at least, in a subgroup of schizophrenics, but it does not provide an explanatory principle for a wider range of schizophrenic difficulties. Whether fundamental differences between subgroups (i.e., the existence of separate groups within the spectrum of schizophrenia) explain this unsatisfactory situation still has to be discussed (Chapter 16).

# V. Slowness of Processing

Yates (1966) sees the basic deficit in schizophrenia as a slowness of processing. Yates excludes the possibility that higher level processing is disturbed, but maintains that the speed of processing from the periphery to central data processing units is slower. In light of the theory by Broadbent, he suggests that the speed of transfer in the information processing channel is slow. Thus, in contrast to the previously mentioned theories, he does not claim that the selection of relevant data is the basis of the schizophrenic deficit. Slow response is indeed a widely observed phenomenon in schizophrenia. However, as was shown in Chapter 4, especially in Section IV, a general slowness of response is an unspecific phenomenon; further, there is evidence that thought-disordered schizophrenics respond more quickly than normal controls under specific circumstances (e.g., primed responses in a word detection task; Manschreck et al., 1988) or that schizophrenics show no altered performance in some tests in which speed of transfer from the periphery (sensory buffer) to the central units is critical (e.g., full-report technique of the span-of-apprehension test). There is further evidence that the assumed slowness of transfer from the periphery to central information processing units is confined to subgroups, possibly to poor premorbid chronic groups, as was demonstrated by the Saccuzzo group with the backward masking paradigm. The poor-premorbid poor-prognosis group does not detect the target before the mask arrives, even after considerable training (Saccuzzo and Braff, 1981, Chapter 4).

Thus, the "slowness of processing" hypothesis may not describe a specific feature and may not be a phenomenon that can be generalized to the total group of schizophrenics.

# VI. Disturbed Lateralized Functions

Beginning with clinical observation and neuropsychological findings, left-hemisphere dysfunction hypotheses were advocated by a number of research workers. In Germany, Kleist (1960) and, later in Canada, Flor-Henry (1969) proposed the left hemisphere as the origin of schizophrenic symptoms. The latter saw evidence in the well-known fact that temporal lobe epileptics with a focus on the left side often have symptoms similar to schizophrenia. (However, Shukla and Katiyar, 1980, and Merrin, 1981, did not see a clear-cut relationship in focal epileptics.) Later, Flor-Henry (cf. 1979) supported his position with results from his own cognitive and psychophysiological studies (e.g., review of Tomer and Flor-Henry, 1989). The work of Flor-Henry was heuristically fruitful since it triggered a large amount of research. Interestingly, in view of the evidence, Tomer and Flor-Henry (1989) modified their position recently (see subsequent text). Although there is some evidence for the involvement of the left hemisphere at several levels of functioning (from information processing to biochemical findings, cf. Chapter 9), there are also unequivocal findings suggesting a disturbance of the right hemisphere. Cutting (1985) in the United Kingdom, after reviewing the cognitive literature, argued in favor of a right-hemisphere deficit. As was discussed in Chapter 9, there is evidence for each of these two possibilities, that is, no single postulate can account for all the results. Interestingly, Tomer and Flor-Henry (1989) stated that neuroleptic medication may be involved in some findings of changed asymmetries in schizophrenics.

Magaro (1980) tried to resolve conflicting results by suggesting that subgroups have different lateralized dysfunctions. Magaro (1980) claimed that the paranoid syndrome has its origin in the right hemisphere and that nonparanoid schizophrenia can be explained as a dysfunction of the left hemisphere. However, this was not confirmed unequivocally with the paranoid group in their own series of experiments that followed (Magaro and Chamrad, 1983). Nevertheless, there are reports of increased activation in the EEG over the left hemisphere for paranoid hallucinating subjects (whatever the reason) or exaggerated right ear advantage in dichotic listening tests (which could signify a high activity left-brain function or low activity right-brain function). However, for other areas of function, no support or controversial claims are reported in the literature (see Chapter 9).

In fact it is almost uncanny that so many groups claim some sort of mild and unusual asymmetric function in medicated patients. The reader should note that recovery of function in unilaterally lesioned animals can be reversed by neuroleptic treatment (e.g., recovery from the neglect syndrome after unilateral frontal damage; Vargo *et al.,* 1989). As discussed already, medication has been recorded as changing attentional asymmetries in schizophrenics (Tomer and Flor-Henry, 1989).

## VII. Positive and Negative Symptoms: Psychological and Neuropsychological Hypotheses

Some of the conflicts arising out of the studies we have discussed are caused by the fact that only a proportion of the schizophrenic subjects examined showed the impairment sought. The idea that this might be due to two illnesses of separate origin, both called schizophrenia, has recently gained widespread attention and popularity. It was suggested that one type of the illness leads to the development of productive or positive symptoms; the other, often treated as a quite independent entity, results in negative symptoms. Although the initial idea can be traced back to J. Hughlings Jackson in the United Kingdom and Kraepelin in Germany at the turn of the century, the study of clusters of such signs and symptoms was only more recently presented in more detail by Strauss and colleagues in the United States (1974). Popularity and interest followed the elaboration by Crow *et al.* in the United Kingdom (1982) and Andreasen in the United States (1982). However, as discussed in Chapter 1, it is still not clear whether the positive and negative syndromes represent truly different entities or different diseases, or whether some of the symptoms are secondary consequences of a long disease process (cf. reviews and critical comments by Lewine, 1985; Sommers, 1985). The now widely used Scale for the Assessment of Negative Symptoms (SANS) developed by Andreasen (1983) classifies the following symptoms with this concept: affective flattening, alogia, avolition/apathy, anhedonia, and attentional impairment. The Scale for the Assessment of Positive Symptoms (SAPS) of Andreasen (1984) groups delusions, hallucinations, bizarre behavior, and positive formal thought disorder with this concept.

In the meantime, a number of theoretical contributions have been made in an attempt to integrate results from several levels of analysis and to try to resolve the issue by looking for evidence on the cognitive and the neuropsychological level.

Naturally if positive and negative symptoms really represent two illnesses with only a limited overlap, as Crow suggested, then they should be associated with different sets of risk markers (Nuechterlein and Dawson, 1984). Such factors should be observable among nonsymptomatic former schizophrenics as much as in their close relatives. These authors, however, have suggested no real proposal of what such features in the first degree relatives should be.

Spring and colleagues (1990) at the Texas Technical University have made such an attempt. (Earlier, together with Zubin, Spring (1977) put forward the influential stress model of vulnerability for schizophrenia; see subsequent text.) Spring *et al.* (1990) suggested that so-called markers for positive symptoms should not only be correlated with the incidence of such symptoms, but should fluctuate with them and, like them, should be influenced by neuroleptic treatment. It follows that markers associated with negative symptoms should fluctuate less and should be less influenced by neuroleptics. Naturally, both types of markers should be present in remitted schizophrenics and their first degree relatives. Herein lies a considerable difficulty. How can one decide which marker (performance deficit) is linked with which symptom in as yet unsymptomatic individuals at risk (first degree relatives of schizophrenics)? Spring's solution lies in equating markers found in relatives with those of the active symptomatic patient. A prominent example is the increased distractability of schizophrenics with positive symptoms that has been reported in so many different situations. Not only does distractability correlate with positive symptoms, but reasonable evidence suggests that neuroleptics reduce both (cf. Chapter 13) and that it is characteristic of (a subgroup of?) first degree relatives of schizophrenics as demonstrated by Spring and others (cf. Chapter 4).

Markers for the negative symptom illness are more difficult to demonstrate. For example, impairments on the CPT or slowed reaction times do appear to correlate with negative symptoms. In contrast to Spring's requirement, they seem to be attenuated by neuroleptic treatment (cf. Chapters 4 and 13). Further, with regard to the performance of relatives, one notes that Nuechterlein's group could only find a deficit on the CPT with degraded stimuli (cf. Chapter 12).

Too few studies have been concerned with the performance of the same subjects on tests indicating risk for negative-symptom and tests indicating risk for positive-symptom illness. It is too early to be sure if there are two populations of high-risk individuals.

The contribution of Spring et al. (1990) should be considered a proposal to reorganize the divergent empirical findings. It should be seen as an attempt to integrate three levels of analysis—clinical symptoms, vulnerability indicators, and information processing—as possible basic deficits of both types of illness.

Here Frith and Done (1988), working with Crow at the Northwick Park Clinic and Research Center in England, go a step further. They are interested in relating positive and negative symptoms to the underlying psychological processes and in relating these, in turn, to a neurobiological level of analysis. In contrast to Spring, they are primarily concerned with actively symptomatic patients and not with remitted patients or subjects at risk.

Dissatisfied with theories of attention, Frith and Done (1988) suggest that schizophrenics with positive symptoms primarily have a disturbance of internal monitoring of their own actions and responses. As a consequence, schizophrenics are less aware that they themselves have initiated the response or action. In other words, there is a "schism" between a collateral internal monitoring system and the system executing the actions. Frith and Done (1988) further suggest that schizophrenics show a failure to integrate feedback from their own actions into the ongoing collateral monitoring process. The task of the monitor is to compare the actual action with the neuronal representation of the "just past" action and the intended action. In other words, the ongoing action is compared with a higher order model of this action. This lack of integration then results in the schizophrenics' interpretation of being under the control of alien forces, a common delusion in schizophrenia and a positive symptom.

In an extension of the hypothesis, Frith and Done (1988) predict that schizophrenics with positive symptoms or type I schizophrenia are less inclined to fail in stimulus-driven processes since these are less dependent on internal monitoring processes. (These are so-called closed-loop processes.) This prediction is interesting, since there is indeed more evidence for a breakdown of non-stimulus-driven processes (open-loop or concept-driven and others) in schizophrenics, as discussed in Chapter 4. We must discuss in Chapter 16 whether this observation is really limited to the positive symptom schizophrenics. However, Frith and Done (1988) confine their argument to the motor component of psychological function. They cite evidence from the literature to support their position. For example, a lack of a reduction in EEG activity to self-generated tones was demonstrated by Braff et al. (1977). Normals showed reduced EEG activity if they themselves triggered a tone compared with when a tone was initiated by the experimenter. Thus self-initiated and non-self-initiated acts are not accompanied by different brain activities in schizophrenics. However, it is not clear from the report of Braff et al. (1977) whether this is limited to positive symptom schizophrenics. Another example, not quoted by the authors, may be the poor eye-tracking performance of schizophrenics. As discussed in Chapter 7, normals show the same poor performance as schizophrenics if feedback cues are reduced. Thus, schizophrenics perform like subjects who have less access to visual feedback from their own performance. Frith and Done (1989) set out to test their theory themselves. They developed a special experiment in which visual feedback was manipulated experimentally. They found that patients with the delusion of alien control performed poorly if feedback was reduced. Thus, patients with a specific positive symptom were affected. However the groups were small. Whether the findings can be generalized remains an open question.

As far as the negative or Type II schizophrenics are concerned, Frith and Done (1988) assume that their main failure is not with internal monitoring of self-generated acts but with initiating those acts. The authors suggest that there are some similarities between the characteristics of schizophrenics with negative symptoms and Parkinson's patients. They lack the ability to generate intentions and initiate acts, but are capable of responding to stimuli. The patient may catch a ball thrown to him but be incapable of throwing it back. However, the theory does not elaborate much on the experimental findings supposedly associated with negative symptoms.

A further interesting point of the theory is that it is one of the rare theories that tries to relate neuropsychological mechanisms with the failures in performance of schizophrenics. Interaction between the prefrontal cortex and septohippocampal system is suggested to be essential to the monitoring process. The authors quote neuropsychological evidence that the former is involved in organizing diverse sources of information and initiating or planning and goal-setting in behavioral sequences (e.g., Goldberg, 1985), whereas the function of the latter can be considered a "comparator" system (Gray, 1982), through which the current sensory information will be compared with the internal model. Frith and Done (1988) assume that the hippocampal–frontal axis shows disturbances of function in positive symptom schizophrenics.

In Figure 15.1 (Gray, 1982), the internal model consists of "plans," that is, intentions, goals, and "stored regularities" (the knowledge about the experienced regularities of events in the past). In the extension of the model by Gray *et al.* (1991), both the "stored regularities" and the "plans" influence the "generator of predictions." (See also Hemsley's, 1987, theory about the failure of schizophrenics to compare sensory events, the "world," with the "stored regularities," as will be discussed in Chapter 16.)

Frith and Done say that an essential feature of negative symptoms is that the patients' intentions are not translated into action, as mentioned earlier. It was therefore supposed that some sort of impairment of the frontal–striatal axis could be involved (see Frith and Done, 1988, for more details). The evidence that this is specifically so for the negative symptoms is limited, yet the analogy with Parkinsonism encourages the hypothesis in this direction. (Note the similarity, although less elaborate, with the hypothesis of other

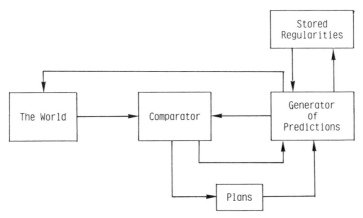

**Figure 15.1** A schematic illustration of the information processing functions and interactions attributed to Gray's (1982) comparator model of septo-hippocampal function (Gray *et al.*, 1991, © Cambridge University Press).

authors concerning the decisive role of the frontal cortex in schizophrenia; e.g., Weinberger, 1987, 1988; Weinberger and Berman, 1988.)

It is worthwhile to try to relate symptoms from the clinic to psychological processes in the laboratory and, in turn, to relate these processes to the effects of experimental neurobiological manipulations. The result has heuristic value both for interpreting the results in the literature and in the sense of offering predictions for testing (e.g., relation of anatomical findings to experimental and clinical symptoms).

However, the weakest point remains the clinically diffuse definition, that is, lack of empirical evidence that the positive–negative label truly describes separate subgroups. A preliminary analysis by Bilder et al. (1985) demonstrated that more than two factors may explain the heterogeneous pattern of symptoms and that the intercorrelation within the positive or the negative group of symptoms as defined by Andreasen (1983, 1984) was low. In other words, the patients with positive symptoms also had more-or-less negative symptoms and some of the symptoms did not belong to their respective concept. Thus, the concept of positive and negative symptoms must be redefined and may represent only degrees of differences and no real dichotomy. Despite these qualifications, the concept is nevertheless an interesting and heuristically fruitful issue valuable for further research.

# VIII. Vulnerability–Stress Model

Based on the general liability/disease model of Falconer (1965), Zubin and Spring (1977) [later modified by Zubin and Steinhauer (1981)] developed a vulnerability–stress model that was and remains very influential. Zubin and Spring worked together at the Institute of Psychiatry in New York. Zubin and Steinhauer are now at the Biometrics Research, Veterans Administration in Pittsburgh.

The general disease model of Falconer (1965) combines genetic and environmental causes. The result of the interaction of both is a liability factor (which is regarded to be normally distributed in the population; cf. Chapter 10). Zubin and colleagues modify this model. The central argument is, in contrast to Falconer, that a variety of several etiological agents are involved and that the interaction of these factors decides the degree of vulnerability. The vulnerability represents the risk of developing an episode. (Schizophrenia is considered to be essentially an episodic disease and not a chronic disease.) The etiological agents are internal biological factors, developmental factors, learning, environment, and genetics. All these factors or a combination of them interact to determine the vulnerability. A vulnerable individual develops a schizophrenic episode if, in addition, he or she experiences much stress. Therefore, the development of schizophrenia depends on two dimensions: the degree of environmental stress and the degree of vulnerability of the individual. This is illustrated in Figure 15.2.

It should be noted that, in contrast to the original model of Falconer, in this model the genetic factor is considered one factor among several. Zubin and colleagues consider the genetic factor as neither necessary nor sufficient, since any combination or interaction of the described etiological agents can cause high vulnerability. The main argument of the authors is that genetic models have "not yet been able to account for the approximately 60% monozygotic twins who are discordant for schizophrenia" (Zubin and Steinhauer, 1981, p. 479). This argument, however, holds only for the assumption that schizophrenia is conceptualized as a dichotomy. Many researchers, however, believe that the discordance for the disease is explained by the continuous nature of the phenotype (and genotype) and that the disease is only the extreme pole on this continuum from mild features to severe symptoms (cf. Chapter 10). These researchers assume that schizophrenia is the result of an interaction between genetically transmitted liability and environment, but that in most cases the liability is not translated into the disease (e.g., Tienari, 1991).

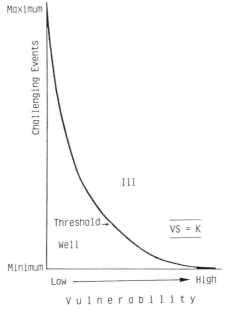

**Figure 15.2** Model of the theoretical interaction of two dimensions on the expression of schizophrenia. Increasing severity of challenging events (stress) is represented on the abscissa and increasing vulnerability on the ordinate. The threshold for expression of the illness is posited by the arrow. For further details, see text (Zubin and Steinhauer, 1981, © Williams and Wilkens).

# References

Andreasen, N. C. (1982). Negative symptoms in schizophrenia: Definition and reliability. *Archives of General Psychiatry, 39*, 784–788.

Andreasen, N. C. (1983). *The scale for the assessment of negative symptoms (SANS).* Iowa City: The University of Iowa Press.

Andreasen, N. C. (1984). *The scale for the assessment of positive symptoms (SAPS).* Iowa City: The University of Iowa Press.

Bilder, R. M., Mukherjee, S., Rieder, R. O., and Pandurangi, A. K. (1985). Symptomatic and neuropsychological components of defect states. *Schizophrenia Bulletin, 11*, 409–419.

Bleuler, E. (1911). *Dementia praecox oder die Gruppe der Schizophrenien.* (Translation: J. Zinkin: Dementia praecox or the group of schizophrenias. International Universities Press, 1950). Leipzig: Deuticke Verlag.

Braff, D. L., Callaway, E., and Naylor, H. (1977). Very short-term memory dysfunction in schizophrenia. *Archives of General Psychiatry, 34*, 25–30.

Broadbent, D. E. (1958). *Perception and communication.* London: Pergamon.

Broadbent, D. E. (1971). *Decision and stress.* London: Academic Press.

Broen, W. E., and Storms, L. H. (1966). Lawful disorganisation: The process underlying a schizophrenic syndrome. *Psychological Review, 73*, 265–279.

Callaway, E., and Naghdi, S. (1982). An information processing model for schizophrenia. *Archives of General Psychiatry, 39*, 339–347.

Chapman, L. J., and Chapman, J. P. (1973). *Disordered thought in schizophrenia.* Englewood Cliffs, NJ: Prentice Hall, Inc.

Crow, T. J., Cross, A. J., Johnstone, E. C., and Owen, F. (1982). Two syndromes in schizophrenia and their pathogenesis. In F. A. Henn and H. A. Nasrallah (Eds.), *Schizophrenia as a brain disease.* New York: Oxford University Press.

Cutting, J. (1985). *The Psychology of Schizophrenia.* Edinburgh: Churchill Livingstone.

Falconer, D. S. (1965). The inheritance of liability to certain diseases estimated from the incidence among relatives. *Annals of Human Genetics, 29*, 51–76.

Flor-Henry, P. (1969). Psychosis and temporal lobe epilepsy. *Epilepsia, 10*, 363–365.

Flor-Henry, P. (1979). Laterality, shifts of cerebral dominance, sinistrality and psychosis. In J. Gruzelier and P. Flor-Henry (Eds.). *Hemisphere asymmetries of function in psychopathology.* Elsevier, North Holland: Biomedical Press.

Frith, C. D., and Done, D. J. (1988). Towards a neuropsychology of schizophrenia. *The British Journal of Psychiatry, 153*, 437–443.

Frith, C. D., and Done, D. J. (1989). Experiences of alien control in schizophrenia reflect a disorder in the central monitoring of action. *Psychological Medicine, 19*, 359–363.

Goldberg, G. (1985). Supplementary motor area structure and function: Review and hypotheses. *The Behavioral and Brain Sciences, 8*, 567–616.

Gray, J. A. (1982). *The neuropsychology of anxiety.* Oxford: Oxford University Press.

Gray, J. A., Feldon, J., Rawlins, J. N. P., Hemsley, D. R., and Smith, A. D. (1990). The neuropsychology of schizophrenia. *The Behavioral and Brain Sciences, 14*, 1–84.

Hemsley, D. R., and Zawada, S. L. (1976). "Filtering" and the cognition deficit in schizophrenia. *The British Journal of Psychiatry, 128*, 456–461.

Hemsley, D. R. (1987). An Experimental Psychological Model for schizophrenia. In H. Häfner, W. F. Gattaz and W. Janzarik (Eds.). *Search for the Causes of Schizophrenia.* Berlin: Springer.

Kahneman, D. (1973). *Attention and Effort.* Englewood Cliffs, NJ: Prentice-Hall.

Kleist, K. (1960). Schizophrenic symptoms and cerebral pathology. *Journal of Mental Science, 106*, 246–255.

Knight, R. A. (1984). Converging models of cognitive deficit in schizophrenia. In W. D.

Spaulding and J. K. Cole (Eds.), *Nebraska symposium on motivation: Theories of schizophrenia and psychosis*, pp. 93–156. Lincoln: University of Nebraska Press.

Kraepelin, E. (1913). *Psychiatrie. Volume 3, Part 2; 8th edition.* (Translation: Dementia praecox and paraphrenia, Edinburgh: Livingstone, 1919). Leipzig: Barth.

Lewine, R. R. J. (1985). Negative symptoms in schizophrenia: Editor's introduction. *Schizophrenia Bulletin, 11*, 361–363.

Magaro, P. A. (1980). *Cognition in schizophrenia and paranoia.* Hillsdale, New Jersey: Erlbaum.

Magaro, P. A., and Chamrad, D. L. (1983). Information processing and lateralization in schizophrenia. *Biological Psychiatry, 18*, 29–44.

Manschreck, T. S., Maher, B. A., Rucklos, M. E., and White, M. T. (1979). The predictability of thought disordered speech in schizophrenic patients. *The British Journal of Psychiatry, 134*, 595–601.

Manschreck, T. C., Maher, B. A., Hoover, T. M., and Ames, D. (1984). The type-token ratio in schizophrenic disorders: Clinical and research value. *Psychological Medicine, 14*, 151–157.

Manschreck, T. C., Maher, B. A., Milavetz, J. J., Ames, D., Weisstein, C. C., and Schneyer, M. L. (1988). Semantic priming in thought disordered schizophrenic patients. *Schizophrenia Research, 1*, 61–66.

McGhie, A., and Chapman, J. (1961). Disorders of attention and perception in early schizophrenia. *The British Journal of Medical Psychology, 34*, 103–116.

Merrin, E. L. (1981). Schizophrenia and brain asymmetry. An evaluation of evidence for dominant lobe dysfunction. *The Journal of Nervous and Mental Disease, 169*, 405–416.

Nuechterlein, K. H., and Dawson, M. E. (1984). Information processing and attentional functioning in the developmental course of schizophrenic disorders. *Schizophrenia Bulletin, 10*, 160–203.

Schneider, W., and Shiffrin, R. M. (1977). Controlled and automatic human information processing: I. Detection, search, and attention. *Psychological Review, 84*, 1–66.

Schwartz-Place, E. J., and Gilmore, G. C. (1980). Perceptual organization in schizophrenia. *The Journal of Abnormal Psychology, 89*, 409–418.

Shakow, D. (1962). Segmental set. *Archives of General Psychiatry, 6*, 1–17.

Sommers, A. A. (1985). "Negative symptoms:" Conceptual and methodological problems. *Schizophrenia Bulletin, 11*, 364–379.

Shukla, G. D., and Katiyar, B. C. (1980). Psychiatric disorders in temporal lobe epilepsy: The laterality effect. *The British Journal of Psychiatry, 137*, 181–182.

Spring, B., Lemon, M., and Fergeson, P. (1990). Vulnerabilities to schizophrenia: Information processing markers. In E. R. Straube and K. Hahlweg (Eds.), *Schizophrenia. Concepts, vulnerability, and intervention*, pp. 97–114. Berlin: Springer.

Strauss, J. S., Carpenter, W. T., Jr., and Bartko, J. J. (1974). The diagnosis and understanding of schizophrenia. Part III. Speculations on the processes that underlie schizophrenic symptoms and signs. *Schizophrenia Bulletin, 11*, 61–69.

Tienari, P. (1991). Results of adoption studies. In C. Eggers (Ed.), *Schizophrenia in youth.* Berlin: Springer.

Tomer, R., and Flor-Henry, P. (1989). Neuroleptics reverse attention asymmetries in schizophrenic patients. *Biological Psychiatry, 25*, 852–860.

Vargo, J. M., Richard-Smith, M., and Corwin, J. V. (1989). Spiroperidol reinstates asymmetries in neglect in rats recovered from left or right dorsomedial prefrontal cortex lesions. *Behavioural Neuroscience, 103*, 1017–1027.

Weinberger, D. (1987). Implications of normal brain development for the pathogenesis of schizophrenia. *Archives of General Psychiatry, 44*, 660–669.

Weinberger, D. R. (1988). Schizophrenia and the frontal lobe. *Trends in Neuroscience, 11*, 367–370.

Weinberger, D. R., and Berman, K. F. (1988). Speculation on the meaning of cerebral metabolic hypofrontality in schizophrenia. *Schizophrenia Bulletin, 14*, 157–168.

Yates, A. J. (1966). Psychological deficit. *Annual Review of Psychology, 17*, 111–144.

Zubin, J., and Spring, B. (1977). Vulnerability—A new view of schizophrenia. *The Journal of Abnormal Psychology, 86*, 103–126.

Zubin, J., and Steinhauer, S. (1981). How to break the logjam in schizophrenia. A look beyond genetics. *The Journal of Nervous and Mental Disease, 8*, 477–492.

# Chapter 16

# An Integrative View of Chapters 1 through 14

## I. Incidence, Heritability, and Environmental Factors

Generally speaking slightly less than 1% of the population of every country, independent of race or culture, will suffer from one form or another of schizophrenic illness during the course of their lifetime (lifetime morbidity risk). With minor local differences, the relatively similar incidence of schizophrenia is confirmed by several surveys by the World Health Organization (WHO) (Figure 16.1; Chapters 1 and 14; review by Häfner, 1987). Considering the variable living conditions and the variable incidence of war, hunger, and natural catastrophe in all these regions, one is tempted to speculate that, if environmental stress were the primary and decisive cause, there would be an effect on the incidence of schizophrenia in these countries. The same argument holds for the stability of first admission rates, for which in some cases records go back over half a century (Häfner, 1987). One may therefore assume that the major reason for this seemingly even distribution is a genetic predisposition that is a human characteristic. Early records of mental illness strongly resembling schizophrenia (e.g., Cutting, 1985) would indicate that humans have been carrying this "heritable component" for a long time. However, most of these lines of reasoning are based on impressions or descriptive statistics and not on empirical controlled observation designed to isolate the factors of interest and measure their relative contribution (i.e., genetic and environmental factors and their interaction).

The requirements for investigations of heritable and environmental factors are fulfilled best by adoption studies. In reports from such studies, the development and behavior of the offspring of schizophrenic mothers or fathers was observed for several years. In all reports, the group of children adopted from affected biological parents developed more disturbances than those adopted from unaffected biological parents, although the rates of a fully developed schizophrenia were lower than in those offspring who lived with their schizophrenic patient (cf. Chapters 10 and 11). Furthermore, the finding that unaffected monozygotic twin partners have more offspring with

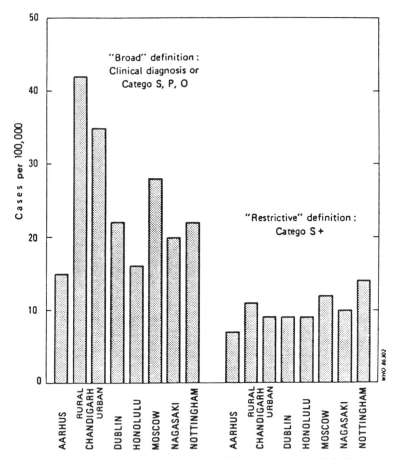

**Figure 16.1**   Incidence rates of schizophrenia per 100,000 population aged 15–54 (both sexes), for the "broad" and for the "restrictive" definition of schizophrenia (from Häfner, 1987).

schizophrenia or schizophrenia-like disturbances than expected also speaks in favor of a genetic component.

Nevertheless, statements on the heritability of schizophrenia are qualified by the fact that only 10–15% of the children of a schizophrenic are likely to suffer from the illness and the probability decreases further if the children are adopted into a healthy family as already mentioned. Clearly the developmental environment also makes a decisive contribution, but does this conflict with the apparently relatively even distribution of schizophrenia around the world? The paradox seems to be more apparent than real. One may speculate that favorable environmental conditions can delay the onset, but obviously in all societies and under all living conditions there seem to be events that sooner or later can trigger a disturbance in a vulnerable individual. However, no specific formative environmental event has been detected so far. Because of the still unclear and probably diffuse nature of the genetic transmission (e.g., the putatively polygenic transmission; Chapter 10) and the polyfactorial nature of environmental influences, no clear statement about the exact nature of the gene–environment interaction is possible.

Discussion of the heritable factors and the trigger role of stress should not exclude the possibility of other influences on the time of onset or severity of the illness, at least in subtypes of the schizophrenia spectrum (e.g., birth complications, viral diseases). This concept will be discussed in more detail later.

Female schizophrenics usually have a later onset for the illness. This could have both a biochemical and an environmental basis (e.g., Häfner, 1987; Goldstein und Tsuang, 1990). On the biochemical side are speculations on the organizational effects of sex hormones on fetal development and also on later brain development (e.g., Seeman and Lang, 1990). On the environmental side are indications that social skills differ (e.g., Mueser *et al.*, 1990) and that premorbid behavior and symptoms are tolerated differently with respect to gender in various social environments (e.g., Goldstein and Kreisman, 1988; Chapter 11).

Of course, to assume that the majority of schizophrenics was predisposed genetically to become so is not to deny the influence of social factors and the family atmosphere. The work of Tienari *et al.* (1984), for example, has shown that only particular children are vulnerable: those who were adopted from a schizophrenic parent. However, the incidence rate was higher in those families (with index offspring) with a disturbed family atmosphere. Tienari (1990) suggests, therefore, that having a heritable predisposition means being more sensitive to environmental insults. The other important message from this extensive study is that a positive psychosocial atmosphere protects against experiences of the poor conditions that are more likely to elicit schizophrenia. Nevertheless, even in a good family atmosphere, the percentage of disturbed, albeit mostly nonschizophrenic individuals, is higher if these are offspring of a schizophrenic biological parent (Tienari *et al.*, 1985). One can assume, therefore, from the outcome of this and similar studies, that the genetic predisposition does not necessarily lead directly to schizophrenia but to a continuum of mild to severe forms of disturbance belonging more-or-less to the schizophrenia spectrum in which schizophrenia is one unusual extreme.

Of course, detailed analysis of familial interactions often shows that a particular member of the family has been the subject of particularly negative experiences. Although so-called double-bind situations or familial schisms were popular concepts among the early researchers in this field, later work has not been able to unequivocally confirm that such situations specifically incite schizophrenia (e.g., Arieti, 1971; Chapter 11). It is also true that the longitudinal study run in California by Goldstein and colleagues showed that parents of children who later developed a schizotypal or schizophrenic syndrome had an unusual style of interaction. They characteristically showed disorganized communication patterns, often highly loaded with affect (e.g., Goldstein, 1987). Why, then, did these children develop a personality disorder or schizophrenic disturbance while the other siblings did not? In fact, the other siblings were not studied, so one does not know what sort of family experience the supposedly healthy children had had. It should be noted that in these studies most probands did not develop a full pattern of schizophrenia, but a spectrum personality disorder. As a whole, the evidence that a particular pattern of interactions is formative for schizophrenia (or schizotypal personality disturbance) is not very strong (see Chapter 11).

As far as the course of the illness is concerned, environmental factors seem to be capable of exerting a stronger influence. Crosscultural studies show that schizophrenia has a more favorable course in some non-Western countries (cf. review of Lin and Kleinman, 1988; Leff et al., 1991), although the incidence of schizophrenia matches that found elsewhere. Assuming that the differences cannot be explained by methodological artifacts, it would seem that some societies do indeed respond differently to one who is or has been ill. Nonetheless, these studies (e.g., Leff, 1991) show that negative interaction features like high expressed emotion (i.e., unfavorable family environments) do occur in these countries and, as elsewhere, are similarly linked to relapse. However, the proportion of relatives showing high expressed emotion seems to be lower in non-Western countries (Wig et al., 1987; Leff, 1991).

If the incidence is the same but the course is variable in different societies, then one might also assume that the sensitivity of the predisposed individual toward the same event is different in the pre-episode phase compared with the post-episode phase, or that the society responds differently to postepisodic handicaps. After the threatening experiences of their first episodes, schizophrenics may be particularly sensitive and vulnerable. The psychotic experience has added to the initial disposing weakness. Unfortunately, for obvious reasons, no one has conducted a prospective and systematic comparison of the quality and frequency of family interactions, of life events, and of stress factors on the vocational level before and after the psychotic episode. Nevertheless, the importance of after-care programs is immediately evident from this and from studies investigating the cause of relapse (e.g., the important role of emotional factors in family interactions as described in Chapters 11 and 13). The supposedly less tolerant attitudes of Western industrialized societies toward a loss in vocational efficiency of the former psychiatric patient may be added to other unfavorable environmental factors as possible differences in the cultural traditional response toward (mentally) deviant behavior.

In conclusion, there is much evidence that environmental factors alter the threshold for mental illness in the predisposed individual and probably play an even more important role in the development of the overt disturbance.

If, however, inheritance plays a role, then one must ask: by what mechanism? There is sufficient evidence that the genetic component cannot be simply dominant or recessive (Chapter 10). One of the assumptions here is that polygenes or a dominant gene within a combination of several genes form the basis for genetic transmission; multifactorial or mixed models seem to be the most likely candidates. (Such models have also been proposed for allergies, epilepsy, high blood pressure, diabetes mellitus and affective disorders; Propping, 1989.) These models, currently in favor with psychiatric genetics, take environmental interaction into account insofar as it may act to release the expression of the illness in the predisposed individual.

The current models also assume that a hidden feature, or features, associated with schizophrenia is distributed continuously in the general population (Chapter 10). They further assume a Gaussian distribution with two thresholds, one for spectrum personality disorders, the other for schizophrenia (cf. Figure 10.3). The psychiatric illness is, according to this model, only "the tip of an iceberg" (Gottesman and Shields, 1982). (The model for affective disorder is similar; Klein *et al.*, 1985.) This in turn may explain why schizophrenia does not "die out" across generations, despite the reduced rate of reproduction of schizophrenics (e.g., Odegard, 1960; see also the critical discussion of this assumption by Saugstad, 1989).

Continuing this argument for an explanation of the hereditary disposition (excluding phenocopies), the offspring of apparently normal or nearly normal parents carrying polygenic components for schizophrenia may receive a combination of genes that makes them more vulnerable to the releasing effects of stressful experience. However the diffuse nature of these models of gene–environment interactions makes it impossible to predict which of the offspring under which conditions risks a breakdown. Nevertheless, there is always a higher incidence of schizophrenia in first degree relatives of schizophrenics (compared with matched controls); this is true even for those not living with the affected relative. Indeed, there are even more cases of relatives with other disturbances. (These disturbances are mostly diffuse in nature, but include personality disorders belonging to the schizophrenic spectrum.)

While on the subject of the features shown by blood relations of schizophrenics, it should not be overlooked that some of these features can be considered advantageous in the society. There are, for example, reports that persons with leading positions in society are frequently found among the relatives of schizophrenics (e.g., Karlson, 1968). Cromwell and co-workers (DeAmicis *et al.*, 1986; Chapter 4) pointed out that nonschizophrenic first degree relatives who showed similarities in test performance to the schizophrenics (redundancy associated deficit) had a higher social status than those with nonconspicuous test performance. Recently Schuldberg *et al.* (1988)

showed that schizotypal subjects scored higher in creativity tests than controls. The German psychiatrist Kretschmer (1958) described schizoid (and manic–depressive) features in an extensive collection of biographical accounts of prominent political leaders and artists (e.g., Robespierre and Rilke). One may speculate that the outstanding ability was a selective advantage for some of the carriers of the polygenic spectrum, a selective advantage, in a neo-Darwinian sense, in the developmental history of humans.

A central problem to schizophrenia research is that, despite a certain number of common features among patients, there is a striking heterogeneity of symptoms. Kraepelin and Bleuler sought unity despite the evident heterogeneity. Genetic research reflects this uncertainty. Polygenic models and, more so, polyfactorial or mixed models (major gene locus, polygenetic background, and environmental factors) are all supported to some extent through results of likelihood statistics. At present there are no additional well-founded indicators available (genetic markers) on which a decision can be based. As a consequence, the experimental search for both the combination of heterogeneous features (polygenetic/polyfactorial) and the search for a single prominent feature with additional heterogeneous background features is plausible.

These two views on schizophrenia research, the search for single basic features as well as the combination of features characterizing schizophrenia (or "the group of schizophrenias," Bleuler, 1911), is the topic of the following sections.

## II. Is There Evidence for a Single Common Experimental Feature?

As considered in Chapter 15, the most widely accepted hypothesis is that the single basic feature of schizophrenics may be described as a form of fundamental disturbance of attention. However, there are three main problems with this statement.

(1) It is a general scientific problem that vague statements, such as "schizophrenics have an attention-disorder problem," are difficult to prove or disprove. Accordingly, Neale and Cromwell (1977) are of the opinion "that this broad use of the term attention does not clarify or increase our understanding of schizophrenic performance" (p. 127).

(2) Tasks with high demands on attentional capacity are more difficult and may therefore uncover only a nonspecific generalized deficit (see introductory remarks in Chapter 2).

(3) Even if one defines attention disorder as a breakdown of stimulus selection in the presence of irrelevant stimuli, one must point out, on the basis of the existing literature, that this is a less ubiquitous failure in schizophrenics than is widely believed (cf. Chapter 4). Consider reports that

used the same experimental paradigm, for example, dichotic shadowing tasks. Dichotic shadowing is regarded as a classical experimental setting in which to examine selective attention performance in the presence of irrelevant stimuli (second channel). As was shown in Chapter 4, the results are equivocal. Under some conditions schizophrenics fail, but under others they show undisturbed selective attention performance. A more detailed analysis reveals that in the majority of cases schizophrenics have less problems if stimulus-driven information processing is required by the dichotic shadowing task. Stimulus-driven processing means that the subject has to follow a predetermined set of stimuli that are defined by their physical characteristics (Lindsay and Norman, 1977). Dichotic shadowing requires a response to stimuli presented to one side of the headset and that those presented to the other side be ignored. This means that schizophrenics are less likely to fail in tasks in which the stimulus material does not need interpretation, further processing, or reorganization in order to reach the goal of the task (see schematic delineation of this type of information processing in Figure 16.2).

However, there are many exceptions. Again, this is most clearly demonstrated with the dichotic shadowing paradigm. If the instruction requires response to material in the one (relevant) channel but also attention to the content of the other (irrelevant) channel (or the specific design allows a deeper processing of the irrelevant material), then schizophrenics fail. It seems that if the irrelevant material reaches a deeper level of processing it cannot easily be rejected. This is reminiscent of an earlier hypothesis by Cromwell and Dokecki (1968) that schizophrenics have difficulty disattending to sensory input that has reached a certain level of processing. This distracts and thus detracts from processing the relevant material.

Such interference becomes even more evident in tasks in which conceptual information processing is involved. This type of task, according to the definition by Bourne *et al.* (1979, p. 229), involves "features and a rule of relationship among these features" (i.e., the whole set of stimuli has to be scrutinized in order to decide the categorial relationship). In Figure 16.3, we represent the set of stimuli to be categorized by $x_1$, $x_2$, and $x_3$. An adequate response is only possible after cognitive reorganization of the material, symbolized by $x_{11}$, $x_{12}$, and $x_{13}$. Compared with pure stimulus-driven

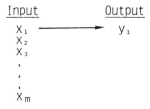

**Figure 16.2** Schematic illustration of "closed-loop" data processing.

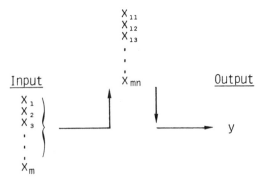

**Figure 16.3** Schematic illustration of "open-loop" data processing. The output depends on the processing of the whole set of data and on matching the result with stored schemata and rules for possible relationships.

selection, in which irrelevant material may be rejected at an early stage, the chance for false responses is high. It seems as though, after full and deep processing of irrelevant material and after reorganization into relevant and irrelevant categories, there is a higher chance for a less efficient result. (Note here the similarity with failures in stimulus-driven selection tasks in which the irrelevant material must be processed more deeply.)

There are numerous examples for a failure of schizophrenics in concept-driven selection, as demonstrated in Chapters 2–4. Schizophrenics and their first degree relatives, for example, do not make use of the differences in redundancy when tested with the Steffy version of the reaction-time task (cf. work by Cromwell and his research group as discussed in Chapter 4). In order to use redundancy, the subjects had to organize the stimulus material into categories of redundant and nonredundant. The reduced variation of the $P_{300}$ to stimuli that belong to different categories of probabilities may be based on the same type of failure, but is less striking since other groups of patients show a similarly reduced $P_{300}$. (The nonspecificity of the finding may indicate that different mechanisms led to the same peripheral response.) Of special interest is the finding of a similarity of $P_{300}$ reduction between schizophrenics and their unaffected siblings, as was discussed in Chapter 6. The common denominator in these tasks is that the subject must make use of the relationships between the elements presented.

Schizophrenics and high-risk children do not show an advantage in short-term recall for stimuli presented in certain prominent positions as opposed to those in nonsalient positions (e.g., primacy effect in the digit-span task with distractors; Oltmanns and co-workers, Chapter 3). In his review and discussion of results of general cognitive psychology, Underwood wrote that "items in early serial position have higher recall than central items because they are processed into categorical memory more effectively" (1976, p. 112). In Chapter 3 on memory performance, we noted further that schizophrenics fail to organize stimulus material spontaneously into categories to improve memory performance.

In Chapter 2, several experiments were discussed in which schizophrenics failed to use contextual information. Hemsley (1987), for example, interprets the results of his own group and related findings as a weakness of the influence of stored contingency rules on current behavior. Similarly, Anscombe (1987) is of the opinion that the failure of schizophrenics is due to a lack of placing incoming material into the context of their background knowledge. On the other hand, the hypothetical reduction of the influence of stored organizational rules on performance can be an advantage in certain situations. Schizophrenics seem to be less "disturbed" by contextual information when selecting a word in a sentence obscured by white noise (Polyakov, 1969; Chapter 2). In the often cited studies of Wells and Leventhal (1984) and Schwarz-Place and Gilmore (1980), schizophrenics perform relatively better just because they perform more independently of the constraints of perceptual contextual (Gestalt) organization.

On the other hand, schizophrenics often fail to organize their speech according to a plan appropriate to the situation (Chapters 1 and 2). It is important to note that the failure in the majority of patients is not due to a basic defect in organizational or abstract and conceptualizing abilities. If schizophrenics are, for example, explicitly instructed to group words into categories, they do so, and improve memory performance (Chapter 3). (Quite another question is how adequate these groupings are.) This seems to suggest that the effect of internal data-organizing structures on behavior is weakened, but not lost. Performance improves if, for example, two proverbs with the same meaning are presented instead of only one. The patient is now capable of interpreting their meaning (i.e., he reorganizes the material in accordance with the common "abstract" meaning). The more structured a clinical interview is, for example, the more the amount of thought disorder presented by the patient is reduced (e.g., Gottschalk–Glaeser procedure; Chapter 2). These and related observations are used in contemporary therapeutic interventions with schizophrenics, for example, in the so-called cognitive training described in Chapter 13.

Thus, schizophrenics are impaired in conceptual data processing (in its broadest sense, i.e., where the stored rules of relationships between input elements play a role) and in specific tasks requiring stimulus-driven information processing in which irrelevant material has to be scrutinized more deeply. This means that the cognitive disturbance of schizophrenics cannot be characterized as being on the controlled-serial or on the automatic-parallel level (in contrast to the theory of Callaway and Naghdi, 1982; Chapter 15). Furthermore, it cannot be characterized as being only on the conceptual level (and not on the stimulus-driven level of processing), even though there is more evidence for a more clear-cut disturbance in the first mode of processing. In order to characterize schizophrenic performance, we therefore need other labels. We propose to use the terms "open-loop" and "closed-loop," terminology borrowed from neuropsychology to describe two different modes of processing (cf. Figures 16.2 and 16.3).

What is the common denominator for the disturbances in open-loop tasks? A decision about a response can only be reached (1) after scrutinizing all the available stimuli and their features more deeply and (2) by finding the best match to the relevant stored rules (constraints).

The types of tasks that illustrate this include the categorical grouping of material for memory, the use of regular intervals (category of redundancy), the use of the relationship of words in a sentence, and the use of perceptual elements in a Gestalt pattern. In these tasks, all available stimuli have to be scrutinized more deeply in order to assess the relationship of the elements (match with stored rules) and to make the adequate response. Some of these tasks need "effort" to reach the goal; other types of perceptual or semantic organization are reached quasiautomatically.

In closed-loop tasks, the stimulus response relationship is immediately evident. Irrelevant material can be excluded from further processing at an early level of processing.

Thus it seems that a stimulus-driven task, in which the instruction or the special design of the experiment demands scrutiny of the irrelevant material more deeply, must be considered a special case of open-loop data processing.

Why, then, are schizophrenics impaired on such tasks? There seem to be two possible explanations:

(1) In view of evidence suggesting that irrelevant material is processed more deeply (in open-loop tasks), one could speculate that more neuronal traces are activated in these types of task. Thus, the chance for the spreading of activation to adjacent neuronal networks is higher in tasks in which more neuronal traces are activated. The chance of a disturbance may therefore be a function of the number of neuronal traces activated, that is, a function of the amount of irrelevant material processed more deeply.

Some evidence seems to support this interpretation. An experiment by Manschreck et al. (1988) illustrated a facilitation of activation with the priming procedure: schizophrenics responded to semantically related words more quickly than the controls. This was explained by a higher facilitation or reduced inhibition of activation within the neuronal network. However, this observation was confined to schizophrenics with thought disorder (see Chapter 2 for more details). The research group of the Chapmans recently confirmed this finding, but without differentiating subgroups (Kwapil et al., 1990). Possibly related are the claims for a lack of prepulse inhibition by the group from Colorado (e.g., Freedman et al., 1983; Chapter 6). This group demonstrated decreased interference in the perception of the second of two stimuli presented in rapid succession in schizophrenics and their relatives. (Although the perceptual findings have been replicated elsewhere, the purported evoked-potential (EP) concomitants still await confirmation; see Chapter 6.) In short, enhanced facilitation or reduced inhibition of neuronal activation may be involved in the deviant performance.

(2) Another explanation of the schizophrenic impairment suggests that the reduced order in information processing is caused by a weakness of the influence of higher level processes on the input material. Each neuronal system can only function appropriately if constraints resulting from established programs guide behavior (cf. Keil, 1981). The demands on internal constraints are higher in open-loop than in closed-loop tasks, in which the response alternatives are more limited. This may therefore account for the increased difficulty of schizophrenics in open-loop tasks. An example from the field of cognitive psychology may be the reduced influence of the stored knowledge of rules (perceptual and semantic constraints) in schizophrenics compared with healthy or psychiatric controls (Hemsley, 1987).

There is obviously evidence for both suggestions we have made. However, the first explanation may be limited more to the performance of particular subgroups (schizophrenics with thought disorder or highly distractable schizophrenics with positive symptoms). Spring *et al.* (1990) proposed that high distractability is characteristic of positive symptom schizophrenics (as discussed in more detail in Chapter 15). Further support for this hypothesis is discussed in Section V.

The relatively better performance of schizophrenics in some specific tasks and the relative independence of schizophrenic performance from context cannot easily be explained by an enhanced activation (or reduced inhibition) in adjacent neuronal traces. It is thus more plausible to suggest that the reduced influence of cognitive constraints (stored rules to organize the input) is the more widespread and perhaps fundamental deficit. (However, it is theoretically possible that the first type of deviance is only a consequence of the second. The spreading of activation in adjacent neuronal networks may be a consequence of the reduced influence from higher centers, i.e., reduced influence of constraints on behavior.)

The explanation put forward here also resembles Frith and Done's (1988) monitoring model, in which inputs are compared with an internal model of the environment. There is, however, a difference of emphasis; Frith and Done prefer to emphasize the effects on motor planning and organization and draw a distinction between positive and negative syndromes. However, as discussed in Chapter 15, in their own experiment (Frith and Done, 1988), the reduced use of feedback was limited to a subgroup within the group of positive-symptom schizophrenics. This may signify that the hypothesis of a reduction of the use of feedback refers only to special cases of schizophrenic impairment.

Nevertheless, the theory of Frith and Done has potentially fruitful elements from a heuristic point of view. Their incorporation of the idea that the hippocampal complex is involved in the matching of incoming information with internal models of the situation and the role of the frontal cortices in intentional and conceptual processes may indeed be relevant to the processes that are proposed to be impaired in schizophrenia. We will come back to this issue in Section VI.

The hypothesis also has some similarity with the set hypothesis of Shakow, especially as elaborated later in his monograph of 1979. He states that the concept of schemata developed in cognitive psychology can be compared with the set concept. Both "schemata" and "sets" prepare the organism for adaptive response by organizing past and present information. He further states that some schemata are determined by experience while others may be innate (Gestalt grouping?).

In conclusion, pronounced difficulties with open-loop tasks, in which incoming information must be matched with stored rules of relationships (organizational rules, concepts), may indeed be a common denominator for a variety of failures of schizophrenics.

However, there are also symptoms and "experimental features" that cannot easily be explained by a reduced influence of conceptual data processing on behavior.

## III. Limits to the Hypothesis of a Failure of Open-Loop Processes

In this section we consider conflicts and possible evidence against the interpretation put forward in the last section. Such contradictions may reflect (1) the heterogeneity of schizophrenia (which will be considered in the next sections), (2) the inadequacy of the basic assumptions, or (3) methodological errors.

Certain tests that play a prominent role in the contemporary experimental literature demonstrate a schizophrenic impairment but seem to be less dependent on abilities required by open-loop processing. Prominent examples are the span-of-apprehension test (SAT), continuous-performance test (CPT), and possibly also the visual masking paradigm (Chapter 4). If, for a moment, one puts aside explanations in terms of subgroup differences or general impairments arising from task difficulty, one must entertain the possibility that a dysfunction of the open-loop match–mismatch of information with stored organized concepts may not be pertinent to all forms of unusual schizophrenic performance.

## A. SAT

Let us first consider the SAT. In Chapter 4 we found that not all experiments support the claim that a deficit in this task represents a disturbance fundamental to schizophrenia. The deficit was also seen in manic patients, and did not always appear in remitted schizophrenics. The task requires the selection of relevant from irrelevant letters; no reorganization, grouping, or categorization is necessary. It can be considered a closed-loop task. If, however, future experimental investigations show that the deficit is specific, and not limited to subgroups, this would then mean that schizophrenics have processing deficits that extend beyond the problems with open-loop tasks.

## B. CPT

In contrast, the CPT shows a well-documented deficit in schizophrenics, although there are some reports that it is more pronounced in those with negative symptoms. The conventional version of the CPT is clearly a stimulus-driven task. The task is to respond to certain sequentially presented letters or digits and to ignore others. It is a sustained attention or vigilance task. No conceptual reorganization of the material is necessary. There are no high demands for the integration of data against a background of knowledge. However, it is interesting to note that the CPT, in its conventional form, does not reveal a deficit in high-risk children. High-risk children only fail if the stimuli are blurred. What may be the reason for this differential deficit? Here the loop between stimulus and response is certainly less closed than in the version with easy-to-identify letters. The demand on internally stored schemata is clearly higher in the degraded version of the CPT. In this version of the task, the emphasis is shifted more strongly onto the probabilistic decision (judgment or criterion) for response. The subject must decide whether it is more probable that a given configuration belongs to the category of all the configurations that could, for example, represent "F" or to the category of all the configurations that could represent "T". This decision problem is depicted in Figure 16.4. Unfortunately, this version of the test is also the more difficult one; thus, both versions of the CPT are not matched for discriminating power in normal healthy controls. Nuechterlein and Dawson (1984) respond that "the 'generalized deficit' described by Chapman and Chapman (1973) may be of theoretical interest and not only a source of psychometric artifact to be controlled" (p. 193). Also, "matching information processing tasks for

**Figure 16.4**  Demonstration of the conflict of two different stored schemata. For example, in the case of ambiguously perceived letters and the stored schemata for "F" and "T."

difficulty level may entail a search for deficits that are not due to processing capacity limitations" (p. 193). Strauss (1978) is also of the opinion that matching tasks for difficulty (discriminating power) within the normal population "may remove the variance that must be studied in order to make valid inferences about the nature of the psychological processes" (p. 318). Nevertheless, the theoretical and methodological difficulties still need clarification.

## C. Masking Paradigm

Basically, the masking paradigm test concerns the recognition of a letter briefly presented before a "mask" of irrelevant letters is shown very shortly afterwards. Impaired schizophrenic performance is especially evident in those with a poor premorbid course, in whom the problem remains even after several repetitions of the task. Schizophrenics have no problem identifying single letters as long as they are presented for a sufficiently long period. This longer critical stimulus duration is particularly evident in the more chronic poor premorbid group. Perhaps the first explanation one might offer is that information processing is slow (cf. Yates hypothesis; Chapter 15), particularly in a subgroup of patients. A second possibility is that the icon itself is deficient. Although most studies show that the icon itself may be intact, Knight *et al.* (1977) did report a slower decay of the icon in subjects who were underinclusive on tests of categorization and who were characterized by a poor premorbid course. Another investigation with a chronic schizophrenic group showed a similarly slow icon decay (Schwartz *et al.*, 1983). Perhaps still more important is the finding that the performance of schizotypal subjects also deviated from that of nonschizotypal groups. In contrast, one of us found that the masking performance of remitted subjects is unimpaired (Zaunbrecher *et al.*, 1990).

Thus, the problem seems to be serious for one type of patient, but conflicting results have been seen in others. Clearly there is a need for more study to show which subgroups (e.g., poor premorbid, chronic) are impaired and what factors proscribe information processing in these subjects on these tasks.

It is, however, possible that some form of conceptual data processing is also involved in this type of task. Knight (1984) interprets the performance in masking and related tasks as showing a "deficiency in perceptual schema formation." This interpretation resembles our discussion of the deficit of high-risk individuals with the identification of degraded letters in the special version of the CPT. There we interpreted the deficit as a failure to match the ambivalent input with stored categories of the features of letters. The deficit may be similar in the masking paradigm. Here the rapidly decaying content (four letters, one relevant, the other irrelevant) of the buffer store has to be compared with stored representations of letters in order to be decoded before the mask appears on the screen. There may, therefore, be a certain demand on conceptual processes (for example, matching with the stored representations of all possible features belonging to the category of the letter "F").

## IV. Biological Markers

The number of potential biological markers for schizophrenia discussed in the literature is great. We can only list a few of the candidates here, some of which are considered again later as serious contenders for features separating subgroups.

Several potential biological markers that have been proposed have not stood the test of time and study. For example, low levels of platelet monoamine oxidase (MAO) can be found associated with many forms of mental dysfunction. Other neurochemical and pharmacological candidates include responsiveness or nonresponsiveness to neuroleptics, the susceptibility to amphetamine-elicited exacerbation or improvement of psychosis, and increases or decreases of dopaminergic activity (or $D_2$ receptors). Anatomical and etiological candidates include the presence or absence of cerebral atrophy, neurological soft signs, frontal or temporal signs, and perinatal problems and family history. Physiological candidates include electrodermal response/nonresponse, reduced $P_{300}$, or the occurrence of abnormal pursuit eye movements (SPEM) with associated saccade irregularities.

Only for SPEM is the analysis at all advanced and promising, although several unsolved questions remain (cf. Chapter 7). The feature has been found in many groups of schizophrenics and subjects at risk. (Interestingly, there are findings that the deviance is less striking in schizophrenic patients with signs of mild cerebral atrophy.) Genetic models for the heritability of the feature and its relative specificity have been described. Holzman and co-workers interpret their findings with first degree relatives as showing that SPEM is an independent manifestation of a genetically linked trait that may sometimes appear as schizophrenia with or without SPEM deviance and sometimes as SPEM deviance without manifestation of schizophrenia. If this is correct then the deviance is a by-product of the pathogenic gene but not necessarily etiologically related to the precipitation of the disorder (cf. Chapter 7; definition of a genetic marker by Iacono, 1983). However, if further evidence shows that it is etiologically linked to the disorder, then one is tempted to speculate on the role of the frontal eye fields, which contribute (among other brain centers) to the control of SPEM (see other evidence presented subsequently that is relevant to a putative frontal lobe involvement in schizophrenia).

## V. Clinical and Experimental Symptoms Distinguishing Subgroups of Schizophrenics

Research workers have tried again and again to resolve the heterogeneity of the schizophrenias in terms of symptoms and psychological, physiological, and pathological processes. The divisions have nearly always been in the form of a dichotomy, separating subjects into those with and those without a particular feature. The mass of results has continually thrown up exceptions, confounding the attempt to define schizophrenia exclusively in terms of one or the other of two rounded concepts. Often attempts have foundered because of a failure to take into account that schizophrenia develops through several stages; the initial stages can be quite different from those after long-term illness or at outcome. Cases with positive symptoms develop negative symptoms, and it is often overlooked that some of these features represent attempts to cope and may be thus only indirectly related to the underlying deficit.

A second frequent problem is the unwillingness to acknowledge that an illness, even with a single cause, can present a diverse range of symptoms that do not necessarily all appear in one patient. (In neurofibromatosis, for example, some of the individuals who are carriers of the gene will develop only a few signs of the illness, the so-called cafe-au-lait spots, whereas others will have severe peripheral nerve tumors.) This risk of diversity on the basis of a single ultimate cause is particularly pertinent for problems of central nervous function. In different individuals, the pattern of neuronal background, types of development, basic personality traits, and the whole complex of interactions between biological characteristics and external events can yield a considerable variety of symptoms.

We shall now briefly consider some of these divisions and try to illustrate their degree of usefulness in accounting for the problems and heterogeneity of schizophrenia.

## A. Paranoid versus Nonparanoid Schizophrenics

We have mentioned the theory of Magaro (1980), described in his book *Cognition and Schizophrenia and Paranoia,* in Chapter 15. One of his main conclusions was that paranoid schizophrenics experience their biggest problems in perceptual processing (i.e., stimulus-driven information processing). He also suggested that nonparanoids are more impaired on conceptual tasks. By this he meant that nonparanoids had difficulty sorting external stimuli in terms of internal schemata when the task required such a categorization for solution. In contrast, paranoid schizophrenics could handle such schemata but often applied them mistakenly. This division of the schizophrenic problem resembles our own description of the psychological process but conflicts since Magaro attributes the differences to different subgroups.

Certainly there are reports that paranoid schizophrenics can have impaired stimulus-driven perception. These impairments seem to be more marked than in nonparanoids. Rappaport and colleagues (1972) reported that untreated paranoids had difficulty detecting signals embedded in white noise. Indeed, paranoid schizophrenics were more disturbed by distractors on the CPT than nonparanoids; they made more false alarm errors (Chapter 4). This seems to relate to the clinical observation that such patients, at the start of the psychotic episode, are bound to notice things that healthy subjects would not.

Even the patient may wonder why it is that he or she notices this and that, although he or she did not want to pay attention to it. (See Chapters 1 and 4; especially the description and interviews of Chapman and McGhie, 1961, which were the starting point for the disturbance-of-attention hypothesis.)

It is, in fact, difficult to exclude the possibility that paranoid schizophrenics show disturbances of rather basic perceptual processes (e.g., target detection). Amazingly this can, if the studies would bear replication, result in even better performance than healthy subjects in resolving spatial frequencies and better than nonparanoids in extrafoveal target detection (Chapter 4). However, these are isolated reports and, therefore, at present, they do not offer a good basis on which to separate subgroups or to eliminate alternative explanations (e.g., differential medication effects).

Given the duration of the illness and the likely symptom changes during this course (e.g., paranoid symptoms tend to disappear in chronic stages of the illness), we cannot be certain whether features such as perceptual disturbances represent a state or a trait characteristic of these subgroups.

In one of our own studies, we tried to take account of this crucial point (Chapter 4; Straube, 1975). We compared the performance of subjects who presently had a diagnosis of paranoid hallucinatory schizophrenia (i.e., positive symptoms were dominant) with patients who had the same diagnosis at admission (i.e., former positive symptom patients who were now non-paranoid and had a chronic course). The paranoid schizophrenics had difficulties on a task requiring them to group simple stimulus configurations in the presence of distractors. The chronic patients had no problems on this task, but both groups showed a bit-by-bit strategy on a Gestalt closure test. Neither group could "see the forest for the trees" (cf. similar result of Cutting and of Schwarz-Place and Gilmore, discussed in Chapter 4). In other words, neither group saw that the perceptual elements were parts of an overall figure. They did not see that the elements were related and belonged to an overall context (e.g., to match stored rules of relationships, as discussed in Section II).

We believe it is important that future studies systematically compare subgroups in which one has developed beyond the symptoms which the other actively shows. Only then can we start to make a judgment about whether there is a genuine subgroup that is not just characterized as a developmental stage of the illness.

However, it should be pointed out that clinical descriptions and longitudinal studies suggest that a genuine subgroup of nonparanoid schizophrenics, that start their clinical course without any paranoid features, exists.

## B. Acute versus Chronic Schizophrenics

It is even more apparent that, in this section, we are likely to be comparing schizophrenics at different stages of their illness. Another problem is encountered here, namely, that subgroup divisions strongly overlap, as much in

research as in the clinical routine. Thus, for example, a schizophrenic with
paranoid features and hallucinations is likely to be acutely ill, probably had a
good premorbid course, and is most likely to show more positive than
negative symptoms. Across patients and across studies, however, neither the
overlap nor the separation is complete (see Figure 16.5).

Despite these inconsistencies, there is enough evidence to allow us to draw

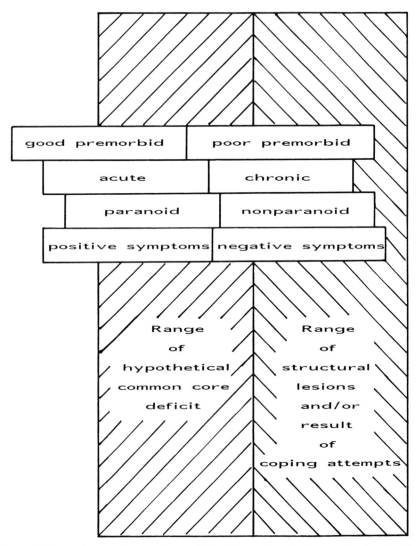

**Figure 16.5**    A schema to illustrate the hypothetical degree of overlap between the characteristic
features of frequently diagnosed subgroups of schizophrenics.

the following conclusions. Acute schizophrenics seem to be able to perform tasks in which divided attention is required. As was discussed in Chapter 4, they are capable of performing two simple tasks at the same time. Chronic schizophrenics usually fail such tests.

The performance of chronic schizophrenics in simple divided attention tasks may be explained by a restriction of the attentional field, as was suggested by Venables as early as 1964. For example, chronic schizophrenics respond more slowly to stimuli located in the periphery of the visual field (Chapter 4), or referential cues influence their judgement less on assessments of stimulus constancy. On the other hand, chronic schizophrenics are less disturbed by distractors than the acutely ill. Here the impairment of acute patients may possibly relate to increased "internal distraction;" acute schizophrenics more often show a loosening of associations on verbal tasks than the chronically ill (Chapter 2). An apparent reduction of sensory input, as seen in tasks with distractors, may even stretch to basic perceptual functions. Chronic schizophrenics often show increased perceptual thresholds. This is sometimes evident when the stimuli are unpleasant. This suggests that a reduction of attention may be a functional change in order to protect themselves from environmental influences that are experienced as unpleasant during a long course of the illness (cf. Chapter 4), that is, some of the symptoms of chronic schizophrenics may be interpreted as attempts to cope (cf. Figure 16.5).

There are also differences on psychophysiological measures. Although some acute schizophrenics are electrodermal nonresponders, many more nonresponders are chronically ill. Chronic schizophrenics often show a slower EEG. This may be, according to some reports, more evident over frontal regions, where relative decreases of blood flow and activation have been recorded, particularly in strongly withdrawn chronic schizophrenics (cf. Chapter 8).

Tomographic signs of mild cerebral atrophy are more likely to be found in chronic patients, based on the number of such reports. Follow-up studies have not found evidence to suggest that this reflects progressive degeneration but this may reflect the sparseness of such studies.

Finally, we should mention an interesting example of information processing that provides a link between the acute–chronic dimension and the potentially associated changes of dopamine (DA) metabolism (Chapter 4). From animal studies we know that disturbances of the latent-inhibition and conditioned-blocking tests of the phenomenon known as "learned inattention" can result from (1) DA release following treatment of the central nervous system with amphetamine (Solomon and Staton, 1982), (2) the induction of increased DA $D_2$ receptors (Crider *et al.*, 1986), and (3) destroying DA terminals in the septum and frontal cortex (Oades *et al.*, 1987). Intriguingly, the research group of Gray and Hemsley at the London Institute of Psychiatry recently showed that latent inhibition was disturbed in acute but not in chronic schizophrenics (Baruch *et al.*, 1988; Jones *et al.*, 1990). As mentioned earlier, in the conditioned-blocking test with teenagers, there is a tendency for more and less blocking to be associated with the excretion of more and less DA metabolites. In schizophrenic teenagers, the tendency is much more exaggerated (Oades, unpublished results). Although patients were medicated, the results would seem to indicate that increased DA activity is associated with a reduced ability to inhibit response to redundant stimuli.

The results we have discussed in this section suggest that there are differences between the performance and function of acute and chronic schizophrenics. Whether these differences reflect two illnesses or two developmental stages of the same illness cannot be stated with any conviction. The results of longitudinal studies will be necessary to form this conclusion, and they are not available. The fact that some differences seem to be a matter of degree leads us to think that we are studying two developmental stages of an illness.

One could also imagine that the reduced levels of activation and reduced input functions reflect secondary protective strategies. After all, in the early stages acute patients are often highly irritable. It is plausible that, in time, they learn ways to reduce this sensitivity. This, in turn, is likely to result in what the observer records as emotional withdrawal (cf. Carpenter et al., 1985). Nevertheless, longitudinal reports suggest that some schizophrenics start with a slow-onset poor-premorbid course, followed by no acute phase, and may continue with an undramatic chronic process-type form of the illness. Therefore, we cannot exclude a truly different type of schizophrenia apart from secondary symptom patterns; their separation is a task for future research.

On the other hand, the emphasis of contemporary research is on the negative symptom type, which is automatically treated as a stable entity. The possibility of developing from one to another phase of illness is, currently, too often overlooked (i.e., the developmental course of the symptoms are not recorded). Chronic syndromes are then considered the most severe form; thus all features of chronic patients are automatically assumed to belong to the hypothetical core syndrome. This assumption overlooks that it is not at all clear which features are primary. Chronic patients may show, in contrast to acute patients, several secondary features, as already discussed.

## C. Schizophrenics with a Good or Poor Premorbid Course

Even more so than with the other syndromes discussed earlier, it has been repeatedly suggested that the early appearance of signs of schizophrenia long before the person falls ill is indicative of a separate illness. Indeed some of the features of this group that emerge from experimental study seem to support the idea. Once again there is a considerable degree of overlap between the features attributed to this subdivision and those attributed to other groups (cf. Figure 16.5). On the other hand, looking at this argument the other way around, it is difficult to be sure that features appearing to be specific to this type of subdivision, do not in fact refer to another subgroup defined by perhaps more relevant criteria.

Subjects with a poor premorbid course (formerly sometimes known as process schizophrenics) have difficulty changing their point of view in problem-solving tasks. They show more perseverative strategies in task solving. This was also true for negative-symptom schizophrenics. Good premorbid patients switched more easily between alternative responses (cf. Chapter 2).

It is also noticeable that the poor premorbid are more impaired than the good premorbid in memory performance (Chapter 3). The performance of the good premorbid but not of the poor premorbid improved when they were given cues to help organize the material to be remembered. This is reminiscent of some of the problems of patients with brain damage. However, there has been a lack of systematic comparison. The memory problems of (a subgroup of) schizophrenics have been viewed as reminiscent of impaired hippocampal function by some authors (for review, see Levin *et al.*, 1989). As we have discussed in Chapter 3, many studies have not adequately taken into account the potential interference of anticholinergic medication on memory performance (cf. review of Spohn and Strauss, 1989).

In studies of masking, poor premorbid subjects perform worse than good premorbid subjects; it is noticeable here that the former group does not improve performance with practice while the latter group can improve. Just as surprising is that the poor premorbid subject experiences no advantage in the partial-report version of the Sperling test, in contrast to the good premorbid subject. Another interesting feature is that the stimulus trace in the sensory buffer (icon) seems to decay more slowly. There is no simple and easy explanation for this. Maybe information processing is slowed down in poor premorbid patients by unknown factors (mild atrophic changes in the brain in this subgroup?).

Some reports imply that there may be more deep rooted structural changes in the brain. Not all studies find that the poor premorbid group is more likely to show mild cerebral atrophy (CT scan) or signs of minor neurological impairment. According to one study, the poor premorbid group was at a greater risk of developing tardive dyskinesia, but this is not uniquely a problem of those with a poor premorbid course. Seen from a different angle, additional studies support the speculation that a poor premorbid course may at least in part be an indication of a separate group. For example, it has been claimed that schizophrenics with dyskinesias and tomographic signs of atrophy tend to be less likely to have a family history of schizophrenia. We must treat these new results with caution, but it is certainly something to consider in future investigations.

In contrast to this, the one feature that does seem to be a well-established characteristic of the group with a poor premorbid course is that they have, in the mid- to long-term, a poor prognosis.

## D. Positive and Negative Symptoms

It has long been evident that schizophrenic symptoms can vary from one to another extreme along the dimension known as productive or florid symptoms, for example, between thought disturbance with bizarre content to speech poverty and mutism or between high to low emotional excitability and flat affect.

Only more recently have groups in Europe and North America attempted to translate and define these symptoms in terms of two basic types of schizophrenic disturbance. The two types were called I and II by Crow *et al.* (1982) or positive and negative (Andreasen, 1982). Crow's type I illness characteristically includes Schneiderian first rank (positive) symptoms, and is seen in the acutely ill with a good prognosis who are likely to respond to neuroleptic treatment (implying increased DA function). The type II illness tends, according to Crow, to be the opposite, with negative symptoms, poor outcome, and possible structural changes in the brain.

One can look through current or past literature and pick out the features that seem to separate subjects with more positive from those with more negative features. (N.B.: It is more correct to say "more" or "less" since one seldom finds a patient with only the one or the other.)

Schizophrenics with predominantly negative symptoms have slowed reaction times (Chapter 4). Subjects with a specific pattern of negative symptoms and with thought disorder tend to be nonresponders (or reduced responders) on the electrodermal component of the orienting response (Chapter 5).

If we look at another psychophysiological measure, the SPEM, it is perhaps surprising to find that impairments are less exaggerated in patients with negative symptoms. This result should be more closely studied, since it implies that some schizophrenic patients with negative features may not have this putative genetic marker (Chapter 7).

If we turn to the biological bases, then in the sense that tomographic signs of atrophy may precede the illness and be associated with a poor prognosis, they are often found in subjects with negative symptoms. Just as we have noted that chronic patients may have passed through an acute stage, it is not surprising that there are some reports of acute patients with positive symptoms and signs of atrophy. Thus, the CT findings may be more a hint toward poor prognosis than toward a specific pattern of symptoms. Reports that negative symptoms may be more associated with frontal (perhaps left-sided) and positive symptoms with temporal (left-sided) structural change require close attention and replication (Chapter 8).

With regard to dopamine, Crow defined his type II group as likely to have a poor neuroleptic response; thus, it is interesting to note that negative symptoms (and signs of atrophy) tend to be associated with signs of reduced DA activity [e.g., reduced metabolites in cerebrospinal fluid (CSF)] and the reverse tends to be true of patients with positive signs (see the following more detailed discussion).

Again, one is tempted to speculate that a nongenetic type of schizophrenia, or one with a weaker genetic load, is associated with a certain type of structural change and with less involvement of the dopamine system in the (still unknown) chain of dysfunctions leading to schizophrenia. However, the concept of negative symptoms seems to embrace a mixture of adaptive behavioral responses as well as features directly related to the roots of the illness and, thus, be too global a category to lead to clear-cut findings (see also Figure 16.5).

With respect to the development of the schizophrenic illness, an interesting observation from the Danish high-risk study emerged, which should be taken into account in future research. They recorded an association between the eventual development of negative symptoms and the "passivity" of the patient earlier in childhood and adolescence. Whether this means that "passive" personalities are more likely to develop protective coping strategies (acquired symptoms) or it represents the premorbid stage in an individual who will develop the fully blown negative symptom illness must remain a matter for speculation at present.

Negative symptoms are the dominant form of expression of schizophrenia in later chronic stages of the illness. However, just as we have said that it is not clear to what extent the symptoms of chronic schizophrenia are of a secondary reactive nature (i.e., acquired for coping with the illness), so it remains an unresolved problem to know which negative symptoms reflect the core illness and which ones are a response to the illness.

A solution must incorporate a closer look at the associations of each symptom, that is, which pattern of (negative) symptoms is correlated with reduced dopaminergic activity, with structural brain changes, with poor neuroleptic response, with low family risk, and with a poor prognosis. With the results of investigations into these questions, we may be able to begin sorting out the true subgroups of schizophrenia. Particularly helpful for the therapy and treatment of such patients would be longitudinal studies illustrating the reactive or coping symptoms.

In particular if, as suggested earlier, some of these reactive symptoms become apparent in the premorbid phase, then prophylactic intervention could help reduce at least the secondary symptoms of the oncoming illness. Such interventions could help reduce the severity of the illness by mitigating some of the conflicts the patient meets in the premorbid phase when signs of the so-called spectrum disorders already appear.

## VI. Findings That May Relate to the Biological Basis of Schizophrenia

## A. Neurotransmitters

Currently there are only two direct ways to see if schizophrenics show signs of changes of DA function in the brain. The one involves analysis of central nervous tissue *postmortem* and the other *in vivo* visualization of radioligand uptake by DA binding sites with positron emission tomography (PET). Controlled PET studies of drug-naive patients in Baltimore showed that schizophrenics had more than twice the number of binding sites of controls (Wong *et al.*, 1986a,b). A study conducted in Paris revealed that acute patients showed 22% more binding than chronic patients (Martinot *et al.*, 1989) but a research team from Stockholm has not found signs of an increase in schizophrenics (e.g., Farde *et al.*, 1987). Methods and procedures differed between these studies, so it is not possible to come to any unequivocal conclusion.

A cooperative study between researchers from Canada, the United States, England, China, and Austria on *postmortem* tissue shows that chronic neuroleptic treatment of patients with a range of illnesses (e.g., Huntington's chorea, Alzheimer's disease, and schizophrenia) can increase DA $D_2$ receptor binding by about 25%. However, a proportion of schizophrenics show a second mode of binding that is more than double that found in other groups (Seeman *et al.*, 1987). Isolated findings from rare untreated patients also suggest that increased binding may occur in some schizophrenics (e.g., Owen *et al.*, 1984). The possibility that these findings still reflect the iatrogenic effects of neuroleptic treatment continue to hamper their interpretation. Only one of the eight subjects in Seeman's study who had never received neuroleptics showed the higher mode of binding reported.

One cannot overlook that some, but not all, schizophrenics show increased numbers of $D_2$ receptors in the brain. It is not easy to interpret this as reflecting an increase or decrease of DA activity; it is not clear that this is the primary DA change (changes of affinity or coupling between binding sites are conceivable and have recently been reported; e.g., Seeman *et al.*, 1989); it is also not clear, when DA changes are evident, whether they are primary or the result of changes of activity in other neurotransmitter systems further along the network or chain of connections. Whether primary or secondary, there are pharmacological and behavioral indications of unusual asymmetric DA function in some schizophrenics (e.g., Reynolds, 1983; Bracha, 1987).

As discussed earlier, there is some evidence that increased DA activity is related to positive symptoms. Crow's group reported (after Crow published his hypothesis in 1980) that there was a significant positive correlation between their measures of $D_2$ receptors and ratings of positive symptoms (e.g., Cross *et al.*, 1983). A number of groups have found that chronic patients with negative symptoms excrete fewer DA metabolites (e.g., homo-vanillic acid) into the CSF and that this correlates inversely with cerebro-ventricle size (i.e., increased atrophy; cf. Chapter 8 and 13). Thus, there are indications that DA systems are up regulated in the presence of positive and down regulated in the presence of negative symptoms. Again we should emphasize that this is a generalization that is not always statistically significant in every small group of patients studied.

Indirect methods also suggest that there is a change of DA function in a considerable proportion of schizophrenics. These methods may be grouped under the rubric of "challenge tests." Challenge of schizophrenic responsiveness to amphetamine (which stimulates DA release) usually shows that those with a larger exacerbation will show more clinical improvement with neuroleptic treatment ($D_2$ antagonism). These patients are less likely to show signs of cerebral atrophy. Those that respond less to amphetamine also respond less to neuroleptics and are more likely to show tomographic signs of cerebral atrophy (e.g., Pandurangi *et al.*, 1989). This supports Crow's hypothesis, but we may note that similar results of amphetamine challenge tests from Van Kammen and colleagues have been used to argue for a state rather than a trait dependency of increased response to amphetamine (Chapter 13).

However, because the evidence for DA dysfunction does not incorporate all subjects, may not be primary, and is not unequivocal, the search goes on for dysfunction in other transmitter systems. Because there is evidence for dysfunction in temporal and frontal lobes of schizophrenics and these regions affect DA activity by way of GABA-ergic and glutamergic pathways, these two amino-acid transmitters are now popular candidates for a source of abnormal activity. Indeed, animal experiments have shown that disturbance of glutamate input to the ventral tegmental area (VTA) can alter motor-related DA changes in the Nucleus accumbens and stress-related DA changes in the frontal cortex (Kalivas *et al.*, 1989). Further, these experiments showed that such manipulations resulted in widespread changes of serotonin metabolism. This is of interest since changes of serotonin metabolism often but irregularly accompany reports of biochemical changes in material from schizophrenics. However, the analysis of amino acids in human tissue is particularly prone to a range of methodological problems and most reports of anomalous function have not survived attempts to replicate them. Nonetheless, one of us has long argued that some of the symptoms of schizophrenia may be attributable to transmitter change elsewhere in the chain of events modulating DA activity (Oades, 1982) and one way of viewing the range of possibilities here is shown in Figure 16.6.

Let us conclude this section by making two points. First studies of DA function have been bedevilled by (1) the confusion caused by the fact that

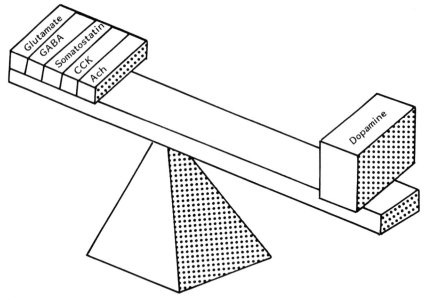

**Figure 16.6** One way to view the physiological balance that regulates dopamine (DA) activity in the brain. The balance can be maintained by treatments that modulate DA activity in one direction or that modulate one transmitter or a combination of transmitters that interact with DA in the other direction and vice versa, such as glutamate, gamma-aminobutyric acid (GABA), somatostatin, cholecystokinin (CCK), and acetylcholine (Ach) (modified after Stevens, 1989).

nearly all patients have been treated with DA agents and (2) the rareness of systematic comparisons of regional distributions in the brain. Both these factors are likely to be overcome in the next few years by the more widespread use of *in vivo* PET studies. Advances will make these methods cheaper, more easily applicable to those who can obtain patients prior to treatment, and will increase the resolution so that brain regions outside the basal ganglia can be studied.

Another point is that increasing evidence of the involvement of temporal and perhaps frontal lobe dysfunction in some of the symptoms of schizophrenia necessarily means that receptors and transmitter function in these areas is disturbed. If there is a structural change, there is bound to be a change of transmitter function. In the nature of things, it is plausible to assume that a change of transmitter function is likely to precede (at least in the majority of cases with no damage to brain tissue during the perinatal period) any structural change. There are indeed indications, from recent studies using new ligands for amino-acid uptake sites, that schizophrenics may show more glutamate-like binding in the frontal lobes and less GABA-like binding in the structures of the temporal lobe (Deakin *et al.*, 1989;

Simpson *et al.*, 1989). Since, in these studies, treatment effects cannot be separated from intrinsic changes, one has to investigate more systematically drug-free groups in the future.

# VII. Structural and Functional Changes

## A. Diffuse Structural Changes

Currently available reports suggest that about one-third of schizophrenics show structural changes in computer tomographic (CT) investigations. The percentage depends very much on the type of sample, as discussed earlier. The percentage seems to be higher in long-term chronic patients, but age does not explain the alterations. Despite this, the now-popular view that "schizophrenia is no longer a functional psychosis" (e.g., Tyrer and Mackay, 1986) is not supported by our review of the literature. Schizophrenia cannot yet be reduced to the findings of diffuse brain atrophies. To date the findings have not proved specific. Patients with affective disorder show about the same range of atrophies. Not all schizophrenics show signs of mild atrophies. The differences from normal controls are often small and require sophisticated analysis. Controversies persist over the best methods.

Balanced against these qualifications one must consider that the missing volume of nervous tissue implied by these results is sometimes considerable. Further, despite controversies and false alarms (particularly abundant in the history of neuropathology) there have been several recent tomographic and *postmortem* histological investigations whose results qualitatively support each other.

The consensus, if one overlooks the exceptions, is that these patients tend to respond poorly to neuroleptic treatment, often (but far from always) show negative symptoms, have less of a family history for schizophrenia, are more likely to have experienced perinatal problems, and have a poor prognosis.

We discussed several times earlier whether these findings reflect a special subgroup of schizophrenia. The existence of many exceptions to our generalization is enough reason to object, but one aspect favoring the subgroup hypothesis is the possibility of a reduced hereditary loading. In this case the problems of perinatal stress (for various reasons including infectious diseases of the mother) and the development of atrophy would constitute the factors placing this group at risk (which does not explain why these patients develop schizophrenia and not affective disorder, but see following text).

The unspecific and diffuse atrophies therefore must be conceptualized as internal stressors (like external stressors) that help to lower the threshold in disposed individuals with reduced genetic loading, who otherwise would not have become schizophrenic (or would have become affectively disordered) as

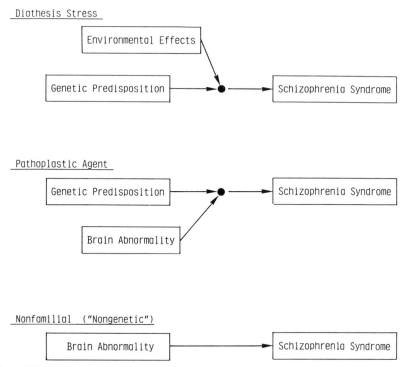

**Figure 16.7**  A model to show the theoretical contributions of various categories of risk factors that can lead to the expression of schizophrenia (modified after Lewine *et al.*, 1990).

discussed in more detail in Section I. In Figure 16.7, this is conceptualized as a "pathoplastic agent" illustrating a proposal by Lewine *et al.*, 1990. Similarly, Leff (1991) proposed two factors that may contribute to lower threshold in the genetically predisposed individual. Both factors are called environmental. One is physical (e.g., brain damage); the other is social (e.g., poor family environment).

Another possibility is that, in some individuals who are genetically not at risk, brain abnormalities occur in regions involved in the genetic form of the illness. This possibility could explain the finding of nongenetic or nonfamilial schizophrenia (Figure 16.7).

## B. Regional Structural and Functional Changes

A number of PET studies of frontal blood flow and glucose metabolism support the hypothesis of frontal changes. An imbalance of frontal activity, either within the structures of the frontal lobes or by comparison with activity elsewhere, is implied. This is particularly evident when information process-ing demands have been placed on cerebral function. The clearest demonstra-tion was with the Wisconsin card-sorting task. Here schizophrenics did not show metabolic activation in the frontal cortex to the extent seen in healthy controls when required to switch strategies for the categorization of stimuli. This feature was also recently reported for unmedicated schizophrenics (Berman *et al.*, 1988). Although quantitatively more apparent in these patients, reduced levels of activation also appear to a lesser degree in the affectively ill (e.g., Cohen *et al.*, 1989).

If we put the results of functional, tomographic, and *postmortem* studies together, the structures implicated in impaired function lie along a frontal–temporal *axis* of communication. They include anterior, dorsolateral, and orbitofrontal areas; the transitional and allocortices of the entorhinalis, amyg-dala, and hippocampus; and polar regions of the temporal neocortex. The number of studies and the small number of patients tested in these studies to date do not enable us to be certain about the type of patient who will develop the one or the other structural change or functional impairment. The origin of these impairments remains unknown. The heterogeneity speaks for different origins.

Nevertheless, the assumption of a disturbance of the frontal–temporal axis of function would fit the hypothesis of a disturbance of open-loop data processing that requires the integration of input data with stored concepts according to acquired rules for data organization. The frontal lobes are involved in planning and forming conceptual approaches to new situations. An important function of temporal and septohippocampal structures is that of matching procedures, that is, matching the input with the appropriate stored models (see Chapter 15).

Finally, there is an indication from results reported in the literature that patients with functional but no overt underlying structural changes constitute a group with a potentially good long-term prognosis. In contrast, when struc-tural changes are manifest, the likelihood that the schizophrenic problem will gradually disappear is reduced.

## C. Lateralized Functional and Structural Changes

Insofar as we are still a long way from fully understanding the normal division of function between the two hemispheres, our understanding of the potential anomaly in the division of function in schizophrenia is poor. Interpretations of studies of schizophrenic function are based on several assumptions that have less-than-secure foundations.

One example here is the assumption that response to many sensory events depends on the major contralateral input. The role of some minor unilateral pathways is poorly understood. (For example, the consequences of unilateral

DA denervation of the basal ganglia in animals has proved more complicated than originally construed.) The special problems involved in this field of research are illustrated by the following questions. (1) Does the detected impairment reflect over- or underfunction (e.g., exaggerated right ear advantage)? (2) Do the changes detected originate in the hemisphere tested or are they (in part) a compensatory process in response to a contralateral dysfunction? (3) Is the detected lateral change a consequence of impaired information transfer from the other hemisphere? (4) Is our understanding of the normal lateralization of a specific function appropriate for the interpretation of a lateralized anomaly? (Both hemispheres are necessary for the full performance of most responses, even if the basic function is lateralized. A lateralized functional deficit thus may be just an epiphenomenon, at least secondary to a more fundamental bilateral weakness.) (5) Could the anomalous lateralization pattern detected arise from pharmacological treatment?

Despite these numerous open questions, there are hints about subgroup differences. Subjects with negative symptoms are often said to show more left-sided problems, but the results are contradictory, and some authors even claim that both positive- and negative-symptom schizophrenics have left-sided problems, but in different locations. For example, one team reported left frontal atrophies in a negative-symptom group and more left temporal atrophies in the positive-symptom group (cf. Chapter 9). The functional changes reported on the left side seem to support an earlier hypothesis developed by Flor-Henry (cf. Chapter 15). However, as he recently has pointed out, the establishment of the true origin of a lateralized deficit is made more complicated by the lateralized functional changes following neuroleptic treatment (Flor-Henry, 1989) and by the lateralized distribution of many neurotransmitters (Chapter 9).

In addition to this, as pointed out in Section II, there is abundant evidence that the cognitive disturbance of schizophrenics involves left-sided (e.g., use of redundant information in a series of stimuli, speech and communication disturbances) as well as right-sided (e.g., Gestalt processing, figure-ground discrimination, face-recognition problems) difficulties without much evidence for subgroup differences.

## VIII. Possible Relationships between Cognitive, Symptomatic, and Neurophysiological Abnormalities in Schizophrenia

We have seen that schizophrenia cannot be characterized simply by the failure of one or two functional elements. Rather, there is an impairment in the integration of the functions of several elements, indeed of several systems. Thus, with the prefrontal cortex viewed as the highest level for the integration of input and the organization of output, it is not surprising that the view that some part of the frontal lobe is the seat of the schizophrenic problem has a certain popularity (e.g., Weinberger, 1988).

As we have discussed in Section II, a putative common failure of schizophrenics is the inability to integrate elements of incoming information into the background of stored rules and then reorganize these elements. If one looks at the way various authors view the normal function of the prefrontal cortex, it is easy to see why the region is seen by many to be involved in the schizophrenic impairment. According to Fuster (1989, p. 185), in the prefrontal cortex "present experience must be matched to previous or anticipated experience. Thus, if necessary, mismatches can be eliminated by corrective action." As Stuss and Benson (1986) put it, the frontal lobes maintain and organize bits of information into meaningful sequences. Luria (1978) sees in patients with frontal damage a bit-by-bit perceptual style, which we also noted in schizophrenics (e.g., Cutting, 1985). Schizophrenics tend to identify and interpret pieces of a picture, rather than put them together to form an overall scene.

Other functions attributed to the frontal, especially the prefrontal areas, point to clinically relevant dysfunctions. Goldberg (1985) argues that the prefrontal areas are involved in goal setting and the planning of behavior. The loss of goal in the language performance of schizophrenics comes immediately to mind. Other features of patients with frontal damage have some similarity with that shown by the chronic negative-symptom schizophrenic: apathy, loss of initiative, and a reduction of emotional tonus ("flat affect"; e.g., Stuss and Benson, 1986). The loss of self-awareness of "frontal patients," that is, the failure to recognize their position in the social milieu (Stuss and Benson, 1986), is paralleled in the schizophrenic failure to be aware of subtle psychosocial interactions and may be related to their problem of perceiving themselves and their own position adequately.

However, we must emphasize an important qualification to the drawing of parallels between the patient with overt frontal brain damage and the schizophrenic. Patients with frontal damage are not, as a result, schizophrenic. The similarity applies only to symptoms but not to the whole pattern of schizophrenia. The disturbance of patients with frontal damage is not as pervasive as that of schizophrenics. They do not have auditory hallucinations or delusions of reference, and seldom show formal thought disorder to the same extent as schizophrenics. Moreover, Weinberger and Berman (1988), in a recent extension of their regional blood flow study, showed that patients with Parkinson's disease displayed the same reduction of blood flow in prefrontal areas while doing the Wisconsin-card-sorting task.

How can these similarities and dissimilarities be resolved? It is obvious from these observations as well as from the findings with schizophrenia, that frontal lobe dysfunction alone cannot explain the full pattern of schizophrenia. (Certain subgroups with negative symptoms may be an exception.) There is a vast amount of evidence that functional and structural changes in the limbic and temporal regions are often accompanied by schizophrenic symptoms. This evidence ranges from "schizophrenic symptoms" in patients with epileptic foci in the temporal lobe (e.g., Diehl, 1989) to numerous reports of structural and functional changes in the temporal and limbic regions of patients with a diagnosis of schizophrenia (Chapters 8 and 13). (It should be noted that this, as for the frontal findings, does not necessarily mean that the reported structural or functional change explains the origin of schizophrenia, but that this indicates an area critical for the schizophrenic disturbances. These alterations still may be secondary or, in some cases, only phenocopies; see Fig. 16.2.)

It is interesting that, based on neurophysiological work, Gray (1982) and others consider the septohippocampal system a neuronal "comparator" (see also Frith and Done, 1988). This system is "a comparator of current sensory information with some internally generated model of the world" (Gray, 1982, p. 441). The model of the world, in our terms, contains the stored rules of relationships (a concept) to which the sensory event must be matched (cf. Gray *et al.*, 1991; Hemsley, 1991).

We stressed in Section II that, in the majority of patients, the sensory input seems to be intact and the centers responsible for concept formation (knowledge of stored rules) are not destroyed. If this assumption is correct, then the primary failure may be in the matching process. Hence we assume that the impaired coordination of prefrontal (conceptual) and temporal–limbic (matching) functions may lie at the root of schizophrenic disturbances in the majority of cases. Thus, we propose here that the prominent clinical and experimental features are not caused by a breakdown of function at a single location but arise through impaired coordination of the frontal and temporal–limbic axes. (Figure 16.8 depicts some relevant functional connections.) Although there are numerous indications for the involvement of structural and functional abnormalities relevant to this interpretation of schizophrenia, there is no definitive candidate for the nature of the biochemical alteration or source of the "lesion."

It is of more than passing interest that there are both mesolimbic and frontal dopamine systems and that alterations of dopamine activity can affect the expression of schizophrenic symptoms. Yet, with the possible exception of a subgroup, the evidence for altered dopamine activity in schizophrenia remains equivocal. Thus, it is reasonable to suppose that a dysfunction in other transmitter systems (e.g., glutamate, GABA) that may interact with dopaminergic function lies closer to the root of the disturbance. That the temporal (limbic) and/or frontal lobes may be the sources of changes in the activity of neural networks using these amino-acid transmitters is indirectly supported by the association we have discussed between damage to these structures (as seen in brain-damaged patients) and similar impairments arising in some schizophrenics.

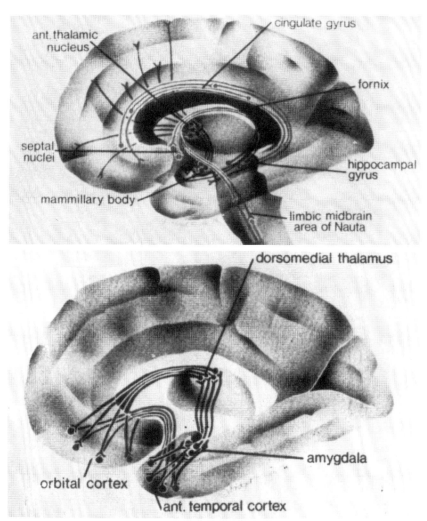

**Figure 16.8** The major connections of two types of limbic circuit in the brain are schematically illustrated. The medial limbic circuit emphasizes the septo-hippocampal connections with diencephalic structures. The basolateral limbic circuit illustrates the direct and indirect interactions (over the mediodorsal thalamus) of the temporal cortex with the frontal cortexes and the amygdala (from Stuss and Benson, 1986).

# References

Andreasen, N. C. (1982). Negative symptoms in schizophrenia: Definition and reliability. *Archives of General Psychiatry*, *39*, 784–788.

Anscombe, R. (1987). The disorder of consciousness in schizophrenia. *Schizophrenia Bulletin*, *13*, 241–260.

Arieti, S. (1971). The origins of development of the pathology of schizophrenia. In M. Bleuler and J. Angst (Eds.). *Die Entstehung der Schizophrenia.* Bern: Huber.

Baruch, I., Hemsley, D. R., and Gray, J. A. (1988). Differential performance of acute and chronic schizophrenics in a latent inhibition task. *Journal of Nervous and Mental Disease, 176,* 598–606.

Berman, K. F., Illowsky, B. P., and Weinberger, D. R. (1988). Physiological dysfunction of dorsolateral prefrontal cortex in schizophrenia. *Archives of General Psychiatry, 45,* 616–622.

Bleuler, E. (1911). *Dementia praecox oder die Gruppe der Schizophrenien.* (Translation: J. Zinkin, 1950. Dementia praecox or the group of schizophrenias. International Universities Press). Leipzig: Deuticke.

Borst, U., and Cohen, R. (1989). Filling the preparatory interval with temporal information or visual noise: crossover effect in schizophrenic and controls. *Psychological Medicine, 19,* 865–874.

Bourne, R. L., Dominowski, E., and Loftus, F. (1979). *Cognitive Processes.* Englewood Cliffs, New Jersey: Prentice Hall.

Bracha, H. S. (1987). Is there a right hemi-hyper-dopaminergic psychosis? *Schizophrenia Research, 2,* 317–324.

Broen, W. E., and Storms, L. H. (1966). Lawful disorganisation: The process underlying a schizophrenic syndrome. *Psychological Review, 73,* 265–279.

Callaway, E., and Naghdi, S. (1982). An information processing model for schizophrenia. *Archives of General Psychiatry, 39,* 339–347.

Carpenter, W. T., Jr., Heinrichs, D. W., and Alphs, L. D. (1985). Treatment of negative symptoms. *Schizophrenia Bulletin, 11,* 440–452.

Chapman, L. J., and Chapman, J. P. (1973). *Disordered thought in schizophrenia.* Englewood Cliffs, New Jersey: Prentice Hall, Inc.

Cohen, R. M., Semple, W. E., Gross, M., Nordahl, T. E., King, A. C., Pickar, D., and Post, M. (1989). Evidence for common alterations in cerebral glucose metabolism in major affective disorders and schizophrenia. *Neuropsychopharmakologie, 2,* 241–254.

Crider, A., Blockel, L., and Solomon, P. R. (1986). A selective attention deficit in the rat following induced dopamine receptor supersensitivity. *Behavioural Neuroscience, 100,* 315–319.

Cromwell, R. L., and Dokecki, P. (1968). Schizophrenic language: A disattention interpretation. In S. Rosenberg and J. H. Koplin (Eds.). *Developments in applied psycholinguistic research.* New York: Macmillan.

Cross, A. J., Crow, T. J., Ferrier, I. N., Johnstone, E. C., McCreadie, R. M., Owen, F., Owens, F. G. C., and Poulter, M. (1983). Dopamine receptor changes in schizophrenia in relation to the disease process and movement disorder. *Journal of Neural Transmission, Suppl. 18,* 265–272.

Crosson, B., and Hughes, C. W. (1988). The role of the thalamus in language: Is it related to schizophrenic thought disorder? *Schizophrenia Bulletin, 13,* 605–621.

Crow, T. J. (1980). Molecular pathology of schizophrenia: More than one disease process? *British Medical Journal, 1,* 66–68.

Crow, T. J., Cross, A. J., Johnstone, E. C., and Owen, F. (1982). Two syndromes in schizophrenia and their pathogenesis. In F. A. Henn and H. A. Nasrallah (Eds.). *Schizophrenia as a brain disease.* New York: Oxford University Press.

Crow, T. J. (1985). The two-syndrome concept: Origins and current status. *Schizophrenia Bulletin, 11,* 471–486.

Cutting, J. (1985). *The psychology of schizophrenia.* Edinburgh: Livingstone.

DeAmicis, L. A., Wagstaff, D. A., and Cromwell, R. L. (1986). Reaction time crossover as a marker of schizophrenia and of higher functioning. *The Journal of Nervous and Mental Disease, 174,* 177–179.

Deakin, J. F. W., Simpson, M. D. C., Gilchrist, A. C., Skan, W. J., Royston, M. C., and Slater, P. (1989). Changes in (3H)-aspartate and (3H)-kainate binding in schizophrenic postmortem brains. *Journal of Neurochemistry*, *52*, 1781–1786.

Diehl, L. W. (1989). Schizophrenic syndromes in epilepsies. *Psychopathology*, *22*, 65–140.

Doty, R. W. (1989). Schizophrenia: A disease of interhemispheric processes at forebrain and brainstem levels? *Behavioural Brain Research*, *34*, 1–33.

Farde, L., Wiesel, F. A., Hall, H., Halldin, C., Stone-Elander, S., and Sedvall, G. (1987). No $D_2$ receptor increase in PET study of schizophrenia. *Archives of General Psychiatry*, *44*, 671–672.

Flor-Henry, P. (1989). Interhemispheric relationships and depression in schizophrenia in the perspective of cerebral laterality. In R. Williams and J. T. Dalby (Eds.). *Depression in Schizophrenics*. New York: Plenum Press.

Freedman, R., Adler, L. E., Waldo, M. C., Pachtman, E., and Franks, R. D. (1983). Neurophysiological evidence for a defect in inhibitory pathways in schizophrenia: Comparison of medicated and drug-free patients. *Biological Psychiatry*, *18*, 537–551.

Frith, C. D., and Done, D. J. (1988). Towards a neuropsychology of schizophrenia. *The British Journal of Psychiatry*, *153*, 437–443.

Frith, C. D., and Done, D. J. (1989). Experiences of alien control in schizophrenia reflect a disorder in the central monitoring of action. *Psychological Medicine*, *19*, 359–363.

Fuster, J. M. (1989). *The prefrontal cortex: Anatomy, physiology, and neuropsychology of the frontal lobe*. (Second Edition). New York: Raven Press.

Goldberg, G. (1985). Supplementary motor area structure and function: Review and hypotheses. *The Behavioral and Brain Sciences*, *8*, 567–616.

Goldstein, M. J. (1987). The UCLA high-risk project. *Schizophrenia Bulletin*, *13*, 505–514.

Goldstein, M. J., and Kreisman, D. (1988). Gender, family environment and schizophrenia. *Psychological Medicine*, *18*, 861–872.

Goldstein, M. J., and Tsuang, M. T. (1990). Gender and schizophrenia: An introduction and synthesis of findings. *Schizophrenia Bulletin*, *16*, 179–184.

Gottesman, I. I., and Shields, J. (1982). *Schizophrenia: The epigenetic puzzle*. Cambridge: Cambridge University Press.

Gray, J. A. (1982). *The neuropsychology of anxiety*. Oxford: Oxford University Press.

Gray, J. A., Feldon, J., Rawlins, J. N. P., Hemsley, D. R., and Smith, A. D. (1991). The neuropsychology of schizophrenia. *Behavioral Brain Sciences*, *14*, 1–84.

Häfner, H. (1987). Epidemiology of schizophrenia. In H. G. Häfner, W. F. Gattaz, and W. Janzarik (Eds.), *Search for the causes of schizophrenia*. Berlin: Springer.

Häfner, H. (1987). Search for the causes of schizophrenia: Summary and outlook. In H. Häfner, W. F. Gattaz, and W. Janzarik (Eds.). *Search for the causes of schizophrenia*. Berlin: Springer.

Hauser, P., Dauphinais, I. D., Berrettini, W., DeLisi, L. E., Gelernter, J., and Post, R. M. (1989). Corpus callosum dimensions measured by magnetic resonance imaging in bipolar affective disorder and schizophrenia. *Biological Psychiatry*, *26*, 659–668.

Hemsley, D. R. (1987). An experimental psychological model for schizophrenia. In H. Häfner, W. F. Gattaz, and W. Janzarik (Eds.). *Search for the causes of schizophrenia*. Berlin: Springer.

Hemsley, D. R. (1991). Perception and cognition in schizophrenia. In R. L. Cromwell and C. R. Snyder (Eds.), *Schizophrenia: Origins, processes, treatment and outcome*. Oxford: Oxford University Press.

Hoffmann, R. E., Stopek, S., and Andreasen, N. C. (1986). A comparative study of manic versus schizophrenic speech disorganization. *Archives of General Psychiatry*, *43*, 831–838.

Iacono, W. G. (1983). Young psychophysiologist award address, 1982. Psychophysiology and genetics. A key to psychopathology research. *Psychophysiology*, *20*, 371–381.

Jeste, D. V., and Lohr, J. B. (1989). Hippocampal pathologic findings in schizophrenia: a morphometric study. *Archives of General Psychiatry*, *46*, 1019–1024.

Jones, S. H., Hemsley, D. R., and Gray, J. A. (1990). The Kamin blocking effect, incidental learning and psychoticism. *The British Journal of Psychology*, *1*, 95–109.

Kalivas, P. W., Duffy, P., and Barrow, J. (1989). Regulation of mesocorticolimbic dopamine system by glutamic acid receptor subtypes. *Journal of Pharmacology and Experimental Therapeutics*, *251*, 378–387.

Karlsson, J. L. (1968). Genealogical studies of schizophrenia. In D. Rosenthal and S. S. Kety (Eds.). *The transmission of schizophrenia*. New York: Pergamon Press.

Keil, F. C. (1981). Constraints on knowledge and cognitive development. *Psychological Review*, *88*, 197–227.

Klein, D. N., Depue, R. A., and Slater, J. F. (1985). Cyclothymia in the adolescent offspring of parents with bipolar affective disorder. *Journal of Abnormal Psychology*, *94*, 115–127.

Knight, R. A., Sherer, M., and Shapiro, J. (1977). Iconic imagery in overinclusive and nonoverinclusive schizophrenics. *The Journal of Abnormal Psychology*, *86*, 242–255.

Knight, R. A. (1984). Converging models of cognitive deficit in schizophrenia. In W. Spaulding and J. K. Cole (Eds.). *Nebraska symposium on motivation, 1983: Theories of schizophrenia and psychosis*. Lincoln: University of Nebraska Press.

Kretschmer, E. (1958). *Geniale Menschen*. Berlin: Springer.

Kuipers, L., and Bebbington, P. (1988). Expressed emotion research in schizophrenia: theoretical and clinical implications. *Psychological Medicine*, *18*, 893–909.

Kwapil, T. R., Hegley, D. C., Chapman, L. J., and Chapman, J. P. (1990). Facilitation of word recognition by semantic priming in schizophrenia. *Journal of Abnormal Psychology*, *99*, 215–221.

Leff, J. (1991). Interaction of environment and personality in the course of schizophrenia. In H. Häfner and W. F. Gattaz (Eds.), *Search for the causes of schizophrenia*. (Vol. II) Berlin: Springer.

Leff, J., Sartorius, N., Jablensky, A., Anker, M., Korten, A., Gulbinat, W., and Ernberg, G. (1991). The International Pilot Study of Schizophrenia: Five-Year Follow-Up Findings. In H. Häfner and W. F. Gattaz (Eds.). *Search for the causes of schizophrenia (Vol. II)*. Berlin: Springer.

Levin, S., Yurgelun-Todd, D., and Craft, S. (1989). Contributions of clinical neuropsychology to the study of schizophrenia. *The Journal of Abnormal Psychology*, *98*, 341–356.

Lewine, R. R. J., Gulley, L. R., Risch, S. C., Jewart, R., and Houpt, J. L. (1990). Sexual dimorphism, brain morphology, and schizophrenia. *Schizophrenia Bulletin*, *16*, 195–203.

Lin, K. M., and Kleinman, A. M. (1988). Psychopathology and clinical course of schizophrenia: A cross-cultural perspective. *Schizophrenia Bulletin*, *14*, 555–568.

Lindsay, P. H., and Norman, D. A. (1972). Human information processing. New York: Academic Press.

Luria, A. R. (1978). *The working brain*. Harmondworth: Penguin Press.

Magaro, P. A. (1980). *Cognition in schizophrenia and paranoia*. Hillsdale: Erlbaum.

Manschreck, T. C., Maher, B. A., Milavetz, J. J., Ames, D., Weisstein, C. C., and Schneyer, M. L. (1988). Semantic priming in thought disordered schizophrenic patients. *Schizophrenia Research*, *1*, 61–66.

Martinot, J. L., Huret, J. D., Peron-Magnan, P., Mazoyer, B. M., Baron, J-C., Caillard, V., Syrota, A., and Loo, H. (1989). Striatal D2 dopaminergic receptor status ascertained in vivo by positron emission tomography and 76Br-bromospiperone in untreated schizophrenics. *Psychiatry Research*, *29*, 357–358.

McCarley, R. W., Faux, S. F., Shenton, M., LeMay, M., Cane, M., Ballinger, R., and Duffy, H. (1989). CT abnormalities in schizophrenia: a preliminary study of their correlations with P300/P200 electrophysiological features and positive/negative symptoms. *Archives of General Psychiatry*, *25*, 207–214.

Mirsky, A. F. (1990). The neuropsychology of attention: Elements of a complex behavior. In E. Perecman (Ed.). *Integrating theory and practice in clinical neuropsychology.* New Jersey: Erlbaum Assoc.

Mueser, K. T., Bellack, A. S., Morrison, R. L., and Wade, J. H. (1990). Gender, social competence, and symptomatology in schizophrenia: A longitudinal analysis. *The Journal of Abnormal Psychology, 99,* 138–147.

Neale, J. M., and Cromwell, R. L. (1977). Attention and schizophrenia. In B. A. Maher (Ed.). *Contributions to the Psychopathology of schizophrenia.* New York: Academic Press.

Nuechterlein, K. H., and Dawson, M. E. (1984). Information processing and attentional functioning in the developmental course of schizophrenic disorders. *Schizophrenia Bulletin, 10,* 160–203.

Oades, R. D. (1982). *Attention and Schizophrenia: Neurobiological Bases.* London: Pitman Press.

Oades, R. D., Rivet, J.-M., Taghzouti, K., Kharouby, M., Simon, H., and LeMoal, M. (1987). Attentional blocking is delayed by depletion of septal dopamine but remains attenuated after frontal depletion. *Brain Research, 406,* 136–146.

Odegard, O. (1960). Marriage rate and fertility in psychotic patients before admissions and after discharge. *International Journal of Social Psychiatry, 6,* 25–33.

Owen, R., Owen, F., Poulter, M., and Crow, T. J. (1984). Dopamine D2 receptors in substantia nigra in schizophrenia. *Brain Research, 299,* 152–154.

Pandurangi, A. K., Goldberg, S. C., Brink, D. D., Hill, M. H., Gulati, A. N., and Hamer, R. M. (1989). Amphetamine challenge test, response to treatment, and lateral ventricle size in schizophrenia. *Biological Psychiatry, 25,* 207–214.

Pfefferbaum, A., Ford, J. M., White, P. M., and Roth, W. T. (1989). P3 in schizophrenia is affected by stimulus modality, response requirements, medication status and negative symptoms. *Archives of General Psychiatry, 46,* 1035–1044.

Polyakov, V. F. (1969). The experimental investigation of cognitive functioning in schizophrenia. In M. Cole and I. Maltzman (Eds.), *Handbook of contemporary Soviet psychology.* New York: Basic Books.

Propping, P. (1989). *Psychiatrische Genetik.* Berlin: Springer.

Rappaport, M., Hopkins, H. K., Silverman, J., and Hall, K. (1972). Auditory signal detection in schizophrenia. *Psychopharmacologia* (Berl.), *24,* 6–28.

Reynolds, G. P. (1983). Increased concentrations and lateral asymmetry of amygdala dopamine in schizophrenia. *Nature, 305,* 527–529.

Sangstad, L. F. (1989). Social class, marriage, and fertility in schizophrenia. *Schizophrenia Bulletin, 15,* 9–44.

Schuldberg, D., French, C., Stone, L., and Heberle, J. (1988). Creativity and schizotypal traits. *The Journal of Nervous and Mental Disease, 176,* 648–657.

Schwartz, B. D., Winstead, D. K., and Adinoff, B. (1983). Temporal integration deficit in visual information processing by chronic schizophrenics. *Biological Psychiatry, 18,* 1311–1320.

Schwartz-Place, E. J., and Gilmore, G. C. (1980). Perceptual organization in schizophrenia. *The Journal of Abnormal Psychology, 89,* 409–418.

Seeman, P., Bzowej, N., Guan, H. C., Bergeron, C., Reynolds, G. P., Bird, E. D., Riederer, P., Jellinger, K., and Tourtellotte, W. W. (1987). Human brain D1 and D2 dopamine receptors in schizophrenia, Alzheimer's, Parkinson's and Huntington's diseases. *Neuropsychopharmakologie, 1,* 5–15.

Seeman, P., Niznik, H. B., Guan, H.-C., Booth, G., and Ulpian, C. (1989). Link between $D_1$ and $D_2$ dopamine receptors is reduced in schizophrenia and Huntington's diseased brain. *Proceedings in Northatlantic Academic Sciences, 86,* 1056–1060.

Seeman, M. V., and Lang, M. (1990). The role of estrogens in schizophrenia gender differences. *Schizophrenia Bulletin, 16,* 185–194.

Shakow, D. (1979). *Adaptation in schizophrenia. The theory of segmental set.* New York: Wiley.

Simpson, M. D. C., Slater, P., Deakin, J. F. W., Royston, M. C., and Skan, W. J. (1989).
    Reduced GABA uptake sites in the temporal lobe in schizophrenia. *Neuroscience Letters*, *107*,
    211–215.
Solomon, P. R., and Staton, D. M. (1982). Differential effects of microinjections of *d*-
    amphetamine into the nucleus accumbens or the caudate putamen on the rat's ability to ignore
    an irrelevant stimulus. *Biological Psychiatry*, *17*, 743–756.
Stevens, J. R. (1989). The search for an anatomic basis of schizophrenia: Review and update. In
    J. Mueller (Ed.), *Neurology and psychiatry: A meeting of minds*, pp. 64–87. Basel: Karger.
Spohn, H. E., and Strauss, M. E. (1989). Relation of neuroleptic and anticholinergic medication
    to cognitive functions in schizophrenia. *The Journal of Abnormal Psychology*, *98*, 367–380.
Spring, B., Lemon, M., and Fergeson, P. (1990). Vulnerabilities to schizophrenia: Information
    processing markers. In E. R. Straube and K. Hahlweg (Eds.). *Schizophrenia. Concepts,
    vulnerability and intervention*. Berlin: Springer.
Strauss, M. E. (1978). The differential and experimental paradigms in the study of cognition in
    schizophrenia. *Journal of Psychiatric Research*, *14*, 316–326.
Straube, E. (1975). Experimente zur Wahrnehmung Schizophrener. *Archiv für Psychiatrie und
    Nervenkrankheiten*, *220*, 139–158.
Stuss, D. T., and Benson, D. F. (1986). *The frontal lobes*. New York: Raven.
Suddath, R. L., Casanova, M. F., Goldberg, T. E., Daniel, D. G., Kelsoe, J. R., and
    Weinberger, D. R. (1989). Temporal lobe pathology in schizophrenia: a quantitative magnetic
    resonance imaging study. *The American Journal of Psychiatry*, *146*, 464–472.
Sutherland, R. J., McDonald, R. J., Hill, C. R., and Rudy, J. W. (1989). Damage to the
    hippocampal formation in rats selectively impairs the ability to learn cue relationships.
    *Behavioral and Neural Biology*, *52*, 331–356.
Tienari, P., Sorri, A., and Naarala, M. (1984). *Interaction of genetic and psychosocial factors in
    schizophrenia*. Paper presented at WPA Regional Symposium, Helsinki.
Tienari, P., Sorri, A., Lahti, I., Naarala, M., Wahlberg, K.-E., Rönkkö, T., Pohjola, J., and
    Moring, J. (1985). The Finnish adoptive family study of schizophrenia. *Yale Journal of
    Biology and Medicine*, *58*, 227–237.
Tienari, P. (1990). *Ergebnisse aus Adoptionsstudien*. Vortrag gehalten auf dem Symposium
    Schizophrenie und Jugend: Ätiologie und therapeutische Konsequenzen, Essen.
Tienari, P. (1991). Results of adoption studies. In C. Eggers (Ed.), *Schizophrenia in youth*.
    Berlin: Springer.
Tomer, R., and Flor-Henry, P. (1989). Neuroleptics reverse attention asymmetries in schizo-
    phrenic patients. *Biological Psychiatry*, *25*, 852–860.
Tyrer, P., and Mackay, A. (1986). Schizophrenia: No longer a functional psychosis. *Trends in
    Neurosciences*, *Nov/Dec*, 537–538.
Underwood, G. (1976). *Attention and memory*. Oxford: Pergamon Press.
Vargo, J. M., Richard-Smith, M., and Corwin, J. V. (1989). Spiroperidol reinstates asymmetries
    in neglect in rats recovered from left or right dorsomedial prefrontal cortex lesions. *Behavioral
    Neuroscience*, *103*, 1017–1027.
Venables, P. H. (1964). Input dysfunction in schizophrenia. In B. A. Maher (Ed.). *Progress in
    Experimental Personality Research*. New York: Academic Press.
Wells, D. S., and Leventhal, D. (1984). Perceptual grouping in schizophrenia. *The Journal of
    Abnormal Psychology*, *93*, 231–234.
Weinberger, D. R. (1988). Schizophrenia and the frontal lobe. *Trends in Neurosciences*, *11*, 367–
    370.
Weinberger, D. R., and Berman, K. F. (1988). Speculation on the meaning of cerebral metabolic
    hypofrontality in schizophrenia. *Schizophrenia Bulletin*, *14*, 157–168.
Wig, N. N., Menon, D. K., Bedi, H., Ghosh, A., Kuipers, L., Leff, J., Korten, A., Day, R.,
    Sartorius, N., Ernberg, G., and Jablensky, A. (1987). Expressed emotion and schizophrenia in

North India. I. Cross-cultural transfer of ratings of relatives' expressed emotion. *The British Journal of Psychiatry*, *151*, 156–173.

Wong, D. F., Gjedde, A., Wagner, H. N. Jr., Dannals, R. F., Douglass, K. H., Link, J. M., and Kuhar, M. J. (1986a). Quantification of neuroreceptors in the living human brain: II. Inhibition studies of receptor density and affinity. *Journal of Cerebral Blood Flow and Metabolism*, *6*, 147–153.

Wong, D. F., Wagner, H. N., Tune, L. E., Dannals, R. F., Pearlson, G. D., Links, J. M., Tamminga, C. A., Brousolle, E. P., Ravert, H. T., Wilson, A. A., Toung, J. K. T., Malat, J., Williams, J. A., O'Tuama, L. A., Snyder, S. H., Kuhar, M. J., and Gjedde, A. (1986b). Positron emission tomography reveals elevated dopamine D2 receptors in drug naive schizophrenics. *Science*, *234*, 1558–1562.

Zaunbrecher, D., Himer, W., and Straube, E. (1990). Sind frühe Stufen der visuellen Informationsverarbeitung bei Schizophrenen gestört? *Der Nervenarzt*, *61*, 418–425.

Zubin, J., and Spring, B. (1977). Vulnerability—A new view of schizophrenia. *The Journal of Abnormal Psychology*, *86*, 103–126.

Zubin, J., and Steinhauer, S. (1981). How to break the logjam in schizophrenia. A look beyond genetics. *The Journal of Nervous and Mental Disease*, *8*, 477–492.

# Chapter 17

# Synopsis

## I. Prevalence

The lifetime prevalence for schizophrenia (less than 1%) is similar all over the world. (Small regional exceptions are reported for northern Sweden, western Ireland, and Finland.) If these frequencies continue to be confirmed then the striking heterogeneity of the illness may be more apparent than real. The distribution of liability in the population may be constant. The diversity of the symptom picture may arise from additional factors such as environmental stress or mild diffuse brain damage.

## II. Age at Onset

Age of onset is earlier in males than in females. The peak of onset for males is between 18 and 25 years; for females it is between 26 and 45 years. There is no obvious reason for this difference.

## III. Genetic Factors

In the majority of cases a genetic basis is assumed, although most schizophrenics have no blood relations with schizophrenia. However, the incidence of personality features belonging to the subclinical spectrum of schizophrenia is higher in the relatives of schizophrenics than in the relatives of control groups. The genetic basis may thus not be apparent in most of the individuals who are potential carriers. The monozygotic twin partner who is not affected with schizophrenia has more offspring (and grandchildren) with schizophrenia than do control twins. Most contemporary theories claim a Gaussian distribution of a genetically transmitted liability.

# IV. Environmental Factors

Since a genetically transmitted liability, in the vast majority of cases, does not lead to schizophrenia, unfavorable conditions must play a role. Unfavorable environmental conditions such as life events or an aversive family atmosphere lower the threshold for the onset of the illness. The incidence of schizophrenia and other mental disturbances is higher in offspring adopted from a biological parent with schizophrenia into a disturbed family atmosphere than in controls, with and without schizophrenic biological parents, adopted into a good family atmosphere. (Nevertheless, the rate of schizophrenia is still higher in the index group than in the control group; this remains so even if the family atmosphere is rated as undisturbed.)

# V. Course of the Illness

The course is very heterogeneous. Nevertheless, all studies confirm that a certain percentage of schizophrenics have a good outcome (about 25%). A poor outcome is seen in 25% or less. The multitude of influences that contributes to the heterogeneity of the symptoms adds variance to the course of the illness. There are consistent indications that the environment plays a role, since the outcome of schizophrenia is reported to be less severe in non-Western less-industrialized societies.

# VI. Clinical Symptoms

Formal thought disorder, auditory hallucinations, delusions, and inappropriate or flat affect are the most prominent schizophrenic symptoms, according to modern diagnostic criteria.

# VII. "Experimental Symptoms"

Disturbance of information processing is the central feature of experimentally assessed symptoms. There is no clear indication of a common underlying mechanism. Several forms of disturbances of information processing may be caused by a mismatch of sensory events with stored rules (knowledge). Deviations can occur at the level of sensory perception (cf. stimulus-driven processing; closed-loop processing) and perhaps more often at the level of conceptual organization (cf. concept-driven processing; open-loop processing). These features may accord with the differentiation of subgroups.

## VIII. Genetic Marker

There is currently only one strong candidate for a genetic marker: deviant smooth pursuit eye movements (SPEM). However, since SPEM deviations are absent in some schizophrenics but present in first degree relatives, the issue is still controversial.

## IX. Structural Brain Abnormalities

Diffuse atrophies, reflected, for example, by enlargement of the ventricles or sulci, are prominent in about one in three patients. They are also found in patients with affective psychosis. Regional alterations are most often reported in limbic (hippocampal) and adjacent temporal structures.

## X. Biochemical and Functional Brain Abnormalities

There is still no clear indication which transmitter system is deviant in schizophrenia. Changes of dopaminergic activity may relate more to the expression of certain symptoms than directly to the etiological factors that gave rise to them. Diffuse brain damage and altered glutamate transmission may be associated.

Regional studies of blood flow and glucose consumption point to changes in the pattern of activation of parts of the frontal lobes in relation to the more posterior cortices.

## XI. Treatment

Currently, the administration of psychopharmacological substances that reduce the activity of the dopamine system in the long run is basic to the treatment of schizophrenics, yet there is no unequivocal demonstration that increased dopamine activity is at the root of the schizophrenic illness (see previous text).

The locus of the antipsychotic effect of medication remains uncertain. At the anatomical level, it is more likely to involve the mesolimbic or cortical system than the basal ganglia. At the biochemical level, although clinical efficacy is generally related to binding to the $D_2$ dopamine receptor, effective atypical neuroleptics such as clozapine are also active at the $D_1$ receptor and modulate serotonergic activity. Treatments also affect, and are affected by, activity of the transmitters glutamate and GABA.

# List of Previous Volumes

*PERSONALITY, PSYCHOPATHOLOGY, AND PSYCHOTHERAPY*
**A Series of Monographs, Texts, and Treatises**
David T. Lykken and Philip C. Kendall, Editors

*Titles initiated during the series editorship of Brendan Maher.

# Index